Treat this book with care and respect.

*It should become part of your personal
and professional library. It will
serve you well at any number
of points during your
professional career.*

Examples of form
Income statement - p. 41
Balance Sheet - p. 42-43
Petty Cash Disbursements p. 50
Payroll Register - p. 76-77

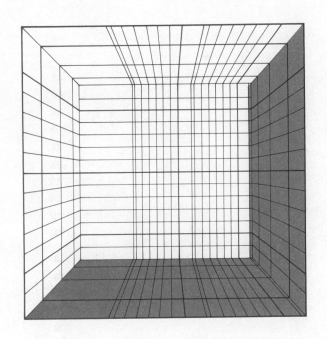

SECRETARIAL ACCOUNTING

10th Edition

PARTS 1~2

A. B. CARSON, PhD, CPA
Professor Emeritus of Accounting
University of California, Los Angeles

ARTHUR E. CARLSON, PhD
Professor of Accounting
School of Business Administration
Washington University, St. Louis

A54-3

Published by

SOUTH-WESTERN PUBLISHING CO.

CINCINNATI   WEST CHICAGO, ILL.   DALLAS   PELHAM MANOR, N.Y.
PALO ALTO, CALIF.   BRIGHTON, ENGLAND

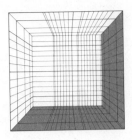

PREFACE

Secretarial Accounting is for students of accounting, business administration, and secretarial science. An understanding of the principles of business accounting is essential for anyone who aspires to a successful career in business, in many of the professions, and in numerous branches of government. Those who manage or operate a business, its owners, its prospective owners, its present and prospective creditors, governmental taxing authorities, and other government agencies have need for various types of information. Accounting systems are designed to fill such needs. The particular practices followed are tailored to meet the requirements and the circumstances in each case. However, the same accounting principles underlie the practices — just as the same principles of structural engineering apply to the construction of a one-car frame garage and of a fifty-floor steel and concrete office building.

This tenth edition of *Secretarial Accounting* continues the pattern of earlier editions — explanations of principles with examples of practices. Numerous forms and documents are illustrated. Because the terminology of accounting is undergoing gradual change, the currently preferred terms are used throughout the textbook. Diagrams and color are used both to facilitate understanding and, in the case of many of the color illustrations, to conform to practice. Because the discussion of accounting practices involves several references to computers, an appendix entitled "Computer-Based Accounting Systems — Design and Use" is included. A new chapter on Accounting Concepts and Practices (Chapter 15) has been added to this edition.

The textbook is organized to facilitate the use of various supplementary learning aids. Each chapter consists of one or more sections. Workbooks containing correlated study assignments are available. Each workbook study assignment (called a *report*) includes an exercise on principles and one or more problems bearing on the material discussed in the related section of the textbook. A compilation of check figures for selected workbook problems is available for distribution to students. Additional accounting problems to be used for either supplementary or remedial work are included following Chapters 5, 10, 15, and 20. Three practice sets (two of which are entirely new) are available: the first involves the accounting records of a professional man (John H. Roberts, a management consultant), the second involves the accounting records of a retail clothing store (Boyd's Clothiers), and the third involves the accounting records of a wholesale paint and varnish business (the partnership of Holling & Renz). These sets provide realistic work designed to test the student's ability to apply the knowledge of accounting principles which has been gained from studying the textbook and completing the workbook assignments. Upon completion of each practice set, a test is used to determine the student's ability to interpret intelligently the records and financial statements of the enterprise. New with this tenth edition is a learning aid entitled Self-Paced Learning Activity Guides (SPLAGs). The SPLAGs were developed to **(1)** provide guides for the completion of the accounting course with minimal instructor direction, and **(2)** provide remedial work whenever trouble spots emerge in the learning process. A comprehensive testing program is provided. Tests are available for use following completion of Chapters 2, 5, 10, 15, and 20.

The authors acknowledge their indebtedness and express their appreciation to the considerable number of accounting instructors, business executives, accountants, and other professional people whose suggestions contributed to the preparation of this textbook.

A. B. Carson

A. E. Carlson

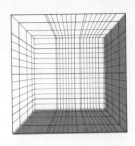

CONTENTS
PARTS 1-2

Chapter 1

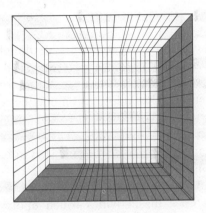

THE NATURE
OF BUSINESS
ACCOUNTING

The purpose of business accounting is to provide information about the financial operations and condition of an enterprise to the individuals, agencies, and organizations who have the need and the right to be so informed. These interested parties normally include the following:

(a) The **owners** of the business — both present and prospective.

(b) The **managers** of the business. (Often, but not always, the owners and the managers are the same persons.)

(c) The **creditors** of the business — both present and prospective. (*Creditors* are those who furnish or supply goods and services "on credit" — meaning that payment need not be made immediately. The creditor category also includes banks and individuals who lend money to the business.)

(d) **Government agencies** — local, state, and national. (For purposes of either regulation or taxation — sometimes both — various governmental agencies must be given certain financial information.)

The preceding four classes of users of information relate to virtually every business enterprise. In connection with many businesses, some or all of the following also make use of relevant information: customers or

1

clients, labor unions, competitors, trade associations, stock exchanges, commodity exchanges, financial analysts, and financial journalists.

The information needed by all of the users is not identical, though most want data regarding either results of operations for a recent period — net income or loss — or financial status as of a recent date, or both. In addition to these requirements, a variety of other information may be wanted. The exact requirement depends upon who wants it and for what purpose. As might be expected, the demand for the greatest quantity and variety of information comes from the managers of the business. They constantly need up-to-the-minute information about many things.

The accountant has the task of accumulating and dispensing needed financial information to users. Since his activities touch upon nearly every phase of business operation and since financial information is communicated in accounting terms, accounting is said to be the "language of business." Anyone intending to engage in any type of business activity is well advised to learn this language.

Since accounting relates to so many phases of business, it is not surprising that there are several fields of specialization in accounting. Some major special fields are tax work, cost accounting, information systems design and installation, and budget preparation. Many accountants have but one employer; whereas others become qualified as public accountants and offer their services as independent contractors or consultants. Some states license individuals as *Public Accountants* or *Registered Accountants*. All states grant the designation *Certified Public Accountant* (CPA) to those who meet various prescribed requirements, including the passing of a uniform examination prepared by the American Institute of Certified Public Accountants. Public accountants perform various functions. One of their major activities is *auditing*. This involves testing and checking the records of an enterprise to be certain that acceptable policies and practices have been consistently followed. In recent years, public accountants have been extending their activities into what is called "management services" — a term that covers a variety of specialized consulting assignments. Specialization is common among members of the accounting profession. Tax work is one important example of specialization. Management services is another.

All of the foregoing comments have related to accounting and accountants in connection with profit-seeking organizations. Since there are thousands of not-for-profit or nonprofit organizations (such as governments, educational institutions, churches, and hospitals) that also need to accumulate information, thousands of accountants are in their employ. These organizations also engage public accountants. While the "rules of the game" are somewhat different for not-for-profit organizations, much of the record keeping is identical with that found in business.

THE ACCOUNTING PROCESS

Business accounting may be defined as the art of analyzing and recording financial transactions and certain business-related economic events in a manner that facilitates classifying and summarizing the information, and reporting and interpreting the results.

Analyzing is the first step. There may be more than one way of looking at something that has happened. The accountant must determine the fundamental significance to the business of each transaction or event in order to record it properly.

Recording traditionally has meant writing something by hand. Much of the record keeping in accounting still is manual, but for years typewriters and many varieties of so-called "bookkeeping machines" (which typically combine the major attributes of typewriters and adding machines or desk calculators) have been in use. Today the recording sometimes takes the form of holes punched in certain places on a card or a paper tape, or of invisible magnetized spots on a special type of tape used to feed information into an electronic computer.

Classifying relates to the process of sorting or grouping like things together rather than merely keeping a simple, diary-like narrative record of numerous and varied transactions and events.

Summarizing is the process of bringing together various items of information to determine or explain a result.

Reporting refers to the process of attempting to communicate the results. In accounting, it is common to use tabular arrangements rather than narrative-type reports. Sometimes, a combination of the two is used.

Interpreting refers to the steps taken to direct attention to the significance of various matters and relationships. Percentage analyses and ratios often are used to help explain the meaning of certain related bits of information. Footnotes to financial reports may also be valuable in the interpreting phase of accounting.

Accounting and bookkeeping

Accounting involves forms and records design, policy making, data analysis, report preparation, and report interpretation. A person involved with or responsible for these functions may be referred to as an accountant. Bookkeeping is the recording phase of the accounting process. The person who records the information in the accounting records may be referred to as a bookkeeper. That term goes back to the time when formal accounting records were in the form of books — pages bound together. While this still is sometimes the case, modern practice favors the use of loose-leaf records and cards and, in some instances, computers. When the language catches up with practice, the designation "record keeper" will replace "bookkeeper." Sometimes the accountant also serves as the bookkeeper — an experience that may be of great value to him.

Accounting elements

If complete accounting records are to be maintained, all transactions and events that affect the basic accounting elements must be recorded. The basic accounting elements are *assets*, *liabilities*, and *owner's equity*.

Assets. Properties of value that are owned by a business are called assets. Properties such as money, accounts receivable, merchandise, furniture, fixtures, machinery, buildings, and land are common examples of business assets. *Accounts receivable* are unwritten promises by customers to pay at a later date for goods sold to them or for services rendered.

It is possible to conduct a business or a professional practice with very few assets. A dentist, for example, may have relatively few assets, such as money, instruments, laboratory equipment, and office equipment. But in many cases, a variety of assets is necessary. A merchant must have merchandise to sell and store equipment on which to display the merchandise, in addition to other assets. A manufacturer must have materials, tools, and various sorts of machinery, in addition to other assets.

Liabilities. An obligation of a business to pay a debt is a business liability. The most common liabilities are accounts payable and notes payable. *Accounts payable* are unwritten promises to pay creditors for property (such as merchandise, supplies, and equipment) purchased on credit or for services rendered. *Notes payable* are formal written promises to pay creditors or lenders specified sums of money at some future time. A business also may have one or more types of *taxes payable*.

Owner's Equity. The amount by which the business assets exceed the business liabilities is termed the owner's equity in the business. The word "equity" used in this sense means "interest in" or "claim of." It would be quite reasonable to call liabilities "creditors' equity," but this is not customary. The terms *proprietorship*, *net worth*, or *capital* are sometimes used as synonyms for owner's equity. If there are no business liabilities, the owner's equity in the business is equal to the total amount of the assets of the business.

In visualizing a business that is owned and operated by one person (traditionally called the proprietor), it is essential to realize that a distinction must be made between his *business* assets and liabilities and any *non-*

business assets and liabilities that he may have. The proprietor will certainly have various types of personal property, such as clothing; it is probable that he will have a home, furniture, and a car. He may own a wide variety of other valuable properties quite apart from his business. Likewise, the proprietor may owe money for reasons that do not pertain to his business. Amounts owed to merchants from whom food and clothing have been purchased and amounts owed to doctors and dentists for services received are common examples. Legally there is no distinction between the proprietor's business and nonbusiness assets nor between the business and nonbusiness liabilities; but since it is to be expected that the formal accounting records for the enterprise will relate to the business only, any nonbusiness assets and liabilities should be excluded. While the term "owner's equity" can be used in a very broad sense, its use in accounting is nearly always limited to the meaning: business assets minus business liabilities.

Frequent reference will be made to the owner's acts of investing money or other property in the business, or to his withdrawal of money or other property from the business. All that is involved in either case is that some property is changed from the category of a nonbusiness asset to a business asset or vice versa. It should be apparent that these distinctions are important if the owner is to be able to judge the financial condition and results of the operations of his business apart from his nonbusiness affairs.

The accounting equation

The relationship between the three basic accounting elements can be expressed in the form of a simple equation:

ASSETS = LIABILITIES + OWNER'S EQUITY

When the amounts of any two of these elements are known, the third can always be calculated. For example, Donna Musgrave has business assets on December 31 in the sum of $28,400. Her business debts on that date consist of $800 owed for supplies purchased on account and $1,000 owed to a bank on a note. The owner's equity element of her business may be calculated by subtraction ($28,400 − $1,800 = $26,600). These facts about her business can be expressed in equation form as follows:

ASSETS	= LIABILITIES	+ OWNER'S EQUITY
$28,400	$1,800	$26,600

In order to increase her equity in the business, Ms. Musgrave must either increase the assets without increasing the liabilities, or decrease the liabilities without decreasing the assets. In order to increase the assets and owner's equity without investing more money or other property in the business, she will have to operate the business at a profit.

For example, if one year later the assets amount to $42,300 and the liabilities to $2,100, the status of the business would be as follows:

ASSETS	= LIABILITIES	+ OWNER'S EQUITY
$42,300	$2,100	$40,200

However, the fact that Ms. Musgrave's equity in the business had increased by $13,600 (from $26,600 to $40,200) does not prove that she had made a profit (often called *net income*) equal to the increase. She might have invested additional money or other property in the business. Suppose, for example, that she invested additional money during the year in the amount of $6,000. In that event the remainder of the increase in her equity ($7,600) would have been due to profit (net income).

Another possibility could be that she had a very profitable year and withdrew assets in an amount less than the amount of profit. For example, her equity might have been increased by $22,000 as a result of profitable operation; and during the year she might have withdrawn a total of $8,400 in cash for personal use. This series of events could account for the $13,600 increase. It is essential that the business records show the extent to which the change in owner's equity is due to the regular operation of the business and the extent to which increases and decreases in owner's equity are due to the owner's acts of investing and withdrawing assets.

Transactions

Any activity of an enterprise which involves the exchange of values is usually referred to as a *transaction*. These values usually are expressed in terms of money. Buying and selling property and services are common transactions. The following typical transactions are analyzed to show that each one represents an exchange of values.

TYPICAL TRANSACTIONS	ANALYSIS OF TRANSACTIONS
(a) Purchased equipment for cash, $950.	Money was exchanged for equipment.
(b) Received cash in payment of professional fees, $250.	Professional service was rendered in exchange for money.
(c) Paid office rent, $200.	Money was exchanged for the right to use property.
(d) Paid an amount owed to a creditor, $575.	Money was given in settlement of a debt that may have resulted from the purchase of property on account or from services rendered by a creditor.
(e) Paid wages in cash, $125.	Money was exchanged for services rendered.
(f) Borrowed $2,500 at a bank giving an 8 percent interest-bearing note due in 30 days.	A liability known as a note payable was incurred in exchange for money.

(g) Purchased office equipment on account, $400.

A liability known as an account payable was incurred in exchange for office equipment.

Effect of transactions on the accounting equation

Each transaction affects one or more of the three basic accounting elements. For example, the purchase of equipment for cash represents both an increase and a decrease in assets. The assets increased because equipment was acquired; the assets decreased because cash was disbursed. If the equipment had been purchased on account, thereby incurring a liability, the transaction would result in an increase in assets (equipment) with a corresponding increase in liabilities (accounts payable). Neither of these transactions has any effect upon the owner's equity element of the equation.

The effect of any transaction on the basic accounting elements may be indicated by addition and subtraction. To illustrate: assume that Stanley Jones, an attorney, decided to go into business for himself. During the first month of this venture (June, 1977), the following transactions relating to his business took place:

An Increase in an Asset Offset by an Increase in Owner's Equity

Transaction (a). Mr. Jones opened a bank account with a deposit of $6,000. This transaction caused his new business to receive the asset cash; and since no business liabilities were involved, the owner's equity element was increased by the same amount. As a result of this transaction, the equation for the business would appear as follows:

ASSETS	=	LIABILITIES + OWNER'S EQUITY
Cash		Stanley Jones, Capital
(a) 6,000		6,000

An Increase in an Asset Offset by an Increase in a Liability

Transaction (b). Mr. Jones purchased office equipment (desk, chairs, file cabinet, etc.) for $3,500 on 30 days' credit. This transaction caused the asset office equipment to increase by $3,500 and resulted in an equal increase in the liability accounts payable. Updating the foregoing equation by this (b) transaction gives the following result:

ASSETS		=	LIABILITIES	+	OWNER'S EQUITY
Cash +	Office Equipment		Accounts Payable		Stanley Jones, Capital
Bal. 6,000					6,000
(b)	+3,500		+3,500		
Bal. 6,000	3,500		3,500		6,000

An Increase in One Asset Offset by a Decrease in Another Asset

Transaction (c). Mr. Jones purchased office supplies (stationery, carbon paper, pencils, etc.) for cash, $530. This transaction caused a $530 increase in the asset office supplies that exactly offset the $530 decrease in the asset cash. The effect on the equation is as follows:

	ASSETS				LIABILITIES + OWNER'S EQUITY	
	Cash +	Office Equipment +	Office Supplies	=	Accounts Payable	Stanley Jones, Capital
Bal.	6,000	3,500			3,500	6,000
(c)	−530		+530			
Bal.	5,470	3,500	530		3,500	6,000

A Decrease in an Asset Offset by a Decrease in a Liability

Transaction (d). Mr. Jones paid $2,000 on account to the company from which the office equipment was purchased. (See Transaction (b).) This payment caused the asset cash and the liability accounts payable both to decrease $2,000. The effect on the equation is as follows:

	ASSETS				LIABILITIES + OWNER'S EQUITY	
	Cash +	Office Equipment +	Office Supplies	=	Accounts Payable	Stanley Jones, Capital
Bal.	5,470	3,500	530		3,500	6,000
(d)	−2,000				−2,000	
Bal.	3,470	3,500	530		1,500	6,000

An Increase in an Asset Offset by an Increase in Owner's Equity Resulting from Revenue

Transaction (e). Mr. Jones received $1,500 cash from a client for professional services. This transaction caused the asset cash to increase $1,500, and since the liabilities were not affected, the owner's equity increased by the same amount. The effect on the equation is as follows:

	ASSETS				LIABILITIES + OWNER'S EQUITY	
	Cash +	Office Equipment +	Office Supplies	=	Accounts Payable	Stanley Jones, Capital
Bal.	3,470	3,500	530		1,500	6,000
(e)	+1,500					+1,500
Bal.	4,970	3,500	530		1,500	7,500

A Decrease in an Asset Offset by a Decrease in Owner's Equity Resulting from Expense

Transaction (f). Mr. Jones paid $300 for office rent for June. This transaction caused the asset cash to be reduced by $300 with an equal reduction in owner's equity. The effect on the equation is as follows:

ASSETS				LIABILITIES + OWNER'S EQUITY	
Cash +	Office Equipment +	Office Supplies	=	Accounts Payable	Stanley Jones, Capital
Bal. 4,970	3,500	530		1,500	7,500
(f) −300					−300
Bal. 4,670	3,500	530		1,500	7,200

Transaction (g). Mr. Jones paid a bill for telephone service, $35. This transaction, like the previous one, caused a decrease in the asset cash with an equal decrease in the owner's equity. The effect on the equation is as follows:

ASSETS				LIABILITIES + OWNER'S EQUITY	
Cash +	Office Equipment +	Office Supplies	=	Accounts Payable	Stanley Jones, Capital
Bal. 4,670	3,500	530		1,500	7,200
(g) − 35					− 35
Bal. 4,635	3,500	530		1,500	7,165

The financial statements

A set of accounting records is maintained to fill a variety of needs. Foremost is its use as source data in preparing various reports including those referred to as *financial statements*. The two most important of these are the *income statement* and the *balance sheet*.

The Income Statement. The income statement, sometimes called a *profit and loss statement* or *operating statement*, shows the *net income* (*net profit*) or *net loss* for a specified period of time and how it was calculated. A very simple income statement relating to the business of Stanley Jones for the first month's operation, June, 1977, is shown below. The information it contains was obtained by analysis of the changes in the owner's equity element of the business for the month. This element went from zero to $7,165. Part of this increase, $6,000, was due to the investment of Mr. Jones. The remainder of the increase, $1,165, must have been due to net income, since Mr. Jones had made no withdrawals. Transaction (e) involved revenue of $1,500; transactions (f) and (g) involved expenses of $300 and $35, respectively. Taken together, these three transactions explain the net income of $1,165.

```
                    STANLEY JONES, ATTORNEY
                         Income Statement
                     For the Month of June, 1977

      Professional fees......................           $1,500

      Expenses:
         Rent expense........................    $300
         Telephone expense...................      35      335

      Net income for month..................           $1,165
```

The Balance Sheet. The balance sheet, sometimes called a *statement of financial condition* or *statement of financial position*, shows the assets, liabilities, and owner's equity of a business at a specified date. A balance sheet for Mr. Jones' business as of June 30, 1977, is shown below. The information it contains was obtained from the accounting equation after the last transaction (g).

```
                       STANLEY JONES, ATTORNEY

                            Balance Sheet

                            June 30, 1977


            Assets                              Liabilities
Cash...................   $4,635     Accounts payable........   $1,500
Office supplies.........      530
Office equipment........    3,500           Owner's Equity

                         _____    Stanley Jones, capital..    7,165

                                     Total liabilities and
Total assets...........   $8,665        owner's equity........   $8,665
```

NOTE: In order to keep the illustrations of transaction analysis, the income statement, and the balance sheet as simple as possible at this point, two expenses were ignored; namely, office supplies used and depreciation of office equipment.

Report No. 1-1

A workbook of study assignments is provided for use with this textbook. Each study assignment is referred to as a report. The work involved in completing Report No. 1-1 requires a knowledge of the principles developed in the preceding textbook discussion. Before proceeding with the following discussion, complete Report No. 1-1 in accordance with the instructions given in the study assignments.

THE DOUBLE-ENTRY MECHANISM

The meanings of the terms asset, liability, and owner's equity were explained in the preceding pages. Examples were given to show how each business transaction causes a change in one or more of the three basic accounting elements. The first transaction (a) shown on page 7 involved an increase in an asset with a corresponding increase in owner's equity. In the second transaction (b), an increase in an asset caused an equal increase in a liability. In the third transaction (c), an increase in one asset was offset by a decrease in another. In each of the transactions illustrated, there was this *dual effect*. This is always true. A change (increase or decrease) in any asset, any liability, or in owner's equity is always accompanied by an offsetting change within the basic accounting elements.

The fact that each transaction has two aspects — a dual effect upon the accounting elements — provides the basis for what is called *double-entry bookkeeping*. This phrase describes a recording system that involves the making of a record of each of the two aspects that are involved in every transaction. Double entry does not mean that a transaction is recorded twice; instead, it means that both of the two aspects of each transaction are recorded.

The technique of double entry is described and illustrated in the following pages. This method of recording transactions is not new. Double entry is known to have been practiced for at least 500 years. This long popularity is easily explained since the method has several virtues. It is orderly, fairly simple, and very flexible. There is no transaction that cannot be recorded in a double-entry manner. Double entry promotes accuracy. Its use makes it impossible for certain types of errors to remain undetected for very long. For example, if one aspect of a transaction is properly recorded but the other part is overlooked, it will soon be found that the records are "out of balance." The bookkeeper then knows that something is wrong and can check his work to discover the trouble and can make the needed correction.

The account   It has been explained previously that the assets of a business may consist of a number of items, such as money, accounts receivable, merchandise, equipment, buildings, and land. The liabilities may consist of one or more items, such as accounts payable and notes payable. A separate record should be kept of each asset and of each liability. Later it will be shown that a separate record should also be kept of the increases and decreases in owner's equity. The form or record kept for each item is known as an *account*. There are many types of account forms in general use. They may be ruled on sheets of paper and bound in book form or kept in a loose-leaf binder, or they may be ruled on cards and kept in a file of some sort. An illustration is shown on page 12 of a *standard form of account* that is widely used.

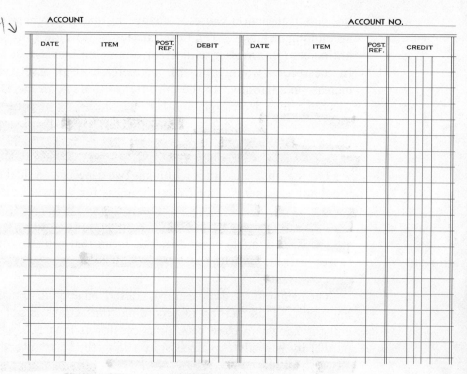

Standard Form of Account

    This account form is designed to facilitate the recording of the essential information regarding each transaction that affects the account. Before any entries are recorded in an account, the title and number of the account should be written on the horizontal line at the top of the form. Each account should be given an appropriate title that will indicate whether it is an asset, a liability, or an owner's equity account. The standard account form is divided into two equal parts or sections which are ruled identically to facilitate recording increases and decreases. The left side is called the debit side, while the right side is called the credit side. The columnar arrangement and headings of the columns on both sides are the same except that the amount column on the left is headed "Debit" while that on the right is headed "Credit." The Date columns are used for recording the dates of transactions. The Item columns may be used for writing a brief description of a transaction when deemed necessary. The Posting Reference columns will be discussed later. The Debit and Credit columns are used for recording the amounts of transactions.

    The three major parts of the standard account form are **(1)** the title (and, usually, the account number), **(2)** the debit side, and **(3)** the credit side. To determine the balance of an account at any time, it is necessary only to total the amounts in the Debit and Credit columns, and calculate the difference between the two totals. To save time, a "T" form of account is commonly used for instructional purposes. It consists of a two-line drawing resembling the capital letter T and is sometimes referred to as a skeleton form of account.

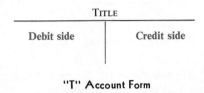

	TITLE	
Debit side		Credit side

"T" Account Form

Debits and credits

To debit an account means to record an amount on the left or debit side of the account. To credit an account means to record an amount on the right or credit side of the account. The abbreviation for debit is Dr. and for credit Cr. (based on the Latin terms *debere* and *credere*). Sometimes the word *charge* is used as a substitute for debit. Increases in assets are recorded on the left side of the accounts; increases in liabilities and in owner's equity are recorded on the right side of the accounts. Decreases in assets are recorded on the right side of the accounts; decreases in liabilities and in owner's equity are recorded on the left side of the accounts. Recording increases and decreases in the accounts in this manner will reflect the basic equality of assets to liabilities plus owner's equity; at the same time it will maintain equality between the total amounts debited to all accounts and the total amounts credited to all accounts. These basic relationships may be illustrated in the following manner:

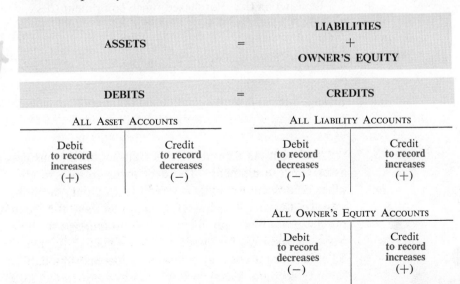

ASSETS	=	LIABILITIES + OWNER'S EQUITY
DEBITS	=	CREDITS

ALL ASSET ACCOUNTS		ALL LIABILITY ACCOUNTS	
Debit to record increases (+)	Credit to record decreases (−)	Debit to record decreases (−)	Credit to record increases (+)

ALL OWNER'S EQUITY ACCOUNTS	
Debit to record decreases (−)	Credit to record increases (+)

Use of asset, liability, and owner's equity accounts

To illustrate the application of the double-entry process, the transactions discussed on pages 7–9 will be analyzed and their effect on the accounting elements will be indicated by showing the proper entries in "T" accounts. As before, the transactions are identified by letters; dates are omitted intentionally.

An Increase in an Asset Offset by an Increase in Owner's Equity

Transaction (a). Stanley Jones, an attorney, started a business of his own and invested $6,000 in cash.

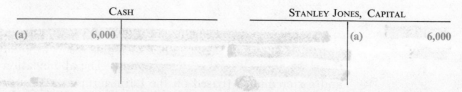

CASH		STANLEY JONES, CAPITAL	
(a) 6,000			(a) 6,000

Analysis: As a result of this transaction the business acquired an asset, cash. The amount of money invested by Mr. Jones represents his equity in the business; thus the amount of the asset cash is equal to the owner's equity in the business. Separate accounts are kept for the asset cash and for the owner. To record the transaction properly, the cash account was debited and Stanley Jones' capital account was credited for $6,000.

An Increase in an Asset Offset by an Increase in a Liability

Transaction (b). Purchased office equipment (desk, chairs, file cabinet, etc.) for $3,500 on 30 days' credit.

OFFICE EQUIPMENT		ACCOUNTS PAYABLE	
(b) 3,500			(b) 3,500

Analysis: As a result of this transaction the business acquired a new asset, office equipment. The debt incurred as a result of purchasing the office equipment on 30 days' credit is a liability, accounts payable. Separate accounts are kept for office equipment and for accounts payable. The purchase of office equipment caused an increase in the assets of the business. Therefore, the asset account Office Equipment was debited for $3,500. The purchase also caused an increase in a liability. Therefore, the liability account Accounts Payable was credited for $3,500.

An Increase in One Asset Offset by a Decrease in Another Asset

Transaction (c). Purchased office supplies (stationery, carbon paper, pencils, etc.) for cash, $530.

CASH			OFFICE SUPPLIES	
(a) 6,000	(c)	530	(c)	530

Analysis: As a result of this transaction the business acquired a new asset, office supplies. However, the addition of this asset was offset by a decrease in the asset cash. To record the transaction properly, Office Supplies was debited and Cash was credited for $530. (It will be noted that this is the second entry in the cash account; the account was previously debited for $6,000 when Transaction (a) was recorded.)

It is proper to record office supplies as an asset at time of purchase even though they will become an expense when consumed. (The procedure in accounting for supplies consumed will be discussed later.)

A Decrease in an Asset Offset by a Decrease in a Liability

Transaction (d). Paid $2,000 "on account" to the company from which the office equipment was purchased. (See Transaction (b).)

CASH			ACCOUNTS PAYABLE	
(a) 6,000	(c)	530	(d) 2,000	(b) 3,500
	(d)	2,000		

Analysis: This transaction resulted in a decrease in the liability accounts payable with a corresponding decrease in the asset cash; hence, it was recorded by debiting Accounts Payable and by crediting Cash for $2,000. (It will be noted that this is the second entry in the accounts payable account and the third entry in the cash account.)

Revenue and expense

The owner's equity element of a business or professional enterprise may be increased in two ways as follows:

(a) The owner may invest additional money or other property in the enterprise. Such investments result in an increase both in the assets of the enterprise and in the owner's equity, but they do not further enrich the owner; he merely has more property invested in the enterprise and less property outside of the enterprise.

(b) Revenue may be derived from sales of goods or services, or from other sources.

As used in accounting, the term *revenue* in nearly all cases refers to an increase in the owner's equity in a business resulting from any transactions involving asset inflows except the investment of assets in the business by its owner. In most cases, the increase in owner's equity due to revenue results from an addition to the assets without any change in the liabilities. Often it is cash that is increased. However, an increase in cash and other assets can occur in connection with several types of transactions that do not involve revenue. For this reason, revenue is defined in terms of the change in owner's equity rather than the change in assets. Any transaction that causes owner's equity to increase, except investments in the business by its owner, involves revenue.

The owner's equity element of a business or professional enterprise may be decreased in two ways as follows:

(a) The owner may withdraw assets (cash or other property) from the business enterprise.

(b) Expenses may be incurred in operating the enterprise.

As used in accounting, the term *expense* in nearly all cases means a decrease in the owner's equity in a business caused by any transactions involving asset outflows other than a withdrawal by the owner. When an expense is incurred, either the assets are reduced or the liabilities are increased. In either event, owner's equity is reduced. If the transaction causing the reduction is not a withdrawal of assets by the owner, an expense is incurred. Common examples of expense are rent of office or store, salaries of employees, telephone service, supplies consumed, and many types of taxes.

If, during a specified period of time, the total increases in owner's equity resulting from revenue exceed the total decreases resulting from expenses, it may be said that the excess represents the *net income* or net profit for the period. On the other hand, if the expenses of the period exceed the revenue, such excess represents a *net loss* for the period. The time interval used in the measurement of net income or net loss can be chosen by the owner. It may be a month, a quarter (three months), a year, or some other period of time. If the accounting period is a year, it is usually referred to as a *fiscal year*. The fiscal year frequently coincides with the *calendar year*.

Transactions involving revenue and expense always cause a change in the owner's equity element of an enterprise. Such changes could be recorded by debiting the owner's equity account for expenses and crediting it for revenue. If this practice were followed, however, the credit side of the owner's equity account would contain a mixture of increases due to revenue and to the investment of assets in the business by the owner, while the debit side would contain a mixture of decreases due to expenses and to the withdrawal of assets from the business by the owner. In order to calculate the net income or the net loss for each accounting period, a careful analysis of the owner's equity account would be required. It is, therefore, better practice to record revenue and expenses in separate accounts. These are called *temporary* owner's equity accounts because it is customary to close them at the end of each accounting period by transferring their balances to a *summary* account. The balance of this summary account then represents the net income or net loss for the period. The summary account is also a temporary account which is closed by transferring its balance to the owner's equity account.

A separate account should be kept for each type of revenue and for each type of expense. When a transaction produces revenue, the amount of the revenue should be credited to an appropriate revenue account. When a transaction involves expense, the amount of the expense should be debited to an appropriate expense account. The relationship of these temporary accounts to the owner's equity account and the application of the debit and credit theory to the accounts are indicated in the following diagram:

ALL OWNER'S EQUITY ACCOUNTS

Debit to record decreases (−)	Credit to record increases (+)

ALL EXPENSE ACCOUNTS		ALL REVENUE ACCOUNTS	
Debit to record increases (+)	Credit to record decreases (−)	Debit to record decreases (−)	Credit to record increases (+)

It is important to recognize that the credit side of each revenue account is serving temporarily as a part of the credit side of the owner's equity account. Increases in owner's equity are recorded as credits. Thus, increases in owner's equity resulting from revenue should be credited to revenue accounts. The debit side of each expense account is serving temporarily as a part of the debit side of the owner's equity account. Decreases in owner's equity are recorded as debits. Thus, decreases in owner's equity resulting from expense should be debited to expense accounts.

Use of revenue and expense accounts

To illustrate the application of the double-entry process in recording transactions that affect revenue and expense accounts, the transactions that follow will be analyzed and their effect on the accounting elements will be indicated by showing the proper entries in "T" accounts. These transactions represent a continuation of the transactions completed by Stanley Jones, an attorney, in the conduct of his business. (See pages 14 and 15 for Transactions (a) to (d).)

An Increase in an Asset Offset by an Increase in Owner's Equity Resulting from Revenue

Transaction (e). Received $1,500 in cash from a client for professional services rendered.

CASH				PROFESSIONAL FEES	
(a)	6,000	(c)	530	(e)	1,500
(e)	1,500	(d)	2,000		

Analysis: This transaction resulted in an increase in the asset cash with a corresponding increase in owner's equity because of revenue from professional fees. To record the transaction properly, Cash was debited and an appropriate account for the revenue was credited for $1,500. Accounts should always be given a descriptive title that will aid in classifying them in relation to the accounting elements. In this case the revenue account was given the title Professional Fees. (It will be noted that this is the fourth entry in the cash account and the first entry in the account Professional Fees.)

A Decrease in an Asset Offset by a Decrease in Owner's Equity Resulting from Expense

Transaction (f). Paid $300 for office rent for one month.

CASH				RENT EXPENSE	
(a)	6,000	(c)	530	(f)	300
(e)	1,500	(d)	2,000		
		(f)	300		

Analysis: This transaction resulted in a decrease in the asset cash with a corresponding decrease in owner's equity because of expense. To record the transaction properly, Rent Expense was debited and Cash was credited for $300. (This is the first entry in the rent expense account and the fifth entry in the cash account.)

Transaction (g). Paid bill for telephone service, $35.

CASH			TELEPHONE EXPENSE	
(a)	6,000	(c)	530	(g)	35
(e)	1,500	(d)	2,000		
		(f)	300		
		(g)	35		

Analysis: This transaction is identical with the previous one except that telephone expense rather than rent expense was the reason for the decrease in owner's equity. To record the transaction properly, Telephone Expense was debited and Cash was credited for $35.

The trial balance

It is a fundamental principle of double-entry bookkeeping that the sum of the assets is always equal to the sum of the liabilities and owner's equity. In order to maintain this equality in recording transactions, the sum of the debit entries must always be equal to the sum of the credit entries. To determine whether this equality has been maintained, it is customary to take a trial balance periodically. A *trial balance* is a list of all of the accounts showing the title and balance of each account. The balance of any account is the amount of difference between the total debits and the total credits to the account. Preliminary to taking a trial balance, the debit and credit amounts in each account should be totaled. This is called *footing* the amount columns. If there is only one item entered in a column, no footing is necessary. To find the balance of an account it is necessary only to determine the difference between the footings by subtraction. Since asset and expense accounts are debited for increases, these accounts normally have *debit balances*. Since liability, owner's equity, and revenue accounts are credited to record increases, these accounts normally have *credit balances*. The balance of an account should be entered on the side of the account that has the larger total. The footings and balances of accounts should be written in small figures just below the last entry. A pencil is generally used for this purpose. If the footings of an account are equal in amount, the account is said to be *in balance*.

The accounts of Stanley Jones are reproduced on page 20. To show the relationship to the fundamental accounting equation, the accounts are arranged in three columns under the headings of Assets, Liabilities, and Owner's Equity. It will be noted that the cash account has been footed and the balance inserted on the left side. The two debits totaled $7,500; the four credits totaled $2,865. Thus, the debit balance was $4,635. The footings and the balance are printed in italics. It was not necessary to foot any of the other accounts because none of them contained more than one entry on either side. The balance of the accounts payable account is shown on the credit side in italics. It was not necessary to enter the balances of the other accounts because there were entries on only one side of those accounts.

ASSETS	=	LIABILITIES	+	OWNER'S EQUITY

CASH		ACCOUNTS PAYABLE	STANLEY JONES, CAPITAL

(a) 6,000	(c) 530	(d) 2,000	(b) 3,500		(a) 6,000
(e) 1,500	(d) 2,000		*1,500*		
4,635 7,500	(f) 300				
	(g) 35				
	2,865				

PROFESSIONAL FEES

(e) 1,500

OFFICE SUPPLIES

(c) 530

RENT EXPENSE

(f) 300

OFFICE EQUIPMENT

(b) 3,500

TELEPHONE EXPENSE

(g) 35

A trial balance of Stanley Jones' accounts is shown below. The trial balance was taken on June 30, 1977; therefore, this date is shown in the third line of the heading. The trial balance reveals that the debit and credit totals are equal in amount. This is proof that in recording Transactions (a) to (g) inclusive the total of the debits was equal to the total of the credits.

Stanley Jones, Attorney
Trial Balance
June 30, 1977

Account	Dr. Balance	Cr. Balance
Cash	4635 00	
Office Supplies	530 00	
Office Equipment	3500 00	
Accounts Payable		1500 00
Stanley Jones, Capital		6000 00
Professional Fees		1500 00
Rent Expense	300 00	
Telephone Expense	35 00	
	9000 00	9000 00

Stanley Jones' Trial Balance

A trial balance is not a formal statement or report. Normally, it is never seen by anyone except the accountant or bookkeeper. It is used to aid in preparing the income statement and the balance sheet. If the trial balance on the preceding page is studied in conjunction with the income statement and balance sheet shown on pages 9 and 10, it will be seen that those statements could have been prepared quite easily from the information that this trial balance provides.

Report No. 1-2

Refer to the study assignments and complete Report No. 1-2 in accordance with the instructions given therein. The work involved in completing the assignment requires a knowledge of the principles developed in the preceding discussion. Any difficulty experienced in completing the report will indicate a lack of understanding of these principles. In such event further study should be helpful. After completing the report, you may continue with the textbook discussion in Chapter 2 until the next report is required.

Chapter 2

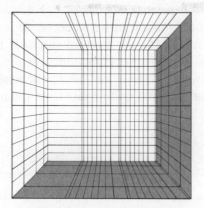

ACCOUNTING PROCEDURE

The principles of double-entry bookkeeping were explained and illustrated in the preceding chapter. To avoid distraction from the fundamentals, the mechanics of collecting and classifying information about business transactions were ignored. In actual practice the first record of a transaction (sometimes called the "source document") is made in the form of a business paper, such as a check stub, receipt, cash register tape, sales ticket, or purchase invoice. The information supplied by source documents is an aid in analyzing transactions to determine their effect upon the accounts.

JOURNALIZING TRANSACTIONS

The first formal double-entry record of a transaction is usually made in a record called a *journal* (frequently in book form). The act of recording transactions in a journal is called *journalizing*. It is necessary to analyze each transaction before it can be journalized properly. The purpose of the journal entries is to provide a chronological record of all transactions completed showing the date of each transaction, titles of accounts to be debited and credited, and amounts of the debits and credits. The journal then provides all the information needed to record the debits and credits in the proper accounts. The flow of data concerning transactions can be illustrated in the following manner:

Transactions are evidenced
by various
SOURCE DOCUMENTS ──────→ The source documents provide the information needed to record the transactions in a
                                                  JOURNAL ──────────────→ The journal provides the information needed to record the debits and credits in the accounts which collectively comprise a
                                                                                                    LEDGER

Source documents

The term source document covers a wide variety of forms and papers. Almost any document that provides information about a business transaction can be called a source document.

SOURCE DOCUMENTS

Examples:	Provide information about:
(a) Check stubs or carbon copies of checks	Cash disbursements
(b) Receipt stubs, or carbon copies of receipts, cash register tapes, or memos of cash register totals	Cash receipts
(c) Copies of sales tickets or sales invoices issued to customers or clients	Sales of goods or services
(d) Purchase invoices received from vendors	Purchases of goods or services

The journal

While the original record of a transaction usually is a source document as explained above, the first formal double-entry record of a transaction is made in a journal. For this reason a journal is commonly referred to as a *book of original entry*. The ruling of the pages of a journal varies with the type and size of an enterprise and the nature of its operations. The simplest form of journal is a *two-column journal*. A standard form of such a journal is illustrated on page 24. It is referred to as a two-column journal because it has only two amount columns, one for debit amounts and one for credit amounts. In the illustration the columns have been numbered as a means of identification in connection with the following discussion.

JOURNAL   PAGE

DATE	DESCRIPTION	POST. REF.	LEFT DEBIT	RIGHT CREDIT	
1					1
2					2
3					3
①	②	③	④	⑤	4
5					5
6					6
7					7
8					8
9					9

Standard Two-Column Journal

Column No. 1 is a date column. The year should be written in small figures at the top of the column immediately below the column heading and need only be repeated at the top of each new page unless an entry for a new year is made farther down on the page. The date column is a double column, the perpendicular single rule being used to separate the month from the day. Thus in writing June 20, the name of the month should be written to the left of the single line and the number designating the day of the month should be written to the right of this line. The name of the month need only be shown for the first entry on a page unless an entry for a new month is made farther down on the page.

Column No. 2 is generally referred to as a description or an explanation column. It is used to record the titles of the accounts affected by each transaction, together with a description of the transaction. Two or more accounts are affected by each transaction, and the titles of all accounts affected must be recorded. Normally the titles of the accounts debited are written first and then the titles of the accounts credited. A separate line should be used for each account title. The titles of the accounts to be debited are generally written at the extreme left of the column, while the titles of the accounts to be credited are usually indented about one-half inch (about 1.3 centimeters). The description should be written immediately following the credit entry, and usually is indented an additional one-half inch. Reference to the journal reproduced on pages 31 and 32 will help to visualize the arrangement of the copy in the Description column. An orderly arrangement is desirable.

Column No. 3 is a posting reference column — sometimes referred to as a folio column. No entries are made in this column at the time of journalizing the transactions; such entries are made only at the time of posting (which is the process of entering the debits and credits in the proper accounts in the ledger). This procedure will be explained in detail later in this chapter.

Column No. 4 is an amount column in which the amount that is to be debited to any account should be written on the same line on which the title of that account appears. In other words, the name of the account to be debited should be written in the Description column and the amount of the debit entry should be written on the same line in the Debit column.

Column No. 5 is an amount column in which the amount that is to be credited to any account should be written on the same line on which the title of that account appears. In other words, the name of the account to be credited should be written in the Description column and the amount of the credit entry should be written on the same line in the Credit column.

Journalizing

Journalizing involves recording the significant information concerning each transaction either **(1)** at the time the transaction occurs or **(2)** subsequently, but in the chronological order in which it and the other transactions occurred. For every transaction the entry should record the date, the title of each account affected, the amounts, and a brief description. The only effect a transaction can have on any account is either to increase or to decrease the balance of the account. Before a transaction can be recorded properly, therefore, it must be analyzed in order to determine:

(a) Which accounts are affected by the transaction.

(b) What effect the transaction has upon each of the accounts involved; that is, whether the balance of each affected account is increased or decreased.

The chart of accounts

In analyzing a transaction preparatory to journalizing it, the accountant or bookkeeper must know which accounts are being kept. When an accounting system is being established for a new business, the first step is to decide which accounts are required. The accounts used will depend upon the information needed or desired. Ordinarily it will be found desirable to keep a separate account for each type of asset and each type of liability, since it is certain that information will be desired in regard to what is owned and what is owed. A permanent owner's equity or capital account should be kept in order that information may be available as to the owner's interest or equity in the business. Furthermore, it is advisable to keep separate accounts for each type of revenue and each kind of expense. The revenue and expense accounts are the temporary accounts that are used in recording increases and decreases in owner's equity from asset movements apart from changes caused by the owner's investments and withdrawals. The specific accounts to be kept for recording the increases and the decreases in owner's equity depend upon the nature and the sources of the revenue and the nature of the expenses incurred in earning the revenue.

A professional person or an individual engaged in operating a small enterprise may need to keep relatively few accounts. On the other hand, a large manufacturing enterprise, a public utility, or any large business may need to keep a great many accounts in order that the information required or desired may be available. Regardless of the number of accounts kept, they can be segregated into the three major classes and should be grouped according to these classes in the ledger. The usual custom is to place the asset accounts first, the liability accounts second, and the owner's equity accounts, including the revenue and the expense accounts, last. It is common practice to prepare a list of the accounts that are to be kept. This list, often in the form of an outline, is called a *chart of accounts*. It has become a general practice to give each account a number and to keep the accounts in numerical order. The numbering usually follows a consistent pattern and becomes a *code*. For example, asset accounts may be assigned numbers that always start with "1," liability accounts with "2," owner's equity accounts with "3," revenue accounts with "4," and expense accounts with "5."

To illustrate: Suppose that on December 1, 1977, L. A. Eason enters the employment agency business under the name of The Eason Employment Agency. He decides to keep his accounts on the calendar-year basis; therefore, his first accounting period will be for one month only, that is, the month of December. It is decided that a two-column journal and a ledger with the standard form of account will be used. Mr. Eason realizes that he will not need many accounts at present because the business is new. He also realizes that additional accounts may be added as the need arises. Following is a chart of the accounts to be kept at the start:

THE EASON EMPLOYMENT AGENCY

CHART OF ACCOUNTS

*Assets**
  111 Cash
  112 Office Supplies
  121 Office Equipment

Liabilities
  211 Accounts Payable

Owner's Equity
  311 L. A. Eason, Capital
  312 L. A. Eason, Drawing

Revenue
  411 Placement Fees

Expenses
  511 Rent Expense
  512 Salary Expense
  513 Traveling Expense
  514 Telephone Expense
  515 Office Supplies Expense
  516 Miscellaneous Expense

*Words in italics represent headings and not account titles.

Journalizing procedure illustrated

To illustrate journalizing procedure, the transactions completed by The Eason Employment Agency through December 31, 1977, will be journalized. A *narrative* of the transactions follows. It provides all of the information that is needed in journalizing the transactions. Some of the transactions are analyzed to explain their effect upon the accounts, with the journal entry immediately following the explanation of the entry. The journal of The Eason Employment Agency with all of the entries recorded is reproduced on pages 31 and 32.

THE EASON EMPLOYMENT AGENCY

NARRATIVE OF TRANSACTIONS

Thursday, December 1, 1977

Mr. Eason invested $3,000 cash in a business enterprise to be known as The Eason Employment Agency.

> As a result of this transaction, the business acquired the asset cash in the amount of $3,000. Since neither a decrease in any other asset nor an increase in any liability was involved, the transaction caused an increase of $3,000 in owner's equity. Accordingly, the entry to record the transaction is a debit to Cash and a credit to L. A. Eason, Capital, for $3,000.

JOURNAL   PAGE 1

	DATE	DESCRIPTION	POST. REF.	DEBIT	CREDIT	
1	1977 Dec. 1	Cash		300000		1
2		L. A. Eason, Capital			300000	2
3		Original investment				3
4		in employment agency.				4

Note that the following steps were involved:

(a) Since this was the first entry on the journal page, the year was written at the top of the Date column.

(b) The month and day were written on the first line in the Date column.

(c) The title of the account to be debited, Cash, was written on the first line at the extreme left of the Description column. The amount of the debit, $3,000, was written on the same line in the Debit column.

(d) The title of the account to be credited, L. A. Eason, Capital, was written on the second line indented one-half inch from the left side of the Description column. The amount of the credit, $3,000, was written on the same line in the Credit column.

(e) The explanation of the entry was started on the next line indented an additional one-half inch. The second line of the explanation was also indented the same distance as the first.

Friday, December 2

Paid office rent for December, $350.

> This transaction resulted in a decrease in owner's equity because of expense, with a corresponding decrease in the asset cash. The transaction is recorded by debiting Rent Expense and by crediting Cash for $350.

5	2	Rent Expense		35000		5
6		Cash			35000	6
7			Paid December rent.			7

> Note: Mr. Eason ordered several pieces of office equipment. Since the dealer did not have in stock what Mr. Eason wanted, the articles were ordered from the factory. Delivery is not expected until the latter part of the month. Pending arrival of the equipment, the dealer loaned Mr. Eason some used office equipment. No entry is required until the new equipment is received.

Monday, December 5

Purchased office supplies from the Adams Supply Co. on account, $261.41.

> In this transaction the business acquired a new asset which represented an increase in the total assets. A liability was also incurred because of the purchase on account. The transaction is recorded by debiting Office Supplies and by crediting Accounts Payable for $261.41. As these supplies are consumed, the amount will become an expense of the business.

8	5	Office Supplies		26141		8
9		Accounts Payable			26141	9
10		Adams Supply Co.				10

Tuesday, December 6

Paid the Consolidated Telephone Co. $32.50 covering the cost of installing a telephone in the office, together with the first month's service charges payable in advance.

> This transaction caused a decrease in owner's equity because of expense and a corresponding decrease in the asset cash. The transaction is recorded by debiting Telephone Expense and by crediting Cash for $32.50.

11	6	Telephone Expense		3250		11
12		Cash			3250	12
13			Paid telephone bill.			13

Wednesday, December 7

Paid $8 for a subscription to a trade journal.

> This transaction resulted in a decrease in owner's equity due to expense and a corresponding decrease in the asset cash. The transaction is recorded by debiting Miscellaneous Expense and by crediting Cash for $8.

14		7 Miscellaneous Expense		800		14
15		Cash			800	15
16		Trade journal sub.				16

Thursday, December 8

Received $200 from James Paynter for placement services rendered.

This transaction resulted in an increase in the asset cash with a corresponding increase in owner's equity because of revenue from placement fees. The transaction is recorded by debiting Cash and by crediting Placement Fees for $200. In keeping his accounts, Mr. Eason follows the practice of not recording revenue until it is received in cash. This practice is common to professional and personal service enterprises.

17		8 Cash		200 00		17
18		Placement Fees			200 00	18
19		James Paynter.				19

Friday, December 9

Paid the World Travel Service $145.30 for an airplane ticket to be used the next week for an employment agency convention trip.

20		9 Traveling Expense		145 30		20
21		Cash			145 30	21
22		Airplane fare, convention.				22

Friday, December 16

Paid Carol Hogan $225 covering her salary for the first half of the month.

Miss Hogan is employed by Mr. Eason as his secretary and bookkeeper at a salary of $450 a month. The transaction resulted in a decrease in owner's equity because of salary expense with a corresponding decrease in the asset cash. The transaction is recorded by debiting Salary Expense and by crediting Cash for $225. (The matter of payroll taxes is purposely ignored at this point. These taxes will be discussed in detail in Chapter 4.)

23		16 Salary Expense		225 00		23
24		Cash			225 00	24
25		Paid secretary's salary.				25

Note: The Posting Reference column has been left blank in the eight preceding journal entry illustrations. This is because the column is not used until the amounts are posted to the accounts in the ledger, a process to be described starting on page 33. Account numbers are shown in the Posting Reference column of the journal illustrated on pages 31 and 32, since the illustration shows how the journal appears *after* the posting has been completed.

The journal entries for the following transactions (as well as for those to this point) are illustrated on pages 31 and 32.

Monday, December 19

Received $500 from Timothy Willis for placement services rendered.

Wednesday, December 21

Mr. Eason withdrew $600 for personal use.

Amounts of cash withdrawn for personal use by the owner of a business enterprise represent a decrease in owner's equity. Although amounts withdrawn might be recorded as debits to the owner's capital account, it is better practice to record withdrawals in a separate account. Doing it in this way makes it a little easier to summarize the decreases in owner's equity caused by the owner's withdrawals. This transaction is recorded in the journal by debiting L. A. Eason, Drawing, and by crediting Cash for $600.

Friday, December 23

Received $650 from Susan Taylor for services rendered.

Tuesday, December 27

Paid $50 membership dues in the American Association of Employment Agencies.

Wednesday, December 28

Received the office equipment ordered December 2. These items were purchased on account from the Walker Office Equipment Co. Cost: $2,948.17. The dealer removed the used equipment that had been loaned to Mr. Eason.

Thursday, December 29

Paid the Adams Supply Co. $261.41 for the office supplies purchased on December 5.

This transaction caused a decrease in the liability accounts payable with a corresponding decrease in the asset cash. The transaction was recorded by debiting Accounts Payable and by crediting Cash for $261.41.

Received $500 from Bradford Davis for placement services rendered.

Friday, December 30

Paid Carol Hogan $225 covering her salary for the second half of the month. (Paid this day since it is the last working day of the month.)

Office supplies used during the month, $45.

By referring to the transaction of December 5 it will be noted that office supplies amounting to $261.41 were purchased and were recorded as an asset. By taking an inventory, counting the supplies in stock at the end of the month, Mr. Eason was able to determine that the cost of supplies used during the month amounted to $45. The expenses for the month of December would not be reflected properly in the accounts if the supplies used during the month were not taken into consideration. Therefore, the cost of supplies used was recorded by debiting the expense account, Office Supplies Expense, and by crediting the asset account, Office Supplies, for $45.

JOURNAL   PAGE *1*

	DATE	DESCRIPTION	POST. REF.	DEBIT	CREDIT	
1	*1977* Dec. 1	Cash	111	3000 00		1
2		L. A. Eason, Capital	311		3000 00	2
3		Original investment				3
4		in employment agency.				4
5	2	Rent Expense	511	350 00		5
6		Cash	111		350 00	6
7		Paid December rent.				7
8	5	Office Supplies	112	261 41		8
9		Accounts Payable	211		261 41	9
10		Adams Supply Co.				10
11	6	Telephone Expense	514	32 50		11
12		Cash	111		32 50	12
13		Paid telephone bill.				13
14	7	Miscellaneous Expense	516	8 00		14
15		Cash	111		8 00	15
16		Trade journal sub.				16
17	8	Cash	111	200 00		17
18		Placement Fees	411		200 00	18
19		James Paynter.				19
20	9	Traveling Expense	513	145 30		20
21		Cash	111		145 30	21
22		Airplane fare-convention.				22
23	16	Salary Expense	512	225 00		23
24		Cash	111		225 00	24
25		Paid secretary's salary.				25
26	19	Cash	111	500 00		26
27		Placement Fees	411		500 00	27
28		Timothy Willis.				28
29	21	L. A. Eason, Drawing	312	600 00		29
30		Cash	111		600 00	30
31		Withdrawn for personal use.				31
32	23	Cash	111	650 00		32
33		Placement Fees	411		650 00	33
34		Susan Taylor.				34
35	27	Miscellaneous Expense	516	50 00		35
36		Cash	111		50 00	36
37		A. A. E. A. dues.				37
38	28	Office Equipment	121	2948 17		38
39		Accounts Payable	211		2948 17	39
40		Walker Office Equip. Co.				40
41				8970 38	8970 38	41

The Eason Employment Agency Journal

(*continued on next page*)

JOURNAL   PAGE 2

	DATE	DESCRIPTION	POST. REF.	DEBIT	CREDIT	
1	1977 Dec. 29	Accounts Payable	211	26141		1
2		Cash	111		26141	2
3		Adams Supply Co.				3
4	29	Cash	111	50000		4
5		Placement Fees	411		50000	5
6		Bradford Davis				6
7	30	Salary Expense	512	22500		7
8		Cash	111		22500	8
9		Paid secretary's salary.				9
10	30	Office Supplies Expense	515	4500		10
11		Office Supplies	112		4500	11
12		Cost of supplies used				12
13		during December.				13
14				1 03141	1 03141	14
15						15
16						16
17						17
18						18
19						19

The Eason Employment Agency Journal (*concluded*)

Note: Some bookkeepers leave a blank line after the explanation of each entry.
This practice is acceptable though not recommended.

Proving the journal

Because a double entry is made for each transaction, the equality of debit and credit entries on each page of the journal may be proved merely by totaling the amount columns. The total of each column is usually entered as a footing immediately under the last entry. When a page of the journal is filled, the footings may be entered just under the last single horizontal ruled line at the bottom of the page as shown in the illustration on page 31. When the page is not filled, the footings should be entered immediately under the last entry as shown in the illustration above.

Report No. 2-1

Refer to the study assignments and complete Report No. 2-1. To complete this assignment correctly, the principles developed in the preceding discussion must be understood. Review the text assignment if necessary. After completing the report, continue with the following textbook discussion until the next report is required.

POSTING TO THE LEDGER; THE
TRIAL BALANCE

The purpose of a journal is to provide a chronological record of financial transactions expressed as debits and credits to accounts. These accounts are kept to supply desired information. Collectively the accounts are described as the *general ledger* or, often, simply as "the ledger." (Frequently, so-called "subsidiary" ledgers are also used. These will be explained and illustrated in Chapter 8.) The account forms may be on sheets of paper or on cards. When on sheets of paper, the sheets may be bound in book form or they may be kept in a loose-leaf binder. Usually a separate page or card is used for each account. The accounts should be classified properly in the ledger; that is, the asset accounts should be grouped together, the liability accounts together, and the owner's equity accounts together. Proper grouping of the accounts in the ledger is an aid in preparing the various reports desired by the owner. Mr. Eason decided to keep all of the accounts for The Eason Employment Agency in a loose-leaf ledger. The numbers shown in the agency's chart of accounts on page 26 were used as a guide in arranging the accounts in the ledger. The ledger of The Eason Employment Agency is reproduced on pages 35–37. Note that the accounts are in numerical order.

Since Mr. Eason makes few purchases on account, he does not keep a separate account for each creditor. When invoices are received for items purchased on account, the invoices are checked and recorded in the journal by debiting the proper accounts and by crediting Accounts Payable. The credit balance of Accounts Payable indicates the total amount owed to creditors. After each invoice is recorded, it is filed in an unpaid invoice file, where it remains until it is paid in full. When an invoice is paid in full, it is removed from the unpaid invoice file and is then filed under the name of the creditor for future reference. The balance of the accounts payable account may be proved at any time by determining the total of the unpaid amounts of the invoices.

Posting

The process of transcribing (often called "entering") information in the ledger from the journal is known as *posting*. All amounts entered in the journal should be posted to the accounts kept in the ledger in order to summarize the results. Such posting may be done daily or at frequent intervals. The ledger is not a reliable source of information until all of the transactions recorded in the journal have been posted.

Since the accounts provide the information needed in preparing financial statements, a posting procedure that insures accuracy in maintaining the accounts must necessarily be followed. Posting from the journal to the ledger involves recording the following information in the accounts:

(a) The date of each transaction.

(b) The amount of each transaction.

(c) The page of the journal from which each transaction is posted.

As each amount in the journal is posted to the proper account in the ledger, the number of that account should be entered in the Posting Reference column in the journal so as to provide a cross-reference between the journal and the ledger. The first entry to be posted from the journal (a segment of which is reproduced below) required a debit to Cash of $3,000. This was accomplished by entering the year, "1977," the month, abbreviated "Dec.," and the day, "1," in the Date column of the cash account (reproduced below); the number "1" in the Posting Reference column (since the posting came from Page 1 of the journal); and the amount, "$3,000.00" in the Debit column. Inasmuch as the number of the cash account is 111, that number was entered in the Posting Reference column of the journal on the same line as the debit of $3,000.00 that was just posted to Cash. The same pattern was followed in posting the credit part of the entry — $3,000 to L. A. Eason, Capital, Account No. 311 (reproduced below).

JOURNAL — PAGE 1

	DATE		DESCRIPTION	POST. REF.	DEBIT	CREDIT	
1	1977 Dec.	1	Cash	111	3000 00		1
2			L. A. Eason, Capital	311		3000 00	2
3			Original investment				3
4			in employment agency.				4

ACCOUNT Cash   ACCOUNT NO. 111

DATE	ITEM	POST. REF.	DEBIT	DATE	ITEM	POST. REF.	CREDIT
1977 Dec. 1		1	3000 00				

ACCOUNT L. A. Eason, Capital   ACCOUNT NO. 311

DATE	ITEM	POST. REF.	DEBIT	DATE	ITEM	POST. REF.	CREDIT
				1977 Dec. 1		1	3000 00

Reference to the journal of The Eason Employment Agency (reproduced on pages 31 and 32) and its ledger (reproduced below and on pages 36 and 37) will indicate that a similar procedure was followed in posting every amount from the journal. Note also that in the ledger, the year "1977" was entered only at the top of each Date column, and that the month "Dec." was entered only with the first posting to an account.

ACCOUNT *Cash*   ACCOUNT NO. *111*

DATE	ITEM	POST. REF.	DEBIT	DATE	ITEM	POST. REF.	CREDIT
1977 Dec. 1		1	3 000 00	1977 Dec. 2		1	350 00
8		1	200 00	6		1	32 50
19		1	500 00	7		1	8 00
23		1	650 00	9		1	145 30
29	2,952.79	2	500 00 / 4 850 00	16		1	225 00
				21		1	600 00
				27		1	50 00
				29		2	261 41
				30		2	225 00 / 1 897 21

ACCOUNT *Office Supplies*   ACCOUNT NO. *112*

DATE	ITEM	POST. REF.	DEBIT	DATE	ITEM	POST. REF.	CREDIT
1977 Dec. 5	216.41	1	261 41	1977 Dec. 30		2	45 00

ACCOUNT *Office Equipment*   ACCOUNT NO. *121*

DATE	ITEM	POST. REF.	DEBIT	DATE	ITEM	POST. REF.	CREDIT
1977 Dec. 28		1	2 948 17				

ACCOUNT *Accounts Payable*   ACCOUNT NO. *211*

DATE	ITEM	POST. REF.	DEBIT	DATE	ITEM	POST. REF.	CREDIT
1977 Dec. 29		2	261 41	1977 Dec. 5		1	261 41
				28	2,948.17	1	2 948 17 / 3 209 58

The Eason Employment Agency Ledger
(*continued on next page*)

ACCOUNT *L. A. Eason, Capital*   ACCOUNT NO. *311*

DATE	ITEM	POST. REF.	DEBIT	DATE	ITEM	POST. REF.	CREDIT
				1977 Dec. 1		1	3000 00

ACCOUNT *L. A. Eason, Drawing*   ACCOUNT NO. *312*

DATE	ITEM	POST. REF.	DEBIT	DATE	ITEM	POST. REF.	CREDIT
1977 Dec. 21		1	600 00				

ACCOUNT *Placement Fees*   ACCOUNT NO. *411*

DATE	ITEM	POST. REF.	DEBIT	DATE	ITEM	POST. REF.	CREDIT
				1977 Dec. 8		1	200 00
				19		1	500 00
				23		1	650 00
				29		2	500 00
							1850 00

ACCOUNT *Rent Expense*   ACCOUNT NO. *511*

DATE	ITEM	POST. REF.	DEBIT	DATE	ITEM	POST. REF.	CREDIT
1977 Dec. 2		1	350 00				

ACCOUNT *Salary Expense*   ACCOUNT NO. *512*

DATE	ITEM	POST. REF.	DEBIT	DATE	ITEM	POST. REF.	CREDIT
1977 Dec. 16		1	225 00				
30		2	225 00				
			450 00				

ACCOUNT *Traveling Expense*   ACCOUNT NO. *513*

DATE	ITEM	POST. REF.	DEBIT	DATE	ITEM	POST. REF.	CREDIT
1977 Dec. 9		1	145 30				

The Eason Employment Agency Ledger (*continued*)

ACCOUNT *Telephone Expense*   ACCOUNT NO. *514*

DATE	ITEM	POST. REF.	DEBIT	DATE	ITEM	POST. REF.	CREDIT
1977 Dec. 6		1	32 50				

ACCOUNT *Office Supplies Expense*   ACCOUNT NO. *515*

DATE	ITEM	POST. REF.	DEBIT	DATE	ITEM	POST. REF.	CREDIT
1977 Dec. 30		2	45 00				

ACCOUNT *Miscellaneous Expense*   ACCOUNT NO. *516*

DATE	ITEM	POST. REF.	DEBIT	DATE	ITEM	POST. REF.	CREDIT
1977 Dec. 7		1	8 00				
27		1	50 00				
			58 00				

The Eason Employment Agency Ledger (*concluded*)

It will be seen from the preceding discussion that there are four steps involved in posting — three involving information to be recorded in the ledger and one involving information to be recorded in the journal. The date, the amount, and the effect of each transaction are first recorded in the journal. The same information is later posted to the ledger. Posting does not involve an analysis of each transaction to determine its effect upon the accounts. Such an analysis is made at the time of recording the transaction in the journal, and posting is merely transcribing the same information in the ledger. In posting, care should be used to record each debit and each credit entry in the proper columns so that the entries will reflect correctly the effects of the transactions on the accounts.

When the posting is completed, the same information is provided in both the journal and the ledger as to the date, the amount, and the effect of each transaction. A cross-reference from each book to the other book is also provided. This cross-reference makes it possible to trace the entry of December 1 on the debit side of the cash account in the ledger to the journal by referring to the page indicated in the Posting Reference column. The entry of December 1 on the credit side of the account for L. A. Eason, Capital, may also be traced to the journal by referring to the page indicated in the Posting Reference column. Each entry in the journal may be traced to the ledger by referring to the account numbers indicated in the Posting

Reference column of the journal. By referring to pages 31 and 32, it will be seen that the account numbers were inserted in the Posting Reference column. This was done as the posting was completed.

The trial balance

The purpose of a trial balance is to prove that the totals of the debit and credit balances in the ledger are equal. In double-entry bookkeeping, equality of debit and credit balances in the ledger must be maintained. A trial balance may be taken daily, weekly, monthly, or whenever desired. Before taking a trial balance, all transactions previously completed should be journalized and the posting should be completed in order that the effect of all transactions will be reflected in the ledger accounts.

Footing Accounts. When an account form similar to the one illustrated on page 36 is used, it is necessary to foot or add the amounts recorded in each account preparatory to taking a trial balance. The footings should be recorded immediately below the last item in both the debit and credit amount columns of the account. The footings should be written in small figures close to the preceding line so that they will not interfere with the recording of an item on the next ruled line. At the same time, the balance, the difference between the footings, should be computed and recorded in small figures in the Item column of the account on the side with the larger footing. In other words, if an account has a debit balance, the balance should be written in the Item column on the debit or left side of the account. If the account has a credit balance, the balance should be written in the Item column on the credit or right side of the account. The balance or difference between the footings should be recorded in the Item column just below the line on which the last regular entry appears and in line with the footing.

Reference to the accounts kept in the ledger shown on pages 35–37 will reveal that the accounts have been footed and will show how the footings and the balances are recorded. When only one item has been posted to an account, regardless of whether it is a debit or a credit amount, no footing is necessary.

Care should be used in computing the balances of the accounts. If an error is made in adding the columns or in determining the difference between the footings, the error will be carried to the trial balance; and considerable time may be required to locate the mistake. Most accounting errors result from carelessness. For example, a careless bookkeeper may write an account balance on the wrong side of an account or may enter figures so illegibly that they may be misread later. Neatness in writing the amounts is just as important as accuracy in determining the footings and the balances.

Preparing the Trial Balance. It is important that the following procedure be followed in preparing a trial balance:

(a) Head the trial balance, being certain to show the name of the individual, firm, or organization, the title, "Trial Balance," and the date. (The date shown is the day of the last transaction that is included in the accounts — usually the last day of a month. Actually, the trial balance might be prepared on January 3, but if the accounts reflected only transactions through December 31, this is the date that should be used.)

(b) List the account titles in order, showing each account number.

(c) Record the account balances in parallel columns, entering debit balances in the left amount column and credit balances in the right amount column.

(d) Add the columns and record the totals, ruling a single line across the amount columns above the totals and a double line below the totals in the manner shown in the illustration below.

A trial balance is usually prepared on ruled paper (though it can be written on plain paper if desired). An illustration of the trial balance, as of December 31, 1977, of the ledger of The Eason Employment Agency is shown below.

Even though the trial balance indicates that the ledger is in balance, there still may be errors in the ledger. For example, if a journal entry has been made in which the wrong accounts were debited or credited, or if an

The Eason Employment Agency
Trial Balance
December 31, 1977

Account	Acct. No.	Dr. Balance	Cr. Balance
Cash	111	2952 79	
Office Supplies	112	216 41	
Office Equipment	121	2948 17	
Accounts Payable	211		2948 17
L. A. Eason, Capital	311		3000 00
L. A. Eason, Drawing	312	600 00	
Placement Fees	411		1850 00
Rent Expense	511	350 00	
Salary Expense	512	450 00	
Traveling Expense	513	145 30	
Telephone Expense	514	32 50	
Office Supplies Expense	515	45 00	
Miscellaneous Expense	516	58 00	
		7798 17	7798 17

Model Trial Balance

item has been posted to the wrong account, the ledger will still be in balance. It is important, therefore, that extreme care be used in preparing the journal entries and in posting them to the ledger accounts.

Report **No. 2-2**	Refer to the study assignments and complete Report No. 2-2. To complete this assignment correctly, the principles developed in the preceding discussion must be understood. Review the text assignment if necessary. After completing the report, continue with the following textbook discussion until the next report is required.

THE FINANCIAL STATEMENTS

The transactions completed by The Eason Employment Agency during the month of December were recorded in a two-column journal (see pages 31 and 32). The debits and credits were subsequently posted to the proper accounts in a ledger (see pages 35–37). At the end of the month a trial balance was taken as a means of proving that the equality of debits and credits had been maintained throughout the journalizing and posting procedures (see page 39).

Although a trial balance may provide much of the information that the owner of a business may desire, it is primarily a device used by the bookkeeper for the purpose of proving the equality of the debit and credit account balances. Although the trial balance of The Eason Employment Agency taken as of December 31 contains a list of all of the accounts and shows the amounts of their debit and credit balances, it does not clearly present all of the information that Mr. Eason may need or desire regarding either the results of operations during the month or the status of his business at the end of the month. To meet these needs it is customary to prepare two types of *financial statements*. One is known as an income statement and the other as a balance sheet or statement of financial position.

The income statement

The purpose of an *income statement* is to provide information regarding the results of operations *during a specified period of time*. It is an itemized statement of the changes in owner's equity resulting from the revenue and expenses of a specific period (month, quarter, year). Such changes are recorded in temporary owner's equity accounts known as revenue and expense accounts. Changes in owner's equity resulting from investments or withdrawals of assets by the owner are not included in the income statement because they involve neither revenue nor expense.

A model income statement for The Eason Employment Agency showing the results of operations for the month ended December 31, 1977, is reproduced below. The heading of an income statement consists of the following:

(a) The name of the business
(b) The title of the statement — Income Statement
(c) The period of time covered by the statement

The Eason Employment Agency
Income Statement
For the Month Ended December 31, 1977

Revenue:		
Placement fees		$185000
Expenses:		
Rent expense	$ 35000	
Salary expense	45000	
Traveling expense	14530	
Telephone expense	3250	
Office supplies expense	4500	
Miscellaneous expense	5800	
Total expenses		108080
Net income		$ 76920

Model Income Statement

The body of an income statement consists of **(1)** an itemized list of the sources and amounts of revenue received during the period and **(2)** an itemized list of the various expenses incurred during the period. It is said that the "heart" of income measurement is the process of *matching* on a *periodic basis* the revenue and expenses of a business. The income statement carries out this matching concept.

The financial statements usually are prepared first on ruled paper. Such handwritten copies may then be typed so that a number of copies will be available for those who are interested in examining the statements. Since the typewritten copies are not on ruled paper, dollar signs are included in the handwritten copy so that the typist will understand just where they are to be inserted. Note that a dollar sign is placed beside the first amount in each column and the first amount below a ruling in each column. The income statement illustrated on page 41 is shown on two-column ruled paper; however, the columns do not have any debit-credit significance.

In the case of The Eason Employment Agency, the only source of revenue was placement fees that amounted to $1,850. The total expenses for the month amounted to $1,080.80. The revenue exceeded the expenses by $769.20. This represents the amount of the net income for the month. If the total expenses had exceeded the total revenue, the excess would have represented a net loss for the month.

The trial balance supplied the information needed in preparing the income statement. However, it can be seen readily that the income statement provides more information concerning the results of the month's operations than was supplied by the trial balance.

	The Eason	
	Balance	
	December	
Assets		
Cash	$2952 79	
Office supplies	216 41	
Office equipment	2948 17	
Total assets		$6117 37

Model Balance Sheet — Account Form (Left Page)

The balance sheet

The purpose of a *balance sheet* is to provide information regarding the status of the assets, liabilities, and owner's equity of a business enterprise *as of a specified date*. It is an itemized statement of the respective amounts of these basic accounting elements at the close of business on the date indicated in the heading.

A model balance sheet for The Eason Employment Agency showing the status of the business when it closed on December 31, 1977, is reproduced below and on page 42. The heading of a balance sheet contains the following:

(a) The name of the business.
(b) The title of the statement — Balance Sheet.
(c) The date of the statement (as of the close of business on that day).

The body of a balance sheet consists of an itemized list of the assets, the liabilities, and the owner's equity, the latter being the difference between the total amount of the assets and the total amount of the liabilities. The balance sheet illustrated is arranged in account form. Note the similarity of this form of balance sheet to the standard account form illustrated on page 12. The assets are listed on the left side and the liabilities and owner's equity are listed on the right side. The information provided by the balance sheet of The Eason Employment Agency may be summarized in equation form as follows:

ASSETS	=	LIABILITIES	+	OWNER'S EQUITY
$6,117.37		$2,948.17		$3,169.20

Model Balance Sheet — Account Form (Right Page)

The trial balance was the source of the information needed in listing the assets and liabilities in the balance sheet. The amount of the owner's equity may be calculated by subtracting the total liabilities from the total assets. Thus, Mr. Eason's equity as of December 31, 1977, is as follows:

Total assets..	$6,117.37
Less total liabilities...	2,948.17
Owner's equity..	$3,169.20

Proof of the amount of the owner's equity as calculated above may be determined by taking into consideration the following factors:

(a) The amount invested in the enterprise by Mr. Eason on December 1 as shown by his capital account.

(b) The amount of the net income of The Eason Employment Agency for December as shown by the income statement.

(c) The total amount withdrawn for personal use during December as shown by Mr. Eason's drawing account.

The trial balance on page 39 shows that Mr. Eason's equity in The Eason Employment Agency on December 1 amounted to $3,000. This is indicated by the credit balance of his capital account. The income statement on page 41 shows that the net income of The Eason Employment Agency for December amounted to $769.20. The trial balance shows that the amount withdrawn by Mr. Eason for personal use during the month amounted to $600. This is indicated by the debit balance of his drawing account. On the basis of this information, Mr. Eason's equity in The Eason Employment Agency as of December 31, 1977, is as follows:

Amount of capital December 1...................................		$3,000.00
Net income for December	$769.20	
Less amount withdrawn for personal use during the month...	600.00	169.20
Capital at close of business December 31.........................		$3,169.20

Report No. 2-3

Refer to the study assignments and complete Report No. 2-3. This assignment provides a test of your ability to apply the principles developed in Chapters 1 and 2 of this textbook. The textbook and the study assignments go hand in hand, each serving a definite purpose in the learning process. Inability to solve correctly any problem included in the report indicates that you have failed to master the principles developed in the textbook. After completing the report, you may proceed with Chapter 3 until the next report is required.

Chapter 3

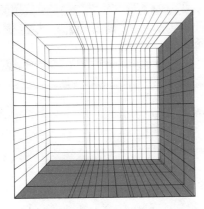

ACCOUNTING FOR CASH

In the preceding chapters the purpose and nature of business accounting, transaction analysis, and the mechanics of double-entry bookkeeping were introduced. Explanations and illustrations were given of **(1)** *journalizing* (recording transactions in a *general journal* — a "book of original entry"), **(2)** *posting* (transcribing the entries to the accounts that, all together, comprise the *general ledger*), **(3)** taking a *trial balance*, and **(4)** using the latter to prepare an *income statement* and a *balance sheet* (two basic and important *financial statements*). This chapter is devoted to a discussion of the handling of and accounting for cash receipts and disbursements, including various considerations that are involved when cash is kept in a commercial bank. (The use of bank "checking accounts" is a near-universal business practice.)

RECORDS OF CASH RECEIPTS AND DISBURSEMENTS; PETTY CASH

The term *cash* has several different, though not totally dissimilar, meanings. In a very narrow sense, cash means currency and coin. In a broader sense, cash includes checks, drafts, and money orders. All of these, as well as currency and coin, are sometimes called "cash items." Usually any reference to the *cash receipts* of a business relates to the receipt of checks, drafts, and money orders payable to the business, as well as to the receipt of currency and coin. The amount of the balance of the cash account, as well as the amount shown for cash in a balance sheet, normally includes cash and cash items on hand plus the amount on deposit in a bank checking account. In some cases the balance sheet figure for cash includes amounts on deposit in more than one bank. In accounting for cash, it is rather rare to make a distinction between "cash on hand" and "cash in bank," but sometimes this is done.

The cash account

This account is debited when cash is increased and credited when cash is decreased. This means that the cash account has a debit balance unless the business has no cash. In the latter case, the account will be *in balance* — meaning that the account has no balance since the total of the debits is equal to the total of the credits.

Cash Receipts. It is vital that an accurate and timely record be kept of cash receipts. When the volume of the receipts is large in both number and amount, a practice designed to reduce the danger of mistake and embezzlement may be followed. When there are numerous receipts of currency and coin from customers paying in person for goods or services just received, it is customary to use a cash register. Such a machine usually provides a listing of amounts recorded as the money is received. A cash register may have the capability of accumulating subtotals that permit classification of amounts — sales by departments, for example. When money comes in by mail (nearly always checks), it is usual for the one remitting to enclose a presupplied form showing name, address, and the amount on the enclosed check or money order. A good example is the top part of a monthly statement the customer has received. (An illustration of such a statement appears on page 194.) Sometimes a written receipt must be prepared. A carbon copy of the receipt provides the initial record of the cash received.

In any case, a record of each amount received should be prepared by someone other than the bookkeeper. The money received (including checks and money orders) is placed in the custody of whoever handles bank deposits and cash on hand. The bookkeeper gets the records to use in preparing proper journal entries for cash receipts. Under such a plan the bookkeeper does not actually handle any cash; instead he enters cash receipts from records prepared by other persons. The procedure of having transactions involving cash handled by two or more persons reduces the danger of fraud and is one of the important features of a system of internal control.

Cash Disbursements. Disbursements may be made in cash or by bank check. When a disbursement is made in cash, a receipt or a receipted voucher should be obtained as evidence of the payment. When a disbursement is made by bank check, it is not necessary to obtain a receipt since the canceled check that is returned by the bank serves as a receipt.

Recording Cash Receipts and Disbursements. In the preceding chapter, transactions involving the receipt and disbursement of cash were recorded in a two-column general journal along with other transactions. If the number of cash transactions is relatively small, the manner of recording that was illustrated is quite satisfactory. If, however, the number of such transactions is large, the repetition entailed in making numerous debit postings or credit postings to the cash account is time-consuming, tedious, and burdensome. A discussion of a journal with special columns is deferred until Chapter 5, and the use of *special journals* is discussed in Chapter 6.

Proving Cash. The process of determining whether the amount of cash (on hand and in the bank) is the amount that should be there according to the records is called *proving cash*. Cash should be proved at least once a week and, perhaps, more often if the volume of cash transactions is large. The first step is to determine from the records what amount of cash should be on hand. The cash balance should be calculated by adding the total of the receipts to the opening balance and subtracting the total of the payments. The result should be equal to the amount of cash on deposit in the bank plus the total of currency, coins, checks, and money orders on hand. Normally, an up-to-date record of cash in bank is maintained — often by using stubs in a checkbook for this purpose. There is space provided on the stubs to show deposits as well as the record of checks drawn, and the resulting balance after each deposit made or check drawn. (See check stubs illustrated on page 60.) The amount of cash and cash items on hand must be determined by actual count.

Cash Short and Over. If the effort to prove cash is not successful, it means that either **(1)** the records of receipts, disbursements, and cash on deposit contain one or more errors, **(2)** the count of cash and cash items was incorrect, or **(3)** a "shortage" or an "overage" exists. If a verification of the records and the cash count does not uncover any error, it is evident that due to some mistake in handling cash, either not enough or too much cash is on hand.

Finding that cash is slightly short or over is not unusual. If there are numerous cash transactions, it is difficult to avoid occasional errors in making change. (There is always the danger of shortages due to dishonesty, but most discrepancies are the result of mistakes.) Many businesses have a ledger account entitled *Cash Short and Over*. If, in the effort to prove cash, it is found that a shortage exists, its amount is treated as a cash disbursement transaction involving a debit to Cash Short and Over. Any overage discovered is regarded as a cash receipt transaction involving a credit to Cash Short and Over. By the end of the fiscal year it is likely that the cash short and over account will have both debits and credits. If the total of the debits exceeds the total of the credits, the balance represents an expense or loss; if the reverse is the case, the balance represents revenue.

The petty cash fund

A good policy for a business enterprise to adopt is one which requires that all cash and cash items which it receives shall be deposited in a bank. When this is done, its total cash receipts will equal its total deposits in the bank. It is also a good policy to make arrangements with the bank so that all checks and other cash items received by the business from customers or others in the usual course of business will be accepted by the bank for deposit only. This will cause the records of cash receipts and disbursements of the business to agree exactly with the bank's record of deposits and withdrawals.

When all cash and cash items received are deposited in a bank, an office fund or *petty cash fund* may be established for paying small items. ("Petty" means small or little.) Such a fund eliminates the necessity of writing checks for small amounts.

Operating a Petty Cash Fund. To establish a petty cash fund, a check should be drawn for the amount that is to be set aside in the fund. The amount may be $25, $50, $100, or any amount considered necessary. The check may be made payable to "Cash," "Petty Cash," "Office Fund," or to the person who will have custody of the fund. When the check is cashed by the bank, the money is placed in a cash drawer, a cash register, or a safe at the depositor's place of business; and a designated individual in the office is authorized to make payments from the fund. The one who is responsible for the fund should be able to account for the full amount of the fund at any time. Disbursements from the fund should not be made without obtaining a voucher or a receipt. A form of petty cash voucher is shown on page 49. Such a voucher should be used for each expenditure unless a receipt or receipted invoice is obtained.

The check drawn to establish the petty cash fund may be recorded in the journal by debiting Petty Cash Fund and by crediting Cash. When it is necessary to replenish the fund, the petty cashier usually prepares a statement of the expenditures, properly classified. A check is then drawn for the exact amount of the total expenditures. This check is recorded in the

```
┌──────────────────────────────────────────────────────────────┐
│              PETTY  CASH  VOUCHER                              │
│                                                                │
│   No. ___4___          Date December 12, 1977                 │
│                                                                │
│   Paid To J. L. Porter                         Amount         │
│                                            ┌──────────────┐    │
│   For Red Cross                            │   10  00     │    │
│                                            └──────────────┘    │
│   Charge To Donations Expense                                 │
│                                                                │
│   Payment Received:                                           │
│                                                                │
│   J. L. Porter          Approved By Arthur Cobb               │
└──────────────────────────────────────────────────────────────┘
```

Petty Cash Voucher

journal by debiting the proper accounts indicated in the statement and by crediting Cash.

The petty cash fund is a revolving fund that does not change in amount unless the fund is increased or decreased. The actual amount of cash in the fund plus the total of the petty cash vouchers or receipts should always be equal to the amount originally charged to the petty cash fund.

This method of handling a petty cash fund is sometimes referred to as the *imprest method*. It is the method most commonly used.

Petty Cash Disbursements Record. When a petty cash fund is maintained, it is good practice to keep a formal record of all disbursements from the fund. Various types of records have been designed for this purpose. One of the standard forms is illustrated on pages 50 and 51. The headings of the Distribution columns may vary with each enterprise, depending upon the desired classification of the expenditures. It should be remembered that the headings represent accounts that eventually are to be charged for the expenditures. The desired headings may either be printed on the form or they may be written in. Often the account numbers instead of account titles are used in the headings to indicate the accounts to be charged.

The petty cashier should have a document for each disbursement made from the petty cash fund. Unless a receipt or receipted invoice is obtained, the petty cashier should prepare a voucher. The vouchers should be numbered consecutively.

A model petty cash disbursements record is reproduced on pages 50 and 51. It is a part of the records of Arthur Cobb, an attorney. Since Mr. Cobb is out of the office much of the time, he considers it advisable to provide a petty cash fund from which his secretary is authorized to make petty cash disbursements not to exceed $20 each. A narrative of the petty cash transactions completed by Dorothy Melvin, Mr. Cobb's secretary, during the month of December follows on page 50.

ARTHUR COBB

NARRATIVE OF PETTY CASH TRANSACTIONS

Dec. 1. Issued check for $100 payable to Dorothy Melvin. She cashed the check, and placed the proceeds in a petty cash fund.

> This transaction was recorded in the journal by debiting Petty Cash Fund and by crediting Cash. A memorandum entry was also made in the Description column of the petty cash disbursements record reproduced below and on page 51.

During the month of December the following disbursements were made from the petty cash fund:

6. Gave Mr. Cobb $14.60 to reimburse him for the amount spent in having his automobile serviced. Petty Cash Voucher No. 1.
7. Gave Mr. Cobb $10 to reimburse him for the amount spent in entertaining a client at lunch. Petty Cash Voucher No. 2.
12. Gave Mr. Cobb $20 for personal use. Petty Cash Voucher No. 3.

> This item was entered in the Amount column provided at the extreme right of the petty cash disbursements record since no special distribution column had been provided for recording amounts withdrawn by the owner for personal use.

12. Gave the Red Cross a $10 donation. Petty Cash Voucher No. 4.
15. Paid $7.50 for typewriter repairs. Petty Cash Voucher No. 5.

PAGE 1   **PETTY CASH DISBURSEMENTS**

DAY	DESCRIPTION	VOU. NO.	TOTAL AMOUNT	Tel. Exp.	Auto. Exp.
	AMOUNTS FORWARDED				
1	Received in fund	100.00 ✓			
6	Automobile repairs	1	14 60		14 60
7	Client luncheon	2	10 00		
12	Arthur Cobb, personal use	3	20 00		
12	Red Cross	4	10 00		
15	Typewriter repairs	5	7 50		
19	Traveling expense	6	7 80		
20	Washing automobile	7	1 75		1 75
22	Postage expense	8	1 25		
23	Salvation Army	9	5 00		
26	Postage stamps	10	10 00		
27	Long distance call	11	3 20	3 20	
			91 10	3 20	16 35
			91 10	3 20	16 35
30	Balance	8.90			
30	Received in fund	91.10			
	Total	100.00			

Arthur Cobb's Petty Cash Disbursements Record (Left Page)

19. Gave Mr. Cobb $7.80 to reimburse him for traveling expenses. Petty Cash Voucher No. 6.
20. Gave Mr. Cobb $1.75 to reimburse him for the amount spent in having his automobile washed. Petty Cash Voucher No. 7.
22. Paid $1.25 for mailing a package. Petty Cash Voucher No. 8.
23. Donated $5 to the Salvation Army. Petty Cash Voucher No. 9.
26. Paid $10 for postage stamps. Petty Cash Voucher No. 10.
27. Gave Mr. Cobb $3.20 to reimburse him for a long distance telephone call made from a booth. Petty Cash Voucher No. 11.
30. Issued check for $91.10 payable to Dorothy Melvin to replenish the petty cash fund.

This transaction was recorded in the journal by debiting the proper accounts and by crediting Cash for the total amount of the expenditures.

Proving the Petty Cash Disbursements Record.   To prove the petty cash disbursements record, it is first necessary to foot all of the amount columns. The sum of the footings of the Distribution columns should equal the footing of the Total Amount column. After proving the footings, the totals should be recorded and the record should be ruled as shown in the illustration. The illustration shows that a total of $91.10 was paid out during December. Since it was desired to replenish the petty cash

FOR MONTH OF *December* 19 77   PAGE *1*

	Post. Exp.	Don. Exp.	Travel Exp.	Misc. Exp.		ACCOUNT	AMOUNT	
1								1
2								2
3								3
4				10 00				4
5						Arthur Cobb, Drawing	20 00	5
6		10 00						6
7				7 50				7
8			7 80					8
9								9
10	1 25							10
11		5 00						11
12	10 00							12
13								13
14	11 25 / 11 25	15 00 / 15 00	7 80 / 7 80	17 50 / 17 50			20 00 / 20 00	14
15								15
16								16
17								17
18								18

Arthur Cobb's Petty Cash Disbursements Record (Right Page)

fund at this time, the following statement of the disbursements for December was prepared:

STATEMENT OF PETTY CASH DISBURSEMENTS FOR DECEMBER

Telephone Expense..	$ 3.20
Automobile Expense..	16.35
Postage Expense..	11.25
Donations Expense...	15.00
Traveling Expense..	7.80
Miscellaneous Expense.......................................	17.50
Arthur Cobb, Drawing..	20.00
Total disbursements.......................................	$91.10

The statement of petty cash disbursements provides the information for the issuance of a check for $91.10 to replenish the petty cash fund. After footing and ruling the petty cash disbursements record, the balance in the fund and the amount received to replenish the fund may be recorded in the Description column below the ruling as shown in the illustration. It is customary to carry the balance forward to the top of a new page before recording any of the transactions for the following month.

The petty cash disbursements record reproduced on pages 50 and 51 is an *auxiliary record* that supplements the regular accounting records. No posting is done from this auxiliary record. The total amount of the expenditures from the petty cash fund is entered in the journal at the time of replenishing the fund by debiting the proper accounts and by crediting Cash. A *compound entry* (one that affects more than two accounts, though the sum of the debits is equal to the sum of the credits) is usually required. The statement of petty cash disbursements provides the information needed in recording the check issued to Dorothy Melvin to replenish the petty cash fund. The entry is posted from the journal.

JOURNAL   PAGE 15

	DATE	DESCRIPTION	POST. REF.	DEBIT	CREDIT	
1	1977 Dec. 30	Telephone Expense		3 20		1
2		Automobile Expense		16 35		2
3		Postage Expense		11 25		3
4		Donations Expense		15 00		4
5		Traveling Expense		7 80		5
6		Miscellaneous Expense		17 50		6
7		Arthur Cobb, Drawing		20 00		7
8		Cash			91 10	8
9		Reimbursement of				9
10		petty cash fund.				10
11						11

The method of recording the check issued by Arthur Cobb on December 30 to replenish the fund is illustrated on the bottom of page 52.

Report No. 3-1 | Refer to the study assignments and complete Report No. 3-1. After completing the report, proceed with the textbook discussion until the next report is required.

BANKING PROCEDURE

A bank is a financial institution that receives deposits, lends money, makes collections, and renders other services, such as providing vaults for the safekeeping of valuables and handling trust funds for its customers. Most banks offer facilities for both checking accounts and savings accounts.

Checking account

It is estimated that 90–95 percent of all money payments in the United States are made by checks. A *check*, a piece of commercial paper, is drawn on a bank and payable on demand. It involves three original parties: **(1)** the *drawer*, the depositor who orders the bank to pay; **(2)** the *drawee*, the bank in which the drawer has money on deposit in a so-called "commercial" account; and **(3)** the *payee*, the person directed to receive the money. The drawer and payee may be the same person, though the payee named in such case usually is "Cash."

A check is *negotiable* (meaning that the right to receive the money can be transferred to someone else) because it complies with the following requirements; it is in writing, is signed by the drawer, contains an unconditional order to pay a specified amount of money, is payable on demand, and is payable to order or bearer. The payee transfers his right to receive the money by *indorsing* the check. If the payee simply signs his name on the back of the check (customarily near the left end), it is called a *blank* indorsement. (This makes the check payable to bearer.) If, as is very common, there are added such words as "For deposit," "Pay to any bank or banker," or "Pay to J. Doe only," it is called a *restrictive* indorsement. A widely used business practice when indorsing checks for deposit is to use a rubber stamp similar to that illustrated on page 55.

Important factors in connection with a checking account are **(1)** opening the account, **(2)** making deposits, **(3)** making withdrawals, and **(4)** reconciling the bank statement.

Opening a Checking Account. To open a checking account with a bank, it is necessary to obtain the approval of an official of the bank and to make an initial deposit. Money, checks, bank drafts, money orders, and other cash items usually will be accepted for deposit, subject to their verification as to amount and validity.

Signature Card. Banks require a new depositor to sign his name on a card or form as an aid in verifying the depositor's signature on checks that he may issue, on cash items that he may indorse for deposit, and on other business papers that he may present to the bank. The form a depositor signs to give the bank a sample of his signature is called a *signature card.* To aid in identification, the depositor's social security number (if any) may also be shown. If desired, a depositor may authorize others to sign his name to checks and to other business forms. Each person who is so authorized is required to sign the depositor's name along with his own signature on a signature card. A signature card is one of the safeguards that a bank uses to protect its own interests as well as the interests of its depositors.

Deposit Ticket. Banks provide depositors with a printed form to use for a detailed listing of items being deposited. This form is called a *deposit ticket.* A model filled-in deposit ticket is reproduced on page 55. This illustration is typical of the type of ticket that most banks provide. Note that the number of the depositor's account is preprinted at the bottom in so-called "MICR" numbers (meaning *magnetic ink character recognition*) that can be "read" by a type of electronic equipment used by banks. This series of digits (which also is preprinted at the bottom of all of the depositor's checks) is actually a code used in sorting and routing deposit slips and checks. In the first set of digits, 0420-0003, the "4" indicates that the bank is in the Fourth Federal Reserve District. The "20" following is what is called a "routing" number. The "3" is a number assigned to the Kenwood National Bank. This numbering method was established by the American Bankers Association (ABA). The second set of digits, 136-92146, is the number assigned by the Kenwood National Bank to the Miller Company's account.

It is very common practice to prepare deposit tickets in duplicate so that one copy, when receipted by the bank teller, may be retained by the depositor. In preparing a deposit ticket, the date should be written in the space provided. Currency (paper money) should be arranged in the order of the denominations, the smaller denominations being placed on top. The bills should all be faced up and top up. Coins (pennies, nickels, dimes, quarters, and half dollars) that are to be deposited in considerable quantities should be wrapped in coin wrappers, which the bank will provide. The name and account number of the depositor should be written

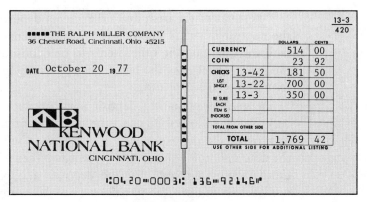

Deposit Ticket

on the outside of each coin wrapper as a means of identification in the event that a mistake has been made in counting the coins. The amounts of cash represented by currency and by coins should be entered in the amount column of the deposit ticket on the lines provided for these items.

Each additional item to be deposited should be listed on a separate line of the deposit ticket as shown in the illustration above. In listing checks on the deposit ticket, the instructions of the bank should be observed in describing the checks for identification purposes. Banks usually prefer that depositors identify checks being deposited by showing the ABA number of the bank on which the check is drawn. The ABA number for the first check listed on the deposit ticket above is $\frac{13-42}{420}$. The number 13 is the number assigned to the city in which the bank is located and the number 42 is assigned to the specific bank. The 420 is the check routing symbol, but only the numerator is used in identifying the deposit.

All checks being deposited must be indorsed. The indorsement on the check illustrated below was by means of a rubber stamp.

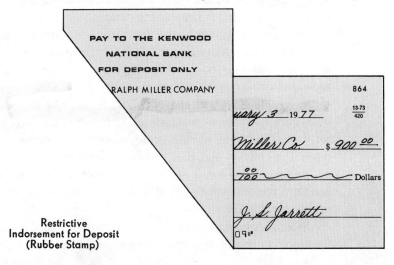

Restrictive
Indorsement for Deposit
(Rubber Stamp)

The total of the cash and other items deposited should be entered on the deposit tickets. The deposit tickets, prepared in duplicate, together with the cash and the other items to be deposited, should be delivered to the receiving teller of the bank. The teller receipts the duplicate copy and returns it to the depositor.

Instead of preparing deposit slips in duplicate, another practice — very widely followed at one time, and still often used — is for the bank to provide the depositor with a *passbook* in which the bank teller enters the date and amount of each deposit together with his initial. This gives the depositor a receipt for the deposit; a duplicate deposit slip is not needed. Of course, the passbook must be brought in (or sent in) to the bank with each deposit.

Instead of providing the depositor with either duplicate deposit tickets or a passbook, the bank may provide him with a machine-printed receipt for each deposit. Some banks use *automatic teller machines* in preparing the receipts. The use of such machines saves the time required to make manual entries in a passbook and eliminates the need for making duplicate copies of deposit tickets. Such machines are not only timesaving, but they also promote accuracy in the handling of deposits. The deposits handled by each teller during the day may be accumulated so that at the end of the day the total amount of the deposits received by a teller is automatically recorded by the machine. This amount may be proved by counting the cash and cash items accepted by a teller for deposit during the day.

Dishonored Checks. A check that a bank refuses to pay is described as a *dishonored check*. A depositor guarantees all items that he deposits and is liable to the bank for the amount involved if, for any reason, any item is not honored when presented for payment. When a check or other cash item is deposited with a bank and is not honored upon presentation to the bank upon which it is drawn, the depositor's bank may charge the amount of the dishonored item to the depositor's account or may present it to the depositor for reimbursement. It is not uncommon for checks that have been deposited to be returned to the depositor for various reasons, as indicated on the debit advice on page 57. The most common reason for checks being returned unpaid is "not sufficient funds" (NSF).

Under the laws of most states, it is illegal for anyone to issue a check on a bank without having sufficient funds on deposit with that bank to cover the check when it is presented for payment. This action is called an *overdraft*. When a dishonored check is charged to the depositor's account, the depositor should deduct the amount from the balance shown on his checkbook stub.

Most checks that turn out to be "bad" or "rubber" (meaning that they "bounce") are not the result of any dishonest intent on the part of the

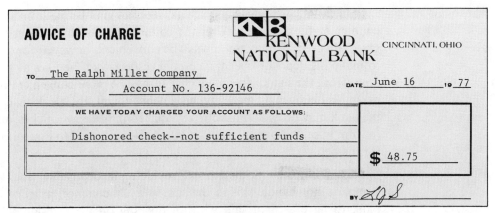

Debit Advice

drawers of such checks. Either the depositor thought that he had enough money in his account when the check was written, or he expected to get a deposit to the bank in time to "cover" the check before it reached the bank for payment. It is commonly considered to be something of a disgrace to the drawer of a check if the bank will not honor (pay) it. In recent years, many banks have made available (for a fee) plans that guarantee that all checks, within prescribed limits as to amount, will be honored even if the depositor's balance is too low. This amounts to a prearrangement with the bank to make a loan to the depositor. These plans have been given names such as "Ready Reserve Account," "Instant Cash," and others. Sometimes arrangements of this sort are parts of larger plans that involve such things as picture checks, no minimum balance, bank statements that list checks paid in numerical order, "check guarantee cards," travelers checks without fee, safe-deposit boxes, and even bank credit cards (discussed in Chapter 6). The bank charges a monthly fee for any or all of these services. Such comprehensive plans are not widely subscribed to by businesses (in contrast to individuals.)

Postdated Checks. Checks dated subsequent to the date of issue are known as *postdated checks*. For example, a check that is issued on March 1 may be dated March 15. The recipient of a postdated check should not deposit it before the date specified on the check. One reason for issuing a postdated check may be that the maker does not have sufficient funds in his bank at the time of issuance to pay it, but he may expect to have a sufficient amount on deposit by the time the check is presented for payment on or after the date of the check. When a postdated check is presented to the bank on which it is drawn and payment is not made, it is handled by the bank in the same manner as any other dishonored check and the payee should treat it as a dishonored check. Generally, it is not considered good practice to issue postdated checks.

Making Deposits by Mail. Bank deposits may be made either over the counter or by mail. The over-the-counter method of making deposits is generally used. It may not always be convenient, however, for a depositor to make his deposits over the counter, especially if he lives at a great distance from the bank. In such a case it may be more convenient for him to make his deposits by mail. When a depositor makes his deposits by mail, the bank may provide him with a special form of deposit ticket, and a form for him to self address which is subsequently returned to him with a receipt for his deposit.

Night Deposits. Some banks provide night deposit service. While all banks do not handle this in the same way, a common practice is for the bank to have a night safe with an opening on the exterior of the bank building. Upon signing a night depository contract, the bank supplies the depositor with a key to the outside door of the safe, together with a bag that has an identifying number and in which valuables may be placed, and two keys to the bag itself. Once the depositor places his bag in the night deposit safe it cannot be retrieved because it moves to a vault in the bank that is accessible to bank employees only. Since only the depositor is provided with keys to his bag, he or his authorized representative must go to the bank to unlock the bag. At that time the depositor may or may not deposit in his account in the bank the funds that he had placed previously in the night deposit safe.

Night deposit banking service is especially valuable to those individuals and concerns that do not have safe facilities in their own places of business and that accumulate cash and other cash items which they cannot take to the bank during regular banking hours.

Making Withdrawals. The amount deposited in a bank checking account may be withdrawn either by the depositor himself or by any other person who has been properly authorized to make withdrawals from the depositor's account. Such withdrawals are accomplished by the use of checks signed by the depositor or by others having the authority to sign checks drawn on the account.

Checkbook. Checks used by businesses commonly come bound in the form of a book with two or three blank checks to a page, perforated so that they may be removed singly. To the left of each one is a *check stub* containing space to record all relevant information about the check (check number, date, payee, amount, the purpose of the check and often the account to be charged, along with the bank balance before the check was issued, current deposits if any, and the resulting balance after the check). The depositor's name and address normally are printed on each check and the MICR numbers are shown along the bottom edge. Often the checks are prenumbered — commonly in the upper right corner.

Sometimes checks come bound in the form of a pad. There may be a blank page after each check for use in making a carbon copy of the check. (The carbon copy is not a check; it is merely a copy of what was typed or written on the check. However, the essential information is supplied to be entered in the formal records.) Sometimes the depositor is provided with a checkbook that, instead of stubs, is accompanied by a small register in which the relevant information is noted. Checks may be provided by the bank (often for a charge) or purchased directly from firms that specialize in the manufacture of check forms.

Writing a Check. If the check has a stub, the latter should be filled in at the time the check is written. If, instead of a stub, a checkbook register is used, an entry for the check should be made therein. This plan insures that the drawer will retain a record of each check issued.

A depositor may personally obtain cash at the time of making a deposit by indicating on the deposit slip the portion of the total of the items listed to be returned to him, with the remainder to constitute the deposit. Alternatively, he may draw a check payable to himself or, usually, just to "Cash."

The purpose for which a check is drawn is often noted in some appropriate area of the check itself. Indicating the purpose on the check provides information for the benefit of the payee and provides a specific receipt for the drawer.

The amount of the check is stated on the check in both figures and words. If the amount shown on the check in figures does not agree with the amount shown in words, the bank usually will contact the drawer for the correct amount or will return the check unpaid.

Care must be used in writing the amount on the check in order to avoid any possibility that the payee or a subsequent holder may change the amount. If the instructions given below are followed in the preparation of a check, it will be difficult to change the amount.

(a) The amount shown in figures should be written so that there is no space between the dollar sign and the first digit of the amount.

(b) The amount stated in words should be written beginning at the extreme left on the line provided for this information. The cents should be written in the form of a common fraction; if the check is for an even number of dollars, use two ciphers or the word "no" as the numerator of the fraction. If a vacant space remains, a line should be drawn from the amount stated in words to the word "Dollars" on the same line with it, as illustrated on the next page.

A machine frequently used to write the amount of a check in figures and in words is known as a *checkwriter*. The use of a checkwriter is desirable because it practically eliminates the possibility of a change in the amount of a check.

Each check issued by a depositor will be returned to him by the bank on which it is drawn after the check has been paid. Canceled checks are returned to the depositor with the bank statement, which is usually rendered each month. Canceled checks will have been indorsed by the payee

Checks and Stubs

and any subsequent holders. They constitute receipts that the depositor should retain for future reference. They may be attached to the stubs from which they were removed originally or they may be filed.

Electronic Processing of Checks. It is now nearly universal practice to use checks that can be processed by MICR (magnetic ink character recognition) equipment. The unique characteristic of such checks is that there is imprinted in magnetic ink along the lower margin of the check a series of numbers or digits in the form of a code that indicates (1) the identity of the Federal Reserve district in which the bank is located and a routing number, (2) the identity of the bank, and (3) the account number assigned to the depositor. Sometimes the check number is also shown. In processing checks with electronic equipment, the first bank that handles a check will imprint its amount in magnetic ink characters to further aid in the processing of the check. The amount will be printed directly below the signature line in the lower right-hand corner of the check.

Checks imprinted with the bank's number and the depositor's number can be fed into MICR machines which will "read" the numbers and cause the checks to be sorted in the desired fashion. If the amounts of the checks are printed thereon in magnetic ink, such amounts can be totaled, and each check can be posted electronically to the customer's account. This process can be carried on at extremely high speed with almost no danger of error.

The two checks reproduced at the top of the preceding page illustrate the appearance of the magnetic ink characters that have been printed at the bottom, as well as check stubs properly completed. (For a further discussion of electronic processing of checks, see Appendix, pages A-11 — A-13.)

Recording Bank Transactions. A depositor should keep a record of the transactions he completes with his bank. The usual plan is to keep this record on the checkbook stubs as shown in the illustration on page 60. It will be noted that the record consists of detailed information concerning each check written and an amount column in which should be recorded **(1)** the balance brought forward or carried down, **(2)** the amount of deposits to be added, and **(3)** the amount of checks to be subtracted. The purpose is to keep a detailed record of deposits made and checks issued and to indicate the balance in the checking account after each check is drawn.

As the amount of each check is recorded in the journal, a check mark may be placed immediately after the account title written on the stub to indicate that it has been recorded. When the canceled check is subsequently received from the bank, the amount shown on the stub may be checked to indicate that the canceled check has been received.

Records Kept by a Bank. The usual transactions completed by a bank with a depositor are:

(a) Accepting deposits made by the depositor.
(b) Paying checks issued by the depositor.
(c) Lending money to the depositor.
(d) Collecting the amounts of various kinds of commercial paper, such as matured bonds, for the account of the depositor.

The bank keeps an account for each depositor. Each transaction affecting a depositor's account is recorded by debiting or crediting his account, depending upon the effect of the transaction. When a bank accepts a deposit, the account of the depositor is credited for the amount of the deposit. The deposit increases the bank's liability to the depositor.

When the bank pays a check that has been drawn on the bank, it debits the account of the depositor for the amount of the check. If the bank makes a collection for a depositor, the net amount of the collection is credited to his account. At the same time the bank notifies the depositor on a form similar to the one shown below that the collection has been made.

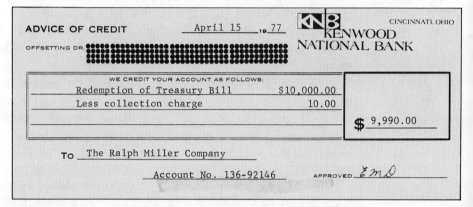

ADVICE OF CREDIT   April 15 ₁₉ 77   KN3 **KENWOOD NATIONAL BANK**   CINCINNATI, OHIO

OFFSETTING DR.

WE CREDIT YOUR ACCOUNT AS FOLLOWS:
Redemption of Treasury Bill $10,000.00
Less collection charge   10.00
$ 9,990.00

To The Ralph Miller Company

Account No. 136-92146   APPROVED _E m O_

Credit Advice

Bank Statement. Once each month a bank renders a statement of account to each depositor. An illustration of a widely used form of bank statement is shown on the next page. It may be mentioned that some banks provide statements that also present information about savings accounts, loan accounts, etc., for those depositors that have such additional accounts. Very commonly, however, a separate statement is furnished for each type of account.

The statement illustrated is for a checking account. It is a report showing **(1)** the balance on deposit at the beginning of the period, **(2)** the amounts of deposits made during the period, **(3)** the amounts of checks honored during the period, **(4)** other items charged to the depositor's account during the period, and **(5)** the balance on deposit at the end of the period. With his bank statement, the depositor also receives all checks paid by the bank during the period, together with any other vouchers representing items charged to his account.

Reconciling the Bank Statement. When a bank statement is received, the depositor should check it immediately with the bank balance record kept on his check stubs. This procedure is known as *reconciling the bank statement*, sometimes called "balancing the statement." The balance shown on the bank statement may not be the same as the amount shown on the check stubs for one or more of the following reasons:

  (a) Some of the checks issued during the period may not have been presented to the bank for payment before the statement was prepared. These are known as *outstanding checks*.

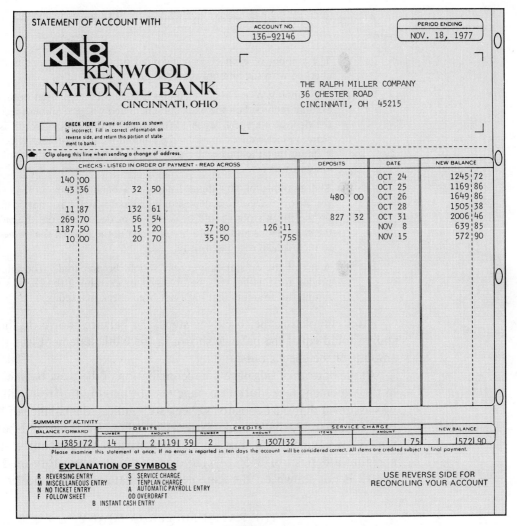

EXPLANATION OF SYMBOLS

R REVERSING ENTRY	S SERVICE CHARGE	USE REVERSE SIDE FOR
M MISCELLANEOUS ENTRY	T TENPLAN CHARGE	RECONCILING YOUR ACCOUNT
N NO TICKET ENTRY	A AUTOMATIC PAYROLL ENTRY	
F FOLLOW SHEET	OD OVERDRAFT	
	B INSTANT CASH ENTRY	

Bank Statement

(b) Deposits made by mail may have been in transit, or a deposit placed in the night depository may not have been recorded by the bank until the day following the date of the statement.

(c) The bank may have credited the depositor's account for an amount collected for him but the depositor may not as yet have noted it on his check stubs — possibly the credit advice had not yet been received.

(d) Service charges or other charges may appear on the bank statement that the depositor has not recorded on the check stubs.

(e) The depositor may have erred in keeping the bank record.

(f) The bank may have erred in keeping its account with the depositor.

If a depositor is unable to reconcile the bank statement, a report on the matter should be made to the bank immediately.

A suggested procedure in reconciling the bank statement is enumerated below:

(a) The amount of each deposit recorded on the bank statement should be checked with the amount recorded on the check stubs.

(b) The amount of each canceled check should be compared both with the amount recorded on the bank statement and with the amount recorded on the depositor's check stubs. When making this comparison it is a good plan to place a check mark by the amount recorded on each check stub to indicate that the canceled check has been returned by the bank and its amount verified.

(c) The amounts of any items listed on a bank statement that represent credits or charges to a depositor's account which have not been entered on the check stubs should be added to or deducted from the balance on the check stubs and should be recorded in the journal that is being used to record cash disbursements.

(d) A list of the outstanding checks should be prepared. The information needed for this list may be obtained by examining the check stubs and noting the amounts that have not been check marked.

After completing the foregoing steps, the balance shown on the check stubs should equal the balance shown in the bank statement less the total amount of the checks outstanding.

At the bottom of this page is a reconciliation of the bank balance shown in the statement reproduced on page 63. In making this reconciliation it was assumed that the depositor's check stub indicated a balance of $757.22 on November 18, that Checks Nos. 416, 419, and 421 had not been presented for payment and thus were not returned with the bank statement, and that a deposit of $456.13 placed in the night depository on November 18 is not shown on the statement. In matching the canceled checks

THE RALPH MILLER COMPANY
Reconciliation of Bank Statement
November 18, 1977

Balance, November 18, per bank statement............		$ 572.90
Add: Deposit, November 18........................		456.13
		$1,029.03
Less checks outstanding, November 18:		
No. 416......................................	$ 85.00	
No. 419......................................	17.40	
No. 421......................................	170.25	272.65
Adjusted bank balance, November 18.................		$ 756.38
Check stub balance, November 18....................		$ 757.22
Less: Bank service charge..........................	$ .75	
Error on stub for Check No. 394................	.09	.84
Adjusted check stub balance, November 18...........		$ 756.38

that were returned with the bank statement against the check stubs, an error on the stub for Check No. 394 was discovered. That check was for $11.87. On its stub, the amount was shown as $11.78. This is called a *transposition* error. The "8" and the "7" were transposed (order reversed). On Stub No. 394 and the others that followed, the bank balance shown was 9 cents too large. The correct amount, $11.87, should be shown on Stub No. 394, and the bank balance shown on the stub of the last check used should be reduced $.09. If Check No. 394 was in payment of, say, a telephone bill, an entry should be made debiting Telephone Expense and crediting Cash. (Alternatively, since such a small amount was involved, the debit might be made to Miscellaneous Expense.)

Service Charges. A service charge may be made by a bank for the handling of checks and other items. The basis and the amount of such charges vary with different banks in different localities. Sometimes a rather elaborate *deposit activity analysis* is involved.

When a bank statement indicates that a service charge has been made, the depositor should record the amount of the service charge by debiting an expense account, such as Miscellaneous Expense, and by crediting Cash. He should also deduct the amount of such charges from the check stub balance.

Keeping a Ledger Account with the Bank. As explained previously, a memorandum account with the bank may be kept on the depositor's checkbook stub. The depositor may also keep a ledger account with the bank if desired. The title of such an account usually is the name of the bank. Sometimes more than one account is kept with a bank in which case each account should be correctly labeled. Such terms as "commercial," "executive," and "payroll" are used to identify the accounts.

The bank account should be debited for the amount of each deposit and should be credited for the amount of each check written. The account should also be credited for any other items that may be charged to the account by the bank, including service charges.

When both a cash account and a bank account are kept in the ledger, the following procedure should be observed in recording transactions affecting these accounts:

CASH		KENWOOD NATIONAL BANK	
Debit	Credit	Debit	Credit
For all receipts of cash and cash items.	(a) For all payments in cash, (b) For all bank deposits,	(a) For all deposits. (b) For collection of amounts for the depositor.	(a) For all checks written, (b) For all service charges, (c) For all other charges, such as for dishonored checks.

Under this method of accounting for cash and banking transactions, the cash account will be in balance when all cash on hand has been deposited in the bank. To prove the balance of the cash account at any time, it is necessary only to count the cash and cash items on hand and to compare the total with the cash account balance. To prove the bank account balance, it will be necessary to reconcile the bank balance in the same manner in which it is reconciled when only a memorandum record of bank transactions is kept on the check stubs.

The cash account can be dispensed with when a bank account is kept in the ledger and all cash receipts are deposited in the bank. When this is done, all disbursements (except small expenditures made from a petty cash fund) are made by check. Daily, or at frequent intervals, the receipts are deposited in the bank. If all cash received during the month has been deposited before the books are closed at the end of the month, the total amount of the bank deposits will equal the total cash receipts for the month. If all disbursements during the month are made by check, the total amount of checks issued will be the total disbursements for the month.

Savings account

When a savings account is opened in a bank, a signature card must be signed by the depositor. A passbook is given to the depositor that must be presented at the bank when making deposits or when making withdrawals. By signing the signature card, the depositor agrees to abide by the rules and the regulations of the bank. These rules and regulations vary with different banks and may be altered and amended from time to time. The principal differences between a savings account and a checking account are that interest is paid by the bank on a savings account and withdrawals from a savings account may be made at the bank or by mail by the depositor or his authorized agent. Interest usually is computed on a quarterly basis. The passbook must be presented òr mailed along with a withdrawal slip when money is withdrawn from the account. Banks do not pay interest on the balances in checking accounts. Depositors use checking accounts primarily as a convenient means of making payments, while savings accounts are used primarily as a means of accumulating funds with interest.

Savings accounts are not too frequently used by businesses. If the assets of a business include money in a bank savings account, there should be a separate account in the ledger with a title and a number that indicate the nature of the deposit. Sometimes the name of the bank is in the title, as, for example, "Kenwood National Bank — Savings Account." When the bank credits interest to the account, the depositor should record the amount in his accounts by a debit to the savings account and by a credit to Interest Earned. The interest is revenue whether withdrawn or not (and is taxed to the depositor when earned).

Report No. 3-2

> Refer to the study assignments and complete Report No. 3-2. This assignment provides a test of your ability to apply the principles developed in the first three chapters of the textbook. After completing the report, you may proceed with the textbook discussion in Chapter 4 until the next report is required.

Chapter 4

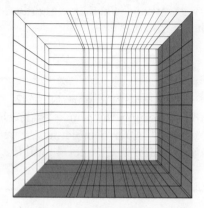

PAYROLL ACCOUNTING

Employers need to maintain detailed and accurate payroll accounting records. Accurate accounting for employees' earnings preserves the legal and moral right of each employee to be paid according to his employment contract and the laws governing such contracts.

Payroll accounting records also provide information useful in the analysis and classification of labor costs. At the same time, payroll accounting information is invaluable in contract discussions with labor unions, in the settlement of company-union grievances, and in other forms of collective bargaining. Clearly, there is virtually no margin for error in payroll accounting.

EARNINGS AND DEDUCTIONS

The first step in determining the amount to be paid to an employee is to calculate the amount of his total or gross earnings for the pay period. The second step is to determine the amounts of any deductions that are required either by law or by agreement. Depending upon a variety of circumstances, either or both of these steps may be relatively simple or quite complicated. An examination of the factors that are involved follows.

**Employer-
employee
relationships**

Not every individual who performs services for a business is considered to be an employee. A public accountant, lawyer, or management consultant who sells his services to a business does not become its employee. Neither does a plumber nor an electrician who is hired to make specific repairs or installations on business property. These people are told what to do, but not how to do it, and the compensation that they receive for their services is called a *fee*. Any person who agrees to perform a service for a fee and is not subject to the control of those whom he serves is called an *independent contractor*.

In contrast, an employee is one who is under the control and direction of his employer with regard to the performance of services. The difference between an independent contractor and an employee is an important legal distinction. The nature and extent of the responsibilities of a contractor and a client to each other and to third parties are quite different from the mutual obligations of an employer and any one of his employees.

**Types of
compensation**

Compensation for managerial or administrative services usually is called *salary*. A salary normally is expressed in terms of a month or a year. Compensation either for skilled or for unskilled labor usually is referred to as *wages*. Wages ordinarily are expressed in terms of hours, weeks, or pieces of accomplishment. The terms salaries and wages often are used interchangeably in practice.

Supplements to basic salaries or wages of employees include bonuses, commissions, cost-of-living adjustments, pensions, and profit sharing plans. Compensation also may take the form of goods, lodging, meals, or other property, and as such is measured by the fair market value of the property or service given in payment for the employee's efforts.

**Determination
of total
earnings**

An employee's earnings commonly are based on the time worked during the payroll period. Sometimes earnings are based on units of output or of sales during the period. Compensation based on time requires a record of the time worked by each employee. Where there are only a few employees, a record of times worked kept in a memorandum book may suffice. Where there are many employees, time clocks commonly are used to record time spent on the job each day. With time clocks, a clock card is provided for each employee and the clock is used to record arrival and departure times. Alternatively, plastic cards or badges with holes punched in them for basic employee data are now being used in computer-based time-keeping systems. Whatever method is used, the total time worked during the payroll period must be computed.

Employees often are entitled to compensation at more than their regular rate of pay for work during certain hours or on certain days. If the employer is engaged in Interstate Commerce, the Federal Fair Labor Standards Act (commonly known as the Wages and Hours Law) provides that all employees covered by the Act must be paid one and one-half times the regular rate for all hours worked over 40 per week. Labor-management agreements often require extra pay for certain hours or days. In such cases, hours worked in excess of eight per day or work on Sundays and specified holidays may be paid for at higher rates.

To illustrate, assume that the company which employs Ronald Slone pays time and a half for all hours worked in excess of 40 per week and double time for work on Sunday. Slone's regular rate is $6 per hour; and during the week ended April 15, he worked nine hours each day Monday through Friday, six hours on Saturday, and four on Sunday. Slone's total earnings for the week ended April 15 would be computed as follows:

```
40 hours @ $6.00............................................................  $240.00
11 hours @ $9.00............................................................    99.00
   (Slone worked 9 hours each day Monday through Friday and 6 hours
   on Saturday — a total of 51 hours. Forty hours would be paid for at the
   regular rate and 11 hours at time and a half.)
4 hours (on Sunday) @ $12.00......................................    48.00
        Total earnings for the week..................................  $387.00
```

An employee who is paid a regular salary may be entitled to premium pay for any overtime. If this is the case, it is necessary to compute the regular hourly rate of pay before computing the overtime rate. To illustrate, assume that Bessie Smith receives a regular salary of $1,000 a month. Ms. Smith is entitled to overtime pay at the rate of one and one-half times her regular hourly rate for any time worked in excess of 40 hours per week. Her overtime pay may be computed as follows:

```
$1,000 × 12 months = $12,000 annual pay
$12,000 ÷ 52 weeks = $230.77 per week
$230.77 ÷ 40 hours = $5.77 per regular hour
$5.77 × 1½ = $8.65 per overtime hour
```

Deductions from total earnings

With few exceptions, employers are required to withhold portions of each employee's total earnings both for federal income tax and for social security taxes. Certain states and cities also require income or earnings tax withholding on the part of employers. Besides these deductions, an agreement between the employer and the employee may call for amounts to be withheld for any one or more of the following reasons:

(a) To purchase United States savings bonds for the employee.
(b) To pay a life, accident, or health insurance premium for the employee.
(c) To pay the employee's union dues.
(d) To add to a pension fund or profit sharing fund.
(e) To pay to some charitable organization.
(f) To repay a loan from the company or from the company credit union.

Social security and tax account number

Each employee is required to have a social security account and tax account number for payroll accounting purposes. A completed Form SS-5, the official form to be used in applying for an account number, follows:

Completed Application for Social Security and Tax Account Number (Form SS-5)

Employees' income tax withheld

Under federal law, employers are required to withhold certain amounts from the total earnings of each employee to be applied toward the payment of the employee's federal income tax. The amount to be withheld is governed by (1) the total earnings of the employee, (2) the number of *withholding allowances* claimed by the employee, (3) the marital status of the employee, and (4) the length of the employee's pay period.

Each federal income taxpayer is entitled to one exemption for himself or for herself and one each for certain other qualified relatives whom he or she supports. The law specifies the relationship that must exist, the extent of support required, and how much the *dependent* may earn in order that an exemption may be claimed. As of 1972, each single taxpayer, or each married taxpayer whose spouse is not also employed, has become entitled to one *special withholding allowance*. A taxpayer and spouse each get an extra exemption for age over 65 years and still another exemption for blindness.

An employed taxpayer must furnish his employer with an Employee's Withholding Allowance Certificate, Form W-4, showing the number of allowances, if any, claimed. The allowance certificate completed by Ronald Marlin Lee is shown on the next page.

Employees with large itemized deductions are permitted to claim *additional withholding allowances*. Each additional withholding allowance will give the taxpayer an additional income tax deduction.

```
┌──────────────────────────────────────────────────────────────────────────────────────────┐
│ Form  W-4          │      Employee's Withholding Allowance Certificate                     │
│                    │                                                                       │
│ Department of the Treasury │        (This certificate is for income tax withholding purposes │
│ Internal Revenue Service   │         only; it will remain in effect until you change it.)    │
├────────────────────────────────────────────────────┬─────────────────────────────────────┤
│ Type or print your full name                        │ Your social security number         │
│   Ronald Marlin Lee                                 │   474-52-4829                       │
│ Home address (Number and street or rural route)     │ Marital status                      │
│   502 Kingsland Avenue                              │  ☐ Single   ☒ Married               │
│ City or town, State and ZIP code                    │ (If married but legally separated, or spouse │
│   St. Louis, MO  63130                              │  is a nonresident alien, check the single │
│                                                     │  block.)                            │
├─────────────────────────────────────────────────────────────────────────────────┬────────┤
│ 1 Total number of allowances you are claiming  . . . . . . . . . . . . . . . . . │   4    │
│                                                                                   │        │
│ 2 Additional amount, if any, you want deducted from each pay (if your employer agrees) . │ $  -0- │
├──────────────────────────────────────────────────────────────────────────────────────────┤
│ I certify that to the best of my knowledge and belief, the number of withholding allowances claimed on this certificate does not exceed the number │
│ to which I am entitled.                                                                    │
│                                                                                            │
│ Signature ▶  Ronald Marlin Lee            Date ▶  January 2,          , 19 77             │
│                                                                         16—83587-1         │
└──────────────────────────────────────────────────────────────────────────────────────────┘
```

Completed Withholding Allowance Certificate (Form W-4)

Any employee desiring to claim one or more additional withholding allowances must estimate his expected total earnings and itemized deductions for the coming year. Generally, the amount of these itemized deductions cannot exceed the amount of itemized deductions (or standard deduction) claimed on the income tax return filed for the preceding year.

The instructions provided for completing Form W-4 include a table, illustrated at the top of the next page, from which the taxpayer can determine the number of additional withholding allowances to which he may be entitled. As shown on Line 1 of the W-4 illustrated above, Mr. Lee claimed four withholding allowances. This was because his estimated earnings and estimated itemized deductions did not qualify him for any additional withholding allowances. (Mr. Lee is married and has two minor children. However, since his wife is also employed, he would not be entitled to a so-called *special* withholding allowance. A special withholding allowance is *one* additional allowance granted to a taxpayer with only one job whose wife or husband does not also work.)

Most employers use the *wage-bracket method* of determining the amount of tax to be withheld. This method involves the use of income tax withholding tables provided by the Internal Revenue Service. Such tables cover monthly, semimonthly, biweekly, weekly, and daily or miscellaneous periods. There are two types of tables: **(1)** single persons and unmarried heads of households, and **(2)** married persons. Copies may be obtained from any local Internal Revenue Service office. A portion of a weekly income tax wage-bracket withholding table for married persons is illustrated on page 74. As an example of the use of this table, assume that Ronald M. Lee (who claims 4 allowances) had gross earnings of $335 for the week ending December 16, 1977. On the line showing the tax on wages

Form W-4   Page 2

Table for Determining Number of Withholding Allowances Based on Itemized Deductions

Estimated salaries and wages	Number of additional withholding allowances for the amount of itemized deductions shown in the appropriate column (See Line i on other side)													
	0		1		2		3		4		5		6*	
Part I Single Employees														
	Under	At least	But less than	At least	But less than	At least	But less than	At least	But less than	At least	But less than	At least	But less than	
Under $10,000	$2,200	$2,200–$2,950		$2,950–$3,700		$3,700–$4,450		$4,450–$5,200		$5,200–$5,950		$5,950–$6,700		
10,000–15,000	2,500	2,500– 3,250		3,250– 4,000		4,000– 4,750		4,750– 5,500		5,500– 6,250		6,250– 7,000		
15,000–25,000	2,800	2,800– 3,550		3,550– 4,300		4,300– 5,050		5,050– 5,800		5,800– 6,550		6,550– 7,300		
25,000–30,000	3,200	3,200– 3,950		3,950– 4,700		4,700– 5,450		5,450– 6,200		6,200– 6,950		6,950– 7,700		
30,000–35,000	4,000	4,000– 4,750		4,750– 5,500		5,500– 6,250		6,250– 7,000		7,000– 7,750		7,750– 8,500		
35,000–40,000	5,000	5,000– 5,750		5,750– 6,500		6,500– 7,250		7,250– 8,000		8,000– 8,750		8,750– 9,500		
40,000–45,000	6,500	6,500– 7,250		7,250– 8,000		8,000– 8,750		8,750– 9,500		9,500–10,250		10,250–11,000		
45,000–50,000**	8,000	8,000– 8,750		8,750– 9,500		9,500–10,250		10,250–11,000		11,000–11,750		11,750–12,500		
Part II Married Employees (When Spouse Is Not Employed)														
Under $15,000	2,900	2,900– 3,650		3,650– 4,400		4,400– 5,150		5,150– 5,900		5,900– 6,650		6,650– 7,400		
15,000–35,000	3,400	3,400– 4,150		4,150– 4,900		4,900– 5,650		5,650– 6,400		6,400– 7,150		7,150– 7,900		
35,000–40,000	3,700	3,700– 4,450		4,450– 5,200		5,200– 5,950		5,950– 6,700		6,700– 7,450		7,450– 8,200		
40,000–45,000	4,300	4,300– 5,050		5,050– 5,800		5,800– 6,550		6,550– 7,300		7,300– 8,050		8,050– 8,800		
45,000–50,000**	5,200	5,200– 5,950		5,950– 6,700		6,700– 7,450		7,450– 8,200		8,200– 8,950		8,950– 9,700		
Part III Married Employees (When Both Spouses Are Employed), and other employees who are holding more than one job														
Under $10,000	3,200	3,200– 3,950		3,950– 4,700		4,700– 5,450		5,450– 6,200		6,200– 6,950		6,950– 7,700		
10,000–12,000	3,700	3,700– 4,450		4,450– 5,200		5,200– 5,950		5,950– 6,700		6,700– 7,450		7,450– 8,200		
12,000–15,000	4,200	4,200– 4,950		4,950– 5,700		5,700– 6,450		6,450– 7,200		7,200– 7,950		7,950– 8,700		
15,000–20,000	5,000	5,000– 5,750		5,750– 6,500		6,500– 7,250		7,250– 8,000		8,000– 8,750		8,750– 9,500		
20,000–25,000	5,600	5,600– 6,350		6,350– 7,100		7,100– 7,850		7,850– 8,600		8,600– 9,350		9,350–10,100		
25,000–30,000	6,200	6,200– 6,950		6,950– 7,700		7,700– 8,450		8,450– 9,200		9,200– 9,950		9,950–10,700		
30,000–35,000	7,100	7,100– 7,850		7,850– 8,600		8,600– 9,350		9,350–10,100		10,100–10,850		10,850–11,600		
35,000–40,000	7,900	7,900– 8,650		8,650– 9,400		9,400–10,150		10,150–10,900		10,900–11,650		11,650–12,400		
40,000–45,000	8,900	8,900– 9,650		9,650–10,400		10,400–11,150		11,150–11,900		11,900–12,650		12,650–13,400		
45,000–50,000**	10,200	10,200–10,950		10,950–11,700		11,700–12,450		12,450–13,200		13,200–13,950		13,950–14,700		

*7 or More Allowances: If your itemized deductions exceed the amount shown in Column 6 (above), you may claim 6 allowances plus one more for each $750 or fraction thereof of itemized deductions in excess of the amounts shown in Column 6 for your salary and wage bracket.

**When annual salary or wage exceeds $50,000, "0" column amounts may be determined as follows: for single employees (Part I)—22% of their annual salary; for married employees whose spouse is not employed (Part II)—15% of their annual salary; and for married employees when both spouses are employed and other employees who are holding more than one job (Part III)—24% of their combined annual salary. An additional withholding allowance may be claimed for each $750 or fraction thereof by which itemized deductions exceed the "0" column amount determined in this manner.

Completed Withholding Allowance Certificate Form W-4 (Back)

of "at least $330, but less than $340," in the column headed "4 withholding allowances," $49.30 is given as the amount to be withheld.

Whether the wage-bracket method or some other method is used in computing the amount of tax to be withheld, the employee is given full benefit for all allowances claimed plus a standard deduction of approximately 15 percent. In any event, the sum of the taxes withheld from an employee's wages only approximates the tax on his actual income derived solely from wages. An employee may be liable for a tax larger than the amount withheld. On the other hand, the amount of the taxes withheld by the employer may be greater than the employee's actual tax liability. In such an event, the employee will be entitled to a refund of the excess taxes withheld, or he may elect to apply the excess to his tax liability for the following year.

Several of the states have adopted state income tax withholding procedures. Some of these states supply employers with withholding allowance

WEEKLY Payroll Period — Employee MARRIED

And the wages are—		And the number of withholding allowances claimed is—										
At least	But less than	0	1	2	3	4	5	6	7	8	9	10 or more
		The amount of income tax to be withheld shall be—										
$100	$105	$14.10	$11.80	$9.50	$7.20	$4.90	$2.80	$.80	$0	$0	$0	$0
105	110	14.90	12.60	10.30	8.00	5.70	3.50	1.50	0	0	0	0
110	115	15.70	13.40	11.10	8.80	6.50	4.20	2.20	.10	0	0	0
115	120	16.50	14.20	11.90	9.60	7.30	5.00	2.90	.80	0	0	0
120	125	17.30	15.00	12.70	10.40	8.10	5.80	3.60	1.50	0	0	0
125	130	18.10	15.80	13.50	11.20	8.90	6.60	4.30	2.20	.20	0	0
130	135	18.90	16.60	14.30	12.00	9.70	7.40	5.10	2.90	.90	0	0
135	140	19.70	17.40	15.10	12.80	10.50	8.20	5.90	3.60	1.60	0	0
140	145	20.50	18.20	15.90	13.60	11.30	9.00	6.70	4.40	2.30	.30	0
145	150	21.30	19.00	16.70	14.40	12.10	9.80	7.50	5.20	3.00	1.00	0
150	160	22.50	20.20	17.90	15.60	13.30	11.00	8.70	6.40	4.10	2.00	0
160	170	24.10	21.80	19.50	17.20	14.90	12.60	10.30	8.00	5.70	3.40	1.40
170	180	26.00	23.40	21.10	18.80	16.50	14.20	11.90	9.60	7.30	5.00	2.80
180	190	28.00	25.20	22.70	20.40	18.10	15.80	13.50	11.20	8.90	6.60	4.30
190	200	30.00	27.20	24.30	22.00	19.70	17.40	15.10	12.80	10.50	8.20	5.90
200	210	32.00	29.20	26.30	23.60	21.30	19.00	16.70	14.40	12.10	9.80	7.50
210	220	34.40	31.20	28.30	25.40	22.90	20.60	18.30	16.00	13.70	11.40	9.10
220	230	36.80	33.30	30.30.	27.40	24.50	22.20	19.90	17.60	15.30	13.00	10.70
230	240	39.20	35.70	32.30	29.40	26.50	23.80	21.50	19.20	16.90	14.60	12.30
240	250	41.60	38.10	34.60	31.40	28.50	25.60	23.10	20.80	18.50	16.20	13.90
250	260	44.00	40.50	37.00	33.60	30.50	27.60	24.70	22.40	20.10	17.80	15.50
260	270	46.40	42.90	39.40	36.00	32.50	29.60	26.70	24.00	21.70	19.40	17.10
270	280	48.80	45.30	41.80	38.40	34.90	31.60	28.70	25.80	23.30	21.00	18.70
280	290	51.20	47.70	44.20	40.80	37.30	33.90	30.70	27.80	25.00	22.60	20.30
290	300	53.60	50.10	46.60	43.20	39.70	36.30	32.80	29.80	27.00	24.20	21.90
300	310	56.00	52.50	49.00	45.60	42.10	38.70	35.20	31.80	29.00	26.10	23.50
310	320	58.40	54.90	51.40	48.00	44.50	41.10	37.60	34.10	31.00	28.10	25.20
320	330	60.80	57.30	53.80	50.40	46.90	43.50	40.00	36.50	33.10	30.10	27.20
330	340	63.60	59.70	56.20	52.80	49.30	45.90	42.40	38.90	35.50	32.10	29.20
340	350	66.40	62.40	58.60	55.20	51.70	48.30	44.80	41.30	37.90	34.40	31.20

*As of the date of printing, the above Weekly Federal Income Tax Withholding Table is the most current available.

Portion of Weekly Federal Income Tax Withholding Table for Married Persons

certificate forms and income tax withholding tables that are similar in appearance to those used by the federal Internal Revenue Service. Note, however, that each state that has an income tax law uses the specific tax rates and dollar amounts for allowances as required by its law. Some states determine the amount to be withheld merely by applying a fixed percentage to the federal withholding amount.

**Employees'
FICA tax
withheld**

Payroll taxes are imposed on almost all employers and employees for old-age, survivors, and disability insurance (OASDI) benefits and health insurance benefits for the aged (HIP) — both under the Federal Insurance Contributions Act (FICA). The base of the tax and the tax rate have been changed several times since the law was first enacted and are subject to change by Congress at any time in the future. For purposes of this chapter, the rate is assumed to be 4.8 percent of the taxable wages paid during the calendar year for OASDI and 1.2 percent for HIP. It is also assumed that

the first $15,000 of the wages paid to each employee in any calendar year is taxable. Any amount of compensation paid in excess of $15,000 is assumed to be exempt from the tax. The employees' portion of the FICA tax must be withheld from their wages by the employer. Although it is true that the base and rate of the tax may be changed at the pleasure of Congress, the accounting principles or methods of recording payroll transactions are not affected.

A few states require employers to withhold a percentage of the employees' wages for unemployment compensation benefits or for disability benefits. In some states and cities, employers are required to withhold a percentage of the employees' wages for other types of payroll taxes. The withholding of income taxes at the state and city level has already been mentioned. Despite the number of withholdings required, each employer must comply with the proper laws in withholding any taxes based on payrolls and in keeping his payroll accounting records.

Payroll records

The needs of management and the requirements of various federal and state laws make it necessary for employers to keep records that will provide the following information:

(a) The name, address, and social security number of each employee.
(b) The gross amount of each employee's earnings, the date of payment, and the period of employment covered by each payroll.
(c) The total amount of gross earnings accumulated since the first of the year.
(d) The amount of any taxes or other items withheld from each employee's earnings.

Regardless of the number of employees or type of business, three types of payroll records usually need to be prepared for or by the employer. They are: **(1)** the payroll register or payroll journal; **(2)** the payroll check with earnings statement attached; and **(3)** the earnings record of the individual employee (on a weekly, monthly, quarterly, or annual basis). These records can be prepared either by *manual* or by *automated* methods.

Payroll Register. A manually prepared payroll register used by Central States Diversified, Inc., for the payroll period ended December 16, 1977, is illustrated on pages 76 and 77. The usual source of information for preparing a payroll register is a time memorandum book, the batch of time clock cards, or a computer print-out. Central States Diversified, Inc., has eight employees, as the illustration shows. Michelle Coxx and Wayne Thomas each claim only one allowance because each has two jobs. Stephen Akos and James Paynter each claim only two withholding allowances because their wives also work. Ole Brandal, John MacArthur and

James O'Donnell each get the special withholding allowance, but none as yet has any children. Regular deductions are made from the earnings of employees for FICA tax, federal income tax, and city earnings tax. In addition, for the pay period ending nearest to the middle of the month, deductions are made for life insurance, private hospital insurance, the company credit union, and (if desired) for the purchase of United States savings bonds.

Ole L. Brandal and Ronald M. Lee have each authorized Central States Diversified, Inc., to withhold $15 on the payday nearest to the middle of each month for United States savings bonds. When the amount withheld reaches the sum of $75, a $100 Series E, United States savings bond is purchased at the bank for each employee and delivered to him.

Only the first $15,000 of earnings received in any calendar year is subject to FICA tax. Mr. Lee's earnings for the week ending December 16 are exempt from the FICA tax because he has already been taxed on earnings totaling $15,000.

After the payroll register has been completed, the amount columns should be footed and the footings proved as follows:

Regular earnings...		$1,635.00
Overtime earnings...		205.00
Gross earnings..		$1,840.00
Deductions:		
FICA tax..	$ 69.90	
Federal income tax....................................	268.60	
City earnings tax......................................	36.80	
Life insurance premiums..............................	31.00	
Private hospital insurance premiums..................	18.00	
Credit union...	20.00	
United States savings bonds..........................	30.00	474.30
Net amount of payroll.................................		$1,365.70

PAYROLL REGISTER

	NAME	EMPLOYEE NO.	NO. OF ALLOW.	MARITAL STATUS	EARNINGS				TAXABLE EARNINGS		
					REGULAR	OVER-TIME	TOTAL	CUMULATIVE TOTAL	UNEM-PLOY COMP.	FICA	
1	Akos, Stephen W.	1	2	M	180 00		180 00	9,250 00	✓	180 00	1
2	Brandal, Ole L.	2	3	M	275 00	65 00	340 00	16,250 00			2
3	Cody, Michelle R.	3	1	S	150 00		150 00	7,600 00		150 00	3
4	Lee, Ronald M.	4	4	M	275 00	60 00	335 00	16,500 00			4
5	MacArthur, John D.	5	3	M	240 00	50 00	290 00	13,750 00		290 00	5
6	O'Donnell, James V.	6	3	M	175 00		175 00	9,000 00		175 00	6
7	Paynter, James R.	7	2	M	180 00	30 00	210 00	10,000 00		210 00	7
8	Thomas, Wayne D.	8	1	S	160 00		160 00	8,050 00		160 00	8
9					1,635 00	205 00	1,840 00	90,400 00		1,165 00	9
					1,635 00	205 00	1,840 00	90,400 00		1,165 00	

Payroll Register — Manually Prepared (Left Page)

After proving the footings, the totals should be entered in ink and the record should be ruled with single and double lines as shown in the illustration. Employees may be paid in cash or by check. Many businesses prepare a check for the net amount of the payroll and deposit it in a special payroll bank account. Individual paychecks are then drawn on that account for the amount due each employee. The employer usually furnishes a statement of payroll deductions to the employee along with each wage payment. Paychecks with detachable stubs, like the one for Ronald M. Lee, illustrated on pages 78 and 79, are widely used. The stub should be detached before the check is cashed, and the stub should be retained by the employee as a permanent record of his earnings and payroll deductions.

Employee's Earnings Record. An auxiliary record of each employee's earnings usually is kept in order to provide the information needed in preparing the various federal, state, and local reports required of employers. A manually prepared employee's earnings record used by Central States Diversified, Inc., for Ronald M. Lee, during the last two quarters of the current calendar year is illustrated on pages 80 and 81. This record may be kept on separate sheets or on cards, which may be filed alphabetically or numerically for ready reference. The information recorded on this form is taken from the payroll register.

Ronald Lee's earnings for the last half of the year up to December 16 are shown on this form. The entry for the pay period ended December 16 is posted from the payroll register illustrated on page 76 and below. It can be seen from Mr. Lee's earnings record that his cumulative earnings passed the $15,000 mark during the week ended November 18. Although his

FOR PERIOD ENDED *December 16*   19 77

	FICA TAX	FEDERAL INC. TAX	CITY TAX	LIFE INS.	PRIV. HOSP. INS.	CREDIT UNION	OTHER		TOTAL	NET PAY	CK. NO.
1	10 80	22 70	3 60	6 00		4 00			47 10	132 90	301
2		55 20	6 80			4 00	Sav. Bonds	15 00	81 00	259 00	302
3	9 00	24 50	3 00		4 00				40 50	109 50	303
4		49 30	6 70	7 50	5 00	4 00	Sav. Bonds	15 00	87 50	247 50	304
5	17 40	43 20	5 80	7 50	5 00	4 00			82 90	207 10	305
6	10 50	18 80	3 50	5 00					37 80	137 20	306
7	12 60	28 30	4 20			4 00			49 10	160 90	307
8	9 60	24 60	3 20	5 00	4 00				48 40	111 60	308
9	69 90	268 60	36 80	31 00	18 00	20 00		30 00	474 30	1,365 70	
	69 90	268 60	36 80	31 00	18 00	20 00		30 00	474 30	1,365 70	

Payroll Register — Manually Prepared (Right Page)

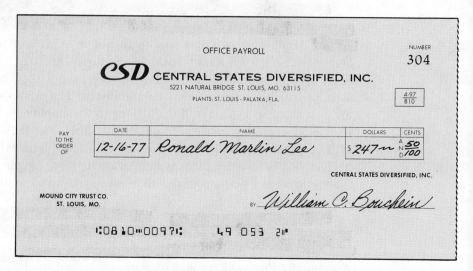

OFFICE PAYROLL

NUMBER
304

CSD CENTRAL STATES DIVERSIFIED, INC.

5221 NATURAL BRIDGE ST. LOUIS, MO. 63115

PLANTS: ST. LOUIS · PALATKA, FLA.

4-97
810

PAY TO THE ORDER OF	DATE	NAME	DOLLARS	CENTS
	12-16-77	*Ronald Marlin Lee*	$ 247	A N D 50/100

CENTRAL STATES DIVERSIFIED, INC.

MOUND CITY TRUST CO.
ST. LOUIS, MO.

BY *William C. Bouchein*

⑆08⑈10⑈0097⑆   49 053 2⑈

Completed Paycheck — Manually Prepared

total earnings for that week amounted to $330, only $40 of such wages was subject to the combined FICA tax of 6 percent, hence only $2.40 was withheld from his wages for that week. For the remainder of the current calendar year, his entire earnings will be exempt from further FICA tax withholding.

The payroll register is a summary of the earnings of all employees for each pay period, while the earnings record is a summary of the annual earnings of each employee. The earnings record illustrated on pages 80 and 81 is designed so that a record of the earnings of the employee for the first half of the year may be kept on one side of the form and a record of the earnings for the last half of the year may be kept on the reverse side of the form. Thus, at the end of the year, the form provides a complete record of the earnings of the employee for the year. It also provides a record of the employee's earnings for each calendar quarter needed by the employer in the preparation of his quarterly returns. These returns will be discussed later in this chapter.

Automated payroll systems

Automated payroll systems may involve the use of small-capacity bookkeeping machines, large-capacity (often electronic) bookkeeping machines, or computer equipment. Both bookkeeping machine payroll systems and computerized payroll systems make it possible to prepare a payroll check with deduction stub, an earnings record, and a payroll register simultaneously. This is an application of the *write-it-once principle*, which recog-

CENTRAL STATES DIVERSIFIED, INC.
ST. LOUIS, MO.

STATEMENT OF EARNINGS

MISC.	HOSPITAL	BONDS	INSURANCE	CR. UNION	PARK	CHARITY	CHECK NO.	DATE
	5.00	15.00	7.50	4.00			304	12-16-77
275.00	60.00		49.30		6.70		87.50	247.50
REGULAR	O'TIME	OTHER	WH. TAX	FICA	CITY	STATE	TOTAL DEDUCTIONS	NET PAY
EARNINGS			TAXES					

NON-NEGOTIABLE

and Deduction Stub

nizes that each time the same information is recopied there is another chance for an error.

Automation Companies and Payroll Accounting. The development of automated accounting methods and computer equipment have led to the establishment of a large number of *automation companies*. Automation companies are business organizations engaged in data processing on a contract basis for other businesses of small and medium size. They either are independently operated or are owned and operated by the major business machine manufacturers, banks, or other financial institutions. Their employees are trained in accounting and information systems work and can set up and operate effective payroll systems for customers.

When payroll accounting is done for a business by an automation company, the preliminary work that the business needs to do usually is quite limited. One or more cards are punched for each employee for each payroll period, with the aid of a keypunch machine and these cards contain necessary information such as:

(a) Employee name
(b) Employee address
(c) Employee social security number
(d) Regular earnings
(e) Overtime earnings
(f) Federal income tax withheld
(g) FICA (OASDI and HIP) tax withheld
(h) Other deductions

Must be Kept for 3 yrs.

EMPLOYEE'S EARNINGS RECORD

1977 PERIOD ENDING	EARNINGS REGULAR	OVER-TIME	TOTAL	CUMULATIVE TOTAL	TAXABLE EARNINGS UNEMPLOY. COMP.	FICA	DEDUCTIONS FICA TAX	FEDERAL INC. TAX	
1	7/8	275 00		275 00	9,555 00		275 00	16 50	34 90	1
2	7/15	275 00	55 00	330 00	9,885 00		330 00	19 80	49 30	2
3	7/22	275 00		275 00	10,160 00		275 00	16 50	34 90	3
4	7/29	275 00	65 00	340 00	10,500 00		340 00	20 40	51 70	4
5	8/5	275 00		275 00	10,775 00		275 00	16 50	34 90	5
6	8/12	275 00		275 00	11,050 00		275 00	16 50	34 90	6
7	8/19	275 00	60 00	335 00	11,385 00		335 00	20 10	49 30	7
8	8/26	275 00		275 00	11,660 00		275 00	16 50	34 90	8
9	9/2	275 00		275 00	11,935 00		275 00	16 50	34 90	9
10	9/9	275 00	55 00	330 00	12,265 00		330 00	19 80	49 30	10
11	9/16	275 00		275 00	12,540 00		275 00	16 50	34 90	11
12	9/23	275 00	60 00	335 00	12,875 00		335 00	20 10	49 30	12
13	9/30	275 00		275 00	13,150 00		275 00	16 50	34 90	13
THIRD QUARTER	3,575 00	295 00	3,870 00			3,870 00	232 20	528 10	
1	10/7	275 00		275 00	13,425 00		275 00	16 50	34 90	1
2	10/14	275 00	60 00	335 00	13,760 00		335 00	20 10	49 30	2
3	10/21	275 00	50 00	325 00	14,085 00		325 00	19 50	46 90	3
4	10/28	275 00		275 00	14,360 00		275 00	16 50	34 90	4
5	11/4	275 00		275 00	14,635 00		275 00	16 50	34 90	5
6	11/11	275 00	50 00	325 00	14,960 00		325 00	19 50	46 90	6
7	11/18	275 00	55 00	330 00	15,290 00		40 00	2 40	49 30	7
8	11/25	275 00	50 00	325 00	15,615 00				46 90	8
9	12/2	275 00		275 00	15,890 00				34 90	9
10	12/9	275 00		275 00	16,165 00				34 90	10
11	12/16	275 00	60 00	335 00	16,500 00				49 30	11
12										12
13										13
FOURTH QUARTER									
YEARLY TOTAL									

SEX	DEPARTMENT	OCCUPATION	SOCIAL SECURITY NO.	MARITAL STATUS	ALLOWANCES
M ✓ F	Maintenance	Service	474-52-4829	M	4

Employee's Earnings Record — Manually Prepared (Left Page)

FOR PERIOD ENDED *December 31*   19 77

	CITY TAX	LIFE INS.	PRIVATE HOSP. INS.	CREDIT UNION	OTHER		TOTAL	NET PAY	CK. NO.	
1	5 50						56 90	218 10	120	1
2	6 60	7 50	5 00	4 00	Sav. Bonds	15 00	107 20	222 80	128	2
3	5 50						56 90	218 10	136	3
4	6 80						78 90	261 10	144	4
5	5 50						56 90	218 10	152	5
6	5 50						56 90	218 10	160	6
7	6 70	7 50	5 00	4 00	Sav. Bonds	15 00	107 60	227 40	168	7
8	5 50						56 90	218 10	176	8
9	5 50						56 90	218 10	184	9
10	6 60						75 70	254 30	192	10
11	5 50	7 50	5 00	4 00	Sav. Bonds	15 00	88 40	186 60	200	11
12	6 70						76 10	258 90	208	12
13	5 50						56 90	218 10	216	13
	77 40	22 50	15 00	12 00		45 00	932 20	2,937 80		
1	5 50						56 90	218 10	224	1
2	6 70	7 50	5 00	4 00	Sav. Bonds	15 00	107 60	227 40	232	2
3	6 50						72 90	252 10	240	3
4	5 50						56 90	218 10	248	4
5	5 50						56 90	218 10	256	5
6	6 50						72 90	252 10	264	6
7	6 60	7 50	5 00	4 00	Sav. Bonds	15 00	89 80	240 20	272	7
8	6 50						53 40	271 60	280	8
9	5 50						40 40	234 60	288	9
10	5 50						40 40	234 60	296	10
11	6 70	7 50	5 00	4 00	Sav. Bonds	15 00	87 50	247 50	304	11
12										12
13										13

	PAY RATE	DATE OF BIRTH	DATE EMPLOYED	NAME - LAST	FIRST	MIDDLE	EMP. NO.
	#275/wk.	7-30-48	1-3-77	Lee,	Ronald	Marlin	4

Employee's Earnings Record — Manually Prepared (Right Page)

NAME	EMPLOYEE NUMBER	NUMBER OF ALLOW.	MARITAL STATUS	EARNINGS				TAXABLE EARNINGS	
				REGULAR	OVERTIME	TOTAL	CUMULATIVE TOTAL	UNEMPLOY-MENT COMP.	FICA
Akos, Stephen W.	1	2	M	180.00		180.00	9,250.00		180.00
Brandal, Ole L.	2	3	M	275.00	65.00	340.00	16,250.00		
Coxx, Michelle R.	3	1	S	150.00		150.00	7,600.00		150.00
Lee, Ronald Marlin	4	4	M	275.00	60.00	335.00	16,500.00		
MacArthur, John D.	5	3	M	240.00	50.00	290.00	13,750.00		290.00
O'Donnell, James V.	6	3	M	175.00		175.00	9,000.00		175.00
Paynter, James R.	7	2	M	180.00	30.00	210.00	10,000.00		210.00
Thomas, Wayne D.	8	1	S	160.00		160.00	8,050.00		160.00
				1,635.00	205.00	1,840.00	90,400.00		1,165.00

Payroll Register — Machine Prepared (Left Page)

These punched cards are picked up by the automation company at regular intervals, and the payroll records desired by the business customer are prepared.

A recent development in payroll accounting is the use of *time sharing*. Several small- to medium-sized businesses may own or rent time on a computer jointly. These businesses contact the computer by telephone over leased lines and carry on their payroll accounting through a typewriter-printer console.

In a manual payroll system, the payroll register normally is prepared first and serves as a journal. The employees earnings records, checks, and stubs are then prepared from the payroll register information. However, in an automated payroll system all three records are prepared simultaneously. Because of this, the order of their preparation is not of any concern to the accountant.

Employer-Operated Payroll Systems. A payroll check with deduction stub, earnings record, and payroll register entry prepared simultaneously on a bookkeeping machine are illustrated above and on the following pages. Assume that these records were prepared by Central States Diversified, Inc., for its employee, Ronald M. Lee, for the same pay period as the manual records previously illustrated on pages 76 to 81, inclusive. Contrast the two types of payroll systems. The primary advantage of the machine system is the saving of time and labor.

REGISTER

	DEDUCTIONS									
FICA TAX	FEDERAL INC. TAX	CITY TAX	LIFE INS.	PRIVATE HOSP. INS.	CREDIT UNION	U.S. SAVINGS BONDS	TOTAL	DATE	NET PAY	CK. NO.
10.80	22.70	3.60	6.00		4.00		47.10	Dec. 16, '77	132.90	301
	55.20	6.80			4.00	15.00	81.00	Dec. 16, '77	259.00	302
9.00	24.50	3.00		4.00			40.50	Dec. 16, '77	109.50	303
	49.30	6.70	7.50	5.00	4.00	15.00	87.50	Dec. 16, '77	247.50	304
17.40	43.20	5.80	7.50	5.00	4.00		82.90	Dec. 16, '77	207.10	305
10.50	18.80	3.50	5.00				37.80	Dec. 16, '77	137.20	306
12.60	28.30	4.20			4.00		49.10	Dec. 16, '77	160.90	307
9.60	26.60	3.20	5.00	4.00			48.40	Dec. 16, '77	111.60	308
69.90	268.60	36.80	31.00	18.00	20.00	30.00	474.30		1,365.70	

Payroll Register — Machine Prepared (Right Page)

In addition to the *write-it-once* features of modern bookkeeping machines, computer-based payroll systems can also provide speed and storage as well as needed adding and multiplying ability. Through the use of computerized equipment, adding and multiplying of payrolls can be speeded up, and information such as wage rates and withholding table amounts can be stored inside the equipment. As one would expect, the cost of computerized payroll equipment is noticeably higher than the cost of more conventional bookkeeping machines. The type of computer-based accounting system well suited to payroll accounting, among other things, is described and illustrated in the appendix to this textbook.

Much of the work usually required to figure employees' gross earnings, deductions, and net pay may be eliminated if the equipment provides sufficient automation, storage capacity, and electronic calculation capability. When conventional electric bookkeeping machines are used, gross earnings are often computed separately on a calculator, and withholding and other tax amounts are either read from tables or worked out manually.

A computer-based payroll accounting system completes all of the major payroll records at once, just as do modern electronic bookkeeping machines. Also, a computer-based payroll accounting system determines automatically:

(a) The presence of the proper earnings record.
(b) The next available posting line.
(c) Whether overtime earnings are due.

EMPLOYEE'S

NAME	RONALD MARLIN LEE
ADDRESS	502 KINGSLAND AVENUE
CITY	ST. LOUIS, MISSOURI 63130
SEX	Male
MARITAL STATUS	Married

NUMBER OF ALLOWANCES   4

EARNINGS				TAXABLE EARNINGS	
REGULAR	OVERTIME	TOTAL	CUMULATIVE TOTAL	UNEMPLOY-MENT COMP.	FICA
275.00		275.00	9,555.00		275.00
275.00	55.00	330.00	9,885.00		330.00
275.00		275.00	10,160.00		275.00
275.00	65.00	340.00	10,500.00		340.00
275.00		275.00	10,775.00		275.00
275.00		275.00	11,050.00		275.00
275.00	60.00	335.00	11,385.00		335.00
275.00		275.00	11,660.00		275.00
275.00		275.00	11,935.00		275.00
275.00	55.00	330.00	12,265.00		330.00
275.00		275.00	12,540.00		275.00
275.00	60.00	335.00	12,875.00		335.00
275.00		275.00	13,150.00		275.00
THIRD QUARTER					
3,575.00	295.00	3,870.00			3,870.00
275.00		275.00	13,425.00		275.00
275.00	60.00	335.00	13,760.00		335.00
275.00	50.00	325.00	14,085.00		325.00
275.00		275.00	14,360.00		275.00
275.00		275.00	14,635.00		275.00
275.00	50.00	325.00	14,960.00		325.00
275.00	55.00	330.00	15,290.00		40.00
275.00	50.00	325.00	15,615.00		
275.00		275.00	15,890.00		
275.00		275.00	16,165.00		
275.00	60.00	335.00	16,500.00		
FOURTH QUARTER					
YEARLY TOTAL					

Employee's Earnings Record — Machine Prepared (Left Page)

(d) Whether there are other earnings.

(e) Whether the FICA limit has been reached.

(f) What tax deductions should be made.

(g) Whether insurance premiums should be deducted.

(h) Whether there are any other deductions to be made.

(i) Whether there are any delinquent deductions to be made.

(j) Whether there is anything else to be done.

EARNINGS RECORD

DEPARTMENT	Maintenance	SOCIAL SECURITY NUMBER	474-52-4829
OCCUPATION	Service	DATE OF BIRTH	July 30, 1948
PAY RATE	$275 Weekly	DATE EMPLOYED	January 3, 1977
EMPLOYEE NO.	4	DATE EMPLOYMENT TERMINATED	

				DEDUCTIONS						
FICA TAX	FEDERAL INC. TAX	CITY TAX	LIFE INS.	PRIVATE HOSP. INS.	CREDIT UNION	U.S. SAVINGS BONDS	TOTAL	DATE	NET PAY	CK. NO.
16.50	34.90	5.50					56.90	July 8, '77	218.10	120
19.80	49.30	6.60	7.50	5.00	4.00	15.00	107.20	July 15, '77	222.80	128
16.50	34.90	5.50					56.90	July 22, '77	218.10	136
20.40	51.70	6.80					78.90	July 29, '77	261.10	144
16.50	34.90	5.50					56.90	Aug. 5, '77	218.10	152
16.50	34.90	5.50					56.90	Aug. 12, '77	218.10	160
20.10	49.30	6.70	7.50	5.00	4.00	15.00	107.60	Aug. 19, '77	227.40	168
16.50	34.90	5.50					56.90	Aug. 26, '77	218.10	176
16.50	34.90	5.50					56.90	Sept. 2, '77	218.10	184
19.80	49.30	6.60					75.70	Sept. 9, '77	254.30	192
16.50	34.90	5.50	7.50	5.00	4.00	15.00	88.40	Sept. 16, '77	186.60	200
20.10	49.30	6.70					76.10	Sept. 23, '77	258.90	208
16.50	34.90	5.50					56.90	Sept. 30, '77	218.10	216
232.20	528.10	77.40	22.50	15.00	12.00	45.00	932.20		2,937.80	
16.50	34.90	5.50					56.90	Oct. 7, '77	218.10	224
20.10	49.30	6.70	7.50	5.00	4.00	15.00	107.60	Oct. 14, '77	227.40	232
19.50	46.90	6.50					72.90	Oct. 21, '77	252.10	240
16.50	34.90	5.50					56.90	Oct. 28, '77	218.10	248
16.50	34.90	5.50					56.90	Nov. 4, '77	218.10	256
19.50	46.90	6.50					72.90	Nov. 11, '77	252.10	264
2.40	49.30	6.60	7.50	5.00	4.00	15.00	89.80	Nov. 18, '77	240.20	272
	46.90	6.50					53.40	Nov. 25, '77	271.60	280
	34.90	5.50					40.40	Dec. 2, '77	234.60	288
	34.90	5.50					40.40	Dec. 9, '77	234.60	296
	49.30	6.70	7.50	5.00	4.00	15.00	87.50	Dec. 16, '77	247.50	304

Employee's Earnings Record — Machine Prepared (Right Page)

Once this system is properly set up, the operator is relieved of manual figuring and of looking up amounts in tables. The primary job is one of feeding in blank payroll accounting record forms and getting these forms back as completed payroll accounting records. (For a further discussion of computer-based accounting systems and procedures, see Appendix, page A-1.)

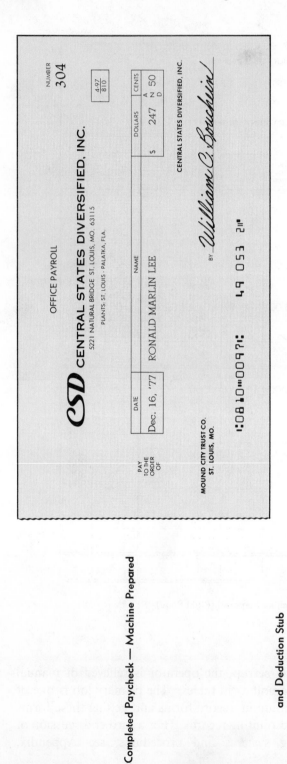

Completed Paycheck — Machine Prepared

and Deduction Stub

Wage and tax statement

Not later than January 31 of each year the law requires employers to furnish each employee from whom income taxes have been withheld the Wage and Tax Statement, Form W-2, showing the total amount of wages paid and the amount of such tax withheld during the preceding calendar year. This statement should be issued 30 days after the last wage payment to a terminating employee. If the employee's wages were subject to FICA tax as well as federal, state, or local income tax, the employer must report total wages paid and the amounts deducted both for income tax and for FICA tax. Information for this purpose should be provided by the employee's earnings record. A completed form W-2 is illustrated below.

	Wage and Tax Statement 1975

| 43-0211630
CENTRAL STATES DIVERSIFIED, INC.
5221 Natural Bridge
St. Louis, MO 63115 | Type or print EMPLOYER'S name, address, ZIP code and Federal identifying number. | Copy C For employee's records

Employer's State identifying number
21-686001 |

Employee's social security number	1 Federal income tax withheld	2 Wages, tips, and other compensation	3 FICA employee tax withheld	4 Total FICA wages
474-52-4829	$2,132.60	$17,050.00	$900.00	$15,000.00

Type or print Employee's name, address, and ZIP code below.	5 Was employee covered by a qualified pension plan, etc.?	6	7
Ronald M. Lee 502 Kingsland Avenue St. Louis, MO 63130	8 State or local tax withheld	9 State or local wages	10 State or locality
	11 State or local tax withheld	12 State or local wages	13 State or locality

Form W-2   This information is being furnished to the Internal Revenue Service.   Department of the Treasury—Internal Revenue Service

Completed Wage and Tax Statement (Form W-2)

The number appearing on the Wage and Tax Statement above the name and address of the employer is an *identification number* assigned to the employer by the Social Security Administration. Every employer of even one person receiving taxable wages must get an identification number within a week of the beginning of such employment. This number must be shown on all reports required of Central States Diversified, Inc., under the Federal Insurance Contributions Act.

Wage and Tax Statements must be prepared in quadruplicate (four copies). Copy A goes to the Internal Revenue Service Center with the employer's return of taxes withheld for the fourth quarter of the calendar year. Copies B and C are furnished to the employee, so that he can send Copy B in with his federal income tax return as required and keep Copy C for his files. Copy D is kept by the employer for his records. In states or cities which have state or city income tax withholding laws, two more copies are furnished. One copy is sent in by the employer to the appropriate state or city tax department, and the other is sent in by the employee with his state or city income tax return.

Accounting for wages and wage deductions

In accounting for wages and wage deductions it is desirable to keep separate accounts for (1) wages earned and (2) wage deductions. Various account titles are used in recording wages, such as Payroll Expense, Salaries Expense, and Salaries and Commissions Expense. The accounts needed in recording wage deductions depend upon what deductions are involved. A separate account should be kept for recording the liability incurred for each type of deduction, such as FICA tax, employees income tax, and savings bond deductions.

Payroll Expense. This is an expense account which should be debited for the total amount of the gross earnings of all employees for each pay period. Sometimes separate

PAYROLL EXPENSE	
Debit	
to record gross earnings of employees for each pay period.	

payroll accounts are kept for the employees of different departments. Thus, separate accounts might be kept for Office Salaries Expense, Sales Salaries Expense, and Factory Payroll Expense.

FICA Tax Payable. This is a liability account which should be credited for (1) the FICA tax withheld from employees' wages and (2) the FICA tax imposed on the employer. The account should be debited for amounts paid to apply on

FICA TAX PAYABLE	
Debit	Credit
to record payment of FICA tax.	to record FICA taxes (a) withheld from employees' wages and (b) imposed on the employer.

such taxes. When all of the FICA taxes have been paid, the account should be in balance.

Employees Income Tax Payable. This is a liability account which should be credited for the total income tax withheld from employees' wages. The account should be

EMPLOYEES INCOME TAX PAYABLE	
Debit	Credit
to record payment of income tax withheld.	to record income tax withheld from employees' wages.

debited for amounts paid to apply on such taxes. When all of the income taxes withheld have been paid, the account will be in balance. A city or state earnings tax payable account is used in a similar manner.

Life Insurance Premiums Payable. This is a liability account which should be credited with amounts withheld from employees' wages for the future payment of life insurance premiums. The account should be debited for the subsequent payment

LIFE INSURANCE PREMIUMS PAYABLE	
Debit	Credit
to record the payment of life insurance premiums withheld.	to record amounts withheld for the future payment of life insurance premiums.

of these premiums to the life insurance company. Accounts for private hospital insurance premiums payable, credit union contributions payable, and savings bond deductions payable are similarly used.

Journalizing Payroll Transactions. The payroll register should provide the information needed in recording wages paid. The payroll register illustrated on pages 82 and 83 provided the information needed in drafting the following general journal entry to record the wages paid on December 16:

```
Dec. 16. Payroll Expense..... (Total Earnings) ........  1,840.00
           FICA Tax Payable...........................            69.90
           Employees Income Tax Payable................           268.60
           City Earnings Tax Payable....................            36.80
           Life Insurance Premiums Payable..............            31.00
           Private Hospital Insurance Premiums Payable....           18.00
           Credit Union Contributions Payable............           20.00
           Savings Bond Deductions Payable...........             30.00
           Cash.................. (Net Pay) .......        1,365.70
           Payroll for week ended December 16
```

It will be noted that the above journal entry involves one debit and eight credits. Regardless of the number of debits and credits needed to record a transaction, the total amount debited must be equal to the total amount credited.

Report

No. 4-1

    Complete Report No. 4-1 in the study assignments and submit your working papers to the instructor for approval. After completing the report, continue with the following textbook discussion until the next report is required.

PAYROLL TAXES IMPOSED ON THE EMPLOYER

    The employer is liable to the government for the taxes which are required by law to be withheld from the wages of employees. These taxes include the federal income tax and the FICA tax which must be withheld from wages paid to employees. Such taxes are not an expense of the employer; nevertheless, the employer is required by law to collect the taxes and he is liable for the taxes until payment is made.

    Certain taxes are also imposed on the employer for various purposes, such as old-age, survivors, and disability insurance benefits; hospital insurance benefits for the aged; and unemployment, relief, and welfare. Most employers are subject to payroll taxes imposed under the Federal

Insurance Contributions Act (FICA) and the Federal Unemployment Tax Act (FUTA). An employer may also be subject to the payroll tax imposed under the unemployment compensation laws of one or more states. These commonly are called "State Unemployment Tax."

Payroll taxes expense

All of the payroll taxes imposed on an employer under federal and state social security laws are an expense of the employer. In accounting for such taxes at least one expense account should be maintained. This account may be entitled Payroll Taxes Expense. It is an expense account which should be debited for all taxes imposed on the employer under federal and state social security laws. Sometimes separate expense accounts are kept for **(1)** FICA Tax Expense,

PAYROLL TAXES EXPENSE
Debit to record FICA, FUTA, and State Unemployment Taxes imposed on the employer.

(2) FUTA Tax Expense, and **(3)** State Unemployment Tax Expense. In small business enterprises it is usually considered satisfactory to keep a single expense account for all federal and state social security taxes imposed on the employer.

Employer's FICA tax

The taxes imposed under the Federal Insurance Contributions Act apply equally to employers and to employees. As explained on page 75, both the rate and base of the tax may be changed by Congress at any time. In this discussion it is assumed that the combined rate is 6 percent which applies both to the employer and to his employees (a total of 12 percent) with respect to taxable wages. Only the first $15,000 of the wages paid to each employee in any calendar year constitutes taxable wages. Any amount of wages paid to an employee during a year in excess of $15,000 is exempt from FICA tax. While the employer is liable to the government both for the tax withheld from his employees' wages and for the tax imposed on the business, only the latter constitutes an expense of the business.

Employer's FUTA tax

Under the Federal Unemployment Tax Act, a payroll tax is levied on employers for the purpose of implementing more uniform administration of the various state unemployment compensation laws. Employers who employ one or more individuals for at least 20 calendar weeks in the calendar year, *or* who pay wages of $1,500 or more in any calendar quarter, are subject to this tax. The federal law imposes a specific rate of tax but allows a substantial credit against this levy if the state in which the employer is located has an unemployment compensation law that meets certain requirements. Since all states have such laws, the rate actually paid by most employers is much less than the maximum legal rate. As in the case of the FICA tax, Congress can and does change the rate from time to time. For the purpose of this discussion, a rate of 3.2 percent with a credit of 2.7 percent available to most employers is used. The difference, 0.5 percent (3.2 — 2.7) is, then, the effective rate. This is applied to the first $4,200 of compensation paid to each employee during the calendar year. It is important to note this limitation in contrast to the $15,000 limit in the case of the FICA tax. It is also important to note that all of the payroll taxes relate to gross wages paid — not to wages earned. Sometimes wages are earned in one quarter or year, but not paid until the following period.

FUTA tax payable

In recording the federal unemployment tax, it is customary to keep a separate liability account entitled FUTA Tax Payable. This is a liability account which should be credited for the tax imposed on employers under the Federal Unemployment Tax Act. The account should be debited for amounts paid to apply on such taxes. When all of the FUTA taxes have been paid, the account should be in balance.

FUTA Tax Payable	
Debit	Credit
to record payment of FUTA tax.	to record FUTA tax imposed on the employer with respect to wages paid.

State unemployment tax

All of the states and the District of Columbia have enacted unemployment compensation laws providing for the payment of benefits to qualified unemployed workers. The cost of administering the state unemployment compensation laws is borne by the federal government. Under the federal law an appropriation is made for each year by the Congress from which grants are made to the states to meet the proper administrative costs of their unemployment compensation laws. As a result of this provision, the entire amount paid into the state funds may be used for the payment of benefits to qualified workers. While in general there is considerable uniformity in the provisions of the state laws, there are many variations in coverage, rates of tax imposed, and benefits payable to qualified workers. The date of payment of unemployment taxes also varies from state to state, and a penalty generally is imposed on the employer for late payment. Not all employers covered by the Federal Unemployment Tax

Act are covered by the unemployment compensation laws of the states in which they have employees. But most employers of one or more individuals are covered by the federal law.

The minimum number of employees specified under state laws varies from 1 to 4. However, in many of the states an employer who is covered by the federal law and has one or more individuals employed within the state is also covered by the state law. Furthermore, under the laws of most states an employer who is covered by the federal law may elect voluntary coverage in states where he has one or more employees, even though he may have less than the number of employees specified by the law in that particular state. In any event, it is necessary for each employer to be familiar with the unemployment compensation laws of all the states in which he has one or more employees, and if such employees are covered, he must keep such records and pay such taxes for unemployment compensation purposes as are prescribed by those laws.

In most states the unemployment benefit plan is financed entirely by taxes imposed on employers. However, in a few states employees are also required to contribute, and the amount of the tax imposed on the employees must be withheld from their wages.

In most states the maximum tax imposed upon employers is 2.7 percent of the first $4,200 of wages paid to each employee in any calendar year. However, under the laws of most states there is a *merit-rating* system which provides a tax-saving incentive to employers to stabilize employment. Under this system an employer's rate may be considerably less than the maximum rate if he provides steady work for his employees.

There are frequent changes in the state laws with respect to coverage, rates of contributions required, eligibility to receive benefits, and amounts of benefits payable. In this discussion, it is assumed that the state tax rate is 2.7 percent of the first $4,200 of wages paid each employee each year.

State unemployment tax payable

In recording the tax imposed under state unemployment compensation laws, it is customary to keep a separate liability account entitled State Unemployment Tax Payable. This is a liability account which

STATE UNEMPLOYMENT TAX PAYABLE	
Debit	Credit
to record state unemployment tax paid.	to record liability for state unemployment tax required of employers.

should be credited for the tax imposed on employers under the state unemployment compensation laws. The account should be debited for the amount paid to apply on such taxes. When all of the state taxes have been paid, the account should be in balance. Some employers who are subject to taxes imposed under the laws of several states keep a separate liability account for the tax imposed by each state.

Journalizing employer's payroll taxes

The payroll taxes imposed on employers may be recorded periodically, such as monthly or quarterly. It is more common to record such taxes at the time that wages are paid so that the employer's liability for such taxes and related expenses may be recorded in the same period as the wages on which the taxes are based. The payroll register illustrated on pages 82 and 83 provides the information needed in recording the FICA tax imposed on Central States Diversified, Inc., with respect to wages paid on December 16. The FICA taxable earnings for the pay period involved amounted to $1,165.00. Assuming that the combined rate of the tax imposed on the employer was 6 percent, which is the same as the rate of the tax imposed on the employees, the tax would amount to $69.90. (This amount will not necessarily be the same as that calculated by multiplying the tax rate times total taxable earnings due to the rounding up of amounts in calculating the tax deduction for each employee.) If only $875.00 of the earnings for the period had been subject to unemployment taxes (none actually were), the federal and state taxes would have been computed as follows:

State unemployment tax, 2.7% of $875.00............................	$23.63
FUTA tax, 0.5% of $875.00..	4.38
Total unemployment taxes..	$28.01

The following general journal entry may be made to record the payroll taxes imposed on the employer with respect to the wages paid on December 16:

Dec. 16.	Payroll Taxes Expense.................................	97.91	
	FICA Tax Payable................................		69.90
	FUTA Tax Payable................................		4.38
	State Unemployment Tax Payable....................		23.63
	Payroll taxes imposed on employer with respect to wages paid December 16.		

Filing returns and paying the payroll taxes

When the cumulative amount withheld from employees' wages for income tax and FICA tax purposes plus the amount of the FICA tax imposed on the employer during the first or second month of any quarter is more than $200, the total must be deposited at a District Federal Reserve Bank or some other United States depositary by the 15th of the following month. If at the end of a quarter the total amount of undeposited taxes is $200 or more, the total amount must be deposited in a federal depositary or Federal Reserve bank on or before the last day of the first month after the end of the quarter. If at the end of a quarter the total amount of undeposited taxes is less than $200, a deposit is not necessary. The taxes may either be paid directly to the Internal Revenue Service along with Form 941 or a deposit may be made.

When the cumulative amount of income and FICA tax is over $200 but under $2,000, the total is required to be deposited by the 15th day of the next month. If this $200–$2,000 limitation is reached in the third month of any quarter, no deposit need be made until the last day of the month following the quarter.

When the cumulative amount is $2,000 or more by the 7th, 15th, 22d, or last day of any month, a deposit must be made within three banking days after that quarter-monthly period.

A completed copy of the Federal Tax Deposit — Withheld Income and FICA Taxes, Form 501, is shown below. The stub is detached by the bank on payment of the taxes due and is the employer's record of the deposit.

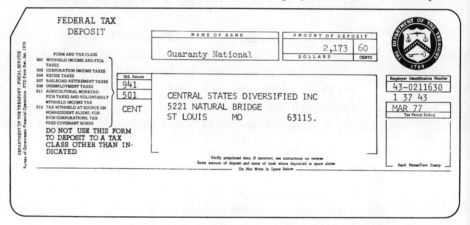

Completed Federal Tax Deposit Form (Form 501)

To illustrate the accounting procedure in recording the payment of employees' income tax and FICA tax withheld, it will be assumed that on February 3 Central States Diversified, Inc., issued a check in payment of the following taxes imposed with respect to wages paid during the month of January:

Employees' income tax withheld from wages...............		$1,274.40
FICA tax:		
Withheld from employees' wages........................	$449.60	
Imposed on employer.................................	449.60	899.20
Amount of check..		$2,173.60

A check for this amount accompanied by the Federal Tax Deposit form, Form 501, was sent to a bank that is qualified as a depositary for federal taxes. (All national banks are qualified.) This transaction may be recorded as indicated by the following general journal entry:

Feb. 3. FICA Tax Payable.............................	899.20	
Employees Income Tax Payable	1,274.40	
Cash..		2,173.60
Remitted $2,173.60 in payment of taxes.		

Further assume that on March 3, $2,165.30 was deposited. This covered income tax withholdings of $1,268.80 during February and the employer's and employees' FICA tax of $896.50 for February. The proper entry was made to record the payment of $2,165.30. Also assume that during March, income tax withholdings amounted to $1,286.50 and FICA tax (employer's and employees'), $904.30 — a total of $2,190.80, which amount was deposited on April 4. The proper entry was made to record the payment of $2,190.80 to the Internal Revenue Service. Finally assume that on April 15, the quarterly return, Form 941, illustrated on page 96 was sent to the nearest Internal Revenue Service Center.

The amount on lines 11 and 13 of the quarterly tax return illustration, $3,829.70, is the sum of the employees' income tax withheld in January ($1,274.40), February ($1,268.80), and March ($1,286.50). The amount on line 14 of this return comes from the total of wages reported on line 8 (the total taxable FICA wages reported on Schedule A) times 12 percent (the combined FICA tax rate for employer and employee). The adjusted total of FICA tax on line 18 is added to the adjusted total of income tax withheld, line 13, to give the amount on line 19, which is the total income tax and FICA tax due to the federal government.

The amount on line 20 of the Form 941 illustration, $6,529.70, is the sum of the tax deposits for February 3 ($2,173.60), March 3 ($2,165.30), and $2,190.80, the balance due to the Internal Revenue Service for which a final deposit was made and listed in Schedule B (not illustrated).

The amount of the tax imposed on employers under the state unemployment compensation laws must be remitted to the proper state office during the month following the close of the calendar quarter. Each state provides an official form to be used in making a return of the taxes due. Assuming that a check for $494.91 was issued on April 30 in payment of state unemployment compensation tax on wages paid during the preceding quarter ended March 31, the transaction may be recorded as indicated by the following journal entry:

```
Apr. 30.  State Unemployment Tax Payable...................   494.91
              Cash.........................................              494.91
                 Paid state unemployment tax.
```

Federal unemployment tax must be computed on a quarterly basis. If the amount of the employer's liability under the Federal Unemployment Tax Act during any quarter is more than $100, the total must be paid to the District Federal Reserve Bank or some other United States depositary on or before the last day of the first month following the close of the quarter. If the amount is $100 or less, no deposit is necessary, but this amount must be added to the amount subject to deposit for the next quarter.

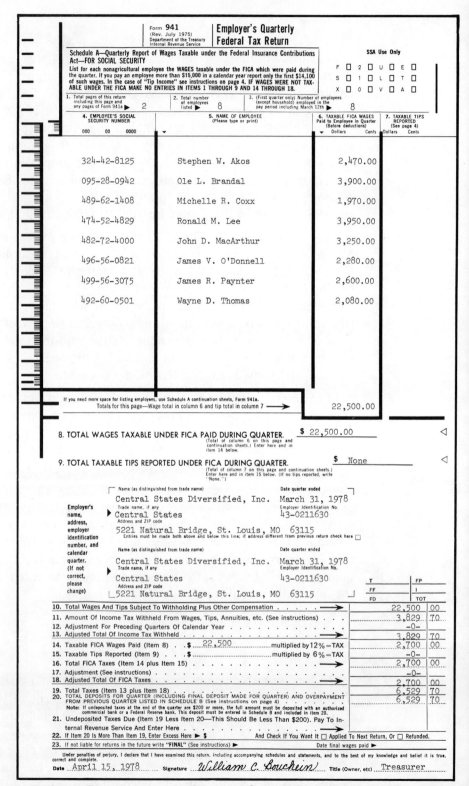

Form **941**
(Rev. July 1975)
Department of the Treasury
Internal Revenue Service

**Employer's Quarterly
Federal Tax Return**

SSA Use Only

Schedule A—Quarterly Report of Wages Taxable under the Federal Insurance Contributions Act—FOR SOCIAL SECURITY

List for each nonagricultural employee the WAGES taxable under the FICA which were paid during the quarter. If you pay an employee more than $15,000 in a calendar year report only the first $14,100 of such wages. In the case of "Tip Income" see instructions on page 4. IF WAGES WERE NOT TAXABLE UNDER THE FICA MAKE NO ENTRIES IN ITEMS 1 THROUGH 9 AND 14 THROUGH 18.

F ☐ 2 U E ☐
S ☐ 1 L T ☐
X ☐ 0 V A ☐

1. Total pages of this return including this page and any pages of Form 941a ▶ **2**

2. Total number of employees listed ▶ **8**

3. (First quarter only) Number of employees (except household) employed in the pay period including March 12th ▶ **8**

4. EMPLOYEE'S SOCIAL SECURITY NUMBER	5. NAME OF EMPLOYEE (Please type or print)	6. TAXABLE FICA WAGES Paid to Employee in Quarter (Before deductions)	7. TAXABLE TIPS REPORTED (See page 4)
000 00 0000		Dollars Cents	Dollars Cents
324-42-8125	Stephen W. Akos	2,470.00	
095-28-0942	Ole L. Brandal	3,900.00	
489-62-1408	Michelle R. Coxx	1,970.00	
474-52-4829	Ronald M. Lee	3,950.00	
482-72-4000	John D. MacArthur	3,250.00	
496-56-0821	James V. O'Donnell	2,280.00	
499-56-3075	James R. Paynter	2,600.00	
492-60-0501	Wayne D. Thomas	2,080.00	

If you need more space for listing employees, use Schedule A continuation sheets, Form 941a.
Totals for this page—Wage total in column 6 and tip total in column 7 ⟶ **22,500.00**

8. TOTAL WAGES TAXABLE UNDER FICA PAID DURING QUARTER. **$ 22,500.00** ◁
(Total of column 6 on this page and continuation sheets.) Enter here and in item 14 below.

9. TOTAL TAXABLE TIPS REPORTED UNDER FICA DURING QUARTER. **$ None** ◁
(Total of column 7 on this page and continuation sheets.) Enter here and in item 15 below. (If no tips reported, write "None.")

Employer's name, address, employer identification number, and calendar quarter. (If not correct, please change)

Name (as distinguished from trade name)
Central States Diversified, Inc.   Date quarter ended **March 31, 1978**
Trade name, if any ▶ **Central States**   Employer Identification No. **43-0211630**
Address and ZIP code **5221 Natural Bridge, St. Louis, MO 63115**
Entries must be made both above and below this line; if address different from previous return check here ☐

Name (as distinguished from trade name)
Central States Diversified, Inc.   Date quarter ended **March 31, 1978**
Trade name, if any ▶ **Central States**   Employer Identification No. **43-0211630**
Address and ZIP code **5221 Natural Bridge, St. Louis, MO 63115**

T		FP
FF		I
FD		TOT

10. Total Wages And Tips Subject To Withholding Plus Other Compensation . . . . . ⟶	22,500	00
11. Amount Of Income Tax Withheld From Wages, Tips, Annuities, etc. (See instructions) . . .	3,829	70
12. Adjustment For Preceding Quarters Of Calendar Year	-0-	
13. Adjusted Total Of Income Tax Withheld . . . . ⟶	3,829	70
14. Taxable FICA Wages Paid (Item 8) . . $ 22,500 ....multiplied by 12% = TAX	2,700	00
15. Taxable Tips Reported (Item 9) . . . $ ....multiplied by 6% = TAX	-0-	
16. Total FICA Taxes (Item 14 plus Item 15) . . . . ⟶	2,700	00
17. Adjustment (See instructions)	-0-	
18. Adjusted Total Of FICA Taxes . . . . ⟶	2,700	00
19. Total Taxes (Item 13 plus Item 18) . . . . ⟶	6,529	70
20. TOTAL DEPOSITS FOR QUARTER (INCLUDING FINAL DEPOSIT MADE FOR QUARTER) AND OVERPAYMENT FROM PREVIOUS QUARTER LISTED IN SCHEDULE B (See instructions on page 4) . . . . . ⟶	6,529	70

Note: If undeposited taxes at the end of the quarter are $200 or more, the full amount must be deposited with an authorized commercial bank or a Federal Reserve bank. This deposit must be entered in Schedule B and included in item 20.

21. Undeposited Taxes Due (Item 19 Less Item 20—This Should Be Less Than $200). Pay To Internal Revenue Service And Enter Here . . . . ⟶

22. If Item 20 Is More Than Item 19, Enter Excess Here ▶ $ And Check If You Want It ☐ Applied To Next Return, Or ☐ Refunded.

23. If not liable for returns in the future write **"FINAL"** (See instructions) ▶ Date final wages paid ▶

Under penalties of perjury, I declare that I have examined this return, including accompanying schedules and statements, and to the best of my knowledge and belief it is true, correct and complete.

Date **April 15, 1978** Signature *William C. Bouchein* Title (Owner, etc) **Treasurer**

Employer's Quarterly Federal Tax Return and Quarterly Report, Schedule A (Form 941)

When paying FUTA tax, it is necessary to complete the Federal Tax Deposit form, Form 508, and to send or take it to the bank with the remittance. This form is not illustrated here, but it is similar in nature to Form 501, previously illustrated on page 94.

The amount of the tax on employers under the Federal Unemployment Tax Act for the entire year must be paid to the District Director of Internal Revenue by the end of the month following the close of the calendar year. An official form (Form 940) is provided to the employer for use in making a report of the taxes due. This form is not illustrated here.

Assuming that a check for $96.10 was issued on January 31 in payment of the tax imposed under the Federal Unemployment Tax Act with respect to wages paid during the preceding year ended December 31, the transaction may be recorded as indicated by the following journal entry:

```
Jan. 31.  FUTA Tax Payable................................    96.10
              Cash...........................................              96.10
                  Paid federal unemployment tax.
```

Report No. 4-2	Complete Report No. 4-2 in the study assignments and submit your working papers to the instructor for approval. After completing the report, you may continue with the textbook discussion in Chapter 5 until the next report is required.

Chapter 5

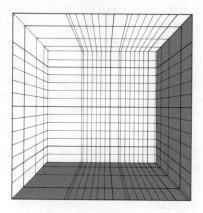

ACCOUNTING FOR A PERSONAL SERVICE ENTERPRISE

A personal service enterprise is one in which the principal source of revenue is compensation for personal services rendered. There are two types of personal service enterprises:

(a) Business enterprises
(b) Professional enterprises

Business enterprises of the personal service type include real estate, insurance, advertising, transportation, storage, entertainment, brokerage, and various others in which the revenue is derived chiefly from personal services rendered. Mercantile enterprises are not classified as personal service enterprises for the reason that their principal source of revenue is from the sale of merchandise rather than from compensation received for services provided.

Professional enterprises include law, medicine, dentistry, public accounting, management consulting, engineering, architecture, art, and education. The principal source of revenue for individuals engaged in such professions is usually the compensation received for the personal services rendered.

The cash basis of accounting for a personal service enterprise

Accounting for revenue on a cash basis means that, in most cases, no record of revenue is made in the accounts until cash is received for the services performed. This may mean that the services are rendered in one period, and the revenue is accounted for in the succeeding period. The business or professional man may well take the view that, in most cases, he has had no revenue until it is received in such form that it can be spent. He cannot "spend" the promise of a customer or client to pay him some money.

The cash basis of accounting for the revenue of a personal service enterprise is widely used. It is acceptable for federal and state income tax purposes. Not only is the receipt of cash accounted for as revenue under this basis; many other types of transactions are accounted for similarly. Any property or service that is accepted in place of cash for services is treated as revenue to the extent of its fair market value at the time received. Revenue is said to be *constructively received* if it is credited to a depositor's account or set apart so that it can be drawn upon. For example, when interest on a savings account is credited to the depositor's account, such interest is considered to be revenue to the depositor even though it is not actually received in cash or is not immediately withdrawn.

Accounting for expenses on the cash basis generally means that expenses are not recorded in the accounts until paid in cash. An expense may be incurred in one period and recorded in the accounts in the succeeding period. In the case of many expenses of a recurring nature, however, this set of circumstances is regarded as a minor objection. If, for example, twelve monthly telephone bills of about the same amount must be paid during each year, little importance is attached to the fact that the bill that is paid and recorded as an expense in January was really for service received in December.

An exception to the cash basis of accounting for expenses is made in connection with most long-lived assets. For example, it would be unreasonable to consider the entire cost of a building or of most equipment to be an expense of the period in which such assets were purchased. If it is expected that an asset will serve for a number of years, its cost (less expected scrap or salvage value, if any) is allocated over its estimated life. The share of cost assigned to each period is described as *depreciation expense*. Such expense cannot be calculated with precise accuracy. Still, an allocation that eventually turns out to have been somewhat in error results in a far more equitable periodic net income (profit) or loss measurement than one that simply considers the cost of such assets to be entirely an expense of the period in which they were purchased.

Another exception to the cash basis of accounting for expenses is sometimes made in connection with supplies purchased and used. If the amount of money involved is substantial and the end of the accounting period finds a considerable quantity of expensive supplies still on hand, an effort is made to determine the cost of those items which are on hand, so that only the cost of the supplies used will be treated as an expense of the period. If both the quantity and the cost of the items on hand at the end of a period are small, the usual practice is to ignore them and to consider the total cost of all items purchased during that accounting period to be an expense of that period.

ACCOUNTING PROCEDURE

As an aid in applying the principles involved in keeping the accounts of a personal service enterprise on the cash basis, a system of accounts for John H. Roberts, a management consultant, will be described. While certain distinctive problems may arise in keeping the accounts of any specific enterprise, it will be found that the principles are generally the same; hence, the system of accounts used by Mr. Roberts may readily be adapted to the needs of any personal service enterprise regardless of whether it is of a professional or a business nature.

Chart of accounts   Mr. Roberts' chart of accounts is reproduced on page 101. Note that all account numbers beginning with 1 relate to assets; 2, liabilities; 3, owner's equity; 4, revenue; and 5, expenses. Account numbers beginning with 0 represent *contra accounts* (meaning "opposite" or "offsetting" accounts) used to show the decrease in the related element. This system of account numbering permits the addition of new accounts as they may be needed without disturbing the numerical order of the existing accounts.

Most of the accounts in the foregoing list have been discussed and their use illustrated in the preceding chapters. Three notable exceptions are: Accumulated Depreciation — Office Equipment (No. 013), Depreciation Expense (No. 517), and Expense and Revenue Summary (No. 321). Each of these will be explained and its use illustrated as the need for the account arises in the narrative of transactions later in the chapter. Except for Depreciation Expense (No. 517), every debit to an expense account arises in connection with a cash disbursement. The cost of all forms and supplies purchased is debited (charged) to Account No. 515. The amount of any unused forms and supplies that may be on hand at the end of the year is ignored because such quantities normally are very small. (Note that there is no asset account for forms and supplies.) The car that Mr. Roberts uses for business purposes is leased. The monthly car rental and the cost

JOHN H. ROBERTS, MANAGEMENT CONSULTANT
CHART OF ACCOUNTS

*Assets**
111 County National Bank
112 Petty Cash Fund
131 Office Equipment
013 Accumulated Depreciation—
     Office Equipment

Liabilities
211 Employees Income Tax Payable
212 FICA Tax Payable

Owner's Equity
311 John H. Roberts, Capital
031 John H. Roberts, Drawing
321 Expense and Revenue Summary

Revenue
411 Professional Fees

Expenses
511 Salary Expense
512 Payroll Taxes Expense
513 Rent Expense
514 Telephone Expense
515 Forms and Supplies Expense
516 Automobile Expense
517 Depreciation Expense
518 Insurance Expense
519 Travel and Entertainment Expense
521 Charitable Contributions Expense
522 Miscellaneous Expense

*Words in italics represent headings and not account titles.

of gasoline, oil, lubrication, washing, and automobile insurance are charged to Automobile Expense, Account No. 516. The cost of all other types of insurance that relate to the enterprise, such as workmen's compensation, "errors and omissions" insurance (normally carried by management consultants), and fire insurance on the office equipment and contents, is charged to Insurance Expense, Account No. 518, when the premiums on the policies are paid.

Books of account

Mr. Roberts uses the following books of account:

(a) General books
    (1) Combined cash journal
    (2) General ledger
(b) Auxiliary records
    (1) Petty cash disbursements record
    (2) Employees' earnings records
    (3) Copies of statements rendered to clients (billings for fees) with collections noted thereon

Combined Cash Journal. The two-column journal could be used to record every transaction of a business enterprise. However, there are likely to be numerous similar transactions that involve the same account or accounts. Outstanding examples are receipts and disbursements of cash. Suppose that in a typical month there are 30 transactions that result in an increase in cash and 40 transactions that involve a decrease in cash. In a two-column journal, this would require writing the word "Cash" (or, perhaps, "County National Bank" if all receipts are deposited in that bank and all payments, except for petty cash, are made by check) 70 times — using a journal line each time. A considerable saving of time and space would result if two columns were added to the journal: one for debits to Cash (or Bank) and the other for credits to Cash (or Bank). The regular Debit and Credit columns in the journal could be used for amounts that go to other accounts. At the end of the month, the "special" columns would each be totaled. The total of the Cash Debit column would be posted as one amount to the debit side of the cash account; the total of the Cash Credit column would be posted as one amount to the credit side of the cash account. Thus, instead of receiving 70 postings, Cash would receive only two (one debit and one credit). Posting would require much less time and the danger of posting error would be reduced.

There is no reason to limit special journal columns to those for cash. If there are other accounts frequently used in the recording of transactions, special columns may be used to assemble all amounts that have the same effect on an account. More space and time may be saved. A journal with such special columns (and always containing a General Debit column and a General Credit column to take care of changes in accounts infrequently involved) is called a *combined cash journal*.

Mr. Roberts uses a combined cash journal as his only book of original entry. This journal, reproduced on pages 106–109, has eight amount columns, two at the left and six at the right of the Description column. The headings of the amount columns (as they read from left to right on the journal page) are as follows:

> County National Bank
>   Deposits 111 Dr.
>   Checks 111 Cr.
>
> General
>   Debit
>   Credit
>
> Professional Fees 411 Cr.
>
> Salary Expense 511 Dr.
>
> Wage Deductions
>   Employees Income Tax Payable 211 Cr.
>   FICA Tax Payable 212 Cr.

The account numbers in the headings of the six special amount columns are an aid in completing the summary posting at the end of each month. Each of the six special columns is justified because there are enough transactions requiring entries in the accounts indicated by the column headings to warrant this arrangement which will save time and labor in the bookkeeping process. A narrative of transactions completed by Mr. Roberts during the month of December, 19--, is given on pages 103–110. These transactions are recorded in the combined cash journal on pages 106–109. Attention is called to the fact that before any transactions were recorded in this journal, a memo notation of the bank balance at the start of the month, $3,120.45, was entered in the Description column just above the words "Amounts Forwarded."

General Ledger. The standard form of account is used in the general ledger of Mr. Roberts' enterprise. The ledger is reproduced on pages 110–

113. In each instance, the balance of the account as of December 1 has been entered. Two accounts are omitted: Expense and Revenue Summary (No. 321) and Depreciation Expense (No. 517). They are not included because neither had a balance on December 1, and neither received any debits or credits as a result of the cash receipt and disbursement transactions in December. These accounts are not used until the end-of-year process of adjusting and closing the accounts takes place. This procedure will be explained and illustrated on pages 118–124.

Auxiliary Records. The auxiliary records included in Mr. Roberts' system of accounts are not reproduced in this chapter. The petty cash disbursements record that is used is almost identical in form to the one illustrated in Chapter 3 on pages 50 and 51. However, the combined cash journal entry to record the reimbursement of the petty cash fund at the end of December is shown (see the first entry of December 30 on pages 108 and 109). Mr. Roberts has two employees: Mr. Edward Hess, a full-time systems programmer, and Ms. Jeanne Haug, a part-time secretary. An employee's earnings record, similar to the one illustrated in Chapter 4 on pages 80 and 81, is maintained for each employee. Mr. Roberts keeps a file for each client which includes, among other things, a copy of the contract or agreement with the client. This agreement stipulates the fee for the assignment and the time of payment (or payments, if the fee is to be paid in installments — which is the usual case). A carbon copy of each statement or billing for fees earned is placed in each client's file. When money is received from a client, the date and amount are noted on the copy of the billing in addition to the formal record made in the combined cash journal.

JOHN H. ROBERTS, MANAGEMENT CONSULTANT

Narrative of Transactions

Friday, December 2

Issued Check No. 211 for $278.10 to Edward Hess, systems programmer, in payment of his salary for week: $325 less income tax withholding, $46.90. (Note: Mr. Hess has been employed since the start of the year. His gross earnings reached $15,000 during the week ended November 26. Since that time, no FICA tax has been withheld.)

Since individual posting of this entry was not required, a check mark was placed in the Posting Reference column of the combined cash journal at the time the transaction was recorded. This is a way of noting that there is nothing in the General Debit and Credit columns on that line.

Issued Check No. 212 for $95.20 to Jeanne Haug, secretary (part-time), in payment of her salary for week: $120 less income tax withholding, $17.60, and FICA tax withholding, $7.20.

Issued Check No. 213 for $300 to W. G. Chance for December office rent.

Monday, December 5

Received a check for $1,000 from J. E. Berra, a client.

Note that the client's name was written in the Description column and that a check mark was placed in the Posting Reference column.

Wednesday, December 7

Issued Check No. 214 for $43.60 to Edward O. Maes, an insurance agent, in payment of the one-year premium on a fire insurance policy covering Mr. Roberts' office equipment and contents.

Friday, December 9

Issued Check No. 215 for $278.10 to Edward Hess and Check No. 216 for $95.20 to Jeanne Haug in payment of salaries for the week. (See explanation relating to Checks Nos. 211 and 212 issued on December 2.)

END-OF-THE-WEEK WORK

(1) Proved the footings of the combined cash journal.

In order to be sure that the debits recorded in the journal are equal to the credits, the journal must be *proved*. Each amount column should be footed and the sum of the footings of the debit columns and the sum of the footings of the credit columns compared. The footings should be recorded in small pencil figures immediately below the last regular entry. If these sums are not the same, the journal entries must be checked to discover and correct any errors that are found. The footings should be proved frequently; when the transactions are numerous, it may be advisable to prove the footings daily. The footings must be proved when a page of the journal is filled to be sure that no error is carried forward to a new page. Proof of the footings is essential at the end of the month before the journal is ruled or any column totals are posted. Below is a proof of the footings of Mr. Roberts' combined cash journal. As is common practice, the footings were proved using an adding machine. The first set of amounts is the totals of the three debit columns, followed by a second set of amounts which is the totals of the four credit columns that had anything in them. (There was nothing in the General Credit column at this point.)

```
                    *
           1,000.00
             343.60
             890.00

           2,233.60*

                    *
           1,090.20
           1,000.00
             129.00
              14.40

           2,233.60*
```

(2) Deposited the $1,000 check from J. E. Berra in the bank, proved the bank balance ($3,030.25), and entered the new balance in the Description column following the second transaction of December 9. **(3)** Posted each entry individually from the General Debit column of the combined cash journal to the proper general ledger accounts. (Note that there were two such postings and that their respective account numbers, 513 and 518, were entered in the Posting Reference column.)

Monday, December 12

Issued Check No. 217 for $69.31 to UARCO Forms Co. in payment for supplies.

Received a check for $9.00 from Edward O. Maes, the insurance agent to whom Mr. Roberts had sent a check (No. 214) a few days earlier in the amount of $43.60 in payment of the premium on a fire insurance policy on his office equipment and contents. The check for $9.00 was accompanied by a letter from Mr. Maes explaining that a clerk in his office had made an error in preparing the invoice for the policy. The correct amount was $34.60 — not $43.60. Mr. Roberts' check for $43.60 had been deposited before the mistake was discovered. Accordingly, Mr. Maes sent his check for $9.00 as a refund of the excess premium.

This insurance premium refund check was recorded in the combined cash journal by a debit to County National Bank, Account No. 111, and a credit to Insurance Expense, Account No. 518, in the amount of $9.00. Since the entry to record Check No. 214 had already been posted as a debit to Insurance Expense, this manner of handling was required. (The trouble resulted from the fact that the clerk in Mr. Maes' office had made a *transposition* error — a mistake well known to bookkeepers and accountants. The intention was to write or type "$34.60," but "$43.60" was written instead. The "3" and the "4" were placed in the wrong order — they were *transposed*.)

Tuesday, December 13

Received a check for $1,200 from G. L. Adams, a client.

Issued Check No. 218 for $315.60 to the County National Bank, a United States depositary, in payment of the following taxes:

Employees' income tax withheld during November.............		$258.00
FICA tax imposed —		
On employees (withheld during November).................	$28.80	
On the employer.......................................	28.80	57.60
Total...		$315.60

This disbursement involved three factors (in addition to the decrease in the bank balance): **(1)** payment of the recorded liability, Employees Income Tax Payable, Account No. 211, of $258.00; **(2)** payment of the recorded liability, FICA Tax Payable, Account No. 212, of $28.80; and **(3)** payment of the unrecorded liability of $28.80, the employer's FICA tax relating to the taxable earnings paid in November. To record the transaction correctly, the first two amounts were debited to the proper liability accounts, and the third amount was debited to Payroll Taxes Expense, Account No. 512. Note that three lines were needed in the combined cash journal.

(The checks from Mr. Adams and Mr. Maes were deposited in the bank, and the check for $315.60, together with a Tax Deposit Form, was presented at the bank in payment of the taxes. The stub attached to the form was filled out and retained as a record of the deposit.)

Wednesday, December 14

Issued Check No. 219 for $1,500 to Mr. Roberts for personal use.

Thursday, December 15

Issued Check No. 220 for $87.60 to the Executive Auto Leasing Co. in payment of one month's rent of the leased automobile used by Mr. Roberts for business purposes.

This disbursement was recorded by a debit to Automobile Expense, Account No. 516.

PAGE 36   COMBINED CASH JOURNAL

	COUNTY NATIONAL BANK		CK. NO.	DAY	DESCRIPTION	POST. REF.	
	DEPOSITS 111 DR.	CHECKS 111 CR.					
1					AMOUNTS FORWARDED *Balance 3,120.45*		1
2		278 10	211	2	Edward Hess	✓	2
3		95 20	212	2	Jeanne Haug	✓	3
4		300 00	213	2	Rent Expense	513	4
5	1000 00			5	J. E. Berra	✓	5
6		43 60	214	7	Insurance Expense	518	6
7		278 10	215	9	Edward Hess	✓	7
8		95 20	216	9	Jeanne Haug	✓	8
9	1000 00	1090 20 69 31	217	12	Forms and Supplies Expense 3,030.25	515	9
10	9 00			12	Insurance Expense	518	10
11	1200 00			13	G. L. Adams	✓	11
12		315 60	218	13	Employees Income Tax Payable	211	12
13					FICA Tax Payable	212	13
14					Payroll Taxes Expense	512	14
15		1500 00	219	14	John H. Roberts, Drawing	031	15
16		87 60	220	15	Automobile Expense	516	16
17		278 10	221	16	Edward Hess	✓	17
18		95 20	222	16	Jeanne Haug	✓	18
19	2209 00	75 00 3511 01	223	16	Charitable Contributions Expense 1,818.44	521	19
20		38 57	224	19	Automobile Expense	516	20
21		15 75	225	19	Miscellaneous Expense	522	21
22		38 65	226	20	Telephone Expense	514	22
23	150 00			21	Mrs. Roberta McDougall	✓	23
24		78 12	227	22	Forms and Supplies Expense	515	24
25		278 10	228	23	Edward Hess	✓	25
26	3709 00	95 20 4055 40	229	23	Jeanne Haug	✓	26
27	3709 00	4055 40			Carried Forward 2,774.05		27

John H. Roberts, Management Consultant — Combined Cash Journal (Left Page)

Friday, December 16

Issued Check No. 221 for $278.10 to Edward Hess and Check No. 222 for $95.20 to Jeanne Haug in payment of salaries for week. (See explanation relating to Checks Nos. 211 and 212 issued on December 2.)

Issued Check No. 223 for $75 to American Red Cross.

END-OF-THE-WEEK WORK

(1) Proved the footings of the combined cash journal. (2) Proved the bank balance $1,818.44). (3) Posted each entry individually from the General Debit and General Credit columns of the combined cash journal to the proper general ledger accounts. When the entry of December 13

FOR MONTH OF *December* 19-- PAGE *36*

	GENERAL		PROFESSIONAL FEES 411 CR.	SALARY EXPENSE 511 DR.	WAGE DEDUCTIONS		
	DEBIT	CREDIT			EMP. INC. TAX PAY. 211 CR.	FICA TAX PAY. 212 CR.	
1							1
2				325 00	46 90		2
3				120 00	17 60	7 20	3
4	300 00						4
5			1000 00				5
6	43 60						6
7				325 00	46 90		7
8				120 00	17 60	7 20	8
9	343 60 / 69 31		1000 00	890 00	129 00	14 40	9
10		9 00					10
11			1200 00				11
12	258 00						12
13	28 80						13
14	28 80						14
15	1500 00						15
16	87 60						16
17				325 00	46 90		17
18				120 00	17 60	7 20	18
19	75 00 2391 11	9 00	2200 00	1335 00	193 50	21 60	19
20	38 57						20
21	15 75						21
22	38 65						22
23			1500 00				23
24	78 12						24
25				325 00	46 90		25
26				120 00	17 60	7 20	26
27	2562 20 2562 20	9 00 9 00	3700 00 3700 00	1780 00 1780 00	258 00 258 00	28 80 28 80	27

John H. Roberts, Management Consultant — Combined Cash Journal (Right Page)

relating to Check No. 218 was posted, debits were made to Employees Income Tax Payable, Account No. 211, and FICA Tax Payable, Account No. 212, which caused those accounts to be in balance. Each of those two accounts was ruled with a double line as illustrated on page 111.

Monday, December 19

Issued Check No. 224 for $38.57 to Wes's Service Station in payment of charges for gasoline, oil, and lubrication purchased on credit during the past month. (All of these purchases related to the leased car used for business purposes.)

Issued Check No. 225 for $15.75 to Apex Typewriter Service in payment of charges for cleaning and repairing office typewriter.

> The amount of this check was charged to Miscellaneous Expense, Account No. 522.

Tuesday, December 20

Issued Check No. 226 for $38.65 to Southwestern Bell Telephone Co. in payment of statement just received showing charges for local service and long distance calls, during the past month. (This telephone bill related exclusively to the phone in Mr. Roberts' office.)

Wednesday, December 21

Received a check for $1,500 from Ms. Roberta McDougall, a client.

PAGE 37   COMBINED CASH JOURNAL

	COUNTY NATIONAL BANK		CK. NO.	DAY	DESCRIPTION	POST. REF.	
	DEPOSITS 111 DR.	CHECKS 111 CR.					
1	3 709 00	4 055 40		23	AMOUNTS FORWARDED *Balance 2,774.05*	✓	1
2		97 80	230	28	*Travel + Entertainment Expense*	519	2
3	900 00			29	*Frank Presker*	✓	3
4		66 83	231	30	*John H. Roberts, Drawing*	031	4
5					*Forms and Supplies Expense*	515	5
6					*Automobile Expense*	516	6
7					*Travel + Entertainment Expense*	519	7
8					*Charitable Contributions Expense*	521	8
9					*Miscellaneous Expense*	522	9
10		278 10	232	30	*Edward Hess*	✓	10
11		95 20	233	30	*Jeanne Haug*	✓	11
12	4 609 00	4 593 33				3,136.12	12
13	(111)	(111)					13

John H. Roberts, Management Consultant — Combined Cash Journal (Left Page) (*concluded*)

Thursday, December 22

Issued Check No. 227 for $78.12 to Systems Supply Co. in payment for supplies purchased.

Friday, December 23

Issued Check No. 228 for $278.10 to Edward Hess and Check No. 229 for $95.20 to Jeanne Haug in payment of salaries for week. (See explanation relating to Checks Nos. 211 and 212 issued on December 2.)

END-OF-THE-WEEK WORK

(1) Proved the footings of the combined cash journal. **(2)** Deposited the $1,500 check from Ms. McDougall and proved the bank balance ($2,774.05). **(3)** Posted each entry individually from the General Debit column of the combined cash journal.

> Because a page of the combined cash journal was filled after Check No. 229 was recorded, the footings of the columns were proved, these footings were recorded as totals on the last line of the page, and the words "Carried Forward" were written in the Description column. The totals were entered in the appropriate columns on the top line of the next page. The bank balance was entered in the Description column of the new page just above the words "Amounts Forwarded."

Wednesday, December 28

Issued Check No. 230 for $97.80 to Sunset Hills Country Club in payment of food and beverage charges for one month.

FOR MONTH OF *December*   19 --   PAGE *37*

	GENERAL		PROFESSIONAL FEES 411 CR.	SALARY EXPENSE 511 DR.	WAGE DEDUCTIONS		
	DEBIT	CREDIT			EMP. INC. TAX PAY. 211 CR.	FICA TAX PAY. 212 CR.	
1	2562 20	9 00	3700 00	1780 00	258 00	28 80	1
2	97 80						2
3			900 00				3
4	15 00						4
5	10 95						5
6	4 30						6
7	23 80						7
8	7 50						8
9	5 28						9
10				325 00	46 90		10
11				120 00	17 60	7 20	11
12	2726 83 / 2726 83	9 00 / 9 00	4600 00 / 4600 00	2225 00 / 2225 00	322 50 / 322 50	36 00 / 36 00	12
13	(✓)	(✓)	(411)	(511)	(211)	(212)	13

John H. Roberts, Management Consultant — Combined Cash Journal (Right Page) *(concluded)*

The amount of this check was charged to Travel and Entertainment Expense, Account No. 519. Mr. Roberts uses the facilities of the club to entertain prospective clients.

Thursday, December 29

Received a check for $900 from Frank Presker, a client.

Friday, December 30

Issued Check No. 231 for $66.83 to replenish the petty cash fund. Following is a summary of the petty cash disbursements for the month of December prepared from the Petty Cash Disbursements Record:

John H. Roberts, Drawing...	$15.00
Forms and Supplies Expense..	10.95
Automobile Expense..	4.30
Travel and Entertainment Expense..................................	23.80
Charitable Contributions Expense..................................	7.50
Miscellaneous Expense...	5.28
Total disbursements..	$66.83

Issued Check No. 232 for $278.10 to Edward Hess and Check No. 233 for $95.20 to Jeanne Haug in payment of salaries for week. (See explanation relating to Checks Nos. 211 and 212 issued on December 2.)

ROUTINE END-OF-THE-MONTH WORK

(1) Proved the footings and entered the totals in the combined cash journal. **(2)** Deposited the $900 check from Mr. Presker and proved the bank balance ($3,136.12). **(3)** Completed the individual posting from the General Debit column of the combined cash journal. **(4)** Completed the summary posting of the six special-column totals of the combined cash journal and ruled the journal as illustrated on pages 108 and 109. (Note that the number of the account to which the total was posted was written in parentheses just below the total, and that check marks were placed below the General Debit and General Credit column totals in parentheses to indicate that these amounts were not posted.) **(5)** Footed the ledger accounts and noted the balances where necessary, as illustrated below and on pages 111–113. **(6)** Prepared a trial balance of the ledger accounts.

Usually a trial balance at the end of a month is prepared using two-column paper. However, because Mr. Roberts has chosen the calendar year for his fiscal year (a common, but by no means universal, practice), the trial balance at the end of December is put in the first two amount columns of a page known as a *work sheet*. The need for and preparation of a work sheet is explained and illustrated on pages 114–117.

ACCOUNT *County National Bank*   ACCOUNT NO. *111*

DATE	ITEM	POST. REF.	DEBIT	DATE	ITEM	POST. REF.	CREDIT
19-- Dec. 1	Balance	✓	3 120 45	19-- Dec. 30		CJ37	4 593 33
30	3,136.12	CJ37	4 609 00 7 729 45				

John H. Roberts, Management Consultant — General Ledger

ACCOUNT *Petty Cash Fund*   ACCOUNT NO. *112*

DATE	ITEM	POST. REF.	DEBIT	DATE	ITEM	POST. REF.	CREDIT
19-- Dec. 1	Balance	✓	100 00				

ACCOUNT *Office Equipment*   ACCOUNT NO. *131*

DATE	ITEM	POST. REF.	DEBIT	DATE	ITEM	POST. REF.	CREDIT
19-- Dec. 1	Balance	✓	10575 60				

ACCOUNT *Accumulated Depreciation - Office Equip.*   ACCOUNT NO. *013*

DATE	ITEM	POST. REF.	DEBIT	DATE	ITEM	POST. REF.	CREDIT
				19-- Dec. 1	Balance	✓	3521 67

ACCOUNT *Employees Income Tax Payable*   ACCOUNT NO. *211*

DATE	ITEM	POST. REF.	DEBIT	DATE	ITEM	POST. REF.	CREDIT
19-- Dec. 13		CD36	258 00	19-- Dec. 1	Balance	✓	258 00
				Dec. 30		CJ37	322 50

ACCOUNT *FICA Tax Payable*   ACCOUNT NO. *212*

DATE	ITEM	POST. REF.	DEBIT	DATE	ITEM	POST. REF.	CREDIT
19-- Dec. 13		CD36	28 80	19-- Dec. 1	Balance	✓	28 80
				Dec. 30		CJ37	36 00

ACCOUNT *John H. Roberts, Capital*   ACCOUNT NO. *311*

DATE	ITEM	POST. REF.	DEBIT	DATE	ITEM	POST. REF.	CREDIT
				19-- Dec. 1	Balance	✓	7285 50

ACCOUNT *John H. Roberts, Drawing*   ACCOUNT NO. *031*

DATE	ITEM	POST. REF.	DEBIT	DATE	ITEM	POST. REF.	CREDIT
19-- Dec. 1	Balance	✓	18755 00				
14		CD36	1500 00				
30		CJ37	15 00				
			20270 00				

John H. Roberts, Management Consultant — General Ledger (*continued*)

ACCOUNT *Professional Fees*   ACCOUNT NO. 411

DATE	ITEM	POST. REF.	DEBIT	DATE	ITEM	POST. REF.	CREDIT
				19-- Dec. 1	Balance	✓	5276000
				30		CJ37	460000
							5736000

ACCOUNT *Salary Expense*   ACCOUNT NO. 511

DATE	ITEM	POST. REF.	DEBIT	DATE	ITEM	POST. REF.	CREDIT
19-- Dec. 1	Balance	✓	2091500				
30		CJ37	222500				
			2314000				

ACCOUNT *Payroll Taxes Expense*   ACCOUNT NO. 512

DATE	ITEM	POST. REF.	DEBIT	DATE	ITEM	POST. REF.	CREDIT
19-- Dec. 1	Balance	✓	177783				
13		CJ36	2880				
			180663				

ACCOUNT *Rent Expense*   ACCOUNT NO. 513

DATE	ITEM	POST. REF.	DEBIT	DATE	ITEM	POST. REF.	CREDIT
19-- Dec. 1	Balance	✓	330000				
2		CJ36	30000				
			360000				

ACCOUNT *Telephone Expense*   ACCOUNT NO. 514

DATE	ITEM	POST. REF.	DEBIT	DATE	ITEM	POST. REF.	CREDIT
19-- Dec. 1	Balance	✓	38560				
20		CJ36	3865				
			42425				

ACCOUNT *Forms and Supplies Expense*   ACCOUNT NO. 515

DATE	ITEM	POST. REF.	DEBIT	DATE	ITEM	POST. REF.	CREDIT
19-- Dec. 1	Balance	✓	136108				
12		CJ36	6931				
22		CJ36	7812				
30		CJ37	1095				
			151946				

John H. Roberts, Management Consultant — General Ledger (*continued*)

ACCOUNT *Automobile Expense* ACCOUNT NO. 516

DATE	ITEM	POST. REF.	DEBIT	DATE	ITEM	POST. REF.	CREDIT
19-- Dec. 1	Balance	✓	1214 95				
15		CJ36	87 60				
19		CJ36	38 57				
30		CJ37	4 30				
			1345 42				

ACCOUNT *Insurance Expense* ACCOUNT NO. 518

DATE	ITEM	POST. REF.	DEBIT	DATE	ITEM	POST. REF.	CREDIT
19-- Dec. 1	Balance	✓	167 38	19-- Dec. 12		CJ36	9 00
7	201.98	CJ36	43 60				
			210 98				

ACCOUNT *Travel and Entertainment Expense* ACCOUNT NO. 519

DATE	ITEM	POST. REF.	DEBIT	DATE	ITEM	POST. REF.	CREDIT
19-- Dec. 1	Balance	✓	1653 26				
28		CJ37	97 80				
30		CJ37	23 80				
			1774 86				

ACCOUNT *Charitable Contributions Expense* ACCOUNT NO. 521

DATE	ITEM	POST. REF.	DEBIT	DATE	ITEM	POST. REF.	CREDIT
19-- Dec. 1	Balance	✓	385 00				
16		CJ36	75 00				
30		CJ37	7 50				
			467 50				

ACCOUNT *Miscellaneous Expense* ACCOUNT NO. 522

DATE	ITEM	POST. REF.	DEBIT	DATE	ITEM	POST. REF.	CREDIT
19-- Dec. 1	Balance	✓	142 82				
19		CJ36	15 75				
30		CJ37	5 28				
			163 85				

John H. Roberts, Management Consultant — General Ledger (*concluded*)

Work at close of the fiscal period

As soon as possible after the end of the fiscal period, the owner (or owners) of an enterprise wants to be provided with (1) an income statement covering the period just ended, and (2) a balance sheet as of the last day of the period. In order to provide these statements, the accountant must consider certain matters that will not have been recorded in routine fashion. (Depreciation of Office Equipment for the past year is the one such matter in the case of Mr. Roberts' enterprise.) Furthermore, the revenue accounts, the expense accounts, and the account showing the owner's withdrawals will have performed their function for the period just ended (in this case, the year) and need to be made ready to receive the entries of the new period. In the language of accountants and bookkeepers, "the books must be adjusted and closed." Actually, it is only the temporary owner's equity accounts — those for revenue, expense, and the owner's drawings — that are closed, but the remark quoted is widely used to describe what takes place at this time.

The End-of-Period Work Sheet. To facilitate **(1)** the preparing of the financial statements, **(2)** the making of needed adjustments in the accounts, and **(3)** the closing of the temporary owner's equity accounts, it is common practice to prepare what is known as a *work sheet*. Because that term is used to describe a variety of schedules and computations that accountants may prepare, the specific type to be discussed here is commonly called an *end-of-period work sheet*. Various forms of this device are used. Because of the nature of Mr. Roberts' enterprise, an eight-column work sheet is adequate. This form is illustrated on page 115. Note that the heading states that it is for the year ended December 31, 19--. The fact that December 30 was the last working day is not important. The income statement will relate to the full year, and the balance sheet will show the financial position as of the last day of the fiscal period.

The first pair of columns of the work sheet was used to show the trial balance taken after the routine posting for the month of December had been completed. Note that the account Depreciation Expense (No. 517) was included in the list of accounts and account numbers even though that account had no balance at this point. The second pair of columns, headed "Adjustments," was used to show the manner in which the expense of estimated depreciation of office equipment for the year affects the accounts. The trial balance shows that the account Office Equipment (No. 131) had a balance of $10,575.60, and that the balance of the account Accumulated Depreciation — Office Equipment (No. 013) was $3,521.67. No new equipment was purchased during the year and there were no sales or retirements of such property during the year. Accordingly, the balances of these two accounts had not changed during the year. The two accounts are closely related: the debit balance of the office equipment account indicates the cost of such assets, and the credit balance of the accumulated depreciation account indicates the amount of such cost that has been charged off as depreciation in past years — that is, to January 1 of the

John H. Roberts, Management Consultant
Work Sheet
For the Year Ended December 31, 19--

	Acct. No.	Trial Balance Debit	Trial Balance Credit	Adjustments Debit	Adjustments Credit	Income Statement Debit	Income Statement Credit	Balance Sheet Debit	Balance Sheet Credit
1 Security National Bank	111	313612						313612	
2 Petty Cash Fund	112	10000						10000	
3 Office Equipment	131	1057560						1057560	
4 Accum. Deprec.—Office Equip.	013		352167		105756				457923
5 Employees Income Tax Pay.	211		32250						32250
6 F.I.C.A. Tax Payable	212		3600						3600
7 John H. Roberts, Capital	311		728550						728550
8 John H. Roberts, Drawing	031	2027000						2027000	
9 Professional Fees	411		5736000				5736000		
10 Salary Expense	511	2314000				2314000			
11 Payroll Taxes Expense	512	180663				180663			
12 Rent Expense	513	360000				360000			
13 Telephone Expense	514	42425				42425			
14 Forms + Supplies Expense	515	151946				151946			
15 Automobile Expense	516	134542				134542			
16 Depreciation Expense	517			105756		105756			
17 Insurance Expense	518	20198				20198			
18 Travel + Entertainment Exp.	519	177486				177486			
19 Charitable Contributions Exp.	521	46750				46750			
20 Miscellaneous Expense	522	16385				16385			
21		6852567	6852567	105756	105756	3550151	5736000	3408172	1222323
22 Net Income						2185849			2185849
23						5736000	5736000	3408172	3408172

John H. Roberts, Management Consultant — End-of-Period Work Sheet current year. The amount of the difference between the two balances, $7,053.93, is described as the *undepreciated cost* of the office equipment. The amount may also be called the *book value* of the equipment. A better description of the difference is "cost yet to be charged to expense."

Since the year had just ended, it was necessary to record as an expense the estimated depreciation for that year. Mr. Roberts estimates that the various items of office equipment have average useful lives of ten years and that any scrap or salvage value at the end of that time is likely to be so small that it can be ignored. Accordingly, estimated depreciation expense for the year was calculated to be $1,057.56 (10 percent of $10,575.60). This expense was due to be recorded in the ledger accounts, but that had to wait. The immediate need was to get the expense entered on the work sheet so that it would be considered when the financial statements were prepared. The record was made on the work sheet as follows: $1,057.56 was written in the Adjustments Debit column on the line for Depreciation Expense, and the same amount was written in the Adjustments Credit column on the line for Accumulated Depreciation — Office Equipment. The Adjustments Debit and Credit columns were totaled.

The next step was to combine each amount in the Trial Balance columns with the amount, if any, in the Adjustments columns and to extend the total into the Income Statement or Balance Sheet columns. Revenue and expense account balances are extended to the Income Statement columns and balance sheet account balances to the Balance Sheet columns. Note that the new amount for Accumulated Depreciation — Office Equipment, $4,579.23 ($3,521.67 + $1,057.56), appears in the Balance Sheet Credit column, and that the depreciation expense of $1,057.56 appears, along with all other expenses, in the Income Statement Debit column. The last four columns were totaled. The total of the Income Statement Credit column exceeded the total of the Income Statement Debit column by $21,858.49 — the calculated net income for the year. That amount, so designated, was placed in the Income Statement Debit column to bring the pair of Income Statement columns into balance. When the same amount ($21,858.49) was placed in the Balance Sheet Credit column, the last pair of columns was brought into balance. The final totals of the last four columns were recorded at the bottom of the work sheet.

The fact that adding the net income for the year, $21,858.49, to the Balance Sheet Credit column caused its total to equal the total of the Balance Sheet Debit column is explained as follows. The amounts for the assets and liabilities in the last pair of columns were up-to-date. The difference between total assets and total liabilities, $8,873.99, was Mr. Roberts' equity in the enterprise at the year's end. The balance of his capital account was $7,285.50 — the amount of his equity at the start of the year (since he had made no additional investments during the year).

His withdrawals during the year, according to the balance in the account John H. Roberts, Drawing, were $20,270.00. How could he start the year with an owner's equity of $7,285.50, make no additional investments, withdraw $20,270.00, and end the year with an owner's equity of $8,873.99? The explanation is that there had been profitable operations during the year that caused the owner's equity element to increase $21,858.49. This can be expressed in the form of the following equation:

OWNER'S EQUITY AT START OF PERIOD	+	NET INCOME FOR THE PERIOD	+	INVESTMENTS	−	WITHDRAWALS	=	OWNER'S EQUITY AT END OF PERIOD
$7,285.50	+	$21,858.49	+	0	−	$20,270.00	=	$8,873.99

Since the correct amounts for assets and liabilities and two of the three factors (owner's equity at start of period and withdrawals) needed to determine the correct amount of the owner's equity as of December 31 were already in the Balance Sheet columns, only the amount of the third factor — the net income for the year — had to be included in order that those columns would reflect the basic equation: Assets = Liabilities + Owner's Equity.

The Financial Statements. The work sheet supplied all of the information needed to prepare an income statement and a balance sheet. These statements for Mr. Roberts' enterprise are shown below and on page 118.

Three features of the balance sheet on page 118 should be noted: **(1)** It is in so-called *report form* — the liabilities and the owner's equity sections are shown below the assets section. An alternative is the so-called *account form* — the assets are at the left, and the liabilities and the owner's equity sections are at the right. (See the balance sheet of The Eason Employment

JOHN H. ROBERTS, MANAGEMENT CONSULTANT
Income Statement
For the Year Ended December 31, 19—

Professional fees............................		$57,360.00
Professional expenses:		
Salary expense...........................	$23,140.00	
Payroll taxes expense....................	1,806.63	
Rent expense.............................	3,600.00	
Telephone expense........................	424.25	
Forms and supplies expense...............	1,519.46	
Automobile expense.......................	1,345.42	
Depreciation expense.....................	1,057.56	
Insurance expense........................	201.98	
Travel and entertainment expense.........	1,774.86	
Charitable contributions expense........	467.50	
Miscellaneous expense....................	163.85	
Total professional expenses............		35,501.51
Net income...............................		$21,858.49

John H. Roberts, Management Consultant — Income Statement

Agency on pages 42 and 43.) **(2)** The assets are classified on the basis of whether they are *current* or *long-lived*. Current assets include cash and any other assets that will be converted into cash within the *normal operating cycle* of the business. This cycle is often a year in length. Mr. Roberts' enterprise does not take into account any current assets other than cash. (The amount shown includes both cash in bank and petty cash.) The long-lived assets are those which are expected to serve for many years. **(3)** All of the liabilities are classified as current, since they must be paid in the near future. Certain types of obligations are classified as long-term, but Mr. Roberts had no debts of this type.

```
            JOHN H. ROBERTS, MANAGEMENT CONSULTANT
                          Balance Sheet
                       December 31, 19--

                             Assets
Current assets:
  Cash............................                          $3,236.12
Long-lived assets:
  Office equipment..................      $10,575.60
  Less accumulated depreciation....        4,579.23         5,996.37
Total assets......................                          $9,232.49
                                                            =========

                          Liabilities

Current liabilities:
  Employees income tax payable......      $    322.50
  FICA tax payable.................            36.00
    Total current liabilities........                     $    358.50

                         Owner's Equity

John H. Roberts, capital:
  Capital, January 1, 19--..........                      $ 7,285.50
  Net income for year...............     $21,858.49
  Less withdrawals.................       20,270.00         1,588.49
  Capital, December 31, 19--........                         8,873.99
Total liabilities and owner's
  equity..........................                         $9,232.49
                                                           =========
```

John H. Roberts, Management Consultant — Balance Sheet

Adjusting Entries for a Personal Service Enterprise. The financial statements must agree with the ledger accounts. To speed up the preparation of the statements, a work sheet was used with the one needed adjustment included. Subsequently this adjustment had to be formally recorded in the accounts. This was accomplished by posting the first journal entry at the top of page 119. The two accounts affected by the entry, Depreciation Expense (No. 517) and Accumulated Depreciation — Office Equipment

(No. 013) are reproduced at the top of page 120 as they appeared after the entry was posted. After this posting was completed, the balance of the depreciation expense account agreed with the amount shown in the income statement, and the balance of the accumulated depreciation account was the same as the amount shown in the balance sheet.

Closing Entries for a Personal Service Enterprise. The revenue and expense accounts and the account for John H. Roberts, Drawing (No. 031) had served their purpose for the year 19––, and the balance of each of these accounts needed to be reduced to zero in order to make the accounts ready for entries in the following year. Since the means of closing a ledger account under the double-entry procedure is to add the amount of the account's balance to the side of the account having the smaller total (so that

COMBINED CASH JOURNAL FOR MONTH OF *December* 19 – –   PAGE *38*

DAY	DESCRIPTION	POST. REF.	GENERAL DEBIT	GENERAL CREDIT	
	AMOUNTS FORWARDED				1
31	*Adjusting Entry*				2
	Depreciation Expense	517	105756		3
	Accumulated Deprec:–Office Equip.	013		105756	4
					5
31	*Closing Entries*				6
	Professional Fees	411	5736000		7
	Expense and Revenue Summary	321		5736000	8
	Expense and Revenue Summary	321	3550151		9
	Salary Expense	511		2314000	10
	Payroll Taxes Expense	512		180663	11
	Rent Expense	513		360000	12
	Telephone Expense	514		42425	13
	Forms and Supplies Expense	515		151946	14
	Automobile Expense	516		134542	15
	Depreciation Expense	517		105756	16
	Insurance Expense	518		20198	17
	Travel + Entertainment Expense	519		177486	18
	Charitable Contributions Expense	521		46750	19
	Miscellaneous Expense	522		16385	20
	Expense and Revenue Summary	321	2185849		21
	John H. Roberts, Capital	311		2185849	22
	John H. Roberts, Capital	311	2027000		23
	John H. Roberts, Drawing	031		2027000	24
			13604756	13604756	25
					26

Net income

John H. Roberts, Management Consultant — Adjusting and Closing Entries

ACCOUNT *Depreciation Expense*   ACCOUNT NO. *517*

DATE	ITEM	POST. REF.	DEBIT	DATE	ITEM	POST. REF.	CREDIT
19-- Dec. 31		CJ38	1 057 56				

ACCOUNT *Accumulated Depreciation - Office Equip.*   ACCOUNT NO. *013*

DATE	ITEM	POST. REF.	DEBIT	DATE	ITEM	POST. REF.	CREDIT
				19-- Dec. 1	Balance	✓	3 521 67
				31		CJ38	1 057 56
							4 579 23

John H. Roberts, Management Consultant — Ledger Accounts After Posting Adjusting Entries

the account will have no balance), each of the temporary owner's equity accounts was closed in this way. The net effect was an increase in the credit balance of the account for John H. Roberts, Capital (No. 311) of $1,588.49 — the excess of his net income for the year, $21,858.49, over his withdrawals for the year, $20,270.00. However, this result was accomplished by means of four entries illustrated in the combined cash journal shown on page 119:

(a) The $57,360 credit balance of Professional Fees, Account No. 411, was closed to (transferred to the credit side of) Expense and Revenue Summary, Account No. 321.

(b) The debit balances of all eleven expense accounts (Nos. 511 through 519 and 521 and 522) which, in total, amounted to $35,501.51, were closed to (transferred to the debit side of) Expense and Revenue Summary (No. 321).

(c) The result of entries **(a)** and **(b)** was a credit balance of $21,858.49 — the net income for the year — in Expense and Revenue Summary (No. 321). This was closed to John H. Roberts, Capital, Account No. 311.

(d) The $20,270 debit balance of John H. Roberts, Drawing, Account No. 031, was closed to John H. Roberts, Capital (No. 311).

As in the case of the adjusting entry, these closing entries were made as of December 31. It should be noted that the work sheet provided all of the data needed to prepare the adjusting and closing entries. The purpose and use of Expense and Revenue Summary, Account No. 321, should be apparent from this illustration. As its name indicates, the account is used to summarize the amounts of expense and revenue which are *reasons* for changes in owner's equity that were *not* the result of investments and withdrawals by the owner.

Ruling the Closed Accounts. After posting the closing entries, all of the temporary owner's equity accounts were in balance (closed), and they were ruled in the manner illustrated below and on pages 122–124.

The following procedures were used:

(a) Where two or more amounts had been posted to either side of an account, the amount columns were footed to be sure that the total debits were equal to the total credits.

(b) A single line was ruled across the debit and credit amount columns immediately below the last amount on the side with the most entries.

(c) The totals of the debit and credit amount columns were entered on the next line in ink.

(d) Double lines were ruled just below the totals. These rulings extended through all but the Item columns.

ACCOUNT *John H. Roberts, Drawing*   ACCOUNT NO. *031*

DATE	ITEM	POST. REF.	DEBIT	DATE	ITEM	POST. REF.	CREDIT
19-- Dec. 1	Balance	✓	18 755 00	19-- Dec. 31		CJ38	20 270 00
14		CJ36	1 500 00				
30		CJ37	15 00				
			20 270 00				
			20 270 00				20 270 00

ACCOUNT *Expense and Revenue Summary*   ACCOUNT NO. *321*

DATE	ITEM	POST. REF.	DEBIT	DATE	ITEM	POST. REF.	CREDIT
19-- Dec. 31		CJ38	35 501 51	19-- Dec. 31		CJ38	57 360 00
31		CJ38	21 858 49				
			57 360 00				
			57 360 00				57 360 00

John H. Roberts, Management Consultant — Closed General Ledger Accounts

(*continued on next page*)

ACCOUNT *Professional Fees*   ACCOUNT NO. 411

DATE	ITEM	POST. REF.	DEBIT	DATE	ITEM	POST. REF.	CREDIT
19-- Dec. 31		CJ38	5736000	19-- Dec. 1	Balance	✓	5276000
				30		CJ37	460000
							5736000
			5736000				5736000

ACCOUNT *Salary Expense*   ACCOUNT NO. 511

DATE	ITEM	POST. REF.	DEBIT	DATE	ITEM	POST. REF.	CREDIT
19-- Dec. 1	Balance	✓	2091500	19-- Dec. 31		CJ38	2314000
30		CJ37	222500				
			2314000				
			2314000				2314000

ACCOUNT *Payroll Taxes Expense*   ACCOUNT NO. 512

DATE	ITEM	POST. REF.	DEBIT	DATE	ITEM	POST. REF.	CREDIT
19-- Dec. 1	Balance	✓	177783	19-- Dec. 31		CJ38	180663
13		CJ36	2880				
			180663				
			180663				180663

ACCOUNT *Rent Expense*   ACCOUNT NO. 513

DATE	ITEM	POST. REF.	DEBIT	DATE	ITEM	POST. REF.	CREDIT
19-- Dec. 1	Balance	✓	330000	19-- Dec. 31		CJ38	360000
2		CJ36	30000				
			360000				
			360000				360000

ACCOUNT *Telephone Expense*   ACCOUNT NO. 514

DATE	ITEM	POST. REF.	DEBIT	DATE	ITEM	POST. REF.	CREDIT
19-- Dec. 1	Balance	✓	38560	19-- Dec. 31		CJ38	42425
20		CJ36	3865				
			42425				
			42425				42425

John H. Roberts, Management Consultant — Closed General Ledger Accounts (*continued*)

ACCOUNT *Forms and Supplies Expense*   ACCOUNT NO. 515

DATE	ITEM	POST. REF.	DEBIT	DATE	ITEM	POST. REF.	CREDIT
19-- Dec. 1	Balance	✓	136 08	19-- Dec. 31		CJ38	1519 46
12		CJ36	69 31				
22		CJ36	78 12				
30		CJ37	10 95				
			1519 46				
			1519 46				1519 46

ACCOUNT *Automobile Expense*   ACCOUNT NO. 516

DATE	ITEM	POST. REF.	DEBIT	DATE	ITEM	POST. REF.	CREDIT
19-- Dec. 1	Balance	✓	1214 95	19-- Dec. 31		CJ38	1345 42
15		CJ36	87 60				
19		CJ36	38 57				
30		CJ37	4 30				
			1345 42				
			1345 42				1345 42

ACCOUNT *Depreciation Expense*   ACCOUNT NO. 517

DATE	ITEM	POST. REF.	DEBIT	DATE	ITEM	POST. REF.	CREDIT
19-- Dec. 31		CJ38	1057 56	19-- Dec. 31		CJ38	1057 56

ACCOUNT *Insurance Expense*   ACCOUNT NO. 518

DATE	ITEM	POST. REF.	DEBIT	DATE	ITEM	POST. REF.	CREDIT
19-- Dec. 1	Balance	✓	167 38	19-- Dec. 12		CJ36	9 00
7	201.98	CJ36	43 60	31		CJ38	201 98
			210 98				210 98
			210 98				210 98

ACCOUNT *Travel and Entertainment Expense*   ACCOUNT NO. 519

DATE	ITEM	POST. REF.	DEBIT	DATE	ITEM	POST. REF.	CREDIT
19-- Dec. 1	Balance	✓	1653 26	19-- Dec. 31		CJ38	1774 86
28		CJ37	97 80				
30		CJ37	23 80				
			1774 86				
			1774 86				1774 86

John H. Roberts, Management Consultant — Closed General Ledger Accounts (*continued*)

ACCOUNT *Charitable Contributions Expense*   ACCOUNT NO. *521*

DATE	ITEM	POST. REF.	DEBIT	DATE	ITEM	POST. REF.	CREDIT
19-- Dec. 1	Balance	✓	385 00	19-- Dec. 31		CJ38	467 50
16		CJ36	75 00				
30		CJ37	7 50				
			467 50				
			467 50				467 50

ACCOUNT *Miscellaneous Expense*   ACCOUNT NO. *522*

DATE	ITEM	POST. REF.	DEBIT	DATE	ITEM	POST. REF.	CREDIT
19-- Dec. 1	Balance	✓	142 82	19-- Dec. 31		CJ38	163 85
19		CJ36	15 75				
30		CJ37	5 28				
			163 85				
			163 85				163 85

John H. Roberts, Management Consultant — Closed General Ledger Accounts (*concluded*)

If an account had only one item on each side, only the double ruling was made. (Note the ruling for Depreciation Expense, Account No. 517.) If an account page is not filled, it may be used for recording the transactions of the following period.

Balancing and Ruling Open Accounts. After the temporary owner's equity accounts were closed, the open accounts (those for assets, liabilities, and John H. Roberts, Capital) were balanced and ruled, where necessary, to prepare them to receive entries in the next fiscal period. Only two of Mr. Roberts' ledger accounts needed to be balanced and ruled: County National Bank, Account No. 111, and John H. Roberts, Capital, Account No. 311. These two accounts are shown on page 125. The procedure in each case was as follows:

(a) The amount of the balance of the account was entered on the side having the smaller total to equalize total debits and total credits. The word "Balance" was written in the Item column.

(b) The columns were footed to prove the equality of the debits and credits.

(c) A single line was ruled across the debit and credit amount columns immediately below the line with the last amount. (This line would have been below the last amount on the side with the most entries, if the number of entries on each side had not been the same.)

(d) The totals of the debit and credit amount columns were entered on the next line in ink.

(e) Double lines were ruled just below the totals extending through all but the Item column.

(f) An entry was made on the next line under date of January 1, with the amount of the balance — so labeled in the Item column — entered in the amount column on the proper side (the debit side for the asset account and the credit side for the owner's equity account). If the account page had been filled, the balance would have been entered at the top of a new account page.

No balancing and ruling was needed in the cases of Petty Cash Fund, Account No. 112, or Office Equipment, Account No. 131, since each of these accounts had only one entry. (These two accounts remained just as illustrated on page 111.) Accumulated Depreciation — Office Equipment, Account No. 013, needed no further attention since it had only two entries, both on the same side. (This account remains as illustrated on page 119.) The two liability accounts, Employees Income Tax Payable (No. 211) and FICA Tax Payable (No. 212) remain as illustrated on page 111, inasmuch as each has had only one entry since previously ruled.

ACCOUNT *County National Bank*   ACCOUNT NO. *111*

DATE	ITEM	POST. REF.	DEBIT	DATE	ITEM	POST. REF.	CREDIT
19-- Dec. 1	Balance	✓	3120 45	19-- Dec. 30		CJ37	4593 33
30	3,136.12	CJ37	4609 00	31	Balance	✓	3136 12
			7729 45				7729 45
			7729 45				7729 45
19-- Jan. 1	Balance	✓	3136 12				

Not Necessary

ACCOUNT *John H. Roberts, Capital*   ACCOUNT NO. *311*

DATE	ITEM	POST. REF.	DEBIT	DATE	ITEM	POST. REF.	CREDIT
19-- Dec. 31		CJ38	2027 00	19-- Dec. 1	Balance	✓	7285 50
31	Balance	✓	887 99	31		CJ38	2185 49
			2914 99				2914 99
			2914 99				2914 99
				19-- Jan. 1	Balance	✓	887 99

John H. Roberts, Management Consultant — Balancing and Ruling Open Accounts

Post-Closing Trial Balance. After posting the closing entries, it is advisable to take a *post-closing trial balance* to prove the equality of the debit and credit balances in the general ledger accounts. The post-closing trial balance of Mr. Robert's ledger is shown at the top of page 126.

The accounting cycle

The steps involved in handling all of the transactions and events completed during an accounting period, beginning with recording in a book of original entry and ending with a post-closing trial balance, are referred to collectively as the *accounting cycle*. This chapter has illustrated a complete accounting cycle. A brief summary of the various steps follows:

(a) Journalizing the transactions.
(b) Posting to the ledger accounts.

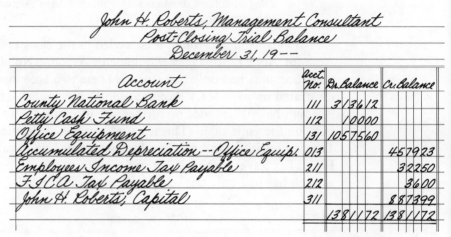

John H. Roberts, Management Consultant
Post-Closing Trial Balance
December 31, 19--

Account	Acct. No.	Dr. Balance	Cr. Balance
County National Bank	111	3136 12	
Petty Cash Fund	112	100 00	
Office Equipment	131	10575 60	
Accumulated Depreciation -- Office Equip.	013		4579 23
Employees Income Tax Payable	211		322 50
F I C A Tax Payable	212		36 00
John H. Roberts, Capital	311		8873 99
		13811 72	13811 72

John H. Roberts, Management Consultant — Post-Closing Trial Balance

(c) Taking a trial balance.
(d) Determining the needed adjustments.
(e) Completing an end-of-period work sheet.
(f) Preparing an income statement and a balance sheet.
(g) Journalizing and posting the adjusting and closing entries.
(h) Ruling the closed accounts and balancing and ruling the open accounts.
(i) Taking a post-closing trial balance.

In visualizing the accounting cycle, it is important to realize that steps (c) through (i) in the foregoing list are performed *as of the last day of the accounting period.* This does not mean that they necessarily are done *on* the last day. The accountant or bookkeeper may not be able to do any of these things until the first few days (sometimes weeks) of the next period. Nevertheless, the work sheet, statements, and entries are prepared or recorded as of the closing date. While the journalizing of transactions in the new period proceeds in regular fashion, it is not usual to post to the general ledger any entries relating to the new period until the steps relating to the period just ended have been completed.

Report No. 5-1

Complete Report No. 5-1 in the study assignments and submit your working papers to the instructor for approval. After completing the report you will then be given instructions as to the work to be done next.

Chapters 1-5

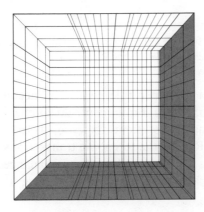

PRACTICAL
ACCOUNTING
PROBLEMS

The following problems supplement those in Reports 1-1 through 5-1 of the Part 1 Study Assignments. These problems are numbered to indicate the chapter of the textbook with which they correlate. For example, Problem 1-A and Problem 1-B correlate with Chapter 1. Loose-leaf stationery should be used in solving these problems. The paper required includes plain ruled paper, two-column journal paper, two-column and three-column statement paper, ledger paper, and work sheet paper.

Problem 1-A   T. B. Curtis is a practicing attorney. As of December 31 he owned the following property that related to his business: Cash, $1,521, office equipment, $2,540; and an automobile, $3,780. At the same time he owed business creditors $1,230.

REQUIRED: **(1)** On the basis of the above information, compute the amounts of the accounting elements and show them in equation form. **(2)** Assume that during the following year there is an increase in Mr. Curtis' business assets of $2,650 and a decrease in his business liabilities of $275. Indicate the changes in the accounting elements by showing them in equation form after the changes have occurred.

Problem 1-B   O. F. Otto, a CPA who has been employed by a large national firm of certified public accountants, decides to go into business for himself. His business transactions for the first month of operations were as follows:

    (a) Mr. Otto invested $15,000 cash in the business.
    (b) Paid office rent for one month, $250.
    (c) Purchased office equipment from the Von Brocken Office Equipment Co. (a supplier), $2,580 on account.

(d) Paid telephone bill, $27.

(e) Received $1,000 for services rendered to Public Finance Co.

(f) Paid $1,500 to the Von Brocken Office Equipment Co., on account.

(g) Received $750 for services rendered to the Kribs Garage.

(h) Paid $500 salary to office secretary.

REQUIRED: **(1)** On a plain sheet of paper rule eight "T" accounts and enter the following titles: Cash, Office Equipment, Accounts Payable, O. F. Otto, Capital, Professional Fees, Rent Expense, Telephone Expense, and Salary Expense. **(2)** Record the foregoing transactions directly in the accounts. **(3)** Foot the accounts and enter the balances where necessary. **(4)** Prepare a trial balance of the accounts, using a sheet of two-column journal paper.

Problem 2-A   Following is a narrative of the transactions completed by Ms. C. V. Little, management consultant, during the first month of her business operations:

Oct.   1. Ms. Little invested $10,000 cash in the business.

   1. Paid office rent, $200.

   3. Purchased office furniture for $1,675.

   3. Paid $24.35 for installation of telephone and for one month's service.

   4. Received $400 from The Premier Linen Service for consulting services rendered.

   5. Purchased stationery and supplies on account from W. K. Woods Stationery Co., $262.49.

   6. Paid $9 for subscription to a professional management magazine (Charge Miscellaneous Expense.)

   8. Paid $65 to Dr. James Bynum, a dentist, for dental service performed for Ms. Little.
       (Note: This is equivalent to a withdrawal of $65 by Ms. Little for personal use. Charge to her drawing account.)

   10. Received $150 from Tropicana Pools, Inc., for professional services rendered.

   12. Paid $85.22 for an airplane ticket for a business trip.

   14. Paid other traveling expenses, $72.40.

   19. Received $450 from Wagner Electric Co. for professional services rendered.

   20. Paid account of W. K. Woods Stationery Co. in full, $262.49.

   31. Paid $500 monthly salary to secretary.

REQUIRED: Journalize the foregoing transactions, using a sheet of two-column journal paper. Number the pages and use both sides of the sheet, if necessary. Select the account titles from the chart of accounts on page 129.

After journalizing the transactions, prove the equality of the debits and credits by footing the amount columns. Enter the footings in pencil immediately under the line on which the last entry appears.

CHART OF ACCOUNTS

Assets
111 Cash
112 Stationery and Supplies
121 Office Furniture

Liabilities
211 Accounts Payable

Owner's Equity
311 C. V. Little, Capital
312 C. V. Little, Drawing

Revenue
411 Professional Fees

Expenses
511 Rent Expense
512 Telephone Expense
513 Traveling Expense
514 Salary Expense
515 Miscellaneous Expense

Problem 2-B   B. H. Sirkin is a certified data processor engaged in practice on his own account. Following is the trial balance of his business taken as of September 30, 19—.

B. H. SIRKIN, CERTIFIED DATA PROCESSOR
Trial Balance
September 30, 19—

Cash.................................	111	2,073.08	
Office Equipment........................	121	1,155.00	
Automobile..............................	122	4,840.00	
Accounts Payable.......................	211		1,737.19
B. H. Sirkin, Capital....................	311		5,526.40
B. H. Sirkin, Drawing....................	312	3,960.00	
Professional Fees........................	411		8,800.00
Rent Expense...........................	511	2,700.00	
Telephone Expense......................	512	193.05	
Electric Expense........................	513	132.00	
Automobile Expense.....................	514	479.38	
Charitable Contributions Expense...........	515	352.00	
Miscellaneous Expense...................	516	179.08	
		16,063.59	16,063.59

A narrative of the transactions completed by Mr. Sirkin during the month of October follows below and on page 130.

NARRATIVE OF TRANSACTIONS FOR OCTOBER

Oct. 1. (Saturday) Paid one month's rent, $300.
   3. Paid telephone bill, $19.20.
   3. Paid electric bill, $15.12.
   5. Received $400 from Associated Grocers for services rendered.
   7. Paid a garage bill, $36.80.
   10. Received $300 from the Breckenridge Hotels for services rendered.
   12. Paid Venture Department Store, $42.30. (Charge to Mr. Sirkin's drawing account.)
   15. Mr. Sirkin withdrew $400 for personal use.
   17. Paid IBM, Inc., $250 on account.
   19. Received $200 from IGA Food Stores for services rendered.
   24. Gave the American Cancer Society $30.

Oct. 26. Paid the Data Processing Management Association $75 for annual membership dues and fees.
   29. Received $125 from Barford Motor Sales Co. for professional services.
   31. Mr. Sirkin withdrew $400 for personal use.

REQUIRED: (1) Journalize the October transactions, using a sheet of two-column journal paper. Number the pages and use both sides of the sheet, if necessary. Foot the amount columns. (2) Open the necessary accounts, using the standard account form of ledger paper. Allow one page for each account. Record the October 1 balances as shown in the September 30 trial balance and post the journal entries for October. (3) Foot the ledger accounts, enter the balances, and prove the balances by taking a trial balance as of October 31. Use a sheet of two-column journal paper for the trial balance.

Problem 2-C

THE R. E. BURLEW AGENCY
Trial Balance
March 31, 19—

Cash	111	6,372.10	
Stationery and Supplies	112	1,238.05	
Office Furniture	121	4,052.40	
Notes Payable	211		1,980.00
Accounts Payable	212		1,415.24
R. E. Burlew, Capital	311		7,737.12
R. E. Burlew, Drawing	312	1,386.88	
Professional Fees	411		3,711.84
Rent Expense	511	330.00	
Telephone Expense	512	47.52	
Salary Expense	513	616.00	
Traveling Expense	514	696.34	
Stationery and Supplies Expense	515	40.55	
Miscellaneous Expense	516	64.36	
		14,844.20	14,844.20

REQUIRED: (1) Prepare an income statement for The R. E. Burlew Agency showing the results of the first month of operations, March. (2) Prepare a balance sheet in account form showing the financial condition of the agency as of March 31. Use a sheet of two-column statement paper for the income statement. Two sheets of two-column statement paper may be used for the balance sheet. List the assets on one sheet and the liabilities and owner's equity on the other sheet.

Problem 3-A   Anne Pollack is an interior designer. The only book of original entry for her business is a two-column journal. She uses the standard form of account in the general ledger. Following is the trial balance of her business taken as of November 30:

ANNE POLLACK, INTERIOR DESIGNER
Trial Balance
November 30, 19—

Cash....................................	111	3,634.28	
Office Equipment.........................	112	800.00	
Accounts Payable........................	211		191.45
Anne Pollack, Capital....................	311		7,371.93
Anne Pollack, Drawing....................	312	5,500.00	
Professional Fees........................	411		11,990.00
Rent Expense............................	511	2,200.00	
Telephone Expense.......................	512	225.60	
Electric Expense.........................	513	143.70	
Salary Expense...........................	514	6,600.00	
Charitable Contributions Expense...........	515	325.00	
Miscellaneous Expense....................	516	124.80	
		19,553.38	19,553.38

NARRATIVE OF TRANSACTIONS FOR DECEMBER

Dec. 1. (Thursday) Paid December office rent in advance, $200.
   1. Paid electric bill, $12.67.
   2. Paid telephone bill, $16.85.
   2. Received a check from Wagner Electric Co. for $500 for services rendered.
   6. Received $400 from Wetterau Grocer Co. for services rendered.
   7. Donated $25 to the Heart Association.
   7. Paid $7.25 for cleaning office.
   8. Received check for $400 from Nooter Corporation for consulting services.
  12. Ms. Pollack withdrew $350 for personal use.
  15. Paid secretary's salary for the half month, $300.
  16. Purchased office furniture on credit from Union Furniture Co., $600.
  19. Paid $5 for having the office windows washed.
  20. Received $200 from Associated General Contractors for services rendered.
  22. Paid traveling expenses while on business, $32.25.
  23. Donated $30 to the United Fund.
  26. Paid Union Furniture Co. $200 on account.
  28. Ms. Pollack withdrew $150 for personal use.
  30. Paid secretary's salary for the half month, $300.

REQUIRED: **(1)** Journalize the December transactions. For the journal use two sheets of two-column journal paper and number the pages. **(2)** Open the necessary ledger accounts. Allow one page for each account and number the accounts. Record the December 1 balances and post the journal entries. Foot the journal. **(3)** Take a trial balance.

Problem 3-B

Gerald W. Renken, an electrician, completed the following transactions with the Merchants Trust and Savings Bank during the month of October:

Oct. 3. (Monday) Balance in bank per record kept on check stubs..........	$6,000.00	
3. Deposit........	4,000.00	
3. Check No. 208..	546.70	
3. Check No. 209..	50.00	
4. Check No. 210..	850.00	
4. Check No. 211..	230.00	
5. Check No. 212..	260.00	
6. Check No. 213..	170.00	
7. Check No. 214..	321.10	
7. Check No. 215..	100.00	
7. Check No. 216..	96.00	
7. Deposit........	569.30	
10. Check No. 217..	968.04	

Oct. 11. Check No. 218..	180.00
11. Check No. 219..	98.10
13. Check No. 220..	859.50
14. Check No. 221..	86.30
14. Check No. 222..	446.49
14. Deposit........	766.28
17. Check No. 223..	250.00
18. Check No. 224..	520.30
21. Check No. 225..	149.90
21. Deposit........	1,492.00
24. Check No. 226..	264.82
25. Check No. 227..	271.66
27. Check No. 228..	545.95
28. Check No. 229..	160.00
31. Check No. 230..	1,269.50
31. Deposit........	1,520.68

REQUIRED: **(1)** A record of the bank account as it would appear on the check stubs. **(2)** A reconciliation of the bank statement for October which indicated a balance of $7,442.87 on October 31, with Checks Nos. 216, 226, 229, and 230 outstanding, and a service charge of $1.35.

Problem 3-C

L. J. Sverdrup, a general contractor, had a balance of $150 in his petty cash fund as of June 1. During June the following petty cash transactions were completed:

June 2. (Thursday) $3.25 for typewriter repairs. Petty Cash Voucher No. 32.
    6. Paid for long-distance telephone call, $3.75. Petty Cash Voucher No. 33.
    8. Gave $20 to the United Fund. Petty Cash Voucher No. 34.
    9. Paid garage for washing car, $2.50. Petty Cash Voucher No. 35.
   12. Gave Mr. Sverdrup's son $5 (Charge L. J. Sverdrup, Drawing.) Petty Cash Voucher No. 36,
   14. Paid for postage stamps, $6, Petty Cash Voucher No. 37.
   17. Paid for newspaper for month, $2.75. Petty Cash Voucher No. 38.
   22. Paid for window washing, $3.75. Petty Cash Voucher No. 39.
   27. Paid $5 to the Parent-Teacher Organization for dues. (Charge L. J. Sverdrup, Drawing.) Petty Cash Voucher No. 40.
   28. Paid for car lubrication, $3.00. Petty Cash Voucher No. 41.
   29. Donated $25 to the American Red Cross. Petty Cash Voucher No. 42.
   30. Rendered report of petty cash expenditures for month and received the amount needed to replenish the petty cash fund.

REQUIRED: **(1)** Record the foregoing transactions in a petty cash disbursements record, distributing the expenditures as follows (a page of work sheet paper may be used):

L. J. Sverdrup, Drawing   Charitable Contributions Expense
Automobile Expense   Miscellaneous Expense
Telephone Expense

(2) Prove the petty cash disbursements record by footing the amount columns and proving the totals. Enter the totals and rule the amount columns with single and double lines. **(3)** Prepare a statement of the petty cash disbursements for June. **(4)** Bring down the balance in the petty cash fund below the ruling in the Description column. Enter the amount received to replenish the fund and record the total.

Problem 4-A   Following is a summary of the hours worked, rates of pay, and other relevant information concerning the employees of The Ozark Lead Co., N. C. Young, owner, for the week ended Saturday, November 5. Employees are paid at the rate of time and one half for all hours worked in excess of 8 in any day or 40 in any week.

No.	Name	Allowances Claimed	M	T	W	T	F	S	Regular Hourly Rate	Cumulative Earnings Jan. 1–Oct. 29
1	Bono, Ben C..............	3	8	8	8	8	8	6	$3.00	$7,212
2	Hauser, Lenore H.........	4	8	9	8	8	8	4	3.25	$8,240
3	Messey, Robert J.........	3	8	8	8	8	8	0	3.10	$8,135
4	Ring, John H.............	1	8	8	8	9	8	4	2.90	$4,857
5	Sparks, Maralynn H......	2	8	8	8	8	8	4	3.15	$5,670
6	Wynn, W. T..............	1	8	8	8	8	4	0	3.40	$6,400

Bono and Ring each have $4.00 withheld this payday for group life insurance. Hauser and Wynn each have $3.50 withheld this payday for private hospital insurance. Sparks has $10 withheld this payday as a contribution to the United Fund.

REQUIRED: **(1)** Using plain ruled paper size 8½″ by 11″, rule a payroll register form similar to that reproduced on pages 76 and 77 and insert the necessary columnar headings. Enter on this form the payroll for the week ended Saturday, November 5. Refer to the Weekly Income Tax Table on page 74 to determine the amounts to be withheld from the wages of each worker for income tax purposes. All of Young's employees are married. Six percent of the taxable wages of each employee should be withheld for FICA tax. Checks Nos. 611 through 616 were issued to the employees. Complete the payroll record by footing the amount columns, proving the footings, entering the totals, and ruling. **(2)** Assuming that the wages were paid on November 9, record the payment on a sheet of two-column journal paper.

Problem 4-B   The River Roads Store employs twelve people. They are paid by checks on the 15th and last day of each month. The entry to record each payroll includes the liabilities for the amounts withheld. The expense and liabilities arising from the employer's payroll taxes are recorded on each payday.

Following is a narrative of the transactions completed during the month of January that relate to payrolls and payroll taxes:

Jan. 15. Payroll for first half of month:

Total salaries..........................		$3,720.00
Less amounts withheld:		
FICA tax............................	$223.20	
Employees' income tax..................	410.90	634.10
Net amount paid........................		$3,085.90

15. Social security taxes imposed on employer:
FICA tax, 6%
State unemployment tax, 2%
FUTA tax, 0.5%

28. Paid $1,520.80 for December's payroll taxes:
FICA tax, $535.60.
Employees' income tax withheld, $985.20.

28. Paid State unemployment tax for quarter ended December 31, $329.40.

28. Paid balance due on FUTA tax for last half of year ended December 31, $150.68.

31. Payroll for last half of month:

Total salaries..........................		$3,800.00
Less amounts withheld:		
FICA tax............................	$228.00	
Employees' income tax..................	440.30	668.30
Net amount paid........................		$3,131.70

31. Social security taxes imposed on employer:
All salaries taxable; rates same as on January 15.

REQUIRED: (1) Journalize the foregoing transactions, using two-column general journal paper. (2) Foot the debit and credit amount columns as a means of proof.

Problem 5-A   Jean Gavin is a certified public accountant engaged in professional practice on her own account. Since her revenue consists entirely of compensation for personal services rendered, she keeps accounts on the cash basis. Her trial balance for the current year ending December 31 appears on page 135.

REQUIRED: (1) Prepare an eight-column work sheet making the necessary entries in the Adjustments columns to record the depreciation of the following assets:

Office equipment, 10%, $441.60
Automobiles, 25%, $2,093

(2) Prepare the following financial statements:

    (a) An income statement for the year ended December 31.

    (b) A balance sheet in report form as of December 31.

JEAN GAVIN, CPA

Trial Balance

December 31, 19—

Cash	111	8,820.63	
Office Equipment	131	4,416.00	
Accumulated Depreciation — Office Equipment	013		441.60
Automobiles	141	8,372.00	
Accumulated Depreciation — Automobiles	014		2,093.00
Accounts Payable	211		1,741.14
Employees Income Tax Payable	212		180.60
FICA Tax Payable	213		193.20
Jean Gavin, Capital	311		13,081.89
Jean Gavin, Drawing	031	20,000.00	
Professional Fees	411		45,814.00
Rent Expense	511	6,000.00	
Salary Expense	512	12,880.00	
Automobile Expense	513	935.80	
Depreciation Expense	514		
Payroll Taxes Expense	515	862.50	
Charitable Contributions Expense	516	550.00	
Miscellaneous Expense	517	708.50	
		63,545.43	63,545.43

Problem 5-B   John Staples operates an airline charter service, specializing in all weather passenger and freight service. A trial balance of his general ledger accounts is reproduced on page 136.

REQUIRED: (1) Prepare an eight-column work sheet making the necessary adjustments to record the depreciation of long-lived assets as shown below.

PROPERTY	RATE OF DEPRECIATION	AMOUNT OF DEPRECIATION
Office equipment	10%	$ 550
Air service equipment	20%	49,660

(2) Prepare an income statement for the year ended December 31. (3) Prepare a balance sheet in report form as of December 31. (4) Using two-column journal paper, prepare the entries required:

    (a) To adjust the general ledger accounts so that they will be in agreement with the financial statements.

    (b) To close the temporary owner's equity accounts on December 31.

Foot the amount columns as a means of proof.

JOHN STAPLES AIR SERVICE
Trial Balance
December 31, 19—

Cash	111	28,939.29	
Office Equipment	1'31	5,500.00	
Accumulated Depreciation — Office Equipment	031		1,100.00
Air Service Equipment	141	248,300.00	
Accumulated Depr. — Air Service Equipment	014		99,320.00
Accounts Payable	211		12,862.00
Employees Income Tax Payable	212		600.00
FICA Tax Payable	213		575.00
John Staples, Capital	311		86,724.83
John Staples, Drawing	031	18,600.00	
Traffic Revenue	411		192,175.28
Rent Expense	511	14,400.00	
Salary Expense	512	36,000.00	
Office Expense	513	2,840.00	
Air Service Expense	514	35,687.12	
Depreciation Expense	515		
Payroll Taxes Expense	516	2,414.00	
Charitable Contributions Expense	517	500.00	
Miscellaneous Expense	518	176.70	
		393,357.11	393,357.11

Problem 5-C   Sue Taylor is the sole proprietor of a dry cleaning establishment called Taylor Cleaners. Since revenue consists of compensation for services rendered, she keeps her accounts on the cash basis. She does not extend credit to customers but operates on a cash-on-delivery basis. The Trial Balance columns of her work sheet for the current year ended December 31 are reproduced on the next page.

REQUIRED: **(1)** Complete the work sheet making the necessary adjusting entries to record the depreciation of long-lived assets as follows:

Office equipment, 10% a year, $300
Cleaning equipment, 8% a year, $688
Delivery trucks, 30% a year, $1,158

(2) Prepare an income statement for the year ended December 31. **(3)** Prepare a balance sheet as of December 31 in report form. **(4)** Using two-column journal paper, prepare the entries required to adjust and close the ledger. Foot the amount columns as a means of proof.

TAYLOR CLEANERS
Work Sheet
For the Year Ended December 31, 19—

Account	Acct. No.	Trial Balance	
		Debit	Credit
Integrity National Bank....................	111	16,265.20	
Office Equipment........................	131	3,000.00	
Accumulated Depreciation — Office Equip...	013		300.00
Cleaning Equipment......................	141	8,600.00	
Accumulated Depreciation — Cleaning Equip.	014		688.00
Delivery Trucks.........................	151	3,860.00	
Accumulated Depreciation — Delivery Trucks.	015		1,158.00
Accounts Payable........................	211		864.61
Employees Income Tax Payable	212		513.90
FICA Tax Payable.......................	213		275.16
Sue Taylor, Capital.....................	311		21,309.04
Sue Taylor, Drawing.....................	031	15,600.00	
Dry Cleaning Revenue....................	411		42,820.60
Pressing Revenue........................	412		18,351.08
Rent Expense...........................	511	9,600.00	
Heat, Light, and Power Expense...........	512	5,641.28	
Salary Expense..........................	513	19,640.00	
Delivery Expense........................	514	1,965.27	
Depreciation Expense....................	515		
Payroll Taxes Expense	516	1,321.51	
Miscellaneous Expense...................	517	787.13	
		86,280.39	86,280.39

Chapter 6

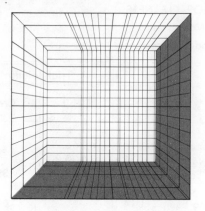

ACCOUNTING FOR MERCHANDISE

In the preceding chapter, accounting and bookkeeping practices suitable for a personal service enterprise were discussed and illustrated. The calculation of net income for the year was made on the so-called "cash basis" except for the matter of depreciation expense. Revenue was not recorded until money was received for the service performed, even though the service may have been performed in a prior period. Similarly, most expenses were not recorded until cash was disbursed for them, even though many of the payments were for things of value received and consumed in a prior period or for things to be received and consumed in a later period. An exception to this practice was made in the matter of depreciation, since it would be unrealistic to consider the entire cost of an asset such as an article of office equipment (expected to be used for many years) to be an expense only of the month or year of purchase. The cost of such long-lived assets is spread as expense over their expected useful lives.

The cash basis, even when slightly modified, is not technically perfect; but it has the virtues of simplicity and ease of understanding. This basis has proved to be quite satisfactory for most personal service enterprises. In the case of business enterprises whose major activity is the purchase and sale of merchandise, however, the cash basis of periodic income calculation usually does not give a meaningful or useful measure of net income or net loss. There are two reasons why this is true: **(1)** Merchandising businesses commonly purchase and often sell merchandise "on account" or "on credit" — meaning that payment is postponed a few days or weeks. The amount of cash paid or collected in any accounting period is almost never the same as the amount of purchases and sales of that period. **(2)** Merchandising businesses normally start and end each period with some goods on hand (commonly called *merchandise inventory*), but the dollar amount is not likely to be the same at both points of time. When either or both of these circumstances exist, the *accrual basis* of accounting must be used.

In the calculation of periodic income under the accrual basis, the focus of the effort is to try to match the *realized revenue* of a period against the expenses reasonably assignable to that period. ("Realized revenue" nearly always means the receipt of cash or a collectible claim to cash arising in return for something of value given up — commonly goods.) In the case of merchants, the process starts with the calculation of what is called *gross margin* (also known as *gross profit*). This is the difference between *net sales* and *cost of goods sold*. Net sales is simply the gross amount of revenue from sales less the sales price of any goods returned by customers because the merchandise has turned out to be unsatisfactory or unwanted for some reason. (Maybe the goods were found to be defective or the wrong color or size.) Sometimes a reduction in the price — an *allowance* — is given to the customer rather than having the goods returned. Cost of goods sold (really *expense* of goods sold) is most simply defined by the following formula:

| COST OF GOODS SOLD | = | MERCHANDISE INVENTORY, BEGINNING OF PERIOD | + | NET PURCHASES | − | MERCHANDISE INVENTORY, END OF PERIOD |

Net purchases is the difference between the cost of goods purchased and the total of **(1)** the cost of goods returned to suppliers and **(2)** the amount of any allowances made by suppliers. To illustrate, consider the following circumstances:

Cost of merchandise (goods) on hand, beginning of period	$12,000
Cost of merchandise purchased during the period	74,000
Cost of goods returned to the supplier for some reason (not ordered, unsatisfactory for some reason, etc.)	2,000
Cash disbursements during the period for goods purchased both in prior periods and the current period	66,000
Sale price of all goods sold and delivered to customers during the current period	95,000
Sale price of goods returned by customers	4,000
Cash received from customers during the period in payment for sales both of prior periods and the current period	78,000
Cost of merchandise (goods) on hand, end of period	15,000

If the *relevant* information in the foregoing array of data is assembled in the proper fashion, the gross margin for the period is calculated to be

$22,000. The conventional means of exhibiting the pertinent amounts is as follows:

Sales..		$95,000
Less sales returns and allowances..................		4,000
Net sales.......................................		$91,000
Cost of goods sold:		
Merchandise inventory, beginning of period........		$12,000
Add: Purchases...............................	$74,000	
Less purchases returns and allowances............	2,000	
Net purchases................................		72,000
Merchandise available for sale...................		$84,000
Less merchandise inventory, end of period.........		15,000
Cost of goods sold.............................		69,000
Gross margin on sales...........................		$22,000

Note that the movement of cash in both directions (to suppliers and from customers) has been ignored as being irrelevant. (It should be mentioned that the manner of accounting for depreciation illustrated in the last chapter was in accordance with the accrual basis of accounting.) Because accrual accounting is widely used, and because one of its major applications relates to the accounting for merchandise transactions, this subject will be examined in some detail.

In recording transactions concerned with merchandising, it is desirable to keep at least the following accounts:

    (a) Purchases
    (b) Purchases Returns and Allowances
    (c) Sales
    (d) Sales Returns and Allowances
    (e) Merchandise Inventory

PURCHASES AND THE PURCHASES JOURNAL

The word *purchase* can refer to the act of buying almost anything or, if used as a noun, to the thing that is bought. In connection with the accounting for a merchandising business, however, the term usually refers to merchandise. A reference to "purchases for the year," unless qualified in some way, would relate to the merchandise (*stock in trade*) that had been bought.

Purchases account

The purchases account is a temporary owner's equity account in which the cost of merchandise purchased is recorded. The account should be debited for the cost of all merchandise purchased during the accounting period. If the purchase was for cash, the cash account should be credited; if on account, Accounts Payable should be credited. The purchases account may also be debited for any transportation charges, such as freight, express, and parcel post charges, that increase the cost of the merchandise purchased.

PURCHASES
Debit to record the cost of merchandise purchased.

Purchases returns and allowances account

This account is a temporary owner's equity account in which purchases returns and allowances are recorded. The account should be credited for the cost of any merchandise returned to creditors or suppliers and for any allowances received from creditors that decrease the cost of the merchandise purchased. The offsetting debit is to Accounts Payable if the goods were purchased on account, or to Cash if a refund is received because the purchase was originally for cash. Allowances may be received from creditors

PURCHASES RETURNS AND ALLOWANCES
Credit to record returns and allowances.

for merchandise delivered in poor condition or for merchandise that does not meet specifications as to quality, weight, size, color, grade, or style.

Although purchases returns and allowances might be credited directly to Purchases, it is better to credit Purchases Returns and Allowances. The accounts will then show both the amount of gross purchases and the amount of returns and allowances. If returns and allowances are large in proportion to gross purchases, a weakness in the purchasing operations is indicated. It may be that better sources of supply should be sought or that purchase specifications should be stated more clearly.

Purchase invoice

A document received by the buyer from the seller that provides information for recording a purchase transaction is known as a *purchase invoice*. An invoice includes the supplier's invoice number, the purchaser's order number, the dates of shipment and billing, the terms of sale, a description of the goods, the quantities shipped, the unit prices, and the total amount of the purchase. A variety of forms and sizes of purchase invoices is in common use.

When both the goods and the invoice have been received, it is customary for the purchaser to assign the incoming invoice a number. (Note that the invoice on page 142 was marked "#37.") Someone must check to see that the invoice is correct as to quantities and unit prices, and that the extensions and total are correct. ("Extensions" are the amounts resulting from multiplying the quantity times the price of each item purchased.) It is common practice for the purchaser to imprint a form on the face of the invoice by means of a rubber stamp. This form provides spaces for the initials of the persons who have verified that the goods were received, and that the prices, extensions, and total are correct. Sometimes there is space to show the number of the account to be debited — Purchases, if the invoice relates to merchandise bought for resale. If everything is found to be in order, the invoice will be paid at the proper time.

Below is a reproduction of a purchase invoice as it would appear after the various aspects of the transaction have been verified and approved.

FINNEY FURNITURE COMPANY   #37 INVOICE

GRAND RAPIDS, MICHIGAN 49501

	DATE May 2, 1977
SOLD TO	**INVOICE NO.** 8712
W. F. BROWN 5401 MADISON ROAD CINCINNATI, OH 45227	**CUST. ORDER NO.** 196
	SHIPPED VIA C & O RR
TERMS 30 days	**DATE SHIPPED** May 2, 1977

QUANTITY		DESCRIPTION	UNIT PRICE	AMOUNT
ORDERED	SHIPPED			
3	3	4119 End Table	26.40	79.20
1	1	662 Dropleaf Table	92.00	92.00
2	2	635 Mhg. Table	58.50	117.00
4	4	2630 Night Stand	27.10	108.40
2	2	2317 Coffee Table	39.80	79.60
				476.20

Date received . 5/5
Received by ··· R.B.
Items o.k. ···· R.B.
Prices o.k. ··· W.H.
Ex. & tot. o.k. W.H.
Acct. no. ····· 511
Appr. for pymt. B.R.

Purchase Invoice

Merchandise may be bought for cash or on account. When merchandise is bought for cash, the transaction results in an increase in purchases and a decrease in the asset cash; hence, it should be recorded by debiting Purchases and by crediting Cash. When merchandise is bought on account, the transaction results in an increase in purchases with a corresponding increase in the liability accounts payable; hence, it should be recorded by debiting Purchases and by crediting Accounts Payable.

Accounts payable

In order that the owner or manager may know the total amount owed to his suppliers (sometimes referred to as "creditors"), it is advisable to keep a summary ledger account for Accounts Payable. This is a liability account. The credit balance of the account at the beginning of the period represents the total amount owed to suppliers. During the period, the account should be credited for the amount of any transactions involving increases and should be debited for the amount of any transactions involving decreases in the amount owed to suppliers. At the end of the period, the credit balance of the account again represents the total amount owed to suppliers.

It is also necessary to keep some record of the transactions completed with each supplier in order that information may be readily available at all times as to the amount owed to each supplier and as to when each invoice should be paid. The following methods of accounting for purchases on account are widely used:

The Invoice Method. Under this method it is customary to keep a chronological record of the purchase invoices received and to file them systematically. All other vouchers or documents representing transactions completed with suppliers should be filed with the purchase invoices. Special filing equipment facilitates the use of this method.

The Ledger Account Method. Under this method it is also customary to keep a chronological record of the purchase invoices received; in addition, an individual ledger account with each supplier is kept. Special equipment may be used in maintaining a permanent file of the invoices and other vouchers or documents supporting the records.

Purchases journal

All of the transactions of a merchandising business can be recorded in an ordinary two-column general journal or in a combined cash journal. However, in many such enterprises purchase transactions occur frequently. If most of the purchases are made on account, such transactions may be recorded advantageously in a special journal called a *purchases journal*. One form of a purchases journal is illustrated on page 144.

It will be noted that in recording each purchase, the following information is entered in the purchases journal:

    (a) Date on which the invoice is received
    (b) Number of the invoice (i.e., the number assigned by the buyer)
    (c) From whom purchased (the supplier)
    (d) Amount of the invoice

When the invoice method of accounting is used for purchases on account, it is not necessary to record the address of the supplier in the purchases journal; neither is it necessary to record the terms in the purchases

PURCHASES JOURNAL   PAGE 9

	DATE	INVOICE NO.	FROM WHOM PURCHASED	POST. REF.	AMOUNT	
1	1977 May 5	37	Finney Furniture Company	✓	476 20	1
2	6	38	L. J. Carter Company	✓	891 63	2
3	12	39	Mathews Manufacturing Co.	✓	1527 90	3
4	27	40	Monroe Brothers	✓	176 211	4
5	31		Purchases Dr.-Accounts Payable Cr.	511 / 231	4657 84	5

Model Purchases Journal

journal. With this form of purchases journal, each transaction can be recorded on one horizontal line.

If an individual ledger account is not kept with each supplier, the purchase invoices should be filed immediately after they have been recorded in the purchases journal. It is preferable that they be filed according to due date in an unpaid invoice file.

If a partial payment is made on an invoice, a notation of the payment should be made on the invoice, and it should be retained in the unpaid invoice file until it is paid in full. It is generally considered a better policy to pay each invoice in full. Paying specific invoices in full simplifies record keeping for both the buyer and the seller. If credit is received because of returns or allowances, a notation of the amount of the credit should also be made on the invoice so that the balance due will be indicated.

When an invoice is paid in full, the payment should be noted on the invoice, which should be transferred from the unpaid invoice file to a paid invoice file.

The unpaid invoice file is usually arranged with a division for each month with folders numbered 1 to 31 in each division. This makes it possible to file the unpaid invoices according to the date they will become due, which facilitates payment of the invoices on or before their due dates. Since certain invoices may be subject to discounts if paid within a specified time, it is important that they be handled in such a manner that payment in time to get the benefit of the discounts will not be overlooked.

The folders in the paid invoice file are usually arranged in alphabetic order, according to the names of suppliers. This facilitates the filing of all paid invoices, and all other vouchers or documents representing transactions with suppliers, in such a manner that a complete history of the business done with each supplier is maintained.

Posting from the Purchases Journal. Under the invoice method of accounting for purchases on account, individual posting from the purchases journal is not required. When this plan is followed, it is customary to place a check mark in the Posting Reference column of the purchases journal at the time of entering each invoice.

At the end of the month the Amount column of the purchases journal should be totaled and the ruling completed as illustrated. The total of the purchases on account for the month should then be posted as a debit to Purchases and as a credit to Accounts Payable. A proper cross-reference should be provided by entering the page of the purchases journal preceded by the initial "P" in the Posting Reference column of the ledger and by entering the account number in the Posting Reference column of the purchases journal. The titles of both accounts and the posting references may be entered on one horizontal line of the purchases journal as shown in the illustration. Posting the total in this manner usually is referred to as *summary posting.*

Regardless of whether the cash basis or the accrual basis of accounting is used, a special account form, called a *balance-column account* form, is widely used. While the standard two-column account form illustrated to this point is still favored by some, the four-column form of balance-column account, illustrated below, has the advantage of providing a place to note the balance of the account. This may be determined and recorded after each transaction, or only at the end of the month. (There is also a three-column form of balance-column account which will be used in subsequent chapters for accounts with individual customers and suppliers.)

The summary posting from W. F. Brown's purchases journal on May 31 is illustrated below:

ACCOUNT *Accounts Payable*   ACCOUNT NO. 231

DATE	ITEM	POST. REF.	DEBIT	CREDIT	BALANCE DEBIT	BALANCE CREDIT
1977 May 31		P9		465784		465784

ACCOUNT *Purchases*   ACCOUNT NO. 511

DATE	ITEM	POST. REF.	DEBIT	CREDIT	BALANCE DEBIT	BALANCE CREDIT
1977 May 31		P9	465784		465784	

General Ledger Accounts After Posting from Purchases Journal

The Ledger Account Method. If an individual ledger account is kept for each supplier, all transactions representing either increases or decreases in the amount owed to each supplier should be posted individually to the proper account. The posting may be done by hand, or posting machines may be used. If the posting is done by hand, it may be completed either directly from the purchase invoices and other vouchers or documents representing the transactions, or it may be completed from the books of original entry. If the posting is done with the aid of posting machines, it will usually be completed directly from the purchase invoices and other vouchers or documents. The ledger account method of accounting for accounts payable is explained in detail in Chapter 8.

| Report No. 6-1 | Refer to the study assignments and complete Report No. 6-1. After completing the report, continue with the textbook discussion until the next report is required. |

SALES AND THE SALES JOURNAL

On page 140 reference was made to the fact that in recording transactions arising from merchandising activities it is desirable to keep certain accounts, including accounts for sales and for sales returns and allowances. A discussion of these accounts, together with a discussion of the sales journal, follows.

Sales account

The sales account is a temporary owner's equity account in which the revenue resulting from sales of merchandise is recorded. The account should be credited for the selling price of all merchandise sold during the accounting period. If sales are for cash, the credit to Sales is offset by a debit to Cash; if the sales are on account, the debit is made to an asset account, Accounts Receivable.

SALES	
	Credit to record the selling price of merchandise sold.

Sales returns and allowances account

This account is a temporary owner's equity account in which sales returns and allowances are recorded. The account should be debited for the selling price of any merchandise returned by customers or for any allowances made to customers that decrease the selling price of the merchandise sold. The offsetting credit is to Accounts Receivable if the goods were sold on account, or to Cash if a refund was made because the sale was originally for cash. Such allow-

SALES RETURNS AND ALLOWANCES	
Debit to record returns and allowances.	

ances may be granted to customers for merchandise delivered in poor condition or for merchandise that does not meet specifications as to quality, weight, size, color, grade, or style.

While sales returns and allowances could be debited directly to Sales, it is better to debit Sales Returns and Allowances. The accounts will then show both the amount of gross sales and the amount of returns and allowances. If returns and allowances are large in proportion to gross sales, a weakness in the merchandising operations is indicated; and the trouble should be determined and corrected.

Retail sales tax

A tax imposed upon the sale of tangible personal property at retail is known as a *retail sales tax*. The tax is usually measured by the gross sales price or the gross receipts from sales. Retail sales taxes are imposed by most states and by many cities. Retail sales taxes may also include taxes imposed upon persons engaged in furnishing services at retail, in which case they are measured by the gross receipts for furnishing such services. The rates of the tax vary considerably but usually range from 1 percent to 6 percent. In most states the tax is a general sales tax. However, in some states the tax is imposed only on specific items, such as automobiles, cosmetics, radio and television sets, and playing cards.

To avoid fractions of cents and to simplify the determination of the tax, it is customary to use a sales tax table or schedule. For example, where the rate is 5 percent the tax may be calculated as shown in the following schedule:

AMOUNT OF SALE	AMOUNT OF TAX
1¢ to 10¢	None
11¢ to 27¢	1¢
28¢ to 47¢	2¢
48¢ to 68¢	3¢
69¢ to 89¢	4¢
90¢ to $1.09	5¢

and so on

The amount of the tax imposed under the schedule approximates the legal rate. Retail sales tax reports accompanied by remittances for the amounts due must be filed periodically, usually monthly or quarterly, depending upon the law of the state or city in which the business is located.

In the case of a retail store operated in a city or state where a sales tax is imposed on merchandise sold for cash or on account, it is advisable to keep an account for Sales Tax Payable. This is a liability account which should be credited for the

SALES TAX PAYABLE	
Debit	Credit
to record payment of tax to the proper taxing authority or for tax on merchandise returned by customers.	to record tax imposed on sales.

amount of the tax collected or imposed on sales. The account should be debited for the amount of the tax paid to the proper taxing authority. A credit balance in the account at any time indicates the amount of the liability to the taxing authority for taxes collected or imposed.

Sales tax accounting may be complicated by such factors as **(1)** sales returns and allowances and **(2)** exempt sales. If the tax is recorded at the time the sale is recorded, it will be necessary to adjust for the tax when recording sales returns and allowances. If some sales are exempt from the tax, it will be necessary to distinguish between the taxable and the nontaxable sales. A common example of nontaxable sales is sales to out-of-state customers.

Sales ticket

The first written record of a sales transaction is called a *sales ticket*. Whether merchandise is sold for cash or on account, a sales ticket should be prepared. When the sale is for cash, the ticket may be printed by the cash register at the time that the sale is rung up. However, some stores prefer to use handwritten sales tickets no matter whether the sale is for cash or on account. Regardless of the method used in recording cash sales, it is necessary to prepare a handwritten sales ticket or charge slip for every sale on account. Such sales tickets are usually prepared in duplicate or in triplicate. The original copy is for the bookkeeping department. A carbon copy is given to the customer. Where more than one salesperson is employed, each is usually provided with a separate pad of sales tickets. Each pad bears a different number that identifies the clerk. The individual sales tickets are also numbered consecutively. This facilitates sorting the tickets by clerks if it is desired to compute the amount of goods sold by each clerk. Reference to the sales ticket illustrated here will show the type of information usually recorded.

Sales Ticket

When merchandise is sold for cash in a state or a city which has a retail sales tax, the transaction results in an increase in the asset cash offset by an increase in sales revenue and an increase in the liability sales tax payable. Such transactions should be recorded by debiting Cash for the amount received and by crediting Sales for the sales price of the merchandise and crediting Sales Tax Payable for the amount of the tax collected. When merchandise is sold on account in such a state or city, the transaction results in an increase in the asset accounts receivable offset by an increase in sales revenue and an increase in the liability sales tax payable. Such transactions should be recorded by debiting Accounts Receivable for the total amount charged to the customer and by crediting Sales for the amount of the sale and crediting Sales Tax Payable for the amount of the tax imposed.

An alternative procedure that is permissible under some sales tax laws is to credit the total of both the sales and the tax to the sales account in the first place. Periodically — usually at the end of each month — a calculation is made to determine how much of the balance of the sales account is presumed to be tax, and an entry is made to remove this amount from the sales account and to transfer it to the sales tax payable account. Suppose, for example, that the tax rate is 5 percent, and that the sales account includes the tax collected or charged, along with the amount of the sales. In this event, 100/105 of the balance of the account is presumed to be the amount of the sales, and 5/105 of the balance is the amount of the tax. If the sales account had a balance of $10,500, the tax portion would be $500 (5/105 of $10,500). A debit to Sales of $500 would remove this tax portion; the credit would be to Sales Tax Payable.

Bank credit card sales

The use of bank credit cards in connection with the retail sales of certain types of goods and service is a common practice. The two most widely used credit cards of this type in the United States are the "Bank-Americard" and the "Master Charge" card. The former was started by the Bank of America in California. That bank now franchises numerous banks in other localities to offer the program. Likewise, several thousand banks participate in the Master Charge program. The two systems have much in common.

Participating banks encourage their depositors and other customers to obtain the cards by supplying the necessary information to establish their credit reliability. When this has been accomplished, a small (approximately 2″ x 3″) plastic card containing (in raised characters so that the card may be used for imprinting) the cardholder's name and an identifying number is issued to the applicant.

Merchants and other businesses are invited to participate in the program. If certain conditions are met, the bank will accept for deposit completed copies of the prescribed form of sales invoices (also sometimes called "tickets," "drafts," or "vouchers") for goods sold or services rendered to cardholders and evidenced by the invoices bearing the card imprints and the buyers' signatures. The bank, in effect, either "buys" the tickets at a discount (commonly 3 percent, though it may be more or less depending upon various factors) immediately, or gives the merchant immediate credit for the full face amount of the tickets, and, once a month, charges the merchant's account with the total amount of the discount at the agreed rate. (The latter practice is more usual.)

For the merchant, bank credit card sales are nearly the equivalent of cash sales. The service is performed or the goods are sold; and the money is secured. It is then up to the bank to collect from the buyer or to bear the loss, if the account proves to be uncollectible.

In most respects, the accounting for bank credit card sales is very much the same as the accounting for regular cash sales. Very often a regular sales ticket is prepared as well as the credit card form of invoice. Usually the transactions are accounted for as sales for the full price with the amount of the discount being treated as an expense when the bank makes the monthly charge.

It will be apparent that bank credit card sales are similar in many respects to the sales made by certain types of businesses that use other forms of retail credit cards — notably those of petroleum companies, and businesses participating in the "Diners Club," "Carte Blanche," and American Express programs.

Accounts receivable

In order that the owner or manager of an enterprise may know the total amount due from charge customers at any time, it is advisable to keep a summary ledger account with Accounts Receivable. This is an asset account. The debit balance of the account at the beginning of the period represents the total amount due from customers. During the period, the account should be debited for the amount of any transactions involving increases and should be credited for the amount of any transactions involving decreases in the amount due from customers. At the end of the period, the debit balance of the account again represents the total amount due from charge customers.

It is also necessary to keep some record of the transactions completed with each customer in order that information may be readily available at all times as to the amount due from each customer. The following methods of accounting for charge sales are widely used:

The Sales Ticket Method. Under this method it is customary to file the charge sales tickets systematically. All other related vouchers or documents representing transactions with customers should be filed with the appropriate sales tickets. Special filing equipment facilitates the use of this method. In some cases a chronological record of the charge sales tickets is kept as a means of control.

The Ledger Account Method. Under this method it is customary to keep a chronological record of the charge sales tickets. An individual ledger account with each customer is also kept. Special equipment may be used in maintaining a permanent file of the charge sales tickets and other vouchers or documents supporting the records.

Under either of these methods of accounting for transactions with charge customers, it is necessary that a sales ticket or charge slip be made for each sale on account. In making a charge sales ticket the date, the name and address of the customer, the quantity, a description of the items sold, the unit prices, the total amount of the sale, and the amount of the sales tax should be recorded.

Sales journal   Transactions involving the sale of merchandise on account can be recorded in an ordinary two-column general journal or in a combined cash journal. However, in many merchandising businesses sales transactions occur frequently, and if it is the policy to sell merchandise on account, such transactions may be recorded advantageously in a special journal. If the business is operated in an area where no sales taxes are imposed, all sales on account can be recorded in a *sales journal* with only one amount column as illustrated below.

SALES JOURNAL   PAGE

	DATE	SALE NO.	TO WHOM SOLD	POST. REF.	AMOUNT	
1						1
2						2
3						3
4						4
5						5
6						6

Sales Journal Without Sales Taxes

At the end of the month, the total of the amount column should be posted as a debit to Accounts Receivable and as a credit to Sales.

The second model sales journal illustrated on page 152 provides three amount columns. This format is most appropriate for use in an area where a sales tax is imposed. The transactions recorded in the journal were completed by W. F. Brown, a retail merchant, during the month of May. His store is located in a state that imposes a tax of 5 percent on the retail sale of all merchandise whether sold for cash or on account.

SALES JOURNAL   PAGE *14*

	DATE	SALE NO.	TO WHOM SOLD	POST REF.	ACCOUNTS RECEIVABLE DR.	SALES CR.	SALES TAX PAYABLE CR.	
1	1977 May 5	240	Alfred Hofflander	✓	279 51	266 20	13 31	1
2	5	241	Louise C. Case	✓	1825 34	1738 42	86 92	2
3	11	242	Elanore S. Buffa	✓	609 95	580 90	29 05	3
4	16	243	C. H. Mason	✓	1544 34	1470 80	73 54	4
5	23	244	C. M. Williams	✓	989 36	942 25	47 11	5
6	26	245	Edward Sedgwick	✓	1517 46	1445 20	72 26	6
7	27	246	E. M. Keithley	✓	639 98	609 50	30 48	7
8					7405 94	7053 27	352 67	
					7405 94	7053 27	352 67	8
9					(121)	(411)	(241)	9

Sales Journal With Sales Taxes

It will be noted that the following information regarding each charge sales ticket is recorded in the sales journal:

(a) Date
(b) Number of the sales ticket
(c) To whom sold (the customer)
(d) Amount charged to customer
(e) Amount of sale
(f) Amount of sales tax

With this form of sales journal, each transaction can be recorded on one horizontal line. The sales ticket should provide all the information needed in recording each sale.

If an individual ledger account is not kept with each customer, the charge sales tickets should be filed immediately after they have been recorded in the sales journal. They are usually filed under the name of the customer. There are numerous types of trays, cabinets, and files on the market that are designed to facilitate the filing of charge sales tickets by customer name. Such devices are designed to save time, to promote accuracy, and to provide a safe means of keeping a record of the transactions with each charge customer.

When a customer makes a partial payment on an account, the amount of the payment should be noted on the most recent charge sales ticket and the new balance should be indicated. Sales tickets paid in full should be receipted and may either be given to the customer or may be transferred to another file for future reference. If a customer is given credit for merchandise returned or because of allowances, a notation of the amount of credit should be made on the most recent charge sales ticket and the new balance should be indicated. If a credit memorandum is issued to a customer, it should be prepared in duplicate and the carbon copy should be attached to the sales ticket on which the amount is noted.

Posting from the Sales Journal. Under the sales ticket method of accounting for sales on account, individual posting from the sales journal is not required. When this plan is followed, it is customary to place a check mark in the Posting Reference column of the sales journal at the time of entering each sale.

At the end of the month the amount columns of the sales journal should be footed in small figures. On a separate sheet of paper the total of the credit columns should then be added. The sum of the totals of the credit columns should equal the total of the debit column. If it does, the totals should be entered in ink and the ruling completed as illustrated. The totals should be posted to the general ledger accounts indicated in the column headings. This summary posting should be completed in the following order:

(a) Post the total of the Accounts Receivable Dr. column to the debit of Accounts Receivable.
(b) Post the total of the Sales Cr. column to the credit of Sales.
(c) Post the total of the Sales Tax Payable Cr. column to the credit of Sales Tax Payable.

A proper cross-reference should be provided by entering the page of the sales journal preceded by the initial "S" in the Posting Reference column of the ledger and by entering the account number immediately below the column total of the sales journal. The proper method of completing the summary posting from W. F. Brown's sales journal on May 31 is shown in the accounts affected as illustrated below.

ACCOUNT *Accounts Receivable*   ACCOUNT NO. *121*

DATE	ITEM	POST. REF.	DEBIT	CREDIT	BALANCE DEBIT	CREDIT
1977 May 31		S14	740594		740594	

ACCOUNT *Sales Tax Payable*   ACCOUNT NO. *241*

DATE	ITEM	POST. REF.	DEBIT	CREDIT	BALANCE DEBIT	CREDIT
1977 May 31		S14		35267		35267

ACCOUNT *Sales*   ACCOUNT NO. *411*

DATE	ITEM	POST. REF.	DEBIT	CREDIT	BALANCE DEBIT	CREDIT
1977 May 31		S14		705327		705327

General Ledger Accounts After Posting from Sales Journal

The Ledger Account Method. If an individual ledger account is kept for each customer, all transactions representing either increases or decreases in the amount due from each customer should be posted individually to the proper account. The posting may be done by hand or posting machines may be used. If the posting is done by hand, it may be completed either directly from the charge sales tickets and other vouchers or documents representing the transactions, or it may be completed from the books of original entry. If the posting is done with posting machines, it will usually be completed directly from the charge sales tickets and other vouchers or documents.

Report No. 6-2

> Refer to the study assignments and complete Report No. 6-2. After completing the report, continue with the textbook discussion until the next report is required.

ACCOUNTING PROCEDURE

The accounting procedure in recording the transactions of a merchandising business is, in general, the same as that involved in recording the transactions of any other enterprise. In a small merchandising business where the number of transactions is not large and all the bookkeeping may be done by one person, a standard two-column general journal or a combined cash journal may be used as the only book of original entry. However, if desired, a purchases journal and a sales journal may be used also. The purchases journal may be used for keeping a chronological record of purchases of merchandise on account, and the sales journal may be used for keeping a chronological record of sales of merchandise on account. All of the accounts may be kept in one general ledger, which may be either a bound book, a loose-leaf book, or a card file. The posting from a two-column journal or from the "General" columns of a combined cash journal may be completed daily or periodically; summary posting from the purchases and sales journals and from the special columns of a combined cash journal is done at the end of the month.

A trial balance should be taken at the end of each month as a means of proving the equality of the debit and credit account balances. The balance of the summary account for Accounts Receivable should be proved periodically, or at least at the end of each month. This may be done by determining the total of the unpaid sales tickets or charge slips that are kept in a customer's file. Likewise, the balance of the summary account for Accounts Payable should be proved periodically, or at least at the end of each month. This may be done by determining the total of the unpaid invoices that are kept in an unpaid invoice file.

This procedure will be illustrated by **(1)** recording a narrative of certain transactions for one month in a purchases journal, a sales journal, and a combined cash journal, **(2)** by posting to the ledger accounts, **(3)** by preparing a schedule of accounts receivable to reconcile the balance of the summary account for Accounts Receivable, and **(4)** by preparing a schedule of accounts payable to reconcile the balance of the summary account for Accounts Payable. (The end-of-month trial balance is not shown since the illustration does not involve all of the accounts in the general ledger.)

Dallas Hubbard is the owner of a small retail business operated under the name of "The Hubbard Store." A purchases journal, a sales journal, and a combined cash journal are used as books of original entry. All of the accounts are kept in a general ledger. Individual ledger accounts with customers and suppliers are not kept; instead, the purchase invoices and the charge sales tickets are filed in the manner previously described. All sales are subject to a retail sales tax of 5 percent, whether for cash or on account. All sales on account are payable by the tenth of the following month unless otherwise agreed. A partial chart of accounts is reproduced below. It includes only the accounts needed to record certain transactions completed during March, 1977, the first month that Mr. Hubbard has owned and operated the business.

THE HUBBARD STORE

PARTIAL CHART OF ACCOUNTS

*Assets**	*Revenue from Sales*
111 Cash	411 Sales
121 Accounts Receivable	041 Sales Returns and Allowances
181 Store Equipment	
Liabilities	*Cost of Goods Sold*
231 Accounts Payable	511 Purchases
241 Sales Tax Payable	051 Purchases Returns and Allowances

Words in italics represent headings and not account titles.

THE HUBBARD STORE

PARTIAL NARRATIVE OF TRANSACTIONS

Thursday, March 3

Purchased store equipment on account from the Metro Store Equipment Co., 1500 Main Street, Lafayette, IN 47901, $1,624.90.

Since this transaction involved a purchase of store equipment, it was recorded in the combined cash journal. (The purchases journal is used only for recording purchases of merchandise on account.)

Friday, March 4

Received invoice dated March 1 from Norton's, 469 Meridian, India-napolis, IN 47906, for merchandise purchased, $215.30. Terms, 30 days net. (Assigned number "1" to this invoice.)

Saturday, March 5

Sold merchandise on account to Elaine C. Peters, 2402 Northwestern, Lafayette, IN 47906, $34.60, tax $1.73. Sale No. 1-1.

Sundry cash sales per cash register tape, $61, tax $3.05. This amount includes sales made to customers who used their BankAmericards. The special vouchers (tickets, slips) prepared are treated the same as checks received for cash sales. Periodically, these vouchers, along with checks and probably some currency and coin, are deposited in the bank. (Early in the following month, and each month thereafter, the bank will charge The Hubbard Store with the agreed percentage of the total amount of the vouchers.)

> Each Saturday the store's total cash sales for the week and related tax are recorded, using the cash register tape as the source of the amounts. This transaction was recorded in the combined cash journal by debiting Cash for the total amount received and by crediting Sales for the selling price of the merchandise and crediting Sales Tax Payable for the amount of the tax imposed on cash sales. This was recorded in the combined cash journal since only sales on account are entered in the sales journal. A check mark was entered in the Posting Reference column to indicate that no individual posting is required.

Monday, March 7

Purchased merchandise from Parks Company, Kokomo, IN 46901, for cash, $96. Check No. 4.

> This transaction was recorded in the combined cash journal since only purchases of merchandise on account are recorded in the purchases journal.

Tuesday, March 8

Sold merchandise on account to W. A. Adams, 908 Oak St., Lafayette, IN 47905, $41, tax $2.05. Sale No. 1-2.

Wednesday, March 9

Gave W. A. Adams credit for merchandise returned, $12, tax 60 cents.

> This transaction increased sales returns and allowances and decreased sales tax payable and accounts receivable. It was recorded in the combined cash journal by debiting Sales Returns and Allowances for the amount of the merchandise returned, by debiting Sales Tax Payable for the amount of the sales tax, and by crediting Accounts Receivable for the total amount of the credit allowed Mr. Adams.

Thursday, March 10

Received invoice (No. 2) dated March 9 from Norton's for merchan-dise purchased, $385. Terms, 30 days net.

Friday, March 11

Sold merchandise on account to Joseph F. Charles, 13 Bexley Rd., Lafayette, IN 47906, $21.80, tax $1.09. Sale No. 2-1.

Saturday, March 12

Sundry cash sales for week, $215.40, tax $10.77.

Received a check for $36.33 from Elaine C. Peters for merchandise sold to her March 5.

Monday, March 14

Received credit for $25.60 from Norton's for merchandise returned by agreement.

> The credit applies to Invoice No. 2, dated March 9. This transaction had the effect of increasing purchases returns and allowances and decreasing accounts payable. It was recorded in the combined cash journal by debiting Accounts Payable and by crediting Purchases Returns and Allowances for the amount of the credit received from Norton's.

Tuesday, March 15

Paid Transit, Inc., freight and drayage on merchandise purchased, $20.50. Check No. 5.

> In the simple set of accounts maintained for The Hubbard Store, no separate account is used to record the cost of freight on merchandise purchases. Instead, the amount is debited to the purchases account. This treatment is acceptable since freight on purchases is really a part of the cost of goods purchased.

Wednesday, March 16

Received invoice (No. 3) dated March 14 from C. E. Arthur & Son, Frankfort, IN 46041, for merchandise purchased, $51. Terms, 30 days net.

Thursday, March 17

Paid Norton's $215.30 in settlement of Invoice No. 1 dated March 1. Check No. 6.

Friday, March 18

Received $30.45 from W. A. Adams for merchandise sold March 8 less merchandise returned March 9.

Saturday, March 19

Sundry cash sales for week, $104.05, tax $5.20.

Monday, March 21

Paid Metro Store Equipment Co. $800 on account. Check No. 7.

Tuesday, March 22

Sold merchandise on account to Joseph F. Charles, $41, tax $2.05. Sale No. 1-3.

Wednesday, March 23

Received invoice (No. 4) dated March 21 from C. E. Arthur & Son for merchandise purchased, $81.20. Terms, 30 days net.

Thursday, March 24

Sold merchandise on account to Elaine C. Peters, $47, tax $2.35. Sale No. 2-2.

Saturday, March 26

Sundry cash sales for week, $103.80, tax $5.19.

Monday, March 28

Sold merchandise on account to W. A. Adams, $34.20, tax $1.71. Sale No. 2-3.

Thursday, March 31

Sundry cash sales, $61.95, tax $3.10.

> Since this is the last day of the month, the amount of cash sales since March 26, including tax, was recorded.

Journalizing   The transactions completed by The Hubbard Store during the month of March were recorded in the combined cash journal reproduced on pages 160 and 161, the purchases journal reproduced on page 159, and the sales journal reproduced on page 159. (The footings of the combined cash journal reflect the amounts of more transactions than are actually recorded. The footings of the purchases journal and of the sales journal reflect only the amounts of the transactions recorded.)

Posting   The accounts affected by the transactions narrated are reproduced on pages 161 and 162. The posting was completed from the books of original entry in the following order; first, the combined cash journal; second, the purchases journal; and third, the sales journal. After the columns of the combined cash journal were footed and the footings were proved, the totals were entered and the rulings were made as illustrated. Each entry in the General Debit and General Credit columns was posted individually to the proper account. The total of each of the six special columns was posted to the account indicated by the column heading. The number of the account to which the posting was made was written below the total. Since the totals of the General Debit and General Credit columns were not posted, a check mark ($\sqrt{}$) was made under each of these columns to so indicate. The total of the single column in the purchases journal was posted as a debit to Purchases and also as a credit to Accounts Payable. The number of each of these accounts was noted in the Posting Reference column beside the total of the Amount column. After the three amount columns of the sales journal were footed and the footings were proved, the totals were entered and the rulings were made as illustrated. Each total was posted to the account indicated by the column heading, and the account number was shown below that total.

PURCHASES JOURNAL   PAGE 1

	DATE	INVOICE NO.	FROM WHOM PURCHASED	POST. REF.	AMOUNT	
1	1977 Mar. 4	1	Norton's	✓	215 30	1
2	10	2	Norton's	✓	385 00	2
3	16	3	C. E. Arthur + Son	✓	51 00	3
4	23	4	C. E. Arthur + Son	✓	81 20	4
5	31		Purchases Dr—Accounts Payable Cr	511 231	732 50	5
6						6
7						7
8						8

The Hubbard Store — Purchases Journal

SALES JOURNAL   PAGE 1

	DATE	SALE NO.	TO WHOM SOLD	POST REF.	ACCOUNTS RECEIVABLE DR.	SALES CR.	SALES TAX PAYABLE CR.	
1	1977 Mar. 5	1-1	Elaine C. Peters	✓	36 33	34 60	1 73	1
2	8	1-2	W. A. Adams	✓	43 05	41 00	2 05	2
3	11	2-1	Joseph F. Charles	✓	22 89	21 80	1 09	3
4	22	1-3	Joseph F. Charles	✓	43 05	41 00	2 05	4
5	24	2-2	Elaine C. Peters	✓	49 35	47 00	2 35	5
6	28	2-3	W. A. Adams	✓	35 91	34 20	1 71	6
7					230 58	219 60	10 98	
7					230 58	219 60	10 98	7
8					(121)	(411)	(244)	8
9								9
10								10

The Hubbard Store — Sales Journal

When more than one book of original entry is used, it is advisable to identify each book by means of an initial (or initials) preceding the page

PAGE *1*   COMBINED CASH JOURNAL

CASH		CK. NO.	DAY	DESCRIPTION	POST. REF.
RECEIPTS 111 DR.	DISBURSEMENTS 111 CR.				
1				AMOUNTS FORWARDED	1
4			3	*Store Equipment*	181 4
5				*Accts. Pay.--Metro Store Equip. Co.*	231 5
10	6405		5	*Cash Sales*	✓ 10
11		9600	4 7	*Purchases*	511 11
12			9	*Sales Ret. + Allow. (W. A. Adams)*	041 12
13				*Sales Tax Payable*	244 13
14	22617		12	*Cash Sales*	✓ 14
15	3633		12	*Elaine C. Peters (on acct.)*	✓ 15
16			14	*Pur. Ret. + Allow. (Norton's)*	051 16
17		2050	5 15	*Purchases (freight)*	511 17
18		21530	6 17	*Norton's*	✓ 18
19	3045		18	*W. A. Adams (on acct.)*	✓ 19
20	10925		19	*Cash Sales*	✓ 20
21		80000	7 21	*Metro Store Equipment Co.*	✓ 21
22	10899		26	*Cash Sales*	✓ 22
31	6505		31	*Cash Sales*	✓ 31
32	277110 277110	170876 170876		1,062.34	32
33	(111)	(111)			33
34					34

The Hubbard Store — Combined Cash Journal (Left Page)

number. The following code was used in conjunction with the page number to indicate the source of each entry in the ledger accounts:

CJ = Combined cash journal
P = Purchases journal
S = Sales journal

Trial balance   After completing the posting to the accounts in the general ledger, the balance of each account was extended to the proper debit or credit balance column. Usually a trial balance then would be prepared to prove the equality of the debit and credit account balances. However, since the illustration did not involve all of the general ledger accounts nor all of the transactions for the month, a trial balance of the general ledger of The Hubbard Store as of March 31, 1977, is not reproduced.

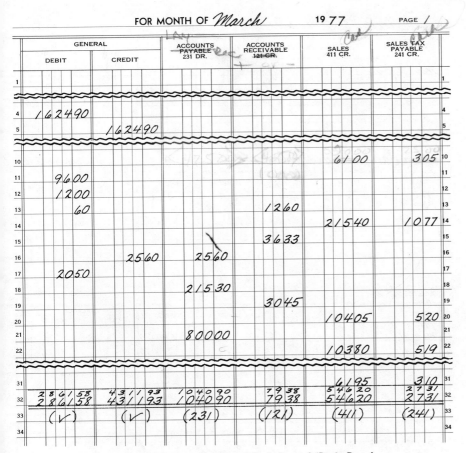

FOR MONTH OF *March*   19 77   PAGE *1*

	GENERAL		ACCOUNTS PAYABLE 231 DR.	ACCOUNTS RECEIVABLE 121 CR.	SALES 411 CR.	SALES TAX PAYABLE 241 CR.	
	DEBIT	CREDIT					
1							1
4	1 624 90						4
5		1 624 90					5
10					61 00	3 05	10
11	96 00						11
12	12 00						12
13	60			12 60			13
14					215 40	10 77	14
15				36 33			15
16		25 60	25 60				16
17	20 50						17
18			215 30				18
19				30 45			19
20					104 05	5 20	20
21			800 00				21
22					103 80	5 19	22
31					41 95	3 10	31
32	2 861 58	4 311 93	1 040 90	79 38	546 20	27 31	32
	2 861 58	4 311 93	1 040 90	79 38	546 20	27 31	
33	(✓)	(✓)	(231)	(121)	(411)	(241)	33
34							34

The Hubbard Store — Combined Cash Journal (Right Page)

ACCOUNT *Cash*   ACCOUNT NO. *111*

DATE	ITEM	POST. REF.	DEBIT	CREDIT	BALANCE DEBIT	BALANCE CREDIT
1977 Mar. 31		CJ1	2 771 10			
31		CJ1		1 708 76	1 062 34	

ACCOUNT *Accounts Receivable*   ACCOUNT NO. *121*

DATE	ITEM	POST. REF.	DEBIT	CREDIT	BALANCE DEBIT	BALANCE CREDIT
1977 Mar. 31		S1	230 58			
31		CJ1		79 38	151 20	

ACCOUNT *Store Equipment*   ACCOUNT NO. *181*

DATE	ITEM	POST. REF.	DEBIT	CREDIT	BALANCE DEBIT	BALANCE CREDIT
1977 Mar. 3		CJ1	1 624 90		1 624 90	

The Hubbard Store — General Ledger Accounts

ACCOUNT *Accounts Payable*   ACCOUNT NO. *231*

DATE	ITEM	POST. REF.	DEBIT	CREDIT	BALANCE DEBIT	BALANCE CREDIT
1977 Mar. 3		CJ1		162490		
31		P1		73250		
31		CJ1	104090			131650

ACCOUNT *Sales Tax Payable*   ACCOUNT NO. *241*

DATE	ITEM	POST. REF.	DEBIT	CREDIT	BALANCE DEBIT	BALANCE CREDIT
1977 Mar. 9		CJ1	60			
31		CJ1		2731		
31		S1		1098		3769

ACCOUNT *Sales*   ACCOUNT NO. *411*

DATE	ITEM	POST. REF.	DEBIT	CREDIT	BALANCE DEBIT	BALANCE CREDIT
1977 Mar. 31		CJ1		54620		
31		S1		21960		76580

ACCOUNT *Sales Returns and Allowances*   ACCOUNT NO. *041*

DATE	ITEM	POST. REF.	DEBIT	CREDIT	BALANCE DEBIT	BALANCE CREDIT
1977 Mar. 9		CJ1	1200		1200	

ACCOUNT *Purchases*   ACCOUNT NO. *511*

DATE	ITEM	POST. REF.	DEBIT	CREDIT	BALANCE DEBIT	BALANCE CREDIT
1977 Mar. 7		CJ1	9600			
15		CJ1	2050			
31		P1	73250		84900	

ACCOUNT *Purchases Returns and Allowances*   ACCOUNT NO. *051*

DATE	ITEM	POST. REF.	DEBIT	CREDIT	BALANCE DEBIT	BALANCE CREDIT
1977 Mar. 14		CJ1		2560		2560

The Hubbard Store — General Ledger Accounts (*concluded*)

Schedule of accounts receivable

A list of customers showing the amount due from each one as of a specified date is known as a *schedule of accounts receivable*. It is usually advisable to prepare such a schedule at the end of each month. An example for The Hubbard Store as of March 31, 1977, is provided below. Such a schedule can be prepared easily by going through the customers' file and listing the names of the customers and the amount due from each. Should the total not be in agreement with the balance of the summary accounts receivable account, the error may be in either the file or the ledger account. The file may be incorrect in that either one or more sales tickets on which collection has been made have not been removed or that one or more uncollected ones are missing. Another possibility is that a memorandum of a partial collection was overlooked in preparing the list. The accounts receivable account could be incorrect, also, because of an error in posting or because of an error in a journal from which the totals were posted. In any event, the postings, journals, and sales tickets must be checked until the reason for the discrepancy is found so that the necessary correction can be made.

W. A. Adams	35 91
Joseph F. Charles	65 94
Elaine C. Peters	49 35
	151 20

The Hubbard Store
Schedule of Accounts Receivable
March 31, 1977

The Hubbard Store — Schedule of Accounts Receivable

Schedule of accounts payable

A list of suppliers showing the amount due to each one as of a specified date is known as a *schedule of accounts payable*. It is usually advisable to prepare such a schedule at the end of each month. An example for The Hubbard Store as of March 31, 1977, is provided on the next page. Such a schedule can be prepared easily by going through the unpaid invoice file and listing the names of the suppliers and the amount due to each. Should the total of the schedule not be in agreement with the balance of the summary accounts payable account, the error may be in either the file or the ledger account. The file may be incorrect in that either one or more paid invoices have not been removed or in that one or more unpaid ones are missing. Another possibility is that a memorandum of a partial payment was overlooked in preparing the list. The accounts payable account could be incorrect, also, because of an error in posting or because of an error in a journal from which the total purchases was posted. In any event, the postings, journals, and invoices must be checked until the reason for the discrepancy is found so that the necessary correction can be made.

The Hubbard Store
Schedule of Accounts Payable
March 31, 1977

C. E. Arthur + Son	132 20
Metro Store Equipment Co.	824 90
Norton's	359 40
	1,316 50

The Hubbard Store — Schedule of Accounts Payable

Merchandise inventory

Apart from the fact that the foregoing illustration did not include any transactions or information about various operating expenses, Mr. Hubbard could not calculate his net income or net loss for the month because the amount of the merchandise inventory at March 31 was not determined. Lacking this information, cost of goods sold could not be calculated. Since there was no inventory at the first of the month, the amount of the month's purchases of merchandise, $849, less the amount of purchases returns and allowances, $25.60, is the cost of the goods that were *available* for sale, $823.40. To calculate the cost of goods *sold*, however, the cost of the goods that remained on hand on March 31 would have to be deducted. The first step would have been to count the items of merchandise in the store at the end of that day. Next, these goods would have to have been assigned a reasonable share of the total purchases cost. Since Mr. Hubbard does not expect to calculate monthly net income (or net loss), he will not "take inventory" until the end of the year. This may be December 31, if he plans to keep his records on a calendar-year basis, or it might be February 28 (or 29), if he wants to use a fiscal year that ends on the last day of February. Whatever the period chosen, a crucial step in the calculation of the periodic net income (or net loss) of a merchandising business under the accrual basis of accounting is the determination of the merchandise inventory at the end of the fiscal period — a point in time that is also the beginning of the next fiscal period.

When the end of the fiscal period does arrive and the cost to be assigned to the merchandise then on hand is calculated, the amount of this calculation will have to be recorded in an asset account. The title of the account usually used is "Merchandise Inventory." This account will be debited; the related credit is made to an account with the title "Expense and Revenue Summary" — a temporary owner's equity account used in summarizing the accounts whose balances enter into the determination of the net income (or loss) for a period. The manner of using the expense and revenue summary account in the end-of-period process of adjusting and closing the books of a retail merchandising business will be explained and illustrated in Chapters 9 and 10.

Report **No. 6-3**	Refer to the study assignments and complete Report No. 6-3. After completing the report, you may proceed with the textbook discussion in Chapter 7 until the next report is required.

Chapter 7

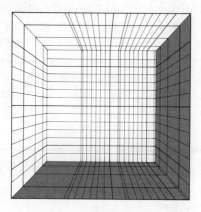

ACCOUNTING FOR NOTES AND INTEREST

A major characteristic of modern business is the extensive use of credit. Each day hundreds of millions of transactions occur that involve the sale of goods or services in return for promises to pay at a later date for what has been received. Sales of this type are said to be "on credit" or "on account"; they are often described as "charge sales." To facilitate such transactions, the use of *credit cards* has become commonplace. The majority of credit transactions do not involve a written promise to pay a specified amount of money. Often the buyer signs a sales slip or sales ticket, but this is done as an acknowledgment of the receipt of the merchandise or service. When "opening an account" the prospective customer may sign a form or document that obligates him to pay for all purchases that he (and, often, members of his family) may make, but this is a general promise to pay if and when something is purchased.

While not nearly so commonplace as transactions that involve "open account" credit, or the use of bank credit cards, *promissory notes* (usually just called *notes*) are sometimes involved. A promise to repay a loan of money nearly always takes the form of a note. The extension of credit for periods of more than 60 days, or when large amounts of money are involved, may entail the use of notes. Such notes nearly always have certain legal characteristics that cause them to be *negotiable instruments*. In order to be considered a negotiable instrument, a promissory note must evidence the following:

(a) Be in writing and signed by the person or persons agreeing to make payment;
(b) Be an unconditional promise to pay a certain amount of money;
(c) Be payable either on demand or at a definite time;
(d) Be payable to the order of a specified person or firm, or to bearer.

A promissory note is illustrated below. It will be observed that this note has all of the characteristics listed on page 166. It should also be understood that to Paul Clark it is a *note payable*, while to Alice Thompson it is a *note receivable*. Paul Clark is known as the *maker* of the note because he is the one who promises to pay. Alice Thompson is called the *payee* of the note because she is the one who is to receive the specified amount of money.

The note illustrated is interest bearing. This is often, though not always, the case. Sometimes no rate of interest is specified, but it is likely that a transaction in which a nominally non-interest-bearing note is involved will entail some interest. For example, a borrower might give a $1,000 note payable in 60 days to a bank in return for a loan of $985. The $15 difference between the amount received and the amount that must be repaid when the note matures will become, in reality, interest expense at maturity. Such a difference is described as *prepaid interest* until the date that the note matures. When a bank is involved in such a transaction, the difference between the amount received and the amount to be repaid may be referred to as *bank discount*.

$ 1,542.50   May 5   19 77

Ninety days *after date* I *promise to pay to the order of* Alice Thompson

One thousand five hundred forty-two 50/100----- *Dollars*

Payable at Citizens Savings Bank

Value received with interest at the rate of 8% per annum from date

No. 5   *Due* Aug. 3, 1977   *Paul Clark*

Model Filled-In Promissory Note

Calculating interest

In calculating interest on notes, it is necessary to take the following factors into consideration:

    (a) The principal of the note
    (b) The rate of interest
    (c) The period of time involved

The principal is the face amount of the note — the amount that the maker promises to pay at maturity, apart from any specified interest. The principal is the base on which the interest is calculated.

The rate of interest is usually expressed in the form of a percentage, such as 7 percent or 9 percent. Ordinarily the rate is an annual percentage rate, but in some cases the rate is quoted on a monthly basis, such as 1½ percent a month. A rate of 1½ percent a month is equivalent to a rate of 18 percent a year payable monthly. When a note is interest bearing but the rate is not specified on the face of the note, it is subject to the legal rate, which varies under the laws of the different states.

The days or months from the date of issue of a note to the date of its maturity (or the interest payment date) is the time for which the interest is to be computed. Thus, if a note is payable in 60 days with interest, each and every day is considered in determining the date due, and the exact number of days is used in calculating interest.

When the time in a note is specified in months, the interest should be calculated on the basis of months rather than days. For example, if a note is payable 3 months from date, the interest should be calculated on the basis of 3 months or ¼ of a year. However, when the due date is specified in a note, the time should be computed by figuring the exact number of days that will elapse from the date of the note to the date of its maturity. The interest should then be computed on the basis of this number of days. For example, if a note is dated March 1 and the due date is specified as June 1, the time should be computed in the manner shown at the right.

Days in March	31
Date of note, March	1
Days remaining in March .	30
Days in April	30
Days in May	31
Note matures on June . . .	1
Total time in days	92

Notice that in this computation the date of maturity was counted but the date of the note was not counted. If the note had specified "3 months after date" instead of June 1, the interest should be computed on the basis of 90 days instead of 92 days.

In the case of long-term notes, the interest may be payable periodically, such as semiannually or annually.

In computing interest it is customary to consider 360 days as a year. Most banks and business firms follow this practice, though some banks and government agencies use 365 days as the base in computing daily interest. In any case, the formula for computing interest is:

PRINCIPAL × RATE × TIME (usually a fraction of a 360-day year) =
AMOUNT OF INTEREST

The 60-Day, 6 Percent Method. There are short cuts that may be used in computing interest on the basis of a 360-day year. The interest on any amount for 60 days at 6 percent can be determined simply by moving the decimal point in the amount two places to the left. The reason for this is that 60 days is ⅙ of a year and the interest on any amount at 6 percent for $\frac{1}{6}$ of a year is the same as the interest at 1 percent for a full year. Thus, the interest on $550 for 60 days at 6 percent is $5.50.

The 60-day, 6 percent method may be used to advantage in many cases even though the actual time may be other than 60 days and the actual rate other than 6 percent. The following examples will serve to illustrate this fact (both involve rates of interest greater than 6 percent, but the same technique would be used for rates less than 6 percent):

FACTORS
(a) Principal of note, $1,000
(b) Time, 30 days
(c) Rate of interest, 8%

FACTORS
(a) Principal of note, $3,000
(b) Time, 120 days
(c) Rate of interest, 9%

CALCULATION
Interest at 6% for 60 days = $10
Interest at 6% for 30 days = $5
Interest at 8% = 1⅓ times $5 or $6.67

CALCULATION
Interest at 6% for 60 days = $30
Interest at 6% for 120 days = $60
Interest at 9% = 1½ times $60 or $90

Sometimes it is helpful to determine the interest for 6 days at 6 percent and to use the result as the basis for calculating the actual interest. The interest on any sum for 6 days at 6 percent may be determined simply by moving the decimal point three places to the left. For example, the interest on $1,000 at 6 percent for 6 days is $1. If the actual time were 18 days instead of 6 days, the interest would be three times $1 or $3. This method differs from the 60-day, 6 percent method only in that 6 days is used in the basic computation instead of 60 days.

Published tables are available for reference use in determining the amount of interest on stated sums at different rates for any length of time. Such tables are widely used by financial institutions and may also be used by other firms.

Accounting for notes receivable

Businesses other than lending institutions (such as commercial banks and savings and loan companies) sometimes have the following types of transactions involving notes receivable:

(a) Note received from customer in return for an extension of time for payment of his obligation
(b) Note collected at maturity
(c) Note renewed at maturity
(d) Note dishonored

Note Received from Customer to Obtain an Extension of Time for Payment. When a customer wishes to obtain an extension of time for the payment of his account, he may be willing to issue a note for all or part of the amount due. A merchant may be willing to accept a note in such a case because the note will be a written acknowledgment of the debt and undoubtedly will bear interest.

Lawrence Moore owes the Ridley Hardware Co. $816.32 on open account. The account is past due and Mr. Ridley insists upon a settlement. Mr. Moore offers to give his 60-day, 8 percent note. Mr. Ridley accepts Mr. Moore's offer; the note is dated April 14. It is recorded in the books of the Ridley Hardware Co. as indicated by the following general journal entry:

```
April 14.  Notes Receivable..................................  816.32
              Accounts Receivable.............................           816.32
              Received note from Lawrence Moore.
```

If, instead of giving a note for the full amount, Mr. Moore gave a check for $16.32 and a note for the balance, the transaction would have been recorded in Mr. Ridley's books as indicated by the following general journal entry:

```
April 14.  Cash............................................   16.32
           Notes Receivable.................................  800.00
              Accounts Receivable.............................           816.32
              Received check and note from Lawrence Moore.
```

(While the foregoing entry is shown in two-column journal form, it actually would be recorded in the combined cash journal or other appropriate book of original entry being used. This observation applies to all illustrations of entries involving the receipt and disbursement of cash.)

Note Collected at Maturity. When a note receivable matures, it may be collected by the holder or it may be left at the bank for collection. If the maker of the note resides in another locality, the note may be forwarded to a bank in that locality for collection. It is customary for banks to charge a fee for making such collections. When the bank makes the collection, it notifies the holder on a form similar to the credit advice shown below, that

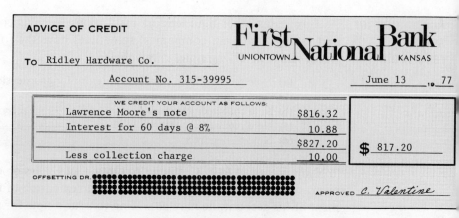

Credit Advice

the net amount has been credited to his account. Usually the maker is notified a few days before the maturity of a note so that he may know the due date and the amount that must be paid.

Suppose Mr. Ridley left Lawrence Moore's note for $816.32 at the First National Bank for collection and on June 13 received the notice of collection reproduced on the opposite page.

The transaction should be recorded as indicated by the following general journal entry:

```
June 13. Cash........................................  817.20
          Collection Expense..............................   10.00
             Notes Receivable................................          816.32
             Interest Earned.................................           10.88
                Received credit for the proceeds of Lawrence Moore's
                note collected by the bank.
```

Note Renewed at Maturity. If the maker of a note is unable to pay the amount due at maturity, he may be permitted to renew all or part of the note. If, instead of paying his note for $816.32 at maturity, Lawrence Moore was permitted to pay the interest and give another note for 60 days at the same rate of interest, the transaction should be recorded in the books of the Ridley Hardware Co. as indicated by the following general journal entry:

```
June 13. Notes Receivable (new note).........................  816.32
          Cash...............................................   10.88
             Notes Receivable (old note).......................          816.32
             Interest Earned.................................           10.88
                Received a new note for $816.32 from Lawrence
                Moore in renewal of his note due today and $10.88
                in cash in payment of the interest on the old note.
```

Note Dishonored. If the maker of a note refuses or is unable to pay or renew it at maturity, the note is said to be *dishonored*. It thereby loses the quality of negotiability which, in effect, means that it loses its legal status as a note receivable. Usually, the amount is transferred from the notes receivable account to the accounts receivable account pending final disposition of the obligation involved. Suppose, for example, that Mr. Ridley was unable to collect a non-interest-bearing note for $400 received a few weeks before from Roger Jones, a customer. (Because of special circumstances, Mr. Ridley had accepted a non-interest-bearing note.) The following entry should be made in the books of the Ridley Hardware Co.:

```
July 18. Accounts Receivable..............................  400.00
          Notes Receivable................................          400.00
             Roger Jones' note dishonored.
```

If the claim against Mr. Jones should turn out to be completely worthless, the $400 will have to be removed from the accounts receivable account and recognized as an uncollectible account loss. The manner of accounting for this type of transaction will be discussed in the next chapter.

Notes receivable register

When many notes are received in the usual course of business, it may be advisable to keep an auxiliary record of such notes that will provide more detailed information than a ledger account. Such an auxiliary record is usually known as a *notes receivable register*. One form of a notes receivable register is reproduced below and on the following page. The notes recorded in the illustration were those received by the L. H. Freeman Co. during the period indicated by the record.

The information recorded in the register is obtained directly from the notes received. The notes are numbered consecutively as they are entered in the register. (This number should not be confused with the maker's number.) The due date of each note is calculated and entered in the proper When Due column. The interest to maturity is calculated and entered in the Interest Amount column. When a remittance is received in settlement of a note, the date is entered in the Date Paid column.

Notes receivable account

The information recorded in the notes receivable account should agree with that entered in the notes receivable register. The account shown on the next page contains a record of the notes that were entered in the notes receivable register of the L. H. Freeman Co. Notice that each note is identified by the number assigned to the note. If the notes are not numbered, each note should be identified by writing the name of the maker in the Item column of the account.

PAGE 2   NOTES RECEIVABLE REGISTER

| | DATE RECEIVED | No. | BY WHOM PAYABLE | WHERE PAYABLE | | DATE MADE | | |
				BANK OR FIRM	ADDRESS	Mo.	Day	Year
	1977							
1	Mar. 7	1	S. J. Olson	First State Bank	Modesto	Mar. 7	'77	1
2	24	2	C. F. Purdy	County National Bank	Denison	Mar. 24	'77	2
3	Apr. 4	3	John A. Beal	City Savings Bank	Westridge	Apr. 4	'77	3
4	21	4	Mrs. C. M. Hollis	Central Trust	Modesto	Apr. 21	'77	4
5	May 23	5	C. F. Purdy	County National Bank	Denison	May 23	'77	5
6								6
7								7

Notes Receivable Register (Left Page)

Proving the notes receivable account

Periodically (usually at the end of each month) the notes receivable account should be proved by comparing the balance of the account with the total of the notes owned as shown by the notes receivable register. A schedule of the notes owned on May 31 is given on page 173.

Notice that the total of this schedule is the same as the balance of the notes receivable account illustrated below.

SCHEDULE OF NOTES OWNED

No. 4...................... $510.00
No. 5......................   350.00
                                      $860.00

ACCOUNT *Notes Receivable*   ACCOUNT NO. *122*

DATE	ITEM	POST. REF.	DEBIT	CREDIT	BALANCE DEBIT	BALANCE CREDIT
1977 Mar. 7	No. 1	CJ3	398 16			
24	No. 2	CJ3	450 00		848 16	
Apr. 4	No. 3	CJ4	692 50			
21	No. 4	CJ4	510 00		2050 66	
May 4	No. 3	CJ5		692 50		
6	No. 1	CJ5		398 16		
23	No. 2	CJ5		450 00		
23	No. 5	CJ5	350 00		860 00	

Indorsement of notes

A promissory note is usually made payable to a specified person or firm, though some notes are made payable to "Bearer." If the note is payable to the order of a specified party, he must *indorse* the note to transfer the promise to pay to another party. The two major types of indorsements are **(1)** the *blank indorsement* and **(2)** the *special indorsement*. When the payee signs only his name on the left end of the back of the note, he is indorsing

NOTES RECEIVABLE REGISTER   PAGE *2*

TIME	WHEN DUE J F M A M J J A S O N D	AMOUNT	INTEREST RATE	INTEREST AMOUNT	DATE PAID	REMARKS
1	60 da. 6	398 16	7%	4 65	May 6	
2	60 da. 23	450 00	8%	6 00	May 23	Renewal for $350
3	30 da. 4	692 50	8%	4 62	May 4	Sent for coll. 5/2
4	90 da. 20	510 00	8%	10 20		
5	60 da. 22	350 00	8%	4 67		Renewal of note No. 2
6						
7						

Notes Receivable Register (Right Page)

it in blank. If, instead, he writes the words "Pay to the order of" followed by the name of a specified party and his signature, he is giving a special indorsement. The legal effect of both types of indorsement is much the same. However, a blank indorsement makes a note payable to the bearer, while a special indorsement identifies the party to whose order payment is to be made.

Under certain circumstances the maker of a note may arrange for an additional party to join in the promise to pay, either as a *cosigner* or as an indorser of the note. In the first instance, this other party signs his name below that of the maker of the note on its face. In the second case, the other party makes a blank indorsement on the back of the note, called an *accommodation indorsement*. In either event the payee of the note has two persons to look to for payment. This presumably adds security to the note.

If a partial payment is made on a note, it is common practice to record the date of the payment and the amount paid on the back of the note. This is called *indorsing the payment*.

Shown below is a reproduction of the back of a promissory note originally made payable to the order of Clark Munn. The maker of the note (whoever he was) was able to get Thelma West to become an accommodation indorser. Later, the payee, Munn, transferred the note to D. F. Fisher by a special indorsement. On April 15, $200 was paid on the note.

Blank Indorsement (Accommodation)

Special Indorsement

Indorsed Payment

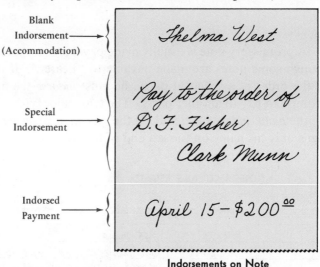

Indorsements on Note

Accounting for notes payable

The following types of transactions involve notes payable:

(a) Note issued to a supplier in return for an extension of time for payment of obligation
(b) Note issued as security for cash loan
(c) Note paid at maturity
(d) Note renewed at maturity

Note Issued to a Supplier in Return for Extension of Time for Payment. When a firm wishes to obtain an extension of time for the payment of an account, a note for all or part of the amount due may be acceptable to the supplier. Assume, for example, that the Ridley Hardware Co. owes

Edward & Co. $547.60 and by agreement on May 12 a check on the First National Bank for $47.60 and a 90-day, 7½ percent interest-bearing note for $500 are issued. This transaction should be recorded in the books of the Ridley Hardware Co. by the following general journal entry:

```
May 12. Accounts Payable...................................  547.60
            Cash...........................................          47.60
            Notes Payable..................................         500.00
            Issued check for $47.60 and note for $500 to Edwards
            & Co.
```

Note Issued as Security for Cash Loan. Many firms experience periods in which receipts from customers in the usual course of business are not adequate to finance their operations. During such periods, it may be necessary to borrow money from banks. Business firms commonly borrow money from banks on short-term notes to help finance their business operations. Assume, for example, that on May 16, M. B. Ridley borrows $4,000 from the First National Bank on a 60-day, 9 percent interest-bearing note. The transaction should be recorded in general journal form as follows:

```
May 16. Cash.........................................  4,000.00
            Notes Payable...............................        4,000.00
            Borrowed $4,000 at the bank on a 60-day, 9%
            note.
```

Commercial banks often deduct interest in advance. If, instead of the transaction described above, Mr. Ridley had issued a $4,000, 60-day, non-interest-bearing note which the bank had discounted at 9 percent, the bank account of the Ridley Hardware Co. would have increased $3,940, and interest expense of $60 would have been recorded as follows:

```
May  6. Cash.........................................  3,940.00
        Interest Expense...............................     60.00
            Notes Payable...............................        4,000.00
            Discounted at 9% a $4,000, 60-day, non-interest-
            bearing note.
```

The $60 debit to Interest Expense at this point is really prepaid interest but, since the amount will become interest expense by the end of the accounting period, it is debited immediately to Interest Expense.

It should be noted that, even though the rate of interest was 9 percent in both cases, the money obtained was more expensive in the second case. In the first case, $4,000 was obtained for 60 days at a cost of $60 — exactly 9 percent. ($60 ÷ $4,000 = 1.5% for 60 days; 9% for 360 days.) In the second case, $60 was paid for the use of $3,940 for 60 days — an *effective rate* of nearly 9.14 percent. ($60 ÷ $3,940 = 1.523% for 60 days; 9.138% for 360 days.)

Note Paid at Maturity. When a note payable matures, payment may be made directly to the holder or to a bank where the note was left for collection. The maker will know who the payee is but he may not know who the holder is at maturity because the payee may have transferred the note to another party or he may have left it with a bank for collection. When a note is left with a bank for collection, it is customary for the bank to mail the maker a notice of maturity. For example, the Lawson Store Equipment Co. might forward a one-month, 7 percent note of M. B. Ridley for $650 (dated July 1) to the First National Bank for collection, and the bank might notify Mr. Ridley by sending a notice similar to the one reproduced below.

First National Bank
UNIONTOWN   KANSAS

YOUR NOTE DESCRIBED BELOW WILL BE DUE ⟶

MAKER - COSIGNER - COLLATERAL	NUMBER	DATE DUE	PRINCIPAL	INTEREST	TOTAL
M. B. Ridley Ridley Hardware Co.	13960	8/1/77	$650.00	$3.79	$653.79

ENDORSER

TO

M. B. Ridley
Ridley Hardware Co.
1600 Elm Street
Uniontown, KS   66779

NOTE: PLEASE BRING THIS NOTICE WITH YOU.   **PAYABLE AT** First National Bank

Notice of Maturity of Note

If, upon receiving this notice, Mr. Ridley issued a check to the bank for $653.79 in payment of the note and interest, the transaction should be recorded in the books of the Ridley Hardware Co. as indicated by the following general journal entry:

```
Aug. 1. Notes Payable.....................................    650.00
        Interest Expense...................................      3.79
            Cash...........................................              653.79
            Paid note issued July 1 to Lawson Store Equipment
            Co., plus interest.
```

PAGE 1   **NOTES PAYABLE REGISTER**

DATE ISSUED	No.	TO WHOM PAYABLE	WHERE PAYABLE BANK OR FIRM	ADDRESS	DATE MADE Mo.	Day	Year
1977 Mar. 14	1	G. C. Hawkes Co.	First State Bank	Modesto	Mar.	14	'77
Apr. 12	2	County National Bank	County National Bank	Denison	Apr.	12	'77
May 2	3	McAllister Brothers	County National Bank	Denison	May	2	'77

Notes Payable Register (Left Page)

A note made payable to a bank for a loan commonly is paid at that bank upon maturity.

Note Renewed at Maturity. If the maker is unable to pay a note in full at maturity, he may arrange to renew all or a part of the note. For example, on August 10 Mr. Ridley might pay the $9.38 interest and $100 on the principal of the note for $500 issued to Edwards & Co. on May 12 and give them a new 60-day, 7½ percent note for $400. This transaction should be recorded as indicated in the following general journal entry:

```
Aug. 10. Notes Payable (old note)...........................    500.00
         Interest Expense...................................      9.38
             Cash...........................................              109.38
             Notes Payable (new note).......................              400.00
             Issued a check for $109.38 and a note for $400 to
             Edwards & Co. in settlement of a note for $500 plus
             interest.
```

Notes payable register

When many notes are issued in the usual course of business, it may be advisable to keep an auxiliary record of such notes that will provide more detailed information than a ledger account. Such an auxiliary record is usually known as a *notes payable register*. One form of such a register is reproduced on the previous page and below. The notes recorded in the illustration were those issued by the L. H. Freeman Co. during the period indicated by the record.

The information recorded in the register may be obtained directly from the note before it is mailed or given to the payee, or from a note stub. Blank notes are usually made up in pads with stubs attached on which spaces are provided for recording such essential information as amount, payee, where payable, date, time, rate of interest, and number. The due date of each note is calculated and entered in the proper When Due column of the register. The interest at maturity is also calculated and entered in the Interest Amount column. When a note is paid, the date is entered in the Date Paid column.

NOTES PAYABLE REGISTER   PAGE 1

	TIME	WHEN DUE													AMOUNT	INTEREST		DATE PAID	REMARKS	
		J	F	M	A	M	J	J	A	S	O	N	D			RATE	AMOUNT			
1	60 da.						13							1 826 14	8%	24 35	May 13	Settlement of Jan. 15 inv.	1
2	90 da.								11					5 000 00	9%	112 50			2
3	30 da.					1								967 35	8%	6 45		Settlement of Mar. 1 inv.	3

Notes Payable Register (Right Page)

Notes payable account

The information recorded in the notes payable account should agree with that recorded in the notes payable register. The following account contains a record of the notes that were entered in the notes payable register of the L. H. Freeman Co.

ACCOUNT *Notes Payable*   ACCOUNT NO. *230*

DATE	ITEM	POST. REF.	DEBIT	CREDIT	BALANCE DEBIT	BALANCE CREDIT
1977 Mar. 14	No. 1	CJ3		1826 14		1826 14
Apr. 12	No. 2	CJ4		5000 00		6826 14
May 2	No. 3	CJ5		967 35		
13	No. 1	CJ5	1826 14			5967 35

Proving the notes payable account

Periodically (usually at the end of each month) the notes payable account should be proved by comparing the balance of the account with the total notes outstanding as shown by the notes payable register. A schedule of the notes outstanding on June 30 is given below. Notice that the total of this schedule is the same as the balance of the notes payable account.

SCHEDULE OF NOTES OUTSTANDING

No. 2.......................... $5,000.00
No. 3..........................   967.35
$5,967.35

Accrued interest receivable

While interest on a note literally accrues day by day, it is impractical to keep a daily record of such accruals. If the life of a note receivable is entirely within the accounting period, no record need be made of interest until the amount is received.

If, however, the business owns some interest-bearing notes receivable at the end of the accounting period, neither the net income for the period nor the assets at the end of the period will be correctly stated unless the interest accrued on notes receivable is taken into consideration. It is, therefore, customary to adjust the accounts by debiting Accrued Interest Receivable and by crediting Interest Earned for the amount of interest that has accrued to the end of the period. The amount of the accrual may be computed by reference to the notes themselves or to the record provided by a notes receivable register. Suppose, for example, that at the end of a fiscal year ending June 30, a business owns four interest-bearing notes. The amount of each note, the date of issue, the rate of interest, the number of days from issue date to June 30, and the interest accrued on June 30 are shown in the schedule at the top of the next page.

SCHEDULE OF ACCRUED INTEREST ON NOTES RECEIVABLE

PRINCIPAL	DATE OF ISSUE	RATE OF INTEREST	DAYS FROM ISSUE DATE TO JUNE 30	ACCRUED INTEREST JUNE 30
$500.00	April 16	7%	75	$ 7.29
300.00	May 4	8%	57	3.80
348.50	May 31	7%	30	2.03
500.00	June 15	7%	15	1.46

Total accrued interest on notes receivable.................$14.58

While the amount involved is so small that some accountants would ignore it on the ground of *immateriality*, technical accuracy requires the following entry, in general journal form, as of June 30:

```
June 30.  Accrued Interest Receivable.......................  14.58
               Interest Earned.................................          14.58
                    Interest accrued on notes receivable as of June 30.
```

In preparing the financial statements at the end of the year, the balance of the interest earned account (which will include the $14.58 interest earned but not yet received) will be reported in the income statement, while the balance of the account with Accrued Interest Receivable will be reported in the balance sheet as a current asset.

Accrued interest payable

Neither the expenses of a period nor the liabilities at the end of the period will be correctly stated unless the interest accrued on notes payable is taken into consideration. The mechanics of calculating the amount of interest accrued on notes payable are the same as in the case of notes receivable. If a notes payable register is kept, it should provide the information needed in computing the amount of interest accrued on notes payable. If the total amount of such accrued interest was calculated to be $126.92, and the fiscal period ended June 30, the proper adjusting entry may be made in general journal form as follows:

```
June 30.  Interest Expense..................................  126.92
               Accrued Interest Payable........................          126.92
                    Interest accrued on notes payable as of June 30.
```

In preparing the financial statements at the end of the year, the balance of the interest expense account (which will include the $126.92 interest incurred but not yet paid) will be reported in the income statement, while the balance of the account with Accrued Interest Payable will be reported in the balance sheet as a current liability.

Report No. 7-1

Complete Report No. 7-1 in the study assignments and submit your working papers to the instructor for approval. Then proceed with the textbook discussion in Chapter 8 until Report No. 8-1 is required.

Chapter 8

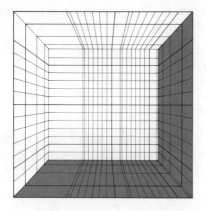

ACCRUAL ACCOUNTING APPLIED TO A RETAIL BUSINESS

A business enterprise that purchases and sells goods on account, maintains a stock of merchandise, and has long-lived assets must account for periodic income or loss on the accrual basis. This is a necessity both for the sake of measuring the success of the business from the standpoint of the owner and in order to comply with federal and state income tax laws. Several of the features of this type of accounting have been introduced in the preceding pages. A more detailed consideration of these procedures and the introduction of the other major practices that constitute accrual accounting will be presented in this and the two following chapters. To make the discussion realistic, it will center around the accounting records of a retail clothing business called Boyd's Clothiers, owned and operated by Lynn C. Boyd. It should be recognized, however, that most of the principles and procedures discussed and illustrated are equally applicable to many other types of businesses.

PRINCIPLES AND PROCEDURES

The discussion will continue to be a blend of accounting principles and bookkeeping practices. It is important to keep in mind that the principles relate to goals and objectives while bookkeeping practices are designed to attain these goals and objectives. Such procedures as double entry and the use of source documents, journals, and ledger accounts are employed to make the record-keeping process complete, orderly, and as error-free as possible. While most accounting principles are broad enough to allow considerable flexibility, it is in the area of bookkeeping procedures that wide latitude is found. Within limits, the records for each business can be styled to meet the particular requirements of the management.

Accrual accounting

The *accrual basis of accounting* consists of recording revenue in the period in which it is earned and expenses in the period in which they are incurred. The receipt or disbursement of cash in the same period may or may not be involved. Revenue is considered to be earned when, in exchange for something of value, money is received or a legal claim to money comes into existence. To a merchant, this normally means the time at which the customer buys the goods and either pays for them or agrees to pay for them. In terms of changes in the accounting elements, revenue arises or accrues when an increase in cash or in a receivable (inflow of assets) causes an increase in owner's equity (except in cases where the increase is due to an investment of assets in the business by the owner). In comparable terms, expense accrues or is incurred when either a reduction in some asset (asset outflow) or an increase in a liability causes the owner's equity to be reduced (except in cases where the owner's withdrawal of assets reduces the owner's equity).

In keeping business records accountants must think in terms of time intervals. They must be sure that revenue and expense are accounted for in the proper accounting period. Within a period, the recognition of many types of revenue and expense at precisely the moment this revenue or expense arises is not so important nor is it usually practicable. For example, the expense of having a salaried employee literally accrues minute by minute during each working day; but if the salary will be paid by the end of the period, no record is made of the expense until it is paid. If, on the other hand, the employee was not paid by the end of the period, the accountant should record the liability and expense at that time. A lag in recording revenue and expense is not serious within the accounting period, but steps must be taken at the end of the period to be sure that all revenue earned and expenses incurred are recorded. These steps consist of making what are called *end-of-period-adjustments* in the accounts. It should be mentioned, however, that adjustments normally are not made for trivial amounts. The *concept of materiality* prevails, which is to ignore matters too small to make any significant difference. Just how small is "too small" is a question that requires judgment on the part of the accountant.

The accrual basis of accounting is widely used because it is suited to the needs of enterprises employing it. It involves the period-by-period matching of revenue with the expenses that caused or aided in producing revenue. The revenue from sales, for example, must be matched against the cost of the goods sold and the various other expenses that were incurred in conducting the business. A simple matching of cash received from customers during a period with the cash paid for goods purchased in that period would be almost meaningless in most cases. The collections might relate to sales of a prior period and the payments to purchases of the current period, or vice versa. The expense related to most long-lived assets does not arise when the property is acquired; the expense occurs as the usefulness of the property is gradually exhausted. The accrual basis recognizes changes in many types of assets and liabilities in computing net income for a specified period — not just changes in the cash account.

The chart of accounts

The importance of classifying accounts in an orderly and systematic manner, identifying each account by assigning it a number to assist in locating it in the ledger, and maintaining a list of the accounts — called a *chart of accounts* — has been discussed and illustrated in preceding chapters. The chart of accounts for the retail business that is used as a basis of the discussion and illustration in this chapter and in the two chapters that follow is shown on page 183.

The pattern of numbers or code shown in the illustration is fairly typical of the arrangement used by many businesses. However, numerous variations are possible. Sometimes letters as well as numbers are made a part of the code. When numbers are used, it is not uncommon for special columns in journals to be headed by just the number, rather than the name, of the account involved. In a system of records that requires numerous accounts, the use of account numbers virtually displaces account names for all but statement purposes. This has been the case for many decades. Furthermore, in recent years account numbers have become essential to the development of a computer-based accounting system. (Note that no account number ends in zero. This is because a zero at the end of a number has no special significance in electronic data processing.)

The nature of many of the accounts included in the chart of accounts for Boyd's Clothiers should be apparent because they have been described in preceding chapters and their use has been illustrated. However, the chart includes certain accounts that are needed in recording several types of transactions and events that have either not yet been considered, or only briefly mentioned. These accounts will be discussed prior to illustrating the accounting records of Boyd's Clothiers.

If this chart of accounts is compared with the accounts in the general ledger illustrated on pages 214–219, it will be noted that the ledger illustration does not include accounts 221, 291, 321, 612, 616, 621, and 622. This is because these accounts are not needed to record routine transactions.

When the matter of adjusting entries and closing entries is discussed and illustrated in the following chapters, these accounts will be shown.

BOYD'S CLOTHIERS

CHART OF ACCOUNTS

*Assets**

Cash
111 First National Bank
112 Petty Cash Fund

Receivables
121 Accounts Receivable
   012 Allowance for Doubtful Accounts

Merchandise Inventory
131 Merchandise Inventory

Prepaid Expenses
141 Prepaid Insurance
151 Supplies

Long-Lived Assets
181 Store Equipment
   018 Accumulated Depreciation —Store Equipment

Liabilities
211 Notes Payable
221 Accrued Interest Payable
231 Accounts Payable
241 Sales Tax Payable
251 FICA Tax Payable
261 Employees Income Tax Payable
271 FUTA Tax Payable
281 State Unemployment Tax Payable
291 Accrued Bank Credit Card Expense

Owner's Equity
311 Lynn C. Boyd, Capital
031 Lynn C. Boyd, Drawing
321 Expense and Revenue Summary

Revenue from Sales
411 Sales
   041 Sales Returns and Allowances

Cost of Goods Sold
511 Purchases
   051 Purchases Returns and Allowances
   052 Purchases Discount

Operating Expenses
611 Rent Expense
612 Depreciation Expense
613 Salaries and Commissions Expense
614 Payroll Taxes Expense
615 Heating and Lighting Expense
616 Supplies Expense
617 Telephone Expense
618 Advertising Expense
619 Bank Credit Card Expense
621 Uncollectible Accounts Expense
622 Insurance Expense
623 Charitable Contributions Expense
624 Miscellaneous Expense

Other Expenses
711 Interest Expense

Words in italics represent headings and not account titles

Accounting for uncollectible accounts receivable

Businesses that sell goods or services on account realize that some of the customers from time to time may not pay all that they owe. The amounts that cannot be collected are called *uncollectible accounts expense*, *bad debts expense*, or *loss from uncollectible accounts*. The last designation is slightly misleading because, while the amounts that cannot be collected are certainly losses, they are losses that may reasonably be expected since they are the direct result of selling on account to encourage a larger volume of sales. The amount of such losses depends to a large degree upon the credit policy of a business. The seller should seek to avoid the two extremes of either having such a "liberal" credit policy that uncollectible accounts become excessive or having such a "tight" credit policy that uncollectible account losses are minimized at the sacrifice of a larger volume of sales and greater net income.

It would be possible to wait until it was certain that the amount due from a customer would never be collected before writing off the amount by a debit to Uncollectible Accounts Expense and by a credit to Accounts Receivable. This procedure is sometimes followed. However, it is considered to be better accounting to estimate the amount of uncollectible account losses that will eventually result from the sales of a period and to treat the estimated amount of expected losses as an expense of that same period. The latter treatment is considered to result in better periodic matching of revenue and expense. The procedure is to use a *contra* account entitled Allowance for Doubtful Accounts (sometimes called Allowance for Bad Debts or Reserve for Bad Debts). This account is contra to the receivable accounts which means its balance will be deducted from the total of the receivable accounts. At the end of the accounting period, an estimate of the expected uncollectible account losses is made, and an adjusting entry is made by debiting Uncollectible Accounts Expense and by crediting Allowance for Doubtful Accounts. To illustrate, suppose that in view of past experience it is expected that there will be a loss of an amount equal to one half of one percent of the sales on account during the year. If such sales amounted to $100,000, the estimated uncollectible account losses would be $500 which should be recorded as follows:

Dec. 31. Uncollectible Accounts Expense.................... 500.00
          Allowance for Doubtful Accounts................   500.00
               Uncollectible accounts expense provision for the year.

The amount of the debit balance in the uncollectible accounts expense account is reported in the income statement as an operating expense. The amount of the credit balance in the allowance for doubtful accounts is reported in the balance sheet as a deduction from the receivables.

Another technique sometimes used in arriving at the end-of-period adjustment for uncollectible accounts involves a detailed analysis of the receivables. This requires "aging" the receivables. Thus, an analysis is made of the accounts to see what proportions are for recent charges — perhaps those less than a month old — and what proportions are 30–60 days old, 61–90 days old, etc. Then, guided by past experience, estimates are made of the probable amounts of each of the age groups that are likely to be uncollectible. (Generally, the longer a charge has been "on the books," the less likely it is that it will ever be collected.) The estimates can be combined (totaled) to arrive at an amount deemed necessary to have as the end-of-period (credit) balance in the Allowance for Doubtful Accounts. An adjustment is made to give the allowance account the indicated balance. To illustrate, assume that after aging the accounts it is determined that $500 will not be collected. If the allowance account has a credit balance of $50, this means that the adjusting entry must be for the amount of $450. This will bring the allowance account to the desired credit balance. The entry would be as follows:

Dec. 31 Uncollectible Accounts Expense............................ 450
        Allowance for Doubtful Accounts........................   450

Many accountants think that this is the best way to be sure that the net amount shown on the balance sheet (that is, gross receivables less allowance for doubtful accounts) is a realistic estimate of "cash realizable value."

It should be apparent that the credit part of the adjusting entry cannot be made directly to one of the receivable accounts because, at the time this entry is made, there is no way of knowing exactly which of the debtors will not pay. Experience gives virtual assurance that some of the amounts due will be uncollectible but only time will reveal which ones.

When it is determined that a certain account will not be collected, an entry should be made to write off the account and to charge the loss against the allowance. Suppose, for example, that on April 22 of the next year, it is determined that $75 owed by Stuart Palmer cannot be collected. Perhaps he died sometime before and it is found that he left no property, or perhaps he became bankrupt, or left town and cannot be traced. Whatever the circumstance, if it is fairly certain that the amount will not be collected, the following journal entry should be made:

Apr. 22. Allowance for Doubtful Accounts.................... 75.00
         Accounts Receivable.............................   75.00
             To write off account of Stuart Palmer found to be
             uncollectible.

Sometimes the allowance for doubtful accounts will show a debit balance at the end of the accounting period. This happens when the total amount of estimated uncollectible customers' accounts for the year is smaller than the total amount of such accounts actually written off during the year. When this condition is encountered, the adjusting entry for estimated uncollectible accounts must **(1)** cover this debit balance, and **(2)** provide for the expected uncollectible-account losses of the coming year.

In still other cases, it may be found that the allowance account has too large a credit balance, which means that the amount of write-offs has not been as large as was expected. Very often, this is handled by making the amount of the adjustment for the year just ended smaller than it otherwise would be. If substantial amounts are involved (either a very large debit balance or too large an accumulated credit balance), it may be necessary to correct the beginning (first-of-period) balance of the allowance account by either **(1)** a debit to the owner's capital account and a credit to Allowance for Doubtful Accounts in an amount sufficient to eliminate the debit balance in the latter and give it a reasonable credit balance, or **(2)** a debit to the allowance account and a credit to the owner's capital in an amount sufficient to remove the excessive portion of the credit balance in the allowance account. (Such entries are examples of what are called "intra-period correcting entries." Entries of this type are made in an effort to correct past income or loss calculations and the consequent misstatement of some asset, contra asset, or liability account. Such entries are not common.) If the beginning-of-period balance in the Allowance for Doubtful Accounts has been corrected, the end-of-period adjusting entry can be made in the normal manner.

The chart of accounts for Boyd's Clothiers includes Allowance for Doubtful Accounts, Account No. 012, and Uncollectible Accounts Expense, Account No. 621, to provide for recording uncollectible accounts expense and subsequent write-offs of the uncollectible accounts.

Accounting for prepaid expenses

The term *prepaid expense* is largely self-explanatory. It refers to something that has been bought that is properly considered an asset when acquired, but which will eventually be consumed or used up and thus become an expense. Prepaid (unexpired) insurance and supplies of various sorts are leading examples. At the end of the period, the portion of such assets that has expired or has been consumed must be determined and an entry made debiting the proper expense accounts and crediting the proper prepaid expense accounts.

The chart of accounts for Boyd's Clothiers includes two prepaid expense accounts, Prepaid Insurance, Account No. 141, and Supplies, Account No. 151. These accounts are classified as assets in the chart of accounts. The prepaid insurance account should be debited for the cost of the insurance purchased. At the end of the year the account should be credited for the portion of the cost that relates to the year then ending with an offsetting debit to Insurance Expense, Account No. 622. The supplies account should be debited for the cost of supplies purchased. At the end of the year the account should be credited for the cost of supplies consumed or used during the year with an offsetting debit to Supplies Expense, Account No. 616.

Accounting for depreciation

Depreciation accounting is the process of attempting to allocate the cost of most long-lived assets to the periods expected to benefit from the use of these assets. Most long-lived assets eventually become useless to the business either because they wear out or because they become inadequate or obsolete. Sometimes all three of these causes combine to make the assets valueless except, perhaps, for some small salvage value as scrap or junk.

Generally, in computing depreciation, no consideration is given to what these assets might bring if they were to be sold. Assets of this type are acquired to be used and not to be sold. During their useful life their resale value is of no consequence unless the business is about to cease. For a going business, the idea is to allocate the net cost of such assets over the years they are expected to serve. By "net cost" is meant original cost less estimated scrap or salvage value. Inasmuch as the possibility of scrap or salvage value is commonly ignored, it is usually the original cost of the assets that is allocated.

It should be apparent that depreciation expense can be no more than an estimate. Usually there is no way of knowing just how long an asset will serve. However, with past experience as a guide, the estimates can be reasonably reliable.

There are several ways of calculating the periodic depreciation write-off. Traditionally, the so-called *straight-line method* has been widely used. With this method, the original cost (or cost less any expected scrap value) of an asset is divided by the number of years the asset is expected to serve to find the amount that is to be considered as depreciation expense each year. It is common practice to express depreciation as a percentage of the original cost of the asset. For example, in the case of an asset with a 10-year life, 10 percent of the original cost should be written off each year; for a 20-year asset, 5 percent should be written off.

There are some depreciation methods that permit larger write-offs in the earlier years of the life of the asset. In 1954 the Internal Revenue Code was revised to permit taxpayers to use certain of these methods in calculating net income subject to tax, though these methods primarily are useful only in the case of new assets. This change in the law stimulated the use of these "reducing-charge" methods. ("Reducing-charge" means a successively smaller write-off each year.) However, the straight-line method has been very popular in the past, and it has a number of virtues including simplicity. Straight-line depreciation is widely used. The straight-line method of accounting for depreciation is used by Boyd's Clothiers.

Depreciation expense is recorded by an end-of-period adjusting entry that involves debiting one or more depreciation expense accounts and crediting one or more accumulated depreciation (sometimes called allowance for depreciation) accounts. The latter accounts are contra accounts — contra to the accounts for the assets that are being depreciated. In theory there would be no objection to making the credits directly to the asset accounts themselves (in the same way that the asset accounts for prepaid expenses are credited to record their decreases). However, in order that the original cost of the assets will be clearly revealed, any portions of this cost written off are credited to the contra accounts. The amounts of the credit balances of the contra accounts are reported in the balance sheet as deductions from the costs of the assets to which they relate.

The credit balances in the accumulated depreciation accounts get larger year by year. When the amounts become equal to the cost of the related assets, no more depreciation may be taken.

The difference between the allowance for doubtful accounts and the accumulated depreciation account should be recognized. Both are credited by adjusting entries at the end of the period. In both cases, the offsetting debits go to expense accounts. In both cases, the balances in the contra accounts are shown in the balance sheet as subtractions from the amounts of the assets to which they relate. However, Allowance for Doubtful Accounts is debited whenever anticipated uncollectibles materialize. The balance of this allowance account does not get continually larger. (If it does, this indicates that the estimate of uncollectible account losses has been excessive.) In contrast, the credit balances of the accumulated depreciation accounts will get larger year by year, often for many years. The credit balances remain in these accounts for as long as the assets to which they relate are kept in service.

Since Boyd's Clothiers has only one class of long-lived assets that is subject to depreciation — store equipment — there is only one contra account, Accumulated Depreciation—Store Equipment, Account No. 018. Depreciation expense is debited to an account so named, Account No. 612.

Purchases discount

Purchase invoices representing purchases on account may be subject to discount if paid within a specified time. Retailers may be allowed a discount by wholesalers on invoices that are paid within a specified time, such as five days, ten days, or fifteen days, from the date of the invoice. This is known as a *cash discount* and it should not be confused with trade discounts allowed by wholesalers.

Trade discounts are the discounts allowed retailers from the list or catalog prices of wholesalers. Such trade discounts are usually shown as deductions on the invoice and only the net amount is recorded as the purchase price. If the invoice is subject to an additional discount for cash, it will be indicated on the invoice under the heading of "Terms." For example, the terms may be specified as "2/10, n/30," which means that if paid within ten days from the date of the invoice a discount of 2 percent may be deducted; otherwise the net amount of the invoice (after any trade discounts) is payable within thirty days. Stated terms of "3/10 EOM" means that if the invoice is paid no later than 10 days after the end of the current month, 3 percent discount may be taken.

To facilitate the payment of invoices in time to be entitled to any discount offered, Ms. Boyd follows the policy of filing each invoice in an unpaid invoice file according to the date it should be paid. It is, therefore, only necessary to refer to the file each day to determine which invoices are due on that date and which may be subject to discount. Any amount of cash discount deducted when paying an invoice should be recorded as a credit to Purchases Discount, Account No. 052. Thus, if an invoice for $140, subject to a discount of 6 percent if paid within ten days, is paid within the specified time, the payment should be recorded by debiting Accounts Payable for $140, by crediting the bank account for $131.60, and by crediting Purchases Discount for $8.40. The purchases discount account has a credit balance and (along with Purchases Returns and Allowances) is reported as a deduction from the gross amount of purchases in the cost of goods sold section of the income statement. Some businesses report the credit balance in the purchases discount account as "other revenue." Although this latter practice is not uncommon, the trend definitely favors the practice of regarding discount earned for prompt payment of purchase invoices as a deduction from the gross amount of purchases rather than as other revenue.

Accounts with suppliers and customers   As previously explained, a record of the amounts due to suppliers for purchases on account and the amounts due from customers for sales on account may be kept without maintaining a separate ledger account for each supplier and for each customer. A file of unpaid vendors' invoices and another of sales slips for sales on account may suffice. Many merchants, however, prefer to keep a separate ledger account for each supplier and for each customer.

Subsidiary Ledgers. When the character of the enterprise and the volume of business are such that it is necessary to keep relatively few accounts, it may be satisfactory to keep all of the accounts together in a single general ledger, which may be bound, loose-leaf, or a set of cards. However, when the volume of business and the number of transactions warrant employment of more than one bookkeeper to keep the records, it may be advisable to subdivide the ledger. In some businesses it is necessary to keep separate accounts with thousands of customers and suppliers. In such cases it usually is considered advisable to segregate the accounts with customers and the accounts with suppliers from the other accounts and to keep them in separate ledgers known as *subsidiary ledgers*.

Three-Column Account Form. A special account form known as the three-column account form is widely used in keeping the individual accounts with customers and suppliers. While the standard account form shown in the illustration on page 12, or the four-column form, illustrated on page 145, may be used satisfactorily for customers' and suppliers' accounts, most accountants favor the use of the *three-column account form* shown below for such accounts. It will be noted that three parallel amount columns are provided for recording debits, credits, and balances. The nature of the account determines whether its usual balance is a debit or a credit. Accounts with customers almost always have debit balances; accounts with suppliers nearly always have credit balances. Following each entry the new balance may be determined and recorded in the Balance column, or if preferred, the balance may be determined and recorded at the end of each month.

NAME

ADDRESS

	DATE	ITEM	POST. REF.	DEBIT	CREDIT	BALANCE	
1							1
2							2
3							3
4							4
5							5
6							6

Three-Column Account Form

Control accounts

When subsidiary ledgers are kept for suppliers and for customers, it is customary to keep *control accounts* for the subsidiary ledgers in the general ledger. Thus, if accounts with suppliers are kept in a subsidiary accounts payable ledger, a control account for accounts payable should be kept in the general ledger; if accounts with customers are kept in a subsidiary accounts receivable ledger, a control account for accounts receivable should be kept in the general ledger. The use of control accounts in the general ledger makes it possible to take a trial balance of the general ledger accounts without reference to the subsidiary ledgers.

Accounts Payable Control. The accounts payable control account provides a summary of the information recorded in the individual accounts with suppliers kept in a subsidiary accounts payable ledger. Transactions affecting suppliers' accounts are posted separately to the individual accounts in the subsidiary ledger. These transactions may also be posted separately, or may be summarized periodically and the totals posted, to the control account in the general ledger. The balance of the accounts payable control account may be proved by preparing a schedule of the individual account balances in the accounts payable ledger.

Accounts with suppliers normally have credit balances. If a supplier's account has a debit balance, the balance may be circled or be written in red ink. In preparing the schedule of accounts payable, the total of the accounts with debit balances should be deducted from the total of the accounts with credit balances, and the difference should agree with the balance of the accounts payable control account.

Accounts Receivable Control. The accounts receivable control account provides a summary of the information recorded in the individual accounts with customers kept in a subsidiary accounts receivable ledger. Transactions affecting customers' accounts are posted separately to the individual accounts in the subsidiary ledger. These transactions may also be posted separately, or may be summarized periodically and the totals posted to the control account in the general ledger. The balance of the accounts receivable control account may be proved by preparing a schedule of the individual account balances in the accounts receivable ledger.

Accounts with customers normally have debit balances. If a customer's account has a credit balance, the balance may be circled or be written in red ink. In preparing the schedule of accounts receivable, the total of the accounts with credit balances should be deducted from the total of the accounts with debit balances and the difference should agree with the balance of the accounts receivable control account.

Posting from the books of original entry

Posting to the individual accounts with suppliers and customers in the respective subsidiary ledgers may be done either from the books of original entry or directly from vouchers or other documents that represent the transactions. When the posting is done from the books of original entry, each item should, of course, be posted separately to the proper account and as the posting is completed the proper cross-reference should be made in the Posting Reference column of the book of original entry and in the Posting Reference column of the ledger account. Under this plan the voucher or other document that represents the transaction may be filed after the transaction is recorded in the appropriate book of original entry. As each transaction is recorded in a book of original entry, care must be taken to enter all of the information that will be needed when posting.

Posting from vouchers or other documents

When the posting is done directly from the vouchers or other documents that represent the transactions, the transactions usually will be recorded first in the proper books of original entry, after which the vouchers or other documents will be referred to the bookkeeper in charge of the suppliers' and customers' accounts for direct posting.

Posting to the individual accounts with suppliers

It is necessary to post all items that represent increases or decreases in the amount owed to each supplier. A list of vouchers or other documents that usually represent transactions completed with suppliers is shown below. The usual posting reference is also indicated.

Voucher or Document	Transaction Represented	Posting Reference
(a) Purchase invoice No. 1	Purchase	P 1
(b) Charge-back invoice No. 1	Return or allowance	CB 1
(c) Check stub No. 1	Payment on account	Ck 1

The purchase invoices and charge-back invoices are usually numbered consecutively as they are received and issued. These numbers should not be confused with the numbers used by the vendor (supplier). The check stubs should be numbered consecutively to agree with the numbers of the checks issued. As the posting is completed, the proper cross-reference should be made in the Posting Reference column of the account and on the voucher or other document. If a loose-leaf ledger is used and accounts with suppliers are kept in alphabetic order, the posting may be indicated by means of a distinctive check mark on the voucher or other document.

Posting to the individual accounts with customers

It is necessary to post all items that represent increases or decreases in the amount owed by each customer. Following is a list of vouchers or other documents that usually represent transactions completed with customers. The usual posting reference is also indicated.

Voucher or Document	Transaction Represented	Posting Reference
(a) Sale ticket No. 1	Sale	S 1
(b) Credit memo No. 1	Return or allowance	CM 1
(c) Remittance received	Collection on account	C

The sales tickets usually are prepared in duplicate or triplicate and are numbered consecutively. Each salesperson may use a different series of numbers. One copy is retained for the use of the bookkeeper and another copy is given to the customer.

Credit memorandums issued to customers in connection with sales returns or allowances are usually prepared in duplicate and are numbered consecutively. One copy goes to the customer and the other copy is retained for the use of the bookkeeper.

Remittances received from customers may consist of cash or cash items, such as checks, bank drafts, and money orders. When the remittance is in the form of cash, it is customary to issue a receipt. The receipt may be issued in duplicate, in which case the duplicate copy will provide the information needed for the purpose of posting to the customer's account. Sometimes receipt stubs are used to record the information for posting purposes. When the remittance is in the form of a check, it is not necessary to issue a receipt as the canceled check will serve as a receipt for the customer.

Posting a credit to the customer's account may be made directly from the check or from a list of checks received. Sometimes all remittances received daily are listed in such a manner as to provide the information needed for posting purposes. When this plan is followed, the bookkeeper need not handle the remittances at all. It is a quite common practice to use a form of monthly statement of account in which the upper portion (containing the customer's name and address) is to be detached and sent in along with the remittance. The amount of the remittance is noted on this slip of paper which then contains all the information needed to post the correct credit to the proper customer's account. If the customer does not send in (or bring in) the top part of the statement, a receipt or memo is prepared to serve the same purpose. This procedure is especially suitable when it is possible to separate the functions of **(1)** handling the cash and cash items, and **(2)** recording the credits to the customers' accounts.

As the posting is completed, the proper cross-reference should be made in the Posting Reference column of the account and on the voucher or other document. If a loose-leaf ledger is used and accounts with customers are kept in alphabetic order, the posting may be indicated by means of a distinctive check mark or by initialing the voucher or other document.

Accountants generally prefer to post from the basic documents rather than from the books of original entry to the individual accounts with suppliers and customers because such procedure provides better control and promotes accuracy. When a purchase invoice is recorded in a purchases journal by one person and is posted directly from the invoice to the proper supplier's account by another person, it is unlikely that both persons will make the same mistake. Even if the posting is done by the person who also keeps the purchases journal, there is less likelihood of making a mistake than when the posting is done from the purchases journal. If a mistake were made in recording the amount of the invoice in the purchases journal, the same mistake would almost certainly be made in posting from the purchases journal to the supplier's account. The same reasoning may be applied to the recording of sales transactions and all other transactions that affect accounts with suppliers and customers.

Statement of account

When merchandise is sold on account, it is customary to render a monthly statement of account to each charge customer. Usually the statements are mailed as soon as they can be completed following the close of each month or at a time during the month determined by the billing cycle. (The use of "billing cycles" is limited, generally, to businesses with hundreds or thousands of customers.) In order that statements may be mailed promptly, some firms follow the policy of including transactions completed up to the 25th of the preceding month or five days before the close of the customer's billing cycle. Such statements are an aid to collection. When a remittance is not received from the customer within the usual credit period, a copy of the statement of account may be referred to the credit department for such action as the credit manager may wish to take. A model filled-in copy of a statement of account is reproduced below. This is a statement of the account of W. D. Ross for the month ended October 31. It shows **(1)** the balance at the beginning of the month amounting to $64.60; **(2)** a charge of $173.25 (for a sale of $165.00 plus tax of $8.25) made on October 24, **(3)** a credit of $150 for cash received on October 27; and **(4)** the balance at the close of the month amounting to $87.85. Note that the customer is asked to tear off the upper portion of the statement and to send it along with his remittance.

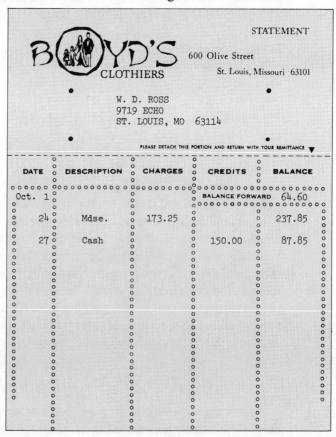

Statement of Account

Report
No. 8-1

Complete Report No. 8-1 in the study assignments and submit your working papers to the instructor for approval. After completing the report, continue with the following textbook discussion until the next report is required.

APPLICATION OF ACCOUNTING PRINCIPLES

The accrual basis of accounting as applied to a merchandising enterprise is illustrated on the following pages by a reproduction of the records of Boyd's Clothiers, owned and operated by Lynn C. Boyd. The records include the following:

BOOKS OF ORIGINAL ENTRY

    Combined cash journal
    Purchases journal
    Sales journal

BOOKS OF FINAL ENTRY

    General ledger
    Accounts receivable ledger
    Accounts payable ledger

AUXILIARY RECORDS

    Petty cash disbursements record
    Checkbook
    Employees' earnings records

Combined cash journal

The form of combined cash journal used is similar to the one illustrated on pages 160 and 161. However, in Boyd's journal the first two amount columns are used in recording banking transactions including deposits, checks, and bank charges. These columns serve the same purpose as though they were headed Cash Receipts and Disbursements. Ms. Boyd follows the practice of depositing all cash receipts in a checking account at the First National Bank and of making all disbursements by check (except for the payment of small items, which may be paid from a petty cash fund, and a few charges made directly by the bank). For these reasons, a bank account rather than a cash account is kept in the general ledger. The posting to the bank account is from the combined cash journal, the account being debited for the total receipts (deposits) and being credited for the total disbursements (checks and bank charges). The journal also differs from the one on pages 106 and 107 in that Boyd's has a Purchases Discount Credit column immediately to the right of the Bank Credit column.

All items entered in the General Debit and Credit columns of the combined cash journal are posted individually to the proper accounts in the general ledger. No individual posting to the general ledger is required from any of the other amount columns. Instead, the totals of these columns are posted at the end of the month.

Purchases journal

The form of purchases journal used is the same as the one illustrated on page 144. It was described in detail in Chapter 6. All transactions involving the purchase of merchandise *on account* are recorded in this journal. Because the posting of the individual credits to the accounts with suppliers is done directly from the purchase invoices, the only posting required from the purchases journal is the total purchases for each month. This involves a debit to Purchases, Account No. 511, and a credit to Accounts Payable, Account No. 231.

Sales journal

The form of sales journal used is the same as the one illustrated on page 152. It was described in detail in Chapter 6. All transactions involving the sale of merchandise *on account* are recorded in this journal. Because the posting of individual charges to the accounts with customers is done directly from the sales tickets, the only posting required from the sales journal is the total sales for each month. This involves a debit to Accounts Receivable, Account No. 121, and credits to Sales, Account No. 411, and to Sales Tax Payable, Account No. 241.

General ledger

A general ledger with the accounts arranged in numerical order is used. A chart of the accounts appears on page 183. The four-column account form is used in the general ledger.

Accounts receivable ledger

An accounts receivable ledger with the accounts for customers arranged in alphabetic order is used. The three-column account form is used in this ledger. Posting to the individual accounts with customers is done directly from the sales tickets or other documents. As each item is posted, the balance is extended immediately so that reference to the account of any customer at any time will reveal without any delay the amount due.

This is important since it is often necessary to determine the status of a particular customer's account before extending additional credit.

Accounts payable ledger

An accounts payable ledger with the accounts for suppliers arranged in alphabetic order is used. The three-column account form also is used in this ledger. Posting to the individual accounts with suppliers is done directly from the invoices or other documents. As each item is posted, the balance is extended immediately so that reference to the account of any supplier at any time will reveal the amount owed to that supplier.

Auxiliary records

As previously stated, certain auxiliary records are used, including a petty cash disbursements record and a checkbook. The form of petty cash disbursements record is similar to that illustrated on pages 50 and 51. A record of deposits made and checks issued is kept on the check stubs as well as in the combined cash journal. At the end of each month, when the summary posting from the combined cash journal has been completed, the balance of the bank checking account in the ledger should be the same as the balance recorded on the check stubs. The earnings records maintained for each of Ms. Boyd's four employees are similar to the one illustrated on pages 80 and 81. (To conserve space, these records are not reproduced in this chapter.)

Accounting procedure

The books of account containing a record of the transactions completed during the month of December are reproduced on pages 208 to 225. These books include the combined cash journal, the purchases journal, the sales journal, the petty cash disbursements record, the general ledger, the accounts receivable ledger, and the accounts payable ledger. Before recording any transactions for December, the balance of the bank checking account was entered in the combined cash journal and the balance in the petty cash fund was entered in the petty cash disbursements record. The balance at the beginning of the month of December is shown in each of the accounts in the general, accounts receivable, and accounts payable ledgers. These balances along with those at the end of the month are summarized in the trial balances and schedules reproduced on pages 225 and 226.

Following is a narrative of the transactions completed during December. Transactions of a type that have not been previously introduced are analyzed to show their effect upon the accounts.

BOYD'S CLOTHIERS

NARRATIVE OF TRANSACTIONS

Monday, December 2

Issued checks as follows:

No. 867, Dolan Realty Co., $700, in payment of December rent.

No. 868, The Penn-Central Railroad Co., $53.18, in payment of freight on merchandise purchased.

No. 869, Aris Glove Co., $330, in payment of invoice of November 5, no discount.

It will be noted that all three checks were recorded in the combined cash journal. Check No. 867 was recorded by debiting Rent Expense, Account No. 611, and by crediting the bank account. Check No. 868 was recorded by debiting Purchases, Account No. 511, and by crediting the bank account. Since the freight charge increases the cost of the merchandise, the purchases account should be debited. Note that the account titles were written in the Description column. The account numbers were inserted in the Posting Reference column when the individual posting was completed at the end of the week.

Check No. 869 was recorded by debiting Accounts Payable and crediting the bank account, the name of the supplier being written in the Description column. A check mark was placed in the Posting Reference column to indicate that checks issued to suppliers are not posted individually from the combined cash journal. Such checks are posted directly to the proper suppliers' accounts in the accounts payable ledger from the information on the check stubs.

Tuesday, December 3

Received the following invoices for merchandise purchased on account:

Daniel Hays Co., Johnstown, NY 12095, $228, per Invoice No. 204 of November 30. Terms, net 30 days.

Hanes Corporation, Winston-Salem, NC 27102, $744, per Invoice No. 205 of November 30. Terms, 8/10 EOM.

Julius Resnick, Inc., 46 E. 32d St., New York, NY 10016, $1,488, per Invoice No. 206 of November 30. Terms, 3/10 EOM.

It will be noted that after receiving the merchandise and checking the invoices, the transactions were recorded in the purchases journal. Check marks were placed in the Posting Reference column to indicate that individual posting is not done from the purchases journal. The invoices were then posted directly to the credit of the three suppliers' accounts in the accounts payable ledger, after which the invoices were filed in an unpaid invoice file according to their due dates.

Wednesday, December 4

Received check from D. P. Walsh, $317.23.

Note that the credit was immediately posted to the customer's account. The remittance was then recorded in the combined cash journal by debiting the bank account and by crediting Accounts Receivable. The name of the customer was written in the Description column. Since the credit had already been posted to the customer's account, a check mark was placed in the Posting Reference column.

Received a notice from the First National Bank that $235.42 had been deducted from the account of Boyd's Clothiers, representing a discount of

3 percent of the net amount of BankAmericard and Master Charge vouchers that had been deposited by Boyd's relating to such sales (less credits issued to customers for returns) during the preceding month.

> Note that this was recorded in the combined cash journal as a debit to Bank Credit Card Expense, Account No. 619, and a credit in the Bank "Checks Cr." column. (Even though the reduction in the Bank balance was not accomplished by issuing a check, the effect was the same. A subtraction of the amount was made on the next check stub.)

Thursday, December 5

Sold merchandise on account as follows:

No. 271A, D. P. Walsh, 113 Grether, St. Louis, MO 63135, $432.39, tax, $21.62.

No. 257B, J. J. Anders, 11939 Rocky, St. Louis, MO 63141, $85.12, tax, $4.26.

No. 235C, J. L. Burnett, 15 Forester, St. Louis, MO 63011, $537.95, tax $26.90.

> Unless otherwise specified, all charge sales are payable on the 10th of the following month. No cash discount is allowed. Note that these transactions were recorded in the sales journal. A check mark was placed in the Posting Reference column to indicate that individual posting is not done from the sales journal. The sales tickets were then posted directly to the proper customers' accounts in the accounts receivable ledger, after which each ticket was filed under the name of the customer for future reference. The numbers of the sales tickets indicate that there are four salespersons identified by the letters A, B, C, and D. Each of these persons uses a separate pad of sales tickets numbered consecutively.

Issued Checks as follows:

No. 870, Brown Shoe Co., $460.60, in payment of invoice of November 27, $470 less discount of $9.40.

No. 871, Damon, Inc., $432.40, in payment of invoice of November 26, $460 less discount of $27.60.

No. 872, El Jay Co., $2,079.20, in payment of invoice of November 29, $2,260 less discount of $180.80.

No. 873, Marx Neuman Co., $784, in payment of invoice of November 27, $800 less discount of $16.

No. 874, Schoeneman, Inc., $1,128, in payment of invoice of November 29, $1,200 less discount of $72.

No. 875, Smart Pants, Inc., $1,258.56, in payment of invoice of November 27, $1,368 less discount of $109.44.

> Each of the six checks was recorded in the combined cash journal by crediting the bank account, crediting Purchases Discount in the column provided, and debiting Accounts Payable for the gross amount. The name of the supplier was written in the description column and a check mark was placed in the Posting Reference column to indicate that the posting to the individual supplier's account in the accounts payable ledger was not made from this journal. The check stubs provided the information for posting. In posting the suppliers' accounts, one line was used for the amount of the check and another for the amount of the discount.

Friday, December 6

Issued checks as follows:

No. 876, Post Publishing Co., $61.04, in payment for circulars to be used for advertising purposes.

No. 877, State Treasurer, $912.14, in payment of sales taxes for November.

Both checks were recorded in the combined cash journal by debiting the proper accounts and by crediting the bank account. Check No. 876 was charged to Advertising Expense and Check No. 877 was charged to Sales Tax Payable. The numbers of the checks were written in the Check No. column and the titles of the accounts to be charged were written in the Description column.

Bought merchandise from Damon, Inc., 16 E. 34th St., New York, NY 10016, $1,150, per Invoice No. 207 of December 4. Terms, 6/10, n/30.

Sold merchandise on account as follows:

No. 259B, J. F. Yager, 5 Brookston Ct., Kirkwood, MO 63122, $106.32, tax $5.32.

Saturday, December 7

Cash (including bank credit card) sales for the week:

SALESPERSON	MERCHANDISE	TAX	TOTAL
A	$ 840.15	$ 42.01	$ 882.16
B	762.18	38.11	800.29
C	1,041.73	52.09	1,093.82
D	628.40	31.42	659.82
	$3,272.46	$163.63	$3,436.09

As each cash sale was completed a sales ticket and a BankAmericard or Master Charge voucher, if necessary, were prepared. This ticket provided the information needed in recording the sale on the cash register when ringing up the amount of cash or vouchers received. As each amount was thus recorded it was added to the previous total of cash sales made by each salesperson on a mechanical accumulator in the register. Usually the total cash sales are recorded daily, but to save time and to avoid unnecessary duplication of entries the total cash sales are here recorded at the end of each week and on the last day of the month. This transaction was recorded in the combined cash journal by debiting the bank account for $3,436.09 and by crediting Sales for $3,272.46 and Sales Tax Payable for $163.63.

Made petty cash disbursements as follows:

Postage stamps, $10. Petty Cash Voucher No. 73.
Messenger fee, $3. Petty Cash Voucher No. 74.

All disbursements from the petty cash fund are recorded in the petty cash disbursements record. This record is ruled so as to facilitate the classification of such expenditures. It will be noted that the cost of the postage stamps was recorded as a charge to Supplies, Account No. 151, and the messenger fees to Miscellaneous Expense, Account No. 624.

END-OF-THE-WEEK WORK

(1) Proved the footings of the combined cash journal. **(2)** Deposited $3,753.32 in the First National Bank and proved the bank balance ($7,621.61). **(3)** Posted each entry individually from the General Debit and Credit columns of the combined cash journal to the proper general ledger accounts. **(4)** Proved the footings of the petty cash disbursements record and proved the balance of the petty cash fund ($87). **(5)** Proved the footings of the sales journal.

Monday, December 9

Issued checks as follows:

No. 878 to Daniel Hays Co., $684, in payment of invoice of November 15, no discount.

No. 879, Hanes Corporation, $684.48, in payment of invoice of November 30, $744 less discount of $59.52.

No. 880, Julius Resnick, Inc., $1,443.36, in payment of invoice of November 30, $1,488 less discount of $44.64.

A customer who had used her Master Charge card to purchase a dress (sales price, $84.95; sales tax, $4.25) two days before, returned it having decided it was the wrong color. Ms. Boyd agreed to take it back and prepared a Master Charge credit voucher for the full amount, $89.20.

Since the original transaction had been handled as a cash sale, the return was recorded in the combined cash journal as a credit of $89.20 in the Bank "Checks Cr." column with a debit of $84.95 to Sales Returns and Allowances, Account No. 041, and a debit of $4.25 to Sales Tax Payable, Account No. 241. (At the time of the next bank deposit, the amount of the credit voucher will be treated as a deduction from the amount of the vouchers being deposited.)

Tuesday, December 10

Issued Check No. 881 for $500.68 to the First National Bank, a U.S. depositary, in payment of the following taxes:

Employees' income tax withheld during November.............		$284.40
FICA tax imposed —		
On employees (withheld during November)................	$108.14	
On the employer......................................	108.14	216.28
Total..		$500.68

This transaction resulted in decreases in FICA tax payable and in employees income tax payable with a corresponding decrease in the bank account; hence, it was recorded in the combined cash journal by debiting FICA Tax Payable for $216.28 and Employees Income Tax Payable for $284.40, and by crediting the bank account for $500.68.

Sold merchandise on account as follows on page 202.

No. 243D, R. D. Williams, 617 Rebecca, St. Charles, MO 63301, $246.05, tax $12.30.

Wednesday, December 11

Received the following remittances from customers:
J. E. Buelt, $300, on account.
L. V. Freeman, $200, on account.
K. E. Vivian, $82.11, in full settlement of account.

Thursday, December 12

Issued Check No. 882 to Damon, Inc., $1,081, in payment of invoice of December 4, $1,150 less discount of $69.
Made the following disbursements from the petty cash fund:
Boy Scouts of America, $5. Petty Cash Voucher No. 75.
Lynn C. Boyd, $10, for personal use. Petty Cash Voucher No. 76.

Friday, December 13

Received the following invoices for merchandise purchased on account:

Aris Glove Co., 10 E. 38th St., New York, NY 10016, $412.50, per Invoice No. 208 of December 10. Terms, net 30 days.

El Jay Co., 411 Anderson, Fairview, NJ 07022, $1,695, per Invoice No. 209 of December 10. Terms, 8/10, n/30.

Huk-a-Poo, Inc., 411 Broadway, New York, NY 10012, $543.75, per Invoice No. 210 of December 11. Terms, 8/10, n/30.

Saturday, December 14

Cash and bank credit card sales for the week:

SALESPERSON	MERCHANDISE	TAX	TOTAL
A	$ 830.12	$ 41.51	$ 871.63
B	1,215.05	60.75	1,275.80
C	728.80	36.44	765.24
D	411.60	20.58	432.18
	$3,185.57	$159.28	$3,344.85

Issued Check No. 883 payable to Payroll for $705.24.

Ms. Boyd follows the policy of paying her employees on the 15th and last day of each month. Since December 15 fell on Sunday, the employees were paid on the 14th. The following statement was prepared from the payroll record:

PAYROLL STATEMENT FOR PERIOD ENDED DECEMBER 15

Total wages and commissions earned during period............		$892.70
Employees' taxes to be withheld:		
Employees' income tax.................................	$133.90	
FICA tax 6% of $892.70...............................	53.56	187.46
Net amount payable to employees.........................		$705.24
Employer's payroll taxes:		
FICA tax, 6% of $892.70..............................		$ 53.56
Unemployment compensation taxes —		
State unemployment tax, 2.7% of $104.80................		2.83
FUTA tax, 0.5% of $104.80...........................		.52
Total...		$ 56.91

None of the earnings of the four employees had reached the $15,000 point. Accordingly, all of the wages and commissions earned during the period are subject to the FICA tax. All but one employee (a part-time employee) had reached the $4,200 State Unemployment and FUTA tax limits in an earlier month. As a result, only $104.80 of wages and commissions earned during the period is subject to these unemployment taxes.

Two entries were required to record the payroll in the combined cash journal — one to record the total earnings of the employees, the amounts withheld for FICA tax and income tax, and the net amount paid; the other to record the social security tax imposed on the employer.

END-OF-THE-WEEK WORK

(1) Proved the footings of the combined cash journal. (2) Deposited $3,837.76 ($3,926.96 — $89.20 credit of December 9) in the First National Bank and proved the bank balance ($6,360.61). (3) Posted each entry individually from the General Debit and Credit columns of the combined cash journal to the proper general ledger accounts. (4) Proved the footings of the petty cash disbursements record and proved the balance of the petty cash fund ($72). (5) Proved the footings of the sales journal.

Tuesday, December 17

Received the following remittances from customers:

J. F. Yager, $213.52, on account.
S. W. Novak, $369.90, in full settlement of account.
C. E. Wuller, $367.57 in full settlement of account.

(Since a page of the combined cash journal was filled at this point, the totals of the amount columns were recorded on the double ruled line at the bottom of the page, after which they were carried forward and entered at the top of the next page.)

Wednesday, December 18

Sold merchandise on credit as follows:

No. 239C, K. E. Vivian, 1830 Patterson Rd., Florissant, MO 63031, $329.90, tax $16.50.

No. 246D, E. E. Palmer, 1129 Mackinac, St. Louis, MO 63141, $68.15, tax $3.41.

No. 277A, W. R. Price, 1629 Rathford Ct., St. Louis, MO 63141, $154.11, tax $7.71.

Thursday, December 19

Issued checks as follows:

No. 884, El Jay Co., $1,559.40, in payment of invoice of December 10, $1,695 less discount of $135.60.

No. 885, Huk-a-Poo, Inc., $500.25, in payment of invoice of December 11, $543.75 less discount of $43.50.

Made petty cash disbursements as follows:

Advertising, $6.29. Petty Cash Voucher No. 77.

Supplies, $8.35. Petty Cash Voucher No. 78.

Miscellaneous expense, $1.75. Petty Cash Voucher No. 79.

Friday, December 20

Issued Charge-Back Invoice No. 291 for $66 to Aris Glove Co., for merchandise returned; to be applied on Invoice No. 208 received December 13.

> This transaction was recorded in the combined cash journal by debiting Accounts Payable and by crediting Purchases Returns and Allowances. It was also posted directly to the account of the Aris Glove Co. in the accounts payable ledger from the charge-back invoice.

Saturday, December 21

Issued Check No. 886 for $1,000 to Ms. Boyd for personal use.

Cash and bank credit card sales for the week:

SALESPERSON	MERCHANDISE	TAX	TOTAL
A	$ 982.50	$ 49.13	$1,031.63
B	801.30	40.07	841.37
C	714.75	35.74	750.49
D	840.05	42.00	882.05
	$3,338.60	$166.94	$3,505.54

END-OF-THE-WEEK WORK

(1) Proved the footings of the combined cash journal. **(2)** Deposited $4,456.53 in the First National Bank and proved the bank balance ($7,757.49). **(3)** Posted each entry individually from the General Debit and Credit columns of the combined cash journal to the proper general ledger accounts. **(4)** Proved the footings of the petty cash disbursements record and proved the balance of the petty cash fund ($55.61). **(5)** Proved the footings of the sales journal.

Monday, December 23

Issued Check No. 887 for $16.80 to United Parcel Service in payment of statement for delivery service for month ended December 15.

> Very few of the customers of Boyd's Clothiers wish to have their purchases delivered. In some special circumstances, Ms. Boyd or one of the employees handles deliveries. In some cases, United Parcel Service is used. Since the monthly amount is small, Miscellaneous Expense is debited when the charge is paid.

Tuesday, December 24

Sold merchandise on credit as follows:

No. 262B, D. P. Walsh, 113 Grether, St. Louis, MO 63135, $18.55, tax $.93.

No. 249D, C. W. Reed, 761 Cella, St. Louis, MO 63124, $191.42, tax $9.57.

No. 256C, L. V. Freeman, 7362 S. Yorkshire, St. Louis, MO 63126, $17.95, tax $.90.

Thursday, December 26

Received the following remittances from customers:

W. R. Price, $100, on account.
C. W. Reed, $300, on account.

Made petty cash disbursements as follows:

Advertising, $4.80. Petty Cash Voucher No. 80.
Supplies, $9.13. Petty Cash Voucher No. 81.
Miscellaneous expense, $2.90. Petty Cash Voucher No. 82.

Friday, December 27

Issued Credit Memorandum No. 12 for $22.58 to W. R. Price for merchandise returned. (Sales price of merchandise, $21.50, tax $1.08.)

Issued Check No. 888 for $421.30 to the Post Publishing Co. in payment of advertising bill.

Received a notice from the First National Bank that $369.90 had been deducted from the account of Boyd's Clothiers, since a check from S. W. Novak deposited a few days before had not been paid by Mr. Novak's bank (not sufficient funds). Mr. Novak's check was enclosed with the notice.

> The amount of the check was debited immediately to Mr. Novak's account in the accounts receivable ledger with the notation "NSF." An entry was made in the

combined cash journal debiting Accounts Receivable with a credit in the Bank "Checks Cr." column. A deduction was made on the following check stub.

Saturday, December 28

Cash and bank credit card sales for the week:

SALESPERSON	MERCHANDISE	TAX	TOTAL
A	$ 795.40	$ 39.77	$ 835.17
B	867.50	43.38	910.88
C	403.10	20.16	423.26
D	642.35	32.12	674.47
	$2,708.35	$135.43	$2,843.78

Issued checks as follows:

No. 889, The Central States Bell Telephone Co., $32.15, for telephone service.

No. 890, The United Gas & Electric Co., $73.28, for gas and electricity.

No. 891, Daniel Hays Co., $228 in payment of invoice of November 30, no discount.

END-OF-THE-WEEK WORK

(1) Proved the footings of the combined cash journal. **(2)** Deposited $3,243.78 in the First National Bank and proved the bank balance, ($9,859.84). **(3)** Posted each entry individually from the General Debit and Credit columns of the combined cash journal to the proper general ledger accounts. **(4)** Proved the footings of the petty cash disbursements record and proved the balance of the petty cash fund ($38.78). **(5)** Proved the footings of the sales journal.

Monday, December 30

Received invoice from Jacob Siegel Co., 4725 N. Broad St., Philadelphia, PA 19141, $1,300, for merchandise purchased per Invoice No. 211 of December 27. Terms, 6/10, n/30.

Tuesday, December 31

Received the following invoices:

Brown Shoe Co., 8300 Maryland Ave., St. Louis, MO 63105, $705 per Invoice No. 212 of December 27. Terms, 2/10, n/30.

El Jay Co., 411 Anderson, Fairview, NJ 07022, $678 per Invoice No. 213 of December 26. Terms, 8/10, n/30.

Hanes Corporation, Winston-Salem, NC 27102, $148.80 per Invoice No. 214 of December 27. Terms, 8/10 EOM.

Marx Neuman Co., 9 W. 57th St., New York, NY 10019, $600 per Invoice No. 215 of December 26. Terms, 2/10, n/30.

Webster Safe & Lock Co., 916 Washington Ave., St. Louis, MO 63101, $562, safe purchased per invoice of December 30. Terms 2/30, n/60.

The first four invoices were recorded in the purchases journal in the usual manner. The invoice received from the Webster Safe & Lock Co. was recorded in the combined cash journal by debiting Store Equipment and by crediting Accounts Payable. In this enterprise the purchases journal is used only for recording invoices covering merchandise purchased on account.

Cash and bank credit card sales:

SALESPERSON	MERCHANDISE	TAX	TOTAL
A	$ 511.70	$25.59	$ 537.29
B	340.65	17.03	357.68
C	320.30	16.02	336.32
D	296.90	14.85	311.75
	$1,469.55	$73.49	$1,543.04

Issued Check No. 892 payable to Payroll for $698.55.

PAYROLL STATEMENT FOR PERIOD ENDED DECEMBER 31

Total wages and commissions earned during period............		$884.20
Employees' taxes to be withheld:		
Employees' income tax..................................	$132.60	
FICA tax, 6% of $884.20..............................	53.05	185.65
Net amount payable to employees........................		$698.55
Employer's payroll taxes:		
FICA tax, 6% of $884.20..............................		$ 53.05
Unemployment compensation taxes —		
State unemployment tax, 2.7% of $103.60................		2.80
FUTA tax, 0.5% of $103.60............................		.52
Total..		$ 56.37

Issued Check No. 893 for $61.22 to replenish the petty cash fund.

STATEMENT OF PETTY CASH DISBURSEMENTS FOR DECEMBER

Lynn C. Boyd, drawing..	$10.00
Supplies...	27.48
Advertising expense...	11.09
Charitable contributions expense....................................	5.00
Miscellaneous expense..	7.65
Total disbursements...	$61.22

Before the above statement was prepared the petty cash disbursements record was proved by footing the amount columns, the totals were entered in ink, and the record was ruled with single and double lines. The balance was then brought down below the double rules. The amount received to replenish the fund was added to the balance and the total, $100, was entered in the Description column.

The amount of the check issued was entered in the combined cash journal by debiting the proper accounts and by crediting the bank account. It should be remembered that no posting is done from the petty cash disbursements record; the proper accounts

PURCHASES JOURNAL   PAGE *32*

	DATE	INVOICE NO.	FROM WHOM PURCHASED	POST. REF.	AMOUNT	
1	19-- Dec. 3	204	Daniel Hays Co	✓	228 00	1
2	3	205	Hanes Corporation	✓	744 00	2
3	3	206	Julius Resnick, Inc.	✓	1488 00	3
4	6	207	Damon, Inc.	✓	1150 00	4
5	13	208	Aris Glove Co.	✓	412 50	5
6	13	209	El Jay Co.	✓	1695 00	6
7	13	210	Huk-a-Poo, Inc.	✓	543 75	7
8	30	211	Jacob Siegel Co.	✓	1300 00	8
9	31	212	Brown Shoe Co.	✓	705 00	9
10	31	213	El Jay Co.	✓	678 00	10
11	31	214	Hanes Corporation	✓	148 80	11
12	31	215	Mary Neuman Co.	✓	600 00	12
13			Purchases Dr.-Accounts Payable Cr.	511/231	9693 05	13
14						14
15						15
16						16
17						17
18						18
19						19
20						20
21						21
22						22
23						23

Boyd's Clothiers — Purchases Journal

will be charged for the petty cash disbursements when the posting is completed from the combined cash journal.

ROUTINE END-OF-THE-MONTH WORK

(1) Proved the footings and entered the totals in the combined cash journal and the sales journal; entered the total in the purchases journal. **(2)** Deposited $1,543.04 in the First National Bank and proved the bank balance ($10,643.11). **(3)** Completed the individual posting from the General Debit and Credit columns of the combined cash journal. **(4)** Completed the summary posting of the columnar totals of the combined cash journal, the purchases journal, and the sales journal to the proper accounts in the general ledger. **(5)** Ruled the combined cash journal, the purchases journal, and the sales journal. **(6)** Prepared a trial balance and schedules of accounts receivable and accounts payable.

SALES JOURNAL   PAGE 44

	DATE	SALE NO.	TO WHOM SOLD	POST. REF.	ACCOUNTS RECEIVABLE DR.	SALES CR.	SALES TAX PAYABLE CR.	
1	19-- Dec. 5	271A	D. P. Walsh	✓	45401	43239	2162	1
2	5	257B	J. J. Anders	✓	8938	8512	426	2
3	5	235C	J. L. Burnett	✓	56485	53795	2690	3
4	6	259B	J. F. Yager	✓	11164	10632	532	4
5	10	243D	R. D. Williams	✓	121988 25835	116178 24605	5810 1230	5
6	18	239C	K. E. Vivian	✓	147823 34640	140783 32990	7040 1650	6
7	18	246D	E. E. Palmer	✓	7156	6815	341	7
8	18	277A	W. R. Price	✓	16182	15411	771	8
9	24	262B	D. P. Walsh	✓	205801 19948	195299 18955	9802 93	9
10	24	249D	C. W. Reed	✓	20099	19142	957	10
11	24	256C	L. V. Freeman	✓	1885	1795	90	11
12					229733 229733	218791 218791	10942 10942	12
13					(121)	(411)	(241)	13
14								14
15								15
16								16
17								17
18								18
19								19
20								20
21								21
22								22
23								23

Boyd's Clothiers — Sales Journal

47 PAGE   COMBINED CASH JOURNAL

	FIRST NATIONAL BANK		PURCHASES DISCOUNT 052 CR.	CK. NO.	DAY	DESCRIPTION	POST. REF.	
	DEPOSITS 111 DR.	CHECKS 111 CR.						
1						AMOUNTS FORWARDED Balance 12,302.83		1
2		700 00		867	2	Rent Expense	611	2
3		53 18		868	2	Purchases	511	3
4		330 00		869	2	Aris Glove Co.	✓	4
5	317 23				4	D. P. Walsh	✓	5
6		235 42			4	Bank Credit Card Expense	619	6
7		460 60	9 40	870	5	Brown Shoe Co.	✓	7
8		432 40	27 60	871	5	Damon, Inc.	✓	8
9		2079 20	180 80	872	5	El Jay Co.	✓	9
10		784 00	16 00	873	5	Mary Neuman Co.	✓	10
11		1128 00	72 00	874	5	Schoeneman, Inc.	✓	11
12		1258 56	109 44	875	5	Smart Pants, Inc.	✓	12
13		61 04		876	6	Advertising Expense	618	13
14		912 14		877	6	Sales Tax Payable	241	14
15	3436 09 / 3753 32	8434 54	415 24		7	Cash + bank credit card sales for wk. 762.61	✓	15
16		684 00		878	9	Daniel Hays Co.	✓	16
17		684 48	59 52	879	9	Hanes Corporation	✓	17
18		1443 36	44 64	880	9	Julius Resnick	✓	18
19		89 20			9	Sales Returns & Allowances	041	19
20						Sales Tax Payable	241	20
21		500 68		881	10	FICA Tax Payable	251	21
22						Employees Income Tax Pay.	261	22
23	300 00				11	J. E. Buelt	✓	23
24	200 00				11	L. V. Freeman	✓	24
25	82 11				11	K. E. Vivian	✓	25
26		1081 00	69 00	882	12	Damon, Inc.	✓	26
27	3344 85				14	Cash + bank credit card sales for wk.	✓	27
28		705 24		883	14	Salaries + Commissions Exp.	613	28
29						FICA Tax Payable	251	29
30						Employees Income Tax Pay.	261	30
31					14	Payroll Taxes Expense	614	31
32						FICA Tax Payable	251	32
33						FUTA Tax Payable	271	33
34						State Unemployment Tax Pay. 6360.61	281	34
35	7680 28 / 213 52	13622 50	588 40		17	J. F. Yager	✓	35
36	369 90				17	S. W. Novak	✓	36
37	367 57				17	C. E. Wuller	✓	37
38	8631 27	13622 50	588 40		17	Carried forward		38

FOR MONTH OF *December* 19 —   PAGE 47

	GENERAL		ACCOUNTS PAYABLE 231 DR.	ACCOUNTS RECEIVABLE 121 CR.	SALES 411 CR.	SALES TAX PAYABLE 241 CR.	
	DEBIT	CREDIT					
1							1
2	70000						2
3	5318						3
4			33000				4
5				31723			5
6	23542						6
7			47000				7
8			46000				8
9			226000				9
10			80000				10
11			120000				11
12			136800				12
13	6104						13
14	91214						14
15	196178		688800	31723	327246	16363	15
16			68400		327246	16363	16
17			74400				17
18			148800				18
19	8495						19
20	425						20
21	21628						21
22	28440						22
23				30000			23
24				20000			24
25				8211			25
26			115000				26
27					318557	15928	27
28	89270						28
29		5356					29
30		13390					30
31	5691						31
32		5356					32
33		52					33
34		283					34
35	350127	24437	1095400	89934	645803	32291	35
35				21352			35
36				36990			36
37				36757			37
38	350127	24437	1095400	185033	645803	32291	38

Boyd's Clothiers — Combined Cash Journal (Right Page)
(*continued on next page*)

48 PAGE   COMBINED CASH JOURNAL

	FIRST NATIONAL BANK		PURCHASES DISCOUNT 052 CR.	CK. NO.	DAY	DESCRIPTION	POST. REF.	
	DEPOSITS 111 DR.	CHECKS 111 CR.						
1	863127	1362250	58840			AMOUNTS FORWARDED		1
2		155940	13560	884	19	El Jay Co.	✓	2
3		50025	4350	885	19	Huk-a-Poo, Inc.	✓	3
4					20	Purchs. R&A-Aris Glove Co.	051	4
5		100000		886	21	Lynn C. Boyd, Drawing	031	5
6	350554				21	Cash+bank credit card sales for wk.	✓	6
7	1213681	1668215	76750	887	23	Miscellaneous Expense 7,157.44	624	7
		1680						
8	10000				26	W.R. Price	✓	8
9	30000				26	C.W. Reed	✓	9
10					27	Sales R&A - W.R. Price	041	10
11						Sales Tax Payable	244	11
12		42130		888	27	Advertising Expense	618	12
13		36990			27	Accounts Rec.- S.W. Novak	121	13
14	284378				28	Cash+bank credit card sales for wk.	✓	14
15		3215		889	28	Telephone Expense	617	15
16		7328		890	28	Heating & Lighting Exp.	615	16
17	1538059	22800	76750	891	28	Daniel Hays Co.	✓	17
		1782358						
18					31	Store Equipment 9,859.84	181	18
19						Accts. Pay.-Webster Safe & Lock Co	231	19
20	154304				31	Cash+bank credit card sales for wk.	✓	20
21		69855		892	31	Salaries+Commissions Exp.	613	21
22						FICA Tax Payable	251	22
23						Employees Income Tax Pay.	261	23
24					31	Payroll Taxes Expense	614	24
25						FICA Tax Payable	251	25
26						FUTA Tax Payable	271	26
27						State Unemployment Tax Pay.	281	27
28		6122		893	31	Lynn C. Boyd, Drawing	031	28
29						Supplies	151	29
30						Advertising Expense	618	30
31						Charitable Contributions Exp.	623	31
32						Miscellaneous Expense 10,643.11	624	32
33	1692363	1858335	76750					33
34	(111)	(111)	(052)					34
35								35
36								36
37								37

Boyd's Clothiers — Combined Cash Journal (Left Page)
(concluded)

FOR MONTH OF *December* 19 —   PAGE 48

GENERAL		ACCOUNTS PAYABLE 231 Dr.	ACCOUNTS RECEIVABLE 121 Cr.	SALES 411 Cr.	SALES TAX PAYABLE 241 Cr.	
DEBIT	CREDIT					
3501 27	244 37	10954 00	1850 33	6458 03	322 91	1
		1695 00				2
		543 75				3
	66 00	66 00				4
1000 00						5
				3338 60	166 94	6
4501 27	310 37	13258 75	1850 33	9796 63	489 85	7
16 80						7
			100 00			8
			300 00			9
21 50			22 58			10
1 08						11
421 30						12
369 90						13
				2708 35	135 43	14
32 15						15
73 28						16
		228 00				17
5437 28	310 37	13486 75	2272 91	12504 98	625 28	18
562 00						18
	562 00					19
				1469 55	73 49	20
884 20						21
	53 05					22
	132 60					23
56 37						24
	53 05					25
	52					26
	2 80					27
10 00						28
27 48						29
11 09						30
5 00						31
7 65						32
7001 07	1114 39	13486 75	2272 91	13974 53	698 77	33
7001 07	1114 39	13486 75	2272 91	13974 53	698 77	33
(✓)	(✓)	(231)	(121)	(411)	(241)	34

Boyd's Clothiers — Combined Cash Journal (Right Page)
(concluded)

PAGE *28*   PETTY CASH DISBURSEMENTS

	DAY	DESCRIPTION	VOU. NO.	TOTAL AMOUNT	031	151	
1		AMOUNTS FORWARDED					1
2	7	Postage stamps *Balance 100.00*	73	10 00		10 00	2
3	7	Messenger fee	74	3 00			3
4	12	Boy Scouts of America *87.00*	75	13 00 / 5 00		10 00	4
5	12	Lynn C. Boyd, personal use *72.00*	76	10 00	10 00		5
6	19	Advertising	77	28 00 / 6 29	10 00	10 00	6
7	19	Supplies	78	8 35		8 35	7
8	19	Miscellaneous expense	79	1 75			8
9	26	Advertising *55.61*	80	44 39 / 4 80	10 00	18 35	9
10	26	Supplies	81	9 13		9 13	10
11	26	Miscellaneous expense	82	2 90			11
12		*38.78*		61 22 / 61 22	10 00 / 10 00	27 48 / 27 48	12
13	31	Balance		38.78			13
14	31	Received in fund		61.22			14
15		Total		100.00			15

Boyd's Clothiers — Petty Cash Disbursements Record (Left Page)

ACCOUNT *First National Bank*   ACCOUNT NO. *111*

DATE		ITEM	POST. REF.	DEBIT	CREDIT	BALANCE DEBIT	BALANCE CREDIT
19-- Dec.	1	Balance	✓			12302 83	
	31		CJ48	16923 63			
	31		CJ48		18583 35	10643 11	

ACCOUNT *Petty Cash Fund*   ACCOUNT NO. *112*

DATE		ITEM	POST. REF.	DEBIT	CREDIT	BALANCE DEBIT	BALANCE CREDIT
19-- Dec.	1	Balance	✓			100 00	

ACCOUNT *Accounts Receivable*   ACCOUNT NO. *121*

DATE		ITEM	POST. REF.	DEBIT	CREDIT	BALANCE DEBIT	BALANCE CREDIT
19-- Dec.	1	Balance	✓			2965 99	
	27		CJ48	369 90			
	31		S44	2297 33			
	31		CJ48		2272 91	3360 31	

ACCOUNT *Allowance for Doubtful Accounts*   ACCOUNT NO. *012*

DATE		ITEM	POST. REF.	DEBIT	CREDIT	BALANCE DEBIT	BALANCE CREDIT
19-- Dec.	1	Balance	✓				59 22

Boyd's Clothiers — General Ledger

FOR MONTH OF *December* 19- -   PAGE 28

DISTRIBUTION OF CHARGES

618	623	624			ACCOUNT	AMOUNT	
							1
							2
		3 00 / 3 00					3
	5 00						4
	5 00	3 00					5
6 29							6
							7
	5 00	1 75 / 4 75					8
6 29 / 4 80							9
							10
11 09	5 00	2 90 / 7 65					11
11 09	5 00	7 65					12
							13
							14
							15

Boyd's Clothiers — Petty Cash Disbursements Record (Right Page)

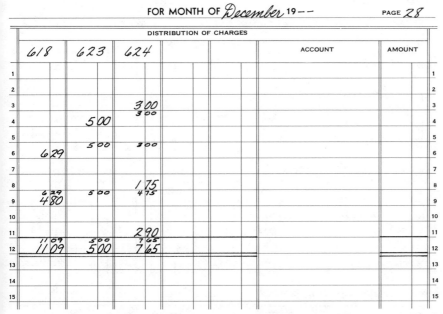

ACCOUNT *Merchandise Inventory*   ACCOUNT NO. 131

DATE	ITEM	POST. REF.	DEBIT	CREDIT	BALANCE DEBIT	BALANCE CREDIT
19-- Dec. 1	Balance	✓			2 763 40	

ACCOUNT *Prepaid Insurance*   ACCOUNT NO. 141

DATE	ITEM	POST. REF.	DEBIT	CREDIT	BALANCE DEBIT	BALANCE CREDIT
19-- Dec. 1	Balance	✓			562 60	

ACCOUNT *Supplies*   ACCOUNT NO. 151

DATE	ITEM	POST. REF.	DEBIT	CREDIT	BALANCE DEBIT	BALANCE CREDIT
19-- Dec. 1	Balance	✓			230 28	
31		CJ48	27 48		257 76	

ACCOUNT *Store Equipment*   ACCOUNT NO. 181

DATE	ITEM	POST. REF.	DEBIT	CREDIT	BALANCE DEBIT	BALANCE CREDIT
19-- Dec. 1	Balance	✓			5 031 60	
31		CJ48	562 00		5 593 60	

Boyd's Clothiers — General Ledger (*continued*)

ACCOUNT *Accumulated Depreciation—Store Equipment*   ACCOUNT NO. 018

DATE		ITEM	POST. REF.	DEBIT	CREDIT	BALANCE DEBIT	BALANCE CREDIT
19-- Dec.	1	Balance	✓				86210

ACCOUNT *Notes Payable*   ACCOUNT NO. 211

DATE		ITEM	POST. REF.	DEBIT	CREDIT	BALANCE DEBIT	BALANCE CREDIT
19-- Dec.	1	Balance	✓				300000

ACCOUNT *Accounts Payable*   ACCOUNT NO. 231

DATE		ITEM	POST. REF.	DEBIT	CREDIT	BALANCE DEBIT	BALANCE CREDIT
19-- Dec.	1	Balance	✓				757200
	31		CJ48		56200		
	31		P32		969305		
	31		CJ48	1348675			434030

ACCOUNT *Sales Tax Payable*   ACCOUNT NO. 241

DATE		ITEM	POST. REF.	DEBIT	CREDIT	BALANCE DEBIT	BALANCE CREDIT
19-- Dec.	1	Balance	✓				91214
	6		CJ47	91214		—0—	—0—
	9		CJ47	425			
	27		CJ48	108			
	31		S44		10942		
	31		CJ47		69877		80286

ACCOUNT *FICA Tax Payable*   ACCOUNT NO. 251

DATE		ITEM	POST. REF.	DEBIT	CREDIT	BALANCE DEBIT	BALANCE CREDIT
19-- Dec.	1	Balance	✓				21628
	10		CJ47	21628		—0—	—0—
	14		CJ47		5356		
	14		CJ47		5356		
	31		CJ48		5305		
	31		CJ48		5305		21322

ACCOUNT *Employees Income Tax Payable*   ACCOUNT NO. 261

DATE		ITEM	POST. REF.	DEBIT	CREDIT	BALANCE DEBIT	BALANCE CREDIT
19-- Dec.	1	Balance	✓				28440
	10		CJ47	28440		—0—	—0—
	14		CJ47		13390		
	31		CJ48		13260		26650

Boyd's Clothiers — General Ledger (*continued*)

ACCOUNT *FUTA Tax Payable*   ACCOUNT NO. 271

DATE	ITEM	POST. REF.	DEBIT	CREDIT	BALANCE DEBIT	BALANCE CREDIT
19-- Dec. 1	Balance	✓				82 96
14		CJ47		52		
31		CJ48		52		84 00

ACCOUNT *State Unemployment Tax Payable*   ACCOUNT NO. 281

DATE	ITEM	POST. REF.	DEBIT	CREDIT	BALANCE DEBIT	BALANCE CREDIT
19-- Dec. 1	Balance	✓				107 77
14		CJ47		283		
31		CJ48		280		113 40

ACCOUNT *Lynn C. Boyd, Capital*   ACCOUNT NO. 311

DATE	ITEM	POST. REF.	DEBIT	CREDIT	BALANCE DEBIT	BALANCE CREDIT
19-- Dec. 1	Balance	✓				25 635 19

ACCOUNT *Lynn C. Boyd, Drawing*   ACCOUNT NO. 031

DATE	ITEM	POST. REF.	DEBIT	CREDIT	BALANCE DEBIT	BALANCE CREDIT
19-- Dec. 1	Balance	✓			22 405 80	
21		CJ48	1 000 00			
31		CJ48	10 00		23 415 80	

ACCOUNT *Sales*   ACCOUNT NO. 411

DATE	ITEM	POST. REF.	DEBIT	CREDIT	BALANCE DEBIT	BALANCE CREDIT
19-- Dec. 1	Balance	✓				18 658 121
31		S44		2 187 91		
31		CJ48		13 974 53		20 274 365

ACCOUNT *Sales Returns and Allowances*   ACCOUNT NO. 041

DATE	ITEM	POST. REF.	DEBIT	CREDIT	BALANCE DEBIT	BALANCE CREDIT
19-- Dec. 1	Balance	✓			2 854 85	
9		CJ47	84 95			
27		CJ48	21 50		2 961 30	

Boyd's Clothiers — General Ledger (*continued*)

ACCOUNT *Purchases*   ACCOUNT NO. 511

DATE	ITEM	POST. REF.	DEBIT	CREDIT	BALANCE DEBIT	BALANCE CREDIT
19-- Dec. 1	Balance	✓			11851272	
2		CJ47	5318			
31		P32	969305		12825895	

ACCOUNT *Purchases Returns and Allowances*   ACCOUNT NO. 051

DATE	ITEM	POST. REF.	DEBIT	CREDIT	BALANCE DEBIT	BALANCE CREDIT
19-- Dec. 1	Balance	✓				165510
20		CJ48		6600		172110

ACCOUNT *Purchases Discount*   ACCOUNT NO. 052

DATE	ITEM	POST. REF.	DEBIT	CREDIT	BALANCE DEBIT	BALANCE CREDIT
19-- Dec. 1	Balance	✓				692204
31		CJ48		76750		768954

ACCOUNT *Rent Expense*   ACCOUNT NO. 611

DATE	ITEM	POST. REF.	DEBIT	CREDIT	BALANCE DEBIT	BALANCE CREDIT
19-- Dec. 1	Balance	✓			770000	
2		CJ47	70000		840000	

ACCOUNT *Salaries and Commissions Expense*   ACCOUNT NO. 613

DATE	ITEM	POST. REF.	DEBIT	CREDIT	BALANCE DEBIT	BALANCE CREDIT
19-- Dec. 1	Balance	✓			1953950	
14		CJ47	89270			
31		CJ48	88420		2131640	

ACCOUNT *Payroll Taxes Expense*   ACCOUNT NO. 614

DATE	ITEM	POST. REF.	DEBIT	CREDIT	BALANCE DEBIT	BALANCE CREDIT
19-- Dec. 1	Balance	✓			170330	
14		CJ47	5691			
31		CJ48	5637		181658	

ACCOUNT *Heating and Lighting Expense*   ACCOUNT NO. 615

DATE	ITEM	POST. REF.	DEBIT	CREDIT	BALANCE DEBIT	BALANCE CREDIT
19-- Dec. 1	Balance	✓			68636	
28		CJ48	7328		75964	

Boyd's Clothiers — General Ledger (*continued*)

ACCOUNT *Telephone Expense*   ACCOUNT NO. *617*

DATE		ITEM	POST. REF.	DEBIT	CREDIT	BALANCE DEBIT	BALANCE CREDIT
19-- Dec.	1	Balance	✓			340 15	
	28		CJ48	32 15		372 30	

ACCOUNT *Advertising Expense*   ACCOUNT NO. *618*

DATE		ITEM	POST. REF.	DEBIT	CREDIT	BALANCE DEBIT	BALANCE CREDIT
19-- Dec.	1	Balance	✓			8219 82	
	6		CJ47	61 04			
	27		CJ48	421 30			
	31		CJ48	11 09		8713 25	

ACCOUNT *Bank Credit Card Expense*   ACCOUNT NO. *619*

DATE		ITEM	POST. REF.	DEBIT	CREDIT	BALANCE DEBIT	BALANCE CREDIT
19-- Dec.	1	Balance	✓			2179 92	
	4		CJ47	235 42		2415 34	

ACCOUNT *Charitable Contributions Expense*   ACCOUNT NO. *623*

DATE		ITEM	POST. REF.	DEBIT	CREDIT	BALANCE DEBIT	BALANCE CREDIT
19-- Dec.	1	Balance	✓			345 00	
	31		CJ48	5 00		350 00	

ACCOUNT *Miscellaneous Expense*   ACCOUNT NO. *624*

DATE		ITEM	POST. REF.	DEBIT	CREDIT	BALANCE DEBIT	BALANCE CREDIT
19-- Dec.	1	Balance	✓			461 20	
	23		CJ48	16 80			
	31		CJ48	7 65		485 65	

ACCOUNT *Interest Expense*   ACCOUNT NO. *711*

DATE		ITEM	POST. REF.	DEBIT	CREDIT	BALANCE DEBIT	BALANCE CREDIT
19-- Dec.	1	Balance	✓			116 09	

Boyd's Clothiers — General Ledger (*concluded*)

NAME *J. J. Anders*
ADDRESS *11939 Rocky, St. Louis, MO 63141*

DATE	ITEM	POST. REF.	DEBIT	CREDIT	BALANCE
19-- Dec. 5		S257B	89 38		89 38

NAME *J. E. Buelt*
ADDRESS *9140 Fox Estates, St. Louis, MO 63126*

DATE	ITEM	POST. REF.	DEBIT	CREDIT	BALANCE
19-- Dec. 1	Dr. Balance	✓			614 86
11		C		300 00	314 86

NAME *J. L. Burnett*
ADDRESS *15 Forester, St. Louis, MO 63011*

DATE	ITEM	POST. REF.	DEBIT	CREDIT	BALANCE
19-- Dec. 5		S235C	564 85		564 85

NAME *L. V. Freeman*
ADDRESS *7362 S. Yorkshire, St. Louis, MO 63126*

DATE	ITEM	POST. REF.	DEBIT	CREDIT	BALANCE
19-- Dec. 1	Dr. Balance	✓			432 40
11		C		200 00	232 40
24		S256C	18 85		251 25

NAME *S. W. Novak*
ADDRESS *216 Hawkesbury, St. Louis, MO 63135*

DATE	ITEM	POST. REF.	DEBIT	CREDIT	BALANCE
19-- Dec. 1	Dr. Balance	✓			369 90
17		C		369 90	—0—
27	N S F	✓	369 90		369 90

NAME *E. E. Palmer*
ADDRESS *1129 Mackinac, St. Louis, MO 63141*

DATE	ITEM	POST. REF.	DEBIT	CREDIT	BALANCE
19-- Dec. 1	Dr. Balance	✓			112 15
18		S246D	71 56		183 71

Boyd's Clothiers — Accounts Receivable Ledger

NAME *W. R. Price*

ADDRESS *1629 Rathford Court, St. Louis, MO 63141*

DATE		ITEM	POST. REF.	DEBIT	CREDIT	BALANCE
19-- Dec.	1	Dr. Balance	✓			142 19
	18		S277a	161 82		304 01
	26		C		100 00	204 01
	27		CM12		22 58	181 43

NAME *C. W. Reed*

ADDRESS *761 Cella, St. Louis, MO 63124*

DATE		ITEM	POST. REF.	DEBIT	CREDIT	BALANCE
19-- Dec.	1	Dr. Balance	✓			314 06
	24		S249D	200 99		515 05
	26		C		300 00	215 05

NAME *K. E. Vivian*

ADDRESS *1830 Patterson Rd., Florissant, MO 63031*

DATE		ITEM	POST. REF.	DEBIT	CREDIT	BALANCE
19-- Dec.	1	Dr. Balance	✓			82 11
	11		C		82 11	—0—
	18		S239C	346 40		346 40

NAME *D. P. Walsh*

ADDRESS *113 Grether, St. Louis, MO 63135*

DATE		ITEM	POST. REF.	DEBIT	CREDIT	BALANCE
19-- Dec.	1	Dr. Balance	✓			317 23
	4		C		317 23	—0—
	5		S271a	454 01		454 01
	24		S262B	19 48		473 49

NAME *C. D. Williams*

ADDRESS *617 Rebecca, St. Charles, MO 63301*

DATE		ITEM	POST. REF.	DEBIT	CREDIT	BALANCE
19-- Dec.	10		S243D	258 35		258 35

Boyd's Clothiers — Accounts Receivable Ledger (*continued*)

NAME *C. E. Wuller*

ADDRESS *10711 St. Mathew Ln., St. Ann, MO 63074*

DATE	ITEM	POST. REF.	DEBIT	CREDIT	BALANCE
19-- Dec. 1	Dr. Balance	✓			36757
17		C		36757	-0-

NAME *J. F. Yager*

ADDRESS *5 Brookston Ct., Kirkwood, MO 63122*

DATE	ITEM	POST. REF.	DEBIT	CREDIT	BALANCE
19-- Dec. 1	Dr. Balance	✓			21352
6		82598	11164		32516
17		C		21352	11164

Boyd's Clothiers — Accounts Receivable Ledger (concluded)

NAME *Aris Glove Co.*

ADDRESS *10 East 38th. St., New York, NY 10016*

DATE	ITEM	POST. REF.	DEBIT	CREDIT	BALANCE
19-- Dec. 1	Cr. Balance	✓			33000
2		Ck869	33000		-0-
13	12/10, n/30	P208		41250	41250
20		CB291	6600		34650

NAME *Brown Shoe Co.*

ADDRESS *8300 Maryland Ave., St. Louis, MO 63105*

DATE	ITEM	POST. REF.	DEBIT	CREDIT	BALANCE
19-- Dec. 1	Cr. Balance	✓			47000
5		Ck870	46060		
5	Discount		940		-0-
31		P212		70500	70500

NAME *Damon, Inc.*

ADDRESS *16 E. 34th St., New York, NY 10016*

DATE	ITEM	POST. REF.	DEBIT	CREDIT	BALANCE
19-- Dec. 1	Cr. Balance	✓			46000
5		Ck871	43240		
5	Discount		2760		-0-
6	12/4 – 6/10, n/30	P207		115000	115000
12		Ck882	108100		
12	Discount		6900		-0-

Boyd's Clothiers — Accounts Payable Ledger

NAME *Daniel Hays Co.*
ADDRESS *Johnstown, N.Y. 12095*

DATE		ITEM	POST. REF.	DEBIT	CREDIT	BALANCE
19-- Dec.	1	Cr. Balance	✓			68400
	3	11/30 - n/30	P204		22800	91200
	9		Ck878	68400		22800
	28		Ck891	22800		—0—

NAME *El Jay Co.*
ADDRESS *411 Anderson, Fairview, N.J. 07022*

DATE		ITEM	POST. REF.	DEBIT	CREDIT	BALANCE
19-- Dec.	1	Cr. Balance	✓			226000
	5		Ck872	207920		
	5	Discount		18080		—0—
	13	12/10 - 8/10, n/30	P209		169500	169500
	19		Ck884	155940		
	19	Discount		13560		—0—
	31	12/26 - 8/10, n/30	P213		67800	67800

NAME *Hanes Corporation*
ADDRESS *Winston-Salem, NC 27102*

DATE		ITEM	POST. REF.	DEBIT	CREDIT	BALANCE
19-- Dec.	3	11/30 - 8/10 EOM	P205		74400	74400
	9		Ck879	68448		
	9	Discount		5952		—0—
	31	12/27 - 8/10 EOM	P214		14880	14880

NAME *Huk-a-Poo, Inc.*
ADDRESS *411 Broadway, New York, N.Y. 10012*

DATE		ITEM	POST. REF.	DEBIT	CREDIT	BALANCE
19-- Dec.	13	12/11 - 8/10, n/30	P210		54375	54375
	19		Ck885	50025		
	19	Discount		4350		—0—

Boyd's Clothiers — Accounts Payable Ledger (*continued*)

NAME *Mary Neuman Co.*
ADDRESS *9 W. 57th St., New York, N.Y. 10019*

DATE	ITEM	POST. REF.	DEBIT	CREDIT	BALANCE
19-- Dec. 1	Cr. Balance	✓			80000
5		Ck873	78400		
5	Discount		1600		—0—
31		P215		60000	60000

NAME *Julius Resnick, Inc.*
ADDRESS *46 E. 32d St., New York, N.Y. 10016*

DATE	ITEM	POST. REF.	DEBIT	CREDIT	BALANCE
19-- Dec. 3	11/30–3/10 EOM	P206		148800	148800
9		Ck880	144336		
9	Discount		4464		—0—

NAME *Schoeneman, Inc.*
ADDRESS *Box 17, Owings Mills, MD 21117*

DATE	ITEM	POST. REF.	DEBIT	CREDIT	BALANCE
19-- Dec. 1	Cr. Balance	✓			120000
5		Ck874	112800		
5	Discount		7200		—0—

NAME *Jacob Siegel Co.*
ADDRESS *4725 N. Broad St., Philadelphia, PA 19141*

DATE	ITEM	POST. REF.	DEBIT	CREDIT	BALANCE
19-- Dec. 30	12/27–6/10, n/30	P211		130000	130000

NAME *Smart Pants, Inc.*
ADDRESS *1407 Broadway, New York, N.Y. 10012*

DATE	ITEM	POST. REF.	DEBIT	CREDIT	BALANCE
19-- Dec. 1	Cr. Balance	✓			136800
5		Ck875	125856		
5	Discount		10944		—0—

Boyd's Clothiers — Accounts Payable Ledger (*continued*)

NAME *Webster, Safe & Lock Co.*
ADDRESS *916 Washington Ave., St. Louis, MO 63101*

DATE	ITEM	POST. REF.	DEBIT	CREDIT	BALANCE
19-- Dec. 31	12/30 – 2/30, n/60	CJ48		56200	56200

Boyd's Clothiers — Accounts Payable Ledger *(concluded)*

Boyd's Clothiers
Trial Balance

Account	Acct. No.	November 30, 19— Dr. Balance	November 30, 19— Cr. Balance	December 31, 19— Dr. Balance	December 31, 19— Cr. Balance
First National Bank	111	1230283		1064311	
Petty Cash Fund	112	10000		10000	
Accounts Receivable	121	296599		336031	
Allow. for Doubt. Accts.	012		5922		5922
Merchandise Inventory	131	2763240		2763240	
Prepaid Insurance	141	56260		56260	
Supplies	151	23028		25776	
Store Equipment	181	503160		559360	
Accum. Depr.–Store Equip.	018		86210		86210
Notes Payable	211		300000		300000
Accounts Payable	231		757200		434030
Sales Tax Payable	241		91214		80286
FICA Tax Payable	251		21628		21322
Employees' Inc. Tax Pay.	261		28440		26650
FUTA Tax Payable	271		8296		8400
State Unemp. Tax Pay.	281		10777		11340
Lynn C. Boyd, Capital	311		2563519		2563519
Lynn C. Boyd, Drawing	031	2240580		2341580	
Sales	411		18658121		20274365
Sales Ret. and Allow.	041	285485		296130	
Purchases	511	11851272		12825895	
Pur. Ret. and Allow.	051		165510		172110
Purchases Discount	052		692204		768954
Rent Expense	611	770000		840000	
Sal. and Comm. Exp.	613	1953950		2131640	
Payroll Taxes Expense	614	170330		181658	
Heating and Light Exp.	615	68636		75964	
Telephone Expense	617	34015		37230	
Advertising Expense	618	821982		871325	
Bank Credit Card Exp.	619	217992		241534	
Charitable Cont. Exp.	623	34500		35000	
Miscellaneous Exp.	624	46120		48565	
Interest Expense	711	11609		11609	
		23389041	23389041	24753108	24753108

Boyd's Clothiers — Trial Balance

Boyd's Clothiers
Schedule of Accounts Receivable

	Nov. 30, 19-	Dec. 31, 19-
J. J. Anders		89 38
J. E. Buelt	614 86	314 86
J. L. Burnett		564 85
L. V. Freeman	432 40	251 25
S. W. Novak	369 90	369 90
E. E. Palmer	112 15	183 71
W. P. Price	142 19	181 43
C. W. Reed	314 06	215 05
K. E. Vivian	82 11	346 40
D. P. Walsh	317 23	473 49
R. D. Williams		258 35
C. E. Wuller	367 57	
J. F. Yager	213 52	111 64
	2966 99	3360 31

Boyd's Clothiers — Schedule of Accounts Receivable

Boyd's Clothiers
Schedule of Accounts Payable

	Nov. 30, 19-	Dec. 31, 19-
Aris Glove Co.	330 00	346 50
Brown Shoe Co.	470 00	705 00
Damon, Inc.	460 00	
El Jay Co.	2260 00	678 00
Hanes Corporation		148 80
Daniel Hays Co.	684 00	
Marx Neuman Co.	800 00	600 00
Schoeneman, Inc.	1200 00	
Jacob Siegel Co.		1300 00
Smart Pants, Inc.	1368 00	
Webster Safe & Lock Co.		562 00
	7572 00	4340 30

Boyd's Clothiers — Schedule of Accounts Payable

Report No. 8-2

Complete Report No. 8-2 in the study assignments and submit your working papers to the instructor for approval. After completing this report, continue with the textbook discussion in Chapter 9 until the next report is required.

Chapter 9

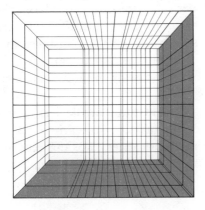

THE PERIODIC SUMMARY

One of the major reasons for keeping accounting records is to accumulate information that will make it possible to prepare periodic summaries of both **(1)** the revenue and expenses of the business during a specified period and **(2)** the assets, liabilities, and owner's equity of the business at a specified date. A trial balance of the general ledger accounts will provide most of the information that is required for these summaries (the income statement and the balance sheet). However, the trial balance does not supply the data in a form that is easily interpreted, nor does it reflect changes in the accounting elements that have not been represented by ordinary business transactions. Therefore, at the end of a fiscal period it is necessary, first, to determine the kind and amounts of changes that the accounts do not reflect and to adjust the accounts accordingly and, second, to recast the information into the form of an income statement and a balance sheet. These two steps are often referred to as "the periodic summary."

END-OF-PERIOD WORK SHEET

It has already been mentioned that an end-of-period work sheet is a device that assists the accountant in three ways. It facilitates **(1)** the preparing of the financial statements, **(2)** the making of needed adjustments in the accounts, and **(3)** the closing of the temporary owner's equity accounts.

In most cases the accountant is under some pressure to produce the income statement and the balance sheet as soon as possible after the period has ended. The end-of-period work sheet is of greatest assistance in helping the accountant meet this need for promptness. The help that the work sheet gives in making adjustments and in closing the accounts is secondary in importance.

Work sheets are not financial statements; they are devices used to assist the accountant in performing certain tasks. Ordinarily it is only the accountant who uses (or even sees) a work sheet. For this reason a work sheet (sometimes called a *working trial balance*) is usually prepared in pencil.

A work sheet for a retail store

While an end-of-period work sheet can be in any one of several forms, a common and widely used arrangement involves ten amount columns. The amount columns are used in pairs. The first pair of amount columns is for the trial balance. The data to be recorded consist of the name, number, and debit or credit balance of each account. Debit balances should be entered in the left-hand column and credit balances in the right-hand column. The second pair of amount columns is used to record needed end-of-period adjustments. The third pair of amount columns is used to show the account balances as adjusted. This pair of amount columns is headed "Adjusted Trial Balance" because its purpose is to show that the debit and credit account balances as adjusted are equal in amount. The fourth pair of amount columns is for the adjusted balances of the expense and revenue accounts. This pair of columns is headed "Income Statement" since the amounts shown will be reported in that statement. The fifth, and last, pair of amount columns is headed "Balance Sheet" and shows the adjusted account balances that will be reported in that statement.

To illustrate the preparation and use of the end-of-period work sheet, the example of the accounts of Boyd's Clothiers will be continued. The journals and ledgers for this business for the month of December were reproduced in the preceding chapter. In this chapter the income statement for the year and the balance sheet at the end of the year will be reproduced, showing the use of a work sheet as a device for summarizing the data to be presented in those statements.

The work sheet for Boyd's Clothiers

The end-of-year work sheet for this business is reproduced on pages 230 and 231. Following is a description and discussion of the steps that were followed in the preparation of this work sheet. Each step should be studied carefully with frequent reference to the work sheet itself.

Trial Balance Columns. The trial balance of the general ledger accounts as of December 31 was entered in the first pair of amount columns. This trial balance is the same as the one shown on page 225 except that all of the account titles were included in the work sheet list even though certain of the accounts had no balances at this point.

The Trial Balance Debit and Credit columns were totaled. The totals should be equal. If not, the cause of any discrepancy must be found and corrected before the preparation of the work sheet can proceed.

Adjustments Columns. The second pair of amount columns on the work sheet was used to record certain entries that were necessary to reflect various changes that had occurred during the year in some of the accounting elements. In this case, adjustments were needed: **(1)** to remove the amount of the beginning-of-year merchandise inventory and to record the amount of the end-of-year inventory; **(2)** to record the amount of interest expense incurred but not paid; **(3)** to record the amount of bank credit card expense for December that will not be deducted from the bank account until early in the following month; **(4)** to record the portions of prepaid insurance expired and of supplies used during the year; **(5)** to record the estimated depreciation expense for the year; and **(6)** to record the estimated amount of expected losses from uncollectible accounts.

Eight complete entries were made in the Adjustments columns to reflect these changes. When an account was debited, the amount was entered on the same horizontal line as the name of the account and in the Adjustments Debit column. Amounts credited were entered, of course, in the Credit column. Each such entry made on the work sheet was identified by a small letter in parentheses to facilitate cross-reference. Following is an explanation of each of the entries:

Entry (a): In order to remove the amount of the beginning inventory of merchandise from the asset account and at the same time to include it in the determination of net income for the current year, Expense and Revenue Summary, Account No. 321, was debited, and Merchandise Inventory, Account No. 131, was credited for $27,632.40. This amount was the calculated cost of the inventory at the end of the preceding year (the beginning of the year under consideration). The amount had been in the merchandise inventory account as a debit since the accounts were adjusted as of December 31 a year ago.

Entry (b): This entry recorded the calculated cost of the merchandise on hand December 31 — often referred to as the year-end inventory. The calculation was based on a physical count of the merchandise in stock at the close of the year. The cost of the merchandise in stock was recorded by debiting Merchandise Inventory, Account No. 131, and by crediting Expense and Revenue Summary, Account No. 321, for $25,074.05.

Boyle's Clothiers
Work Sheet
For the Year Ended December 31, 19—

Line	Account	Acct. No.	Trial Balance Debit	Trial Balance Credit	Adjustments Debit	Adjustments Credit	Adj. Trial Balance Debit	Adj. Trial Balance Credit	Income Statement Debit	Income Statement Credit	Balance Sheet Debit	Balance Sheet Credit
1	First National Bank	111	10643.11				10643.11				10643.11	
2	Petty Cash Fund	112	100.00				100.00				100.00	
3	Accounts Receivable	121	3360.31				3360.31				3360.31	
4	Allowance for Doubtful Accts.	012		59.22		(d) 250.98		310.20				310.20
5	Merchandise Inventory	131	27632.40		(a) 25074.05	(a) 27632.40	25074.05				25074.05	
6	Prepaid Insurance	141	562.60			(c) 281.30	281.30				281.30	
7	Supplies	151	257.76			(b) 197.76	60.00				60.00	
8	Store Equipment	181	5593.60				5593.60				5593.60	
9	Accum. Deprec.—Store Equip.	018		862.10		(f) 503.16		1365.26				1365.26
10	Notes Payable	211		3000.00				3000.00				3000.00
11	Accrued Interest Payable	221				(e) 37.33		37.33				37.33
12	Accounts Payable	231		4340.30				4340.30				4340.30
13	Sales Tax Payable	241		802.86				802.86				802.86
14	FICA Tax Payable	251		213.22				213.22				213.22
15	Employees Income Tax Pay.	261		266.50				266.50				266.50
16	F.U.T. Tax Payable	271		84.00				84.00				84.00
17	State Unemployment Tax Pay.	281		113.40				113.40				113.40
18	Accrued Bank Credit Card Exp. Pay.	291				(d) 209.62		209.62				209.62
19	Lynn C. Boyle, Capital	311		25635.19				25635.19				25635.19
20	Lynn C. Boyle, Drawing	031	23415.80				23415.80				23415.80	
21	Exp. and Rev. Summary	321			(a) 27632.40	(a) 25074.05	27632.40	25074.05	27632.40	25074.05		
22	Sales	411		202743.65				202743.65		202743.65		
23	Sales Returns and Allow.	044	2961.30				2961.30		2961.30			
24	Purchases	511	128258.95				128258.95		128258.95			
25	Purchases Returns and Allow.	051		1721.10				1721.10		1721.10		
26	Purchases Discount	052		7689.54				7689.54		7689.54		
27	Rent Expense	611	8400.00				8400.00		8400.00			
28	Depreciation Expense	612			(f) 503.16		503.16		503.16			
29	Sal. and Commissions Exp.	613	21316.40				21316.40		21316.40			

Boyd's Clothiers — Ten Column Work Sheet

	Acct.										
1	Payroll Taxes Expense	614	181658			181658			181658		
2	Heating and Lighting Exp.	615	75964			75964			75964		
3	Supplies Expense	616		(4) 19776		19776			19776		
4	Telephone Expense	617	37230			37230			37230		
5	Advertising Expense	618	871325			871325			871325		
6	Bank Credit Card Expense	619	241534	(a) 20962		262496			262496		
7	Uncollectible Accounts Exp.	621		(a) 25098		25098			25098		
8	Insurance Expense	622		(a) 28130		28130			28130		
9	Charitable Contributions Exp.	623	35000			35000			35000		
10	Miscellaneous Expense	624	48565			48565			48565		
11	Interest Expense	711	11609	(a) 3733		15342			15342		
12			24753108	5418660	5418660	27360622	27360622	20507805	23722834	6852817	3637788
13	Net Income								3215029		3215029
14									23722834	23722834	6852817	6852817

Entry (*c*): This entry recorded the accrued interest expense that had been incurred but not paid by debiting Interest Expense, Account No. 711, and by crediting Accrued Interest Payable, Account No. 221, for $37.33. The December 31 trial balance shows that Notes Payable had a credit balance of $3,000. This related to an 8 percent, 6-month note dated November 5. From November 5 to December 31 was 56 days. Interest at the rate of 8 percent per year on $3,000 for 56 days is $37.33.

Entry (*d*): This entry recorded the expense of the deduction that will be made by the bank during January for BankAmericard and Master Charge vouchers deposited during December. These amounted to $6,987.27. The bank will deduct 3 percent of this amount from the checking account. Since the amount, $209.62 (3 percent of $6,987.27), is really an expense for the year just ended, this adjustment gets it into the calculation of the net income for the past year. The adjustment was recorded by a debit to Bank Credit Card Expense, Account No. 619, and a credit to Accrued Bank Credit Card Expense, Account No. 291.

Entry (*e*): This entry recorded the insurance expense for the year by debiting Insurance Expense, Account No. 622, and by crediting Prepaid Insurance, Account No. 141, for $281.30. The December 31 trial balance shows that Prepaid Insurance had a debit balance of $562.60. This amount was the cost of a two-year policy dated January 2 of the year under consideration. By December 31 one year had elapsed and, thus, one half of the premium paid had become an expense.

Entry (*f*): This entry recorded the calculated cost of the supplies used during the year by debiting Supplies Expense, Account No. 616, and by crediting Supplies, Account No. 151, for $197.76. The December 31 trial balance shows that Supplies had a debit balance of $257.76. This amount was the sum of the cost of any supplies on hand at the start of the year, plus the cost of supplies purchased during the year. A physical count of the supplies on hand December 31 was made and the cost determined to be $60. Thus, supplies that cost $197.76 ($257.76 − $60) had been used during the year.

Entry (*g*): This entry recorded the calculated depreciation expense for the year by debiting Depreciation Expense, Account No. 612, and by crediting Accumulated Depreciation — Store Equipment, Account No. 018, for $503.16. The December 31 trial balance shows that Store Equipment had a debit balance of $5,593.60. This balance represented the $5,031.60 cost of various items of property that had been owned the entire year plus the $562 cost of the safe that was purchased on December 31. Ms. Boyd follows the policy of not calculating any depreciation on assets that have been owned for less than a month. Thus, depreciation expense for the year on store equipment relates to property that had been owned for the entire year. Its cost was $5,031.60. This equipment is being depreciated at the rate of 10 percent a year. Ten percent of $5,031.60 is $503.16.

Entry (h): This entry recorded the estimated uncollectible accounts expense for the year by debiting Uncollectible Accounts Expense, Account No. 621, and by crediting Allowance for Doubtful Accounts, Account No. 012, for $250.98. Guided by past experience, Ms. Boyd estimated that uncollectible accounts losses will be approximately one percent of the total sales on account for the year. Investigation of the records revealed that such sales amounted to $25,098.13. One percent of this amount is $250.98.

After making the required entries in the Adjustments columns of the work sheet, the columns were totaled to prove the equality of the debit and credit entries.

Adjusted Trial Balance Columns. The third pair of amount columns of the work sheet was used for the *adjusted trial balance*. To determine the balance of each account after making the required adjustments, it was necessary to take into consideration the amounts recorded in the first two pairs of amount columns. When an account balance was not affected by entries in the Adjustments columns, the amount in the Trial Balance columns was extended directly to the Adjusted Trial Balance columns.

When an account balance was affected by an entry in the Adjustments columns, the balance recorded in the Trial Balance columns was increased or decreased, as the case might be, by the amount of the adjusting entry. For example, Accumulated Depreciation — Store Equipment was listed in the Trial Balance Credit column as $862.10. Since there was an entry of $503.16 in the Adjustments Credit column, the amount extended to the Adjusted Trial Balance Credit column was found by addition to be $1,365.26 ($862.10 + $503.16). Prepaid Insurance was listed in the Trial Balance Debit column as $562.60. Since there was an entry of $281.30 in the Adjustments Credit column, the amount to be extended to the Adjusted Trial Balance Debit column was found by subtraction to be $281.30 ($562.60 − $281.30).

There is one exception to the procedure just described that relates to the debit and the credit on the line for Expense and Revenue Summary, Account No. 321, in the Adjustments columns. While the $2,558.35 excess of the $27,632.40 debit (the amount of the beginning-of-year merchandise inventory) over the $25,074.05 credit (the amount of the end-of-year merchandise inventory) could be extended to the Adjusted Trial Balance Debit column, it is better to extend both the debit and the credit amounts into the Adjusted Trial Balance columns. The reason is that both amounts are used in the preparation of the income statement and, accordingly, it is helpful to have both amounts appear in the Income Statement columns. Therefore, both amounts are shown in the Adjusted Trial Balance columns.

The Adjusted Trial Balance columns were totaled to prove the equality of the debits and credits.

Income Statement Columns. The fourth pair of amount columns of the work sheet was used to show the amounts that will be reported in the income statement. The manner of extending the debit and credit amounts on the line for Expense and Revenue Summary was mentioned previously. The amounts for sales, purchases returns and allowances, and purchases discount were extended to the Income Statement Credit column. The amounts for sales returns and allowances, purchases, and all of the expenses were extended to the Income Statement Debit column.

The Income Statement columns were totaled. The difference between the totals of these columns is the amount of the increase or the decrease in owner's equity due to net income or net loss during the accounting period. If the total of the credits exceeds the total of the debits, the difference represents the increase in owner's equity due to net income; if the total of the debits exceeds the total of the credits, the difference represents the decrease in owner's equity due to net loss.

Reference to the Income Statement columns of Boyd's Clothiers work sheet will show that the total of the credits amounted to $237,228.34 and the total of the debits amounted to $205,078.05. The difference, amounting to $32,150.29, was the amount of the net income for the year.

Balance Sheet Columns. The fifth pair of amount columns of the work sheet was used to show the amounts that will be reported in the balance sheet. The Balance Sheet columns were totaled. The difference between the totals of these columns also is the amount of the net income or the net loss for the accounting period. If the total of the debits exceeds the total of the credits, the difference represents a net income for the accounting period; if the total of the credits exceeds the total of the debits, the difference represents a net loss for the period. This difference should be the same as the difference between the totals of the Income Statement columns.

Reference to the Balance Sheet columns of the work sheet will show that the total of the debits amounted to $68,528.17 and the total of the credits amounted to $36,377.88. The difference of $32,150.29 represented the amount of the net income for the year.

Completing the Work Sheet. The difference between the totals of the Income Statement columns and the totals of the Balance Sheet columns should be recorded on the next horizontal line below the totals. If the difference represents net income, it should be so designated and recorded in the Income Statement Debit and in the Balance Sheet Credit columns. If, instead, a net loss has been the result, the amount should be so designated and entered in the Income Statement Credit and in the Balance Sheet

Debit columns. Finally, the totals of the Income Statement and Balance Sheet columns, after the net income (or net loss) has been recorded, are entered, and a double line is ruled immediately below the totals.

Proving the Work Sheet. The work sheet provides proof of the arithmetical accuracy of the data that it summarizes. The totals of the Trial Balance columns, the Adjustments columns, and the Adjusted Trial Balance columns must be equal. The amount of the difference between the totals of the Income Statement columns must be exactly the same as the amount of the difference between the totals of the Balance Sheet columns.

The reason why the same amount must be inserted to cause both the Income Statement columns and the Balance Sheet columns to be in balance was mentioned in Chapter 5. Stated slightly differently, the explanation is found in the basic difference between the balance sheet accounts and the income statement accounts, and in an understanding of the real nature of net income (or net loss). The reality of net income is that the assets have increased, or that the liabilities have decreased, or that some combination of both events has taken place during a period of time. Day by day most of these changes have been recorded in the asset and liability accounts in order that they may be kept up to date. However, the effect of the changes on the owner's equity element is not recorded in the permanent owner's equity account. Instead, the changes are recorded in the temporary owner's equity accounts — the revenue and expense accounts.

Thus, at the end of the period after the accounts have been adjusted, each of the asset and liability accounts reflects the amount of that element *at the end of the period*. If, however, there have been no capital investments during the period and any withdrawals have been charged to a drawing account, the balance of the owner's capital account is the amount of the equity *at the beginning of the period*. (All of the changes in owner's equity are shown in the revenue and expense accounts and in the drawing account.)

As applied to the work sheet, this must mean that the Balance Sheet column totals are out of balance by the amount of the change in owner's equity that is due to net income or net loss for the period involved. If there was net income, the assets, in total, are either that much larger, or the liabilities are that much smaller, or some combination of such changes has resulted. In other words, the asset and liability accounts reflect the net income of the period, but the owner's capital account at this point does not. It is only after the temporary accounts are closed at the end of the period and the amount of the net income for the period has been transferred to the owner's capital account that the latter account reflects the net income of the period.

The owner's capital account lacks two things to bring its balance up to date (as are the balances of the asset and liability accounts): **(1)** the decrease due to any withdrawals during the period which is reflected in the debit balance of the drawing account and **(2)** the increase due to any net income for the period. On the work sheet the debit balance of the drawing account is extended to the Balance Sheet Debit column. Thus, all that is needed to cause the Balance Sheet columns to be equal is the amount of the net income for the year — the same amount that is the difference between the totals of the Income Statement columns.

<table>
<tr><td>

Report No. 9-1

</td><td>

Complete Report No. 9-1 in the study assignments and submit your working papers to the instructor for approval. After completing the report, continue with the following textbook discussion until the next report is required.

</td></tr>
</table>

THE FINANCIAL STATEMENTS

The financial statements usually consist of **(1)** an income statement and **(2)** a balance sheet. The purpose of an income statement is to summarize the results of operations during an accounting period. The income statement provides information as to the sources of revenue, types of expenses, and the amount of the net income or the net loss for the period. The purpose of a balance sheet is to provide information as to the status of a business at a specified date. The balance sheet shows the kinds and amounts of assets and liabilities and the owner's equity in the business at a specified point in time — usually at the close of business on the last day of the accounting period.

The income statement

A formal statement of the results of the operation of a business during an accounting period is called an *income statement*. Other titles commonly used for this statement include *profit and loss statement, income and expense statement, revenue and expense statement, operating statement,* and *report of earnings.* Whatever the title, the purpose of the statement or report is to show the types and amounts of revenue and expenses that the business had during the period involved, and the resulting net income or net loss for this accounting period.

Importance of the Income Statement. The income statement is now generally considered to be the most important financial statement of a business. A business cannot exist indefinitely unless it has profit or net income. The income statement is essentially a "report card" of the enterprise. The statement provides a basis for judging the overall effectiveness of the management. Decisions as to whether to continue a business, to expand it, or to contract it are often based upon the results as reported in the income statement. Actual and potential creditors are interested in income statements because one of the best reasons for extending credit or for making a loan is that the business is profitable.

Various government agencies are interested in income statements of businesses for a variety of reasons. Regulatory bodies are concerned with the earnings of the enterprises they regulate, because a part of the regulation usually relates to the prices, rates, or fares that may be charged. If the enterprise is either exceptionally profitable or unprofitable, some change in the allowed prices or rates may be needed. Income tax authorities — federal, state, and local — have an interest in business income statements. Net income determination for tax purposes differs somewhat from the calculation of net income for other purposes, but, for a variety of reasons, the tax authorities are interested in both sets of calculations.

Form of the Income Statement. The form of the income statement depends, in part, upon the type of business. For merchandising businesses, the so-called "ladder type" is commonly used. This name is applied because the final net income is calculated on a step-by-step basis. The amount of gross sales is shown first with sales returns and allowances deducted. The difference is *net sales*. Cost of goods sold is next subtracted to arrive at *gross margin* (sometimes called *gross profit*). The portion of the statement down to this point is sometimes called the "trading section." Operating expenses are next listed, and the total of their amounts is subtracted to arrive at the amount of the *operating income*. Finally, the amounts of any "other" revenue are added and any "other" expenses are subtracted to arrive at the final amount of net income (or net loss).

It is essential that the statement be properly headed. The name of the business (or of the individual if it is a professional practice or if the business is operated in the owner's name) should be shown first. The name of the statement is then shown followed by the period of time that the statement covers. It is common practice to state this as, for example, "For the Year Ended December 31, 1977" (or whatever the period and ending date happen to be).

The income statement presented to the owner (or owners) of a business, and to potential creditors or other interested parties is usually in typewritten form. Very often, however, the accountant prepares the original statement in pencil or ink on ruled paper. This is used by the typist in preparing typewritten copies. The income statement for Boyd's Clothiers

BOYD'S CLOTHIERS

Income Statement

For the Year Ended December 31, 19--

Operating revenue:			
Sales......................................			$202,743.65
Less sales returns and allowances....			2,961.30
Net sales..............................			$199,782.35
Cost of goods sold:			
Merchandise inventory, January 1.......		$ 27,632.40	
Purchases.............................	$128,258.95		
Less: Purch. ret. and allow. $1,721.10			
Purchases discounts.. 7,689.54	9,410.64		
Net purchases.........................		118,848.31	
Merchandise available for sale.........		$146,480.71	
Less merchandise inv., December 31...		25,074.05	
Cost of goods sold...................			121,406.66
Gross margin on sales....................			$ 78,375.69
Operating expenses:			
Rent expense...........................		$ 8,400.00	
Depreciation expense...................		503.16	
Salaries and commissions expense.......		21,316.40	
Payroll taxes expense..................		1,816.58	
Heating and lighting expense..........		759.64	
Supplies expense......................		197.76	
Telephone expense.....................		372.30	
Advertising expense...................		8,713.25	
Bank credit card expense..............		2,624.96	
Uncollectible accounts expense.........		250.98	
Insurance expense.....................		281.30	
Charitable contributions expense.......		350.00	
Miscellaneous expense.................		485.65	
Total operating expenses.............			46,071.98
Operating income........................			$ 32,303.71
Other expenses:			
Interest expense......................			153.42
Net income..............................			$ 32,150.29

Boyd's Clothiers — Income Statement

for the year ended December 31, 19--, is shown above. The information needed in preparing the statement was obtained from the work sheet shown on pages 230 and 231.

Income Statement Analysis. There are various procedures employed to assist in the interpretation of income statements. One device is to present income statements for two or more comparable periods in comparative form. If the figures for two periods are shown in adjacent columns, a third column showing the amount of increase or decrease in each element may be shown. This will call attention to changes of major significance.

Another analytical device is to express all, or at least the major, items on the statement as a percent of net sales and then to compare these percentages for two or more periods. For example, if the net sales of $199,782.35 for Boyd's Clothiers for the year just ended are treated as 100 percent, the cost of goods sold which amounted to $121,406.66 was equal to 60.77 percent of net sales; the gross margin on sales which amounted to $78,375.69 was equal to 39.23 percent of net sales; operating expenses which amounted to $46,071.98 were equal to 23.06 percent of net sales; operating income (gross margin less operating expenses) which amounted to $32,303.71 was equal to 16.17 percent of net sales; and net income which amounted to $32,150.29 was equal to 16.09 percent of net sales. A comparison of these percentages with the same data for one or more prior years would reveal trends that would surely be of interest, and perhaps of real concern, to the management of the business.

The balance sheet

A formal statement of the assets, liabilities, and owner's equity in a business at a specified date is known as a *balance sheet*. The title of the statement had its origin in the equality of the elements, that is, in the balance between the sum of the assets and the sum of the liabilities and owner's equity. Sometimes the balance sheet is called a *statement of assets and liabilities*, a *statement of condition*, or a *statement of financial position*. Various other titles are used occasionally.

Importance of the Balance Sheet. The balance sheet of a business is of considerable interest to various parties for several reasons. The owner or owners of a business are interested in the kinds and amounts of assets and liabilities, and the amount of the owner's equity or capital element.

Creditors of the business are interested in the financial position of the enterprise, particularly as it pertains to the claims they have and the prospects for prompt payment. Potential creditors or possible lenders are concerned about the financial position of the business. Their decision as to whether to extend credit or to make loans to the business may depend, in large part, upon the condition of the enterprise as revealed by a balance sheet.

Persons considering buying an ownership interest in a business are greatly interested in the character and amount of the assets and liabilities, though this interest is probably secondary to their concern about the future earnings possibilities.

Finally, various regulatory bodies are interested in the financial position of the businesses that are under their jurisdiction. Examples of regulated businesses include banks, insurance companies, public utilities, railroads, and airlines.

Form of the Balance Sheet. Traditionally, balance sheets have been presented either in *account form* or in *report form*. When the account form is followed, the assets are listed on the left side of the page (or on the left of two facing pages) and the liabilities and owner's equity are listed on the right. This form is similar to the debit-side and credit-side arrangement of the standard ledger account. The balance sheet of Boyd's Clothiers as of December 31, 19––, in account form is reproduced on pages 242 and 243. The data for the preparation of the statement were secured from the work sheet.

When the report form of the balance sheet is followed, the assets, liabilities, and owner's equity elements are exhibited in that order on the page. The balance sheet of John H. Roberts, Management Consultant, was shown in report form on page 117. This arrangement is generally superior when the statement is typed on regular letter-size paper (8½″ x 11″).

Whichever form is used, it is essential that the statement have the proper heading. This means that three things must be shown: **(1)** The name of the business must be given (or the name of the individual if the business or professional practice is carried on in the name of an individual), followed by **(2)** the name of the statement — usually just "Balance Sheet," and finally **(3)** the date — month, day, and year. Sometimes the expression "As of Close of Business December 31, 1977" (or whatever date is involved) is included. It must be remembered that a balance sheet relates to a particular moment of time.

Classification of Data in the Balance Sheet. The purpose of the balance sheet and of all other financial statements and reports is to convey as much information as possible. This aim is furthered by some classification of the data being reported. As applied to balance sheets, it has become almost universal practice to classify both assets and liabilities as between those that are considered "current" and those that are considered "noncurrent" or "long-lived."

Current Assets. *Current Assets* include cash and all other assets that may be reasonably expected to be realized in cash or sold or consumed during the normal operating cycle of the business. In a merchandising business the current assets usually will include cash, receivables (such as accounts receivable), merchandise inventory, and temporary investments. Prepaid expenses, such as unexpired insurance and unused supplies, are also generally treated as current assets. This is not because such items will be realized in cash, but because they will probably be consumed in a relatively short time.

The asset cash may be represented by one or more accounts, such as bank checking accounts, bank savings accounts, or a petty cash fund.

Reference to Boyd's Clothiers balance sheet will show that cash is listed at $10,743.11. Reference to the work sheet will show that this is made up of two items: the balance in the checking account at the First National Bank, $10,643.11, and the amount of the petty cash fund, $100.

Temporary investments refer to those assets that have been acquired with money that would otherwise have been temporarily idle and unproductive. Such investments usually take the form of corporate stocks, bonds, or notes, or any of several types of government bonds. Quite often the policy is to invest in securities that can be liquidated in a short time with little chance of loss. So-called *marketable securities* are often favored. Assets of the same type may be owned by a business for many years, and, under such circumstances, they would not be classified as temporary investments. It is the matter of intention that indicates whether the investments are to be classified as temporary and included in the current assets or considered as long-term investments and either included in the long-lived asset classification or in a separate classification entitled *Permanent Investments*.

Reference to the balance sheet of Boyd's Clothiers on pages 242 and 243 reveals that the current assets of this business consisted of cash, accounts receivable, merchandise inventory, prepaid insurance, and supplies.

Long-Lived Assets. Property that is used in the operation of a merchandising business may include such assets as land, buildings, office equipment, store equipment, and delivery equipment. Such assets are called *long-lived assets*. Of these assets only land is really permanent; however, all of these assets have a useful life that is comparatively long.

Reference to the balance sheet of Boyd's Clothiers will show that the long-lived assets of the business consist of store equipment. The amount of the accumulated depreciation is shown as a deduction from the cost of the equipment. The difference represents the *undepreciated cost* of the equipment — the amount that will be written off as depreciation expense in future periods.

Current Liabilities. *Current liabilities* include those obligations that will be due in a short time and paid with monies provided by the current assets. As of December 31, the current liabilities of Boyd's Clothiers consisted of notes payable, accrued interest payable, accounts payable, sales tax payable, FICA tax payable, employees income tax payable, FUTA tax payable, state unemployment tax payable and accrued bank credit card expense.

Long-Term Liabilities. *Long-term liabilities* (sometimes called *fixed liabilities*) include those obligations that will not be due for a relatively long time. The most common of the long-term liabilities is mortgages payable.

A mortgage payable is a debt or an obligation that is secured by a *mortgage*, which provides for the conveyance of certain property upon failure to pay the debt at maturity. When the debt is paid, the mortgage becomes void. It will be seen, therefore, that a mortgage payable differs little from an account payable or a note payable except that the creditor holds the mortgage as security for the payment of the debt. Usually debts secured by mortgages run for a longer period of time than ordinary notes payable or accounts payable. A mortgage payable should be classified as a long-term liability if the maturity date extends beyond the normal operating cycle of the business (usually a year). Boyd's Clothiers has no long-term liabilities.

Owner's Equity. As previously explained, accounts relating to the owner's equity element may be either permanent or temporary owner's equity accounts. The permanent owner's equity accounts used in recording the operations of a particular enterprise depend upon the type of legal organization, that is, whether the enterprise is organized as a sole proprietorship, as a partnership, or as a corporation.

BOYD'S
Balance
December

Assets

Current assets:

Cash....................................		$10,743.11
Accounts receivable....................	$ 3,360.31	
Less allowance for doubtful accounts.	310.20	3,050.11
Merchandise inventory..................		25,074.05
Prepaid insurance......................		281.30
Supplies...............................		60.00
Total current assets...............		$39,208.57

Long-lived assets:

Store equipment........................		$ 5,593.60
Less accumulated depreciation........		1,365.26
Total long-lived assets.............		4,228.34

Total assets............................	$43,436.91

Boyd's Clothiers — Balance Sheet (Left Side)

In the case of a sole proprietorship, one or more accounts representing the owner's interest or equity in the assets may be kept. Reference to the chart of accounts, shown on page 183, will reveal that the following accounts are classified as owner's equity accounts:

Account No. 311, Lynn C. Boyd, Capital
Account No. 031, Lynn C. Boyd, Drawing
Account No. 321, Expense and Revenue Summary

Account No. 311 reflects the amount of Ms. Boyd's equity. It may be increased by additional investments or by the practice of not withdrawing cash or other assets in an amount as large as the net income of the enterprise; it may be decreased by withdrawals in excess of the amount of the net income or by sustaining a net loss during one or more accounting periods. Usually there will be no changes in the balance of this account during the accounting period, in which case the balance represents the owner's investment in the business as of the beginning of the accounting period and until such time as the books are closed at the end of the accounting period.

Account No. 031 is Ms. Boyd's drawing account. This account is charged for any withdrawals of cash or other property for personal use. It is a temporary account in which is kept a record of the owner's personal

```
CLOTHIERS
Sheet
31, 19---
                              Liabilities
Current liabilities:

  Notes payable..........................    $ 3,000.00
  Accrued interest payable...............        37.33
  Accounts payable.......................      4,340.30
  Sales tax payable......................        802.86
  FICA tax payable.......................        213.22
  Employees income tax payable...........        266.50
  FUTA tax payable.......................         84.00
  State unemployment tax payable.........        113.40
  Accrued bank credit card expense.......        209.62
                                            ----------
    Total current liabilities...........                $ 9,067.23
                              Owner's Equity

Lynn C. Boyd, capital:

  Capital, January 1.....................    $25,635.19
  Net income............................. $32,150.29
    Less withdrawals.....................  23,415.80    8,734.49
                                           ----------   ---------
  Capital, December 31..................                34,369.68
                                                       ----------
Total liabilities and owner's equity.....              $43,436.91
                                                       ==========
```

Boyd's Clothiers — Balance Sheet (Right Side)

drawings during the accounting period. Ordinarily such drawings are made in anticipation of earnings rather than as withdrawals of capital. The balance of the account, as shown by the trial balance at the close of an accounting period, represents the total amount of the owner's drawings during the period.

Reference to the work sheet shown on pages 230 and 231 will reveal that the balance of Ms. Boyd's drawing account is listed in the Balance Sheet Debit column. This is because there is no provision on a work sheet for making deductions from owner's equity except by listing them in the Debit column. Since the balance of the owner's capital account is listed in the Balance Sheet Credit column, the listing of the balance of the owner's drawing account in the Debit column is equivalent to deducting the amount from the balance of the owner's capital account.

Account No. 321 is used only at the close of the accounting period for the purpose of summarizing the temporary owner's equity accounts. Sometimes this account is referred to as a *clearing account*. No entries should appear in the account before the books are closed at the end of the accounting period.

The owner's equity section of the balance sheet of Boyd's Clothiers is arranged to show the major changes that took place during the year in the owner's equity element of the business. Ms. Boyd's interest in the business amounted to $25,635.19 at the beginning of the period. Her interest was increased $32,150.29 as the result of profitable operations, and decreased $23,415.80 as the result of withdrawals during the year. Thus, the owner's equity element of the business on December 31 amounted to $34,369.68.

Balance Sheet Analysis. The information provided by a balance sheet can be analyzed in several ways to assist in judging the financial position and soundness of the business. A few of the major analytical procedures will be briefly considered.

A balance sheet as of one date may be compared with a balance sheet as of another date to determine the amount of the increase or the decrease in any of the accounts or groups of accounts. Sometimes balance sheets as of two or more dates are prepared in comparative form by listing the amounts as of different dates in parallel columns. Thus, if balance sheets as of the close of two succeeding calendar years are compared, it is possible to determine the amount of the increase or the decrease during the intervening period in any of the accounts or groups of accounts involved. If such a comparison reveals an increase in accounts receivable, it may indicate that collections during the later period were not as favorable as they were during the preceding period. If the comparison reveals an increase in accounts payable, it may indicate an inability to pay current bills because of insufficient cash. If the comparison reveals an increase in the current assets without a corresponding increase in the liabilities, it may indicate an improved financial position or status.

Too much emphasis should not be placed upon an increase or a decrease in cash. Some individuals are inclined to judge the results of operations largely by the cash balance. This practice may be misleading. The net results of operations can be properly determined only by comparison of all the assets and the liabilities. The ability of a business to meet its current obligations may be determined largely by an analysis of its current assets, particularly those assets that are sometimes referred to as the quick assets. *Quick assets* include cash and all other current assets that are readily realizable in cash, such as temporary investments in the form of marketable securities.

The relation of an account, a group of accounts, or an accounting element to another account, group of accounts, or accounting element may be referred to as the *ratio*. For example, if the total current assets amount to twice as much as the total current liabilities, the ratio is said to be 2 to 1. Ratios may be expressed in percentages or on a unit basis. Fractions of units may be expressed by means of common fractions or decimals as, for example, $7\frac{3}{4}$ to 1 or 7.75 to 1.

In an enterprise in which capital invested is a material revenue-producing factor, such as is the case in a merchandising enterprise, the ratio of the current assets to the current liabilities may be important. Reference to the balance sheet shown on pages 242 and 243 reveals that the total current assets amount to $39,208.57 and the total current liabilities amount to $9,067.23, a ratio of over 4 to 1. The total assets amount to $43,436.91 and the total liabilities amount to $9,067.23, a ratio of nearly 5 to 1. These ratios are sufficiently high to indicate a very favorable financial position.

Banks often consider the ratio of current assets to current liabilities when considering the advisability of making a loan. It is not expected that the long-lived assets will be sold to realize sufficient funds with which to pay a short-term loan. If the balance sheet seems to indicate that a sufficient amount of cash will not be realized from the collection of accounts receivable or from the sales of service or merchandise to repay a loan at maturity, the bank may consider the loan inadvisable. The excess of the amount of the current assets over the amount of the current liabilities is called *net current assets* or *working capital*.

It is difficult to estimate what the proper ratio of current assets to current liabilities should be, because of the variations in enterprises and industries. A 2 to 1 ratio of current assets to current liabilities may be more than sufficient in some enterprises but entirely insufficient in others. In the milk distributing business, for example, a 1 to 1 ratio of current assets to current liabilities is considered satisfactory. The reasons are that very little capital is tied up in inventory, the amount of accounts receivable is comparatively small, and the terms on which the milk is purchased from farmers are such that settlements are slow and comparatively large amounts are due to farmers at all times. Another reason is that a large amount of capital is invested in long-lived assets, such as equipment for treating the milk and for delivering it to customers.

Generally speaking, the ratio of the current assets to the current liabilities should be maintained in a range from 2 to 1 to 5 to 1. While a standard ratio cannot be established for all enterprises, a knowledge of the working capital requirements of a particular enterprise will be helpful in determining what the ratio of current assets to current liabilities should be.

A comparison of the relationships between certain amounts in the income statement and certain amounts in the balance sheet may be informative. The leading example of this type is the ratio of net income to owner's equity in the business. The owner's equity of Boyd's Clothiers was $25,635.19 on January 1. The net income for the year of $32,150.29 was over 125 percent of this amount. A comparison of this ratio with the ratio of net income to capital invested in prior years should be of interest to the owner. It may also be of interest to compare the ratio of the net income of Boyd's Clothiers to the amount of capital invested by Ms. Boyd with the same ratio for other stores of comparable nature and size. It is important to note, however, that the net income of Boyd's Clothiers was computed without regard to any salary or other compensation for the services of Ms. Boyd. In comparing the results of operations of Boyd's Clothiers with those of other retail clothing businesses, some appropriate adjustment of the data might be needed to make the comparison valid.

Inventory turnover

A merchant is usually interested in knowing the rate of *inventory turnover* for each accounting period. This has reference to the number of times the merchandise available for sale is turned during the accounting period. The rate of turnover is found by dividing the cost of goods sold for the period by the average inventory. Where an inventory is taken only at the end of each accounting period, the average inventory for the period may be found by adding the beginning and ending inventories together and dividing by two. The turnover of Boyd's Clothiers for the year ended December 31 may be computed as follows:

Beginning inventory	$ 27,632.40
Ending inventory	25,074.05
Cost of goods sold for the period	121,406.66

$$\$27,632.40 + \$25,074.05 \div 2 = \$26,353.23, \text{ average inventory}$$
$$\$121,406.66 \div \$26,353.23 = 4.6, \text{ rate of turnover}$$

This calculation indicates that, on the average, the merchandise turns over about once every 2½ months. A careful analysis of the theory involved in computing the rate of turnover will indicate that the greater the sales the smaller the margin need be on each dollar of sales in order to produce a satisfactory dollar amount of gross margin.

**Report
No. 9-2**

> Complete Report No. 9-2 in the study assignments and submit your working papers to the instructor for approval. After completing the report, you may continue with the textbook discussion in Chapter 10 until the next report is required.

Chapter 10

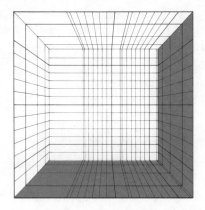

ADJUSTING AND CLOSING ACCOUNTS AT END OF ACCOUNTING PERIOD

As explained in the preceding chapter, the adjustment of certain accounts at the end of the accounting period is required because of changes that have occurred during the period that are not reflected in the accounts. Since the purpose of the temporary owner's equity accounts is to assemble information relating to a specified period of time, at the end of the period the balances of these accounts must be removed to cause the accounts to be ready to perform their function in the following period. In other words, accounts of this type must be "closed."

ADJUSTING ENTRIES

In preparing the work sheet for Boyd's Clothiers (reproduced on pages 230 and 231), adjustments were made to accomplish the following purposes:

(a) To transfer the amount of the merchandise inventory at the beginning of the accounting period to the expense and revenue summary.
(b) To record the calculated cost of the merchandise inventory at the end of the accounting period.
(c) To record the amount of interest accrued on notes payable.
(d) To record the amount of accrued bank credit card expense.
(e) To record the amount of insurance premium expired during the year.

(f) To record the cost of supplies used during the year.

(g) To record the estimated amount of depreciation of long-lived assets (store equipment) for the year.

(h) To record the amount of losses from uncollectible accounts expected to result from the sales on account made during the year.

The effect of these adjustments was reflected in the financial statements reproduced on pages 238, 242, and 243. To bring the ledger into agreement with the financial statements, the adjustments should be recorded in the proper accounts. It is customary, therefore, at the end of each accounting period to journalize the adjustments and to post them to the accounts.

Journalizing the adjusting entries

Adjusting entries may be recorded in either a general journal or a combined cash journal. If the entries are made in a combined cash journal, the only amount columns used are the General Debit and Credit columns. A portion of a page of a combined cash journal showing the adjusting entries of Boyd's Clothiers is reproduced below. It should be noted that when the adjusting entries are recorded in the combined cash journal, they are entered in exactly the same manner as they would be entered in

COMBINED CASH JOURNAL FOR MONTH OF *December* 19 —— PAGE *49*

DAY	DESCRIPTION	POST. REF.	GENERAL DEBIT	GENERAL CREDIT
	AMOUNTS FORWARDED			
31	*Adjusting Entries*			
	Expense and Revenue Summary	321	27 63240	
	Merchandise Inventory	131		27 63240
	Merchandise Inventory	131	25 07405	
	Expense and Revenue Summary	321		25 07405
	Interest Expense	711	3733	
	Accrued Interest Payable	221		3733
	Bank Credit Card Expense	619	20962	
	Accrued Bank Credit Card Expense	291		20962
	Insurance Expense	622	28130	
	Prepaid Insurance	141		28130
	Supplies Expense	616	19776	
	Supplies	151		19776
	Depreciation Expense	612	50316	
	Accum. Deprec.-Store Equip.	018		50316
	Uncollectible Accounts Expense	621	25098	
	Allowance for Doubtful Accounts	012		25098
			54 18660	54 18660

Boyd's Clothiers — Adjusting Entries

a general journal. Since the heading "Adjusting Entries" explains the nature of the entries, a separate explanation of each adjusting entry is unnecessary. The information needed in journalizing the adjustments was obtained from the Adjustments columns of the work sheet reproduced on pages 230 and 231. The account numbers were not entered in the Posting Reference column at the time of journalizing; they were entered as the posting was completed.

Posting the adjusting entries

The adjusting entries should be posted individually to the proper general ledger accounts. The accounts of Boyd's Clothiers that were affected by the adjusting entries are reproduced below and on pages 251 and 252. The entries in the accounts for December transactions that were posted prior to posting the adjusting entries are the same as appeared in the accounts reproduced on pages 214–219. The number of the combined cash journal page on which the adjusting entries were recorded was entered in the Posting Reference column of the general ledger accounts affected, and the account numbers were entered in the Posting Reference column of the combined cash journal as the posting was completed. This provided a cross-reference in both books.

ACCOUNT *Allowance for Doubtful Accounts*   ACCOUNT NO. 012

DATE	ITEM	POST. REF.	DEBIT	CREDIT	BALANCE DEBIT	BALANCE CREDIT
19-- Dec. 1	Balance	✓				5922
31		CJ49		25098		31020

ACCOUNT *Merchandise Inventory*   ACCOUNT NO. 131

DATE	ITEM	POST. REF.	DEBIT	CREDIT	BALANCE DEBIT	BALANCE CREDIT
19-- Dec. 1	Balance	✓			2763240	
31		CJ49		2763240		
31		CJ49	2507405		2507405	

ACCOUNT *Prepaid Insurance*   ACCOUNT NO. 141

DATE	ITEM	POST. REF.	DEBIT	CREDIT	BALANCE DEBIT	BALANCE CREDIT
19-- Dec. 1	Balance	✓			56260	
31		CJ49		2830	2830	

Boyd's Clothiers — General Ledger Accounts After Posting Adjusting Entries

ACCOUNT *Supplies*   ACCOUNT NO. *151*

DATE	ITEM	POST. REF.	DEBIT	CREDIT	BALANCE DEBIT	BALANCE CREDIT
19-- Dec. 1	Balance	✓			230 28	
31		CJ48	27 48		257 76	
31		CJ49		197 76	60 00	

ACCOUNT *Accumulated Depreciation – Store Equipment*   ACCOUNT NO. *018*

DATE	ITEM	POST. REF.	DEBIT	CREDIT	BALANCE DEBIT	BALANCE CREDIT
19-- Dec. 1	Balance	✓				862 10
31		CJ49		503 16		1365 26

ACCOUNT *Accrued Interest Payable*   ACCOUNT NO. *221*

DATE	ITEM	POST. REF.	DEBIT	CREDIT	BALANCE DEBIT	BALANCE CREDIT
19-- Dec. 31		CJ49		37 33		37 33

ACCOUNT *Accrued Bank Credit Card Expense*   ACCOUNT NO. *291*

DATE	ITEM	POST. REF.	DEBIT	CREDIT	BALANCE DEBIT	BALANCE CREDIT
19-- Dec. 31		CJ49		209 62		209 62

ACCOUNT *Expense and Revenue Summary*   ACCOUNT NO. *321*

DATE	ITEM	POST. REF.	DEBIT	CREDIT	BALANCE DEBIT	BALANCE CREDIT
19-- Dec. 31		CJ49	2763 40			
		CJ49		2507 05		

ACCOUNT *Depreciation Expense*   ACCOUNT NO. *612*

DATE	ITEM	POST. REF.	DEBIT	CREDIT	BALANCE DEBIT	BALANCE CREDIT
19-- Dec. 31		CJ49	503 16		503 16	

Boyd's Clothiers — General Ledger Accounts After Posting Adjusting Entries (*continued*)

ACCOUNT _Supplies Expense_   ACCOUNT NO. 616

DATE	ITEM	POST. REF.	DEBIT	CREDIT	BALANCE DEBIT	BALANCE CREDIT
19-- Dec. 31		CJ49	19776		19776	

ACCOUNT _Bank Credit Card Expense_   ACCOUNT NO. 619

DATE	ITEM	POST. REF.	DEBIT	CREDIT	BALANCE DEBIT	BALANCE CREDIT
19-- Dec. 1	Balance	✓			217992	
4		CJ47	23542		241534	
31		CJ49	20962		262496	

ACCOUNT _Uncollectible Accounts Expense_   ACCOUNT NO. 621

DATE	ITEM	POST. REF.	DEBIT	CREDIT	BALANCE DEBIT	BALANCE CREDIT
19-- Dec. 31		CJ49	25098		25098	

ACCOUNT _Insurance Expense_   ACCOUNT NO. 622

DATE	ITEM	POST. REF.	DEBIT	CREDIT	BALANCE DEBIT	BALANCE CREDIT
19-- Dec. 31		CJ49	28130		28130	

ACCOUNT _Interest Expense_   ACCOUNT NO. 711

DATE	ITEM	POST. REF.	DEBIT	CREDIT	BALANCE DEBIT	BALANCE CREDIT
19-- Dec. 1	Balance	✓			11609	
31		CJ49	3733		15342	

Boyd's Clothiers — General Ledger Accounts After Posting Adjusting Entries (*concluded*)

Report No. 10-1	Complete Report No. 10-1 in the study assignments and submit your working papers to the instructor for approval. Continue with the following textbook discussion until Report No. 10-2 is required.

CLOSING PROCEDURE

After the adjusting entries have been posted, all of the temporary owner's equity accounts should be closed. This means that the accountant must remove ("close out") **(1)** the balance of every account that enters into the calculation of the net income (or net loss) for the accounting period and **(2)** the balance of the owner's drawing account. The purpose of the closing procedure is to transfer the balances of the temporary owner's equity accounts to the permanent owner's equity account. This could be accomplished simply by debiting or crediting each account involved with an offsetting credit or debit to the permanent owner's equity account. However, it is considered better practice to transfer the balances of all accounts that enter into the net income or net loss determination to a summarizing account called Expense and Revenue Summary (sometimes called *Income Summary*, *Profit and Loss Summary*, or just *Profit and Loss*). Then, the resulting balance of the expense and revenue summary account (which will be the amount of the net income or net loss for the period) is transferred to the permanent owner's equity account.

The final step in the closing procedure is to transfer the balance of the owner's drawing account to the permanent owner's equity account. After this is done, only the asset accounts, the liability accounts, and the permanent owner's equity account have balances. If there has been no error, the sum of the balances of the asset accounts (less balances of any contra accounts) will be equal to the sum of the balances of the liability accounts plus the balance of the permanent owner's equity account. The accounts will agree exactly with what is shown in the balance sheet as of the close of the period. Reference to the balance sheet of Boyd's Clothiers reproduced on pages 242 and 243 will show that the assets, liabilities, and owner's equity as of December 31 may be expressed in equation form as follows:

$$\text{ASSETS} = \text{LIABILITIES} + \text{OWNER'S EQUITY}$$

$$\$43,436.91 \qquad \$9,067.23 \qquad \$34,369.68$$

Journalizing the closing entries

Closing entries, like adjusting entries, may be recorded in either a general journal or a combined cash journal. If the entries are made in a combined cash journal, only the General Debit and Credit columns are used. A portion of a page of a combined cash journal showing the closing entries for Boyd's Clothiers is reproduced below. Since the heading

COMBINED CASH JOURNAL FOR MONTH OF *December* 19 —— PAGE *50*

	DAY	DESCRIPTION	POST. REF.	GENERAL DEBIT	GENERAL CREDIT
1		AMOUNTS FORWARDED			
2	31	Closing Entries			
3		Sales	411	20274365	
4		Purchases Returns + Allowances	051	172110	
5		Purchases Discount	052	768954	
6		Expense and Revenue Summary	321		21215429
7		Expense and Revenue Summary	321	17744565	
8		Sales Returns + Allowances	041		296130
9		Purchases	511		12825895
10		Rent Expense	611		840000
11		Depreciation Expense	612		50316
12		Salaries and Commissions Exp.	613		2131640
13		Payroll Taxes Expense	614		181658
14		Heating and Lighting Expense	615		75964
15		Stationery and Supplies Expense	616		19776
16		Telephone and Telegraph Expense	617		37230
17		Advertising Expense	618		871325
18		Bank Credit Card Expense	619		262496
19		Uncollectible Accounts Expense	621		25098
20		Insurance Expense	622		28130
21		Charitable Contributions Expense	623		35000
22		Miscellaneous Expense	624		48565
23		Interest Expense	711		15342
24		Expense and Revenue Summary	321	3215029	
25		Lynn C. Boyd, Capital	311		3215029
26		Lynn C. Boyd, Capital	311	2341580	
27		Lynn C. Boyd, Drawing	031		2341580
				44516603	44516603

Boyd's Clothiers — Closing Entries

"Closing Entries" explains the nature of the entries, a separate explanation of each closing entry is not necessary. The information required in preparing the closing entries was obtained from the work sheet illustrated on pages 230 and 231.

The first closing entry was made to close the sales, purchases returns and allowances, and purchases discount accounts. Since these accounts have credit balances, each account must be debited for the amount of its balance in order to close it. The debits to these three accounts are offset by a credit of $212,154.29 to Expense and Revenue Summary.

The second closing entry was made to close the sales returns and allowances, purchases, and all of the expense accounts. Since these accounts have debit balances, each account must be credited for the amount of its balance in order to close it. The credits to these accounts are offset by a debit of $177,445.65 to Expense and Revenue Summary.

Since the posting of the first two adjusting entries and the first two closing entries causes the expense and revenue summary account to have a credit balance of $32,150.29 (the net income for the year), the account has served its purpose and must be closed. The third closing entry accomplishes this by debiting the expense and revenue summary account with an offsetting credit to Lynn C. Boyd, Capital, for $32,150.29.

The fourth closing entry was made to close the Lynn C. Boyd drawing account. Since this account has a debit balance, it must be credited to close it. The offsetting entry is a debit of $23,415.80 to Lynn C. Boyd, Capital.

The account numbers shown in the Posting Reference column were not entered at the time of journalizing the closing entries — they were entered as the posting was completed.

Posting the closing entries

Closing entries are posted in the usual manner and proper cross-references are provided by using the Posting Reference columns of the combined cash journal and the ledger accounts. After all the closing entries have been posted, the accounts affected appear as shown on pages 256-261. Note that as each account was closed, the "no balance" symbol "—0—" was placed in each column.

It may be observed that the first two adjusting entries described and illustrated earlier in the chapter actually qualify both as "adjusting" and as "closing" entries. They serve to adjust the merchandise inventory account by removing the amount of the beginning inventory and by recording the amount of the ending inventory. They facilitate the closing process in that they cause two amounts that enter into the calculation of net income or net loss to be entered in the Expense and Revenue Summary. It matters little which descriptive term is applied; the important thing is to be sure that needed adjustments are made and that the temporary owner's equity accounts are closed as of the end of the accounting period.

ACCOUNT *Lynn C. Boyd, Capital*   ACCOUNT NO. 311

DATE	ITEM	POST. REF.	DEBIT	CREDIT	BALANCE DEBIT	BALANCE CREDIT
19-- Dec. 1	Balance	✓				2563519
31		CJ50		3215029		
31		CJ50	2341580			3436968

ACCOUNT *Lynn C. Boyd, Drawing*   ACCOUNT NO. 031

DATE	ITEM	POST. REF.	DEBIT	CREDIT	BALANCE DEBIT	BALANCE CREDIT
19-- Dec. 1	Balance	✓			2240580	
21		CJ48	100000			
31		CJ48	1000		2341580	
31		CJ50		2341580	—0—	—0—

ACCOUNT *Expense and Revenue Summary*   ACCOUNT NO. 321

DATE	ITEM	POST. REF.	DEBIT	CREDIT	BALANCE DEBIT	BALANCE CREDIT
19-- Dec. 31		CJ49	2763240			
31		CJ49		2507405		
31		CJ50		2121542 9		
31		CJ50	17744565			
31		CJ50	3215029		—0—	—0—

Boyd's Clothiers — Partial General Ledger

ACCOUNT *Sales*   ACCOUNT NO. 411

DATE		ITEM	POST. REF.	DEBIT	CREDIT	BALANCE	
						DEBIT	CREDIT
19-- Dec.	1	Balance	✓				1865812 1
	31		S44		218791		
	31		CJ48		1397453		20274365
	31		CJ50	20274365		—0—	—0—

ACCOUNT *Sales Returns and Allowances*   ACCOUNT NO. 041

DATE		ITEM	POST. REF.	DEBIT	CREDIT	BALANCE	
						DEBIT	CREDIT
19-- Dec.	1	Balance	✓			285485	
	9		CJ47	8495			
	27		CJ48	2150		296130	
	31		CJ50		296130	—0—	—0—

ACCOUNT *Purchases*   ACCOUNT NO. 511

DATE		ITEM	POST. REF.	DEBIT	CREDIT	BALANCE	
						DEBIT	CREDIT
19-- Dec.	1	Balance	✓			1185 1272	
	2		CJ47	5318			
	31		P32	969305		12825895	
	31		CJ50		12825895	—0—	—0—

ACCOUNT *Purchases Returns and Allowances*   ACCOUNT NO. 051

DATE		ITEM	POST. REF.	DEBIT	CREDIT	BALANCE	
						DEBIT	CREDIT
19-- Dec.	1	Balance	✓				165510
	20		CJ48		6600		172110
	31		CJ50	172110		—0—	—0—

Boyd's Clothiers — Partial General Ledger (*continued*)

ACCOUNT *Purchases Discount*   ACCOUNT NO. *052*

DATE		ITEM	POST. REF.	DEBIT	CREDIT	BALANCE	
						DEBIT	CREDIT
19-- Dec.	1	Balance	✓				692204
	31		CJ48		76750		768954
	31		CJ50	768954		—0—	—0—

ACCOUNT *Rent Expense*   ACCOUNT NO. *611*

DATE		ITEM	POST. REF.	DEBIT	CREDIT	BALANCE	
						DEBIT	CREDIT
19-- Dec.	1	Balance	✓			770000	
	2		CJ47	70000		840000	
	31		CJ50		840000	—0—	—0—

ACCOUNT *Depreciation Expense*   ACCOUNT NO. *612*

DATE		ITEM	POST. REF.	DEBIT	CREDIT	BALANCE	
						DEBIT	CREDIT
19-- Dec.	31		CJ49	50316		50316	
	31		CJ50		50316	—0—	—0—

ACCOUNT *Salaries and Commissions Expense*   ACCOUNT NO. *613*

DATE		ITEM	POST. REF.	DEBIT	CREDIT	BALANCE	
						DEBIT	CREDIT
19-- Dec.	1	Balance	✓			1953950	
	14		CJ47	89270			
	31		CJ48	88420		2131640	
	31		CJ50		2131640	—0—	—0—

Boyd's Clothiers — Partial General Ledger (*continued*)

ACCOUNT *Payroll Taxes Expense*   ACCOUNT NO. 614

DATE		ITEM	POST. REF.	DEBIT	CREDIT	BALANCE DEBIT	BALANCE CREDIT
19-- Dec.	1	Balance	✓			1703 30	
	14		CJ47	56 91			
	31		CJ48	56 37		1816 58	
	31		CJ50		1816 58	—0—	—0—

ACCOUNT *Heating and Lighting Expense*   ACCOUNT NO. 615

DATE		ITEM	POST. REF.	DEBIT	CREDIT	BALANCE DEBIT	BALANCE CREDIT
19-- Dec.	1	Balance	✓			686 36	
	28		CJ48	73 28		759 64	
	31		CJ50		759 64	—0—	—0—

ACCOUNT *Supplies Expense*   ACCOUNT NO. 616

DATE		ITEM	POST. REF.	DEBIT	CREDIT	BALANCE DEBIT	BALANCE CREDIT
19-- Dec.	31		CJ49	197 76		197 76	
	31		CJ50		197 76	—0—	—0—

ACCOUNT *Telephone Expense*   ACCOUNT NO. 617

DATE		ITEM	POST. REF.	DEBIT	CREDIT	BALANCE DEBIT	BALANCE CREDIT
19-- Dec.	1	Balance	✓			340 15	
	28		CJ48	32 15		372 30	
	31		CJ50		372 30	—0—	—0—

Boyd's Clothiers — Partial General Ledger (*continued*)

ACCOUNT *Advertising Expense*   ACCOUNT NO. *618*

DATE	ITEM	POST. REF.	DEBIT	CREDIT	BALANCE DEBIT	BALANCE CREDIT
19-- Dec. 1	Balance	✓			821982	
6		CJ47	6104			
27		CJ48	42130			
31		CJ48	1109		871325	
31		CJ50		871325	—0—	—0—

ACCOUNT *Bank Credit Card Expense*   ACCOUNT NO. *619*

DATE	ITEM	POST. REF.	DEBIT	CREDIT	BALANCE DEBIT	BALANCE CREDIT
19-- Dec. 1	Balance	✓			217992	
4		CJ47	23542		241534	
31		CJ49	20962		262496	
31		CJ50		262496	—0—	—0—

ACCOUNT *Uncollectible Accounts Expense*   ACCOUNT NO. *621*

DATE	ITEM	POST. REF.	DEBIT	CREDIT	BALANCE DEBIT	BALANCE CREDIT
19-- Dec. 31		CJ49	25098		25098	
31		CJ50		25098	—0—	—0—

ACCOUNT *Insurance Expense*   ACCOUNT NO. *622*

DATE	ITEM	POST. REF.	DEBIT	CREDIT	BALANCE DEBIT	BALANCE CREDIT
19-- Dec. 31		CJ49	28130		28130	
31		CJ50		28130	—0—	—0—

Boyd's Clothiers — Partial General Ledger *(continued)*

ACCOUNT *Charitable Contributions Expense*   ACCOUNT NO. 623

DATE		ITEM	Post. Ref.	DEBIT	CREDIT	BALANCE	
						DEBIT	CREDIT
19-- Dec.	1	Balance	✓			34500	
	31		CJ48	500		35000	
	31		CJ50		35000	—0—	—0—

ACCOUNT *Miscellaneous Expense*   ACCOUNT NO. 624

DATE		ITEM	Post. Ref.	DEBIT	CREDIT	BALANCE	
						DEBIT	CREDIT
19-- Dec.	1	Balance	✓			46120	
	23		CJ48	1680			
	31		CJ48	765		48565	
	31		CJ50		48565	—0—	—0—

ACCOUNT *Interest Expense*   ACCOUNT NO. 711

DATE		ITEM	Post. Ref.	DEBIT	CREDIT	BALANCE	
						DEBIT	CREDIT
19-- Dec.	1	Balance	✓			11609	
	31		CJ49	3733		15342	
	31		CJ50		15342	—0—	—0—

Boyd's Clothiers — Partial General Ledger (*concluded*)

Trial balance after closing

A trial balance of the general ledger accounts that remain open after the temporary owner's equity accounts have been closed is usually referred to as a *post-closing trial balance*. The purpose of the post-closing trial balance is to prove that the general ledger is in balance at the beginning of a new accounting period. It is advisable to know that such is the case before any transactions for the new accounting period are recorded.

The post-closing trial balance should contain the same accounts and amounts as appear in the Balance Sheet columns of the work sheet, except that **(1)** the owner's drawing account is omitted because it has been closed, and **(2)** the owner's capital account has been adjusted for the amount of the net income (or net loss) and the amount of his drawings.

A post-closing trial balance of the general ledger of Boyd's Clothiers is shown below. Some accountants advocate that the post-closing trial balance should be dated as of the close of the old accounting period, while others advocate that it should be dated as of the beginning of the new accounting period. In this illustration the trial balance is dated December 31, the end of the period.

Boyd's Clothiers

Post-Closing Trial Balance

December 31, 19--

Account	Acct. No.	Dr. Balance	Cr. Balance
First National Bank	111	10 643 11	
Petty Cash Fund	112	100 00	
Accounts Receivable	121	3 360 31	
Allowance for Doubtful Accounts	012		310 20
Merchandise Inventory	131	25 074 05	
Prepaid Insurance	141	281 30	
Supplies	151	60 00	
Store Equipment	181	5 593 60	
Accumulated Depr.—Store Equipment	018		1 365 26
Notes Payable	211		3 000 00
Accrued Interest Payable	221		37 33
Accounts Payable	231		4 340 30
Sales Tax Payable	241		802 86
FICA Tax Payable	251		213 22
Employees Income Tax Payable	261		266 50
FUTA Tax Payable	271		84 00
State Unemployment Tax Payable	281		113 40
Accrued Bank Credit Card Expense	291		209 62
Lynn C. Boyd, Capital	311		34 369 68
		45 112 37	45 112 37

Boyd's Clothiers — Post-Closing Trial Balance

Reversing entries for accrual adjustments

Many accountants reverse the adjusting entries for accruals. The purpose of such reversing entries (sometimes called "readjusting entries") is to make possible the recording of the transactions of the succeeding accounting period in a routine manner and to assure that the proper amount of revenue will be credited to the period in which earned and that the proper amount of expenses will be charged to the period in which incurred.

A case in point is the matter of interest expense. When cash is disbursed in payment of interest, the routine manner of recording the transaction is to debit Interest Expense and to credit Cash (or Bank). If any portion of such interest was accrued in the preceding accounting period and the adjusting entry had not been reversed at the beginning of the current accounting period, the amount debited to Interest Expense would not represent the proper amount of expense incurred in the current period. If, however, the adjusting entry at the end of the preceding period had been reversed, the interest expense account would be credited for the amount accrued and, after recording the interest paid in the current period as a debit to Interest Expense, the balance of the account would represent the correct amount of the interest expense for the current period.

Journalizing the reversing entries

Reversing entries, like adjusting and closing entries, may be recorded in either a general journal or a combined cash journal. If the entries are made in a combined cash journal, the only amount columns used are the General Debit and Credit columns. A portion of a page of a combined cash journal showing the reversing entries of Boyd's Clothiers is reproduced below. Usually the reversing entries are made immediately after closing the books at the end of an accounting period. However, it is customary to date the entries as of the first day of the succeeding accounting period. Thus, the reversing entries for Boyd's Clothiers are dated January 1. Since the heading "Reversing Entries" explains the nature of the entries, a separate explanation of each reversing entry is unnecessary. Following is a discussion of each of the reversing entries.

COMBINED CASH JOURNAL FOR MONTH OF *January* 19 —   PAGE *51*

DAY	DESCRIPTION	POST. REF.	GENERAL DEBIT	GENERAL CREDIT
	AMOUNTS FORWARDED			
1	*Reversing Entries*			
	Accrued Interest Payable	221	37.33	
	Interest Expense	711		37.33
	Accrued Bank Credit Card Expense	291	209.62	
	Bank Credit Card Expense	619		209.62
			246.95	246.95

Boyd's Clothiers — Reversing Entries

Accrued Interest Payable. Reference to the adjusting entries for Boyd's Clothiers reproduced on page 249 will reveal that Interest Expense, Account No. 711, was debited and Accrued Interest Payable, Account No. 221, was credited for $37.33 to record the interest accrued on an 8 percent interest-bearing note for $3,000 issued November 5. To reverse the adjusting entry it was necessary to debit Accrued Interest Payable, Account No. 221, and to credit Interest Expense, Account No. 711, for $37.33. The accounts affected by this entry are reproduced below.

ACCOUNT *Accrued Interest Payable*   ACCOUNT NO. *221*

DATE	ITEM	POST. REF.	DEBIT	CREDIT	BALANCE DEBIT	BALANCE CREDIT
19-- Dec. 31		CJ49		37 33		37 33
19-- Jan. 1		CJ51	37 33		—0—	—0—

ACCOUNT *Interest Expense*   ACCOUNT NO. *711*

DATE	ITEM	POST. REF.	DEBIT	CREDIT	BALANCE DEBIT	BALANCE CREDIT
19-- Dec. 1	Balance	✓			1 16 09	
31		CJ49	37 33		1 53 42	
31		CJ50		1 53 42	—0—	—0—
19-- Jan. 1		CJ51		37 33		37 33

**Boyd's Clothiers — Accrued Interest Payable and Interest Expense
After Posting of Reversing Entry**

It will be noted that after posting the reversing entry, the account Accrued Interest Payable has a zero balance and the account Interest Expense has a credit balance of $37.33. If the note for $3,000 plus interest is paid when due on May 5, the payment will be $3,120 (principal of note $3,000, plus interest at 8 percent for 6 months, $120). To record the payment it is necessary only to debit Notes Payable, Account No. 211, for $3,000 and Interest Expense, Account No. 711, for $120 and to credit First National Bank, Account No. 111, for $3,120. After posting this entry, the interest expense account will have a debit balance of $82.67 ($120 minus $37.33). This balance represents the amount of interest expense incurred in the year in which the note matures. If the adjusting entry had not been reversed, it would be necessary to make an analysis before recording the payment on May 5 in order to determine the amount of interest expense incurred in the preceding year and the amount of interest expense incurred in the current year. This would reveal that it would be necessary to debit Accrued Interest Payable for $37.33 and Interest Expense for $82.67 so that each year might be charged with the correct interest expense. When the adjustment is reversed, the need for this analysis is eliminated.

The reversal procedure is particularly useful if the year-end adjustment for interest expense incurred but not paid related to interest accrued on several interest-bearing obligations. When the adjustment is reversed, all future payments of interest can be debited to the interest expense account without any concern as to when each amount paid was incurred. The portion of any payments that is an expense of the new period will automatically emerge as the balance of the interest expense account.

Accrued Bank Credit Card Expense. In the adjusting entries for Boyd's Clothiers, Bank Credit Card Expense, Account No. 619, was debited and Accrued Bank Credit Card Expense, Account No. 291, was credited for $209.62 to record the amount of the expense for December which the bank will not deduct from Boyd's checking account until early in January. The reversing entry (as of January 1) was a debit to the accrual account (No. 291) and a credit to the expense account (No. 619) for the same amount. Because the debit balance of the expense account (including the December expense not yet paid) had been closed, the result of the reversing entry was to remove the credit balance in the liability account and give the expense account a credit balance of $209.62. Below and on page 266 are the accounts after the reversing entry has been posted.

ACCOUNT *Accrued Bank Credit Card Expense*   ACCOUNT NO. 291

DATE	ITEM	POST. REF.	DEBIT	CREDIT	BALANCE DEBIT	BALANCE CREDIT
19-- Dec. 31		CJ49		209 62		209 62
19-- Jan. 1		CJ51	209 62		—0—	—0—

Boyd's Clothiers — Accrued Bank Credit Card Expense
After Posting of Reversing Entry

ACCOUNT *Bank Credit Card Expense*   ACCOUNT NO. *619*

DATE	ITEM	POST. REF.	DEBIT	CREDIT	BALANCE DEBIT	BALANCE CREDIT
19-- Dec. 1	Balance	✓			217992	
4		CJ47	23542		241534	
31		CJ49	20962		262496	
31		CJ50		262496	—0—	—0—
19-- Jan. 1		CJ51		20962		20962

Boyd's Clothiers — Bank Credit Card Expense
After Posting of Reversing Entry

The regular entry to record the bank's deduction for this expense is a debit to Bank Credit Card Expense and a credit to the bank account. If such an entry is made in early January for the calculated amount, $209.62, the expense account will be in balance. This is what is wanted — the amount is an expense of the year just ended, not the new year. If the reversing entry had not been made, the accountant would have had to remember that the January debit was to be different from the other eleven months. This is not a serious problem, but it is better whenever possible not to disturb the regular routine of recording transactions. Reversing entries for accrued expenses and revenue help accomplish this objective.

The accounting cycle

The steps involved in handling the effect of all transactions and events completed during an accounting period, beginning with entries in the books of original entry and ending with the reversing entries, collectively comprise the *accounting cycle*. In Chapter 5 (pages 125 and 126) nine steps were listed. A tenth step — journalizing and posting the reversing entries — needs to be added if the accrual basis of accounting is being followed.

Income and self-employment taxes

The discussion of accounting for the revenue and expenses of a business enterprise has included frequent references to income tax considerations. It is important to note that an unincorporated business owned by one person is not taxed. The owner — not the business — is subject to income taxes. However, the amounts of business revenue and business expenses must be reported on the owner's personal tax return regardless of the amount of money or other property that has actually been withdrawn from the business during the year. As mentioned earlier, in the case of a sole proprietorship, there is no legal distinction between the business and its owner.

In order to bring a large class of self-employed individuals into the federal social security program, the law requires all self-employed persons (except those specifically exempted) to pay a self-employment tax. The rate of tax is 2 percent more than the prevailing FICA rate, but the base of the "self-employment income tax" is the same as the base for the FICA tax. (If it is assumed that the combined FICA tax rate is 6 percent, the self-employment income tax rate would be 8 percent on the assumed base of $15,000.) The actual rate and base of the tax may be changed by Act of Congress at any time. In general, *self-employment income* means the net income of a trade or business conducted by an individual or a partner's distributive share of the net income of a partnership whether or not any cash is distributed. Earnings of less than $400 from self-employment are ignored.

A taxable year for the purpose of the tax on self-employment income is the same as the taxpayer's taxable year for federal income tax purposes. The self-employment tax is reported along with the regular federal income tax. For calendar-year taxpayers, the tax return and full or final payment is due on April 15 following the close of the year. Like the personal income tax, the self-employment tax is treated as a personal expense of the owner. If the taxes are paid with business funds, the amount should be charged to the owner's drawing account.

**Report
No. 10-2**

> Complete Report No. 10-2 in the study assignments and submit your working papers to the instructor for approval. You will then be given instructions as to the work to be done next.

Chapters 6-10

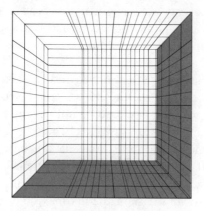

PRACTICAL ACCOUNTING PROBLEMS

Problem 6-A   Ms. Elinor Spiller decides to open a dress shop under the name of Elinor's Shop. The books of original entry include a purchases journal, a sales journal, and a combined cash journal. This problem involves the use of the purchases journal and the combined cash journal only. The following selected transactions were completed during the month of October:

Oct. 1. Invested $8,000 in the business.

1. Received Invoice No. 262 dated Sept. 29 from Mini Midi Maxi, Inc., for merchandise purchased, $95.50. Terms, 30 days net.

3. Received Invoice No. 263 dated Sept. 29 from Terre Brothers for merchandise purchased, $232.41. Terms, 10 days net.

5. Purchased a cash register for cash, $124.75. (Debit Furniture and Fixtures.)

6. Received Invoice No. 264 dated October 4 from Boes, Inc., for merchandise purchased, $126.80. Terms, 30 days net.

10. Purchased merchandise for cash, $61.65.

11. Received Invoice No. 265 dated October 8 from Mini Midi Maxi, Inc., for merchandise purchased, $161.30. Terms, 30 days net.

12. Paid Terre Brothers $232.41 in full for Invoice No. 263, dated Sept. 29.

13. Returned defective merchandise to Mini Midi Maxi, Inc., $32.50.

17. Received invoice dated October 15 from the American Showcase Co. for showcases purchased, $1,843.12. Terms, 15 days net.

24. Received Invoice No. 266 dated October 18 from Terre Brothers for merchandise purchased, $286.74. Terms, 10 days net.

Oct. 25. Purchased merchandise for cash, $136.18.
    31. Received Invoice No. 267 dated October 26 from Kay Francis for merchandise purchased, $52.40. Terms, 30 days net.

REQUIRED: **(1)** Record each transaction in the proper journal using the following accounts:

111 Cash	311 Elinor Spiller, Capital
151 Furniture and Fixtures	511 Purchases
231 Accounts Payable	051 Purchases Returns and Allowances

For the purchases journal, use a sheet of paper ruled like that shown in the illustration on page 144. For the combined cash journal, use a sheet of paper like that shown in the illustration on pages 160 and 161. (The Check No. column will not be used in this problem.) Number the pages of the journals. **(2)** Prove the combined cash journal by footing the amount columns; then total and rule this journal. Total the purchases journal and rule. **(3)** Open the necessary accounts using the four-column form of ledger paper. Post the combined cash journal and purchases journal entries for October, foot the accounts, and enter the balances. **(4)** Take a trial balance as of October 31, using a sheet of two-column journal paper.

Problem 6-B   A. K. Lein decides to open a men's clothing store under the name of The Southgate Store. The books of original entry include a sales journal, a purchases journal, and a combined cash journal. This problem involves the use of the sales journal and combined cash journal only. The following selected transactions were completed during the month of July:

July 1. Invested $10,000 in the business.
    2. Sold merchandise on account to J. D. Mead, $65.10, tax $3.26. Sale No. 304.
    5. Sold merchandise on account to B. A. Moore, $69.45, tax $3.47. Sale No. 305.
    6. J. D. Mead returned goods for credit. Sales price $16.40, tax 82 cents.
    9. Sold merchandise on account to H. C. Bock, $83.12, tax $4.16. Sale No. 306.
    13. Received $51.14 from J. D. Mead on account.
    14. Sold merchandise on account to R. G. Fear, $50.40, tax $2.52. Sale No. 307.
    19. A customer returned some merchandise purchased earlier in the day for cash. Sales price, $12.25, tax 61 cents.
    21. Received $87.28 from H. C. Bock on account.
    26. Sold merchandise on account to G. M. Decker, $30.60, tax $1.53. Sale No. 308.
    28. Sold merchandise on account to J. R. Metcalf, $18.80, tax 94 cents. Sale No. 309.
    30. Total cash sales for month, $681.50, tax, $34.08.

REQUIRED: (1) Record each transaction in the proper journal using the following accounts:

111 Cash	311 A. K. Lein, Capital
121 Accounts Receivable	411 Sales
241 Sales Tax Payable	041 Sales Returns and Allowances

For the sales journal, use a sheet of paper ruled like that shown at the top of page 152. For the combined cash journal, use a sheet of paper like that shown in the illustration on pages 160 and 161. (The Check No. column will not be used in this problem.) Number the pages of the journals. (2) Prove the combined cash journal by footing the amount columns; then total and rule this journal. (3) Prove the sales journal by footing the amount columns and determining that the totals of the debit and credit columns are equal in amount. Enter the totals and rule. (4) Open the necessary accounts using the four-column form of ledger paper. Post the sales journal and combined cash journal entries for July, foot the accounts, and enter the balances. (5) Take a trial balance as of July 31, using a sheet of two-column journal paper.

Problem 6-C   Helen M. Harris operates a retail business under the name of The HMH Store. She keeps a purchases journal, a sales journal, and a two-column general journal as books of original entry. The four-column form of general ledger is used. Individual accounts with customers and suppliers are not kept in ledger form; however, the purchase invoices and sales tickets are filed in such a manner that the amounts due to suppliers and due from customers may be determined at any time. All charge sales are payable by the tenth of the following month. The trial balance taken as of March 31, 19—, is reproduced at the top of page 271.

NARRATIVE OF TRANSACTIONS FOR APRIL

Apr. 1. (Friday) Paid the rent for April in advance, $650.
    2. Paid the following bills:
        Gas and electric bill, $49.60.
        Telephone bill, $29.85.
    4. Received Invoice No. 81 dated April 1 from G. B. Jenkins, 13 Holly Drive, St. Louis, MO 63048, for merchandise purchased, $225. Terms, 30 days net.
    4. Sold merchandise on account to W. N. St. John, 10204 Whitlock, St. Louis, MO 63114, $29.25, tax $1.46. Sale No. 51.
    6. Sold merchandise on account to the Breckenridge Inn, 1351 Dunn Road, St. Louis, MO 63135, $90.75, tax $4.54. Sale No. 52.
    8. Sundry cash sales, $196, tax $9.80.

THE HMH STORE
Trial Balance
March 31, 19—

Cash	111	4,926.00	
Accounts Receivable	121	7,410.00	
Merchandise Inventory	131	48,400.00	
Store Equipment	181	2,540.00	
Accounts Payable	231		7,743.42
Sales Tax Payable	241		169.24
Helen M. Harris, Capital	311		14,403.34
Helen M. Harris, Drawing	031	3,000.00	
Sales	411		106,300.00
Sales Returns and Allowances	041	935.00	
Purchases	511	58,700.00	
Purchases Returns and Allowances	051		468.00
Rent Expense	611	1,950.00	
Advertising Expense	621	530.00	
Heating and Lighting Expense	631	275.00	
Telephone Expense	641	158.00	
Miscellaneous Expense	651	260.00	
		129,084.00	129,084.00

Apr. 9. Paid the following suppliers on account:
Chatman Bros., $165.30.
Sexton & Co., $274.20.

11. Received the following remittances to apply on account:
Marriott Hotel, $83.25.
J. W. Weiler, $40.
Ms. B. K. Cheek, $62.70.

12. Received Invoice No. 82 dated April 9 from Rose & Stroble, Columbus, OH 43216, for merchandise purchased, $385. Terms, 30 days net.

13. Paid $169.24 to State Treasurer for March sales tax.

13. Made sales on account as follows:
No. 53, Ms. M. J. Calais, Baden, MO 63147, $96.15, tax $4.81.
No. 54, Marriott Hotel, Lambert Field, St. Louis, MO 63134, $63, tax $3.15.
No. 55, Ms. J. P. Stephan, 4148 Parc Chalet, St. Louis, MO 63114, $77, tax $3.85.

14. Paid $29 for newspaper advertising.

15. Sundry cash sales, $156.75, tax $7.84.

16. Helen M. Harris withdrew $500 for personal use.

18. Made sales on account as follows:
No. 56, C. L. Beggs, 318 E. Claymont, St. Louis, MO 63011, $79.10, tax $3.96.
No. 57, Ms. R. E. Morris, 3818 Connecticut, St. Louis, MO 63111, $34.80, tax $1.74.
No. 58, Breckenridge Inn, 1351 Dunn Road, St. Louis, MO 63135, $82.66, tax $4.13.

Apr. 19. Received Invoice No. 83 dated April 16 from Chatman Bros., Cincinnati, OH 45227, for merchandise purchased, $252.40. Terms, 30 days net.

20. Gave the Breckenridge Inn credit for $14.70 for merchandise returned. (Sales price, $14, tax 70 cents.)

21. Received credit from Chatman Bros. for $19.60 for merchandise returned.

22. Sundry cash sales, $173.40, tax $8.67.

23. Received Invoice No. 84 dated April 22 from Sexton & Co., Detroit, MI 48237, for merchandise purchased, $95.20. Terms, 30 days net.

25. Made sales on account as follows:

     No. 59, J. W. Weiler, 332 Portica, St. Louis, MO 63017, $49.95, tax $2.50.

     No. 60, Marriott Hotel, Lambert Field, St. Louis, MO 63134, $82.56, tax $4.13.

25. Allowed credit for $4.83 to C. L. Beggs for merchandise returned. (Sales price, $4.60, tax 23 cents.)

27. Paid Edison Bros. $75.45 on account.

27. Received $137.38 from Breckenridge Inn to apply on account.

28. Purchased store equipment on account from the Stern Fixture Co., 800 N. 7, St. Louis, MO 63101, $150. Terms, 60 days net.

28. Paid freight and drayage on merchandise purchased, $30.

30. Sundry cash sales, $164.50, tax $8.23.

30. Helen M. Harris withdrew $450 for personal use.

REQUIRED: (1) Journalize the April transactions. Total the purchases journal and rule; foot the sales journal, enter the totals, and rule. Prove each page of the two-column journal by footing the debit and credit columns. (2) Open the necessary general ledger accounts, using the trial balance on page 271 as a guide. Record the April 1 balances as shown in the March 31 trial balance, complete the individual posting from the two-column journal, and complete the summary posting from the purchases and sales journals. Enter the account balances. (3) Take a trial balance using a sheet of two-column journal paper.

Problem 7-A   Ms. F. M. Nations is a dealer in mirrors and glassware. In accounting for notes received from customers in return for extensions of time in paying their obligations, she uses a notes receivable register similar to the one reproduced on pages 172 and 173. Following is a narrative of transactions involving notes received from customers during the current year:

Mar. 7. Received from George Lucas a 60-day, 7% note (No. 1) for $800 dated March 5 and payable at First National Bank, Willow Springs.

Apr. 27. Received from John J. Neel a 90-day, 6% note (No. 2) for $600 dated April 26 and payable at Second National Bank, Lemay.

May   4. Received a check for $809.33 from George Lucas in payment of his note due today plus interest.

20. Received from Edward F. Ford a 60-day, 8% note (No. 3) for $650 dated May 19 and payable at Meachem Park Trust Company, Meachem Park.

July 18. Received a check for $658.67 from Edward F. Ford in payment of his note due today plus interest.

25. Received a check for $609 from John J. Neel in payment of his note due today plus interest.

Sept. 3. Received from W. P. Clark a 90-day, 7% note (No. 4) for $900 dated September 2 and payable at Kirkwood State Bank, Kirkwood.

Dec.   2. Received a check from Kirkwood State Bank for $905.75 in payment of the W. P. Clark note due yesterday plus interest less a $10 collection charge.

REQUIRED: **(1) Prepare entries in two-column journal form to record the foregoing transactions. Foot the amount columns as a means of proof. (2) Make the required entries in a notes receivable register to provide a detailed auxiliary record of the notes received by Ms. F. M. Nations.**

Problem 7-B   J. C. Hess operates a department store. Sometimes he finds it necessary to issue notes to suppliers to obtain extensions of time for payment of their accounts. Unless otherwise stated, all such notes are made payable at the Jefferson County Bank, Jefferson. Following is a narrative of transactions involving notes issued by Mr. Hess during the current year:

Feb.   1. Borrowed $1,000 from the bank on a 90-day, 8% note (No. 1).

Mar.   7. Issued a 60-day, 7% note (No. 2) for $625 to Black & Decker Co.

Apr. 21. Issued a 60-day, 6% note (No. 3) for $720 to J. E. Andrews & Sons.

May   2. Issued a check for $1,020 to the bank in payment of note due today plus interest.

6. Gave Black & Decker Co. a check for $7.29 in payment of the interest and a new note (No. 4) for $625, due in 60 days, with interest at 7%, in settlement of the note due today.

June 20. Issued a check for $727.20 to J. E. Andrews & Sons in payment of note due today plus interest.

July   1. Borrowed $3,000 from the bank on a 90-day, 8% note (No. 5).

5. Issued a check for $632.29 to Black & Decker Co. in payment of note due today plus interest.

Sept. 29. Gave Jefferson County Bank a check for $60 in payment of the interest and a new note (No. 6) for $3,000, due in 60 days with interest at 8%, in settlement of the note due today.

Nov. 28. Issued a check for $3,040 to the bank in payment of note due today plus interest.

REQUIRED: **(1)** Prepare entries in two-column journal form to record the foregoing transactions. Foot the amount columns as a means of proof. **(2)** Make the required entries in a notes payable register, similar to the one reproduced on pages 176 and 177, to provide a detailed auxiliary record of the notes issued.

There are no Practical Accounting Problems for Chapter 8.

Problem 9-A   Ward Wentworth is in the business of retail heating and cooling. Merchandise is sold for cash and on account. On the next page is a reproduction of the Trial Balance columns of his work sheet for the year ended December 31.

REQUIRED: Prepare a ten-column work sheet making the necessary entries in the Adjustments columns to record the following:

(1) Merchandise inventory, end of year, $20,406.40.
(2) Accruals:
Interest accrued on notes payable, $29.34.
Accrued bank credit card expense, $165.40.
(3) Prepaid expenses:
Prepaid insurance unexpired, $448.
Supplies on hand, $96.
(4) Depreciation:
Store equipment, 10% a year, $704.
(5) Uncollectible accounts expense:
Increase allowance for doubtful accounts $128 to provide for estimated loss.

Problem 9-B   Refer to the work sheet for Ward Wentworth (based on Problem 9-A) and from it prepare the following financial statements:

(1) An income statement for the year ended December 31.
(2) A balance sheet in account form as of December 31.

WARD WENTWORTH
Work Sheet
For the Year Ended December 31, 19—

Account	Acct. No.	Trial Balance Debit	Trial Balance Credit
Marshall & Ilsley Bank.....................	111	8,745.44	
Petty Cash Fund.........................	112	100.00	
Accounts Receivable......................	121	9,158.40	
Allowance for Doubtful Accounts..........	012		79.55
Merchandise Inventory...................	131	17,164.80	
Prepaid Insurance.......................	141	896.00	
Supplies................................	151	288.00	
Store Equipment........................	161	7,040.00	
Accumulated Depreciation—Store Equipment	016		704.00
Notes Payable..........................	211		3,500.00
Accrued Interest Payable.................	221		
Accounts Payable.......................	231		10,674.70
Sales Tax Payable.......................	241		828.00
FICA Tax Payable.......................	251		540.00
Employees Income Tax Payable...........	261		590.00
FUTA Tax Payable......................	271		86.00
State Unemployment Tax Payable.........	281		122.60
Accrued Bank Credit Card Expense........	291		
Ward Wentworth, Capital...............	311		42,317.69
Ward Wentworth, Drawing..............	031	12,000.00	
Expense and Revenue Summary...........	321		
Sales.................................	411		82,296.00
Sales Returns and Allowances............	041	286.40	
Purchases..............................	511	57,970.00	
Purchases Returns and Allowances.........	051		294.90
Rent Expense...........................	611	4,800.00	
Advertising Expense.....................	612	624.00	
Salaries Expense........................	613	19,200.00	
Payroll Taxes Expense...................	614	1,320.00	
Insurance Expense.......................	615		
Supplies Expense.......................	616		
Depreciation Expense....................	617		
Uncollectible Accounts Expense...........	618		
Charitable Contributions Expense..........	619	400.00	
Bank Credit Card Expense...............	621	1,827.60	
Miscellaneous Expense...................	622	168.00	
Interest Expense........................	711	44.80	
		142,033.44	142,033.44

Note: Problems 9-B and 10-A are also based on Ward Wentworth's work sheet. If these problems are to be solved, the work sheet prepared in Problem 9-A should be retained for reference until after they are solved, when the solutions of all three problems may be submitted to the instructor.

Problem 10-A   Refer to the work sheet for Ward Wentworth (based on Problem 9-A) and draft the general journal entries required:

(1) To adjust the general ledger accounts so that they will be in agreement with the financial statements.
(2) To close the temporary owner's equity accounts on December 31.
(3) To reserve the accrual adjustments as of January 1.

Problem 10-B
(Complete cycle
problem)

Kathy Dirkers operates a merchandising business as a sole owner. She calls her business "Kathy's Boutique." She keeps a purchases journal, sales journal, combined cash journal, and general ledger. While a petty cash fund is maintained, no payments are made from the fund in December. For her combined cash journal, she uses nine-column paper (9 columns divided — 3 left, 6 right) with headings arranged as follows:

Bank
   (1) Deposits Dr.
   (2) Checks Cr.
   (3) Purchases Discount Cr.

General
   (4) Debit
   (5) Credit
   (6) Accounts Payable Dr.
   (7) Accounts Receivable Cr.
   (8) Sales Cr.
   (9) Sales Tax Payable Cr.

The four-column form of ledger ruling is used. Individual accounts with customers and suppliers are not kept in ledger form; however, the purchase invoices and sales tickets are filed in such a manner that the amounts owed to suppliers and due from customers can be determined at any time. At the end of the eleventh month of this year, her trial balance appeared as shown on page 277.

NARRATIVE OF TRANSACTIONS FOR DECEMBER

Dec. 1. (Thursday) Purchased merchandise from Borowsky Bros., Cedar Rapids, IA 52401, $1,800, Invoice No. 21, dated November 30. Terms, 6/10, n/30.
   2. Paid the December rent, $900. Check No. 64.
   2. Paid the telephone bill, $48. Check No. 65.
   3. Paid Curlee Co. $1,685 in full of December 1 balance. Check No. 66.
   5. Sold merchandise on account to M. T. Clark, 901 Clayton Rd., St. Louis, MO 63117, $150, tax $7.50. Sale No. 121.
   6. Purchased merchandise from the James Co., Jamestown, NY 14701, $1,320. Invoice No. 22, dated December 5. Terms, 30 days.
   7. Received $225 from Vernelle Cone in full settlement of her account.

KATHY'S BOUTIQUE
Trial Balance
November 30, 19—

Clayton Bank	111	14,093.70	
Petty Cash Fund	112	100.00	
Accounts Receivable	121	12,711.70	
Allowance for Doubtful Accounts	012		194.90
Merchandise Inventory	131	58,240.00	
Prepaid Insurance	141	1,330.00	
Supplies	151	224.00	
Store Equipment	181	5,320.00	
Accumulated Depreciation — Store Equipment	018		1,064.00
Notes Payable	211		3,360.00
Accrued Interest Payable	221		
Accounts Payable	231		4,507.60
Sales Tax Payable	241		926.20
Employees Income Tax Payable	251		334.90
FICA Tax Payable	261		278.40
FUTA Tax Payable	271		79.30
State Unemployment Tax Payable	281		106.70
Accrued Bank Credit Card Expense	291		
Kathy Dirkers, Capital	311		94,525.75
Kathy Dirkers, Drawing	031	12,600.00	
Expense and Revenue Summary	321		
Sales	411		234,304.00
Sales Returns and Allowances	041	353.90	
Purchases	511	176,960.00	
Purchases Returns and Alllowances	051		395.10
Purchases Discount	052		308.00
Rent Expense	611	9,900.00	
Advertising Expense	612	6,750.00	
Salaries and Commissions Expense	613	36,200.00	
Payroll Taxes Expense	614	2,483.80	
Miscellaneous Expense	615	501.25	
Insurance Expense	616		
Supplies Expense	617		
Depreciation Expense	618		
Uncollectible Accounts Expense	619		
Bank Credit Card Expense	621	2,577.30	
Interest Expense	711	39.20	
		340,384.85	340,384.85

Dec. 8. Paid Borowsky Bros. $1,692 in settlement of their invoice of November 30, less 6% discount. Check No. 67.

8. Received $222.45 from LaVerne Becht in full settlement of her account.

9. Sold merchandise on account to Isabel Godair, Fenton, MO 63026, $57.30, tax $2.87. Sale No. 122.

Dec. 9. Received a notice from Clayton Bank that $352.25 had been deducted from the account of Kathy's Boutique, representing a discount of 3 percent on the amount net of returns of BankAmericard and Master Charge vouchers that had been deposited during November.

10. Purchased merchandise from the Thayer Mfg. Co., Kansas City, MO 64019, $483.20. Invoice No. 23, dated December 9. Terms, 30 days.

12. Sold merchandise on account to Fae Underwood, Irondale Estates, St. Louis, MO 63101, $150.40, tax $7.52. Sale No. 123.

13. Issued Check No. 68 to Clayton Bank, a U.S. Depositary, in payment of the following taxes:

(a) Employees' income tax withheld during November....			$334.90
(b) FICA tax:			
	On employees (withheld during November)........	$139.20	
	On the employer.............................	139.20	278.40
Total...			$613.30

14. Sold merchandise on account to Marian Bock, 873 Cliff St., Ferguson, MO 63135, $145, tax $7.25. Sale No. 124.

15. Issued Check No. 69 payable to State Treasurer for $926.20 for November sales tax.

17. Kathy Dirkers withdrew $300 for personal use. Check No. 70.

19. Gave Fae Underwood credit for $52.50 because a part of the merchandise sold her on the twelfth was returned. (Sales price, $50, tax $2.50)

20. Sold merchandise on account to M. T. Clark, 901 Clayton Rd., St. Louis, MO 63117, $85, tax $4.25. Sale No. 125.

21. Purchased merchandise from Barbie Brooks, Inc., Cincinnati, OH 45202, $1,096.50. Invoice No. 24, dated December 20. Terms, 8/10, n/30.

22. Received $105.42 from Fae Underwood for balance of Sale No. 123.

23. Paid bill for advertising, $300. Check No. 71.

26. Sold merchandise on account to Joan Aach, 195 Johnson St., St. Louis, MO 63130, $225.75, tax $11.29. Sale No. 126.

26. Purchased merchandise from Borowsky Bros., Cedar Rapids, IA 52401, $1,541.90. Invoice No. 25, dated December 23. Terms, 2/10, n/30.

26. Received a check for $100 from M. T. Clark to apply on account.

27. Sold merchandise on account to Fae Underwood, Irondale Estates, St. Louis, MO 63101, $235.50, tax $11.78. Sale No. 127.

27. Sent the Thayer Mfg. Co. a check for $200 to apply on account. Check No. 72.

28. Sold merchandise on account to Linda Boyd, 812 Sixth St., Kirksville, MO 63501, $92.50, tax $4.63. Sale No. 128.

28. Purchased store equipment from the Mattoon Supply Co., Mattoon, IL 61938, $520. Terms, 60 days net.

29. Received $60.17 from Isabel Godair in payment of Sale No. 122.

29. Received credit from Borowsky Bros. for $60 because a part of the merchandise purchased on the twenty-sixth was returned by agreement.

29. Sold merchandise on account to Isabel Godair, Fenton, MO 63026, $122.50, tax $6.13. Sale No. 129.

Dec. 30. Sundry cash and bank credit card sales for month, $14,414.80, tax $720.74.

30. Issued Check No. 73 payable to Payroll for $2,606.70.

PAYROLL STATEMENT FOR MONTH ENDED DECEMBER 31

Total wages and commissions earned during period..........		$3,300.00
Employees' taxes to be withheld		
(a) Employees' income tax............................	$495.30	
(b) FICA tax @ 6%...................................	198.00	693.30
Net amount payable to employees........................		$2,606.70
Employer's payroll taxes:		
(a) FICA tax @ 6%...................................		$ 198.00
(b) UC taxes —		
State @ 2.7%.................................	$ 89.10	
Federal @ 0.5%..............................	16.50	105.60
Total...		$ 303.60

(In addition to recording the amounts withheld from employees' wages for income tax purposes and for FICA tax, the social security tax imposed on the employer should also be recorded.)

REQUIRED: **(1)** Journalize the December transactions. **(2)** Open the necessary general ledger accounts and record the December 1 balances, using the November 30 trial balance as the source of the needed information. Complete the individual and summary posting from the books of original entry. **(3)** Take a trial balance of the general ledger accounts. **(4)** Prepare a ten-column work sheet making the required adjustments from the information given below. Number the pages of the journals as follows:

Purchases Journal........ Page 34
Sales Journal............ Page 46
Combined Cash Journal.. Pages 49–51

(a) Merchandise inventory, end of year, $81,900.

(b) Accruals:
Interest accrued on notes payable, $33.60.
Accrued bank credit card expense, $357.65.

(c) Prepaid expenses:
Prepaid insurance unexpired, $886.
Supplies on hand, $70.

(d) Depreciation:
Store equipment, 10% a year, $532.

(e) Uncollectible accounts expense:
Increase allowance for doubtful accounts $295.90 to provide for estimated loss.

(5) Prepare an income statement for the year ending December 31 and a balance sheet in report form as of December 31. (6) Record the adjusting entries in the combined cash journal and post. (7) Record the closing entries in the combined cash journal and post. (8) Place "no balance" symbols in the accounts that are in balance after the adjusting and closing entries have been posted. (9) Take a post-closing trial balance. (10) Record the necessary reversing entries as of January 1 in the combined cash journal. Place "no balance" symbols in the accounts that are closed.

Chapter 11

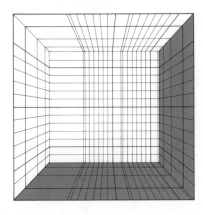

ACCOUNTING FOR PURCHASES

In Chapter 6, mention was made of the fact that the word "purchase" usually is taken to mean the purchase of merchandise. However, the word is often used in the broader sense to refer to the buying of many sorts of property. In this chapter the broader meaning applies, though much of the discussion relates to the purchase of merchandise.

PURCHASING PROCEDURE

Merchandise for resale and other property for use in the operation of a business enterprise may be purchased either for cash or on account. In one enterprise the buying may be done by the owner or by an employee, and it may require only part-time attention. In a large enterprise a purchasing department may be maintained with a manager and staff who will devote their entire time to buying activities. The successful operation of such a purchasing department requires an efficient organization as well as the proper equipment.

The purchase requisition
A form used to request the purchasing department to purchase merchandise or other property is known as a *purchase requisition*. Such requests may come from any department of an enterprise. Purchase requisitions should be numbered consecutively to prevent the loss or misuse of

281

any of the forms. Usually they are prepared in duplicate with the original going to the purchasing department and the duplicate copy being retained in the department originating the requisition.

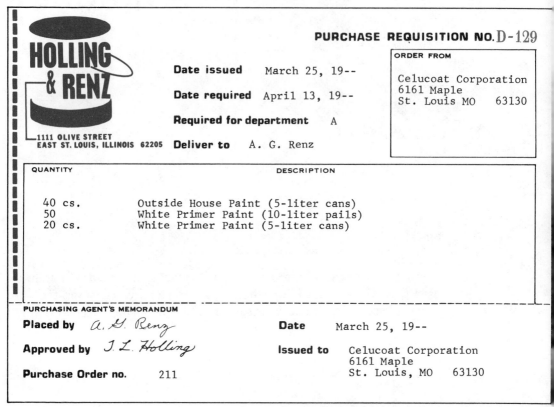

PURCHASE REQUISITION NO. D-129

HOLLING & RENZ

1111 OLIVE STREET
EAST ST. LOUIS, ILLINOIS 62205

Date issued   March 25, 19--

Date required   April 13, 19--

Required for department   A

Deliver to   A. G. Renz

ORDER FROM

Celucoat Corporation
6161 Maple
St. Louis MO   63130

QUANTITY	DESCRIPTION
40 cs.	Outside House Paint (5-liter cans)
50	White Primer Paint (10-liter pails)
20 cs.	White Primer Paint (5-liter cans)

PURCHASING AGENT'S MEMORANDUM

Placed by   a. G. Renz

Approved by   J. L. Holling

Purchase Order no.   211

Date   March 25, 19--

Issued to   Celucoat Corporation
6161 Maple
St. Louis, MO   63130

Purchase Requisition

A purchase requisition is reproduced above. The requisition specifies merchandise wanted in Department A. The merchandising business conducted by Holling & Renz is organized into two departments. Requisitions for merchandise originate with the heads of these two departments. After the purchase requisition shown in the illustration was approved by Holling, an order was placed with the Celucoat Corporation, manufacturers of paints and varnishes, as indicated by the purchasing agent's memorandum at the bottom of the form. The purchase requisition, when approved, is the purchasing department's authority to order the merchandise or other property described in the requisition.

The purchase order

A written order by the buyer for merchandise or other property specified in the buyer company's purchase requisition is known as a *purchase order*. A purchase order may be prepared on a printed stock form, on a specially designed form, or on an order blank furnished by a supplier of goods or services. Purchase orders should be numbered consecutively. Usually they are prepared with multiple copies. The original copy goes to the *supplier* or *vendor* — the person or firm from whom the merchandise or other property is ordered. Sometimes the duplicate copy also goes to the supplier. If this is the case, this copy — called the "acknowledgment copy" — will have a space for the supplier to sign to indicate his

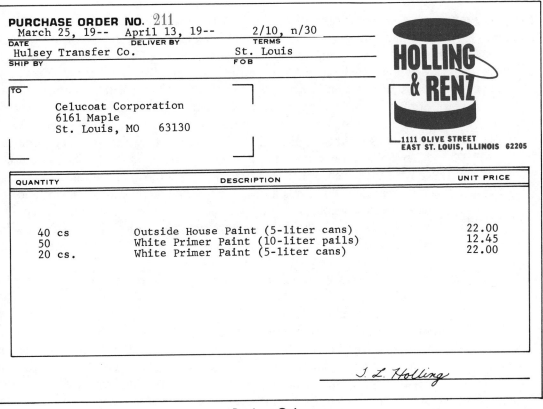

PURCHASE ORDER NO. 211		
March 25, 19-- April 13, 19--	2/10, n/30	
DATE DELIVER BY	TERMS	
Hulsey Transfer Co.	St. Louis	HOLLING & RENZ
SHIP BY	FOB	

TO

Celucoat Corporation
6161 Maple
St. Louis, MO   63130

1111 OLIVE STREET
EAST ST. LOUIS, ILLINOIS 62205

QUANTITY	DESCRIPTION	UNIT PRICE
40 cs	Outside House Paint (5-liter cans)	22.00
50	White Primer Paint (10-liter pails)	12.45
20 cs.	White Primer Paint (5-liter cans)	22.00

J. L. Holling

Purchase Order

acceptance of the order. Such acceptance creates a formal contract. The signed acknowledgment copy is then returned to the ordering firm. Sometimes a copy of the purchase order is sent to the department of the company that requisitioned the purchase. In many organizations a copy of the purchase order is sent to the receiving clerk. The procedure followed by some firms requires that the accounting department receive a copy of the purchase order to provide a basis for verifying the charges made by the supplier. A variety of practices are followed with respect to requisitioning purchases, placing orders, checking goods received and charges made, recording purchases, and paying suppliers. Each organization adopts procedures best suited to its particular needs.

A purchase order is reproduced on page 283. The quantity and the description of the merchandise ordered are the same as were specified in the purchase requisition reproduced on page 282. The unit prices shown in the purchase order are those quoted by the supplier and it is expected that the merchandise will be billed at such prices.

The purchase invoice

A business form prepared by the seller that lists the items shipped, their cost, and the method of shipment is commonly referred to as an *invoice*. From the viewpoint of the seller, it is considered a *sales invoice;* from the viewpoint of the buyer, it is considered a *purchase invoice.*

A purchase invoice may be received by the buyer before or after delivery of the merchandise or other property ordered. As invoices are received, it is customary to number them consecutively. These numbers should not be confused with the suppliers' numbers, which represent their sale numbers. After being numbered, each purchase invoice should be checked with a copy of the purchase order to determine that the quantity, the description, the prices, and the terms agree and that the method of shipment and the date of delivery conform to the instructions and specifications. A separate approval form may be used, or approval may be stamped on the invoice by means of a rubber stamp. If a separate approval form is used, it may be stapled to or be pasted on the invoice form.

An example of a purchase invoice is reproduced on page 285. A rubber stamp was used to imprint the approval form on the face of the invoice. When the merchandise is received, the contents of the shipment may be checked by the receiving clerk with a copy of the purchase order, or he may prepare a separate *receiving report*. In the latter event, the receiving report and the purchase order must be checked by a clerk in either the purchasing department or the accounting department. After the prices and extensions are verified, the purchase invoice is recorded by entering it in the *invoice register* and then posting it to the account of the proper creditor in the accounts payable ledger. The invoice is then held in an unpaid invoice file until it is paid.

Back Orders. Sometimes the supplier is unable to ship immediately a part or all of the merchandise ordered. However, an invoice may be immediately sent for the complete order, indicating on it what has been back ordered and when such items will be shipped. Reference to the purchase invoice reproduced on the opposite page will indicate that while

40 cases of outside house paint were ordered, only 30 were shipped immediately by the Celucoat Corporation. Notice of this shortage was indicated on the invoice. In this instance, only the items shipped were billed.

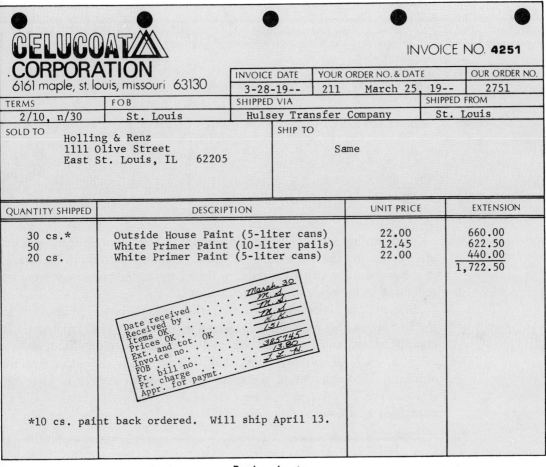

Purchase Invoice

Trade Discounts. Many manufacturers and wholesalers quote list prices (printed) which are subject to trade discounts. This makes possible the publication of catalogs with quotations of prices that will not be subject to frequent changes. Some firms, such as those dealing in hardware and jewelry, publish catalogs listing thousands of items. Such catalogs are costly, and considerable loss might be involved when price changes occur if it were not for the fact that discount rates may be changed without changing the list or catalog prices. This practice also has the advantage of permitting retail dealers to display catalogs to their customers without revealing what the items of merchandise cost the dealers.

When an invoice is subject to a trade discount, the discount is usually shown as a deduction from the total amount of the invoice. For example, if the invoice shown on page 285 had been subject to a trade discount of 10 percent, the discount might be stated in the body of the invoice in the manner shown below:

QUANTITY SHIPPED	DESCRIPTION	UNIT PRICE	EXTENSION
30 cs.*	Outside House Paint (5-liter cans)	22.00	660.00
50	White Primer Paint (10-liter pails)	12.45	622.50
20 cs.	White Primer Paint (5-liter cans)	22.00	440.00
			1,722.50
		Less 10% discount	172.25
			1,550.25
*10 cs. paint back ordered. Will ship April 13.			

In recording such an invoice the amount to be entered is the net amount after deducting the trade discount; trade discounts should not be entered in the accounts of either the seller or the buyer, as they represent merely a reduction in the price of the merchandise.

Sometimes a series or chain of trade discounts is allowed. For example, the list prices may be subject to discounts of 25, 10, and 5 percent. In computing the total discount where two or more trade discounts are allowed, each discount is computed separately on the successive net amounts. For example, if the gross amount of an invoice is $100 and discounts of 25, 10, and 5 percent are allowed, the net amount should be computed as follows:

Gross amount of invoice...	$100.00
Less 25%...	25.00
Balance..	$ 75.00
Less 10%...	7.50
Balance..	$ 67.50
Less 5%..	3.38
Net amount	$ 64.12

In recording this invoice only the net amount, or $64.12, should be entered.

Cash Discounts. Many firms follow the practice of allowing cash discounts as an inducement for prompt payment of invoices. The terms of payment should be clearly indicated on the invoice. It will be noted that the terms specified on the invoice reproduced on page 285 are "2/10, n/30." This means that a discount of 2 percent will be allowed if payment is made within 10 days from the date of the invoice (March 28), that is, if payment is made by April 7.

Should the invoice be paid on or before April 7, 2 percent of $1,722.50, or $34.45, may be deducted and a check for $1,688.05 may be issued in full settlement of the invoice. After April 7 no discount will be allowed, and the total amount, or $1,722.50, must be paid not later than 30 days after the date of the invoice, that is, by April 27.

Cash discounts usually are ignored at the time of recording purchase invoices, even though it may be the policy of a firm to pay all invoices in time to get the benefit of any cash discounts offered. For example, the invoice reproduced on page 285 should be recorded by debiting the proper account or accounts and by crediting Accounts Payable for $1,722.50. The discount taken at time of payment on or before April 7 will be entered at the time of recording the check issued in settlement of the invoice. At the end of the period and credit balance of the purchases discount account is shown in the income statement as a deduction from the cost of goods purchased. Sometimes purchases discount is regarded as "other revenue" but this treatment is not logical and is disappearing from practice.

A minor complication arises in treating purchases discount as a reduction in purchase cost when purchases are accounted for on a departmental basis. While it would be possible to have two or more purchases discount accounts and to analyze each discount taken to determine the department (or departments) to which it relates, such a procedure could be very time-consuming. The resulting accuracy might not be worth the trouble. An acceptable alternative is to record all purchases discount in a single account whose balance, as a part of the closing process, is allocated among the departmental cost of goods sold accounts in proportion to the net purchases of the departments. (The nature and use of cost of goods sold accounts will be explained and illustrated in Chapters 17 and 18.)

Sometimes an invoice is subject to both trade and cash discounts. In such cases the trade discount should be deducted from the gross amount of the invoice before the cash discount is computed and deducted. For example, if the invoice reproduced on page 285 were subject to a trade discount of 10 percent and the terms were 2/10, n/30, the net amount payable within 10 days from the date of the invoice should be computed in the following manner:

Amount of invoice...	$1,722.50
Less trade discount, 10%.......................................	172.25
Amount subject to cash discount.................................	$1,550.25
Less cash discount, 2%..	31.00
Net amount payable..	$1,519.25

Usually an entire invoice must be paid for within the time specified in order to obtain the benefit of any cash discount offered. However, in some instances, the purchaser may be allowed the usual cash discount for partial payment of an invoice within the time specified. Thus, if, instead of paying the entire invoice of the Celucoat Corporation, Holling & Renz had made a payment of $800 on the invoice by April 7, the Celucoat Corporation might agree to allow them the cash discount of 2 percent. In such case the amount of the discount should be computed in the following manner:

```
100% = amount for which Holling & Renz should receive credit
100% − 2% = 98%
98% = $800
$800 ÷ 98% = $816.33
$816.33 − $800 = $16.33 discount
```

This transaction should be recorded on the books of Holling & Renz by debiting Accounts Payable for $816.33, by crediting Purchases Discount for $16.33, and by crediting the bank account for $800.

Terms. The terms commonly used in connection with purchase invoices are interpreted as follows:

30 days	The amount of the invoice must be paid within 30 days from its date.
2/10, n/30	A discount of 2% will be allowed if payment is made within 10 days from the date of the invoice; otherwise, the total amount of the invoice must be paid within 30 days from its date.
2/EOM, n/60	A discount of 2% will be allowed if payment is made before the end of the month; otherwise, the total amount of the invoice must be paid within 60 days of its date.
4/10 EOM	A discount of 4% will be allowed if payment is made within 10 days after the end of the current month.
COD	Collect on delivery. The amount of the invoice must be paid at the time the merchandise is delivered.
FOB Shipping Point	Free on board at point of origin of the shipment. Under such terms the buyer must pay all transportation costs and assume all risks from the time the merchandise is accepted for shipment by the carrier.
FOB Destination	Free on board at destination of the shipment. The seller will pay the transportation costs and will assume all responsibility for the merchandise until it reaches the carrier's delivery point at destination.

Miscellaneous forms

In addition to the forms previously discussed, there are a number of miscellaneous forms, such as bills of lading, freight bills, drayage bills, and credit memorandums, that may be used in connection with the purchase of merchandise or other property. It is important that the function of these forms be understood in order that they may be properly processed.

Bills of Lading. The desired method of shipment is usually specified on the purchase order and the actual method of shipment is indicated on the purchase invoice. When shipment is made by railroad, highway freight, or air, the shipper is given a receipt that is known as a *bill of lading*.

A bill of lading is prepared in triplicate. The first copy is referred to as the original, the second copy as the shipping order, and the third copy as the memorandum. The freight agent signs all three copies, returning the original and the memorandum to the shipper and retaining the shipping order. The shipper in turn may send either the original or the memorandum copy to the buyer and retain the other copy for his files.

The merchandise or other property is delivered to the freight agent in cases, cartons, bundles, or packages; hence, the description in the bill of lading may differ from the description in the purchase invoice. In addition to describing the merchandise in the bill of lading, the number of packages and the weight of each are indicated. The freight rate depends upon the type of merchandise being shipped, the distance it is being

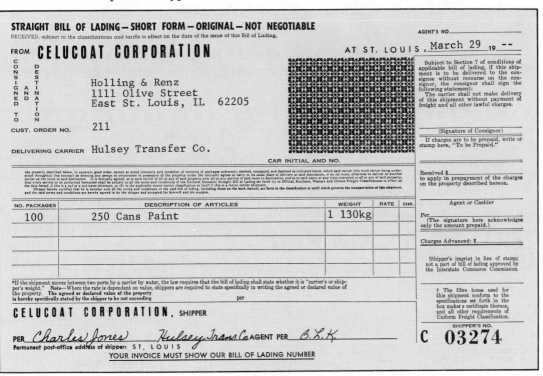

Straight Bill of Lading

shipped, and the weight of the shipment. The rate per 100 kilograms on a carload (CL) is lower than the rate on less than a carload (LCL).

A model filled-in bill of lading is reproduced above. This is known as a *straight bill of lading*, under the terms of which title to the merchandise passed to Holling & Renz when the merchandise was delivered to the transportation company. When Holling & Renz present a copy of this bill of lading to the local agent of the carrier, they will be entitled to receive the merchandise.

COD Purchases. Merchandise or other property may be purchased on COD terms, that is, *collect on delivery* or *cash on delivery*. COD shipments may be received by parcel post, express, or freight. When such shipments are received by parcel post or express, the recipient must pay for the property at the time of delivery. The bill may include transportation charges and COD fees. In any event, the total amount paid represents the cost of the property purchased.

When COD shipments are made by freight, the amount to be collected by the transportation company should be entered immediately below the description of the merchandise on the bill of lading. A copy of the sales invoice may be inserted in an envelope which can be pasted to the outside of the package, carton, or case. The transportation company will then collect the amount specified, plus a COD collection fee, at the time of delivering the merchandise, and will in turn remit to the shipper.

Freight Bills. At the time merchandise or other property is delivered to a transportation company for shipment, an agent of the transportation

			1	ORIGINAL FREIGHT BILL		NUMBER 385745	
TO	Holling & Renz 1111 Olive Street East St. Louis, IL 62205			CODE 3	TERMINAL St. Louis		SHIPPER NO. C 03274
FROM	Celucoat Corporation 6161 Maple St. Louis, MO 63130			FOR OFFICE USE ONLY CL NAME PRO DIV DATE March 29			
	HULSEY TRANSFER CO.			Broadway at Poplar, St. Louis, Missouri 63102			
PIECES	DESCRIPTION			WEIGHT	RATE	PREPAID	COLLECT
100	250 Cans Paint			1130kg	1.54		17.40
					C. O. D. AMOUNT		
	ARTICLES LISTED HAVE BEEN RECEIVED IN GOOD CONDITION BY *m.s.* DATE March 30				FEE DRIVER COLLECT		

Freight Bill

*Note that the weight is shown in kilograms (abbreviated "kg") and that the rate is the charge per 100 kilograms. A kilogram is slightly more than 2.2 pounds.

company prepares a *waybill* — a document which describes the shipment, shows the point of origin and destination, and indicates any special handling that may be required. The original is forwarded to the agent of the transportation company at the station to which the shipment is directed. When the shipment arrives at the destination, a bill for the transportation charges called a *freight bill* is prepared. Sometimes the recipient of the shipment is required to pay the bill before the property can be obtained.

A reproduction of a freight bill is presented on the preceding page. A comparison of this freight bill with the bill of lading reproduced on page 289 will show that it contains the same description of the shipment. In addition, however, the freight charges are shown.

Trucking companies usually make what is known as "store-to-door delivery." Freight shipments made by railroad or airline may also be delivered to the recipient's place of business at no extra charge. In case such service is not rendered by the transportation company, it may be necessary for the recipient to employ a drayage company to transport the merchandise from the freight station to the place of business. In such a case, the drayage company will submit a bill (a *drayage bill*) for its services.

Credit Memorandums. Ordinarily the buyer expects to receive the merchandise or other property ordered and to pay for it at the agreed

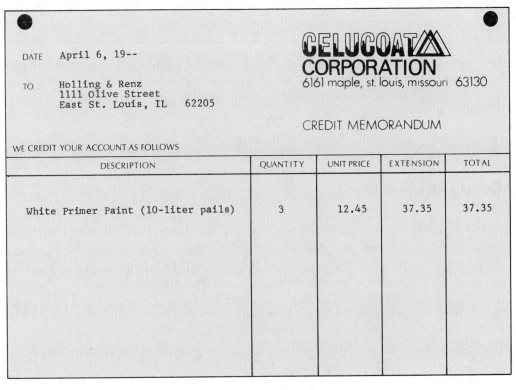

| WE CREDIT YOUR ACCOUNT AS FOLLOWS | | | | |
DESCRIPTION	QUANTITY	UNIT PRICE	EXTENSION	TOTAL
White Primer Paint (10-liter pails)	3	12.45	37.35	37.35

DATE   April 6, 19--

TO   Holling & Renz
      1111 Olive Street
      East St. Louis, IL   62205

CELUCOAT CORPORATION
6161 maple, st. louis, missouri 63130

CREDIT MEMORANDUM

Credit Memorandum

price in accordance with the terms specified in the purchase invoice. However, part or all of the merchandise or other property may be returned to the supplier for various reasons, such as those listed on the next page.

(a) It may not conform to the specifications in the purchase order.

(b) A mistake may have been made in placing the order and the supplier may give permission for it to be returned.

(c) It may have been delayed in shipment and, thus, the buyer cannot dispose of it. This sometimes happens with seasonal goods.

If the merchandise received is unsatisfactory or the prices charged are not in accord with an existing agreement or with previous quotations, an adjustment may be made that is referred to as an *allowance*.

When merchandise is to be returned to the supplier for credit, a charge-back invoice is usually issued by the buyer for the purchase price of the merchandise returned. Upon receipt of the merchandise, the supplier will usually issue a credit memorandum for the amount of the credit allowed. A model filled-in credit memorandum is reproduced on page 291. This form indicates that the Celucoat Corporation has given Holling & Renz credit for the return of three 10-liter pails of white primer paint.

Report No. 11-1

Complete Report No. 11-1 in the study assignments and submit your working papers to the instructor for approval. Then continue with the following textbook discussion until Report No. 11-2 is required.

ACCOUNTING PRACTICE

The practices followed in accounting for purchases must be tailored to conform to the nature of the business, the volume of purchases of all sorts, and the type and amount of information that is wanted. The discussion and illustration that follow explain a procedure that has wide application in accounting for purchases.

Invoice register

In many firms all incoming invoices covering purchases on account, whether they represent purchases of merchandise, supplies, or other property, are recorded in one book of original entry. Many firms also prefer to keep the merchandise accounts on a departmental basis in order that more information may be available and that better control may be exercised.

Property purchased may consist of: **(1)** merchandise bought for resale; **(2)** supplies, such as letterheads and envelopes for office use, catalogs and circulars for advertising purposes, wrapping paper and twine for use in wrapping and shipping, and cleaning supplies; or **(3)** long-lived assets, such as office equipment, store equipment, and delivery equipment, bought for use in operating the business.

The use of a properly designed columnar register facilitates the recording in one book of account of all incoming invoices covering purchases on account, regardless of whether they represent purchases of merchandise, supplies, or long-lived assets. Such a register also facilitates a proper classification of essential data and makes summary posting possible. A register of this type is often called an *invoice register*.

When all incoming invoices covering purchases on account are recorded in an invoice register, regardless of whether the invoices represent the purchase of merchandise or other property, provision should be made for a proper classification of the debits and the credits. If the merchandise accounts are kept on a departmental basis, a separate column should be provided for recording the merchandise purchased for each department. The use of special columns for this purpose will facilitate summary posting. General Ledger Debit and Credit columns should also be provided for recording items that must be posted individually to the general ledger accounts. If individual accounts with suppliers are kept in a subsidiary ledger, a summary or control account for accounts payable must be kept in the general ledger.

The procedure in recording all incoming invoices covering purchases on account in an invoice register and of keeping the merchandise accounts on a departmental basis will be illustrated **(1)** by showing the chronological recording of a group of selected transactions in an invoice register, **(2)** by showing the direct posting of the purchase invoices to the individual accounts of suppliers kept in a subsidiary accounts payable ledger, and **(3)** by showing the posting from the invoice register to the proper general ledger accounts.

Holling & Renz are engaged in the wholesale paint and varnish business. Two departments are maintained — Department A, paint, and Department B, varnish. Separate merchandise accounts are kept for each department in order that the gross margin on sales for each department may be computed separately. In addition to separate departmental purchases accounts and sales accounts, separate departmental accounts are kept for freight charges and for returns and allowances. Only one account is kept for sales discounts and one other account for purchases discounts. The balances of these two latter accounts are allocated in the adjusting and closing process at the end of the period. A list of the above-mentioned accounts with appropriate account numbers is shown on page 295.

INVOICE REGISTER FOR MONTH OF *April* 19___   PAGE *34*

	PURCHASES DEPT. A	DEPT. B	GL ACCT. NO.	GL AMOUNT	✓	DAY	DATE OF INV.	INV. NO.	NAME	✓	ACCOUNTS PAYABLE	✓	GL ACCT. NO.	GL AMOUNT	✓
1									AMOUNTS FORWARDED						
2	172250					1	3/30	151	Glucoat Corporation		172250	✓			
3		109600				1	3/29	152	Mid-States Paint Co.		109600	✓			
4			161	11590	✓	1	3/31	153	Orchard Paper Co.		11590	✓			
5			171	28760	✓	5	4/1	154	Commercial Machine Co.		28760	✓			
6	1200					5	3/29	152	Mid-States Paint Co.(Corrected Invc)		1200	✓			
7	136200		541	1378	✓	6	4/3	155	Sports Point Industries		137578	✓			
8		32860	551	394	✓	6	4/4	156	Point City, Inc.		33254	✓			
9			163	9600	✓	6	4/5	157	S. G. Adams Co.		9600	✓			
10			191	49620	✓	6	4/3	158	Business Interiors, Inc.		49620	✓			
11			271	400	✓	8	4/5	157	S. G. Adams Co. (Corrected Invc)		400	✓	163	400	✓
31	46 4230	61 1534		1 49617							54 02981			400	
31	46 4230	61 1534		1 49617							54 02981			400	
32	(511)	(521)		(✓)							(277)			(✓)	

Holling & Renz — Invoice Register

411 Sales — Department A
    041 Sales Returns and Allowances — Department A
421 Sales — Department B
    042 Sales Returns and Allowances — Department B
    043 Sales Discount
511 Purchases — Department A
    051 Purchases Returns and Allowances — Department A
521 Purchases — Department B
    052 Purchases Returns and Allowances — Department B
    053 Purchases Discount
541 Freight In — Department A
551 Freight In — Department B

The form of the invoice register used by Holling & Renz is illustrated on page 294. A narrative of the transactions that have been entered in the invoice register follows. It will be helpful to check each transaction and to note how it was entered in the invoice register.

HOLLING & RENZ

Narrative of Transactions

Friday, April 1

Received the following purchase invoices:

No. 151, Celucoat Corporation, St. Louis, MO 63130; paint, $1,722.50; terms, March 30 — 2/10, n/30; freight collect.

No. 152, Mid-States Paint Co., Crestwood, MO 63126; varnish, $1,096; terms, March 29 — 2/10, n/30; freight collect.

No. 153, Orchard Paper Co., St. Louis, MO 63119; store supplies (Account No. 161) $115.90; terms, March 31 — 30 days.

No. 154, Commercial Machine Co., St. Louis, MO 63112; store equipment (Account No. 171) $287.60; terms, April 1 — n/30.

Tuesday, April 5

Received a corrected purchase invoice from Mid-States Paint Co. for $1,108. (See Purchase Invoice No. 152.)

Wednesday, April 6

Received the following purchase invoices:

No. 155, Spatz Paint Industries, Maplewood, MO 63102; paint, $1,362; terms, April 2 — 2/10, n/60; freight prepaid and added to invoice, $13.78.

No. 156, Paint City, Inc., St. Louis, MO 63103; varnish, $328.60; terms, April 4 — 1/10, n/30; freight prepaid and added to invoice, $3.94.

No. 157, S. G. Adams Co., St. Louis, MO 63103; office supplies (Account No. 163) $96; terms, April 5 — 30 days.

No. 158, Business Interiors, Inc., Kansas City, KS 66110; office equipment (Account No. 191) $479.40; terms, April 2 — 2/10, n/30; freight prepaid and added to invoice, $16.80.

Friday, April 8

Received a corrected purchase invoice from S. G. Adams Co. for $92. (See Purchase Invoice No. 157.)

(The transactions for April 9 through April 30 are omitted.)

> Since postings to suppliers' accounts in the subsidiary accounts payable ledger will be made directly from copies of the invoices, a check mark was placed in the Check (√) column beside the Accounts Payable column as each item was entered in the invoice register.

Corrected Purchase Invoices. If a corrected purchase invoice is received before the original invoice has been entered in the invoice register, the original invoice may be discarded and the corrected invoice may be entered in the usual manner. If a corrected purchase invoice is received after the original invoice has been entered in the invoice register and has been posted to the individual account of the supplier, the corrected invoice may be entered in the invoice register if the amount of the corrected invoice is more than the amount of the original invoice. The increase should be recorded by debiting the proper account and by crediting Accounts Payable. (See Invoice No. 152.) The amount of the increase should also be posted to the credit of the proper supplier's account in the subsidiary accounts payable ledger.

If the amount of the corrected invoice is less than the amount of the original invoice, the decrease should be recorded by debiting Accounts Payable and by crediting the proper account. The entry can be recorded in the invoice register if General Ledger Debit and Credit columns are provided. (See Invoice No. 157.) If the needed columns are not provided in the invoice register, the entry must be made in the general journal. The amount of the decrease should be posted to the debit of the proper supplier's account in the subsidiary accounts payable ledger. The corrected invoice should be attached to the original invoice.

Proving the Invoice Register. The invoice register may be footed and the footings may be proved at any time by comparing the sum of the debit footings with the sum of the credit footings. The footings of Holling & Renz's invoice register were proved as of April 30 in the following manner:

Column Headings	Debit	Credit
Purchases, Dept. A	$46,422.30	
Purchases, Dept. B	6,115.34	
General Ledger	1,496.17	
Accounts Payable		$54,029.81
General Ledger		4.00
Totals	$54,033.81	$54,033.81

It is very common practice to make the proof simply by using an adding machine to see that the totals of the debit columns and the totals of the credit columns are the same. The adding machine tape would appear as follows:

```
                            *
            46,422.30
             6,115.34
             1,496.17

            54,033.81*

                            *
            54,029.81
                 4.00

            54,033.81*
```

Ledgers   The ledgers used by Holling & Renz include a general ledger with four-column ruling and a subsidiary accounts payable ledger with three-column ruling. The accounts affected by the transactions recorded in the invoice register reproduced on page 294 are shown in skeleton form on pages 299–301.

Posting Procedure. Posting to Holling & Renz's general ledger and accounts payable ledger involves both individual posting and summary posting.

After each purchase invoice was entered in the invoice register, it was immediately posted to the proper supplier's account in the accounts payable ledger. The posting was done directly from the invoice, the invoice number being inserted in the Posting Reference column of the accounts payable ledger.

While the posting to suppliers' accounts may be done from the invoice register, there are certain advantages in posting directly from the purchase invoices. For example, the invoice provides all the information needed in posting, whereas, if the posting were done from the invoice register, it would be necessary to enter in the invoice register all the information needed in posting, regardless of whether or not it served any other purpose. Furthermore, if an error were made in entering an invoice in the invoice register, it would probably be carried over into the accounts payable ledger through the posting, whereas if the posting is done directly from the invoice, it is not likely that the same error would be made twice.

Posting directly from incoming invoices to the suppliers' accounts in the accounts payable ledger is not only efficient; it also provides a sound method of internal check and control. One bookkeeper may record the invoices in the invoice register and complete such posting as is required from the invoice register to the general ledger accounts, while another bookkeeper may post directly from the invoices to the suppliers' accounts in the accounts payable ledger. Thus the work is divided between two employees. Proof of the accuracy of their work is obtained periodically by preparing a schedule of accounts payable and comparing its total with the balance of the accounts payable control account kept in the general ledger.

Posting to the accounts of suppliers in the accounts payable ledger may be done either by hand or by machine. The use of posting machines for this purpose may be appropriate where there are a large number of accounts and a large number of transactions involved. Such machines frequently are electronic and capable of being programmed.

Individual Posting. Each invoice entered in the Accounts Payable Credit column of the invoice register was posted individually to the proper supplier's account in the accounts payable ledger shown on pages 300 and 301. In the case of invoices involving prepaid transportation charges, the amounts of the merchandise or other property purchased and the transportation charges were posted separately. In posting the invoice of April 2 received from Spatz Paint Industries, the amount of the merchandise, $1,362, and the prepaid freight charge, $13.78, were posted separately to the account of Spatz Paint Industries. The reason for doing this is that the transportation charges are never subject to discount; only the amount of the merchandise purchased may be subject to discount.

It was also necessary to post individually each item entered in the General Ledger Debit and Credit columns of the invoice register. Usually this posting is completed daily. As each item was posted, a check mark was placed in the Check ($\sqrt{}$) column following the proper Amount column of the invoice register, and the number of the invoice was entered in the Posting Reference column of the ledger account.

Summary Posting. Summary posting is usually completed at the end of each month and involves the following procedure:

    (a) The total of the column headed Purchases, Dept. A, was posted to the debit of Purchases — Department A, Account No. 511, in the general ledger.

    (b) The total of the column headed Purchases, Dept. B, was posted to the debit of Purchases — Department B, Account No. 521, in the general ledger.

    (c) The total of the column headed Accounts Payable was posted to the credit of Accounts Payable, Account No. 271, in the general ledger.

As the total of each column was posted, the account number was written in parentheses immediately below the total in the invoice register and the page number of the invoice register was written in the Posting Reference

General Ledger (Partial)

ACCOUNT STORE SUPPLIES   ACCOUNT No. 161

DATE		ITEM	POST. REF.	DEBIT	CREDIT	BALANCE DEBIT	BALANCE CREDIT
19—Apr.	1	Balance	√			52.11	
	1		IR34	115.90		168.01	

ACCOUNT OFFICE SUPPLIES   ACCOUNT No. 163

DATE		ITEM	POST. REF.	DEBIT	CREDIT	BALANCE DEBIT	BALANCE CREDIT
19—Apr.	1	Balance	√			78.40	
	6		IR34	96.00		174.40	
	8		IR34		4.00	170.40	

ACCOUNT STORE EQUIPMENT   ACCOUNT No. 171

DATE		ITEM	POST. REF.	DEBIT	CREDIT	BALANCE DEBIT	BALANCE CREDIT
19—Apr.	1	Balance	√			2,874.80	
	1		IR34	287.60		3,162.40	

ACCOUNT OFFICE EQUIPMENT   ACCOUNT No. 191

DATE		ITEM	POST. REF.	DEBIT	CREDIT	BALANCE DEBIT	BALANCE CREDIT
19—Apr.	1	Balance	√			4,911.70	
	6		IR34	496.20		5,407.90	

ACCOUNT ACCOUNTS PAYABLE   ACCOUNT No. 271

DATE		ITEM	POST. REF.	DEBIT	CREDIT	BALANCE DEBIT	BALANCE CREDIT
19—Apr.	1	Balance	√				9,537.74
	8		IR34	4.00			9,533.74
	30		IR34		54,029.81		63,563.55

ACCOUNT PURCHASES — DEPARTMENT A   ACCOUNT No. 511

DATE		ITEM	POST. REF.	DEBIT	CREDIT	BALANCE DEBIT	BALANCE CREDIT
19—Apr.	1	Balance	√			371,621.92	
	30		IR34	46,422.30		418,044.22	

ACCOUNT   PURCHASES — DEPARTMENT B   ACCOUNT No. 521

DATE		ITEM	POST. REF.	DEBIT	CREDIT	BALANCE DEBIT	BALANCE CREDIT
19— Apr.	1	Balance	✓			45,070.15	
	30		IR34	6,115.34		51,185.49	

ACCOUNT   FREIGHT IN — DEPARTMENT A   ACCOUNT No. 541

DATE		ITEM	POST. REF.	DEBIT	CREDIT	BALANCE DEBIT	BALANCE CREDIT
19— Apr.	1	Balance	✓			3,143.59	
	6		IR34	13.78		3,157.37	

ACCOUNT   FREIGHT IN — DEPARTMENT B   ACCOUNT No. 551

DATE		ITEM	POST. REF.	DEBIT	CREDIT	BALANCE DEBIT	BALANCE CREDIT
19— Apr.	1	Balance	✓			804.12	
	6		IR34	3.94		808.06	

Accounts Payable Ledger (Partial)

NAME   S. G. ADAMS CO.
ADDRESS   ST. LOUIS, MO 63103

DATE		ITEM	POST. REF.	DEBIT	CREDIT	BALANCE
19— April	1	Cr. Balance	✓			124.80
	6	4/5 — 30 ds.	Inv. 157		96.00	220.80
	8	Corrected invoice	Inv. 157	4.00		216.80

NAME   BUSINESS INTERIORS, INC.
ADDRESS   KANSAS CITY, KS 66110

DATE		ITEM	POST. REF.	DEBIT	CREDIT	BALANCE
19— April	6	4/2 — 2/10, n/30	Inv. 158		479.40	
	6	Freight Prepaid	Inv. 158		16.80	496.20

NAME   CELUCOAT CORPORATION
ADDRESS   ST. LOUIS, MO 63130

DATE		ITEM	POST. REF.	DEBIT	CREDIT	BALANCE
19— April	1	Cr. Balance	✓			2,489.25
	1	Mdse. 3/30 — 2/10, n/30	Inv. 151		1,722.50	4,211.75

NAME   COMMERCIAL MACHINE CO.
ADDRESS   ST. LOUIS, MO 63112

DATE		ITEM	POST. REF.	DEBIT	CREDIT	BALANCE
19—						
April	1	4/1 — n/30	Inv. 154		287.60	287.60

NAME   MID-STATES PAINT CO.
ADDRESS   CRESTWOOD, MO 63126

DATE		ITEM	POST. REF.	DEBIT	CREDIT	BALANCE
19—						
April	1	Cr. Balance	✓			192.50
	1	Mdse. 3/29 — 2/10, n/30	Inv. 152		1,096.00	1,288.50
	5	Corrected invoice	Inv. 152		12.00	1,300.50

NAME   ORCHARD PAPER CO.
ADDRESS   ST. LOUIS, MO 63119

DATE		ITEM	POST. REF.	DEBIT	CREDIT	BALANCE
19—						
April	1	Cr. Balance	✓			45.65
	1	3/31 — 30 ds.	Inv. 153		115.90	161.55

NAME   PAINT CITY, INC.
ADDRESS   ST. LOUIS, MO 63103

DATE		ITEM	POST. REF.	DEBIT	CREDIT	BALANCE
19—						
April	1	Cr. Balance	✓			1,258.35
	6	Mdse. 4/4 — 1/10, n/30	Inv. 156		328.60	
	6	Freight Prepaid	Inv. 156		3.94	1,590.89

NAME   SPATZ PAINT INDUSTRIES
ADDRESS   MAPLEWOOD, MO 63102

DATE		ITEM	POST. REF.	DEBIT	CREDIT	BALANCE
19—						
April	1	Cr. Balance	✓			349.56
	6	Mdse. 4/2 — 2/10, n/60	Inv. 155		1,362.00	
	6	Freight prepaid	Inv. 155		13.78	1,725.34

column of the general ledger as a cross-reference. A check mark was placed in parentheses below the totals of the General Ledger Debit and Credit columns in the invoice register to indicate that those totals were not posted.

Cash purchases

Holling & Renz follow the practice of entering only purchases on account in their invoice register. Cash purchases are entered in the record of checks issued, by debiting the proper departmental purchases accounts and by crediting the bank account. Usually cash purchases are not posted to the individual accounts of creditors. However, if it is desired to post cash purchases to the individual accounts of creditors, such transactions may be entered both in the invoice register and in the record of checks issued. In other words, invoices received in connection with cash purchases *may* be recorded in the same manner as invoices for purchases on account.

COD purchases

When property is purchased on COD terms, the total amount paid represents the cost of the property. Since payment must be made before possession of the property can be obtained, it is customary to treat such transactions the same as cash purchases. Thus the check issued in payment of a COD purchase is entered in the check record by debiting the proper account and by crediting the bank account. The proper account to debit depends upon the kind of property purchased. If merchandise is purchased, the proper departmental purchases account should be debited for the cost of the merchandise and the proper departmental transportation account should be debited for the amount of any transportation charges paid. If long-lived assets are purchased, the proper equipment account should be debited for the total cost, including COD fees and any transportation charges. If supplies are purchased, the proper supplies account should be debited for the total cost of the supplies, including COD fees and any transportation charges.

Transportation charges

Express and freight charges may be prepaid by the shipper or may be paid by the buyer at the time of delivery. Parcel post charges must be prepaid by the shipper. Store-to-door delivery of freight shipments may be made by the transportation companies. However, when freight shipments are not delivered to the buyer's place of business by the transportation company, the buyer must either call for the goods at a nearby freight station or must employ a trucker to deliver the goods.

Transportation Charges Prepaid. If the transportation charges are prepaid by the shipper, the amount may or may not be added to the invoice, depending upon the terms of sale. If the shipper has quoted prices FOB destination, it is understood that the prices quoted include transportation charges either to the buyer's place of business or to a nearby freight station and that no additional charge will be made for any transportation charges paid by the shipper.

If the shipper has quoted prices FOB shipping point, it is understood that the prices quoted do not include the transportation charges and that the buyer will be expected to pay the transportation costs. If shipment is made prepaid, the transportation charges will be added to the invoice, and the shipper will be reimbursed by the buyer when the invoice is paid.

Transportation Charges Collect. If prices are quoted FOB shipping point and shipment is made collect, the buyer must pay the transportation charges before obtaining possession of the shipment. Such transportation charges represent an addition to the cost of the merchandise or other property purchased. The method of recording the transportation charges in this case is the same as if the charges had been prepaid by the shipper and added to the invoice.

If prices are quoted FOB destination but for some reason shipment is made collect, the buyer must pay the transportation charges before he can obtain possession of the shipment. In such cases the transportation charges paid by the buyer should be recorded as a debit to the account of the creditor from whom the merchandise or other property was ordered. In other words, the payment of the transportation charges in such case should be treated the same as a partial payment of the amount due the shipper.

Transportation Accounts. As explained in Chapter 6, transportation charges applicable to merchandise purchased may be recorded by debiting the purchases account. However, it is common practice to record transportation charges on incoming merchandise in a separate account, which may be entitled Freight In or Transportation In. This account is treated as a subdivision of the purchases account and the balance must be taken into consideration in computing the cost of goods sold at the close of each accounting period.

The merchandise accounts of Holling & Renz are kept on a departmental basis, with separate accounts for Purchases and for Freight In being kept for Departments A and B. The only time transportation charges are entered in the invoice register is when they are prepaid by the shipper and are added to the invoice. For example, in recording Invoice No. 155, the freight prepaid amounting to $13.78 was charged to Freight In — Department A, Account No. 541. In recording Invoice No. 156, the freight prepaid amounting to $3.94 was charged to Freight In — Department B, Account No. 551. On all shipments sent freight collect, the transportation charges will be entered in the check record. For example, when the freight charges applicable to Invoice No. 151 are paid, the amount of the check issued will be entered in the check record as a debit to Freight In — Department A, Account No. 541, and as a credit to the bank account.

Transportation charges applicable to long-lived assets, such as office equipment, store equipment, or delivery equipment, should be treated as an addition to the cost of such equipment. For example, in entering the invoice of April 2 from Business Interiors, Inc., in the invoice register of Holling & Renz, the total amount of the invoice, $496.20, including transportation charges amounting to $16.80, was charged to Office Equipment, Account No. 191. It is immaterial whether the freight charges are prepaid by the shipper and added to the invoice or whether shipment is made collect. If the freight is prepaid and added to the invoice, the total cost, including the invoice price and the transportation charges, may be recorded as a debit to the office equipment account in one amount. On the other hand, if shipment is made freight collect, the amount of the invoice and the amount of the freight charges must be posted as separate debits to the office equipment account.

Parcel Post Insurance. Merchandise or other property mailed parcel post may be insured against loss or damage in transit. Such insurance may be purchased from the government through the post office, or it may be purchased from private insurance companies. If the cost of insurance is charged to the customer and is added to the invoice, it represents an addition to the cost of the merchandise or other property purchased. Thus, if an invoice is received for merchandise purchased and the merchandise is billed at a total cost of $125 plus postage of $1.50 and insurance of 40 cents, the total cost of the merchandise is $126.90.

The cost of insurance is seldom recorded separately on the books of the buyer, but either is charged directly to the purchases account or is included with transportation charges and is charged to Freight In.

The purchaser may indicate in placing an order that the merchandise is not to be insured. When this is indicated, the purchaser implies a willingness to assume the risk for any loss or damage sustained to the merchandise in transit. Title to merchandise ordinarily passes to the purchaser when it is placed in the hands of the post office for delivery.

Purchases returns and allowances

When a credit memorandum is received as a result of merchandise returned for credit or because of an allowance made by the seller, it should be recorded by debiting Accounts Payable and by crediting the proper purchases returns and allowances account. The individual account of the supplier should also be debited for the amount of the credit memorandum. For example, if a credit memorandum for $165 is received from Paint City, Inc., for varnish returned, it should be recorded as follows:

Accounts Payable...................................... 165.00
Purchases Returns and Allowances — Department B...... 165.00

This amount should also be posted to the debit of the individual account of Paint City, Inc., in the subsidiary accounts payable ledger.

Computerized processing of purchasing records

If a business has a very large volume of purchases, it may be feasible to adopt some type of computerized purchasing system. It has been noted that purchasing involves several steps: requisitioning, issuing purchase orders, receiving, inspection, storing; checking suppliers' invoices with respect to prices, extensions, and footings; handling returns and allowances, determining the proper amounts to be charged and credited to the proper accounts; maintaining detailed records of accounts payable, and making timely payments to suppliers. In this process, various calculations must be made and various source documents, forms, and records must be prepared. In some cases, the information on certain source documents (for example, purchase orders and suppliers' invoices) can be punched into cards, written on magnetic tapes, or prepared in type suitable for optical scanning. These cards, tapes, or source documents can be fed into computers that will make the necessary calculations and verifications and classify the information to provide certain needed records, such as an invoice register that gives a breakdown showing the amounts to be charged and credited to the proper accounts. Because of the relationship between purchasing and inventory and between purchasing and cash disbursements, it is likely that the system will include both inventory and cash disbursement procedures.

(For a further discussion of computer-based accounting systems, see Appendix, page A-1.)

Report No. 11-2

Complete Report No. 11-2 in the study assignments and submit your working papers to the instructor for approval. Then continue with the textbook discussion in Chapter 12 until Report No. 12-1 is required.

Chapter 12

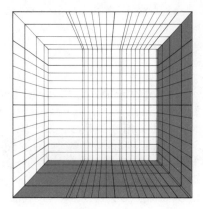

ACCOUNTING FOR SALES

The organization of a sales department and the procedure in handling orders received may vary widely depending upon many factors, such as the nature of the merchandise sold, the volume of sales, the methods of selling, and the terms. Each order received must be interpreted, the terms determined, the credit approved, a sales invoice prepared, goods packed and shipped or delivered, and collection made before the sales transaction is entirely completed.

TERMS OF SALE: PROCESSING ORDERS RECEIVED

The terms on which merchandise is sold affect the procedure in handling orders and in recording the sales transactions. Goods may be sold under any of the following conditions:

(a) For cash (including sales involving bank credit cards)
(b) On account
(c) COD

(d) On approval
(e) Will call sales
(f) On installment
(g) On consignment

Cash sales Some businesses sell merchandise for cash only, while others sell merchandise either for cash or on account. A variety of practices are followed in the handling of cash sales. If such transactions are numerous, it is probable that one or more types of cash register will be used. In many cases the original record of the sale is made in the register. Often, registers that have the capability of accumulating more than one total are used. This means that by using the proper key, each amount that is "punched in" the register can be classified in the desired manner — perhaps by type of merchandise, by department, or by salesperson. Where sales taxes are involved, the amount of the tax may be separately recorded. In many retail establishments, the procedure in handling cash sales is for the salesclerks to prepare sales tickets in duplicate or in triplicate. Usually one copy is given to the customer and another copy is sent to the accounting department for analysis and recording purposes. Sometimes the preparation of the sales tickets involves the use of a type of cash register that provides means for the tickets (and any copies) to be inserted in the register in such a way that the amount being recorded is printed on the tickets. At the end of each day the cash received is checked with the record that the register provides. The receipts may also be checked with the total of the cash-sale tickets, if the system makes use of the latter.

In the discussion and illustration of the accounting for a retail merchant in Chapters 8–10, it was noted that sales to customers using their bank credit cards could be accounted for as cash sales.

Sales on account

Sales on account are often referred to as "charge sales" because the seller exchanges merchandise for the buyer's promise to pay which, in accounting terms, means that the asset accounts receivable is increased by a debit or charge. Selling goods on account is common practice at both the wholesale and retail levels of the distribution process. Firms that sell goods on account should investigate the financial reliability of those to whom they sell. A business of some size may have a separate credit department whose major function is to establish credit policies and to pass upon requests for credit from persons and firms who wish to buy goods on account. Seasoned judgment is needed to avoid a credit policy that is so stringent that profitable business may be refused, or a credit policy that is so liberal that uncollectible account losses may become excessive.

Generally, no goods are delivered until the salesclerk has been assured that the buyer has established credit — that there is an account for this customer with the company. In the case of many retail businesses, customers with established credit are provided with *credit cards* or *charge plates*. These cards or plates not only provide evidence that the buyer has an account; they also are used in mechanical devices to print the customer's name and other identification on the sales tickets or sales invoices (and copies). (This type of credit card should not be confused with bank credit cards and other types of credit card plans that are in operation.) In the case of *wholesale* merchants who commonly secure a large portion of their orders by mail, by phone, or by telegraph, this confirmation of the buyer's status can be handled as a matter of routine before the goods are delivered. There is no pressing problem in this respect because the buyer is not personally waiting for the merchandise.

COD sales

Merchandise or other property may be sold on COD terms. Under this arrangement payment must be made at the time the goods are delivered by the seller or the agent. The agent may be an employee of the seller, a messenger, the post office, an express company, a railroad company, a trucking company, a steamship company, an airline, or any common carrier.

In wholesale merchandising, COD sales are usually recorded in the same manner as charge sales. When such sales are made to out-of-town customers, the merchandise is usually delivered by parcel post, express, or freight.[1] If shipment is made by parcel post or express, the post office or the express company will collect for the merchandise before giving the customer possession of it and, in turn, will remit to the seller by means of a money order or check. When this remittance is received by the seller, it is handled in the same manner as a remittance received from any other customer in full or part payment of his account.

By way of contrast, in retail merchandising, COD sales are usually recorded as cash sales. The COD sales tickets are segregated each day and a COD list is prepared for control purposes. The merchandise is then delivered to the customer and the sale price is collected upon delivery. When the money is turned in by the driver or other agent of the seller, he is given credit for the collection on the COD list and the sale is then recorded in the same manner as a cash sale. If, for any reason, the customer refuses to accept the merchandise, it is returned to stock and the sale is canceled. It should be understood that, under this plan of handling COD sales, title to the merchandise does not pass to the customer until the goods are delivered and collection has been made; therefore, the merchandise is considered to be a part of the inventory of the seller until a remittance is received. Usually, retail merchants who sell merchandise on COD terms make their own deliveries and collections; however, delivery may be made through the postal service or any common carrier.

---

[1]The method of making COD shipments by freight and of collecting for the merchandise before delivery was explained in the preceding chapter under the heading of COD Purchases.

Sales on approval

When sales are made on approval, the customer is given the right to return the goods within a specified time. Accordingly, the sale is not complete until it is known whether the customer will retain the goods or return them. Such sales may be handled as ordinary charge sales, and any returns may be handled as ordinary sales returns. On the other hand, sales on approval may be handled the same as ordinary cash sales. Under this plan a memorandum record of the sale is kept until it is definitely known that the goods will be retained by the customer. The customer must either pay for the goods or return them by a specified date. If the sale is not recorded until a remittance is received, it may be treated the same as an ordinary cash sale.

Will call sales

Sales on approval should not be confused with *will call sales*. Will call sales may be made for cash or on account, but in either case the customer agrees to call for the goods. Sometimes a deposit is made by the buyer with the understanding that merchandise will be held until some future date, at which time he will call for the merchandise or at his request the merchandise will be delivered to him. Accounting for such deposits is not uniform, but the usual plan is to record the deposits in the same manner as cash sales. When this plan is used, a charge sales ticket is prepared for the balance due and is recorded by debiting a special accounts receivable control account and by crediting the proper sales account. Individual accounts with such customers may be kept in a special subsidiary ledger, sometimes referred to as a *will call ledger*.

Instead of calling for the merchandise, the customer may request delivery on a COD basis. In this case a COD slip is made for the proper amount. When the remittance is received, it is recorded in the same manner as if the customer had called for the merchandise and paid cash.

At the end of the accounting period, the total amount due from customers who have made deposits on will call sales is treated in the same manner as ordinary accounts receivable. The cost of the merchandise that is being held for future delivery is not included in the inventory because it is considered to be the property of the customer.

Installment sales

The term *installment sales* is applied to a variety of arrangements in which the purchaser of goods (and sometimes services) makes a so-called "down payment" and agrees to pay the remainder of the sales price in fractional, periodic amounts over an extended period of time. It would be more accurate to call such arrangements "installment payments." From the standpoint of the seller, such transactions often amount to cash (or bank credit card) sales. Frequently, some type of financial institution is a party to the transaction at the outset. The seller gets the money immediately; thus the buyer becomes a borrower who must make payments to a bank or finance company. Interest is always involved. In other cases, the seller does acquire a receivable, but soon "sells" it to a financial institution. (Often, the seller must guarantee the collectibility of the receivable.) In some cases, the seller "carries the account" and the buyer makes periodic payments directly to the business from whom the goods were purchased. Usually, the payments include an interest component.

If the seller does carry the account, it is desirable to use a special form of subsidiary ledger account that is designed to facilitate recording installment transactions. The subsidiary accounts comprise what is called an "installment ledger" that contains the details of the general ledger account titled *Installment Accounts Receivable*. At one time, the accounting for installment sales entailed a somewhat complicated procedure that was based on the idea that no gross margin on such sales should be taken into income calculations until the money was received. Each dollar collected, whether from down payment or periodic installments, was considered to be partly a recovery of the cost of what was sold and partly gross margin. If the collection period extended over several years, the recognition of the gross margin on the sale would be spread over those years. This procedure, called the "installment method," is no longer considered to be an acceptable accounting practice except in special and unusual circumstances. Normal practice is to regard installment sales in the same manner as regular sales on account. That is, to consider that gross margin is realized at the "point of sale." For income tax purposes, however, the installment method may be used. Using this method in the calculation of taxable income permits the postponement of payment of taxes until the year that the money is received.

Consignment sales

The term "consignment sales" refers to an arrangement in which one business, known as the *consignor*, ships goods to another business, known as the *consignee*, without any change in the legal ownership of the goods. The consignee acts as an agent for the consignor and attempts to sell the goods — usually at prices specified by the consignor. The consignee receives an agreed commission, which is deducted from the proceeds of the sales when remittance of the amount due is made to the consignor. Sometimes, each party keeps a type of formal memoranda accounts for consignment transactions. In other cases, no formal records are made until the goods have been sold. Consignment selling is not a widespread practice.

Procedure in handling incoming purchase orders

Sales by wholesale merchants usually are made in response to purchase orders received by mail, telephone, telegram, or cablegram. Purchase orders received by mail may be written on the purchase order form, letter-head, or other stationery of the buyer or on an order blank furnished by the seller. An illustration of a typical Purchase Order form was shown on page 283. It is probable that upon receiving this order, a rubber stamp impression with spaces to show date received, credit approval, approval of prices shown, and date of billing would be placed on its face. In the process of handling the order, the persons involved would make appropriate notations. Orders received by telephone should be carefully recorded on forms provided for that purpose. The procedure in handling purchase orders varies widely with different firms; nevertheless, it is important that there be a well-organized plan for handling orders. The purpose of such a plan should be to promote efficiency and to maintain an internal check that will tend to prevent mistakes in handling orders. The following five steps constitute the heart of such a plan:

(1) **Interpretation.** Each purchase order received should be interpreted as to (a) identity of the customer and (b) quantity and description of items ordered. Orders may be received from old or new customers. Sometimes it is difficult to identify a new customer, particularly where there has been no previous correspondence with him or where he has not been contacted by the seller's representative. In some cases the identity of the items ordered involves considerable difficulty because customers frequently are careless in describing the merchandise wanted. Different items of merchandise may be specified by name, stock number, or code word. Care should be used to make sure that the stock number or the code word agrees with the description of the item. Code words are commonly used in ordering by telegram or cablegram.

(2) **Transportation.** In handling each purchase order, it is necessary to determine how shipment will be made and how the transportation charges will be handled. Shipment may be made by parcel post, express, or freight. Parcel post packages may be insured. Express shipments may be made by rail or air. Freight shipments may be made by rail, air, truck, or water.

The transportation charges must be prepaid on shipments made by parcel post. The transportation charges on express and freight shipments may be prepaid by the shipper or may be paid by the customer upon receipt of the shipment. When transportation charges are prepaid by the shipper, they may or may not be added to the invoice, depending upon whether prices have been quoted FOB shipping point or FOB destination.

If shipment is to be made by freight, it is also necessary to determine the routing of the shipment. The buyer may specify how he prefers to have shipment made. When the buyer does not indicate any preference, the shipper must determine whether to make shipment by rail, truck, air, or water, and also frequently must make a choice of transportation companies to be used. Shipment to certain points may be made via a variety of different trucking companies, airlines, or railroads.

(3) Credit Approval. All purchase orders received that involve credit in any form should be referred to the credit department for approval before being billed or shipped. COD orders should also be approved by the credit department, because some customers have a reputation for not accepting COD shipments which are then returned at the seller's expense. Customers who abuse the COD privilege may be required thereafter to send cash with the order, either in full or part payment. Some firms follow a policy of requiring part payment in cash with all orders for merchandise to be shipped COD.

(4) Check for Accuracy of Purchase Orders. The unit prices specified on purchase orders should be checked, the proper extensions should be made, and the total should be recorded. The clerks performing this function usually use either mechanical or electronic calculating machines.

(5) Billing. The next step in the handling of an order is billing or preparing the sales invoice. In the case of a manufacturer or a wholesale merchant, the sales invoice is usually prepared on a typewriter, billing machine, or computer-printer. Sales invoices should be numbered consecutively. By using carbon paper or some other duplicating device, additional copies may be prepared. At least three copies usually are considered necessary: the original copy going to the customer as an acknowledgment of his order, a copy going to the accounting department for recording purposes, and a copy going to the shipping department as authority for packing and shipping the merchandise. The copy of the sales invoice reproduced at the top of the next page is based on an order taken by phone from the Central Hardware Company.

Additional copies of the sales invoice may also be used for the following purposes:

(a) One copy may go to the salesperson in whose territory the sale is made.
(b) One copy may go to a branch office, if the sale is made in a territory served by such an office.
(c) One copy may serve as a label to be pasted on the carton or package in which shipment is made. Usually this copy is perforated so that only that part containing the name and the address of the customer is used.

Discounts   Any trade discounts allowed on sales are usually shown as a deduction in arriving at the total of the sales invoice. Such discounts should not be

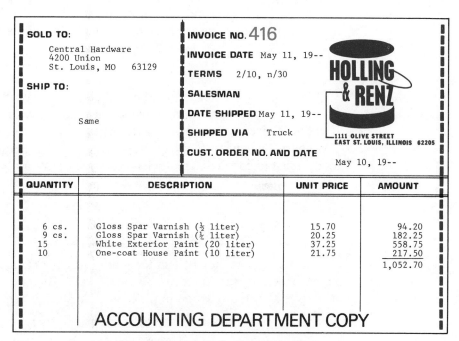

<table>
<tr><td>SOLD TO:
Central Hardware
4200 Union
St. Louis, MO   63129

SHIP TO:

Same</td><td>INVOICE NO. 416

INVOICE DATE May 11, 19--

TERMS   2/10, n/30

SALESMAN

DATE SHIPPED May 11, 19--

SHIPPED VIA   Truck

CUST. ORDER NO. AND DATE
May 10, 19--</td></tr>
</table>

QUANTITY	DESCRIPTION	UNIT PRICE	AMOUNT
6 cs.	Gloss Spar Varnish (½ liter)	15.70	94.20
9 cs.	Gloss Spar Varnish (¼ liter)	20.25	182.25
15	White Exterior Paint (20 liter)	37.25	558.75
10	One-coat House Paint (10 liter)	21.75	217.50
			1,052.70

HOLLING & RENZ
1111 OLIVE STREET
EAST ST. LOUIS, ILLINOIS 62205

ACCOUNTING DEPARTMENT COPY

Copy of Sales Invoice for Accounting Department

entered in the accounts of the seller, as they represent merely a reduction in the selling price of the merchandise.

Any cash discounts offered should be indicated in the terms. Retail merchants seldom allow cash discounts, but wholesale merchants commonly allow cash discounts as an inducement for prompt payment of sales invoices. Cash discounts should be ignored at the time of recording sales invoices, for it cannot be known at that time whether the customers will pay the invoices in time to get the discounts offered. Any cash discount that is deducted from an invoice by the customer when making a remittance can be regarded by the seller either as an expense or as a reduction in gross sales (similar to sales returns and allowances). Some accountants accept the view that sales discounts are expenses, but to most accountants it seems more logical to regard such discounts as a reduction of sales price. Accordingly, the debit balance of the sales discount account is shown as a subtraction from sales in the income statement.

A minor complication arises in treating sales discounts as a reduction of sales when the latter are accounted for on a departmental basis. While it would be possible to have two or more sales discount accounts and to analyze each discount taken to determine the department (or departments) to which it relates, such a procedure would be burdensome. In most cases the resulting accuracy would not be worth the trouble involved. An acceptable alternative is to record all sales discounts in a single account and, in preparing the income statement, to allocate the amount of such discounts in proportion to the net sales of the departments.

Returns and allowances   Merchandise may be returned by the customer for credit or he may ask for an allowance representing a reduction in the price of the merchandise. If credit is given for merchandise returned or an allowance is made, it is customary to issue a credit memorandum for the amount involved. A model filled-in copy of a credit memorandum was reproduced on page 291.

Report No. 12-1   Complete Report No. 12-1 in the study assignments and submit your working papers to the instructor for approval. Then continue with the following textbook discussion until Report No. 12-2 is required.

ACCOUNTING PROCEDURE

When the merchandise accounts are kept on a departmental basis and all sales invoices covering charge sales are recorded in a columnar sales record, often called a *sales register*, provision should be made for a proper classification of the debits and the credits. Separate columns should be provided for recording the charge sales of each department so as to facilitate periodic summary posting of the totals. General Ledger Debit and Credit columns should also be provided for recording items that must be posted individually to the general ledger accounts. If individual accounts with customers are kept in a subsidiary ledger, a summary or control account for accounts receivable must be kept in the general ledger.

The procedure of recording all charge sales invoices in a sales register and of keeping the merchandise accounts on the departmental basis will be illustrated **(1)** by showing the chronological recording of a narrative of selected transactions in the sales register, **(2)** by showing the direct posting from copies of the sales invoices to the individual accounts of customers kept in a subsidiary accounts receivable ledger, and **(3)** by showing the posting from the sales register to the proper general ledger accounts.

Holling & Renz is a partnership engaged in the wholesale paint and varnish business. Separate departments are maintained as follows:

Department A — Paint
Department B — Varnish

Separate departmental accounts are kept for sales and for sales returns and allowances as follows:

411 Sales — Department A
     041 Sales Returns and Allowances — Department A
421 Sales — Department B
     042 Sales Returns and Allowances — Department B

All charge sales are made on uniform terms of 2/10, n/30. Unless otherwise specified, freight and express shipments are made on a basis of transportation charges collect. In the case of parcel post shipments, the postage is prepaid and added to the invoice as an additional charge to the customer. As each invoice is entered in the sales register, the amount of postage prepaid is credited to Postage Stamps, Account No. 164, in the General Ledger column.

Sales register

The form of the sales register used by Holling & Renz is illustrated on page 316. All of their sales are made to dealers. The merchandise is intended for resale. Accordingly, Holling & Renz do not have to collect retail sales taxes. A narrative of the transactions that have been entered in the sales register follows. It will be helpful to check each transaction and to note how it was entered in the sales register.

HOLLING & RENZ

NARRATIVE OF TRANSACTIONS

Saturday, April 2

Made charge sales as follows:

No. 418, Glaze Hardware Co., paint, $419.90; varnish, $403.20; freight collect.

No. 419, Morgan Paint Co., paint, $1,688.60; varnish, $75.50; express collect.

No. 420, Laclede Hardware Co., paint, $890.40; express collect.

No. 421, Fischer Paints, varnish, $247.70; postage added to invoice, $34.65.

No. 422, Affton Paints, varnish, $135.20; insured parcel post, $14.80.

SALES REGISTER FOR MONTH OF *April* 19 — PAGE 65

ACCT. NO. (DEBIT GL)	AMOUNT (DEBIT GL)	√	ACCOUNTS RECEIVABLE	√	DAY	NAME	SALE NO.	SALES DEPT. A	SALES DEPT. B	ACCT. NO. (CREDIT GL)	AMOUNT (CREDIT GL)	√
			82310	√	2	Sloge Hardware Co.	418	41990	40320			
			176410	√	2	Morgan Paint Co.	419	168860	7550			
			89040	√	2	Laclede Hardware Co.	420	89040				
			28235	√	2	Fischer Paints	421		24770	164	3465	√
			15000	√	2	Upton Paints	422		13520	164	1480	√
			675	√	6	Fischer Paints	421		675			
			76250	√	7	Caldwell Paint Co.	423	69120	7130			
			37960	√	7	Morgan Paint Co.	424	28080	9880			
042	3880	√	2240	√	7	Upton Paints	425		6120			
421	1200	√	1200	√	8	Morgan Paint Co.	424			131	1200	√
31	5050 / 5080		5290625 / 5290625					4481370 / 448370	809190 / 808190		6145 / 6145	
32	(√)		(131)					(411)	(421)		(√)	

Holling & Renz — Sales Register

Wednesday, April 6

Sent Fischer Paints a corrected invoice for Sale No. 421, amounting to $289.10. (The original postage charge was correct but the varnish was underpriced $6.75.)

Thursday, April 7

Made charge sales as follows:

No. 423, Caldwell Paint Co., paint, $691.20; varnish, $71.30; freight collect.

No. 424, Morgan Paint Co., paint, $280.80; varnish, $98.80; freight collect.

No. 425, Affton Paints, varnish, $61.20; less credit for varnish returned, $38.80. Note that Accounts Receivable is debited for the difference between the new amount of varnish sold and the amount of varnish returned.

Friday, April 8

Sent Morgan Paint Co. a corrected invoice for Sale No. 424; paint, $280.80; varnish, $86.80. In the sales register note that Sales, Department B (Account No. 421) was debited for $12 and that Accounts Receivable (Account No. 131) was credited for a like amount.

(The transactions for April 8 through April 30 are omitted.)

Since postings to the customers' accounts in the subsidiary accounts receivable ledger will be made directly from copies of the sales invoices, a check mark was placed in the Check ($\sqrt{}$) column beside the Accounts Receivable column as each item was entered in the sales register.

Corrected Sales Invoices. If an error in the preparation of a sales invoice is discovered and a corrected sales invoice is prepared before the original invoice has been entered in the sales register, the original invoice may be canceled and the corrected one may be entered in the usual manner.

If a corrected sales invoice is prepared after the original sales invoice has been entered in the sales register and has been posted to the individual account of the customer, the corrected invoice may be entered in the sales register if the amount of the corrected invoice is more than the amount of the original invoice. (See Sale No. 421.) The increase should be recorded by debiting Accounts Receivable and by crediting the proper departmental sales account. The amount of the increase should also be posted to the debit of the proper customer's account in the subsidiary accounts receivable ledger.

If the amount of the corrected invoice is less than the amount of the original invoice, the decrease should be recorded by debiting the proper departmental sales account and by crediting Accounts Receivable. (The entry can be made in the sales register if General Ledger Debit and Credit columns are provided; if not, the entry must be made in the general journal.) The amount of the decrease should also be posted to the credit of the proper customer's account in the subsidiary accounts receivable ledger. (See Sale No. 424.)

A copy of the corrected invoice should be attached to the copy of the original invoice.

Proving the Sales Register. The sales register may be footed and the footings may be proved at any time by comparing the sum of the debit footings with the sum of the credit footings. The footings of Holling & Renz's sales register were proved as of April 30 by the use of an adding machine. The tape appeared as follows:

```
                                    *
                   50.80
               52,906.25

               52,957.05*

                                    *
               44,813.70
                8,081.90
                   61.45

               52,957.05*
```

Ledgers

The ledgers used by Holling & Renz include a general ledger with four-column ruling and a subsidiary accounts receivable ledger with three-column ruling. The accounts affected by the transactions entered in the sales register reproduced on page 316 are shown in skeleton form on pages 319 and 320. The March 31 balances are recorded in the accounts as of April 1. An accounts receivable control account is kept in the general ledger.

Posting Procedure. The use of a general ledger and an accounts receivable ledger involves both individual posting and summary posting. After each sales invoice was entered in the sales register, it was immediately posted to the proper customer's account in the accounts receivable ledger. The posting was done directly from the invoice, the invoice number being inserted in the Posting Reference column.

While the posting to customers' accounts might be done from the sales register, there are certain advantages in posting directly from the sales invoice. For example, the invoice provides all the information needed in posting, whereas, if the posting were done from the sales register, it would be necessary to enter in the sales register all the information needed in posting whether or not it served any other purpose. Furthermore, if an error had been made in entering an invoice in the sales register, it would probably be carried over into the accounts receivable ledger through the posting; whereas, if the posting were done directly from the invoice, it is not likely that the same error would be made twice.

General Ledger (Partial)

ACCOUNT   **ACCOUNTS RECEIVABLE**   ACCOUNT No. 131

DATE		ITEM	POST. REF.	DEBIT	CREDIT	BALANCE DEBIT	BALANCE CREDIT
19-- Apr.	1	Balance	√			16,154.67	
	8		SR65		12.00	16,142.67	
	30		SR65	52,906.25		69,048.92	

ACCOUNT   **POSTAGE STAMPS**   ACCOUNT No. 164

DATE		ITEM	POST. REF.	DEBIT	CREDIT	BALANCE DEBIT	BALANCE CREDIT
19-- Apr.	1	Balance	√			215.60	
	2		SR65		34.65	180.95	
	2		SR65		14.80	166.15	

ACCOUNT   **SALES — DEPARTMENT A**   ACCOUNT No. 411

DATE		ITEM	POST. REF.	DEBIT	CREDIT	BALANCE DEBIT	BALANCE CREDIT
19-- Apr.	1		√				659,451.40
	30		SR65		44,813.70		704,265.10

ACCOUNT   **SALES — DEPARTMENT B**   ACCOUNT No. 421

DATE		ITEM	POST. REF.	DEBIT	CREDIT	BALANCE DEBIT	BALANCE CREDIT
19-- Apr.	1	Balance	√				61,607.30
	8		SR65	12.00			61,595.30
	30		SR65		8,081.90		69,677.20

ACCOUNT   **SALES RETURNS AND ALLOWANCES — DEPARTMENT B**   ACCOUNT No. 042

DATE		ITEM	POST. REF.	DEBIT	CREDIT	BALANCE DEBIT	BALANCE CREDIT
19-- Apr.	1	Balance	√			942.60	
	7			38.80		981.40	

Accounts Receivable Ledger (Partial)

NAME   AFFTON PAINTS
ADDRESS CENTERVILLE, MO 63633

DATE		ITEM	POST. REF.	DEBIT	CREDIT	BALANCE
19--						
April	1	Dr. Balance				478.25
	2	Mdse.	S422	135.20		
	2	Postage	S422	14.80		628.25
	7	Mdse.	S425	22.40		650.65

NAME   CALDWELL PAINT CO.
ADDRESS ST. LOUIS, MO 63129

DATE		ITEM	POST. REF.	DEBIT	CREDIT	BALANCE
19--						
April	1	Dr. Balance				312.40
	7	Mdse.	S423	762.50		1,074.90

NAME   FISCHER PAINTS
ADDRESS LOGAN, MO 63950

DATE		ITEM	POST. REF.	DEBIT	CREDIT	BALANCE
19--						
April	1	Dr. Balance				680.10
	2	Mdse.	S421	247.70		
	2	Postage	S421	34.65		962.45
	6	Corrected invoice	S421	6.75		969.20

NAME   GLAZE HARDWARE
ADDRESS ST. LOUIS, MO 63115

DATE		ITEM	POST. REF.	DEBIT	CREDIT	BALANCE
19--						
April	1	Dr. Balance				1,042.30
	2	Mdse.	S418	823.10		1,865.40

NAME   LACLEDE HARDWARE CO.
ADDRESS ST. LOUIS, MO 63114

DATE		ITEM	POST. REF.	DEBIT	CREDIT	BALANCE
19--						
April	1	Dr. Balance				121.90
	2	Mdse.	S420	890.40		1,012.30

NAME   MORGAN PAINT CO.
ADDRESS ST. LOUIS, MO 63113

DATE		ITEM	POST. REF.	DEBIT	CREDIT	BALANCE
19--						
April	1	Dr. Balance				309.80
	2	Mdse.	S419	1,764.10		2,073.90
	7	Mdse.	S424	379.60		2,453.50
	8	Corrected invoice	S424		12.00	2,441.50

Posting directly from the sales invoices to the customers' accounts in the accounts receivable ledger is not only efficient, but it also provides a sound method of internal check and control. One bookkeeper may enter the invoices in the sales register and may complete the posting required from the sales register to the general ledger accounts, while another bookkeeper may post directly from the sales invoices to the customers' accounts in the accounts receivable ledger. Thus the work is divided between two employees. Proof of the accuracy of their work is obtained periodically by preparing a schedule of accounts receivable and comparing its total with the balance of the accounts receivable control account that is kept in the general ledger.

Posting to the accounts of customers in the accounts receivable ledger may be done either manually or with a machine. A large volume of transactions makes it feasible to use posting machines or, in some cases, electronic equipment. This is discussed further on page 324.

Some firms use the *microfilm* method of accounting for charge sales. Under this method it is customary to keep a chronological record of charge sales in the same manner as in other methods of accounting. An individual account of the transactions with each customer is also kept until the end of the month when it is photographed. The film is then filed as a permanent record of the business done with each customer, while the individual account becomes the customer's monthly statement.

Individual Posting. Each sales invoice entered in the Accounts Receivable Debit column of the sales register was posted individually to the proper customer's account in the accounts receivable ledger shown on the opposite page. In the case of sales invoices involving prepaid transportation charges, the amount of the merchandise sold and the amount of the prepaid transportation charges were posted separately. For example, in posting Sales Invoice No. 421, Fischer Paints was debited separately for the amount of the merchandise sold, $247.70, and for the amount of the postage, $34.65. The reason for posting the transportation charges as separate items is that these amounts are never subject to discount; only the amount of the merchandise sold is subject to discount.

It was also necessary to post each item in the General Ledger Debit and Credit columns of the sales register. Usually this posting is completed daily. As each such item was posted, a check mark was placed in the Check ($\sqrt{}$) column beside the proper amount, and the page number of the sales register was entered in the Posting Reference column of the affected general ledger account.

Summary Posting. The summary posting from the sales register is usually completed at the end of each month and involves the procedure shown on the following page.

(a) The total of the column headed Accounts Receivable was posted to the debit of Accounts Receivable, Account No. 131, in the general ledger.

(b) The total of the column headed Sales, Dept. A was posted to the credit of Sales — Department A, Account No. 411, in the general ledger.

(c) The total of the column headed Sales, Dept. B was posted to the credit of Sales — Department B, Account No. 421, in the general ledger.

As the total of each column was posted, the account number was written in parentheses immediately below the total in the sales register and the page of the sales register was written in the Posting Reference column of the general ledger as a cross-reference. A check mark was placed in parentheses below the totals of the General Debit and Credit columns in the sales register to indicate that those totals were not posted.

Cash sales

Holling & Renz follow the practice of entering charge sales only in their sales register. Cash sales are entered in the record of cash receipts by debiting the bank account and by crediting the proper departmental sales accounts. Cash sales are not posted to the individual accounts of customers. In a wholesale business there are relatively few cash sales as most of the business is usually done on a charge basis.

COD sales

Holling & Renz follow the practice of recording COD sales in the same manner as charge sales. Since they are engaged in a wholesale business, a relatively large percentage of their sales is made to out-of-town customers; hence, several days may elapse from the date of sale until the date a remittance is received. COD sales are therefore recorded in the sales register in the same manner as ordinary sales. When the remittance is received from the post office, express company, trucking company, railroad company, or other common carrier, it is entered in the record of cash receipts in the same manner as other remittances received from customers to apply on account.

Transportation charges

In the case of parcel post shipments, the postage must be prepaid. If such packages are insured, the total amount of the postage and the insurance is added to the invoice. Holling & Renz follow the practice of making all express and freight shipments with transportation charges collect, unless the customer requests that they be prepaid and added to the invoice. Since most shipments are made collect, it is not considered necessary to provide a special column in the sales register for recording express and freight charges prepaid; instead, they are entered in the General Ledger Credit column as a credit to Freight Out, Account No. 6119.

When the express and freight charges are prepaid, the payments are entered in the record of checks issued by debiting Freight Out and by crediting the bank account. The freight out account should be in balance after all posting is completed at the end of the month, provided all prepaid express and freight charges have been charged to customers' accounts. If, however, any shipments are made FOB destination, the freight charges represent a selling expense. In this case the freight out account will have a debit balance, which represents the amount of such expense incurred.

Where numerous shipments are made by parcel post, express, and freight and the transportation charges are prepaid and charged to customers, it is advisable to provide a special credit column in the sales register for entering the transportation charges. All prepaid transportation charges on outgoing shipments that are added to the invoices and charged to customers should be entered in this column. At the end of the month when the summary posting is completed, the total of the column should be posted to the credit of Freight Out.

Sales returns and allowances

When a credit memorandum is issued to a customer for the price of merchandise returned for credit or because of an allowance made on merchandise sold, it should be recorded by debiting the proper sales returns and allowances account and by crediting Accounts Receivable. The individual account of the customer should also be credited for the amount of the credit memorandum. For example, if a credit memorandum for $63.40 is issued to the Harris Lumber Co. for some varnish returned for credit, it should be recorded as indicated in the following general journal entry:

```
Sales Returns and Allowances — Department B.................  63.40
    Accounts Receivable........................................        63.40
        Issued credit memorandum to Harris Lumber Co.
```

The amount should also be posted to the credit of the individual account of the Harris Lumber Co. in the subsidiary accounts receivable ledger.

If transactions involving the issuance of credit memorandums are numerous, a special sales returns and allowances register may be used to advantage. The design of such a register would be similar to that of the sales register reproduced on page 316, except that there should be columns provided on the debit side for recording departmental sales returns and allowances and a column provided on the credit side for recording accounts receivable. The effect of an entry to record credit allowed for merchandise returned is the reverse of an entry to record merchandise sold; therefore, if a special register is used, its columnar arrangement should be the reverse of the columnar arrangement of the sales register.

Computerized processing of sales records

If a business has a very large volume of sales, it may be feasible to adopt some type of computerized sales system. It has been noted that selling involves several steps: receiving and interpreting orders, assembling the orders, shipping, billing, handling returns and allowances, determining the proper amounts to be charged and credited to the proper accounts, and maintaining a record of accounts receivable. In this process, various calculations must be made and various source documents, forms, and records must be prepared. In some cases, the information on certain source documents (incoming purchase orders, for example) can be punched into cards, written on magnetic tapes, or prepared in type suitable for optical scanning. The cards, tapes, or source documents can be fed into computers that will make the necessary calculations and verifications, and classify the information to provide certain needed records such as a sales register that gives a detailed breakdown of the amounts to be charged and credited to the proper accounts. Computer equipment may be used to prepare sales invoices, to keep the accounts receivable ledger, and to facilitate the preparation of customers' monthly statements. It is probable that computer equipment also will be used to obtain detailed analyses of sales (by products or product line, by different classes of customers, by regions, etc.). Because of the relationship between sales and inventory and between sales and cash receipts, it is likely that the system will include both inventory and cash receipts records. (For a further discussion of computer-based accounting systems, see Appendix, page A-1.)

Report No. 12-2

Complete Report No. 12-2 in the study assignments and submit your working papers to the instructor for approval. Then continue with the textbook discussion in Chapter 13 until Report No. 13-1 is required.

Chapter 13

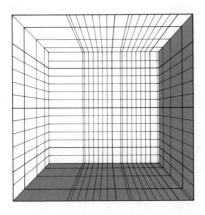

ACCOUNTING FOR INVENTORY AND PREPAID EXPENSES

Merchandise inventory and prepaid expenses have an important characteristic in common: both represent costs incurred in one accounting period that are expected in part to benefit the following period. Because the benefit is expected to be realized within a relatively short time, these assets are considered to be current rather than long-lived. In most cases, the dollar amount of merchandise inventory is much larger than that for prepaid expenses. For this reason, accounting for merchandise inventory poses a much greater problem and receives much more care and attention.

MERCHANDISE INVENTORY

One of the major reasons for keeping accounting records is to make it possible to determine the net income (or net loss) of a business on a periodic basis. If the business is engaged in the purchase and sale of merchandise, it is essential that the cost of all merchandise available for sale during the accounting period (goods on hand at the start of the period plus net purchases) be apportioned in a reasonable manner between the expense called cost of goods sold and the asset commonly called merchandise inventory. The routine bookkeeping procedure involved in accounting for merchandise, using accounts for purchases, purchases returns and allowances, purchases discount, and merchandise inventory, has been discussed and illustrated in preceding chapters. The problem of determining the quantity of goods on hand at the end of the period and of assigning cost to these goods remains to be considered.

Taking a physical inventory

In many cases there is no record that shows the quantity and the cost of the merchandise on hand. Lacking such a record, the first step in attempting to apportion merchandise costs between sold and unsold goods consists of counting the goods that are on hand (or otherwise measuring their quantity) at the end of the period. This process is called *taking an inventory* or *taking a physical inventory*.

Taking a physical inventory of a stock of merchandise can be a sizable task. Frequently it must be done after regular business hours. Some firms cease operations for a few days to take inventory. The ideal time to count the goods is when the quantity on hand is at its lowest level. A fiscal year may be selected so as to start and end at the time that the stock of goods is normally at its lowest level. This is known as a *natural business year*. Such a year is used by many businesses for accounting purposes.

It would be desirable if all goods on hand could be inventoried within a few hours. Sometimes extra help is employed so as to take the inventory in as short a time as possible. Even if this is done, however, the taking of an inventory may require several days. If regular business is carried on during this time, special records must be kept of additions to and subtractions from the stock during the inventory-taking period. In this way the quantities of goods that were on hand at the end of the last day of the fiscal period can be determined.

Various procedures are followed in taking an inventory so as to be sure that no items are missed and that no items are included more than once. It is customary for persons taking inventory to work in pairs; one counts the items and "calls out" the information to the other who records it. Usually such information is recorded on a form commonly known as an *inventory sheet*. The sheet is arranged with space to show the description of each type of item, the quantity on hand, the cost per unit, and the extension — the amount that results from multiplying the quantity by the unit cost. (The cost per unit can be determined and the extensions completed after the count is finished.) Inventory sheets commonly provide spaces **(1)** to note the date of the inventory count, **(2)** to record the location of the items listed, and **(3)** to record the names or initials of the person who did the calling, the person who recorded the quantities, the person who entered the unit costs, the person who made the extensions, and the person who checked the information. A reproduction of part of an inventory sheet of a furniture store is shown on page 327. Two extension columns are provided so that subtotals may be separated from item extensions.

Description	Quantity	Unit	Unit Cost	Extensions	
Table Lamp	20	ea.	31 80	636 00	
Wall Rack	18	ea.	5 85	105 30	
Bookcase	7	ea.	52 10	364 70	
End Table	13	ea.	19 60	254 80	
Desk	6	ea.	63 90	383 40	
Total					2,642 10

INVENTORY   *May 31,*   19 _77_   Page _1_

Sheet No. _1_

Called by _A. H. B._   Department _A_

Entered by _H. N._   Location _Storeroom_

Costed by _W. R. D._

Extended by _W. R. D._

Examined by _R. W. O._

Inventory Sheet

In taking a physical inventory, care must be exercised to be sure that only the goods that are the property of the firm are included. Goods that have been sold and are awaiting delivery and goods held on consignment must not be included in the count. It is also important to be sure to include goods that are owned on the date of the inventory but which may not be in the store or warehouse. Examples are goods out on consignment and goods which may have been recorded as purchases but which have not been received. Such goods are said to be *in transit* (on their way in a freight car, truck, ship, or airplane). Goods which have arrived but have not yet been unloaded must also be included.

Assigning cost to the inventory

After the quantities of goods that are owned at the end of the accounting period have been determined, the next step is to decide how much cost should be assigned to each unit. At first thought, this might seem to be an easy, though perhaps a time-consuming job. If all purchases of the same article had been made at the same price per unit, reference to any purchase invoice covering such items would show the unit cost. The unit cost times the number of units in the inventory would give the total cost to be assigned to those units. However, it is frequently the case that identical articles have been purchased at different times at different costs per unit. The question then arises as to which unit cost should be assigned to the goods in the inventory. Often there is no way of knowing exactly which price was paid for the specific goods that are on hand. As a workable solution to this problem, one of several different bases of cost apportionment must be adopted. The most common bases are **(1)** first-in, first-out costing, **(2)** weighted average costing, and **(3)** last-in, first-out costing.

First-In, First-Out Costing. A widely used method of allocating cost between goods sold during an accounting period and goods on hand at the end of that period has been to assume that the first goods bought were the first goods sold. Accordingly, the items on hand at the end of the period are considered to be those most recently purchased. This is known as the *first-in, first-out* method, frequently referred to as the "fifo" method. To illustrate how this method works, assume the following circumstances with respect to a particular article of merchandise:

On hand at start of period, 400 units assigned a cost of $3.05 each $1,220.00
Purchased during period:
    First purchase, 300 units @ $3.20 each 960.00
    Second purchase, 700 units @ $3.40 each 2,380.00
    Last purchase, 600 units @ $3.50 each 2,100.00

Total cost of 2,000 units available for sale $6,660.00

On hand, end of period, 500 units

If it is assumed that the first units purchased were the first ones sold, then the 500 units left at the end of the period were among those purchased last at a cost of $3.50 each. Accordingly, the total cost to be assigned to these units would be $1,750 (500 units × $3.50). The cost assigned to the units sold would be $4,910 ($6,660 − $1,750).

First-in, first-out costing became popular because of two features: **(1)** Whenever the flow of merchandise can be controlled, the merchant will see to it that the older goods are moved out first. Thus, fifo costing is often in harmony with what has actually happened. **(2)** Fifo costing assigns the most recent purchase costs to the ending inventory. The amount of that inventory is shown on the balance sheet among the current assets. Accordingly, some accountants contend, very current inventory cost should be shown.

Another reason for the continuing widespread use of fifo costing is the reluctance of accountants to change a long followed method of accounting, for such a change would destroy the comparability of their income calculations over a period of years. Consistency is important in accounting. Firms that have used the fifo method for a long time are reluctant to abandon it.

Weighted Average Costing. Another method of allocating merchandise cost between goods sold and those in the inventory is on the basis of the average cost of identical units. In the example above, the total cost of the 2,000 units that were available for sale during the period was $6,660. Dividing $6,660 by 2,000 units results in a weighted average cost of $3.33 per unit. This is described as a *weighted average* because both the quantities involved and the unit costs are taken into consideration. On a weighted average cost basis, the 500 units in the ending inventory would be assigned a total cost of $1,665 (500 × $3.33). The cost assigned to the units sold would be $4,995 ($6,660 − $1,665).

There is a logical appeal to the use of the weighted average basis to allocate cost between goods sold and goods on hand. In this example, one fourth (500) of the total units available (2,000) were unsold. The weighted average cost basis assigns one fourth ($1,665) of the total cost ($6,660) to these goods.

Last-In, First-Out Costing. A third method of allocating cost between goods sold and goods on hand is to assume that all of the sales in the period were of the goods most recently purchased. This is called the *last-in, first-out* or "lifo" method. As applied to the data shown on the opposite page, this would mean that the 500 units on hand at the end of the period would be assumed to include the 400 units that were on hand at the start of the period with an assigned cost of $3.05 per unit plus 100 of the units from the first purchase at their actual cost of $3.20 each. Therefore, the cost assigned to the inventory would be calculated as follows:

400 units @ $3.05................	$1,220.00
100 units @ $3.20................	320.00
Total........................	$1,540.00

The cost assigned to the units sold would be $5,120 ($6,660 − $1,540).

Sometimes the lifo method has been justified on the grounds that the physical movement of goods in some businesses is actually last-in, first-out. This is rarely the case, but the method has become popular for other reasons. One persuasive argument for the use of lifo is that the method matches the cost of the items purchased most recently against the current sales revenue. In many cases in which the lifo method is used, the calculated amount called "cost of goods sold" is really the *cost to replace the goods sold*. When this amount is subtracted from sales revenue, the resulting gross margin figure is not inflated or deflated by gain or loss due merely to price changes. In the opinion of many accountants, this is proper and desirable.

Another argument in favor of the lifo method is that a going business must keep a minimum or base quantity of inventory on hand at all times. While this portion of the inventory is considered to be a current asset, it is, in reality, more like a long-lived asset. Because long-lived assets are carried at original cost, it is logical to assign original cost to the base amount of inventory. Lifo accomplishes this result for the most part.

Probably the major reason for the growing popularity of the lifo method is the fact that when prices are rising, net income calculated by using the lifo method is smaller than the amount that would result from using either the fifo or the weighted average method. As a result, the related income tax is smaller. The reverse would be true if prices were falling, but periods of falling prices have been few and brief in the past two centuries.

The lifo method is used by firms in many industries. Procedures have been developed to apply the "lifo principle" to situations in which the goods sold are not literally replaced. (High-fashion merchandise is an example.) Index numbers are used to adjust costs to a lifo basis.

Opponents of the lifo method contend that its use causes old, out-of-date inventory costs to be shown in the balance sheet. The theoretical and practical merits of fifo and lifo are the subject of much debate.

Comparison of Methods. To compare the results obtained by the use of the three cost-allocation methods discussed, assume that the 1,500 units that were sold brought $7,000 and that operating expenses for the period were $1,500. (The amount of the revenue from sales and the amount of operating expenses will not be affected by the method used to apportion cost between goods sold and goods on hand.) The tabulation below contrasts calculated net income and the cost assigned to the ending inventory under each of the three cost allocation methods. It must be remembered, however, that the example relates to a period in which costs and prices were rising.

	FIFO COSTING	WEIGHTED AVERAGE COSTING	LIFO COSTING
Sales................................	$7,000	$7,000	$7,000
Cost assigned to goods sold..............	4,910	4,995	5,120
Gross margin.......................	$2,090	$2,005	$1,880
Operating expenses....................	1,500	1,500	1,500
Net income........................	$ 590	$ 505	$ 380
Cost assigned to ending inventory.........	$1,750	$1,665	$1,540

Note that in all cases, the total cost of goods available for sale ($6,660) was apportioned between goods sold and goods on hand at the end of the period. For example, under fifo costing, $4,910 is apportioned to cost of goods sold and $1,750 to ending inventory. It is common practice to describe the methods that have been discussed as methods of inventory valuation. It should be apparent, however, that a process of valuing the cost of goods sold also is involved. The term valuation is somewhat misleading, since what is involved is really *cost apportionment*.

Cost or market, whichever is lower

There is a well-established tradition in accounting that unrealized profits should not be recorded except in very unusual cases. If the value of an asset increases, no formal record of the fact is entered on the books because the gain has not been actually realized. Nevertheless, in many cases, if the value or usefulness of an asset declines, it is generally considered proper to recognize that an expense or a loss has been incurred and to record the fact even though the loss has not yet been realized. This is in keeping with what is called the *rule of conservatism*. The practice of assigning "cost or market, whichever is lower" to the items that comprise the inventory of merchandise at the end of an accounting period is an important application of the rule of conservatism. In this connection, "cost" means the amount calculated using either the fifo or the weighted average method. "Market" means the cost to replace. It is the prevailing price in the market in which the goods must be purchased — not the prevailing price in the market in which they are normally sold — that is involved. An improved statement of the practice is *cost or cost to replace, whichever is lower*.

The lower of cost or market rule is not applied if inventory cost is calculated on a lifo basis. The reason is that the lifo method is usually adopted because of its possible income tax advantage. The tax law does not permit the use of the lower of "lifo cost" or market for tax purposes. Lifo users must follow the tax rule for all business income calculations and report its use on all annual financial statements.

To illustrate the application of the lower of cost or market rule to the previous example, suppose that the replacement cost or market price of the items in question was $3.30 on the last day of the period. This is less than the fifo cost per unit ($3.50) or the weighted average cost per unit ($3.33). Accordingly, the 500 units in the ending inventory would be assigned a total cost of $1,650 (500 × $3.30) and the cost of goods sold would be $5,010 ($6,660 − $1,650). Gross margin and net income would be reduced accordingly. Actually the cost of goods sold figure would then include an amount that can be described as a loss due to a decline in the replacement cost of unsold goods. This is often termed a "holding loss" because it results from holding the goods during a period of price decline.

Since the merchandise will probably be sold for considerably more than either market or cost (however calculated), the reason for following such a conservative practice may be questioned. (Not all businesses do follow the lower of cost or market rule. Some firms assign cost — fifo or weighted average — to the ending inventory even if market is less.) The purpose in using the "cost or market, whichever is lower" rule is to carry the goods into the next period with an assigned cost that will result in no less than an average or normal percentage of margin when the units are sold in the new period. If replacement cost has fallen, competition may cause some reduction in selling price.

To adhere strictly to the rule, the lower of cost or market should be used for each item in the inventory; it is not simply a matter of using the lower of total cost or total replacement cost of the entire inventory. Special applications of the rule have been developed to take care of nonreplace-able, damaged, or shopworn goods.

In determining the cost to be assigned to goods in an inventory, it is proper to assign to the goods on hand a fair share of any transportation costs that have been incurred on goods purchased. In other words, cost means cost at the buyer's place of business, not cost at the supplier's ship-ping point. In some cases, transportation charges are an important part of the total cost of merchandise acquired.

In calculating the cost to be assigned to goods on hand, the matter of purchases discounts should not be overlooked. It may be that the unit costs entered on the inventory sheets exclude cash discounts. If purchases discounts are regarded as a reduction of cost (and this practice is recom-mended), the amount of cost assigned to the ending inventory should reflect purchases discounts taken. It is not necessary to adjust every unit cost figure for discounts. The total cost before cash discounts can be calculated and this amount can then be reduced by a percentage determined by the re-lationship of purchases discounts to purchases for the year. For example, if purchases (less purchases returns and allowances) for the year amounted to $100,000 and purchases discounts taken were $2,000, the latter would be equal to 2 percent of purchases. If the calculated fifo or weighted average cost (exclusive of discounts) of the ending inventory was $20,000, the corrected cost amount would be $19,600 ($20,000 less 2% of $20,000). This $19,600 amount would then be assigned to the ending inventory unless the lower of cost or market basis was being followed and the replace-ment cost of the goods was less than $19,600.

Estimated allocation of merchandise cost

The taking of a physical inventory may be such a sizable task that it is not attempted more than once a year. If so-called *interim* income state-ments and balance sheets are to be prepared, the portions of the cost of goods available for sale during the interim period to be allocated to goods sold during the period and to goods on hand at the end of the period must be estimated. One way of doing this uses a gross margin approach. The amount of sales during the period is reduced by what is considered to be the normal percentage of gross margin (gross profit) to determine the estimated cost of goods sold. Deducting this amount from the total cost of goods available for sale gives the estimated amount of the ending inventory.

To illustrate, assume that a firm normally has a gross margin of 40 per-cent on sales. At the start of its fiscal year, the balance in the merchandise inventory account was $50,000. Net purchases for the first month of the year amounted to $45,000. Net sales for the month amounted to $80,000. **(1)** What was the estimated cost of the goods that were sold during the month? **(2)** What was the estimated amount of the merchandise inventory at the end of the month?

    (a) Since gross margin is assumed to have been 40% of sales, cost of goods sold is assumed to have been 60% of sales (100% − 40%).
    Therefore, the estimated cost of goods sold = 60% of $80,000 (net sales for the month), or $48,000.

    (b) Cost of goods available for sale was $95,000 (opening inventory of $50,000 plus net purchases of $45,000).
    The estimated inventory at the end of the month would be equal to goods available for sale, $95,000, less estimated cost of goods sold, $48,000, or $47,000.

Such computed amounts are only reasonable if the normal gross margin on sales has prevailed during the immediate past period and is expected to prevail during the following periods when the goods in the inventory will be sold. This type of calculation can be used to check the general reasonableness of the amount of an inventory that has been computed on the basis of a physical count. Any sizable difference in the two calculations might serve to call attention to a possible mistake in the count, in costing the items, or a marked change in the actual realized rate of gross margin. The gross margin procedure can also be used to estimate the cost of an inventory that may have been destroyed by fire or other casualty. Such a calculation might be useful in negotiating an insurance settlement.

The retail method of inventory

Many retail merchants use a variation of the gross margin method to calculate cost of goods sold and ending inventory for interim-statement purposes. The procedure employed is called the *retail method of inventory*. Its use requires keeping records of the prices at which purchased goods are marked to sell. This information, together with the record of the cost of goods purchased, will make it possible to compute the ratio between cost and retail prices. When the amount of retail sales is subtracted from the retail value of all goods available for sale, the result is the estimated retail value of the ending inventory. Multiplying this amount by the ratio of cost to selling price gives the estimated cost of the ending inventory.

Following is an example of the calculation of the estimated cost of an ending inventory of merchandise by the retail method:

	COST	RETAIL
Inventory, start of period	$ 34,000	$ 50,000
Net purchases during period	71,000	100,000
Merchandise available for sale	$105,000	$150,000
Less sales for period		110,000
Inventory, end of period, at retail		$ 40,000

Ratio of cost to retail prices of merchandise available for sale
($105,000 ÷ $150,000)............................   70%

Estimated inventory, end of period, at cost (70% of $40,000).. $ 28,000

The foregoing example was simplified by assuming that there were no changes in the prices at which the goods were marked to sell. In practice, such changes as additional mark-ups, mark-up cancellations, and mark-downs are commonplace and the calculation must take such adjustments into consideration.

In addition to using the retail method in estimating the cost of inventory for interim-statement purposes, the cost-retail ratio that is developed can be used to convert the amount of a physical inventory which originally has been priced at retail to its approximate cost.

Perpetual inventories

Firms that deal in certain types of merchandise sometimes find it feasible to keep up-to-date records of the quantities and costs of goods on hand at all times. Such records are known as *perpetual inventories*. The general ledger account for Merchandise Inventory under such a system is somewhat like the account for Cash or Bank; chronological records of additions (purchases) and subtractions (sales) are maintained. The balance of the account at any time shows the cost of goods that should be on hand.

When a perpetual inventory is kept, the merchandise inventory account in the general ledger is usually a control account. A subsidiary ledger with an account for each type of goods is maintained. These accounts are often in the form of cards which provide spaces to show additions, subtractions, and the balance after each change. Goods sold can be assigned cost on either a fifo, a weighted average, or a lifo basis. The day-to-day costing of sales on either the weighted average or lifo basis will give results that differ somewhat from those obtained when lifo or weighted average costing is applied at the end of the period. (The results will be the same if the fifo basis is used.) Perpetual inventories do not eliminate the need for taking periodic physical inventories. The records must be checked from time to time to discover and correct any errors. However, it is not always necessary to count everything at almost the same time. The stock can be counted and the records verified by groups of items, by departments, or by sections as time permits, so long as the inventory is completely verified within a single accounting period.

A business that sells a wide variety of comparatively low-cost goods (such as a limited-price variety store) will not find it practical to keep a perpetual inventory. In contrast, a business that sells relatively few high-cost items (an automobile dealer, for example) can maintain such a record without incurring excessive clerical cost.

Many types of businesses often keep supplementary or auxiliary records of goods in terms of quantities only. These are called *stock records*. Stock records serve as a guide in purchasing operations, help to reveal any shortages, and provide information as to the goods on hand as a basis for assigning merchandise cost for interim-statement purposes.

Perpetual inventory records in computer-based accounting systems

Some businesses with very large volumes of transactions and inventories composed of substantial numbers of different items have found it advantageous to use computer systems in keeping their perpetual inventory records. Some of these computer systems have very large data storage capacities and have the capability of retrieving any item of stored information in fractions of a second. Each item in the inventory is given a code number. By means of punched cards, magnetic tapes, and disc packs, data relating to the amounts of additions to and subtractions from each inventory item are fed into the computer. It makes the necessary addition or subtraction and computes the new balance in each case. In response to coded instructions, the status of any particular inventory item can be determined at will. Whenever desired, the machine will provide a listing of the status of all of the items in the inventory. Computer capacity can be purchased or leased sufficient to maintain records for inventories of many thousands of different items. (For a further discussion of computer-based accounting systems, see Appendix, page A-1.)

Report No. 13-1

Complete Report No. 13-1 in the study assignments and submit your working papers to the instructor for approval. Then continue with the following textbook discussion until Report No. 13-2 is required.

PREPAID EXPENSES

Office supplies, store supplies, advertising supplies, fuel, and other supplies purchased may not be wholly consumed in the period in which they are acquired. The premiums on insurance policies covering merchandise, equipment, and buildings may be prepaid, but the terms of the policies may extend beyond the current accounting period. Rent and interest may be paid in advance, but the expenses may not be wholly incurred in the same accounting period. The cost of unused supplies on hand at the close of an accounting period and the portion of such prepayments that will benefit future periods should be treated as current assets because the benefits will be realized within a comparatively short time. Current assets of this type are known as *prepaid expenses*.

When accounts are kept on the accrual basis, it is necessary to adjust certain of them at the close of each accounting period for the following:

(a) The amounts of any supplies or services purchased during the period that were recorded as assets at time of purchase and that were consumed or used during the period.

(b) The amounts of any supplies or services purchased during the period that were recorded as expenses at time of purchase and that were not consumed or used during the period.

Asset method of accounting for supplies and prepayments

Supplies, such as office supplies, store supplies, advertising supplies, fuel, and postage, which may not be wholly consumed in the accounting period in which they are acquired, are usually recorded as assets at the time of purchase.

Office Supplies. Office supplies include letterheads and envelopes, pencils, carbon paper, adding machine tape, notebooks, typewriter ribbons, rubber bands, paper clips, and other miscellaneous supplies that are normally consumed in the operation of an office. Transactions arising from the purchase of such supplies on account should be entered in the invoice register. When such supplies are purchased for cash, the transactions should be entered in the record of checks issued. In either case, the purchases are posted to the account for office supplies in the general ledger.

At the end of each accounting period, an inventory of the office supplies on hand is taken and an adjusting entry is made to record the amount of the office supplies consumed during the period. For example, if on December 31 the office supplies account has a debit balance of $842.96 and an inventory reveals that the cost of the supplies on hand amounts to $350, it is assumed that the supplies expense during the period was $492.96. The following adjusting entry would be made:

```
Office Supplies Expense.....................................  492.96
    Office Supplies...........................................          492.96
        Office supplies consumed during period.
```

After this entry is posted, the office supplies account will have a debit balance of $350, which should be reported in the balance sheet as a current asset. The account for office supplies expense will have a debit balance of $492.96, which should be reported in the income statement as an operating expense.

Store Supplies.   Store supplies include wrapping paper and twine, corrugated board, paper bags and other containers, cleaning supplies, and other miscellaneous supplies that are normally consumed in the operation of a store. Transactions arising from the purchase of such supplies should be recorded in the same manner as transactions arising from the purchase of office supplies; that is, purchases should be recorded by debiting Store Supplies and by crediting either Accounts Payable or the bank account, depending upon whether the purchases are made on account or for cash.

At the end of each accounting period, an inventory of the store supplies on hand is taken and an adjusting entry is made to record the amount of the store supplies consumed during the period. For example, if on December 31 the store supplies account has a debit balance of $578.13 and an inventory reveals that the cost of the supplies on hand amounts to $275, it is assumed that the supplies expense during the period was $303.13. The following adjusting entry would be made:

Store Supplies Expense......................................	303.13	
Store Supplies..		303.13
Store supplies consumed during period.		

After this entry is posted, the store supplies account will have a debit balance of $275, which should be reported in the balance sheet as a current asset. Store Supplies Expense will have a debit balance of $303.13, which should be reported in the income statement as an operating expense.

Advertising Supplies.   Advertising supplies include catalogs, circulars, price lists, order blanks, and other miscellaneous supplies that are normally consumed in an advertising program. Transactions arising from the purchase of such supplies should be recorded in the same manner as transactions arising from the purchase of other types of supplies; that is, purchases should be recorded by debiting Advertising Supplies and by crediting either Accounts Payable or the bank account, depending upon whether the purchases are made on account or for cash.

At the end of each accounting period, an inventory of the advertising supplies on hand is taken and an adjusting entry is made to record the amount of the advertising supplies consumed during the period. For example, if on December 31 the advertising supplies account has a debit balance of $724.50 and an inventory reveals that the cost of the supplies on hand amounts to $250, it is assumed that the supplies expense during the period was $474.50. The following adjusting entry would be made:

Advertising Supplies Expense..............................	474.50	
Advertising Supplies.....................................		474.50
Advertising supplies consumed during period.		

After this entry is posted, the advertising supplies account will have a debit balance of $250, which should be reported in the balance sheet as a current asset. The account for advertising supplies expense will have a debit balance of $474.50, which should be reported in the income statement as an operating expense.

Postage Stamps. The cost of postage stamps purchased is usually recorded by debiting Postage Stamps and by crediting the bank account. Some of the stamps may be used on parcel post packages and others on ordinary mail. If stamps used on parcel post packages are billed to the customer, the entry to record the sale will include a credit to the postage stamps account. Usually no record is kept of the stamps used on ordinary mail each day, but periodically the stamps on hand are counted and their value is determined. The difference between the amount of the unused stamps on hand and the debit balance of the postage stamps account represents the amount of the stamps used and not billed to customers.

If the account for postage stamps is debited **(1)** for the amount of the stamps on hand at the beginning of the month, $37, and **(2)** for the amount of stamps purchased during the month, $182.60, and is credited for the amount of the stamps used on parcel post packages during the month, $60, the account will have a debit balance of $159.60 at the end of the month. If, at that time, the amount of the stamps on hand is found to be $44.10, the difference, or $115.50, represents the amount of the stamps that appear to have been used and not billed to customers during the month. The following adjusting entry would be made:

```
Postage Expense......................................    115.50
     Postage Stamps......................................              115.50
          Amount of stamps used on ordinary mail.
```

After this is posted, the account for postage stamps will have a debit balance of $44.10, which should be reported in the balance sheet as a current asset. The postage expense account will have a debit balance of $115.50, which should be reported as an operating expense in the income statement.

A business may meet its postage requirements by **(1)** buying postage stamps, **(2)** making a deposit under the postal permit system for a certain amount of postage, or **(3)** using a postage meter. In the latter case, a certain amount of postage is paid for and the meter is set so that the postage may be used as needed. Regardless of whether postage stamps are purchased, whether a deposit is made under the permit system, or whether metered postage is purchased, the accounting procedure can be the same. The prepaid postage can be charged to an account with postage stamps, and when the stamps are used or the postage is consumed, the amount should be charged to the proper expense account.

Insurance. A variety of risks are entailed in the operation of a business. Property such as buildings, furniture, machinery, supplies, and merchandise inventory may be damaged or destroyed by fire, water, earthquake, or windstorm. Many types of property, especially money, may be stolen by burglars (and sometimes employees). State laws impose liability on the part of an employer to employees for injury or death arising out of the employees' work. The hazards connected with the ownership and operation of motor vehicles are well known. Accidents to persons unconnected with the business but occurring on business premises pose the threat of lawsuits and, possibly, large settlements. Loss of income as a result of the interruption of business operations because of a fire or a flood is a possibility.

It is possible to obtain insurance against the types of losses enumerated above and certain others not mentioned. A contract under which an insurance company (the insurer) agrees to protect the business (the insured) from loss is known as an *insurance policy*. A separate insurance policy relating to each type of risk could be obtained. In recent years, however, the practice of obtaining one policy covering most or all of the risks has become commonplace. Such contracts are described as "package," "blanket," or "multi-peril" policies. In total, the cost of such types of insurance is lower than a collection of policies for separate individual risks.

The amount that the insured is required to pay for such protection is known as the *premium*. The premium is usually stated as a specified rate per $1,000 of insurance for one or more years. (Rates for workmen's compensation and automobile insurance are subject to change each year even though the coverage is a part of a policy that includes other matters. The rate for the other features may be for a three-year period. The premium for three-year coverages is usually 2.7 times the one-year rate — a type of "quantity discount.") Since insurance is usually purchased for a period of one or more years and the premium must be paid in advance by the insured, the amount paid is usually charged to an account for prepaid insurance. This account is classified as a current asset.

Expired Insurance. The portion of an insurance premium that is prepaid decreases day by day, but it is not customary to keep a daily record of expired insurance. Instead the usual plan is to record at the close of each accounting period (usually a year but sometimes a month), the total amount of the prepayment that has expired during the period just ended. The expired amount is recorded as an expense. If the management of the business does not see a need for any "breakdown" of the insurance expense, an end-of-year adjusting entry such as the following would suffice:

Insurance Expense...	312.62	
Prepaid Insurance..		312.62
Insurance expired during the year.		

The amount was determined by referring to the policy (or policies) and calculating the portion of the premium that related to the year just ended. The amount of the premium for each major type of coverage will be shown on the face of the policy. If more detail about the expense were wanted (which would mean that there would be two or more insurance expense accounts), it would be possible to analyze the total and to classify it into, perhaps, delivery equipment insurance expense, fire insurance expense (with subclassifications relating to building, to furniture and fixtures, and to merchandise), workmen's compensation insurance expense, and public liability insurance expense. (It has been noted in other connections that accounts can be established to provide as much detail as needed.)

If a business has several insurance policies, it may be useful to maintain an auxiliary record known as an "Insurance Policy Register." This record provides spaces to show the date and number of each policy, name of the insurer, type and amount of coverage, total term, expiration date, total premium, and columns to show the premium applicable to each month. Usually a separate page is used for each year.

Canceled Insurance. Either the insurance company or the insured may cancel an insurance policy at any time before expiration of the policy. If a policy is canceled, the insured is entitled to receive a refund of that part of the premium applicable to the unexpired period. The amount of the refund will depend upon whether the policy is canceled by direct action of the insurance company or at the request of the insured. When the policy is canceled directly by the insurance company, the premium for the expired period is computed on a pro rata basis. When the policy is canceled at the request of the insured, the premium for the expired period is usually computed on a *short-term rate* basis. To record the amount refunded, it is only necessary to debit the bank account and to credit the prepaid insurance account.

If the policy or a part of it is canceled on a short-term basis, there could be what is sometimes regarded as a "loss" involved. For example, suppose that a three-year policy was purchased on January 1 and that the premium was $592. If the policy is canceled by the insured on September 30 and the insurance company refunds $428.85, there is, seemingly, a loss of $15.15 computed as follows: at the date of cancellation, the policy had 27 months to run — three fourths of the total original life of 36 months. On a pro rata basis, the premium relating to this portion was 3/4 of $592 or $444. However, the insurance company refunded $428.85 — a loss of $15.15. Another way of looking at the matter would be to assume that there really was no loss, but that the real cost for the nine months the insurance was in force was $163.15 ($592 — $428.85). In any case, the "loss" would not be separately accounted for. When the end-of-year adjustment is made and the unexpired premium relating to the policies still in force has been calculated, the adjustment of the prepaid insurance account will cause the "loss" (if it is so considered) to be a part of the total debit Insurance Expense.

Prepaid Interest. When a note payable to a bank is discounted (interest deducted from the face value of the note), it is usual to regard the amount of the discount as "prepaid" interest. If the note matures in a later accounting period, it is common practice to debit Prepaid Interest for the amount of the discount (part of the entry made when the note is issued and the proceeds are received). Prepaid interest is classified as a current asset.

At the end of the accounting period the amount of the interest expense relating to the period just ended should be calculated and an adjusting entry should be made to transfer that portion of the interest from the prepaid interest account to an interest expense account. For example, on December 1 a note for $10,000 due in three months with interest at 9 percent was issued to a bank, and the interest amounting to $225 was deducted by the bank. On December 31 it was determined that one third of the interest expense was related to the period then ended; therefore, the following adjusting entry was made:

```
Interest Expense......................................... 75.00
     Prepaid Interest.......................................          75.00
          Prepaid interest transferred to Interest Expense.
```

After this entry is posted, the prepaid interest account will have a debit balance of $150, which should be reported in the balance sheet as a current asset. The debit balance of the interest expense account should be reported in the income statement under the heading of "Other Expenses."

One advantage of using the asset method of accounting for prepaid expenses is that the adjusting entries that are required at the end of the period are of the write-off type. Such adjustments do not need to be reversed at the start of the new period.

Expense method of accounting for prepaid expense

Supplies and services that may not be wholly consumed in the period in which they are purchased may be recorded as expenses at the time of purchase. Under this method of accounting, it is necessary to adjust the accounts at the end of each accounting period in order that the unused portions may be recorded as assets. For example, if office supplies purchased during an accounting period are charged to the account for office supplies expense, it will be necessary to adjust the account at the end of the period for the cost of the supplies on hand. If Office Supplies Expense had been charged for a total of $250 during the period and an inventory taken at the end of the period showed that the supplies on hand amounted to $95, it would be necessary to make the following adjusting entry:

Office Supplies..	95.00	
Office Supplies Expense..		95.00
Office supplies on hand.		

After this entry is posted, the account for office supplies expense will have a debit balance of $155, which should be reported in the income statement as an operating expense. The account for office supplies will have a debit balance of $95, which should be reported in the balance sheet as a current asset.

When the expense method of accounting is followed, the adjustments made at the end of the period may be called *deferral adjustments* — they defer expenses to the next period. Adjustments of this type should be reversed at the start of the new period. In such case, the effect of the adjusting, closing, and reversing procedure is to remove the unused or unexpired amount from an expense account at the end of the period, to transfer the remaining amount to the expense and revenue summary account, and, at the start of the new period, to transfer back to the expense account the amount of expense that had been deferred.

The asset method and the expense method of accounting for prepaid expenses give the same final result. In the asset method, an amount that will eventually become the expenses of current and future periods is first put into an asset account, and at the end of each period, a proper portion is transferred to an expense account. In the expense method, the original amount is first put into an expense account. At the end of each accounting period the portion that is then an expense of future periods is moved into an asset account and subsequently brought back into the expense account by a reversing entry at the start of the new period.

Report **No. 13-2**	Complete Report No. 13-2 in the study assignments and submit your working papers to the instructor for approval. Then continue with the textbook discussion in Chapter 14 until Report No. 14-1 is required.

Chapter 14

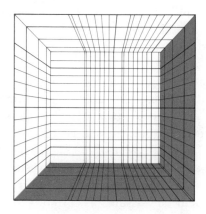

ACCOUNTING FOR TANGIBLE LONG-LIVED ASSETS

Many types of business assets are acquired with the expectation that they will remain in service for a number of accounting periods. Assets of this type are called *long-lived assets* or *fixed assets*. (The descriptions *plant assets* and *capital assets* are used sometimes.) Such assets can be classified in various ways. From a legal standpoint all property is either *real property* or *personal property*. Real property (realty or real estate) includes land and anything attached to the land; personal property includes everything else that can be owned other than real property. In nearly all cases, any real property owned by a business is considered to be a long-lived asset. (Real estate acquired as a short-term investment is an exception.) Many kinds of personal property are classified as long-lived assets. Furniture, equipment, motor vehicles, machinery, patents, and copyrights are common examples of personal property that is owned and used by a business for a number of accounting periods.

Another way of classifying long-lived assets is on the basis of tangibility. All real property is tangible (has physical substance). The same is true of such personal property as furniture, equipment, and machinery. Major examples of *intangible* long-lived assets are patents, copyrights, leases,

343

franchises, trademarks, and goodwill. All of these are assets because they are expected to bring future economic benefit and (all but goodwill) have a legal status that allows them to be classed as property. (The subject of goodwill will be considered in Chapter 16.)

Sometimes businesses own interests in other incorporated businesses in the form of capital stock, bonds, or long-term notes. Not infrequently, government bonds or notes are also owned. It is logical to classify such assets as intangibles; however, because of their special nature, they are usually classified as investments. If it is expected that such assets will be owned for a long time, they will be considered long-term investments and will be shown in the balance sheet under some such heading. If investments are temporary in nature, they should be classified as current assets.

For accounting purposes, a common classification of long-lived assets is on the basis of how the original cost of the property is handled in the process of determining net income period by period. The cost of land used only as a site for a store, a factory, a warehouse, or a parking lot is normally left undisturbed in the accounts as long as the land is owned. Because land does not lose its capability to serve for these uses, it does not depreciate. Assets such as buildings, furniture, and equipment are usually called *depreciable assets*, because their value or usefulness is diminished as time passes. In determining net income period by period, a portion of the cost of such assets is charged off as depreciation expense. In a similar fashion, the cost of such intangible properties as patents, copyrights, and leaseholds is gradually charged off as expense to the periods benefited by the ownership of the assets. As applied to these assets, however, the periodic write-off is termed *amortization* (in contrast to *depreciation* of certain tangible assets). Actually, the meaning of the word amortization is broad enough to include depreciation, but customarily the write-off of the cost of most tangible long-lived assets is called depreciation, while the write-off of the cost of intangibles is called amortization.

Finally, certain long-lived assets whose physical substance is consumed in the operation of a business are called *wasting assets*. Common examples include mines, stands of timber, and oil and gas wells. As might be expected, an effort is made to allocate the cost of such property to the periods in which its removal or exhaustion occurs. In this case, the periodic write-off is called *depletion*.

The subject of wasting assets and their depletion will be considered briefly at the end of the chapter. Because land, buildings, and various types of equipment are more common, the major features of accounting for these latter types of property will be considered first. For the sake of brevity, such items will be referred to simply as "long-lived assets," though it should be understood that those discussed in this chapter are all in the "tangible" category.

LAND, BUILDINGS, AND EQUIPMENT

Long-lived assets may be purchased for cash or on account. The amount at which long-lived assets should be recorded initially is the total of all outlays needed to put them in place ready for use. This total may include the purchase price, transportation charges, installation costs, and any other costs that are incurred up to the point of placing the assets in service. In some cases interest may be included in the cost. For example, if money is borrowed for the purpose of constructing a building or other facilities, it is considered sound accounting to add the interest incurred during the period of construction to the cost of such building or facilities. It is important that the cost of depreciable assets be properly accounted for, because the total cost becomes the basis for the periodic depreciation write-off.

Transactions involving the purchase of long-lived assets may be recorded in the appropriate book of original entry by debiting the proper asset accounts and by crediting the bank account for the amount paid, or by crediting the proper liability account, such as Accounts Payable, Notes Payable, or Mortgages Payable, for the obligations incurred.

Additions or improvements representing an increase in the value of long-lived assets should be recorded by debiting the proper asset accounts and by crediting the bank account or the proper liability account. For example, if an addition to a building is constructed, the total cost incurred should be debited to the building account. In the same manner, such improvements as the installation of partitions, shelving, hardwood or tile floors, a sprinkler system, an air conditioning system, or any other improvements that increase the usefulness of the property, should be recorded by debiting the proper asset accounts for the cost of the improvements. The cost of landscaping grounds surrounding an office or factory building, constructing new driveways, or planting trees and shrubbery represent improvements in the land which enhance its value. Assessments for street improvements, sidewalks, sewers, flood prevention, or parks also represent improvements in, or enhancement of the value of the land. Such costs and assessments should be recorded by debiting the land account.

Depreciation   The central task in attempting to determine net income or loss on a periodic basis is to allocate revenue to the period in which it is earned and to assign expenses to the periods that are benefited. Long-lived assets frequently last for many years and, accordingly, benefit a number of periods. The process of determining and recording the depreciation of most long-lived assets is carried on in an effort to assign their cost to the periods that they benefit or serve.

Causes of Depreciation. Depreciation is the loss of usefulness of an asset. There are two major types of depreciation:

Physical Depreciation. This term refers to the loss of usefulness because of deterioration from age and from wear. This type of depreciation is generally continuous, though not necessarily uniform from period to period. Assets exposed to the elements may wear out at a fairly regular rate. Assets not exposed to the elements may slowly deteriorate whether in use or not, but the speed at which they deteriorate often is related to the extent to which they are used.

Functional Depreciation. This term refers to loss of usefulness because of inadequacy or obsolescence. The growth of a business may result in some of its long-lived assets becoming inadequate. The assets remain capable of doing the job for which they were acquired, but the job has become too big for them. Assets may become obsolete because of a change in the demand for products or services, or because of the development of new methods, equipment, or processes which either reduce costs, or increase quality, or both.

Calculating the Amount of Depreciation for a Period. The net cost of an asset should be apportioned over the periods the asset is expected to serve. Net cost means original cost less scrap or salvage value. Scrap or salvage value is difficult, if not impossible, to predict in most cases. Unless such value is expected to be a significant fraction of original cost, it usually is ignored (considered to be zero). Scrap or salvage value normally is a significant fraction of original cost in the case of automobiles and trucks. The major problem connected with depreciation accounting, however, is to attempt to foretell either how many periods the asset will serve or how many units of service the asset will provide. If it were possible to know that a machine would operate for 100,000 hours, it would be easy to decide that 5 percent of its net cost should be charged to the first year in which it was used 5,000 hours. Likewise, a certain knowledge that an asset would last 10 years and equally serve each of those years would solve the problem of how to apportion its cost. Unfortunately, there is no way of knowing exactly how long an asset will last or exactly what its output will be. All that can be done is to make estimates based upon past experience. In attempting to make such estimates, the accountant may be assisted by information relating to assets previously owned by the business or be guided by the experience of others. Statistics supplied by trade associations and government agencies (such as the Internal Revenue

Service) may help. Opinions of engineers or appraisal companies may be sought. Past experience with respect to physical depreciation may be a very good guide for the future. Past events, however, are not much help in attempting to predict depreciation caused by inadequacy or obsolescence. Uncertainty surrounds all depreciation calculations.

Methods of Calculating Depreciation. There are several different ways of calculating the amount of depreciation to be recorded each period. The most commonly used methods are the following:

   (a) Straight-line method.
   (b) Declining-balance method.
   (c) Sum-of-the-years-digits method.

A fourth method, based on the estimated productive capacity of the asset, will be described, though it is not used as frequently as the other three methods mentioned.

Depreciation may be taken into consideration in calculating income subject to federal and state income taxes. A business is not required to calculate depreciation in the same way for both income tax and business accounting purposes. However, because depreciation can be only an estimate, many firms adopt depreciation practices that are acceptable for income tax determination purposes. This does not impose severe limitations since the tax laws generally allow any method that is reasonable and consistently followed.

Straight-Line Method. When the *straight-line* method is used, the net cost of an asset is apportioned equally over its estimated useful life in terms of months or years. For example, assume that a frame building cost $37,500 and it is expected that with reasonable "upkeep," it can be used for 25 years. At the end of that time, it is expected that the building will have to be torn down. It is hoped that proceeds from the sale of used building materials, such as lumber, plumbing fixtures, and electrical fixtures, will be as much as the cost of demolition. These considerations lead to the conclusion that the scrap or salvage value should be considered to be zero. The amount of depreciation each year, then, would be $1,500. This is computed as follows:

$$\frac{\$37,500 - \$0}{25} = \$1,500$$

The annual rate of depreciation would be 4 percent ($1,500 ÷ $37,500).

A month is usually the shortest period that is considered in depreciation accounting. An asset purchased before the fifteenth of the month is considered to have been owned for the full month. An asset purchased after the middle of the month is not considered to have been acquired until the first of the next month.

The difference between the cost of an asset and the total amount of such cost that has been charged off as depreciation as of a certain date is its *undepreciated cost* (sometimes called *book value*) at that time. When the straight-line method is used, the undepreciated cost of the asset decreases uniformly period by period. Shown on a graph, the undepreciated cost over a number of periods is a downward-sloping, but perfectly straight line. That is how the method got its name.

The straight-line method of calculating depreciation closely reflects the facts in many cases. The method's outstanding advantage is its simplicity. Since depreciation is based upon estimates in any case, many business people and accountants believe that the use of more complicated procedures is not warranted. The calculation of depreciation on a straight-line basis is still the most widely followed practice.

Depreciation can be calculated on each individual asset or on each group of substantially identical assets. It is possible to calculate a *group* or *composite rate* to be applied to a number of assets that may include various related types of property. For example, suppose that the general ledger account Office Furniture included the following:

ITEM	QUANTITY	ESTIMATED LIFE, YEARS	TOTAL COST
Desks	12	20	$3,600
Chairs...........	20	15	1,500
Tables...........	5	12	400
Filing Cabinets ...	20	20	1,800
			$7,300

Further suppose that it is estimated that the salvage values of the several items in the group will average 10 percent of original cost. (It might be contended that this is small enough to ignore, but this estimated salvage value is included in the illustration.) The composite or group rate of depreciation would be 4.9726 percent computed as follows:

ITEM	COST	SALVAGE VALUE	DEPRECIABLE COST	ESTIMATED LIFE	ANNUAL DEPRECIATION
Desks...........	$3,600	$360	$3,240	20	$162
Chairs..........	1,500	150	1,350	15	90
Tables..........	400	40	360	12	30
Filing Cabinets...	1,800	180	1,620	20	81
	$7,300	$730	$6,570		$363

$$\$363 \div \$7,300 = 4.9726$$

The rate would be rounded to 5 percent. As long as the relative proportions of the items in the groups stay about the same, and no reason arises to alter the estimated life of any of the items, the composite rate of 5 percent can be applied to the group total to determine the annual depreciation write-off.

When depreciation is calculated on the basis of a group or composite rate, no attempt is made to relate the depreciation to specific units. No depreciation is recorded in the subsidiary record (if any) for each individual unit. Therefore, when disposition is made of a unit, its original cost, less any salvage or trade-in value, is charged to the accumulated depreciation account for the appropriate group. No gain or loss is recognized upon the disposition of a unit. (The group method is an averaging device. It is expected that some units will have lives shorter than the average, and some will serve longer.)

Declining-Balance Method. Many long-lived assets require repairs and parts replacements to keep them in service. Such expenses usually increase as the assets grow older. Some accountants believe that depreciation expense should be higher in early years to offset the higher repair and maintenance expenses of the later years. Another reason advanced in support of a depreciation method that gives a greater write-off at first is the contention that many, if not most, assets contribute proportionately more to the business during the years that the assets are comparatively new. For these reasons, it may be desirable to calculate depreciation in a way that will give larger write-offs in the early years of the life of the unit. One way to accomplish this result is to apply a fixed or uniform rate to the undepreciated cost of the property each year. As the undepreciated cost diminishes year by year, the depreciation charges are successively smaller. This method is called the *declining-balance* or the *fixed percentage of diminishing value* method.

There is a formula which can be used to calculate a rate which will leave a predetermined amount at the end of a predetermined number of years.[1] This rate must be applied each year to the difference between original cost and amounts already written off. (There must always be some salvage or scrap value involved; any rate less than 100 percent will never reduce the original amount to zero.)

In practice, however, the rate used is rarely calculated by a formula. Instead, a rate equal to the maximum allowed for federal income tax purposes is used. Depending upon certain conditions being met, the maximum allowed is either twice the straight-line rate (generally the case if assets are acquired new), $1\frac{1}{2}$ times the straight-line rate or $1\frac{1}{4}$ times the straight-line rate. In the discussion that follows, twice the straight-line rate is used. (Because a rate is used that is double the straight-line

---

[1]The formula is:

$$\text{Rate} = 1 - \sqrt[n]{s \div c}$$

when n = number of years of estimated life, s = estimated salvage value, and c = original cost.

rate, the method is sometimes referred to as the "double-declining-balance method" or the "200 percent method.")

Suppose, for example, that an asset with a cost of $1,000 and an expected life of 5 years is to be depreciated on the declining-balance basis. It was new when acquired. Assume that the company wishes to handle depreciation in the same way for both income tax and business accounting purposes. Accordingly, since the straight-line rate would be 20 percent (100% ÷ 5 years), the company would use a declining-balance rate of 40 percent (2 × 20%). The annual depreciation, the balance in the accumulated depreciation account, and the undepreciated cost at the end of each year would be as shown below.

YEAR	ANNUAL DEPRECIATION	ACCUMULATED DEPRECIATION END OF YEAR	UNDEPRECIATED COST END OF YEAR
0......			$1,000.00
1......	$400.00	$400.00	600.00
2......	240.00	640.00	360.00
3......	144.00	784.00	216.00
4......	86.40	870.40	129.60
5......	51.84	922.24	77.76

For income tax purposes, the declining-balance rate can be abandoned at any time without permission, and the undepreciated cost at that date, less any estimated salvage value, can be written off in equal installments over the estimated remaining life. For example, suppose, that in the foregoing illustration at the end of the third year when the asset had an undepreciated cost of $216, it appeared likely that the salvage value would be zero. Accordingly, $108 (½ of $216) depreciation could be taken for each of the two remaining years. If the expected salvage value was approximately $75 or $80, however, there would be no reason to depart from the declining-balance procedure.

Sum-of-the-Years-Digits Method. Another method of writing off smaller amounts of depreciation year by year is known as the *sum-of-the-years-digits* method. This method is similar in effect to the declining-balance method. However, with the "years-digits" method, a write-down to the exact amount of estimated salvage value (which might be, and often is, zero) is possible. The write-off each year is based on a schedule of fractions obtained by listing the digits that represent the years of the estimated life of the asset and adding these digits to get a denominator for all of the fractions. The largest digit is used as the numerator for the first year, the next largest digit as the numerator for the second year, etc. For example, suppose that the estimated life of the asset is 5 years. 5 + 4 + 3 + 2 + 1 = 15. Therefore, write off 5/15 of the net cost (original cost less estimated salvage value) the first year, 4/15 the second year, 3/15 the third year, etc. As applied to an asset costing $1,000, with an estimated salvage value of $100, the results would be as follows:

Year	Annual Depreciation	Accumulated Depreciation End of Year	Undepreciated Cost End of Year
0......			$1,000.00
1......	$300.00	$300.00	700.00
2......	240.00	540.00	460.00
3......	180.00	720.00	280.00
4......	120.00	840.00	160.00
5......	60.00	900.00	100.00

(This method became popular when the Internal Revenue Act passed in 1954 specifically allowed its use in depreciating new assets acquired after December 31, 1953.)

Comparison of Methods. The following tabulation contrasts the results of using straight-line, declining-balance, and sum-of-the-years-digits depreciation methods for an asset costing $1,000 with a ten-year estimated life and an estimated salvage value of $100:

Year	Straight-Line Method Depreciation Charge	Straight-Line Method Undepreciated Cost End of Year	Declining-Balance Method Depreciation Charge	Declining-Balance Method Undepreciated Cost End of Year	Sum-of-The-Years-Digits Method Depreciation Charge	Sum-of-The-Years-Digits Method Undepreciated Cost End of Year
0...		$1,000.00		$1,000.00		$1,000.00
1...	$90.00	910.00	$200.00	800.00	$163.64	836.36
2...	90.00	820.00	160.00	640.00	147.27	689.09
3...	90.00	730.00	128.00	512.00	130.91	558.18
4...	90.00	640.00	102.40	409.60	114.55	443.63
5...	90.00	550.00	81.92	327.68	98.18	345.45
6...	90.00	460.00	65.54	262.14	81.82	263.63
7...	90.00	370.00	52.43	209.71	65.45	198.18
8...	90.00	280.00	41.94	167.77	49.09	149.09
9...	90.00	190.00	33.55	134.22	32.73	116.36
10...	90.00	100.00	26.84	107.38	16.36	100.00

The annual depreciation charge under the straight-line method was determined by dividing the net cost of $900 ($1,000 − $100) by 10.

In using the declining-balance method in the preceding comparison, salvage value was ignored (since it was a "built-in" factor) and twice the straight-line rate was applied to the undepreciated cost at the start of each year. With a ten-year life, the straight-line rate was 10 percent, so twice this, or 20 percent, was used. In this case, the undepreciated cost at the end of ten years ($107.38) was very close to the estimated salvage value stated at the outset of the comparison. If this were not the case, the declining-balance procedure could have been dropped at some point and in the years remaining, equal charges could have been made to write off all but the estimated salvage value.

In using the sum-of-the-years-digits method in the preceding comparison, salvage value was taken into consideration. The sum of the digits one through ten is 55. Therefore, under the years-digits method, the charge for the first year was 10/55 of the net cost, 9/55 in the second year, and so on.

Effect of Different Depreciation Methods on Net Income Calculation. Over a number of years, the *total* of the amounts of the calculated annual net incomes (deducting, perhaps, net losses in some years) will be about the same regardless of the method of depreciation used. For any one year, however, the method of depreciation used may make a significant difference in the amount of the calculated net income. For example, consider the case of a new business with a number of new depreciable assets which have just been acquired at a cost of $50,000, with an estimated life of 10 years and an estimated scrap value of $5,000. Suppose that, for the first year, revenue was $125,000 and all costs and expenses except depreciation amounted to $100,000. Following is a comparison of three very condensed income statements of the new business showing the net income for the first year after applying each of the depreciation methods so far discussed. (To check the depreciation calculation, refer to Year 1 of the previous comparison and multiply by 50 since that example was based on a $1,000 asset and this illustration assumes that the depreciable assets cost $50,000.)

	STRAIGHT-LINE DEPRECIATION METHOD USED		DECLINING-BALANCE DEPRECIATION METHOD USED		SUM-OF-THE-YEARS-DIGITS DEPRECIATION METHOD USED	
Revenue..........		$125,000		$125,000		$125,000
Costs and expenses except depreciation....	$100,000		$100,000		$100,000	
Depreciation.....	4,500	104,500	10,000	110,000	8,182	108,182
Net income....		$ 20,500		$ 15,000		$ 16,818

Note that the calculated amount of net income in the first case is over one-third greater than the amount in the second case. When such differences may result from the choice of depreciation methods, and it is recalled that the choice of method of allocating cost between goods sold and inventory on hand may make an important difference, it is apparent that periodic business income calculation is not an exact science, but rather an art involving careful judgment based on an understanding of acceptable alternatives and the consequences of their use.

Units-of-Output Method. Another method of calculating the amount of depreciation for each period is the *units-of-output* or *units-of-production* method. If it is possible to estimate the number of units of service or output that can be secured from an asset, then it is logical to allocate the net cost of the asset to the periods it serves on the basis of the use or output during each period. Obviously such a measure of service does not exist in the case of many assets. In the case of certain types of machinery, equipment, and vehicles, however, the units-of-output method may be used.

For example, a company may have found from experience that it usually can obtain 70,000 miles of service from certain types of trucks before they become so worn out that the need for extensive repairs and replacements makes it advisable for the company to dispose of them. Suppose a new truck of this type is purchased. The cost of the truck (apart from tires, which are separately depreciated on the basis of shorter lives) is $6,000. The company expects that the truck can be traded in for $1,800 after 70,000 miles. The estimated net cost to be charged to operations during the life of the truck is, therefore, $4,200. The estimated depreciation per mile is 6 cents ($4,200 ÷ 70,000 miles). If the truck were driven 22,000 miles the first year, the depreciation charge for that year with respect to that truck would be $1,320 (22,000 × .06).

Report No. 14-1	Complete Report No. 14-1 in the study assignments and submit your working papers to the instructor for approval. Then continue with the textbook discussion until Report No. 14-2 is required.

ACCOUNTING PROCEDURE

The number of accounts for tangible long-lived assets that will be kept in the general ledger will depend upon the number of such assets, the type of information required by the management, and, in the case of all but land, the sort of depreciation procedure that is to be followed. If there are very few long-lived assets, a separate account for each one with a related depreciation account (except for land, which is not subject to depreciation) can be kept in the general ledger. In such a case, the periodic depreciation for each one would be calculated and recorded separately.

If the business has a considerable number of depreciable long-lived assets, it is likely that there will be relatively few accounts for them in the general ledger. Summary accounts will be kept for each major class of assets, such as one account for buildings, one for machinery and equipment, one for office furniture and equipment, and one for delivery trucks. Each of these summary accounts will have a related accumulated depreciation account. It is highly desirable that such summary accounts be supported by some sort of supplementary or subsidiary records of the items that comprise the general ledger account totals. If depreciation is calculated on a *unit basis* (meaning a separate calculation and record of depreciation for each unit), it is common practice to maintain a subsidiary record of each unit. Such records are commonly in the form of cards. Space is provided on each card to show the details about the asset, including the cost of the unit (which supports the debit in the general ledger asset account), and the amount of depreciation taken each period. (These entries support the credits in the general ledger accumulated depreciation accounts.) Space is also provided to record matters relating to the disposition of the asset. A typical long-lived asset record card of this type is shown below. (Note that while salvage value was considered in arriving at the amount of annual depreciation, $48, the rate was this amount in relation to the original cost of $300.) Following is a narrative of the transactions that were recorded on the card:

January 6, 1975. Purchased Olivetti Underwood Typewriter, No. 6200625, from the Office Supply Co., City, for $300.

December 31, 1975. Depreciation of typewriter at annual rate of 16 percent of cost, $48. (A salvage value of $60 and a five-year life are estimated.)

December 31, 1976. Depreciation of typewriter at annual rate of 16 percent of cost, $48.

July 1, 1977. Sold typewriter for $210 cash.

LONG-LIVED ASSET RECORD

Description   Typewriter   Account   Office Equipment

Age when acquired   New   Estimated salvage value $60

Estimated life   5 years   Rate of annual depreciation based on cost 16%

COST				DEPRECIATION RECORD			
Date Purchased	Description		Amount	Year	Rate	Amount	Total To Date
1975				1975	16%	48 00	48 00
Jan. 6	Olivetti Underwood Typewriter		300 00	1976	16%	48 00	96 00
	#6200625			1977	16%	24 00	120 00
	Office Supply Company			19			
	City			19			
				19			
				19			
				19			
				19			

SOLD, EXCHANGED, OR DISCARDED						19			
Date	Explanation	Amount Realized	More than / Less than	Undepr. Cost	Accum. Depr.	19			
1977						19			
July 1	Sold	210 00		30 00	120 00	19			
						19			

Long-Lived Asset Record

Before the sale of the typewriter on July 1, 1977 was recorded, depreciation for the half year, amounting to $24, was recorded by debiting Depreciation of Office Equipment and by crediting Accumulated Depreciation — Office Equipment. The amount of this depreciation was also entered on the record card. The sale was then recorded as indicated by the following general journal entry:

Bank...	210.00	
Accumulated Depreciation — Office Equipment.................	120.00	
Office Equipment...		300.00
Gain on Sale of Office Equipment...........................		30.00
Sold Olivetti Underwood typewriter #6200625.		

The sale was also entered on the record card, after which the card was transferred from a file of assets owned to a file of assets sold, exchanged, or discarded. Such an asset record, when properly kept, will provide all the information needed in claiming the proper amount of depreciation of long-lived assets as a deduction from gross income in the annual income tax returns. The gain resulting from the sale of the typewriter for $30 more than its undepreciated cost represents taxable income, which must be reported in the income tax return for the year in which the sale was made.

In some accounting systems, no effort is made to calculate separately the periodic depreciation on each unit. Instead, depreciation is calculated for groups of assets. The grouping is usually by similar types of assets and similarity of average length of life. If this procedure is followed, there will be relatively few summary asset and related accumulated depreciation accounts in the general ledger, and there are not likely to be very extensive subsidiary records. No record is kept of the periodic depreciation on each unit; depreciation is calculated for each group as a whole, using an average or composite rate. Even if the group procedure is followed, however, it is desirable to have some sort of an individual record for each asset that will show its acquisition date, cost, location, and date and nature of disposition.

Recording depreciation

It has been seen that depreciation usually is recorded at the end of the period, along with other necessary adjusting entries. One or more depreciation expense accounts may be debited, and one or more accumulated depreciation accounts may be credited. The number of each of these accounts that will be used will depend upon the degree of detail that is desired in the general ledger accounts and for the periodic statements. Usually there is one depreciation expense account for each major type of asset, such as Depreciation of Buildings, Depreciation of Furniture and Fixtures, and Depreciation of Delivery Equipment. A business that classifies expenses on a departmental basis may use a considerable number of depreciation expense accounts.

In the normal course of events, the only entries in the accumulated depreciation accounts are those made at the end of each period to record the depreciation for the period then ended. When some disposition is made of a depreciable asset (such as its sale, exchange, retirement, or destruction by fire), depreciation should be recorded for the interval between the date of the last regular adjustment of the accounts and the date of the disposition of the asset. (Usually the depreciation is calculated to the nearest full month.)

Disposition of long-lived assets

A long-lived asset may be disposed of in any one of the following ways:

(a) It may be discarded or retired.
(b) It may be sold.
(c) It may be exchanged or traded in for property of like kind or for other property.

If the record of the cost of, and any depreciation on, the asset being removed is a part of some long-lived asset group records, no gain or loss will be recognized when the asset is removed. The cost of the item must be credited to the proper (group) asset account. The cost less any amount received for the item is charged to the proper (group) accumulated depreciation account. The discussion in the paragraphs that follow relates to assets that have been depreciated on a unit basis.

Discarding or Retiring Long-Lived Assets. A long-lived asset may be discarded or retired whether or not it has been fully depreciated. If it has been fully depreciated, no gain or loss will be realized. If it has not been fully depreciated, the undepreciated cost of the discarded asset will represent a loss. Such a loss may be the result of underestimating the depreciation of the asset for the period of time that it has been in use, or it may be the result of obsolescence. Often it is better to scrap an obsolete machine and to buy a new one even though a loss is realized on the old machine.

On July 16, Holling & Renz discarded parcel post scales that had no exchange or sale value. The long-lived asset record indicated that the scales originally had cost $80 and that depreciation amounting to a total of $60 had been recorded as a credit to the accumulated depreciation — store equipment account.

This event involved a loss of $20 because that was the amount of the undepreciated cost of the asset that was discarded. The transaction should be recorded as indicated by the following general journal entry:

```
Loss on Discarded Store Equipment...........................  20.00
Accumulated Depreciation — Store Equipment...................  60.00
   Store Equipment..........................................          80.00
      Discarded parcel post scales.
```

When this entry is posted, the debit of $60 to the accumulated depreciation account and the credit of $80 to the store equipment account will remove the amounts relating to the parcel post scales from the balances of these accounts. The debit of $20 to Loss on Discarded Store Equipment records the realized loss.

When a long-lived asset is discarded after it has been fully depreciated, no gain or loss will result from the transaction, but the amounts relating to the discarded asset should be eliminated from the account balances by debiting the accumulated depreciation account and by crediting the asset account for the original cost of the asset.

Selling Long-Lived Assets. If a long-lived asset is sold, it is necessary to know its undepreciated cost before the proper amount of any gain or loss resulting from the transaction can be determined. The undepreciated cost of an asset is the difference between its cost and the amount of depreciation recorded. Thus, if an adding machine that cost $200 depreciates at the rate of 10 percent a year and the annual depreciation is recorded by debiting Depreciation of Office Equipment and by crediting Accumulated Depreciation — Office Equipment, the undepreciated cost of the adding machine at the end of three years will be $140, the difference between the cost price of the adding machine and the credit balance of the accumulated depreciation account. When a long-lived asset is sold at its undepreciated cost, no gain or loss results from the transaction; when it is sold for more than its undepreciated cost, the difference represents a gain; when it is sold for less than its undepreciated cost, the difference represents a loss.

Assuming that the adding machine was sold at the end of three years for $150 cash, the transaction should be recorded as indicated by the following general journal entry:

```
Bank.......................................................  150.00
Accumulated Depreciation — Office Equipment................   60.00
   Office Equipment........................................         200.00
   Gain on Sale of Office Equipment........................          10.00
      Sold adding machine.
```

When this entry is posted, the debit of $60 to the accumulated depreciation account will offset the amount recorded previously as a credit to the accumulated depreciation account because of the estimated depreciation of the adding machine over a period of three years. The amount credited to Office Equipment will offset the purchase price previously recorded as a debit to Office Equipment. These entries have the effect of completely eliminating the amounts relating to the old adding machine from the office equipment and accumulated depreciation accounts. The gain realized from the sale of the adding machine for $10 more than its undepreciated cost is reported as a "Gain on Sale of Office Equipment." This gain should be listed under the heading of "Other Revenue" in the income statement.

If the adding machine referred to was sold at the end of three years for $110 instead of $150, there would be a loss of $30 instead of a gain of $10. The transaction should be recorded as indicated by the following general journal entry:

```
Bank......................................................   110.00
Accumulated Depreciation — Office Equipment.................    60.00
Loss on Sale of Office Equipment............................    30.00
    Office Equipment.......................................              200.00
        Sold adding machine.
```

When this entry is posted, the debit of $60 to the accumulated depreciation account and the credit of $200 to the office equipment account will eliminate the amounts relating to the old adding machine from these accounts. The loss resulting from the sale of the old adding machine for $30 less than its undepreciated cost will be reported as a "Loss on Sale of Office Equipment." This loss should be listed under the heading of "Other Expenses" in the income statement.

Exchange or Trade-In of Long-Lived Assets. A long-lived asset may be exchanged or traded in for other property. While in a simple trade each party must expect to benefit, it is not likely that either would record any gain. In most cases, the asset acquired would be assigned a cost equal to the undepreciated cost of the asset given.

If one asset is traded in on the purchase of another, the *trade-in allowance* may be equal to, greater than, or less than the undepreciated cost of the asset turned in. If the allowance is greater, a gain results; if less, a loss is sustained. However, gains or losses of this sort are not always "recognized." To simplify the preparation of income tax returns, it is common practice to record trade-ins in a way that conforms to the tax regulations. These regulations state that no gain or loss is recognized if property held for productive use is exchanged for property *of like kind* acquired for similar use. The cost (the tax laws call it the "basis") of the new property acquired is the undepreciated cost of the old property exchanged for it, plus the additional cash paid.

For example, suppose that a delivery truck that cost $4,200 has been owned for three years. Depreciation in the amount of $1,220 has been taken each year — a total of $3,660. Thus, the undepreciated cost of the truck is $540 ($4,200 − $3,660). If this truck is traded in on a new one to be used for a similar purpose and $4,500 is paid in cash, the cost of the new truck is $5,040 ($4,500 + $540). The transaction should be recorded as indicated in the following general journal entry:

Delivery Equipment (new truck)	5,040.00	
Accumulated Depreciation — Delivery Equipment	3,660.00	
Delivery Equipment (old truck)		4,200.00
Bank		4,500.00
Purchased a new truck.		

When this journal entry is posted, the cost of the old truck will be eliminated from the delivery equipment account and that account will be charged for the cost of the new truck, a figure which constitutes the basis for future depreciation charges. The amount of the depreciation of the old truck will also be eliminated from the accumulated depreciation account. No gain or loss is recognized in recording the transaction. This method of accounting conforms to the income tax regulations.

Some accountants prefer to take into consideration the amount of the exchange allowance rather than the undepreciated cost of an asset given in exchange in determining the cost of the new asset acquired. However, if this practice is followed, it will be necessary to make special calculations when preparing the annual income tax return. These calculations can become quite complicated where there are frequent transactions involving the exchange of long-lived assets. It is, therefore, generally preferable from a practical standpoint to follow the income tax regulations in recording such transactions.

In any transaction involving an exchange in which property is exchanged for property *not of like kind*, any gain or loss resulting from the transaction should be recorded, since it must be taken into consideration in preparing the income tax return.

For example, suppose that the $175 cost of a typewriter was charged to the office equipment account and depreciation on the typewriter amounting to $35 had been credited to the accumulated depreciation account each year for two years. At the end of two years the typewriter was traded in on a new cash register costing $450. The trade-in allowance amounted to $130, the balance, $320, being paid in cash. Since this transaction did not involve an exchange of property for other property of like kind, any gain realized or loss involved would be recognized for income tax purposes. Because $130 was allowed for an asset that had an undepreciated cost of $105 ($175 − $70), the transaction involved a gain of $25. The transaction should be recorded as indicated in the following general journal entry:

Store Equipment	450.00	
Accumulated Depreciation — Office Equipment	70.00	
Office Equipment		175.00
Bank		320.00
Gain on Sale of Office Equipment		25.00
Purchased a new cash register.		

When this entry is posted, the debit of $70 to the accumulated depreciation account will offset the amount recorded previously as a credit to that account because of the estimated depreciation of the typewriter over a period of two years. The amount credited to Office Equipment will offset the purchase price of the typewriter previously recorded as a debit to that account. These entries have the effect of completely eliminating the amounts relating to the old typewriter from the office equipment account and the accumulated depreciation account. The gain realized on the old typewriter is recorded as a credit to Gain on Sale of Office Equipment. Had the trade-in allowance been less than the undepreciated cost of the typewriter, the difference would have represented a loss to be charged to Loss on Sale of Office Equipment.

Fully depreciated long-lived assets

A long-lived asset is said to be fully depreciated when the recorded depreciation is equal to the cost of the asset. When an asset is fully depreciated, no further depreciation should be recorded. Since the rate of depreciation is based on its estimated useful life, an asset may be continued in use after it is fully depreciated. In this case, the cost of the asset and an equal amount of accumulated depreciation are usually retained in the accounts. When a fully depreciated asset is scrapped, the cost of the asset and the total amount of depreciation should be removed from the accounts. Such an adjustment involves a debit to the proper accumulated depreciation account and a credit to the proper long-lived asset account for the cost of the asset.

In some states a taxable value is placed on a fully depreciated long-lived asset if the asset is continued in use. Under such circumstances, the taxable value of the fully depreciated asset should be stated in the long-lived asset record as a guide in preparing the property tax schedule. The taxable values of fully depreciated long-lived assets and the undepreciated costs of other long-lived assets should be listed so that the total taxable value of the long-lived assets may be determined.

Depreciation in the statements

Most accountants and business-people consider depreciation to be an operating expense and so classify it in the income statement. There may be as much subclassification as the management desires. Depreciation of delivery equipment, for example, may be classed as a selling expense, while depreciation of office furniture and equipment may be classed as an office or general administrative expense.

In view of the close relationship between long-lived asset accounts and their accumulated depreciation accounts, the preferred practice in the preparation of balance sheets is to show the amount of the accumulated depreciation as a deduction from the cost of the asset. The difference, representing undepreciated cost, is extended to be included in the asset total.

Accumulated depreciation accounts, like allowances for doubtful accounts, are sometimes called asset valuation accounts. An accumulated depreciation account, however, only values the asset in a very limited and remote sense. The difference between the cost of the asset and the balance of the accumulated depreciation account is not expected to have any relation to the market value of the asset. Such assets are not intended for sale. What they might bring, if sold, is usually of small consequence. Those who understand accounting interpret the difference between the gross amount of the long-lived assets and the related accumulated depreciation accounts as being simply costs not yet charged to operations. Some companies so describe this difference in their balance sheets.

Wasting assets

The term *wasting asset* is applied to real property which is acquired for the purpose of removing or extracting the valuable natural resource on or in the property. Stands of timber, mines, oil wells, gas wells, or land acquired in the belief that the property contains minerals, oil, or gas that can be extracted, are examples of this type of asset. The adjective "wasting" is applied because, in most cases, it is expected that the valuable product eventually will be removed or exhausted so as to leave the property relatively valueless. In the case of many types of mines and wells, only the valuable material below the surface is owned. The land, as such, may not be owned by the mining, oil, or gas company.

Depletion. The consumption or exhaustion of wasting assets is called *depletion*. Apart from income tax considerations, the accounting problem is to apportion the cost of such assets to the periods in which they are consumed. The procedure is very similar to that involved in computing depreciation on a units-of-output basis. The cost of the property is reduced by estimated salvage or residual value, if any, and the difference is divided by the estimated number of units that the property contains. The result is the depletion expense per unit. This amount times the number of units removed and sold during the period will give the depletion expense for the period.

The example on page 362 is used to illustrate both the method of computing depletion and the proper accounting procedure.

A coal mine is acquired at a cost of $300,000. No salvage value is expected. The estimated number of units available for production is 1,000,000 tons. During the current year 145,000 tons of coal are mined and sold.

COMPUTATION OF AMOUNT OF DEPLETION EXPENSE

$300,000 ÷ 1,000,000 tons = 30¢ per ton
145,000 tons × 30¢ per ton = $43,500, amount of depletion expense

The depletion may be recorded by means of the following general journal entry:

Depletion Expense..	43,500	
Accumulated Depletion — Coal Mine........................		43,500
Depletion based on 145,000 tons of coal at a unit rate of 30¢ a ton.		

The difference between the cost of the mine and the amount of the accumulated depletion is the undepleted cost of the property.

Cost of coal mine...	$300.000
Less accumulated depletion.......................................	43,500
Undepleted cost of mine...	$256,500

It is customary to show the accumulated depletion as a deduction from the property account in the balance sheet to indicate the undepleted cost of the property. Depletion Expense is a temporary account that is closed into Expense and Revenue Summary at the end of the accounting period. It should be reported as an operating expense in the income statement. It is an expense that may be deducted in calculating taxable income.

From time to time the estimate of the quantity of the resource that remains in the property has to be changed. The usual practice is to make a new calculation of the depletion per unit, starting with the most recently determined undepleted cost of the property and dividing that amount (less estimated salvage value, if any) by the number of units extracted during the current year plus the current estimate of the number of units remaining. For example, the mine mentioned in the previous illustration had an undepleted cost of $256,500 at the start of the second year. During that year 200,000 tons were extracted and at the end of the year the engineers estimate that 700,000 tons remain. The calculation of the revised depletion expense per unit would be as follows:

$$\frac{\$256,500}{200,000 \text{ tons} + 700,000 \text{ tons}} = 28\tfrac{1}{2}¢ \text{ per ton}$$

200,000 tons × 28½¢ = $57,000, depletion expense for the second year

Depletion Expense for Federal Income Tax Purposes. Special rules govern the amount of the deduction for depletion expense that can be taken for federal income tax purposes. The taxpayer may compute the amount in the manner explained in the preceding paragraphs which is known as *cost depletion*. However, certain taxpayers who own and operate oil and gas wells and certain types of mines may take deductions equal to certain specified percentages (which vary from 5 percent to 22 percent) of the amount of the sales of the period subject to stated maximum and minimum limits. This procedure is commonly known as *percentage depletion*. It is limited to 50 percent of the taxable income exclusive of any depletion deduction.

**Report
No. 14-2**

> Complete Report No. 14-2 in the study assignments and submit your working papers for approval. Then continue with the textbook discussion in Chapter 15 until Report No. 15-1 is required.

Chapter 15

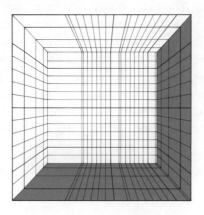

ACCOUNTING CONCEPTS AND PRACTICES

The structure that underlies modern business accounting is a blend of various assumptions, conventions, requirements, compromises, and restraints. Because these matters are so interrelated, it is not possible to array them in an unquestioned order of importance. This fact must be remembered in the discussion that follows. In the organization of this chapter, the various matters are grouped according to (1) those that can be regarded as *concepts* and (2) those that may be classed as *practices*. However, it will become apparent that each category overlaps the other.

BASIC CONCEPTS IN FINANCIAL ACCOUNTING

The basic concepts in financial accounting include: (1) the business entity, (2) periodicity and matching with the related matter of realization, (3) transaction-based records including the requirement that historical cost be shown in the accounts, and (4) the going-concern assumption.

The business entity

As applied to business accounting, what is called the *entity concept* involves identifying the business to which the records (or financial statements) relate without regard to legal considerations of who actually owns the property and who is liable for the debts. In connection with the discussions and illustrations of the accounts of a single-owner business (a sole proprietorship), it was stressed that while the owner may possess various properties, only the property used in the business was taken into account. Likewise, the record of liabilities excluded any of the proprietor's debts of a nonbusiness or personal nature. Consequently, there was no accounting for any type of revenue and expense not connected with business operations. Of course, the business could be considered to include various, perhaps wholly unrelated, profit-seeking activities if the owner so desired. Thus, the "accounting entity" could consist of the assets used by the business and the liabilities incurred on behalf of the business, even though, legally, the property belonged to the owner and he or she was personally liable for the debts.

In the case of business partnerships (discussed in the next chapter), the separate entity is almost a legal reality. Property can be owned by a partnership. However, with limited exceptions, the debts of the firm may become personal liabilities of each of the partners. It is in the case of business corporations (also discussed in the next chapter) that the business entity is a legal reality. Corporations can own property, incur debt, sue, and be sued. The debts of a corporation are not debts of its owners (stockholders). This is one of the reasons for the popularity of the corporate form of business organization.

Probably the greatest extension of the entity concept is in the case of one corporation owning most or all of another (or, perhaps, several others). While each corporation is a legal entity and each has a separate set of records, their individual financial statements are combined to present what is known as a *consolidated income statement* and a *consolidated balance sheet*. From the viewpoint of the stockholders of the so-called "parent" corporation, there is, in effect, just one entity. (Because of various factors such as intercorporate transactions and problems resulting from cases where a subsidiary corporation is less than 100 percent owned by the parent, the process of preparing consolidated statements may be very complicated.)

Periodicity and matching; realization

Central to business accounting is the requirement that income determination be made on a *periodic* basis. This usually means annually, and in addition, sometimes for shorter periods, such as every quarter or every month. (Any period shorter than a year is described as an *interim* period.) This periodic determination requirement causes most of the problems associated with income measurement. Realized revenue must be *matched* with expense on a periodic basis. *Realization* of revenue generally means the receipt of cash or a claim to cash in exchange for goods or services. Were it not for the periodic requirement, realization would not have been considered to have occurred until cash had been received for goods or services provided. However, calculating income for specified periods may pose a problem if the goods or services are provided in one period and the collection of the money does not occur until a following period. In order to achieve a reasonable matching, either the cost (and expense) associated with a sale of goods or services will have to be deferred to the period of collection, or the acquisition of an account receivable will have to be considered as evidence of realized revenue to be matched with the expired costs (expenses) that relate to the period in which the sale was made. This latter process, recognizing the acquisition of a claim to cash as evidence of realized revenue, is nearly always followed rather than trying to defer "proper" amounts of cost (and expenses) to the period of the cash collection. It should be apparent, however, that the "claim to cash" recognition approach raises the problem of how to treat uncollectible accounts receivable so as to conform to the matching objective. It has already been explained that the solution is to estimate the amount of uncollectible receivables at the end of each period and include this amount in the income calculation for the same period in which the receivables arose.

It is in connection with the expense aspect of income measurement that the periodic-income-determination requirement poses the largest problems. Two outstanding examples were discussed in the immediately-preceding chapters: **(1)** the question of apportioning merchandise cost between cost of goods sold and end-of-period inventory and **(2)** the problem of allocating the cost of most long-lived assets — depreciation. Lesser examples are in connection with prepaid expenses and the accrual of some expenses such as interest expense. It should be apparent that all of these complications would not exist if there were no periodic income determination and, thus, no matching requirement. The basis of accounting frequently referred to as the accrual basis has evolved from these compelling requirements.

Transaction-based records; historical cost in the accounts

Fundamental to business accounting is the idea that, in most cases, there is nothing to account for until a transaction occurs. Closely allied to this notion is the requirement that the amount to be recorded when the transaction involves the acquisition of an asset is the acquisition cost, or *historical cost*, of that asset. This is not to deny the fact that many acquisitions may be regarded as involving real gains. (It always has been presumed that both parties to an exchange must have placed a higher value on what they were getting than on what they were giving.) However, the amount of the gain may be difficult to measure and may never materialize. For at least these reasons, historical cost usually remains in the accounts, except that it may be written off (often amortized) as the economic value of the asset expires or diminishes. Add to this **(1)** the requirement that there must be realization of revenue in the income-measurement process, **(2)** the tradition of conservatism in accounting (to be discussed in a later section), and **(3)** the importance of having the dollar amounts in the accounts rest upon *objective, verifiable evidence*, and the case for the historical-cost basis of accounting is very strong. The greatest weakness of historical-cost accounting arises from the circumstance of the decreasing value of money. This subject will be considered in a section at the end of this chapter.

The going-concern assumption

A well-established tradition in business accounting is that in the absence of strong reason to believe otherwise, the business should be assumed to have a continuing, indefinite life. This is called the *going-concern assumption*, or *concept of continuity*. Several arguments are offered in support of this assumption. Corporations can have virtually perpetual existence. In the other two forms of business organizations, proprietors and partners will die, but the businesses involved can be continued by others — perhaps by those who inherit the business, by remaining partners, or by those to whom the business may be sold. It is argued that, in most cases, the owners and managers of a business intend and hope that the business will continue indefinitely. They usually make decisions with a view to maintaining the existence of the business, often in the hope of expanding it.

The reality of the economic world doesn't give full support to the going-concern assumption. Business failures are commonplace. The "infant mortality rate" among new businesses is especially high. However, the alternative to assuming that a business will continue indefinitely would be to make an estimate of its probable life. What would be a reasonable estimate? Two years? Five years? Ten years? Whatever the estimated life, it would mean that the acquisition of a depreciable asset with a potential useful life greater than the expected life of the business might seem inadvisable. If long-lived assets were acquired, the nature of depreciation calculations could be affected. The estimated life of the business rather than the estimated useful life of the asset might become the controlling element. In addition, the longer a business does survive, the greater is the chance for its continued existence, thus some depreciation rates might have to be revised and rerevised. Since this alternative option to a continuity assumption is so unattractive (perhaps unworkable), the going-concern assumption seems the more sensible alternative.

Report No. 15-1	Complete Report No. 15-1 in the study assignments and submit your working papers to the instructor for approval. Then continue with the textbook discussion until Report No. 15-2 is required.

ACCOUNTING PRACTICES

In an attempt to serve the interests of various groups of people concerned with a business' affairs as reported in its periodic financial statements, several practices have become well established in the business accounting process. Some of these practices have grown out of the concepts that have been discussed. Others are intended to help make accounting reports easier to understand. Many involve a compromise between partially-conflicting objectives. Four of the most important of these practices are discussed in the paragraphs that follow.

The rule of conservatism

The customs, concepts, and conventions of modern business accounting involve a tendency (some say a bias) toward *conservatism*. Generally, this means that when two or more acceptable ways of allocating the cost of an asset between benefiting periods can be used, the one that causes assets and periodic income to be smaller usually is chosen. The widely-used "cost or market, whichever is lower" method for assigning a value to the end-of-period merchandise inventory will cause both the inventory and the income for the period just ended to be smaller than otherwise. As applied to depreciation, if equally good reasons exist to use either a ten-year or a twelve-year estimated life for a depreciable asset, most accountants would use the shorter life. For the years just ahead, both the income of each of the periods and the undepreciated cost of the asset at the end of each period will be smaller than if the longer life were used. When the question arises whether to immediately charge something to expense or instead treat it as an asset to be amortized, the expense-it-now option usually is followed.

Probably the most all-encompassing example of the rule of conservatism stems from the historical-cost and realization principles which do not permit "writing up" assets even if they are thought at a later date to be worth more than the accounts show. Some accountants contend that refusing to show current or present values for all assets causes many balance sheets to be almost worthless. However, if such write-ups were to become accepted practice, either accountants would have to be trained as appraisers or appraisers would have to be employed. It is questionable whether the values thus determined would qualify as "objective, verifiable evidence." Historical costs, generally, do meet this test. Further, either the amount of the write-up would have to be considered as income even though there were no inflows of cash or receivables (or other assets), or provision would have to be made in the accounts to record *unrealized income*. In the opinion of many accountants and business executives, so-called "unrealized income" is not income at all. Price-level adjustments of accounting data (to be discussed later) might provide one solution to the cost-versus-current value issue.

The conservative rule or practice is thought to have become deeply imbedded in accounting for two major reasons: **(1)** If unquestioned absolute accuracy in accounting is not possible, there is probably less danger of damaging the interests of existing and prospective owners and creditors by following conservative practices. **(2)** While income tax regulations do not require that most items be handled in the same way for tax purposes as in the accounts, a tax approach is easier to defend if it corresponds with what was done in the accounts. Since it is usually desirable to minimize or, at least, defer income taxes, conservative accounting practices serve the interests of the business in accomplishing this objective.

Consistency in accounting

It has already been noted that the problems posed by the periodicity and matching requirements (which are fundamental to business accounting) preclude the attainment of absolute accuracy in the calculation of periodic income. Couple this practical reality with the further fact that the users of financial statements invariably want to make comparisons between current and past results, and the desirability of having *consistency* from period to period becomes apparent. One example is found in the matter of the choice of an accounting method for merchandise inventory. Regardless of whether fifo or lifo is considered best, it is not difficult to imagine the possible consequence of switching from one to the other each year. This switching might make any comparison of the results of operations for several years almost meaningless. Frequent changes of the depreciation method could produce a similar undesirable result. Stated loosely, the rule is: "If you can't be completely certain of your choice of method, at least use it consistently."

The consistency principle or practice must not be carried to such an extreme that it is taken to mean that a method of accounting once adopted must never be changed. Changing circumstances may require a change in accounting method, but it is not expected that numerous and substantial changes will be needed each year. When important changes are made, it is essential that the financial statements clearly indicate (by footnote or otherwise) the changes made and the reasons therefore. Sometimes data are included in the explanation to show what the result might have been if the change had not been made. The act of providing an explanation of what was done, and why, is an example of compliance with the *full disclosure principle.*

Full disclosure in accounting reports

For at least the following three reasons the full disclosure principle must be observed in the preparation of accounting reports:

(a) Financial statement users want to know which of the various "generally accepted" accounting principles and practices have been used.
(b) There is a danger that significant facts about what has taken place during the period under review will somehow get "buried" among all the other information that the report contains or else remain undisclosed.
(c) There has been an increasing demand from users of financial reports for more information about the business.

To meet the full disclosure requirement, a number of procedures have evolved. The use of explanatory notes, either in the body of financial statements or as footnotes has become widespread. (Mention was made earlier of the importance of disclosing any important changes in an accounting method.) What is termed the "all-inclusive" type of income statement has become widely used. Such a statement not only shows the composition of the income (loss) from regular operations for the period, but, in addition, any unusual gains or losses that occurred. (At one time, gains and losses of the latter type commonly were included in a supplementary statement or schedule of changes in the owners' equity. In this location, such items were easily overlooked.)

The annual reports of large corporations often include an assortment of tables and graphs intended to emphasize significant trends in their corporate business affairs. Often statistical data of a nonfinancial nature are included, such as the number of employees or the number of units produced. Annual reports of this type always include a message from the company president or board chairman that draws attention to important things that happened during the year, including any major changes in management personnel and a general forecast (usually rather optimistic) for the year or years ahead.

In the interest of full disclosure, it has been proposed that annual reports should include a financial (forecast) budget so that interested parties can have an idea of "what's coming." However, this procedure might reveal information useful to competitors and since the reported plans may not work out, both business managers and accountants fear that such a procedure might do more harm than good. Another proposed requirement for multi-line companies is that more detail about product lines or major segments of the business be supplied. This, too, is generally opposed by business executives on the grounds that it might help competitors. In addition, the allocation of expenses that is required by product-line reporting is apt to be on extremely arbitrary grounds. Just how far full disclosure should go is an unsettled issue.

The doctrine of materiality

In the field of law there is a maxim called *de minimis non curat lex* which means that the law is not concerned with trifles. The same can be said of accounting. In accounting, what is called the *doctrine of materiality* means that the principles of accrual accounting need not be followed in the case of amounts that are too small to make any real difference. For example, even though a waste basket that cost $5 may be expected to be useful for many years, it is not necessary to account for it as an asset to be depreciated. Simply treat the expenditure as, perhaps, miscellaneous expense. It is an almost universal practice for each business to establish some "cut-off point" that the accountant should follow in recording such expenditures. In the case of a small business, the point might be $25 or $50; larger businesses may have a higher limit. Consistency of treatment is, of course, necessary.

In the matter of certain year-end adjustments, the amount involved may dictate whether an adjustment should even be made. For example, it would be absurd to bother with accrued interest (payable or receivable) in the amount of $2.65 or to record the fact that $15 of the supplies expense account balance (amounting to more than $400) actually related to supplies that were still on hand.

Probably the most important application of the materiality doctrine is in connection with the financial statements. Full disclosure does not require that a petty cash fund of $100 be shown by itself rather than lumped together with cash in bank, or that the detail be shown for prepaid expenses whose total is equal to one percent of total assets. In fact, the interests of full disclosure are best served by preparing financial statements and schedules that are not so filled with detail that the significant matters may be obscured. This is called *adequate disclosure*.

Another widespread practice that is followed in the interest of eliminating the immaterial aspects of financial statements is to eliminate cents; instead, each amount is rounded to the nearest dollar. (In order to stress the importance of arithmetic accuracy, this treatment has not been illustrated to this point in the book. Starting in Chapter 19, all financial statements will show dollars only.) The financial statements of very large companies frequently show amounts to the nearest $1,000.

The price-level question

This topic cannot be classed either as an established concept or as a practice, but since it has such an important bearing on both it is included in this chapter.

For several decades, the question of whether changes in the value of the dollar should be recognized in the accounting process has been discussed and debated. Hundreds of millions of words have been spoken and written on the subject. It is difficult to deny the contention that it seems unreasonable (some say absurd) to go along always assuming that "a dollar is a dollar" even though it is well known that the purchasing power of the dollar is constantly changing — nearly always declining. The impact of this is greatest in the case of long-lived assets. Quite apart from the question of whether the amounts reported on a balance sheet should approximate current market values of the assets as opposed to historical cost, is the problem that the amounts shown as the costs of long-lived assets may be a mixture of some dollars spent, perhaps, 25 years ago, some 20 years ago, some 10 years ago, and some more recently. Almost certainly, the value of the dollar was not the same at those different times. The amount charged to depreciation expense would be, in consequence, a mixture of different-valued dollars. To a lesser extent, all this may apply to shorter-lived assets whose costs become expenses within a shorter period of time; for example, inventories. Another point is that the dollars of revenue for a single period represent, generally, similar purchasing power, while the dollars of expense deducted may be a diverse mixture. This results in violations of both the matching and consistency principles.

This situation might be corrected if, either in the formal accounts or in work sheets used to assemble data for financial statements, adjustments were made to convert or adjust all past dollars involved to dollars of end-of-period purchasing power. Some sort of *price-level* or *purchasing-power index* would have to be used. Various federal government agencies prepare and continually update certain indexes. The best known is the *Consumers Price Index* (CPI), prepared by the Bureau of Labor Statistics. Another is the *Gross National Product Implicit Price Deflator* prepared by the Department of Commerce. (It is considered by many to be a better index.) If necessary, special types of indexes can be prepared.

To illustrate how an index may be used, consider the following: An expenditure of $15,000 made ten years ago is involved. The price index being used stood at 120 at that time; at the end of the recent accounting period it was 204. This means that, on the average, what $1.20 would buy ten years before would cost $2.04 at the end of the recent period. Worked by logical steps, it is found that the index increased 70 percent (204 − 120 = 84; 84 ÷ 120 = .7 or 70%). Therefore increase the $15,000 by 70 percent, or $10,500, to $25,500. Accomplished by a short cut: multiply the $15,000 by 204 and divide the product by 120. The result, $25,500, is the same.

In spite of a succession of recommendations made as the result of studies by individuals, boards, committees, and commissions urging some sort of price-level adjustments in financial accounting and reporting, historical-cost accounting and reporting remains the rule. A number of reasons are given to explain why this is true. The major reasons are the following:

(a) Users of price-level-adjusted statements might be more confused than enlightened. Historical-cost statements, it is argued, are hard enough to understand.

(b) Federal and state income tax laws do not allow price-level adjustments in determining taxable income.

(c) Among those favoring some sort of price-level adjustments, opinion is divided on questions such as the following:

   1. What index should be used?

   2. Should all businesses use the same index?

   3. How should adjustments be made (if at all) to amounts of long-term debt and owners' equity?

   4. What about losses from holding monetary assets (cash and short-term receivables) during inflation?

(d) Surveys of the opinions of financial analysts have shown that few of them want to see a change from historical-cost accounting.

(e) Business executives, generally, oppose the change. Understandably, they do not favor any departure from existing conservative accounting practices that might make their companies "look bad." Under conditions of ever-increasing prices (which seem to be the rule), price-level adjustment of certain expenses (notably, depreciation) would cause net income to be less. That, in the case of corporations, might mean that dividends would have to be reduced, a step that surely would make stockholders unhappy. Further, lower reported net income undoubtedly would decrease the value of stock holdings. If product prices could be and were raised to offset higher costs, this would add to inflation. However, if the tax laws are changed to permit the beneficial use of price-level adjustments in calculating taxable income, the opposition of business people may vanish.

It certainly is to be hoped that the time never comes when inflation is so severe that accounting data either will have to be price-level adjusted or be worthless. Far short of that, the interests of sensible accounting calculations may bring about the practice of price-level adjustments.

Report No. 15-2

Complete Report No. 15-2 in the study assignments and submit your working papers for approval. Then continue with the textbook discussion in Chapter 16 until Report No. 16-1 is required.

Chapters 11-15

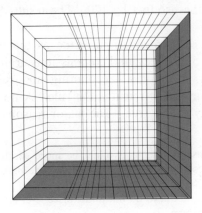

PRACTICAL
ACCOUNTING
PROBLEMS

Problem 11-A Schuyler Hoslett, is a wholesale distributor of office furniture and supplies. The merchandise accounts are kept on the departmental basis, Dept. A comprising furniture and Dept. B all other merchandise. The following general ledger accounts are affected by this problem:

171 Store Equipment	531 Purchases — Dept. A
181 Office Equipment	541 Purchases — Dept. B
261 Accounts Payable	551 Freight In — Dept. A
	561 Freight In — Dept. B

Following is a narrative of purchases made during February:

Feb. 1. (Tuesday) No. 306, The Yawman & Erbe Co., Pittsburgh; desks, $431.20; terms, January 27 — 2/10, n/30; Penn-Central freight collect.

1. No. 307, Steno Supply Co., Cleveland; memo books, $52.95; terms, January 28 — 2/10, n/30.

1. No. 308, Great Lakes Office Supply Co., Chicago; ledger outfits, $182.60; terms, January 28 — 2/10, n/60; postage prepaid and added to invoice, $8.40.

1. No. 309, Mohawk Chair, Inc., Syracuse; chairs, $123.50; terms January 28 — 3/10, n/30; Penn-Central freight collect.

1. No. 310, Heywood Furniture Co., Grand Rapids; tables, $195.75; terms, January 27 — 30 days; Michigan Central freight collect.

14. No. 311, The Chestnut Bros. Co., Kansas City; tables, $180; terms, February 11 — 30 days; Missouri Pacific freight prepaid and added to invoice, $12.20.

14. No. 312, Parker's, Janesville; desk sets, $224.80; terms, February 10 — 30 days; express prepaid and added to invoice, $15.25.

21. No. 313, The Yawman & Erbe Co., Pittsburgh; filing cabinets (for their own store use), $326; terms, February 18 — 2/10, n/30; Penn-Central freight collect.

21. Received a corrected purchase invoice, dated January 27, from Heywood Furniture Co., Grand Rapids, $185.75. (See Purchase Invoice No. 310.)

21. No. 314, High Point Furniture Co., High Point; desks, $650; terms, February 19 — 30 days.

28. No. 315, Olivetti Underwood Corporation, Buffalo; typewriter (for their own office use), $225; terms, February 26 — 30 days.

REQUIRED: As the accountant for the business, **(1)** enter each invoice in an invoice register similar to the one reproduced on page 294 and post directly to the proper supplier's account in a subsidiary accounts payable ledger. **(2)** Complete the individual posting from the invoice register to the general ledger, and update the account balances. **(3)** Foot, prove the footings, enter the totals, and rule the invoice register. **(4)** Complete the summary posting, and update the account balances. **(5)** Prove the balance of the accounts payable account by preparing a schedule of accounts payable as of February 28. Use four-column ledger paper for the general ledger and three-column ledger paper for the accounts payable ledger.

Problem 12-A   Edwin Prokasky is a wholesale distributor of musical instruments. The merchandise accounts are kept on the departmental basis. Following is a list of the general ledger accounts that are affected by this problem with the September 1 balances indicated:

133 Accounts Receivable, $3,729.50
411 Sales — Dept. A, $16,295.24.
    041 Sales Returns and Allowances — Dept. A, $725.00.
421 Sales — Dept. B, $14,342.84
    042 Sales Returns and Allowances — Dept. B, $327.20.
619 Freight Out, $658.60 (Cr.).

As of September 1, the accounts receivable had debit balances as follows:

Crandall & Seymour, 211 Main Street, Beloit; $800.
Holt Bros., 462 Spruce Street, Peoria; $685.50.
Hughes' Department Store, 1241 Main Street, Rockford; $721.90.
Mitchell & Son, 1622 Division Street, DeKalb; $684.54.
Taylor's Department Store, 2531 Virginia Avenue, Elgin, $837.56.

All charge sales are subject to a discount of 3% if paid within ten days from date of invoice, net 30 days.

The narrative of the September charge sales begins below:

Sept. 1. (Thursday) Sale No. 362, Taylor's Department Store; Dept. A, $146.20.

2. Sale No. 363, Mitchell & Son; Dept. B, $182.60; express prepaid and added to invoice, $8.25.

5. Sale No. 364, Crandall & Seymour; Dept. A, $95.50; Dept. B, $64.80.

8. Sale No. 365, T. J. Carmody, 2518 Blair, Geneva; Dept. A, $162.40.

10. Sale No. 366, Holt Bros.; Dept. A, $138.20; Dept. B, $26.10; freight prepaid and added to invoice, $10.50.

13. Sale No. 367, Taylor's Department Store; Dept. A, $230; Dept. B, $193.50.

15. Sale No. 368, Lapp & Bradshaw Furniture Store, 221 Green Street, Batavia; Dept. B, $85.60; express prepaid and added to invoice, $5.32.

16. Sale No. 369, Hughes' Department Store; Dept. A, $94.50; Dept. B, $86.20.

16. Sent T. J. Carmody a corrected invoice for Sale No. 365 amounting to $184.60.

20. Sale No. 370, Weston's Hi-Fi Shop, 422 Bloomfield Street, Belvidere; Dept. A, $225.

22. Sent Lapp & Bradshaw Furniture Store a corrected invoice for Sale No. 368 amounting to $96.52.

27. Sale No. 371, Taylor's Department Store; Dept. A, $64.20; parcel post charges added to invoice, $4.42.

28. Sale No. 372, Mitchell & Son; Dept. A, $75; Dept. B, $76.80; less credit for merchandise returned, Dept. A, $9.20.

30. Sale No. 373, Crandall & Seymour; Dept. B, $154.30; freight prepaid and added to invoice, $6.57.

REQUIRED: (1) Using four-column ledger paper, open the necessary general ledger accounts and enter the September 1 balances. (2) Using three-column ledger paper, open the necessary accounts receivable ledger accounts and enter the September 1 balances. (3) Using a sales register similar to the one reproduced on page 316, enter the charge sales for September and post directly to the proper customers' accounts. (4) Complete the individual posting from the sales register to the general ledger accounts and update the account balances. (5) Foot, prove the footings, enter the totals, and rule the sales register; complete the summary posting and update the account balances. (6) Prove the balance of the accounts receivable account by preparing a schedule of the accounts receivable as of September 30.

Problem 13-A   The Nations Company is in the wholesale hardware business. Stock record cards are kept of all merchandise handled. The data with respect to Article Y were assembled from their stock record cards and appeared as shown below and on the following page.

On hand at beginning of period, 800 units.
First purchase during period, 900 units @ $30.00.

Second purchase during period, 600 units @ $25.00.
Last purchase during period, 650 units @ $32.00.
In stock at end of period, 590 units.

REQUIRED: Assuming that the units in stock at the beginning of the period were assigned a cost of $28 each under the fifo method, or $29.00 each under the lifo method, compute (1) the total cost of the units in stock at the end of the period and (2) the total cost of the units sold during the period under (a) the fifo method and (b) the lifo method of cost assignment.

Problem 13-B   Barber & Hawley operate a mail-order house as partners. Metered postage is used on parcel post packages. As required, deposits are made for postage under the postal permit system. Postage stamps are purchased for other purposes. All prepaid postage is charged to Postage Stamps, Account No. 154, and periodically the postage used is charged to the following expense accounts:

619 Freight Out (Parcel Post)
624 Advertising Postage Expense
639 General Postage Expense

Before adjusting entries had been made on June 30, the postage stamps account had a debit balance of $2,040.

REQUIRED: (1) Open the necessary accounts and enter the balance of the postage stamps account before adjustment. (2) Assuming that (a) during the month of June the postage used on parcel post packages amounted to $702 and on advertising matter, $636, and (b) that on June 30 the unused stamps on hand amounted to $225 and the unused metered postage amounted to $360, make the required adjusting entry in general journal form to record all postage expense for the month. (3) Post.

Problem 13-C   Beginning on January 3 of the current year, 19A, Suellen Keller goes into the distribution of soft drinks. In accounting for insurance, the following accounts are used:

155 Prepaid Insurance
621 Merchandise Insurance Expense
631 Store Equipment Insurance Expense
641 Office Equipment Insurance Expense

All premiums paid for insurance policies are charged to the prepaid insurance account. At the end of each month the expired insurance is charged to the proper expense accounts and credited to Prepaid Insurance. The firm keeps an auxiliary record of insurance in the form of an insurance policy file.

Following is a record of the insurance transactions completed during the current year (19A):

Jan.   3. Paid the premiums on the following insurance policies: No. 47022 dated January 1, Sentry Accident, Fire & Life Insurance Co.; merchandise, $50,000; term, one year; premium, $624.60.
No. 61224 dated January 1, Voyagers' Mutual Insurance Company of Iowa; merchandise, $8,000; term, three years; premium, $360.
No. 724830 dated January 1, Brokers' Mutual Insurance Co.; office equipment, $3,000; term, one year; premium, $36.
No. 26144 dated January 1, Confectioners' Mutual Fire Insurance Co.; store equipment, $2,500; term, one year; premium, $27.

Feb.   2. Paid $225 premium on Policy No. 142019 dated February 1, Bankers' Fire Insurance Co.; merchandise, $15,000; term, one year.

Mar.   7. Paid $63 premium on Policy No. 40362 dated March 1, McKinley Mutual Fire Insurance Co.; merchandise, $2,500; term, three years.

Sept. 12. Received a check for $66 from the Bankers' Fire Insurance Co. representing a refund on Policy No. 142019 canceled by Ms. Keller as of September 1.

Nov. 10. Paid $72 premium on Policy No. 23610 dated November 1, Belleville Mutual Fire Insurance Co.; store equipment, $5,000; term, one year.

REQUIRED: (1) Journalize the transactions involving the premiums paid on insurance policies purchased during January. (2) Prepare a journal entry to record the amount of the insurance expired during January. (3) Continue the work required each month to record any new insurance policies purchased during the month and to record the total insurance expired during the month. In recording the transactions for September, it will also be necessary to prepare a journal entry to record the amount refunded on September 12 on Policy No. 142019. (4) Open an account for Prepaid Insurance, Account No. 155. Post the debit and credit entries affecting the prepaid insurance account from the general journal. After completing each posting to the prepaid insurance account, determine the balance, and enter it in the proper balance column. (5) Prove the final balance of the Prepaid Insurance account by computing the total unexpired premium on the three unexpired policies: No. 61224, 24 months to run; No. 40362, 26 months to run; and No. 23610, 10 months to run.

Problem 14-A   On February 1 of the current year, 19A, Meyers & Anderson begin the wholesale distribution of air-conditioning equipment as partners. In accounting for their long-lived assets, the following accounts are used:

171 Office Equipment
017 Accumulated Depreciation — Office Equipment
181 Store Equipment
018 Accumulated Depreciation — Store Equipment

191 Delivery Equipment
019 Accumulated Depreciation — Delivery Equipment
231 Accounts Payable
617 Depreciation of Office Equipment
618 Depreciation of Store Equipment
619 Depreciation of Delivery Equipment

Transactions involving the purchase of long-lived assets on account are recorded in an invoice register from which they are posted to the proper general ledger accounts. Accounts with suppliers are kept in a subsidiary accounts payable ledger and the posting to these accounts is done directly from the invoices and other documents representing transactions completed with suppliers. The following is a narrative of transactions involving the purchase of long-lived assets during the year ended December 31, 19A:

Feb. 2. Invoice No. 348; purchased cabinet file for office use from The Steelcase Co.; $250; terms, February 1 — 30 days. Estimated useful life, 10 years. Estimated trade-in value at end of 10 years, $50.

Mar. 7. Invoice No. 362; purchased a small truck for delivery purposes from Molding Motors, Inc.; $3,600; terms, March 4 — 30 days. Estimated useful life, 4 years. Estimated trade-in value at end of 4 years, $400.

April 8. Invoice No. 379; purchased an office table from The National Furniture Co.; $160; terms, April 7 — 30 days. Estimated useful life, 20 years. No salvage value.

July 12. Invoice No. 404; purchased showcases from S. C. Jones Co.; $540; terms, July 11 — 2/10, n/30. Estimated useful life, 15 years. No salvage value.

Aug. 18. Invoice No. 421; purchased used double-pedestal desk for use in storeroom from Snyder Store Equipment Co.; $180; terms, August 16 — 2/10, n/30. Estimated useful life, 20 years. No salvage value.

Sept. 19. Invoice No. 442; purchased used Olivetti Underwood typewriter, No. 5837852-11, from Olivetti Underwood Corporation; $175; terms, September 17 — 30 days. Estimated useful life, 5 years. Estimated trade-in value at end of 5 years, $25.

REQUIRED: (1) Using an invoice register similar to the one reproduced on page 294, record the foregoing transactions. (2) Foot the amount columns, prove the footings, enter the totals, and rule the invoice register. (3) Determine the annual rate of depreciation (straight-line method) applicable to each of the long-lived assets purchased, compute the amount of the depreciation accumulated during the current year ended December 31, 19A, and prepare an entry in general journal form to record the depreciation. (4) Assume that on January 7, 19C, after recording twenty-two months' depreciation, the delivery truck purchased on March 7, 19A was traded in for a new truck, with $1,800 in cash being paid. Prepare a general journal entry to record the transaction. (No gain or loss to be recognized.)

Problem 14-B   Buer Enterprises, Inc., owns a gravel pit that had been purchased a few years before for $50,000. The accountant has been calculating depletion on the basis of 9 cents for every cubic yard of gravel excavated. At the beginning of the current year the balance of the accumulated depletion account was $3,870. During the first four months of this year (19A) 30,000 cubic yards of gravel were excavated, and on May 2, 19A, the pit was sold for $46,800 cash.

REQUIRED: Prepare entries in general journal form, to record **(1)** the depletion accumulated for the first four months of the year, and **(2)** the sale of the gravel pit, recognizing any gain or loss on the sale.

Problem 15-A   Anderson's Delicatessen, owned and operated by James A. Anderson, is in the process of separating the assets and liabilities of the business enterprise from Mr. Anderson's personal assets and liabilities as of December 31, 1977. Mr. Anderson has solicited your help.

REQUIRED: (a) From the list of assets, liabilities, income, and withdrawals given below and on page 381, separate out those that clearly relate to Anderson's Delicatessen and prepare a balance sheet as of December 31, 1977 in report form. (b) The separation of Anderson's Delicatessen assets and liabilities from James A. Anderson's assets and liabilities is an adaptation of what accounting concept?

Cash in business bank account in Manchester Bank..............	$14,900
Cash in personal bank account in Clayton Bank.................	32,465
Accounts receivable owed to James A. Anderson.................	6,742
Accounts receivable owed to Anderson's Delicatessen.............	15,680
Allowance for doubtful accounts:	
on Anderson's Delicatessen accounts receivable...............	725
on James A. Anderson's accounts receivable..................	610
Merchandise inventory of Anderson's Delicatessen...............	55,420
Prepaid insurance:	
James A. Anderson..	350
Anderson's Delicatessen...................................	425
Supplies	
Anderson's Delicatessen...................................	55
James A. Anderson.......................................	40
Store Equipment......................................	3,870
Accumulated depreciation thereon............................	1,640
Business delivery truck....................................	4,100
Accumulated depreciation thereon............................	2,250
Mr. Anderson's personal automobile..........................	4,500
Store building (which Mr. Anderson owns as a personal asset (net))..	8,500
Notes payable to outsiders by James A. Anderson...............	3,000

Notes payable to outsiders by Anderson's Delicatessen.   4,500
Accrued interest payable on above notes:
    Anderson's Delicatessen.   42
    James A. Anderson.   27
Accounts payable to outsiders by:
    James A. Anderson.   2,750
    Anderson's Delicatessen.   6,425
Sales tax owed by delicatessen.   1,230
Withheld business taxes payable.   620
Mortgage due on Mr. Anderson's home.   16,750
Net Income of Anderson's Delicatessen for 1977.   18,250
James A. Anderson's withdrawals for 1977.   16,750

Problem 15-B   In order to determine what the effect of price-level adjustment might be on depreciation expense if certain circumstances existed, consider the following: Depreciation expense (based on historical cost) for a year just ended was $28,000. Analysis of this amount discloses that:

   $ 8,000 relates to assets purchased when the price-level index was   70.
     6,000   "   "   "   "   "   "   "   "   " 140.
   14,000   "   "   "   "   "   "   "   "   " 168.
   At the close of the year just ended, the index was 210.

REQUIRED: Adjust the three amounts for price-level change. Show the total and how each component was calculated.

Chapter 16

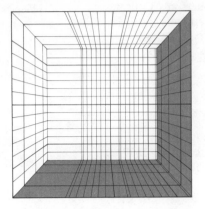

ACCOUNTING FOR OWNER'S EQUITY

The assets of a business are subject to the claims of its creditors and of its owners. The claims of the creditors are known as the liabilities of a business. The dollar amount of the difference between the assets and the liabilities of a business is the amount of the equity of the owner or owners in the assets.

THE SINGLE PROPRIETORSHIP

When there is only one owner, the amount of his interest in the business is called owner's equity. At one time, the term *proprietorship* was widely used to indicate owner's equity. Sometimes the designations *net worth* or *capital* are used. The word "Capital" commonly follows the name of the owner as a part of the title of the account that shows the amount of the owner's equity element of the business.

In small merchandising enterprises and in personal service enterprises the single proprietorship form of organization predominates. The medical and dental professions, for example, are composed largely of individuals who are engaged in practice as sole owners. One reason for the popularity of the single proprietorship form of operation is that it is easily organized, involving no formal or legal agreement with others as to ownership or conduct. Anyone may engage in a lawful enterprise merely by complying with state and local laws.

Organization of a single proprietorship

When engaging in an enterprise as a sole owner, an individual decides the amount that he will invest and the nature of the property that he will invest. The original investment may consist of cash only, or of cash and any other property that he owns, such as merchandise, office equipment, store equipment, or delivery equipment. The property invested usually is segregated from any other property that may be owned by the proprietor. An individual may engage in more than one enterprise and may operate each enterprise separately as a single proprietorship. In such cases, it may be desirable to keep separate records of the activities of each enterprise.

In comparison with other forms of business organization, the single proprietorship offers certain advantages, such as:

(a) Simplicity of organization.
(b) Freedom of initiative and industry.
(c) Fewer government reports required.
(d) Strong incentive to individual enterprise.

The single proprietorship form of organization has some disadvantages, of which the following are the most significant:

(a) The amount of available capital may be limited.
(b) The amount of available credit may be restricted.
(c) The proprietor is solely responsible for all debts incurred.

Accounting procedure

In general, the accounting procedure in recording the ordinary operating transactions of an enterprise is not affected by the type of ownership. Whether an enterprise is operated as a single proprietorship by an individual, as a partnership by two or more partners, or as a corporation by stockholders through directors and officers has little bearing on the accounting procedure in recording the routine transactions in connection with the ordinary operations of the business. However, the owner's equity accounts required depend largely upon the type of ownership.

Owner's Equity Accounts. There are two types of owner's equity accounts: **(1)** permanent and **(2)** temporary.

In a single proprietorship, the owner's capital account is the only permanent owner's equity account. The account is usually given the name of the owner of the enterprise followed by "Capital" or "Proprietor."

The temporary owner's equity accounts are those in which increases and decreases in owner's equity arising from the transactions completed during an accounting period are recorded. The owner's drawing or personal account and all of the revenue and expense accounts are temporary owner's equity accounts. At the end of each year, it is customary to close the temporary revenue and expense accounts by transferring their balances to one or more summary accounts. In a service enterprise, the only summary account may be Expense and Revenue Summary. In a merchandising type of enterprise, there also may be a summary account Cost of Goods Sold. In the closing process, this latter account is debited for **(1)** the amount of the merchandise inventory at beginning of the year and **(2)** the amount of the purchases for the year; it is credited for **(1)** the amount of purchases returns and allowances for the year, **(2)** the amount of purchase discounts for the year, and **(3)** the amount of the merchandise inventory at end of the year. The balance of the account, representing the cost of goods sold during the year, is in turn transferred to the debit of Expense and Revenue Summary. The balances of all expense and revenue accounts are also transferred to Expense and Revenue Summary whose balance then represents the net income or net loss for the year. The cost of goods sold account and the expense and revenue summary account are the most temporary of all accounts; they are used only at the end of the year in summarizing the revenue and expense accounts.

Opening Entries. An individual may invest cash and other property in a single proprietorship enterprise. Certain liabilities may attach to the property invested. If the investment consists solely of cash, the opening entry will involve a debit to Cash or the bank account and a credit to the owner's capital account for the amount invested.

If cash and other property, such as office equipment, store equipment, or other equipment, are invested, the opening entry will involve a debit to Cash or the bank account for the amount of cash invested, debits to appropriate equipment accounts for the amounts of the other property items invested, and a credit to the owner's capital account for the total amount of the investment.

If, at the time of organizing an enterprise, there are any liabilities, such as accounts payable, notes payable, or mortgages payable applicable to the property invested, appropriate liability accounts should be credited and the owner's capital account should be credited only for the excess of the amount of the assets invested over the total amount of the liabilities.

EXAMPLE: Wilma Sullivan decides to engage in a merchandising business and invests cash, $4,500, office equipment, $1,200 and store equipment, $800. She owes $300 on the office equipment. The opening entry in general journal form to record Ms. Sullivan's investment is:

Bank[1]	4,500.00	
Office Equipment	1,200.00	
Store Equipment	800.00	
Accounts Payable		300.00
Wilma Sullivan, Capital		6,200.00
Investment in business.		

---

[1]The bank account is debited for the amount of cash invested for the reason that it is the usual custom of business firms to deposit all cash receipts in the bank and to make all disbursements by check. Under this plan a cash account need not be kept in the general ledger. Instead, all receipts may be debited to the bank account and all disbursements may be credited to the bank account. It should be understood, however, that a cash account and one or more bank accounts may be kept in the general ledger, if desired.

Some small business enterprises are started and operated for a time with very scanty records. No journals or ledgers are used. The record of cash receipts and disbursements is kept on check stubs. The amounts of accounts receivable and payable can be found only by consulting files of uncollected charge-sale slips and unpaid bills. At the end of a period, various calculations relating to inventory, doubtful accounts, expired insurance, depreciation, and accruals are made in informal fashion and the several bits of information are pieced together to prepare an income statement and a balance sheet. These statements are often incorrect. Conditions and facts may have been overlooked. Business papers may have been lost. The absence of double-entry records means that one method of checking the mathematical accuracy of the figures assembled is not available.

While such informal accounting practices may barely suffice when the enterprise is small and transactions are few, the time will come when a formal accounting system is needed. To get this started, it is necessary to prepare a balance sheet from the information at hand and to use this as the basis for an opening journal entry to record the assets, liabilities, and owner's equity of the enterprise.

For example, assume that M. J. Price has been operating a business without any formal, double-entry accounting records. After several months he decides that proper records are necessary. With the help of an accountant, he constructs the balance sheet reproduced below for his business. The information supplied by the balance sheet is used in preparing the general journal entry shown below the statement.

M. J. PRICE
Balance Sheet
December 31, 1977

Assets			Liabilities		
Cash................		$ 1,750.00	Notes payable........	$1,500.00	
Accounts receivable....	$2,800.00		Accounts payable......	2,200.00	
Less allow. for doubtful accounts..........	300.00	2,500.00	Total liabilities........		$ 3,700.00
Mdse. inventory.......		6,670.00			
Store equipment.......	$4,000.00		*Owner's Equity*		
Less accumulated depreciation........	400.00	3,600.00	M. J. Price, capital.....		10,820.00
Total assets..........		$14,520.00	Total liabilities and owner's equity.......		$14,520.00

Jan. 1.	Bank...	1,750.00		
	Accounts Receivable............................	2,800.00		
	Merchandise Inventory..........................	6,670.00		
	Store Equipment...............................	4,000.00		
	Notes Payable..............................		1,500.00	
	Accounts Payable............................		2,200.00	
	Allowance for Doubtful Accounts...............		300.00	
	Accumulated Depreciation — Store Equipment.....		400.00	
	M. J. Price, Capital............................		10,820.00	
	Opening a set of books.			

After the necessary accounts in the general ledger have been opened, the debits and the credits of the opening journal entry should be posted in the usual manner. As a result of such posting each asset account is debited and each liability account is credited for the respective amounts shown in the balance sheet. These amounts represent the balances of the accounts. The accounts for allowances for doubtful accounts and accumulated depreciation are credited for their balances. Mr. Price's capital account is credited for his equity in the business. The balances of the accounts with customers in the accounts receivable ledger may be entered directly from a schedule of accounts receivable. The balances of the accounts with suppliers in the accounts payable ledger may be entered directly from a schedule of accounts payable.

Proprietary Transactions Completed During the Accounting Period. Certain types of transactions may be referred to as proprietary transactions because they affect either the owner's drawing account or his capital account. The following are typical proprietary transactions:

(a) Periodic withdrawals of cash for personal use of owner.

(b) Payment of owner's personal or family bills with business cash.

(c) Withdrawal of cash or other assets by the owner intended as a partial liquidation of the business.

(d) Investment of cash or other assets by owner intended as a permanent increase in assets and owner's equity.

Cash withdrawn periodically by the owner for personal use usually is charged to the owner's drawing or personal account on the assumption that such amounts represent withdrawals in anticipation of income. Such withdrawals are sometimes regarded as salary or compensation for personal services rendered; however, they represent charges to the owner's drawing or personal account and should not be treated as an operating expense of the enterprise.

The payment of personal or family bills or accounts with business funds should be recorded as a withdrawal of cash by the owner. It is quite common for an individual engaged in a business or professional enterprise as a sole owner to pay all personal and family or household bills by issuing checks against the same bank account as that used for business expenditures of the enterprise. However, care should be used in recording all checks issued, and those representing personal or family expenditures should be charged to the owner's drawing or personal account. Those representing business expenditures should be charged to the proper expense, asset, or liability accounts.

An owner may, at any time, withdraw a portion of the cash or other assets invested in the business, or additional investments in the business in the form of cash or other property may be made. Withdrawals that are considered to be decreases in the permanent invested capital should be charged to the capital account; investments in the business should be credited to the capital account.

Disposition of the Balance of the Expense and Revenue Summary Account at End of Accounting Period. It is customary to close the temporary owner's equity accounts at the end of each year. As the temporary accounts are closed, their balances usually are transferred to an account entitled Expense and Revenue Summary. The difference between the amount of debits and the amount of credits to this summary account represents the amount of the net income or the net loss for the year. If the summary account has a credit balance, it represents net income; if the account has a debit balance, it represents net loss. The simplest way to dispose of the balance of the expense and revenue summary account at the end of the accounting period is to transfer its balance to the owner's capital account by means of a journal entry. If the expense and revenue summary account has a credit balance, the journal entry will involve a debit to Expense and Revenue Summary and a credit to the owner's capital account for the amount of the net income. If the summary account has a debit balance, the journal entry will involve a debit to the owner's capital account and a credit to Expense and Revenue Summary for the amount of the net loss.

Closing the Owner's Drawing Account. The owner's drawing account usually is closed at the end of each year by transferring its balance to the owner's capital account. The drawing account usually has a debit balance, and it may be closed by means of a journal entry debiting the owner's capital account and crediting the drawing account for the amount of its balance.

After transferring the balances of the expense and revenue summary account and the owner's drawing account to the owner's capital account, the balance of the owner's capital account represents the owner's equity in the enterprise at the end of the year.

Owner's Equity Section of the Balance Sheet. The method of exhibiting the equity of the owner of the business in the balance sheet is shown on pages 43, 118, and 243. There may be some variation in the account titles used by different enterprises. However, the final results should be the same since the balance sheet is an exhibit of the accounting elements: **(1)** the assets, **(2)** the liabilities, and **(3)** the owner's equity. The owner's equity section of the balance sheet should be arranged to show the owner's equity in the business at the beginning of the accounting period, the net increase or the net decrease of the equity during the period, and the amount at the end of the period.

Report
No. 16-1

> Complete Report No. 16-1 in the study assignments and submit your working papers to the instructor for approval. Then continue with the following textbook discussion until Report No. 16-2 is required.

THE PARTNERSHIP

When two or more individuals engage in an enterprise as co-owners, the organization is known as a partnership. This form of organization is prevalent in practically all types of enterprises. However, it is more popular among personal service enterprises than among merchandising enterprises. For example, the partnership form of organization is quite common in the legal and public accounting professions.

Organization of a partnership

The Uniform Partnership Act states that "a partnership is an association of two or more persons who carry on, as co-owners, a business for profit." The partners may, by agreement, unite their capital, labor, skill, or experience in the conduct of a business for their mutual benefit. While under certain circumstances a partnership may be formed by means of an oral or an implied agreement, it is desirable that a partnership agreement be evidenced by a written contract. A written agreement containing the various provisions under which a partnership is to operate is known as a *partnership agreement*. There is no standard form of partnership agreement, but there are certain provisions that are essential, such as:

(a) Date of agreement.
(b) Names of the partners.
(c) Kind of business to be conducted.
(d) Length of time the partnership is to run.
(e) Name and location of the business.
(f) Investment of each partner.
(g) Basis on which profits or losses are to be shared by the partners.
(h) Limitation of partners' rights and activities.
(i) Salary allowances to partners.
(j) Division of assets upon dissolution of the partnership.
(k) Signatures of the partners.

The conventional form of partnership agreement is reproduced on page 389.

In comparison with the single proprietorship form of organization, the partnership form offers certain advantages, such as those listed on page 390:

PARTNERSHIP AGREEMENT

THIS CONTRACT, made and entered into on the first day of July, 19--, by and between T. L. Holling of East St. Louis, Illinois, and A. G. Renz of the same city and state.

WITNESSETH: That the said parties have this day formed a partnership for the purpose of engaging in and conducting a wholesale paint and varnish business in the city of East St. Louis under the following stipulations which are a part of this contract:

FIRST: The said partnership is to continue for a term of twenty-five years from July 1, 19--.

SECOND: The business is to be conducted under the firm name of Holling & Renz, at 1111 Olive St., East St. Louis, Illinois.

THIRD: The investments are as follows: T. L. Holling, cash, $60,000; A. G. Renz, cash $40,000. These invested assets are partnership property.

FOURTH: Each partner is to devote his entire time and attention to the business and to engage in no other business enterprise without the written consent of the other partner.

FIFTH: During the operation of this partnership, neither partner is to become surety or bondsman for anyone without the written consent of the other partner.

SIXTH: Each partner is to receive a salary of $18,000 a year, payable $750 in cash on the fifteenth day and last business day of each month. At the end of each annual fiscal period, the net income or the net loss shown by the income statement, after the salaries of the two partners have been allowed, is to be shared as follows: T. L. Holling, 60 percent; A. G. Renz, 40 percent.

SEVENTH: Neither partner is to withdraw assets in excess of his salary, any part of the assets invested, or assets in anticipation of net income to be earned, without the written consent of the other partner.

EIGHTH: In the case of the death or the legal disability of either partner, the other partner is to continue the operations of the business until the close of the annual fiscal period on the following June 30. At that time the continuing partner is to be given an option to buy the interest of the deceased or incapacitated partner at not more than 10 percent above the value of the deceased or incapacitated partner's proprietary interest as shown by the balance of his capital account after the books are closed on June 30. It is agreed that this purchase price is to be paid one half in cash and the balance in four equal installments payable quarterly.

NINTH: At the conclusion of this contract, unless it is mutually agreed to continue the operation of the business under a new contract, the assets of the partnership, after the liabilities are paid, are to be divided in proportion to the net credit to each partner's capital account on that date.

IN WITNESS WHEREOF, the parties aforesaid have hereunto set their hands and affixed their seals on the day and year above written.

T. L. Holling _____ (Seal)

A. G. Renz _____ (Seal)

Partnership Agreement

(a) The ability and the experience of the partners are combined in one enterprise.
(b) More capital may be raised because the resources of the partners are combined.
(c) Credit may be improved because each general partner is personally liable for partnership debts.

There are some disadvantages that are peculiar to the partnership form of organization, including the following:

(a) Each partner is individually liable for all of the debts of the partnership. The liability of each partner is not limited to a pro rata share of the partnership debts; he is personally liable for all of the debts of the business to the same extent as if he were the sole owner. Under the laws of some states, certain partners may limit their liability. At least one partner, however, must be a general partner who is responsible for all of the debts of the partnership.
(b) A partner cannot transfer his interest in the partnership without the consent of the other partners.
(c) Termination of the partnership agreement, bankruptcy of the firm, or death of one of the partners dissolves the partnership.

Accounting procedure

In accounting for the operations of a partnership, it is necessary to keep a separate capital account for each partner. It is also customary to keep a separate drawing or personal account for each partner. While no new principles are involved in keeping these accounts, care should be used in preparing the opening entry and in recording any transactions thereafter that affect the respective interests of the partners.

Opening Entries. When two or more individuals engage in an enterprise as partners, each may invest cash and other property. Certain liabilities may be assumed by the partnership, such as accounts payable, notes payable, and mortgages payable. In opening the books for a partnership, it is customary to prepare a separate journal entry to record the investment of each partner. The proper asset accounts should be debited for the amounts invested, the proper liability accounts should be credited for the amounts of obligations assumed, and each partner's capital account should be credited for his equity in the assets. The opening entries for Holling & Renz based on the partnership agreement reproduced on page 389 may be made in general journal form as follows:

Bank..	60,000.00	
T. L. Holling, Capital.....................................		60,000.00
T. L. Holling invested $60,000 in cash.		
Bank..	40,000.00	
A. G. Renz, Capital......................................		40,000.00
A. G. Renz invested $40,000 in cash.		

If, instead of investing $60,000 in cash only, Holling were to invest office equipment valued at $2,600 on which he owes $800, delivery equipment valued at $2,900 on which he owes $700 represented by a mortgage, and $56,000 in cash, the proper opening entry in general journal form to record his investment should be as follows:

Bank...	56,000.00	
Office Equipment....................................	2,600.00	
Delivery Equipment..................................	2,900.00	
Accounts Payable..................................		800.00
Mortgage Payable..................................		700.00
T. L. Holling, Capital................................		60,000.00
T. L. Holling's investment in partnership.		

Sometimes two or more individuals who have been engaged in business as sole owners form a partnership for the purpose of combining their businesses. Their respective balance sheets may be the basis for the opening entries to record the investments of such partners. For example, on April 1, E. S. Walker and S. W. Edwards form a partnership under the firm name of Walker and Edwards to continue the conduct of the businesses which they have been operating as sole owners. They agree to invest the assets shown in their respective balance sheets. It is also agreed that the partnership shall assume the liabilities shown in their respective balance sheets. Each partner is to receive credit for his equity in the assets invested by him, and the profits and losses are to be shared on a 50-50 basis. In case of dissolution, the assets are to be distributed between the partners in the ratio of their capital interests at the time of dissolution. The balance sheets reproduced on page 392 were made a part of the partnership agreement.

Since the partnership is taking over the long-lived assets at their undepreciated cost, the cost of such property should be adjusted for prior accumulated depreciation up to the date of the transfer. Thus, the cost of the store equipment contributed by Walker should be adjusted for the depreciation accumulated prior to the organization of the partnership. The adjusted value is the difference between the cost of $1,200 and the accumulated depreciation of $319, or $881. Likewise, the cost of the office equipment and the store equipment contributed by Edwards should be adjusted for the depreciation accumulated prior to the organization of the partnership. The adjusted value of the office equipment is $1,050 and of the store equipment is $1,100.

Since it cannot be determined now which of the accounts receivable may later prove to be uncollectible in whole or in part, the amount of the accounts receivable cannot be adjusted for the accumulated allowance for doubtful accounts. It is, therefore, necessary to record the full amount of the accounts receivable as a debit and the amount of the allowance for doubtful accounts as a credit in journalizing each partner's investment in the books of the partnership.

The proper entries in general journal form to record the partners' investments are shown under the statements below.

E. S. WALKER
Balance Sheet
March 31, 1977

Assets			Liabilities		
Cash................		$ 2,033.00	Notes payable........	$1,000.00	
Accounts receivable....	$1,771.32		Accounts payable......	3,231.60	
Less allow. for doubtful			Total liabilities........		$ 4,231.60
accounts..........	137.52	1,633.80			
Mdse. inventory.......		7,875.86			
Store equipment.......	$1,200.00		**Owner's Equity**		
Less accumulated depreciation........	319.00	881.00	E. S. Walker, capital...		8,192.06
			Total liabilities and		
Total assets..........		$12,423.66	owner's equity......		$12,423.66

S. W. EDWARDS
Balance Sheet
March 31, 1977

Assets			Liabilities		
Cash................		$ 1,136.30	Notes payable........	$2,000.00	
Accounts receivable....	$1,700.00		Accounts payable......	4,243.00	
Less allow. for doubtful			Total liabilities........		$ 6,243.00
accounts..........	200.00	1,500.00			
Mdse. inventory.......		9,517.22	**Owner's Equity**		
Supplies.............		91.90	S. W. Edwards, capital..		8,152.42
Office equipment......	$1,400.00				
Less accumulated depreciation	350.00	1,050.00			
Store equipment.......	$1,500.00				
Less accumulated depreciation........	400.00	1,100.00			
			Total liabilities and		
Total assets..........		$14,395.42	owner's equity......		$14,395.42

April 1.	Bank..	2,033.00	
	Accounts Receivable..............................	1,771.32	
	Merchandise Inventory............................	7,875.86	
	Store Equipment.................................	881.00	
	Notes Payable..............................		1,000.00
	Accounts Payable............................		3,231.60
	Allowance for Doubtful Accounts.................		137.52
	E. S. Walker, Capital...........................		8,192.06
	E. S. Walker's investment in partnership.		
1.	Bank..	1,136.30	
	Accounts Receivable..............................	1,700.00	
	Merchandise Inventory............................	9,517.22	
	Supplies...	91.90	
	Office Equipment.................................	1,050.00	
	Store Equipment.................................	1,100.00	
	Notes Payable..............................		2,000.00
	Accounts Payable............................		4,243.00
	Allowance for Doubtful Accounts.................		200.00
	S. W. Edwards, Capital..........................		8,152.42
	S. W. Edwards' investment in partnership.		

Had the long-lived assets of Walker and Edwards been taken over by the partnership at other than their undepreciated cost, the assets should be recorded in the books of the partnership at the value agreed upon. For example, if it had been agreed that the store equipment invested by Walker was to be valued at $1,000 instead of its undepreciated cost, Store Equipment should be debited for $1,000 instead of $881, and Walker's capital account should be credited for $8,311.06 instead of $8,192.06. Thus, the undepreciated cost of the store equipment as shown in Walker's balance sheet of March 31 would be ignored and the store equipment would be recorded on the books of the partnership at the value agreed upon by the partners. Such agreed value represents the cost of the store equipment to the partnership.

It will be observed that the ratio of the partners' investments in the partnership ($8,192.06 to $8,152.42) is not exactly the same as their profit-and-loss-sharing ratio (50% each). The basis on which profits and losses are to be shared is a matter of agreement between the partners, and it is not necessarily the same as their investment ratio. It should be recognized that there are factors other than the assets invested that may enter into a profit-and-loss-sharing agreement. For example, one partner may contribute most of the assets but may render no services, while the other partner may contribute less in assets but may devote full time to the activities of the partnership.

Admitting a New Partner. A new partner may be admitted to a partnership by agreement among the existing partners. For example, Walker and Edwards may admit R. B. James as a partner and agree to share profits and losses on the basis of their capital interests. If his investment consisted of cash only, the proper entry to admit him to the partnership would involve a debit to the bank account and a credit to his capital account for the amount invested. If James has been operating a business of his own as a sole owner and his business is taken over by the partnership, his balance sheet will serve as a basis for preparing the opening entry. Assume that, as of July 1, James was admitted to the partnership. The assets listed in his balance sheet are taken over, his liabilities are assumed, and he is given credit for his equity in the assets of his business. His balance sheet is shown at the top of the next page.

The proper entry in general journal form to admit James as a partner is shown beneath the balance sheet.

The admission of a new partner calls for the dissolution of the old partnership and the creation of a new partnership. A new partnership agreement that includes all of the necessary provisions should be drawn.

Goodwill. Some business organizations consistently are able to earn profits that are very large in relation to the amount of the recorded assets.

R. B. JAMES
Balance Sheet
June 30, 1977

Assets			Liabilities		
Cash..............		$ 1,917.81	Notes payable........	$2,900.00	
Accounts receivable....	$4,580.00		Accounts payable......	2,419.65	
Less allow. for doubtful			Total liabilities........		$ 5,319.65
accounts...........	345.43	4,234.57			
Mdse. inventory.......		8,747.26	Owner's Equity		
			R. B. James, capital....		9,579.99
			Total liabilities and		
Total assets..........		$14,899.64	owner's equity.......		$14,899.64

July 1. Bank..	1,917.81	
Accounts Receivable..............................	4,580.00	
Merchandise Inventory............................	8,747.26	
Notes Payable................................		2,900.00
Accounts Payable..............................		2,419.65
Allowance for Doubtful Accounts.................		345.43
R. B. James, Capital............................		9,579.99
R. B. James admitted to partnership.		

This unique earning power may be due to exceptional management, good location, or one or more of several other factors. When such a condition exists, the business is said to possess *goodwill*. Since goodwill is difficult to measure and may not prove to be permanent, accountants do not favor its formal recognition as an asset unless it has been purchased.

For example, suppose that Walker and Edwards purchased the business of R. B. James for $13,082.18 cash, acquiring all of his business assets except cash and assuming his business liabilities. If the undepreciated cost ($12,981.83; that is, $4,234.57 plus $8,747.26) of the assets purchased from James was considered to be their fair value, Walker and Edwards paid $5,420.00 more for the business than the net value of the assets acquired. This amount may be considered to be the price paid for the goodwill of James' business. The transaction may be recorded as follows:

July 1. Accounts Receivable..............................	4,580.00	
Merchandise Inventory............................	8,747.26	
Goodwill...	5,420.00	
Notes Payable................................		2,900.00
Accounts Payable..............................		2,419.65
Allowance for Doubtful Accounts.................		345.43
Bank..		13,082.18
Purchased R. B. James' business.		

It is permissible to record goodwill if a new partner is taken into a firm and is allowed a capital interest in excess of the net assets he invests. For example, suppose that instead of purchasing James' business, Walker and Edwards had agreed to take him into the firm as a partner and to give him a capital interest of $15,000 for his business (including his business cash). James' investment may be recorded as follows:

July 1. Bank.. 1,917.82
　　　Accounts Receivable............................ 4,580.00
　　　Merchandise Inventory.......................... 8,747.26
　　　Goodwill....................................... 5,420.00
　　　　Notes Payable...............................　　　　　　 2,900.00
　　　　Accounts Payable............................　　　　　　 2,419.65
　　　　Allowance for Doubtful Accounts...............　　　　　 345.43
　　　　R. B. James, Capital..........................　　　　 15,000.00
　　　　　R. B. James admitted to partnership.

Goodwill is considered to be an *intangible long-lived asset*. When good-will is recorded in the accounts, it is usually reported in the balance sheet as the last item in the asset section.

Compensation of Partners. The compensation of partners (other than their shares of profits) may be in the nature of salaries, royalties, com-missions, bonuses, or other compensation. The amount of each partner's compensation and the method of accounting for it should be stated in the partnership agreement. For example, in the partnership agreement shown on page 389, it is stated that each partner is to receive a salary of $1,500 a month. When all partners receive the same salaries and when profits and losses are shared equally, it is immaterial whether the salaries are treated as an expense of the partnership or as withdrawals of anticipated profits. Under the federal income tax law, salaries or other compensation paid to partners for services rendered may not be claimed as a deduction from gross income in the income tax information return of the partnership un-less such salaries are guaranteed. In this latter event, the amounts may be treated as deductions. (The partners, of course, must report such income in their individual returns.) However, apart from income tax considera-tions, the partnership agreement may provide that partners' salaries are to be treated as operating expenses in computing the net income or the net loss to be shared by the partners.

If partners' salaries are not treated as an expense of the partnership, it is not necessary to keep a salary account for each partner. Thus, amounts with-drawn by the partners as compensation for services may simply be charged to their respective drawing accounts. If partners' salaries are treated as operating expenses, it is usually advisable to keep a separate salary ac-count for each partner. For example, the salaries specified in the partner-ship agreement between T. L. Holling and A. G. Renz are to be treated as operating expenses. If the salaries are paid regularly, such as monthly or semimonthly, it will be necessary only to debit each partner's salary ac-count and to credit the bank account. Instead of paying partners' salaries regularly in cash, they may be credited to the partners' drawing accounts. The partners may then draw against such salaries at will. Under this plan the proper entry to record each partner's salary on each payday is to debit his salary account and to credit his drawing account for the proper amount.

Allocation of Partnership Profits and Losses. The partnership agreement should specify the basis on which profits and losses are to be shared by the partners. In the absence of any agreement between the partners, profits and losses must be shared equally regardless of the ratio of the partners' investments. If the partnership agreement specifies how profits are to be shared, but does not specify how losses are to be shared, the losses must be shared on the same basis as that indicated for the profits.

After closing the temporary accounts into Expense and Revenue Summary at the end of the accounting period, the balance of the summary account represents either net income or net loss. If the account has a credit balance, it represents net income; if the account has a debit balance, it represents net loss.

The balance of the expense and revenue summary account should be allocated in accordance with the partnership agreement. If the account has a credit balance, the entry to close the account requires a debit to Expense and Revenue Summary and credits to either the partners' drawing or capital accounts for the proper share of the net income in each case. Because the partners may formally or informally agree that they will not withdraw any of their permanent investments without mutual consent, it may be preferable to credit their drawing accounts with their respective shares of net income. Any credit balances in partners' drawing or personal accounts can then be reduced by withdrawals without restriction.

Dissolution of a Partnership. Dissolution of a partnership may be brought about through bankruptcy or the death of one of the partners. No partner can retire from the partnership before its termination without the consent of the remaining partners. To do so would constitute a violation of the partnership agreement and would make the retiring partner liable to the remaining partners for any loss resulting from his retirement.

By agreement, a partner may retire and be permitted to withdraw assets equal to, greater than, or less than the amount of his capital interest in the partnership. The book value of a partner's interest is shown by the credit balance of his capital account after all profits or losses have been allocated in accordance with the agreement and the books are closed. Should the retiring partner withdraw cash or other assets equal to the credit balance of his capital account, the transaction will have no effect upon the capital of the remaining partners.

Suppose, for example, that sometime after R. B. James had been taken into the partnership of Walker and Edwards, he expressed a desire to retire and his partners agreed to his withdrawal of cash equal to the amount of his equity in the assets of the partnership. After closing the temporary owner's equity accounts into Expense and Revenue Summary, and after allocating the net income and closing the partners' drawing accounts, assume that the partners' capital accounts had credit balances as follows:

E. S. Walker...	$ 7,000.00
S. W. Edwards...	9,000.00
R. B. James...	12,000.00

This indicates that the book value of James' interest in the partnership amounts to $12,000. If this amount is withdrawn in cash, the entry in general journal form to record the transaction on the books of the partnership is as follows:

R. B. James, Capital....................................	12,000.00	
Bank...		12,000.00
R. B. James retired, withdrawing $12,000 in settlement of his equity.		

While the transaction involves a decrease in the asset Cash with a corresponding decrease in the total capital of the partnership, it does not affect the equity of the remaining partners. Walker still has an equity of $7,000 and Edwards an equity of $9,000 in the partnership assets.

If a retiring partner agrees to withdraw less than the book value of his interest in the partnership, the effect of the transaction will be to increase the capital accounts of the remaining partners. To record such a transaction it is necessary to debit the retiring partner's account for the amount of its credit balance, to credit the assets withdrawn, and to credit the difference to the capital accounts of the remaining partners.

Thus, if James had agreed to withdraw only $10,000 in settlement of his interest in the partnership, the transaction should be recorded in the books of the partnership as follows:

R. B. James, Capital....................................	12,000.00	
Bank...		10,000.00
E. S. Walker, Capital................................		875.00
S. W. Edwards, Capital..............................		1,125.00
R. B. James retired, withdrawing $10,000 in settlement of his equity.		

The difference between James' equity in the assets of the partnership and the amount of cash withdrawn is $2,000. This difference is divided between the remaining partners on the basis stipulated in the partnership agreement, the ratio of their capital interests after allocating net income and closing their drawing accounts. Thus, Walker is credited for 7/16 of $2,000, or $875, while Edwards is credited for 9/16 of $2,000, or $1,125.

If a partner is permitted to withdraw more than the book value of his interest in the partnership, the effect of the transaction will be to decrease the capital accounts of the remaining partners. Thus, if Walker and Edwards had agreed to James' withdrawal of $14,000 in settlement of his interest in the partnership, the transaction should be recorded in the books of the partnership as shown at the top of the next page.

R. B. James, Capital..................................	12,000.00	
E. S. Walker, Capital..................................	875.00	
S. W. Edwards, Capital..............................	1,125.00	
Bank...		14,000.00

    R. B. James retired, withdrawing $14,000 in settlement of his equity.

The excess of the amount of cash withdrawn over James' equity in the partnership is divided between the remaining partners on the basis stipulated in the partnership agreement. Thus, Walker is debited for 7/16 of $2,000, or $875, while Edwards is debited for 9/16 of $2,000, or $1,125.

When a partner retires from the business his interest may be purchased by one or more of the remaining partners or by an outside party. If he sells his interest to one of the remaining partners, his equity is merely transferred to the other partner. Thus, if instead of withdrawing cash in settlement of his equity in the partnership, James sells his interest to Walker, the entry to record the transaction on the books of the partnership is as follows:

R. B. James, Capital..................................	12,000.00	
E. S. Walker, Capital..............................		12,000.00

    E. S. Walker purchased R. B. James' interest in the partnership.

The amount paid to James by Walker is a personal transaction not recorded on the books of the partnership and is immaterial to the firm. Any gain or loss resulting from the transaction is a personal gain or loss of the withdrawing partner and not of the firm. Thus, whatever the amount involved, the credit in James' account had to be moved to the credit of Walker.

Owners' Equity Section of a Partnership Balance Sheet. The method of showing the equity of the partners in the balance sheet of a partnership is similar to that of a single proprietorship, except that the equity of each partner should be shown separately. On the next page is an illustration of the owners' equity section of a balance sheet for a partnership whose accounts are kept on a calendar year basis.

Report No. 16-2.

> Complete Report No. 16-2 in the study assignments and submit your working papers to the instructor for approval. Then continue with the textbook discussion until Report No. 16-3 is required.

Owners' Equity

Mildred Mason
     Capital, January 1, 1977 . . . . $46,790.15
     Net income
     (5/8 of $26,543.80) . . . $16,589.88
     Less withdrawals 10,426.20   6,163.68

     Capital, December 31, 1977 . . . . $52,953.83

Katherine Arnold
     Capital, January 1, 1977 . . . . $39,671.60
     Net income
     (3/8 of $26,543.80) . . . $ 9,953.92
     Less withdrawals 8,134.80   1,819.12

     Capital, December 31, 1977 . . . .   41,490.72

Total owners' equity $94,444.55

THE CORPORATION

A private corporation is an artificial person created by law for a specific purpose. A corporation differs from a single proprietorship or a partnership with respect to organization, ownership, and distribution of net income or net loss.

In contrast to a partnership, the corporate form of organization has several advantages. The most important of these are that:

(a) Except in very unusual cases, the owners (stockholders) have no personal liability for the debts of the corporation.
(b) The shares of ownership are easily transferred from one person to another.
(c) The corporation has a perpetual life that is independent of the lives of its owners.

The outstanding disadvantage of the corporate form of organization is that the net income of a corporation is taxed and any cash dividends resulting from that income are also taxable to the stockholders.

Organization of a corporation

In order to incorporate an enterprise, a charter must be obtained from the state in which the corporation is to be formed. The persons who file articles of incorporation are known as the *incorporators*. Such persons must be competent to contract, some or all of them must be citizens of the state in which the articles are filed, and usually each incorporator is required to be a subscriber for one or more shares of the capital stock. All of the incorporators must sign the articles.

The procedure in incorporating an enterprise must conform to the laws of the state in which it is desired to incorporate. The laws of the different states vary considerably in their provisions relating to the organization of corporations. Persons desiring to incorporate a business should acquaint themselves with the laws of the particular state in which they wish to incorporate, as it will be necessary to comply with the laws of that state. The following excerpts from the laws of one of the states will illustrate a typical procedure to be observed in forming a corporation:

"Private corporations may be created by the voluntary association of three or more persons for the purposes authorized by law and in the manner hereinafter mentioned.

"A charter must be prepared, setting forth:

1. The name of the corporation;
2. The purpose for which it is formed;
3. The place or places where the business is to be transacted;
4. The term for which it is to exist;
5. The number of directors or trustees, and the names and residences of those who are appointees for the first year; and
6. The amount of the capital stock, if any, and the number of shares into which it is divided.

"It must be subscribed by three or more persons, two of whom must be citizens of this State, and must be acknowledged by them, before an officer duly authorized to take acknowledgments of deeds.

"The articles of incorporation shall also set forth the minimum amount of capital with which the corporation will commence business, which shall not be less than $1,000. The articles of incorporation may also contain any provision which the incorporators may choose to insert for the management of the business and for the conduct of the affairs of the corporation, and any provisions creating, defining, limiting, and regulating the powers of the corporation, the directors and the stockholders, or any class of the stockholders.

"The affidavit of those who executed the charter shall be furnished to the Secretary of State, showing:

1. The name, residence, and post office address of each subscriber to the capital stock of such company;
2. The amount subscribed by each, and the amount paid by each;
3. The cash value of any property received, with its description, location, and from whom and the price at which it was received; and
4. The amount, character, and value of labor done, and from whom and the price at which it was received."

The Charter. After the articles of incorporation have been filed, and other conditions, such as the payment of incorporation fees, have been fulfilled, the document is examined by a court or an administrative officer. If the instrument is satisfactory and the other requirements have been met, a license, a certificate of incorporation, or a charter is issued and recorded or filed as required by the particular statute of the state concerned. While, as previously stated, the provisions of law governing corporate organization vary in different states, in general they include such matters as the name, purpose, duration, location, and capitalization.

Ownership of a Corporation. Ownership in a corporation is represented by *capital stock*. To make it possible to have many owners — often with different ownership interests — the capital stock is divided into *shares*. The persons forming a corporation (the incorporators) and others who wish to become owners *subscribe* for shares. Each agrees to buy a certain number of shares for a certain amount per share. Often payment is to be made in cash. Sometimes the subscription is paid for by transferring assets other than cash to the corporation.

Subscriptions to the capital stock of a corporation may be made before or after incorporation. A subscription made before incorporation is an agreement to subscribe for stock. It is a contract entered into between the subscriber and the incorporator or promoter and not between the subscriber and the corporation. The corporation, as such, does not exist until after the articles of incorporation have been filed with the proper state official and approved. A subscription for capital stock after incorporation is a contract between the subscriber and the corporation.

Stockholders. All parties owning shares of stock in a corporation are known as *stockholders* (sometimes called *shareholders*). In order to possess all of the rights of a stockholder of record, the party owning stock must have his ownership properly recorded on the books of the corporation. If stock is acquired from a previous stockholder, the transfer is not complete until it is recorded on the appropriate record of the corporation. Until this takes place, the new shareholder cannot have a *certificate of stock* issued in his name, he cannot vote at a stockholder's meeting, nor can he share in any dividends declared by the board of directors.

Directors. The stockholders elect a *board of directors* that is charged with the management and direction of corporate affairs. It would be impractical for all of the stockholders of a large corporation to meet periodically or at special times to decide upon questions in connection with the direction and management of company affairs. For this reason the stockholders elect a board of directors that is responsible to the stockholders for the proper management of corporate affairs. The directors are the legal agents of the corporation.

A board of directors usually consists of three or more stockholders. Where the board is unusually large in number, it is customary to appoint an *executive committee* of from three to five members of the board, which is given authority to administer the affairs of the corporation.

Officers. The board of directors elects the officers. Usually a president, vice-president, secretary, and treasurer are elected as executive officers. One person may hold two positions; for instance, the same person may serve both as secretary and treasurer or as vice-president and treasurer. All of the officers are responsible to the board of directors and receive their instructions from the board. The officers have no authority other than to perform the duties required by the bylaws of the corporation and the statutes of the state. Generally they are liable for fraud or misrepresentation, or for exceeding the rights and powers conferred upon them by the bylaws of the company or the statutes of the state.

Capital Stock. The charter obtained by a business corporation specifies the amount of capital stock that it is authorized to issue. The state of incorporation authorizes a corporation to issue a certain number of shares of stock, and it is illegal for a company to issue a greater number of shares than is authorized in its charter. A certificate of stock issued to Peter C. Hill by The Whitson Company, Inc., is reproduced on page 403. The fact that the certificate illustrated has such a low number ("2") must mean that it represents the original issue of these shares. (At a later point the matter of a transfer of shares entailing the cancellation of a certificate and the issuance of another to a new owner will be discussed.)

Capital stock may or may not have *par value*. Par value is a technical legal matter. Its practical significance is not very great in most cases. In general, par represents the smallest amount that the corporation can accept in exchange for a share of stock at the time it is originally issued without the buyer of the stock incurring some liability to the corporation. In many states par-value stock cannot be sold originally by the corporation for less than par value. In most states it is possible for corporations to issue stock that has no par value.

If the corporation issues only one type of capital stock, it is called *common stock*. The stockholders own the corporation "in common." Among other things, the stockholders have the right to vote for directors and upon certain other matters, including the right to share in any distributions (called *dividends*) resulting either from profitable operations, or from the fact that the corporation is being dissolved. In all cases these rights are in direct proportion to the number of shares of stock owned.

Some corporations have more than one class or type of stock. The classes differ with respect to the rights which go with the ownership of

Certificate of Stock

the stock. In addition to common stock, a corporation may have one or more types of *preferred stock*. Stock of this type may entitle the owner to receive a limited share of the earnings before the common stockholders receive any dividends and may involve a first or "prior" claim upon assets in the event that the corporation is dissolved. Sometimes preferred stock has a "preference" as to both dividends and assets. Frequently, preferred stockholders do not have voting rights.

If a corporation has only one class of common stock outstanding, the *book value* per share of such stock is equal to the total owners' equity of the corporation (assets less liabilities) divided by the number of shares outstanding. If the corporation also has preferred stock outstanding, the book value per share of common stock will be the total owners' equity less the portion that is allocated to the preferred stock divided by the number of shares of common stock outstanding.

It is not to be expected that the book value per share and the *market value* per share will be the same. The latter is influenced by a number of factors, particularly the corporation's chances for success in the future. Market value is easy to determine if the corporation's stock is listed and actively traded on an organized stock exchange. If not, market value can only be estimated. It would be most improbable that the par value (if any), the book value, and the market value of the stock of a corporation were the same amounts at any one point in time.

Transactions unique to a corporation

The day-to-day operating transactions of a corporation are similar to those of a single proprietorship or of a partnership business of a like nature. Certain transactions involving the owners' equity of a business are unique if the enterprise is incorporated. Examples of such transactions include:

(a) Capital stock subscriptions.

(b) Amounts received to apply on capital stock subscriptions.

(c) Issuance of capital stock to subscribers.

(d) Transfer of capital stock from one stockholder to another stockholder.

(e) Declaration and payment of dividends.

Accounts unique to a corporation

A list of the major accounts that are unique to the corporate form of organization is shown below.

ACCOUNT	CLASSIFICATION
Capital Stock	Owners' equity
Subscriptions Receivable	Asset
Capital Stock Subscribed	Owners' equity
Retained Earnings (sometimes called *Earnings Retained in the Business*; at one time commonly called *Earned Surplus*)	Owners' equity
Dividends Payable	Liability

One of the features of accounting for corporate owners' equity is the distinction that usually is maintained in the records between owners' equity that results from investments by stockholders (often described as *paid-in capital*) and that which results from retention of earnings (profitable operations coupled with a moderate dividend policy). In the case of certain types of corporate transactions, this distinction as to the source of the owners' equity is not evident, but in most cases the difference is reflected in the accounts. When the corporation exchanges its stock for cash or other property equal in amount to the par value of the shares issued, the transaction should be recorded by debiting the proper asset account and by crediting Capital Stock. If there is more than one type of capital stock, there should be an account for each type.

Sometimes a corporation obtains *subscriptions* to its stock in which each subscriber agrees to buy a certain number of shares at an agreed price (possibly par, if the stock has par value) and to pay for the shares at or within a specified time, either in full at one time or in installments over a period of time. If, for example, a subscription were received for 100 shares at a price of $50 each (assumed to be the par value of the shares in this case), the transaction should be recorded by debiting Subscriptions Receivable and by crediting Capital Stock Subscribed for $5,000. Collections on the subscription should be debited to Cash (or whatever is accepted in lieu of cash) and credited to Subscriptions Receivable. When the subscription is paid in full, the stock will be issued and an entry should be made debiting Capital Stock Subscribed and crediting Capital Stock for $5,000. As long as Subscriptions Receivable has a balance representing an amount that is expected to be collected, the account is treated as an asset and should be so shown on the balance sheet. Capital Stock Subscribed is an owners' equity account, the balance of which indicates the amount that eventually will be added to Capital Stock.

At the end of each accounting period, the balance of the expense and revenue summary account is transferred to the retained earnings account. If a corporation is operated at a loss, the amount of the net loss which is transferred from the expense and revenue summary account to the retained earnings account might result in the retained earnings account having a debit balance. In such event, this balance is termed a *deficit* and it will appear as a deduction in the owners' equity section of the corporation's balance sheet.

A decision on the part of the directors of a corporation to pay a dividend is commonly referred to as a *declaration of dividends*. When dividends are declared and such dividends are payable in cash at a later date, it is customary to record the declaration by debiting Retained Earnings and by crediting Dividends Payable. The dividends payable account will have a credit balance until all dividends declared have been paid in full. When dividends are paid immediately upon being declared, there is no need for setting up an account with Dividends Payable. Usually the dividends are not paid until some time after being declared by the directors. In the meantime, the dividends declared represent a liability of the corporation.

Accounting procedure

Following is a narrative of corporate transactions with illustrative general journal entries:

(a) The Whitson Company, Inc., was incorporated with an authorized issue of 500 shares of common capital stock, par value $100 per share. At the time of incorporation, subscriptions had been received as follows:

J. H. Whitson	250 shares
Peter C. Hill	125 shares
Esther Johnson	125 shares

The stock was subscribed for at par value and one half of the subscription price was paid in cash, the balance to be paid on demand.

To record this transaction it is necessary (1) to record the stock subscriptions received, and (2) to record the cash received to apply on the subscription price. These entries may be made in general journal form as illustrated at the top of the next page.

(1)

Subscriptions Receivable...............................	50,000.00	
Capital Stock Subscribed.............................		50,000.00

        Received subscriptions to capital stock at par as follows:
            J. H. Whitson, 250 shares
            Peter C. Hill, 125 shares
            Esther Johnson, 125 shares

(2)

Bank...	25,000.00	
Subscriptions Receivable.............................		25,000.00

        Received cash on account of subscriptions to capital
        stock as follows:
            J. H. Whitson, $12,500
            Peter C. Hill, $6,250
            Esther Johnson, $6,250

(b) Received cash from subscribers to capital stock in settlement of balances due as follows:

J. H. Whitson...	$12,500.00
Peter C. Hill...	6,250.00
Esther Johnson...	6,250.00

This transaction involves an increase in the asset cash and a decrease in the asset subscriptions receivable. The transaction may be recorded in general journal form as follows:

Bank...	25,000.00	
Subscriptions Receivable.............................		25,000.00

        Received cash in settlement of the balance due from
        subscribers to capital stock as follows:
            J. H. Whitson, $12,500
            Peter C. Hill, $6,250
            Esther Johnson, $6,250

(c) Issued certificates of stock to the following subscribers who had remitted their subscriptions in full:

J. H. Whitson...	250 shares
Peter C. Hill...	125 shares
Esther Johnson...	125 shares

Usually certificates of stock are not issued until subscriptions are remitted in full. In this case the subscribers have remitted their subscriptions in full and the stock certificates have been issued. The transactions may be recorded in general journal form as follows:

Capital Stock Subscribed.............................	50,000.00	
Capital Stock[2].......................................		50,000.00

        Capital stock issued to subscribers as follows:
            J. H. Whitson, 250 shares
            Peter C. Hill, 125 shares
            Esther Johnson, 125 shares

After posting the above entry, the capital stock account will have a credit balance of $50,000, the par value of the capital stock outstanding.

---

[2]When both common stock and preferred stock are authorized in the charter of a corporation, separate accounts should be kept for each class of stock. A memorandum entry of the number of shares authorized should be entered in the Item column of each capital stock account.

(d) J. H. Whitson returned his stock certificate for 250 shares and requested that 50 shares be transferred to T. F. Pfeffer and that a new certificate for 200 shares be issued to himself.

This transaction indicates that Whitson has sold 50 shares of his stock to Pfeffer. Transferring capital stock from one stockholder to another involves the cancellation of an old certificate and the issuance of new certificates for the proper numbers of shares. In this case, it is necessary to cancel the original certificate for 250 shares issued to Whitson and to issue two new certificates, one to Pfeffer for 50 shares and one to Whitson for 200 shares. This transaction has no effect upon the assets, liabilities, or capital of the corporation. It is merely a transfer of stock between stockholders and the only entry required is a transfer entry in the capital stock records kept by the corporation.

(e) The board of directors at its annual meeting held on June 15 voted to pay a cash dividend of $6 per share, the dividend to be paid on July 1 to stockholders of record June 15.

The board of directors has the right to decide when dividends shall be paid to stockholders. After dividends have been declared, they constitute a liability of the corporation, and this liability should be recorded at the time that the dividend is declared. The transaction may be recorded in general journal form as follows:

```
June 15. Retained Earnings.............................  3,000.00
            Dividends Payable...........................            3,000.00
               Dividend declared by the directors.
```

Dividends may be paid immediately upon being declared or at some later date. Large corporations usually do not pay dividends until sometime after the date of declaration. The directors usually specify that the dividends shall be paid to the stockholders *of record* as of a certain date. This means that only stockholders whose stock is recorded in their names on that date are entitled to receive dividends. Any stockholder who acquires stock after that date is not entitled to share in the dividend previously declared. To record the payment of the dividend declared in transaction **(e)**, it is necessary to debit Dividends Payable and to credit the bank account as in the following general journal entry:

```
July 1. Dividends Payable...............................  3,000.00
            Bank........................................            3,000.00
               Paid dividend declared June 15.
```

This transaction has the effect of decreasing the liability dividends payable $3,000 with a similar decrease in the asset cash. After the transaction is posted, the dividends payable account will have no balance.

Incorporating a Single Proprietorship. The legal steps involved in incorporating a single proprietorship are the same as in organizing a new corporation. Usually the sole proprietor becomes the principal stockholder in the corporation and transfers the assets of his business to the corporation in exchange for capital stock. The business liabilities may also be assumed by the corporation. The same books of account may be continued or an entirely new set of records may be installed. Suppose, for example, that The Foster Company, Inc., was organized to take over the business formerly conducted by D. E. Foster as a single proprietorship. Foster subscribes for 200 shares of the capital stock at $100 per share and transfers his equity in his business ($15,300) to apply on his subscription. Just before the transfer at the end of the year, the balance sheet of the business appeared as reproduced below:

D. E. FOSTER
Balance Sheet
December 31, 1977

Assets			Liabilities		
Cash		$ 4,750.00	Notes payable	$1,000.00	
Accounts receivable	$3,800.00		Accounts payable	3,200.00	
Less allow. for doubtful accounts	400.00	3,400.00	Total liabilities		$ 4,200.00
Mdse. inventory		7,950.00			
Office equipment	$1,600.00		**Owner's Equity**		
Less accumulated depreciation	400.00	1,200.00	D. E. Foster, capital		15,300.00
Store equipment	$1,200.00				
Less accumulated depreciation	300.00	900.00			
Delivery equipment	$2,900.00				
Less accumulated depreciation	1,600.00	1,300.00			
Total assets		$19,500.00	Total liabilities and owner's equity		$19,500.00

If Foster intends to continue to use the same set of books with only those modifications needed because of the change to the corporate form of enterprise, the entries to record his subscription and its partial payment by the transfer of his business assets and liabilities to the corporation should be as follows:

Subscriptions Receivable	20,000.00	
Capital Stock Subscribed		20,000.00
D. E. Foster subscribed for 200 shares of stock at par.		
D. E. Foster, Capital	15,300.00	
Subscriptions Receivable		15,300.00
Assets and liabilities of D. E. Foster transferred to corporation at book value.		

When the foregoing entries are posted, Foster's capital account will have no balance. The corporate accounts listed below will take the place of Foster's capital account in the general ledger.

Capital Stock
Subscriptions Receivable
Capital Stock Subscribed

If, instead of using the same books of account that were used by Foster, a new set of books is installed by the corporation, a general journal entry should be made to record the transfer of the accounts of the single proprietorship to the corporation. If the long-lived assets are being taken over at their undepreciated cost, it is customary to record them in the books of the corporation at their net value after making adjustment for prior accumulated depreciation. If the long-lived assets are being taken over at any value other than their undepreciated cost, they should be recorded on the books of the corporation at the value agreed upon. Such value represents the cost of the assets to the corporation. The accounts of Foster may be transferred to The Foster Company, Inc., by means of a general journal entry entered on the books of the corporation as follows:

Bank...	4,750.00	
Accounts Receivable...................................	3,800.00	
Merchandise Inventory................................	7,950.00	
Office Equipment.....................................	1,200.00	
Store Equipment......................................	900.00	
Delivery Equipment...................................	1,300.00	
Notes Payable.....................................		1,000.00
Accounts Payable....................................		3,200.00
Allowance for Doubtful Accounts.....................		400.00
Subscriptions Receivable............................		15,300.00
Assets and liabilities of D. E. Foster transferred to corporation at book value.		

Assuming that Foster paid the balance due on his subscription and that a stock certificate for 200 shares was issued to him, the transactions should be recorded on the books of the corporation as follows:

Bank...	4,700.00	
Subscriptions Receivable.............................		4,700.00
Cash received from D. E. Foster in settlement of balance due on subscription to capital stock.		
Capital Stock Subscribed.............................	20,000.00	
Capital Stock.......................................		20,000.00
Issued 200 shares of common capital stock to D. E. Foster.		

Incorporating a Partnership. A partnership may be terminated by incorporation, and the partners may become stockholders of the corporation. The same books of account may be continued or a new set of books may be installed by the corporation. Suppose, for example, that The Lawson Company, Inc., is organized with an authorized capital of $50,000 to take over the business formerly conducted by Lawson and Lawson, partners. The partners subscribe for capital stock of the corporation as follows:

Laura Lawson, 300 shares @ $50 a share.........................	$15,000.00
Florence Lawson, 200 shares at @ $50 a share.....................	10,000.00

Lawson and Lawson, as individuals, are to receive credit toward their subscriptions for their respective equities in the assets of the partnership.

The balance sheet following on the next page for the partnership was prepared just prior to the time of incorporating the business (April 1, 1977):

LAWSON AND LAWSON
Balance Sheet
March 31, 1977

Assets			Liabilities		
Cash.................		$ 6,600.00	Notes payable........	$2,000.00	
Notes receivable.......	$ 750.00		Accounts payable......	3,738.75	
Accounts receivable....	3,800.00		Total liabilities........		$ 5,738.75
	$4,550.00				
Less allow. for doubtful					
accounts.........	300.00	4,250.00	**Owners' Equity**		
Mdse. inventory.......		9,800.00	Laura Lawson, capital...	$8,246.50	
Office equipment......	$1,600.00		Florence Lawson, capital.	8,364.75	
Less accumulated de-			Total owners' equity....		16,611.25
preciation........	500.00	1,100.00			
Delivery equipment.....	$1,200.00				
Less accumulated de-					
preciation........	600.00	600.00			
			Total liabilities and		
Total assets..........		$22,350.00	owners' equity.......		$22,350.00

The subscriptions to the capital stock should be recorded as indicated in the following general journal entry:

Subscriptions Receivable.............................	25,000.00	
Capital Stock Subscribed............................		25,000.00
Received subscriptions to capital stock as follows:		
Laura Lawson, 300 shares		
Florence Lawson, 200 shares		

If the books of the partnership are to be continued in use by the corporation, the transfer of the partners' equities to the corporation may be made by means of the following general journal entry:

Laura Lawson, Capital...............................	8,246.50	
Florence Lawson, Capital.............................	8,364.75	
Subscriptions Receivable............................		16,611.25
Assets and liabilities of Lawson and Lawson transferred		
to corporation at book value.		

When this entry is posted, the partners' accounts will have no balance. If, instead of using the same books of account as were used by Lawson and Lawson, a new set of books is installed by the corporation, a general journal entry on the books of the corporation is required to transfer the accounts of the partnership to the corporation. This journal entry is:

Bank..	6,600.00	
Notes Receivable.....................................	750.00	
Accounts Receivable..................................	3,800.00	
Merchandise Inventory................................	9,800.00	
Office Equipment.....................................	1,100.00	
Delivery Equipment...................................	600.00	
Notes Payable......................................		2,000.00
Accounts Payable...................................		3,738.75
Allowance for Doubtful Accounts.....................		300.00
Subscriptions Receivable............................		16,611.25
Assets and liabilities of Lawson and Lawson transferred		
to corporation at book value.		

It will be noted that the long-lived assets of Lawson and Lawson are recorded on the books of the corporation at their undepreciated cost after making adjustments for prior accumulated depreciation. Had the long-lived assets been taken over at any value other than their undepreciated cost, they should be recorded on the books of the corporation at the value agreed upon.

Assuming that Lawson and Lawson paid the balance due on their subscriptions and that stock certificates were issued to them, the transactions should be recorded on the books of the corporation as follows:

```
Bank...................................................   8,388.75
    Subscriptions Receivable.............................             8,388.75
        Received cash from subscribers as follows:
        Laura Lawson, $6,753.50
        Florence Lawson, $1,635.25

Capital Stock Subscribed..............................  25,000.00
    Capital Stock.......................................            25,000.00
        Issued common capital stock to subscribers.
```

Owners' Equity Section of a Corporation Balance Sheet. The difference between the amounts of the assets and of the liabilities of a corporation is called either "capital" or "stockholders' equity" and is so described in the balance sheet of the corporation. Generally, the amount resulting from the issuance of capital stock and the amount resulting from undistributed earnings are shown. At the end of the first year of operations, the owners' equity section of the balance sheet of The Lawson Company, Inc., appeared as follows:

Stockholders' Equity

Capital stock (1,000 shares authorized; 500 shares issued).....................	$25,000.00
Retained earnings...................................	8,000.00
Total stockholders' equity...........................	$33,000.00

It should be understood that because of differences in capital structure, there may be considerable variation in the capital section of balance sheets prepared for different corporations. If more than one kind of capital stock is issued, each kind should be listed separately. There may be retained earnings (accumulated income) or a deficit (accumulated losses) at the end of the year. A deficit should be shown as a deduction from the amount resulting from the issuance of the capital stock in arriving at the net stockholders' equity of a corporation.

Report No. 16-3

Complete Report No. 16-3 in the study assignments and submit your working papers to the instructor for approval. Then continue with the textbook discussion in Chapter 17 until Report No. 17-1 is required.

Chapter 17

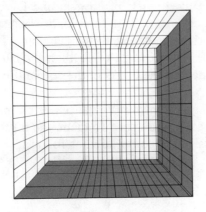

ACCRUAL ACCOUNTING APPLIED TO A WHOLESALE BUSINESS

In a wholesale merchandising enterprise, the merchandise handled is usually purchased directly from manufacturers, importers, or producers and is sold to retailers and distributors, who in turn sell to consumers at retail prices. The wholesaler usually buys in sizable quantities and has storage facilities to enable him to carry a large stock of merchandise. Goods may be purchased for cash or on account and, likewise, the goods may be sold for cash or on account. A large percentage of the wholesale business involves the use of credit.

Factors affecting accounting records used

The books of account and the auxiliary records of a wholesale business will vary depending upon a number of factors, such as the following:

(a) Type of business organization.
(b) Volume of business.
(c) Office equipment used.
(d) Information desired by the management and others concerned with the operation of the business.

Type of Business Organization. A wholesale merchandising enterprise may be conducted as a single proprietorship, a partnership, or a corporation. So far as the single proprietorship and the partnership forms of organization are concerned, there are no distinctive records to be kept. With the corporate form of organization, however, certain corporate records, such as a minute book, a stock certificate record, and a stock-holders ledger, may be kept. The type of organization will also affect the accounts that are kept. In the case of a single proprietorship, it may be necessary to keep two accounts for the proprietor — one for recording his capital and the other for recording his personal transactions. In the case of a partnership, it is necessary to keep separate accounts for each partner. In the case of a corporation, it is necessary to keep separate accounts for capital stock, retained earnings, and dividends payable.

Volume of Business. The volume of business is an important factor in determining the types of records and the number of accounts to be maintained. Obviously, the records and the accounts of a firm with annual sales of a million dollars or more will differ considerably from one with annual sales of only $50,000 a year. In a big business with numerous departments, there will be a demand for more financial and statistical information for management and a greater need for adequate control.

When manual methods are used, there is a fairly direct relationship between the size of a business and the number of persons engaged in keeping its accounting records. When several persons are required, the work must be divided in some logical fashion. Generally, this means that a separate record or book of original entry will be kept for each major type of business transaction, and that the books of final entry (the ledgers) will be subdivided. For example, one journal may be provided to record purchases, another journal to record sales, another to record cash receipts, another to record checks drawn, and a general journal to record transactions that cannot be recorded in the special journals. It is likely that there will be one or more subsidiary ledgers to record the details about some of the elements that are shown in summary in certain of the general ledger accounts. Each employee engaged in accounting activity will specialize in keeping one of these records.

A functional division of the accounting activity has, among others, the following advantages:

(a) Provides for better internal check and control.
(b) Makes possible an equitable distribution of work among several employees.
(c) Provides for a more detailed classification of transactions in the books of original entry.
(d) Makes possible periodic summary posting to the general ledger.

Office Equipment. The accounting system is certain to be affected by the use of various types of office equipment. In recent years there has been a great expansion in the use of modern accounting, calculating, and other office machines. In the modern office of a big business enterprise, it is not uncommon to find a large share of the bookkeeping work being done with the aid of electro-mechanical and electronic devices, including posting machines, accounting machines, and photographic equipment. Many large companies are using computers and other auxiliary data processing equipment.

Regardless of the extent to which equipment is used in the accounting department, the fundamental principles involved in keeping the accounts continue to apply. A knowledge of accounting theory on the part of those employed in the accounting department is just as essential as if no machines were used.

Information Desired. The accounting system must be designed to provide management and others concerned with the operation of a business with the desired information. The management will wish to know where the business stands financially from time to time, as well as the results of operations for given periods of time. The accounting department may be required to supply much information of a statistical nature as well as the usual accounting reports. For example, the manager of the purchasing department may expect the accounting department to keep detailed stock records of all merchandise handled. The accounts must be kept so as to provide all the information needed for all of the various tax reports required by the federal, state, and local governments. In recent years there has been a tremendous increase in the number of tax reports and in the amount of tax information that must be furnished. Many large firms have found it necessary to organize a tax accounting department separate from the general accounting department.

ACCOUNTING PROCEDURE

Holling and Renz are partners who conduct a wholesale paint and varnish business. Paint is handled in Department A, varnish in Department B. Such merchandise is purchased on account from various manufacturers. The terms of purchase may vary considerably. Most of the firms from whom Holling & Renz buy allow discounts ranging from 1 to 3 percent for cash in from 10 to 30 days. Holling & Renz sell the merchandise to local dealers and distributors both on account and for cash. On charge sales their terms usually are 2 percent discount for cash in 10 days, net 30 days, frequently expressed as 2 percent, 10 days, net 30; or in an abbreviated form as 2/10, n/30.

The records maintained by Holling & Renz consist of the following:

(a) Books of original entry

(1) Invoice register
(2) Sales register
(3) Record of cash receipts
(4) Record of checks drawn
(5) General journal

(b) Books of final entry

(1) General ledger
(2) Subsidiary ledgers
    a. Accounts receivable ledger
    b. Accounts payable ledger
    c. Operating expense ledger

(c) Auxiliary records

(1) Petty cash disbursements record
(2) Check stubs
(3) Stock record
(4) Long-lived asset record

Invoice register

A comparison of Holling & Renz's invoice register reproduced on page 294 with the invoice register reproduced on page 436 will reveal that they are identical. This form of invoice register was described in detail in Chapter 11.

Sales register

A comparison of Holling & Renz's sales register reproduced on page 316 with the sales register reproduced on page 437 will reveal that they are identical. This form of sales register was described in detail in Chapter 12.

Record of cash receipts

Holling & Renz keep a multicolumn record of cash receipts. Reference to their record of cash receipts reproduced on page 438 will reveal that General Ledger Debit and Credit columns are provided. In addition, special debit amount columns are provided for (1) Sales Discount and (2) Bank. Special credit amount columns are provided for (1) Accounts Receivable, (2) Sales, Department A, and (3) Sales, Department B. All cash and cash items are recorded by debiting the bank account immediately. This practice usually is followed where it is the custom to deposit all cash receipts in a bank and to make all disbursements (other than petty cash) by check.

Proving the Record of Cash Receipts. The record of cash receipts may be footed and the footings may be proved daily or periodically by comparing the sum of the debit footings with the sum of the credit footings. When a page is filled, the amount columns should be footed, the footings should be proved, and the totals should be carried forward to the top of the next page. It is customary to start a month at the top of a new page.

Posting from the Record of Cash Receipts. Completing the posting from the record of cash receipts involves both individual posting and summary posting. Individual posting is required from the General Ledger Debit and Credit columns. This posting usually is done daily. As each such item is posted, a check mark should be entered in the Check ($\sqrt{}$) column following the Amount column of the record of cash receipts. The initials "CR" and the page number of the record of cash receipts then should be entered in the Posting Reference column of the proper general ledger account preceding the amount posted.

The summary posting usually is completed at the end of each month and involves the following procedure:

(a) The total of the column headed Sales Discount should be posted as a debit to Sales Discount, Account No. 043, in the general ledger.

(b) The total of the column headed Bank should be posted as a debit to Federal National Bank, Account No. 111, in the general ledger.

(c) The total of the column headed Accounts Receivable should be posted as a credit to Accounts Receivable, Account No. 131, in the general ledger.

(d) The total of the column headed Cash Sales, Dept. A, should be posted as a credit to Sales — Department A, Account No. 411, in the general ledger.

(e) The total of the column headed Cash Sales, Dept. B, should be posted as a credit to Sales — Department B, Account No. 421, in the general ledger.

As the total of each column is posted, the account number should be written in parentheses immediately below the total in the record of cash receipts. The page number of the record of cash receipts then should be entered in the Posting Reference column of the proper general ledger account as a cross-reference. A check mark should be placed in parentheses below the totals of the General Ledger Debit and Credit columns to indicate that these totals are not posted.

Record of checks drawn

Holling & Renz keep a multicolumn record of checks drawn. Reference to the record of checks drawn reproduced on pages 439 and 440 will reveal that General Ledger Debit and Credit columns are provided. In addition, special debit amount columns are provided for (1) Operating Expenses and (2) Accounts Payable. Special credit amount columns are provided for (1) Purchases Discount and (2) Bank.

Proving the Record of Checks Drawn. The record of checks drawn may be footed and the footings may be proved daily or periodically by comparing the sum of the debit footings with the sum of the credit footings. When a page is filled, the amount columns should be footed, the footings should be proved, and the totals should be carried forward to the top of the next page. It is customary to start a month at the top of a new page.

Posting from the Record of Checks Drawn. Completing the posting from the record of checks drawn involves both individual posting and summary posting. Individual posting is required from the General Ledger Debit and Credit columns. This posting usually is done daily. As each item is posted, a check mark should be entered in the Check ($\sqrt{}$) column following the Amount column of the record of checks drawn. The initials "CD" and the page number of the record of checks drawn then should be entered in the Posting Reference column of the ledger account to the left of the amount posted.

Individual posting is also required from the Operating Expenses Debit column. This posting usually is done daily. As each item is posted, a check mark should be entered in the Check ($\sqrt{}$) column following the Amount column of the record of checks drawn. The initials "CD" and the page number of the record of checks drawn then should be entered in the Posting Reference column of the proper operating expense ledger account to the left of the amount posted.

The summary posting usually is completed at the end of each month and involves the following procedure:

(a) The total of the column headed Operating Expenses should be posted as a debit to Operating Expenses, Account No. 611, in the general ledger.

(b) The total of the column headed Accounts Payable should be posted as a debit to Accounts Payable, Account No. 271, in the general ledger.

(c) The total of the column headed Purchases Discount should be posted as a credit to Purchases Discount, Account No. 053, in the general ledger.

(d) The total of the column headed Bank should be posted as a credit to Federal National Bank, Account No. 111, in the general ledger.

As the total of each column is posted, the account number should be written in parentheses immediately below the total in the record of checks drawn. The page number of the record of checks drawn then should be entered in the Posting Reference column of the proper general ledger account as a cross-reference. A check mark should be placed in parentheses below the totals of the General Ledger Debit and Credit columns to indicate that these totals are not posted.

General journal

Holling & Renz use a multicolumn general journal. Reference to the general journal reproduced on page 441 will reveal that General Ledger Debit and Credit columns are provided. In addition, special debit amount columns are provided for (1) Operating Expenses and (2) Accounts Payable. Special credit amount columns are provided for (1) Accounts Payable and (2) Accounts Receivable. The general journal is used for recording all transactions that cannot be recorded in the special journals. Adjusting, closing, and reversing entries also are recorded in the general journal.

Proving the General Journal. The general journal may be footed and the footings may be proved daily or periodically by comparing the sum of the debit footings with the sum of the credit footings. When a page is filled, the amount columns should be footed, the footings should be proved, and the totals should be carried forward to the top of the next page. It is customary to start a month at the top of a new page.

Posting from the General Journal. Completing the posting from the general journal involves both individual posting and summary posting. Individual posting is required from the General Ledger Debit and Credit columns. This posting usually is done daily. As each item is posted, a check mark should be entered in the Check (√) column following the Amount column of the general journal. The initial "G" and the page number of the general journal then should be entered in the Posting Reference column of the proper general ledger account to the left of the amount posted.

Individual posting is also required from the Operating Expenses Debit column. As each item is posted, a check mark should be entered in the Check (√) column following the Amount column of the general journal. The initial "G" and the page number of the general journal then should be entered in the Posting Reference column of the proper operating expense ledger account to the left of the amount posted.

The summary posting usually is completed at the end of each month and involves the following procedure:

    (a) The total of the debit column headed Operating Expenses should be posted as a debit to Operating Expenses, Account No. 611, in the general ledger.

(b) The total of the debit column headed Accounts Payable should be posted as a debit to Accounts Payable, Account No. 271, in the general ledger.

(c) The total of the credit column headed Accounts Payable should be posted as a credit to Accounts Payable, Account No. 271, in the general ledger.

(d) The total of the credit column headed Accounts Receivable should be posted as a credit to Accounts Receivable, Account No. 131, in the general ledger.

As the total of each column is posted, the account number should be written in parentheses immediately below the total in the general journal. The page number of the general journal then should be entered in the Posting Reference column of the proper general ledger account as a cross-reference. A check mark should be placed in parentheses below the totals of the General Ledger Debit and Credit columns to indicate that these totals are not posted.

General ledger

Holling & Renz use a general ledger with four-column ledger account ruling. The accounts are arranged in this ledger in numerical order. A chart of accounts is reproduced on page 420. It will be noted that the chart includes several accounts not previously used in this presentation. A brief discussion of each of these accounts follows.

Government Bonds, Account No. 121. This account is used to record the cost of the United States government bonds owned by Holling & Renz. From time to time, the partners find that the firm's bank balance is larger than necessary. In order to supplement earnings from regular operations, the excess cash is temporarily invested in certain types of government bonds which have a high degree of safety even though the rate of return is comparatively low. Whenever the money is needed, the bonds can be sold or redeemed with little risk of loss. Because there is no present intention to hold the same bonds for a long period of time, they are regarded as a temporary investment and classified as a current asset of the firm. In the end-of-period adjustment process, any interest accrued on the bonds is recorded as a debit to Account No. 122 (with a credit to Interest Earned, Account No. 711).

Sales Discount, Account No. 043. It is the practice of most wholesale businesses to offer their customers cash discounts for prompt payment of purchases on account. As previously mentioned, Holling & Renz allow a discount of 2 percent if an amount due is paid within ten days from date of purchase. When a sale on account is made, the customer is billed for the gross amount due. If a remittance is received within the discount period, the entry to record it involves debits to Federal National Bank and Sales

Discount with a credit to Accounts Receivable. In preparing the income statement at the end of the fiscal year, the amount of sales discount is prorated on the basis of the amount of sales, less sales returns and allowances, of each department. While sales discount could be treated as an expense, a preferred treatment is to consider it (like sales returns and allowances) as a reduction of sales revenue in calculating the amount of net sales.

Freight In — Department A and Freight In — Department B, Accounts Nos. 541 and 551. These accounts are charged with the amount of freight

HOLLING & RENZ

CHART OF GENERAL LEDGER ACCOUNTS

*Assets**
Cash
111 Federal National Bank
112 Petty Cash Fund

Temporary Investments
121 Government Bonds
122 Accrued Interest Receivable

Receivables
131 Accounts Receivable
　013 Allowance for Doubtful Accounts

Merchandise Inventory
141 Merchandise Inventory — Department A
151 Merchandise Inventory — Department B

Supplies and Prepayments
161 Store Supplies
162 Advertising Supplies
163 Office Supplies
164 Postage Stamps
165 Prepaid Insurance

Long-Lived Assets
171 Store Equipment
　017 Accumulated Depreciation — Store Equipment
181 Delivery Equipment
　018 Accumulated Depreciation — Delivery Equipment
191 Office Equipment
　019 Accumulated Depreciation — Office Equipment

Liabilities
211 FICA Tax Payable
221 FUTA Tax Payable
231 State Unemployment Tax Payable
241 Employees Income Tax Payable
251 Notes Payable
261 Accrued Interest Payable
271 Accounts Payable

Owners' Equity
311 T. L. Holling, Capital
　031 T. L. Holling, Drawing
321 A. G. Renz, Capital
　032 A. G. Renz, Drawing
331 Expense and Revenue Summary

Revenue from Sales
411 Sales — Department A
　041 Sales Returns and Allowances — Department A
421 Sales — Department B
　042 Sales Returns and Allowances — Department B
　043 Sales Discount

Cost of Goods Sold
511 Purchases — Department A
　051 Purchases Returns and Allowances — Department A
521 Purchases — Department B
　052 Purchases Returns and Allowances — Department B
　053 Purchases Discount
541 Freight In — Department A
551 Freight In — Department B
561 Cost of Goods Sold — Department A
571 Cost of Goods Sold — Department B

Operating Expenses
611 Operating Expenses

Other Revenue
711 Interest Earned

Other Expenses
811 Interest Expense
821 Charitable Contributions Expense

Words in italics represent headings and not account titles.

paid by Holling & Renz on incoming shipments of merchandise. The balances of these accounts are treated as additions to the cost of merchandise purchased and are so reported in the income statement.

Cost of Goods Sold — Department A and Cost of Goods Sold — Department B, Accounts Nos. 561 and 571. These two accounts are similar to Expense and Revenue Summary in that they are used at the end of the accounting period in the closing process. Such accounts are used to summarize the elements that enter into the calculation of the cost of goods sold by each department. The debit balances of the merchandise inventory accounts (representing the beginning inventories), the purchases accounts, and the freight in accounts, together with the credit balances of the purchases returns and allowances accounts and the purchases discount account, are closed to the respective cost of goods sold accounts. When the amounts of the ending inventories are recorded, the respective cost of goods sold accounts are credited. The balance of each of these accounts then represents the cost of goods sold for the indicated department. These balances then are closed to the expense and revenue summary account.

Charitable Contributions Expense, Account No. 821. This account is not new, but classifying it as an "other expense" differs from the treatment in the case of Boyd's Clothiers. In the Boyd chart of accounts (see page 183) this expense was classified as an "operating expense." There is a difference of opinion among accountants as to which is the preferred classification of charitable contributions expense.

Accounts receivable ledger

Holling & Renz use an accounts receivable ledger with balance-column account ruling. The accounts are arranged in this ledger in alphabetic order. A control account for accounts receivable (Account No. 131) is kept in the general ledger. At the end of each month it is customary to prepare a schedule of the accounts receivable, the total of which should be the same as the balance of the accounts receivable control account.

Posting to the customers' accounts in the accounts receivable ledger may be done either from the books of original entry or directly from vouchers or other documents that represent the transactions. The accountant for Holling & Renz follows the latter practice.

Accounts payable ledger

Holling & Renz use an accounts payable ledger with balance-column account ruling. The accounts are arranged in this ledger in alphabetic order. A control account for accounts payable (Account No. 271) is kept in the general ledger. At the end of each month it is customary to prepare a schedule of the accounts payable, the total of which should be the same as the balance of the accounts payable control account.

Posting to suppliers' accounts in the accounts payable ledger may be done either from the books of original entry or directly from vouchers or other documents that represent the transactions. The accountant for Holling & Renz follows the latter practice.

Operating expense ledger

Holling & Renz use an operating expense ledger with balance-column account ruling. The accounts are arranged in this ledger in numerical order. A chart of the accounts appears below. A control account for operating expenses (Account No. 611) is kept in the general ledger. At the end of each month it is customary to prepare a schedule of the operating expenses, the total of which should be the same as the balance of the operating expenses control account.

All posting to the operating expense accounts is done from the books of original entry. As each item is posted, the page of the journal from which it is posted is entered in the Posting Reference column of the account.

HOLLING & RENZ

CHART OF OPERATING EXPENSE LEDGER ACCOUNTS

Selling Expenses

6111 Advertising Expense
6112 Store Clerks Salary Expense
6113 Truck Drivers Wage Expense
6114 A. G. Renz, Salary Expense
6115 A. G. Renz, Traveling Expense
6116 Truck Gas and Oil Expense
6117 Truck Repairs Expense
6118 Garage Rent Expense
6119 Freight Out
6121 Merchandise Insurance Expense
6122 Delivery Equipment Insurance Expense
6123 Store Equipment Insurance Expense
6124 Store Supplies Expense
6125 Postage Expense (Selling)
6126 Depreciation of Store Equipment
6127 Depreciation of Delivery Equipment
6128 Miscellaneous Selling Expense

Administrative Expenses

6131 Rent Expense
6132 T. L. Holling, Salary Expense
6133 Office Salaries Expense
6134 Light and Water Expense
6135 Telephone Expense
6136 Uncollectible Accounts Expense
6137 Property Tax Expense
6138 Office Supplies Expense
6139 Postage Expense (Administration)
6141 Office Equipment Insurance Expense
6142 Depreciation of Office Equipment
6143 Payroll Taxes Expense
6144 Miscellaneous General Expense

Auxiliary records

Holling & Renz keep certain auxiliary records. These are as follows: a petty cash disbursements record, a long-lived asset record, check stubs, and a stock record. Their record of petty cash disbursements for June is reproduced on pages 442 and 443. The form of the long-lived asset record is not shown. (Since Holling & Renz use the group method of depreciation accounting, the long-lived asset record does not show the periodic depreciation of each unit.) A discussion of check stubs and the stock record follows.

Check Stubs. Holling & Renz use a checkbook bound with two checks to a page with stubs attached. The purpose of the stubs is **(1)** to provide spaces for recording the current bank balance, deposits, and the information needed to keep the records of checks drawn, and **(2)** to post to the accounts of suppliers in the accounts payable ledger. Space is also provided on the stubs of the checks to record the account number of the account to be debited.

Stock Record. Holling & Renz keep a stock record as a means of control and as an aid to good business management. Such a record may serve several purposes. It indicates when the supply of any item is low and its replenishment is needed. A physical count should be made at least once a year even if the stock record is maintained, because the record shows the quantity that should be on hand and indicates the need for closer control if a substantial discrepancy is discovered. With a stock record, such as the one shown below, it is not essential that a physical count of the entire inventory be made at the same time. Businesses that want *interim* financial statements (monthly or quarterly) can base their calculation of cost of goods sold and of inventory at the statement date upon information provided by a stock record. (A complete physical count at the end of

STOCK RECORD									
DATE	INV. NO.	RECEIVED	ISSUED	BALANCE	DATE	INV. NO.	RECEIVED	ISSUED	BALANCE
19— May 1				1062					
5	104		30	1032					
9	108		40	992					
10	821	100		1092					
16	CM 881	4		1096					
18	111		60	1036					
20	114		40	996					
25	CB 14		5	991					
27	839	50		1041					
ARTICLE		DESCRIPTION		MINIMUM		DEPARTMENT			
Oil-Base Paint		White Primer 1 ea. 10-liter pail		1000		A			

Stock Record

each month or each quarter may not be practical, and calculations based upon estimates may not be sufficiently reliable.)

One form of stock record is shown on the preceding page. The information needed in keeping such a record is obtained from the purchase invoices, sales invoices, charge-back invoices, and credit memorandums. In recording receipts, sales, returns, and balances, only quantities are entered. Minimum quantities are indicated and, whenever the quantity in stock reaches the minimum, more of the item is ordered.

Accounting procedure illustrated

The accounts of Holling & Renz are being kept on the basis of a fiscal year ending June 30. Their books of original entry (invoice register, sales register, record of cash receipts, record of checks drawn, and general journal) are reproduced on pages 436 to 441, inclusive. The only auxiliary record reproduced is the petty cash disbursements record, pages 442 and 443. The general and subsidiary ledgers are not reproduced in this illustration. Following is a narrative of the June transactions that are shown recorded in the illustrations.

HOLLING & RENZ

WHOLESALE DEALERS IN PAINT AND VARNISH

NARRATIVE OF TRANSACTIONS

Wednesday, June 1

Issued Check No. 830 for $550 to T. R. Walsh in payment of the June rent.

Received a check for $681.10 from Don V. Davis for our invoice of May 23 for $695, less 2 percent discount.

Before the check received from Don V. Davis was recorded, it was reconciled by referring to his account in the accounts receivable ledger. The account showed that on May 23 he had been charged for merchandise amounting to $695. A discount of 2 percent is allowed for cash in ten days. The amount of his remittance was therefore verified in the following manner:

Merchandise sold..	$695.00
Less 2% discount..	13.90
Net amount due..	$681.10

When the check was found to be for the proper amount, it was posted immediately to the credit of the account with Don V. Davis in the accounts receivable ledger. The amount of the check, $681.10, was entered on one line and the amount of the discount,

$13.90, on the next line. The check was then entered in the record of cash receipts by debiting the bank account for the amount of the check, $681.10, by debiting Sales Discount for the amount of the discount, $13.90, and by crediting Accounts Receivable for the total of the invoice, $695. A check mark was placed in the Check ($\sqrt{}$) column following the amount entered in the Accounts Receivable column to indicate that the posting to Don V. Davis' account had been completed.

Made charge sale as follows:

No. 104, Don V. Davis, St. Louis, Missouri; paint, $322.70; varnish, $181.80; terms, 2/10, n/30.

The information needed by the bookkeeper in recording each sale is obtained from a carbon copy of the sales invoice prepared by the billing clerk. As this invoice was entered in the sales register, a check mark was placed in the Check ($\sqrt{}$) column following the Accounts Receivable Debit column to indicate that the invoice would be posted directly to the account of Don V. Davis. The invoice was then posted to Mr. Davis' account in the accounts receivable ledger. A copy of the sales invoice was used to make appropriate entries on the affected stock record cards — the date, invoice number, quantity issued, and balance remaining. (Refer to Stock Record form illustrated on page 423.)

Holling & Renz follow the practice of depositing at the end of each day all checks and other cash items received during the day.

Thursday, June 2

Issued checks as follows:

No. 831, U.S. Paint Co. $1,021.12, in payment of its invoice of May 24 for $1,052.70, less 3 percent discount.

No. 832, M.F.A. Insurance Co., $205, in payment of bill for one-year policy on delivery truck.

As these checks were entered in the record of checks drawn, check marks were placed in the Check ($\sqrt{}$) column following the amounts entered in the Accounts Payable and General Ledger Debit columns to indicate that the checks would be posted directly from the check stubs to the proper accounts in the subsidiary ledgers. In posting to the account of U.S. Paint Company, the amount of the check, $1,021.12, was entered on one line and the amount of the discount, $31.58, was entered on the next line.

Friday, June 3

Received the following invoices:

Celucoat Corporation, St. Louis, Missouri; paint, $691.20; terms, June 2 — 2/10, n/30.

Phelan-Faust Paint Manufacturing Co., St. Louis, Missouri; varnish, $473; terms, June 2 — 3/10, n/30.

Sunbrite Supply Co., St. Louis, Missouri; office supplies, $46.70; terms, June 3 — n/30.

As these invoices were received they were numbered consecutively, beginning with No. 741, and were entered in the invoice register. Check marks were placed in the Check ($\sqrt{}$) column following the Accounts Payable Credit column to indicate that the invoices would be posted directly to the proper creditors' accounts in the accounts payable ledger. These invoices were used to make appropriate entries on the affected stock record cards — the date, invoice number, quantity received, and new balance.

Saturday, June 4

Issued Check No. 833 for $1,400.03 to Celucoat Corporation in payment of its invoice of May 25 for $1,428.60, less 2 percent discount.

Received the following invoices:

Celucoat Corporation, St. Louis, Missouri; paint, $450.40; terms, June 4 — 2/10, n/30; shipped directly to Kaplan Lumber Co., St. Charles, Missouri, freight collect.

> Holling & Renz are agents for Celucoat Corporation. However, they do not necessarily carry in stock the entire line of that corporation's paint. When an order is received for items that are not carried in stock, an order is placed with the supplier with instructions to ship directly to the customer, transportation charges collect. After the invoice was recorded in the invoice register and was posted to the account of Celucoat Corporation in the accounts payable ledger, the invoice was referred to the billing clerk with instructions to bill the Kaplan Lumber Co. (See related charge sale No. 107 of June 6.)

U.S. Paint Company, St. Louis, Missouri; varnish, $680; terms, June 3 — 3/10, n/30.

Steelcote Paper Products, St. Louis, Missouri; office supplies, $52; terms, June 4 — n/30.

END-OF-THE-WEEK WORK

(1) Footed the amount columns in the invoice register and record of checks drawn and proved the footings. **(2)** Proved the bank balance in the following manner:

Balance, June 1	$5,439.01*
Total receipts June 1–4 per record of cash receipts	681.10
Total	$6,120.11
Less total checks issued June 1–4 per record of checks drawn	3,176.15
Balance, June 4	$2,943.96

*Indicated by General Ledger Account No. 111 not reproduced in this illustration.

(3) Completed the individual posting from the books of original entry to the general ledger and to the operating expense ledger accounts.

Monday, June 6

Received a check for $921.20 from Famous-Barr Co. for merchandise sold on May 27 amounting to $940, less 2 percent discount.

Made charge sales as follows:

No. 105, St. John Hardware, St. John, Missouri; paint, $369.50; terms, 2/10, n/30.

No. 106, Morris Hardware, St. Louis, Missouri; paint, $172.30; postage, $2.05; terms, 2/10, n/30.

In entering Sales Invoice No. 106 in the sales register, the postage was charged to the customer's account and was credited to Postage Stamps, Account No. 164. In posting this invoice to the account of Morris Hardware Co. in the accounts receivable ledger, the amount of the merchandise sold, $172.30, was entered on one line, and the amount of the postage prepaid, $2.05, was entered on the next line.

No. 107, Kaplan Lumber Co., St. Charles, Missouri; paint, $600.60; terms, 2/10, n/30; shipped directly from factory, freight collect.

The paint billed to the Kaplan Lumber Co. on Sales Invoice No. 107 was shipped directly by Celucoat Corporation on June 3, and an invoice was received by Holling & Renz on June 4.

Issued Check No. 834 for $984.94 to Phelan-Faust Paint Manufacturing Co. in payment of its invoice of May 27 for $1,015.40, less 3 percent discount.

Tuesday, June 7

Issued Credit Memorandum No. 892 to Don V. Davis, $21.30, for paint returned.

The paint returned had been billed on Sales Invoice No. 104. The return transaction was recorded in the general journal, after which the credit memorandum was posted directly to the account of Don V. Davis in the accounts receivable ledger. The stock record was adjusted accordingly.

Made the following cash sales:

No. 151, Badger Paint Stores; paint, $545.40.
No. 152, M. J. Rosen; paint, $344.20.

At the end of each day the carbon copies of the cash sales tickets are analyzed to determine the total sales by departments, after which an entry is made in the record of cash receipts debiting the Bank for the total amount of cash received and crediting Cash Sales by departments for the total sales made in each department.

Issued the following checks:

No. 835, $50, payable to Cash. (Cashed the check at the bank and purchased $50 worth of stamps.)
No. 836, Banner Paint Co., $327.19, in payment of its invoice of May 30 for $330.50, less 1 percent discount.
No. 837, Celucoat Corporation, $419.64, in payment of merchandise purchased May 30 amounting to $428.20, less 2 percent discount.

Wednesday, June 8

Issued Credit Memorandum No. 893 to Atlas Hardware, $10.60, for varnish returned.

Received the following checks:

Wittenberg Lumber Co., $1,074.08, in payment of merchandise sold May 30 amounting to $1,096, less 2 percent discount.

Atlas Hardware, $707.40, in payment of merchandise sold May 10.

Made the following cash sales:

No. 153, W. E. Brubaker; paint $440; varnish, $234.80.
No. 154, C. R. Wannen; paint $212.60.

Made petty cash disbursements as follows:

Typewriter repairs, $5.50. Voucher No. 56.
500 advertising letters, $9.90. Voucher No. 57.

Issued charge-back Invoice No. 15 to Celucoat Corporation, $63.40, for paint returned; paint purchased May 30.

This transaction was recorded in the general journal, after which the charge-back invoice was posted directly to the account of Celucoat Corporation in the accounts payable ledger.

Issued the following checks:

No. 838, Celucoat Corporation, $700.60, in payment of balance due on merchandise purchased May 30 for $778.30, less 2 percent discount.

In computing the amount of the check to be issued it was necessary to refer to the account of Celucoat Corporation and to make the following calculations:

Merchandise purchased May 30	$778.30
Less merchandise returned for credit June 8	63.40
Amount subject to discount	$714.90
Less 2% discount	14.30
	$700.60

No. 839, Phelan-Faust Paint Manufacturing Co., $600.53, in payment of its invoice of May 30, $619.10, less 3 percent discount.

Thursday, June 9

Received the following invoices:

Vane-Calvert Paint Co., St. Louis, Missouri; varnish, $56.80; terms, June 8 — 1/10, n/30; delivered to United Lumber Co., City.

Celucoat Corporation, St. Louis, Missouri; paint, $1,157.20; terms, June 8 — 2/10, n/30.

Office Equipment Co., St. Louis, Missouri; calculator, $602.85; terms, June 9 — n/30.

Friday, June 10

Made charge sales as follows:

No. 108, Warson Village Hardware, Warson Village, Missouri; paint, $546.80; terms, 2/10, n/30; express collect.

No. 109, County Lumber Co., Jennings, Missouri; paint, $475.90; varnish, $711.70; terms, 2/10, n/30; express collect.

No. 110, Famous-Barr Co., St. Louis, Missouri; paint, $3,313,80; varnish, $113.70; terms, 2/10, n/30.

No. 111, United Lumber Co., St. Louis, Missouri; varnish, $76.40; terms, 2/10, n/30.

The varnish billed to the United Lumber Co. on Sales Invoice No. 111 was delivered directly by the Vane-Calvert Paint Co. on June 9 and an invoice was received on June 9.

Issued Credit Memorandum No. 894 to St. John Hardware, $65.20, for paint returned. Since the paint was defective, it was returned immediately to Celucoat Corporation for credit at cost, $48.40. Issued charge-back Invoice No. 16.

Both of these transactions were recorded in the general journal. It will be noted that St. John Hardware was given credit for the wholesale price of the paint, while Celucoat Corporation was charged for the manufacturer's price.

Issued Check No. 840 to The Daily Post for $19.60 in payment of an advertisement in the Sunday edition of June 5.

Received the following checks:

United Lumber Co., $850, in full settlement for merchandise sold May 5.

Zephyr Hardware, $773.42, in full settlement of our invoice of May 31, $789.20, less 2 percent discount.

Saturday, June 11

Issued Check No. 841 for $178.16 to the Federal National Bank in payment of a dishonored check of the Forest Park Lumber Co. Its check was returned unpaid by the bank on which it was drawn with a notice stating the reason as "not sufficient funds."

The dishonored check was originally received for a sales invoice issued May 19 for $181.80, less 2 percent discount. Holling & Renz have arranged with the bank for all dishonored checks to be presented to them for reimbursement. When the dishonored check of the Forest Park Lumber Co. was presented, Mr. Holling issued Check No. 841 in settlement and wrote A. L. Jinks, President of the Forest Park Lumber Co., advising him that his check of May 31 had been returned unpaid and had been charged back to his account.

Received the following invoices:

Sunbrite Supply Co., St. Louis, Missouri; advertising supplies, $69.40; terms, June 11 — n/30.

Celucoat Corporation, St. Louis, Missouri; paint, $1,218.60; terms, June 10 — 2/10, n/30.

Glidden Co., St. Louis, Missouri; paint, $414.80; terms, June 10 — 3/10, n/30; delivered directly to Famous-Barr Co., City.

Morris Paper Co., St. Louis, Missouri; store supplies, $42.45; terms, June 10 — n/30.

Vane-Calvert Paint Co., St. Louis, Missouri; varnish, $54.20; terms, June 10 — 1/10, n/30; shipped by the supplier to Beyers Lumber Co., Olivette, Missouri; express collect.

Issued the following checks:

No. 842, Celucoat Corporation, $677.38, in payment of its invoice of June 2 for $691.20, less 2 percent discount.

No. 843, Phelan-Faust Paint Manufacturing Co., $458.81, in payment of its invoice of June 2 for $473, less 3 percent discount.

Received a check for $473.54 from Don V. Davis, in settlement of the balance of our invoice of June 1; merchandise, $483.20, less 2 percent discount.

END-OF-THE-WEEK WORK

(1) Footed the amount columns in all the books of original entry and the petty cash disbursements record and proved the footings. (2) Proved the bank balance as follows:

Balance, June 1..	$ 5,439.01
Total receipts for the period June 1–11 per record of cash receipts......	7,257.74
Total...	$12,696.75
Less total checks issued during period June 1–11 per record of checks drawn..	7,593.00
Balance, June 11..	$5,103.75

(3) Completed the individual posting from the books of original entry to the general ledger and the operating expense ledger accounts.

Monday, June 13

Made charge sales as follows:

No. 112, Beyers Lumber Co., Olivette, Missouri; paint, $162; varnish, $72.80; postage, $2.86; terms, 2/10, n/30. (The varnish was shipped directly from the factory, express collect. See the related transaction of June 11.)

No. 113, Hoffman Paint Co., Rock Hill, Missouri; paint, $117.70; varnish, $186.40; terms, 2/10, n/30.

No. 114, Famous-Barr Co., St. Louis, Missouri; paint, $584; terms, 2/10, n/30; delivered directly from factory on June 11, freight collect.

No. 115, Brod-Dugan Co., Clayton, Missouri; paint, $3,809.10; terms, 2/10, n/30.

Received the following check:

E. E. Wilson, $882.60, in full settlement of account.

Made the following cash sale:

No. 155, R. J. Powell; paint, $555.20; varnish, $74.80.

Issued the following checks:

No. 844, Celucoat Corporation, $441.39, in payment of merchandise purchased June 4 for $450.40, less 2 percent discount.

No. 845, U.S. Paint Co., $659.60, in payment of its invoice of June 3, $680, less 3 percent discount.

Tuesday, June 14

Issued Check No. 846 for $166.18 to the Lion Oil Co. in payment of gasoline and oil supplied during May.

Paid $5.80 out of the petty cash fund for repairs on truck. Voucher No. 58.

Sent a corrected invoice to the Warson Village Hardware, Warson Village, Missouri; for $99.70.

> On Sales Invoice No. 94 dated May 25 the paint, through an error, was billed at $97.90.
> In recording this transaction in the sales register, it was necessary only to debit Accounts Receivable and to credit Sales — Department A for $1.80, which represented the increased amount of the corrected invoice. Since the transaction related to Sale No. 94, that number was entered in the Sale No. column of the sales register.

Wednesday, June 15

Made petty cash disbursements as follows:

Water bill, $9.50. Voucher No. 59.
1M shipping tags, $6.80. Voucher No. 60.
100 sheets carbon paper, $2.20. Voucher No. 61.
Painting window sign, $7.50. Voucher No. 62.

Made the following cash sales:

No. 156, Affton Hardware; paint, $139.60.
No. 157, Badger Paint Stores; varnish, $271.80.

Received the following checks:

St. John Hardware, $362.11, in settlement of balance due on merchandise sold June 6; merchandise, $369.50, less 2 percent discount.

Morris Hardware, $170.90, for merchandise sold June 6, $172.30, less 2 percent discount, plus postage $2.05.

Kaplan Lumber Co., $588.59, in payment of merchandise sold June 6 for $600.60, less 2 percent discount.

Central Hardware, $390.20, in payment of merchandise sold. May 17.

Mr. Holling reported that he had clipped interest coupons, amounting to $150, from government bonds owned and had deposited them in the Federal National Bank.

This transaction was recorded in the record of cash receipts.

Issued Check No. 847 for $770.40 to the Federal National Bank, a United States depositary, in payment of the following taxes:

Employees' income tax (withheld during May)		$387.60
FICA tax imposed —		
On employees (withheld during May)	$191.40	
On employer	191.40	382.80
Total		$770.40

Issued Check No. 848 payable to Payroll for $2,805.50.

Holling & Renz follow the policy of paying their employees on the 15th and the last day of each month. They are subject to the taxes imposed under the Federal Insurance Contributions Act for old-age benefits and hospital insurance, and under the Federal Unemployment Tax Act for unemployment insurance purposes. They are also required to make contributions to the state unemployment compensation fund. They are required to withhold a percentage of their employees' wages both for old-age and hospital insurance benefits and for income tax purposes. In addition to the wages paid to employees, the Holling & Renz partnership agreement provides that each partner is to receive a salary of $1,500 a month, payable semimonthly. While the salaries of the partners constitute an operating expense of the business, they do not represent "wages" as defined in the social security and income tax laws; hence, such salaries are not subject to the FICA tax imposed upon employers and employees. Neither are such salaries subject to withholding for employees' income tax.

Each payday the bookkeeper is supplied with a report prepared by the payroll clerk showing the total amount of wages and salaries earned during the pay period, the amount of the payroll deductions, and the net amount of cash needed for payroll purposes. The report for June 15 appears on the next page.

A check made payable to Payroll was issued for the net amount payable. This check was then cashed at the Federal National Bank and currency and coins in the right denominations needed to pay each employee were obtained. The bookkeeper was instructed by Messrs. Holling and Renz to deposit their salaries in their individual bank accounts and to furnish them with duplicate copies of the deposit tickets.

The payroll check is entered in the record of checks drawn by debiting the proper salary accounts for the earnings, by crediting the proper liability accounts for the taxes withheld, and by crediting the bank account for the amount of the check issued. The payroll taxes imposed on the employer are recorded in the general journal by debiting Payroll Taxes Expense and by crediting the proper liability accounts for the taxes imposed. (Inasmuch as payroll taxes are imposed on a calendar-year basis and none of the employees had earnings in excess of the limits to June 30, all wages and salaries paid in June were subject to tax.)

The double waved lines appearing at this point in the records illustrated indicate omission of the transactions completed on the days between June 15 and 30.

Thursday, June 30

Received the following invoices (numbered consecutively beginning with 768):

PAYROLL STATEMENT FOR PERIOD BEGINNING JUNE 1
AND ENDING JUNE 15

| | | DEDUCTIONS | | |
CLASSIFICATION	TOTAL EARNINGS	FICA TAX	EMPLOYEES' INCOME TAX	NET AMOUNT PAYABLE
Salaries of store clerks..........	$ 780.00	$46.80	$107.20	$ 626.00
Wages of truck driver...........	350.00	21.00	32.30	296.70
Office salaries.................	465.00	27.90	54.30	382.80
Partners' salaries:				
T. L. Holling...............	750.00	None	None	750.00
A. G. Renz.................	750.00	None	None	750.00
	$3,095.00	$95.70	$193.80	$2,805.50

Employer's payroll taxes:		
FICA tax, 6% of $1,595.................................		$ 95.70
Unemployment compensation tax —		
State unemployment tax, 2.7% of $1,595.................	$43.07	
FUTA tax, 0.5% of $1,595............................	7.98	51.05
Total...		$146.75

Vane-Calvert Paint Co., St. Louis, Missouri; varnish, $152.40; terms, June 30 — 1/10, n/30.

Celucoat Corporation, St. Louis, Missouri; paint, $2,844.60; terms, June 29 — 2/10, n/30.

U.S. Paint Co., St. Louis, Missouri; varnish, $1,141.30; terms, June 28 — 3/10, n/30.

Office Equipment Co., St. Louis, Missouri; one checkwriter, $95, less credit for exchange allowance on old checkwriter, $5; terms, June 29 — n/30.

The original cost of the old checkwriter was $45. Since the group method of accounting for depreciation is used, the accumulated depreciation account must be charged with the cost of the old checkwriter less the $5 trade-in allowance. This transaction was recorded in the invoice register by debiting Office Equipment, Account No. 191, for $95, the cost of the new checkwriter; by debiting Accumulated Depreciation — Office Equipment, Account No. 019, for $40, the difference between the cost and the trade-in allowance on the old checkwriter; by crediting Office Equipment, Account No. 191, for $45, the original cost of the old checkwriter; and by crediting Accounts Payable for $90, the balance due the Office Equipment Co.

John J. Baker, attorney at law, advises that he is unable to collect the $55 owed by Raymond Hall, and Mr. Holling has instructed that the account be charged off.

This transaction is recorded in the general journal by debiting Allowance for Doubtful Accounts, Account No. 013, and by crediting Accounts Receivable for $55. It is then posted immediately as a credit to the account of Raymond Hall in the accounts receivable ledger.

Made charge sales as follows:

No. 139, Joe Miller Lumber Co., Centerville, Missouri; varnish, $105; terms, 2/10, n/30.

No. 140, Branneky and Sons, St. Ann, Missouri; paint, $1,725.90; varnish, $1,195.30; terms, 2/10, n/30; freight collect.

No. 141, County Lumber Co., Jennings, Missouri; paint, $732.40; varnish, $445.25; terms, 2/10, n/30; shipped by prepaid express, $7.35.

> It will be noted from the entry in the sales register that the express prepaid on the merchandise sold to the County Lumber Co. at Jennings, Missouri, was credited to Freight Out, Account No. 6119. Since this account is kept in the subsidiary operating expense ledger, it is also necessary to credit the freight to the general ledger control account for Operating Expenses, Account No. 611. The double posting is provided for by drawing a diagonal line in the Account No. column.

As a part of the foregoing transaction, paid $7.35 out of the petty cash fund for express charges on merchandise shipped to the County Lumber Co., Jennings, Missouri. Voucher No. 67.

Beyers Lumber Co. has advised that the paint and varnish shipped directly from the factory on June 24 arrived by express collect, $5.75, even though a delivered price had been quoted them. Mr. Holling, therefore, directed that a credit memorandum (No. 897) be issued to Beyers Lumber Co. for the amount of the express charges.

> This transaction was recorded in the general journal by debiting Freight Out, Account No. 6119, in the Operating Expenses column, and by crediting Accounts Receivable for $5.75. The credit memorandum was also posted directly to the account of Beyers Lumber Co. in the accounts receivable ledger.

Made petty cash disbursement of $1.30, for long-distance telephone call made from a booth by Mr. Renz. Voucher No. 68.

Issued the following checks:

No. 868, Pine Street Garage, $30, in payment of May storage.

No. 869, Vane-Calvert Paint Co., $30.69, in payment of its invoice of June 22, $31, less 1 percent discount.

No. 870, Hulsey Transfer Co., $115.35, in payment of freight and drayage on incoming merchandise received during June.

> According to Mr. Holling's instructions, freight and drayage on incoming merchandise should be distributed on a basis of the cost of the merchandise purchased for each department during the month. On this basis, Freight In — Department A should be charged for $102.55 and Freight In — Department B should be charged for $12.80.

Issued Check No. 871 payable to Payroll for $2,805.50.

> The payroll for the second half of June was the same as that for the first half of the month. Refer to payroll statement, page 433.

Issued Check No. 872 for $94.55 payable to Petty Cash to replenish the petty cash fund. The petty cash disbursements for June are shown at the top of the next page.

STATEMENT OF PETTY CASH DISBURSEMENTS FOR JUNE

Acct. No.	Account	Amount
163	Office Supplies...	$ 2.20
6111	Advertising Expense..................................	9.90
6117	Truck Repairs Expense...............................	5.80
6119	Freight Out..	9.60
6128	Miscellaneous Selling Expense........................	8.65
6134	Light and Water Expense.............................	9.50
6135	Telephone Expense..................................	3.60
6144	Miscellaneous General Expense.......................	45.30
	Total disbursements................................	$94.55

END-OF-THE-MONTH WORK

(1) Footed the amount columns, proved the footings, entered the totals, and ruled each of the books of original entry and the petty cash disbursements record. **(2)** Proved the bank balance as illustrated below:

Balance, June 1..	$ 5,439.01
Total receipts for June per record of cash receipts..................	41,327.35
Total...	$46,766.36
Less total checks issued during June per record of checks drawn....	39,112.17
Balance, June 30...	$ 7,654.19

(3) Completed the individual posting from the books of original entry to the general ledger and to the operating expense ledger accounts. **(4)** Completed the summary posting of the totals of the special columns of each of the books of original entry to the general ledger accounts. **(5)** Prepared a trial balance and schedules of accounts receivable, accounts payable, and operating expenses.

Step **(5)** would be completed as a part of the normal routine at the end of each month. However, since the end of June is also the end of the fiscal year for Holling & Renz, the procedure is varied slightly. The preparation of the general ledger trial balance and the schedule of operating expenses is combined with the preparation of the end-of-year work sheets used to assist in producing the income statement for the year and the balance sheet as of June 30. This process is described and illustrated in the following chapter. (The schedules of accounts receivable and accounts payable are shown on page 472.)

INVOICE REGISTER FOR MONTH OF *June* 19—— PAGE 38

Line	DEPT. A	DEPT. B	ACCT. NO.	AMOUNT	✓	DAY	DATE OF INV.	INV. NO.	NAME	ACCOUNTS PAYABLE	✓	ACCT. NO.	AMOUNT	✓
1									AMOUNTS FORWARDED					
2	69120					3	6/2	741	Celucoat Corporation	69120	✓			
3		47300				3	6/2	742	Phelan-Faust Paint Mfg. Co.	47300	✓			
4			163	4670	✓	3	6/3	743	Lambrite Supply Co.	4670	✓			
5	45040					4	6/4	744	Celucoat Corporation	45040	✓			
6		68000				4	6/3	745	U.S. Paint Company	68000	✓			
7			163	5200	✓	4	6/4	746	Staback Paper Products	5200	✓			
8		5680				9	6/8	747	Vano-Calvert Paint Co.	5680	✓			
9	115720					9	6/8	748	Celucoat Corporation	115720	✓			
10			191	60285	✓	9	6/9	749	Office Equipment Co.	60285	✓			
11			162	6940	✓	11	6/11	750	Lambrite Supply Co.	6940	✓			
12	121860					11	6/10	751	Celucoat Corporation	121860	✓			
13	41480					11	6/10	752	Widdow Co.	41480	✓			
14			161	4245	✓	11	6/10	753	Morris Paper Co.	4245	✓			
15		5420				11	6/10	754	Vano-Calvert Paint Co.	5420	✓			
	393220	126400		81340	(✓)				600960					
33		15240				30	6/30	768	Vano-Calvert Paint Co.	15240	✓			
34	284460					30	6/29	769	Celucoat Corporation	284460	✓			
35		114130				30	6/28	770	U.S. Paint Co.	114130	✓			
36			019	9500	✓	30	6/29	771	Office Equipment Co.	9000	✓	191	4500	✓
37				4000	✓									
38	2916290	406780		108360						3426930			4500	
39	(511)	(521)		(✓)						(27)			(1)	

Holling & Renz — Invoice Register

SALES REGISTER FOR MONTH OF June 19—   PAGE 45

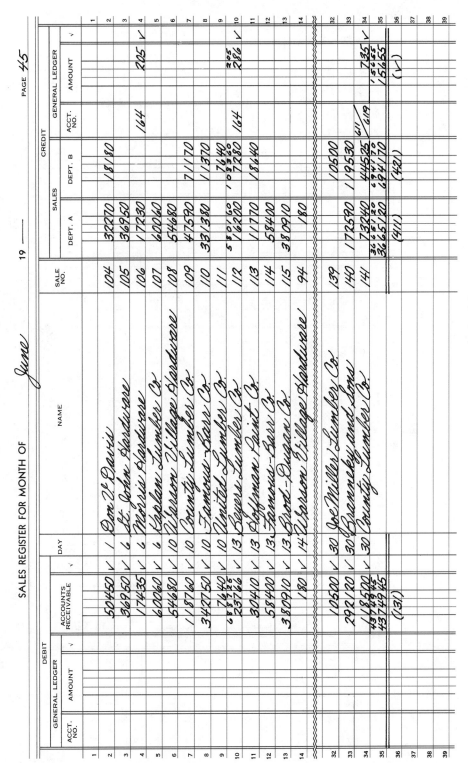

		DEBIT					CREDIT			
		General Ledger Acct. No.	General Ledger Amount	Accounts Receivable	DAY	NAME	SALE NO.	SALES Dept. A	SALES Dept. B	Credit Acct. No. / General Ledger Amount
1				50450 ✓	1	Dan N. Davis	104	32270	18180	
2				36950 ✓	6	Lt. John Hardware	105	36950		
3				17435 ✓	6	Morris Hardware	106	17230		164 / 205 ✓
4				60060 ✓	6	Kaplan Lumber Co.	107	60060		
5				54680 ✓	10	Warson Village Hardware	108	54680		
6				118760 ✓	10	County Lumber Co.	109	47590	71170	
7				342750 ✓	10	Famous-Barr Co.	110	331380	11370	
8				7640 ✓	10	United Lumber Co.	111		7640	
9				235760 ✓	13	Beyers Lumber Co.	112	16200	7280	164 / 205, 286 ✓
10				30410 ✓	13	Hoffman Paint Co.	113	11770	8640	
11				58400 ✓	13	Famous-Barr Co.	114	58400		
12				380910 ✓	13	Brod-Dugan Co.	115	380910		
13				180 ✓	14	Warson Village Hardware	94	180		
32				10500 ✓	30	Joe Miller Lumber Co.	139		10500	
33				292120 ✓	30	Granneby and Sons	140	172580	119530	
34				418500 ✓	30	County Lumber Co.	141	73240	44525	611 / 735 ✓ , 619 / 15655
35				4374945				3665120	694170	151655
				(131)				(411)	(421)	(√)

RECORD OF CASH RECEIPTS FOR MONTH OF June 19__   PAGE 66

ACCT. NO.	GEN. LEDGER AMOUNT	✓	SALES DISCOUNT	✓	BANK NET AMOUNT	DAY	RECEIVED FROM — DESCRIPTION	ACCOUNTS RECEIVABLE	✓	CASH SALES DEPT. A	CASH SALES DEPT. B	ACCT. NO.	GEN. LEDGER AMOUNT	✓
							AMOUNTS FORWARDED							
			1390		68110	1	Don W. Davis	69500	✓					
			1980		92120	6	Famous-Barr Co.	94000	✓					
					88960	7	Cash Sales			88960				
			2192		107408	8	Wittenberg Lumber Co.	109600	✓					
					70740	8	Atlas Hardware	70740	✓					
					88740	8	Cash Sales			65260	23480			
					85000	10	United Lumber Co.	85000	✓					
			1578		77342	10	Zahburg Hardware	78920	✓					
			966		47354	11	Don W. Davis	48320	✓					
					88260	13	E. E. Wilson	88260	✓					
					63000	13	Cash Sales			55520	7480			
					41140	15	Cash Sales			13960	27180			
			739		3621	15	St. John Hardware	36950	✓					
			345		17090	15	Morris Hardware	17435	✓					
			1201		58859	15	Kaplan Lumber Co.	60060	✓					
					39020	15	Central Hardware	39020	✓					
					15000	15	Interest on government bonds					711	15000	✓
			62631		4132735			3690416		361210	128740		15000	
			62631		4132735			3690416		361210	128740		15000	
			(043)		(111)			(131)		(411)	(421)		(✓)	

Holling & Renz — Record of Cash Receipts

RECORD OF CHECKS DRAWN FOR MONTH OF *June* 19—   PAGE 77

DEBIT GENERAL LEDGER ACCT. NO.	DEBIT GENERAL LEDGER AMOUNT	DEBIT OPERATING EXPENSES ACCT. NO.	DEBIT OPERATING EXPENSES AMOUNT	DEBIT ACCOUNTS PAYABLE	DAY	DRAWN TO THE ORDER OF	CREDIT GENERAL LEDGER ACCT. NO.	CREDIT GENERAL LEDGER AMOUNT	CREDIT PUR-CHASES DISC.	CK. NO.	BANK NET AMOUNT
						AMOUNTS FORWARDED					
		6131	55000 ✓		1	J. C. Walsh				830	55000
				105270 ✓	2	U. S. Paint Co.			3158	831	102112
165	20500 ✓				2	M. F. Q. Insurance Co.				832	20500
				142860 ✓	4	Celucoat Corporation			2857	833	140003
				101540 ✓	6	Phelan-Faust Paint Mfg. Co.			3046	834	94944
164	5000				7	Cash (for stamps)				835	5000
				33050 ✓	7	Bonner Paint Co.			331	836	3279
				42820 ✓	7	Celucoat Corporation			856	837	41944
				71490 ✓	8	Celucoat Corporation			1430	838	70060
				61910 ✓	8	Phelan-Faust Paint Mfg. Co.			1857	839	60053
		6111	1960 ✓		10	The Daily Post				840	1960
131	18180 ✓				11	Federal National Bank	043	364 ✓		841	17816
				69120 ✓	11	Celucoat Corporation			1382	842	67738
			54960	47300 ✓	11	Phelan-Faust Paint Mfg. Co.		364	1419	843	45881
				45040 ✓	13	Celucoat Corporation			901	844	44139
				68000 ✓	13	U. S. Paint Co.			2040	845	65960
		6116	16618 ✓		14	Lion Oil Co.				846	16618
241	38760 ✓				15	Federal National Bank	211	9570 ✓		847	77040
211	38280 ✓						244	19380 ✓			
		6112	78000 ✓		15	Payroll	211	9570		848	280550
		6113	35000 ✓				244	19380			
		6114	75000 ✓								
		6132	75000 ✓								
		6133	46500 ✓								
		6118	3000 ✓		30	Pine Street Garage				868	3000
				3100 ✓	30	Pine-Calvert Paint Co.			31	869	3069
136650		395128		3517280		Carried forward		377867	61574		3409677

Holling & Renz — Record of Checks Drawn

RECORD OF CHECKS DRAWN FOR MONTH OF *June* 19 — PAGE *78*

	DEBIT									CREDIT				
	GENERAL LEDGER			OPERATING EXPENSES			ACCOUNTS PAYABLE	DAY	DRAWN TO THE ORDER OF	GENERAL LEDGER			PUR-CHASES DISC.	CK. NO.	BANK NET AMOUNT
	ACCT. NO.	AMOUNT	√	ACCT. NO.	AMOUNT	√	√			ACCT. NO.	AMOUNT	√			
1		136650			3951 28		35172 80	30	AMOUNTS FORWARDED		377867		61514		3609677
2	541	10265	√					30	Hulsey Transfer Co.					870	11535
3	551	1280	√												
4				6112	78000	√		30	Payroll	211	9570	√		871	280650
5				6113	35000	√				244	19380	√			
6				6114	75000	√									
7				6132	76000	√									
8				6133	46500	√									
9	163	220	√	6111	990	√		30	Petty Cash					872	9455
10				6117	580	√									
11				6119	960	√									
12				6128	865	√									
13				6134	950	√									
14				6135	360	√									
15		143605		6114	4530	√	35172 80				406817		61514		3911217
16		1484405			7138 63		35172 80				406817		61514		3911217
17		(√)			(611)		(271)				(√)		(053)		(111)
18															
19															
20															
21															
22															
23															
24															
25															
26															
27															
28															
29															

GENERAL JOURNAL FOR MONTH OF June 19 — PAGE 43

DEBIT							DAY	DESCRIPTION	CREDIT				
OPERATING EXPENSES			ACCOUNTS PAYABLE		GENERAL LEDGER				GENERAL LEDGER			ACCOUNTS PAYABLE	ACCOUNTS RECEIVABLE
ACCT. NO.	AMOUNT	✓		✓	ACCT. NO.	AMOUNT ✓			ACCT. NO.	AMOUNT	✓	✓	✓
								AMOUNTS FORWARDED					
					041	2130	7	Don V. Davis, CM 892					2130 ✓
					04R	1060	8	Atlas Hardware, CM 893					1060 ✓
			6340 ✓				8	Celucraft Corporation, CB 15	051	6340	✓		
					041	6520	10	St. John Hardware, CM 894					6520 ✓
			4840 ✓				10	Celucraft Corporation, CB 16	051	4840	✓		
			9770						211	9670	✓		9770
6143	14675 ✓						15	Payroll Taxes	221	798	✓		
									231	4307	✓		
					013	5500 ✓	30	Raymond Hall					5500 ✓
6119	575 ✓						30	Beyers Lumber Co., CM 897					575 ✓
6143	14675 ✓						30	Payroll Taxes	211	9670	✓		
									221	798	✓		
									231	4307 ✓			
29225			25750			27160				61445			21390
(611)			(271)			(✓)				(✓)			21320
										(✓)			(131)

Holling & Renz — General Journal

PAGE *23*   PETTY CASH DISBURSEMENTS

	DAY	DESCRIPTION	VOU. NO.	TOTAL AMOUNT		6111	6117	
1		AMOUNTS FORWARDED *Balance 100.00*						1
2	8	*Typewriter repairs*	56	5 50				2
3	8	*Advertising letters*	57	9 90 / 15 40		9 90 / 9 90		3
4	14	*Repairs on truck*	58	5 80			5 80	4
5	15	*Water bill*	59	9 50				5
6	15	*Shipping tags*	60	6 80				6
7	15	*Carbon paper*	61	2 20				7
8	15	*Painting window sign*	62	7 50				8
13	30	*Express charges*	67	7 35				13
14	30	*Phone call*	68	1 30				14
15				94 55 / 94 55		9 90 / 9 90	5 80 / 5 80	15
16	30	*Balance* 5.45						16
17		*Received in fund* 94.55						17
18		100.00						18
19								19
20								20
21								21
22								22
23								23
24								24
25								25
26								26
27								27
28								28
29								29
30								30
31								31
32								32
33								33
34								34
35								35
36								36
37								37
38								38
39								39
40								40
41								41
42								42

Holling & Renz — Petty Cash Disbursements (Left Page)

FOR MONTH OF *June* 19 ——   PAGE *23*

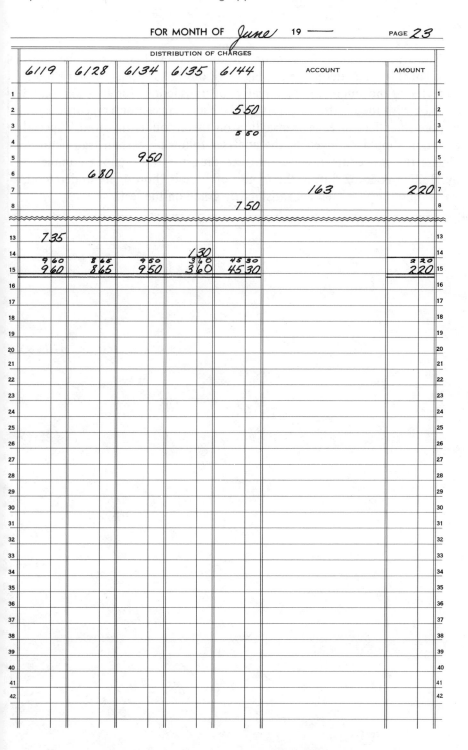

DISTRIBUTION OF CHARGES

	6119	6128	6134	6135	6144	ACCOUNT	AMOUNT	
1								1
2					5 50			2
3					5 50			3
4								4
5			9 50					5
6		6 80						6
7						163	2 20	7
8					7 50			8
13	7 35							13
14				1 30				14
15	9 60	8 65	9 50	3 60	45 30		2 20	15
15	9 60	8 65	9 50	3 60	45 30		2 20	15
16								16
17								17
18								18
19								19
20								20
21								21
22								22
23								23
24								24
25								25
26								26
27								27
28								28
29								29
30								30
31								31
32								32
33								33
34								34
35								35
36								36
37								37
38								38
39								39
40								40
41								41
42								42

Holling & Renz — Petty Cash Disbursements (Right Page)

**Report
No. 17-1**

The study assignments contain an analysis test that should be completed at this time. Before beginning work on the test, this chapter should be reviewed thoroughly. The narrative of transactions for June should be checked with the illustrations to see how each transaction is recorded and to note the effect of each transaction on the accounts involved. Special attention should be given to the analyses following certain transactions. Unless the procedure involved in recording the transactions completed by Holling & Renz during the month of June is thoroughly understood, you cannot hope to make a satisfactory grade on the test.

Chapter 18

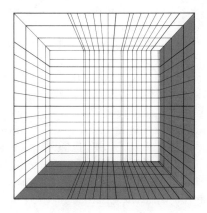

ACCOUNTING PROCEDURE AT END OF YEAR

One of the several reasons for maintaining a set of accounting records is to make it possible to prepare periodic financial reports. At the very least, an income statement for the fiscal year and a balance sheet as of the close of that year are needed. Long experience has shown that one of the fastest ways to produce these statements is **(1)** to use the information provided by the accounts — as reflected by the year-end trial balance taken after the regular posting has been completed, **(2)** to determine the needed adjustments, and **(3)** to bring these amounts together in a manner that facilitates statement preparation. The device most commonly used is the work sheet (or, sometimes, work *sheets*). A work sheet can be described in modern terminology as one means of processing data.

SUMMARY AND SUPPLEMENTARY YEAR-END WORK SHEETS

A simple eight-column work sheet for a personal service enterprise was discussed and illustrated in Chapter 5. A ten-column work sheet for a retail merchandising business was introduced in Chapter 9. Following is a discussion and illustration of a ten-column summary work sheet supplemented by a three-column operating expenses work sheet. The illustrations relate to the firm of Holling & Renz, wholesale distributors of paint and varnish. In the preceding chapter, a partial narrative of transactions for this firm for the month of June, 19— (the last month of the fiscal year) was given. These transactions were shown as recorded in the books of original entry and in certain of the auxiliary records. The books of original entry were reproduced as they would appear after both the individual and the summary posting had been completed. Neither the general ledger accounts nor the accounts in each of the three subsidiary ledgers (accounts receivable, accounts payable, and operating expenses) were reproduced. However, it may be assumed that trial balances of all ledgers were taken, and that everything was found to be in order. That is, the general ledger was found to be in balance, and the total of the account balances in each subsidiary ledger was found to agree with the balance of the related control account in the general ledger.

Summary end-of-year work sheet

This work sheet is reproduced on pages 448 and 449. It is identical in form to that used for Boyd's Clothiers reproduced on pages 230–231. The first step in its preparation was to write the proper heading at the top, to insert the proper headings in the space provided at the top of each of the five pairs of amount columns, and to list the general ledger account titles and numbers in the spaces provided at the left. Note that, with one exception, the title and number of every general ledger account was listed even though certain of the accounts had no balances at the time the trial balance was taken. (Refer to the Chart of Accounts given on page 420 for the complete list.) The one exception was Expense and Revenue Summary, Account No. 331. That account is used in the formal process of adjusting and closing the books, but it is not needed on the work sheet. Note also that in the cases of Cost of Goods Sold — Department A, Account No. 561, and Cost of Goods Sold — Department B, Account No. 571, three lines were allowed in each case to accommodate the several debits and credits that will be involved. (The purpose of each cost of goods sold account is to provide a means of bringing together all the elements that are involved in calculating the amount of this cost: (1) beginning inventory, (2) purchases, (3) purchases returns and allowances, (4) purchases discount, (5) freight in, and (6) ending inventory.)

The account balances were entered in the first pair of columns and these columns were totaled to prove their equality.

Adjustment of the Merchandise Accounts. Eleven entries were made in the adjustments columns on the work sheet to show the calculation of the cost of goods sold for each department and to adjust the merchandise inventory accounts.

Entry (a): The amount of the beginning inventory for Department A, $174,494.10, was transferred to Cost of Goods Sold — Department A by a debit to that account (No. 561) and by a credit to Merchandise Inventory — Department A, Account No. 141.

Entry (b): The amount of the beginning inventory for Department B, $17,380.40, was transferred to Cost of Goods Sold — Department B by a debit to that account (No. 571) and by a credit to Merchandise Inventory — Department B, Account No. 151.

Entry (c): The amount of the purchases for the year for Department A, $569,910.40, was transferred to Cost of Goods Sold — Department A by a debit to that account (No. 561) and by a credit to Purchases — Department A, Account No. 511.

Entry (d): The amount of the purchases for the year for Department B, $61,359.50, was transferred to Cost of Goods Sold — Department B by a debit to that account (No. 571) and by a credit to Purchases — Department B, Account No. 521.

Entry (e): The amount of the purchases returns and allowances for the year for Department A, $2,668.15, was transferred to the proper cost of goods sold account by a debit to Purchases Returns and Allowances — Department A, Account No. 051, and by a credit to Cost of Goods Sold — Department A, Account No. 561.

Entry (f): The amount of the purchases returns and allowances for the year for Department B, $173.95, was transferred to the proper cost of goods sold account by a debit to Purchases Returns and Allowances — Department B, Account No. 052, and by a credit to Cost of Goods Sold — Department B, Account No. 571.

Entry (g): The amount of the purchases discount taken during the year, $10,892.65, was prorated between the cost of goods sold accounts in proportion to the amount of the purchases (less returns and allowances) of the two departments. Purchases (less returns and allowances) of Department A were $567,242.25 ($569,910.40 − $2,668.15). Purchases (less returns and allowances) of Department B were $61,185.65 ($61,359.50 − $173.95). Thus the total purchases (less returns and allowances) amounted to $628,427.90. Of this total, 90.3 percent were those of Department A, and 9.7 percent were those of Department B. Therefore, $9,836.06 was credited to Cost of Goods Sold — Department A, Account No. 561, and $1,056.59 to Cost of Goods Sold — Department B, Account No. 571, with a debit of $10,892.65 to Purchases Discount, Account No. 053.

Entry (h): The amount of the freight in on Department A purchases for the year, $4,590.54, was transferred to Cost of Goods Sold — Department

Holling & King
Work Sheet
For the Year Ended June 30, 19 —

#	Account	Acct. No.	Trial Balance Debit	Trial Balance Credit	Adjustments Debit	Adjustments Credit	Adj. Trial Balance Debit	Adj. Trial Balance Credit	Income Statement Debit	Income Statement Credit	Balance Sheet Debit	Balance Sheet Credit
1	Federal National Bank	111	765419				765419				765419	
2	Petty Cash Fund	112	10000				10000				10000	
3	Government Bonds	121	500000				500000				500000	
4	Accrued Interest Receivable	122			(l) 1250		1250				1250	
5	Accounts Receivable	131	1939510				1939510				1939510	
6	Allowance for Doubtful Accts.	013		1642		(a) 264204		265846				265846
7	Merchandise Inventory - Dept. A	141	1749410		(b) 1836030	(a) 1749410	1836030				1836030	
8	Merchandise Inventory - Dept. B	151	1738040		(b) 2068815	(a) 1738040	2068815				2068815	
9	Store Supplies	161	169874			(b) 153874	16000				16000	
10	Advertising Supplies	162	44783			(a) 29783	15000				15000	
11	Office Supplies	163	167052			(c) 141552	25500				25500	
12	Postage Stamps	164	125832			(c) 122271	3561				3561	
13	Prepaid Insurance	165	120248			(h) 74304	45944				45944	
14	Store Equipment	171	312590				312590				312590	
15	Accum. Deprec. - Store Equip.	017		73148		(h) 31259		104407				104407
16	Delivery Equipment	181	549580				549580				549580	
17	Accum. Deprec. - Delivery Equip.	018		286235		(o) 137395		423630				423630
18	Office Equipment	191	533760				533760				533760	
19	Accum. Deprec. - Office Equip.	019		88960		(p) 46398		135358				135358
20	F.I.C.A. Tax Payable	211		38280				38280				38280
21	F.U.T.C. Tax Payable	221		4788				4788				4788
22	State Unemployment Tax Pay.	231		25842				25842				25842
23	Employees Income Tax Pay.	241		38760				38760				38760
24	Notes Payable	251		450000				450000				450000
25	Accrued Interest Payable	261				(m) 5900		5900				5900
26	Accounts Payable	271		855060				855060				855060
27	J.L. Holling, Capital	311		11432881				11432881				11432881
28	J.L. Holling, Drawing	031	2148615				2148615				2148615	

Account	No.	Trial Balance Dr.	Trial Balance Cr.	Adjustments Dr.	Adjustments Cr.	Income Statement Dr.	Income Statement Cr.	Balance Sheet Dr.	Balance Sheet Cr.
A.S. Renz, Capital	321		7309547						7309547
A.S. Renz, Drawing	032	1613720						1613720	
Sales – Department A	411		73302530				73302530		
Sales Ret. & Allow. – Dept. A	041	1144260				1144260			
Sales – Department B	421		7892120				7892120		
Sales Ret. & Allow. – Dept. B	042	123150				123150			
Sales Discount	043	783528				783528			
Purchases – Department A	511	56991040			(a) 56991040				
Purchases Ret. & Allow. – Dept. A	051		266815	(a) 266815					
Purchases – Department B	521	6135950			(b) 6135950				
Purchases Ret. & Allow. – Dept. B	052		17395	(b) 17395					
Purchases Discount	053		1089265	(a)(b) 1089265					
Freight In – Department A	531	459054			(a) 459054				
Freight In – Department B	551	77158			(b) 77158				
Cost of Goods Sold – Dept. A	561			(a) 7449410 / 56991040 / 459054	(a) 266815 / 983606	55113053			
Cost of Goods Sold – Dept. B	571			(b) 7138040 / 6135950 / 77158	(b) 17395 / 105659	5759279			
Operating Expenses	611	9215195		(ot-X) 1001040		10216235			
Interest Earned	711		16250		(L) 1250		16250		
Interest Expense	811	5000		(L) 5900		10900			
Charitable Contributions Exp.	821	65500				65500			
		103182268	103182268	105837162	105837162	73215905	81210900	29085294	21090299
Net Income						7994925			7994925
						81210900	81210900	29085294	29085294

Holling & Renz — Ten Column Work Sheet

A by a debit to that account (No. 561) and by a credit to Freight In —
Department A, Account No. 541.

Entry (i): The amount of the freight in on Department B purchases for
the year, $771.58, was transferred to Cost of Goods Sold — Department B
by a debit to that account (No. 571) and by a credit to Freight In —
Department B, Account No. 551.

Entry (j): The cost assigned to the June 30 merchandise inventory of
Department A, $185,360.30, was debited to that account (No. 141) with
an offsetting credit to Cost of Goods Sold — Department A, Account
No. 561. Holling & Renz use the first-in, first-out method of accounting for
inventory. A physical count of the goods on hand at the year's end had
been made. Reference to recent purchase invoices provided unit costs for
the various items. (While it would be quite reasonable to slightly reduce
the inventory cost because of purchase discounts taken and to slightly
increase the amount because of freight in, the amounts of both of these are
small in relation to the cost of the goods, and they partially offset each
other. For these reasons, they are ignored in calculating the cost to be assigned to the inventory.) Each time a physical inventory is taken, the quantities found to be on hand are compared with the stock records. The latter
are corrected if any discrepancy is discovered.

Entry (k): The cost assigned to the June 30 merchandise inventory of
Department B, $20,688.15, was debited to that account (No. 151) with an
offsetting credit to Cost of Goods Sold — Department B, Account No. 571.
(The description of the procedure followed in connection with the inventory cost assignment in Department A likewise applies to Department B.)

At this point the amount of the cost of goods sold for each department
was determined by subtracting the sum of the three credits from the sum
of the three debits to each of the cost of goods sold accounts. The amounts,
$551,130.53 for Department A and $57,592.79 for Department B, were
extended to the Adjusted Trial Balance Debit column.

Adjustment of the Interest Accounts. In order to have the calculation
of the net income for the year reflect the correct amounts of both interest
earned and interest expense, accruals of both types had to be taken into
consideration.

On June 30, Holling & Renz owned five $1,000, 6 percent United States
treasury bonds. Semiannual interest totaling $150 had been collected on
June 15. Since that date, interest for 15 days amounting to $12.50 had
accrued.

Entry (l): On the work sheet the accrued interest receivable on June 30,
$12.50, was debited to that account (No. 122) and credited to Interest
Earned, Account No. 711.

Holling & Renz had only one note payable outstanding on June 30. It was a $4,500, 90-day, 8 percent note, dated May 2. On June 30, 59 days' interest amounting to $59 had accrued.

Entry (m): The accrued interest payable was recorded on the work sheet by debiting Interest Expense, Account No. 811, and by crediting Accrued Interest Payable, Account No. 261, for $59. At this point, work on the summary end-of-year work sheet was suspended temporarily.

Supplementary work sheet for operating expenses   To provide the desired information, the income statement that was to be prepared had to be supplemented by a schedule of operating expenses. The accounting records of Holling & Renz include a subsidiary operating expenses ledger which is controlled by the account, Operating Expenses (No. 611), in the general ledger. A considerable number of the operating expense accounts required end-of-year debit adjustments (with, of course, a summary debit to the general ledger control account). These adjustments involved offsetting credits to various general ledger accounts.

In order to assemble all of the information needed both for the income statement and for the supporting schedule of operating expenses, as well as to facilitate the recording of adjustments in the general ledger and subsidiary ledger accounts (which must be done later), an operating expenses work sheet was used. As will be seen, it is very closely tied in with the summary work sheet. This operating expenses work sheet is reproduced on page 452. Note that it was given an appropriate heading that included the period involved. This work sheet needed only three amount columns: (1) to show the account balances when the trial balance was taken, (2) to provide space for certain adjustments, and (3) to show the adjusted amounts. In every case only debits were involved. The titles and numbers of all of the accounts in the subsidiary operating expenses ledger were placed in the columns provided. (Refer to the Chart of Accounts given on page 422 for the complete list.) It will be observed that a considerable number of the accounts had no balance when the trial balance was taken. The balance of each account (that had a balance) was entered in the Trial Balance Debit column. That column was totaled. If its total, $92,151.95, had not agreed with the balance shown for Operating Expenses, Account No. 611 (the control account), on the summary work sheet, it would have been necessary to discover and correct the discrepancy before the preparation of either work sheet could proceed.

All of the adjustments that follow (for depreciation, supplies used, insurance expired, and the doubtful accounts provision) involved both the summary and the supplementary work sheet. One or more operating expense accounts were debited on the operating expenses work sheet, and one or more general ledger accounts were credited on the summary work sheet.

Holling & Renz
Operating Expenses Work Sheet
For the Year Ended June 30, 19—

Account	Acct. No.	Trial Balance Debit	Adjustments Debit	Adj. Trial Bal. Debit
Advertising Expense	6111	323935	(n) 29783	353718
Store Clerks' Salary Expense	6112	1872000		1872000
Truck Drivers' Wage Expense	6113	840000		840000
A. G. Renz, Salary Expense	6114	1800000		1800000
A. G. Renz Traveling Expense	6115	131810		131810
Truck Gas and Oil Expense	6116	158319		158319
Truck Repairs Expense	6117	25755		25755
Garage Rent Expense	6118	36000		36000
Freight Out	6119	2207		2207
Merchandise Insurance Exp.	6121		(u) 35052	35052
Delivery Equip. Insurance Exp.	6122		(u) 28820	28820
Store Equip. Insurance Exp.	6123		(u) 3870	3870
Store Supplies Expense	6124		(s) 153874	153874
Postage Expense (Selling)	6125		(t) 58690	58690
Depreciation of Store Equipment	6126		(w) 31259	31259
Depreciation of Delivery Equip.	6127		(v) 137395	137395
Miscellaneous Selling Expense	6128	28614		28614
Rent Expense	6131	660000		660000
J. L. Holling, Salary Expense	6132	1800000		1800000
Office Salaries Expense	6133	1116000		1116000
Light and Water Expense	6134	14358		14358
Telephone Expense	6135	25128		25128
Uncollectible Accounts Expense	6136		(u) 264204	264204
Property Tax Expense	6137	51635		51635
Office Supplies Expense	6138		(s) 141552	141552
Postage Expense (Administration)	6139		(t) 63581	63581
Office Equip. Insurance Exp.	6141		(u) 6562	6562
Depreciation of Office Equipment	6142		(p) 46398	46398
Payroll Taxes Expense	6143	296880		296880
Miscellaneous General Expense	6144	32554		32554
		9215195	1001040	10216235

Holling & Renz — Operating Expenses Work Sheet

Depreciation Expense. Holling & Renz use the group method of accounting for long-lived assets and their depreciation. In the general ledger, three long-lived asset accounts (with related accumulated depreciation accounts) are kept: store equipment, delivery equipment, and office equipment. In the operating expenses ledger, three depreciation expense accounts (that correspond to the asset classifications) are kept. Depreciation is not considered on assets owned for less than one month. The schedule reproduced below was prepared to determine the estimated depreciation expense for the year.

Based upon the calculations shown on the schedule, the following adjustments were made on the work sheets — the debits on the operating expenses work sheet and the credits on the summary work sheet:

Entry (n): Depreciation of Store Equipment, Account No. 6126, was debited, and Accumulated Depreciation — Store Equipment, Account No. 017, was credited for $312.59.

SCHEDULE OF DEPRECIATION EXPENSE
FOR THE YEAR ENDED JUNE 30, 19—

ASSET	COST	ANNUAL (STRAIGHT-LINE) RATE OF DEPRECIATION	DEPRECIATION FOR THE YEAR
Store Equipment	$3,125.90	10%	$ 312.59
Delivery Equipment	5,495.80	25	1,373.95
Office Equipment	4,639.75*	10	463.98

*It may be noted that the balance of the office equipment account shown on the work sheet on page 448 is $5,337.60. That is because the costs of a desk calculator purchased on June 9 and of a checkwriter purchased on June 30 are included. However, since those assets have been owned for less than one month, no depreciation is taken on them.

Entry (o): Depreciation of Delivery Equipment, Account No. 6127, was debited, and Accumulated Depreciation — Delivery Equipment, Account No. 018, was credited for $1,373.95.

Entry (p): Depreciation of Office Equipment, Account No. 6142, was debited, and Accumulated Depreciation — Office Equipment, Account No. 019, was credited for $463.98.

Supplies Expense. The general ledger of Holling & Renz includes four asset accounts for supplies — store supplies, advertising supplies, office supplies, and postage stamps. When purchased, the supplies are recorded as assets. An inventory of unused supplies (and postage stamps) is taken at the end of the year so that the cost of the supplies used can be calculated and charged to the proper operating expense accounts. The following schedule was prepared to determine the needed adjustments. (Note that with the exception of postage stamps, which were based on an exact count, the amounts shown for each of the three other types of supplies were "round amounts" determined by count of unopened packages and boxes of the affected items which were assigned approximate costs of recent purchases of such supplies.)

SCHEDULE OF SUPPLIES USED

FOR THE YEAR ENDED JUNE 30, 19--

ASSET	ACCOUNT BALANCE JUNE 30, 19--	AMOUNT ON HAND JUNE 30, 19--	EXPENSE FOR YEAR
Store Supplies	$1,698.74	$160.00	$1,538.74
Advertising Supplies	447.83	150.00	297.83
Office Supplies	1,670.52	255.00	1,415.52
Postage Stamps	1,258.32	35.61	1,222.71*

*Memorandum records kept by the shipping clerk indicate that $586.90 should be treated as a selling expense and the remainder, $635.81, as an administrative expense.

Based upon the calculation, the following adjustments were made on the work sheets:

Entry (q): Store Supplies Expense, Account No. 6124, was debited, and Store Supplies, Account No. 161, was credited for $1,538.74.

Entry (r): Advertising Expense, Account No. 6111, was debited, and Advertising Supplies, Account No. 162, was credited for $297.83.

Entry (s): Office Supplies Expense, Account No. 6138, was debited, and Office Supplies, Account No. 163, was credited for $1,415.52.

Entry (t): Postage Expense (Selling), Account No. 6125, was debited for $586.90; Postage Expense (Administration), Account No. 6139, was debited for $635.81; and Postage Stamps, Account No. 164, was credited for $1,222.71.

Insurance Expense. Prepaid insurance premiums are recorded by Holling & Renz in the same manner as supplies. At the time of payment of a premium, the amount paid is recorded as an asset. The prepaid insurance account (No. 165) in the general ledger is debited. At the end of the fiscal year, June 30, calculations are made to determine the fraction of the total term of each policy that has elapsed during the year. That fraction of the original premium is an expense of the year. Each such amount is classified according to the type of asset insured to determine the proper total amount to be charged to each insurance expense account. The operating expenses ledger of Holling & Renz includes insurance expense accounts for the insurance on merchandise, the delivery truck, store equipment, and office equipment.

The summary of insurance expense on page 455 was prepared from a file of information relating to insurance policies.

SCHEDULE OF INSURANCE EXPENSE

FOR THE YEAR ENDED JUNE 30, 19--

Type of Property Insured	Expense for Year
Merchandise..	$350.52
Delivery Truck.......................................	288.20
Store Equipment......................................	38.70
Office Equipment.....................................	65.62
Total...	$743.04

Based upon this summary, the following adjustment was made on the work sheets:

Entry (u): Merchandise Insurance Expense, Account No. 6121, was debited for $350.52; Delivery Equipment Insurance Expense, Account No. 6122, was debited for $288.20; Store Equipment Insurance Expense, Account No. 6123, was debited for $38.70; Office Equipment Insurance Expense, Account No. 6141, was debited for $65.62; and Prepaid Insurance, Account No. 165, was credited for $743.04.

Doubtful Accounts. Holling & Renz use the allowance method of accounting for doubtful accounts. Past experience indicates that accounts that have turned out to be uncollectible averaged ½ of 1 percent of sales on account. For the year ended June 30, 19--, sales on account totaled $528,407.30. One half of one percent of this amount is $2,642.04. The following entry was made on the work sheets:

Entry (v): Uncollectible Accounts Expense, Account No. 6136, was debited, and Allowance for Doubtful Accounts, Account No. 013, was credited for $2,642.04.

Completing the operating expenses work sheet

It will be noted that only one of the thirteen debits in the Adjustments column of this work sheet had to be added to a previous debit balance in the account — the $297.83 debit to Advertising Expense, Account No. 6111. This was added to the $3,239.35 shown in the Trial Balance column, and their sum, $3,537.18, was extended into the Adjusted Trial Balance column. In every other case, either the unadjusted amount or the amount of the adjustment was extended into the last column.

The Adjustments and Adjusted Trial Balance columns were totaled. Since only debits were involved in this work sheet, the total of the Adjusted Trial Balance column, $102,162.35, had to be equal to the sum of the totals of the first two columns ($92,151.95 + $10,010.40).

A double rule was made below the three totals.

Completing the summary work sheet   To complete the adjustments on the summary work sheet, the balance of the control account for operating expenses had to be increased to reflect the total of all of the debits to the operating expenses that had been made on the supplementary work sheet. Accordingly, that total, $10,010.40, was entered on the line for Operating Expenses, Account No. 611, in the Adjustments Debit Column. Note that the debit was identified as "(n–v)," since it was offset by credits to nine general ledger accounts made when adjustments (n) through (v) were entered on the work sheets to adjust the operating expense accounts.

The Adjustments columns were totaled to prove their equality. The amounts in the Trial Balance columns, altered where indicated by amounts in the Adjustments columns, were extended to the Adjusted Trial Balance columns. The latter were totaled to prove their equality. Each amount in the Adjusted Trial Balance columns was extended to the proper Income Statement or Balance Sheet column. The last four columns were totaled. It was found that the Income Statement Credit column exceeded the Debit column by $79,949.95, and that the Balance Sheet Debit column exceeded the Credit column by the same amount. "Net Income" was written on the next line at the left, and the amount was placed in the two proper places. The Income Statement and Balance Sheet columns were totaled to prove that each pair was in balance. Double rules were made below the final totals in all ten columns.

The summary work sheet then could be used to prepare the income statement for the fiscal year (shown on page 467) and the balance sheet as of the last day of that year (shown on page 471). The supplementary work sheet provided the information for the schedule of operating expenses (shown on page 469).

Report No. 18-1

Complete Report No. 18-1 in the study assignments. Do not submit the report at this time. Since Reports Nos. 18-1 and 18-2 are related, you should retain the working papers until you have completed both reports. Continue with the textbook discussion until Report No. 18-2 is required.

ADJUSTING, CLOSING, AND REVERSING ENTRIES

The most important function of the end-of-year work sheet (or work sheets) is to facilitate the preparation of the income statement and the balance sheet as soon as possible after the end of the accounting period. Having completed the work sheets illustrated and discussed in the preceding pages, the accountant for Holling & Renz would next prepare the financial statements. A secondary function of the work sheets is to aid in the process of formally recording the adjusting and closing entries in the books. However, for the purpose of organization of subject matter in this textbook, adjusting, closing, and reversing entries will be considered next. The financial statements will be illustrated and discussed in Chapter 19.

Journalizing the adjusting entries

The adjusting entries had to be recorded in the general journal. The page of the general journal containing the adjusting entries as of June 30, 19--, is reproduced on page 458. In the form of general journal used by Holling & Renz, a special Debit column is provided for charges to the accounts in the operating expenses subsidiary ledger. Journalizing the adjusting entries involved the use of this column as well as the General Ledger Debit and Credit columns. Several features of these entries should be noted: **(1)** The titles of the accounts involved appear only as a part of the explanation of the entries. The identification of the accounts was accomplished by entering the account numbers in the space provided for this purpose when the journalizing was done, *not* as a step in the posting. **(2)** The entries are made in the same order as shown alphabetically, (a) through (v), on the work sheets (pages 448, 449, and 452). While this order was not essential, the danger of omitting an entry was slightly reduced by using the work sheets as a guide in journalizing the entries. **(3)** In order to be sure that the total of the debits equaled the total of the credits, and because the total of the Operating Expenses Debit column had to be posted, the three columns were footed, the totals were entered, and the usual rulings were made.

Posting the adjusting entries

As the individual amounts in the General Ledger Debit and Credit columns were posted to the accounts (indicated by the account numbers), a check mark (√) was made to the right of each amount in the column provided. A check mark was made in parentheses below the total of each of those two columns to indicate that, in this case, the amount was *not* posted anywhere. In the case of the entries in the Operating Expenses Debit column, a check mark was placed to the right of each amount as it was posted. The number "611" was placed in parentheses below the total of that column to indicate that the amount, $10,010.40, was posted as a debit to Operating Expenses, Account No. 611, in the general ledger. In both the general ledger and the operating expenses ledger, the page of

GENERAL JOURNAL FOR MONTH OF *June* 19——   PAGE 44

DEBIT — OPERATING EXPENSES			DEBIT — ACCTS. PAY.	DEBIT — GENERAL LEDGER			DAY	DESCRIPTION	CREDIT — GENERAL LEDGER			CREDIT — ACCTS. PAY.	CREDIT — ACCTS. REC.
ACCT. NO.	AMOUNT	√	√	ACCT. NO.	AMOUNT	√	√		ACCT. NO.	AMOUNT	√	√	√
							30	*Adjusting Entries*					
				561	1744940	√		To Transfer Beg. Inv. to Cost of Goods Sold - Depts. A and B	141	1744940			
				571	1738040	√		of Goods Sold - Depts. A and B	151	1738040			
				561	5699040	√		To Transfer purchases to Cost of Goods Sold - Depts. A and B	511	5699040			
				571	6135950	√		of Goods Sold - Depts. A and B	521	6135950			
				051	2668.15	√		To Transfer pur. ret. & allow. to	561	2668.15			
				052	17395	√		Cost of Goods Sold - Depts. A and B	571	17395			
				053	1089265	√		To allocate pur. disc. to Cost	561	983606			
								of Goods Sold - Depts. A and B	571	105659			
				561	459054	√		To Transfer freight-in to Cost	541	459054			
				571	77158	√		of Goods Sold - Depts. A and B	555	77158			
				141	18536030	√		To record ending inventory	561	18536030			
				151	2068815	√		Depts. A and B	571	2068815			
				122	1250	√		Accrued interest receivable	711	1250			
				811	5900	√		Accrued interest payable	261	5900			
617	31259							Depr. of store equipment	017	31259			
627	137395							Depr. of delivery equipment	018	137395			
642	46398							Depr. of office equipment	019	46398			
624	153874							Store supplies used	161	153874			
611	29783							Advertising supplies used	162	29783			
638	141552							Office supplies used	163	141552			
625	58690							Postage stamps used	164	12227			
639	6358												
631	36052							Insurance expired	165	74304			
622	28820												
623	3870												
644	6562												
636	264204							Provision for doubtful accts.	013	264204			
	1058361.22				1058361.22					1058361.22			
	1001040				1048361.22	(√)				1058357.162	(√)		
	(611)												

Holling & Renz — Adjusting Entries

the general journal (G44) was placed in the Posting Reference column as each posting was made.

Journalizing the closing entries

The page of the general journal showing the closing entries as of June 30, 19--, is reproduced on page 460. Certain features of these entries should be noted: **(1)** Each closing entry was made in conventional form — the names of the accounts both to be debited and to be credited were given. The names of the accounts to be credited were slightly indented. As in the case of the adjusting entries, however, the numbers of the accounts were entered at the time of journalizing. The check marks were made later as the posting was completed. **(2)** The order of the closing entries follows a logical sequence. The revenue accounts are closed first, followed by the expense accounts. The third entry closes the expense and revenue summary account by dividing the income ($79,949.95) between T. L. Holling and A. G. Renz in a 60-40 ratio as their partnership agreement specifies. The last two closing entries transfer the amount of each partner's withdrawals to his capital account. The amount columns were footed to prove the equality of the debits and credits.

It should be noted that, while there was a credit of $102,162.35 to close Operating Expenses, Account No. 611, the individual credits to close the thirty accounts in the operating expenses subsidiary ledger were not shown. One reason is that the form of the journal page does not accommodate credits to the operating expenses accounts, because these accounts rarely are credited (except when they are closed). The occasional transaction that requires a credit to an operating expense account can be handled by noting *both* the number of the control account (611) and the number of the subsidiary ledger account in the account number column provided just to the left of the General Ledger Credit column. The amount of the credit will then be posted as a credit to both accounts. It must be understood, however, that the operating expense accounts in the subsidiary ledger *must be closed.* The manner of doing so is illustrated by the reproduction of the account for Advertising Expense, Account No. 6111, shown on page 461. The accountant knows that when a general ledger control account is closed, all accounts in a ledger that is subsidiary to that control account also must be closed. Knowing this, the space and time required to list all of the subsidiary ledger accounts, numbers, and balances (thirty in the case at hand) is not warranted.

Posting the closing entries

The postings were made to the general ledger accounts indicated. A check mark was placed in the column provided in the general journal as each posting was made. The page of the general journal (G 45) was noted

GENERAL JOURNAL FOR MONTH OF _June_ 19——   PAGE 45

OPERATING EXPENSES ACCT. NO.	OPERATING EXPENSES AMOUNT	DEBIT GENERAL LEDGER ACCT. NO.	DEBIT GENERAL LEDGER AMOUNT	DEBIT ACCOUNTS PAYABLE	DAY	DESCRIPTION	CREDIT GENERAL LEDGER ACCT. NO.	CREDIT GENERAL LEDGER AMOUNT	CREDIT ACCOUNTS PAYABLE	CREDIT ACCOUNTS RECEIVABLE
						AMOUNTS FORWARDED				
					30	Closing Entries				
		411	7330 25 30			Sales — Department A				
		421	789 21 20			Sales — Department B				
		711	1 62 50			Interest Earned				
						Expense & Revenue Summary	331	8121 09 00		
		331	7321 59 05			Expense & Revenue Summary				
						Sales R. and A. — Dept. A	041	114 42 40		
						Sales R. and A. — Dept. B	042	12 31 70		
						Sales Discount	043	78 35 28		
						Cost of Goods Sold — Dept. A	561	5511 30 53		
						Cost of Goods Sold — Dept. B	571	575 92 79		
						Operating Expenses	611	1021 62 35		
						Interest Expense	811	1 09 00		
						Charitable Cont. Expense	821	6 55 00		
		331	799 49 25			Expense & Revenue Summary				
						J.L. Holling, Capital	311	479 69 97		
						A.G. Renz, Capital	321	319 79 98		
		311	21 48 61 5			J.L. Holling, Capital				
						J.L. Holling, Drawing	031	21 48 61 5		
		321	16 13 72 0			A.G. Renz, Capital				
						A.G. Renz, Drawing	032	16 13 72 0		
			166 18 41 35					166 18 41 35		
			(✓)					(✓)		

Holling & Renz — Closing Entries

in the Posting Reference column of the account involved. As mentioned in the preceding paragraph, the balance of each account in the subsidiary operating expenses ledger was closed in the manner indicated by the entry on the last line of the illustration of the account for Advertising Expense shown below. (Note that "G 45" was entered in the Posting Reference column, since that is the page of the general journal that called for the closing entry in the operating expenses control account.) The other twenty-nine operating expense accounts were closed in a similar fashion.

ACCOUNT *Advertising Expense*   ACCOUNT NO. *6111*

DATE	ITEM	POST REF.	DEBIT	CREDIT	BALANCE	
June 1	Dr. Balance	✓			3209 85	1
10		CD 77	19 60		3229 45	2
30		CD 78	9 90		3239 35	3
30		G 44	297 83		3537 18	4
30		G 45		3537 18	—O—	5
						6
						7
						8
						9
						10
						11
						12

Closed Subsidiary Operating Expense Ledger Account

The expense and revenue summary account and the two cost of goods sold accounts after the adjusting and closing entries had been posted are reproduced on page 462. Remember that all three of these accounts are summarizing accounts that are used only at the end of the accounting period. (In some accounting systems, cost of goods sold accounts are used throughout the year, if such cost is known at the time of sale. This is possible if so-called *perpetual inventories* are maintained. While Holling & Renz keep stock records, these records show physical quantities only. In the accounting system of Holling & Renz, the cost of goods sold accounts are used only at the end of the fiscal year.)

Post-closing trial balance   After the closing entries were posted, a trial balance of the general ledger accounts that remained open was taken to prove the equality of the debit and credit balances. This post-closing trial balance of the general ledger of Holling & Renz is reproduced on page 463.

ACCOUNT *Expense and Revenue Summary*   ACCOUNT NO. *331*

DATE	ITEM	POST. REF.	DEBIT	CREDIT	BALANCE DEBIT	BALANCE CREDIT
19-- June 30		J45		8121 09 00		
30		J45	7321 59 05			7994995
30	To Close	J45	7994995		—0—	—0—

ACCOUNT *Cost of Goods Sold—Department A*   ACCOUNT NO. *561*

DATE	ITEM	POST. REF.	DEBIT	CREDIT	BALANCE DEBIT	BALANCE CREDIT
19-- June 30	Beg. Inventory	J44	1744 9410			
30	Purchases	J44	5699 1040			
30	Purchases R+A	J44		2668 15		
30	Purchases Disc.	J44		9836 06		
30	Freight In	J44	4590 54			
30	End. Inventory	J44		1853 6030	5511 3053	
30	Exp. + Rev. Summary	J45		5511 3053	—0—	—0—

ACCOUNT *Cost of Goods Sold—Department B*   ACCOUNT NO. *571*

DATE	ITEM	POST. REF.	DEBIT	CREDIT	BALANCE DEBIT	BALANCE CREDIT
19-- June 30	Beg. Inventory	J44	1738 040			
30	Purchases	J44	6135 950			
30	Purchases R+A	J44		173 95		
30	Purchases Disc.	J44		1056 59		
30	Freight In	J44	771 58			
30	End. Inventory	J44		2068 815	5759 279	
30	Exp. + Rev. Summary	J45		5759 279	—0—	—0—

Closed General Ledger Summary Accounts

Holling & Renz
Post Closing Trial Balance
June 30, 19--

Account	Acct. No.	Dr. Balance	Cr. Balance
Federal National Bank	111	765419	
Petty Cash Fund	112	10000	
Government Bonds	121	500000	
Accrued Interest Receivable	122	1250	
Accounts Receivable	131	1939510	
Allowance for Doubtful Accounts	013		265846
Merchandise Inventory-Department A	141	1853630	
Merchandise Inventory-Department B	151	2068815	
Store Supplies	161	16000	
Advertising Supplies	162	15000	
Office Supplies	163	25500	
Postage Stamps	164	3561	
Prepaid Insurance	165	45944	
Store Equipment	171	312590	
Accumulated Depreciation-Store Equip.	017		104407
Delivery Equipment	181	549580	
Accumulated Depreciation-Del. Equip.	018		423630
Office Equipment	191	533760	
Accumulated Depreciation-Office Equip.	019		135358
F I C A Tax Payable	211		38280
F U T A Tax Payable	221		4788
State Unemployment Tax Payable	231		25842
Employees Income Tax Payable	241		38760
Notes Payable	251		450000
Accrued Interest Payable	261		5000
Accounts Payable	271		855060
T. L. Holling, Capital	311		1408 1263
A. G. Renz, Capital	321		8893825
		25322959	25322959

Holling & Renz — Post Closing Trial Balance

Not all accountants feel that it is necessary to prepare a post-closing trial balance in the form illustrated. Some think that it is sufficient merely to use an adding machine tape to list and total **(1)** the amounts of the debit balances and **(2)** the amounts of the credit balances to be sure that the totals are the same. If this proves to be the case, the tapes usually are thrown away. (The cause of any discrepancy would have to be located and remedied if the ledger was found not to be in balance). However, many accountants feel that it is desirable to prepare the post-closing trial balance in the form illustrated and file it with various other records.

Reversing entries

Two adjusting entries of the "accrual type" had been made as of June 30, 19—. One was for accrued interest receivable ($12.50), and the other for accrued interest payable ($59). In order that interest collections and payments may be handled in routine fashion in the new period, the accountant for Holling & Renz follows the practice of reversing accrual adjustments. A reproduction of part of the first page of the general journal

GENERAL JOURNAL FOR MONTH OF   *July*   19 ——

GENERAL LEDGER			DAY	DESCRIPTION	GENERAL LEDGER		
ACCT. NO.	AMOUNT	√			ACCT. NO.	AMOUNT	√
				AMOUNTS FORWARDED			
711	1250	√	1	*To reverse adjusting entries*	122	1250	
261	5900	√		*for accrued interest*	811	5900	

Holling & Renz — Reversing Entries

for the next month (July, 19—, the first month of the next fiscal year) is given below. The first entries for the new period are the reversals of the previous accrual adjustments.

Report No. 18-2

Complete Report No. 18-2 in the study assignments and submit Reports Nos. 18-1 and 18-2 for approval. Continue with the textbook discussion in Chapter 19 until Report No. 19-1 is required.

Chapter 19

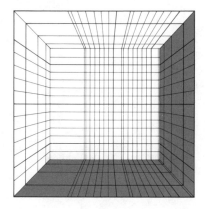

THE ANNUAL REPORT

The term *annual report* as applied to a business usually refers to the financial statements and schedules relating to the accounting (fiscal) year of the enterprise. The report generally includes an income statement, a balance sheet, and a statement of changes in financial position. The nature and preparation of the last-mentioned statement is discussed and illustrated later in this chapter. In the case of business corporations with many stockholders (thousands, even hundreds of thousands, in some cases), the annual report may be a thirty- to forty-page printed publication — sometimes in full color with numerous pictures of the company's products, plants, officers, and various graphs and statistics in addition to the financial statements. In reports of this type, it is customary to include a letter addressed to the stockholders signed by the president of the corporation and, sometimes, by the chairman of the board of directors also. The letter is printed in the report booklet and constitutes a verbal report — often described as "highlights" of the year. Such annual reports invariably include a reproduction of the *opinion* (sometimes referred to as the *Auditor's Report*) of the CPA firm that performed the audit.

Annual reports of the elaborate type just mentioned are not used if the business has few owners. In the case of a partnership, it is probable that no one other than the partners and, possibly, one or two of the officials at their bank will ever see their reports. The annual report of Holling & Renz consists of the following statements and schedules:

Income Statement for the Year
   Schedule of Cost of Goods Sold
   Schedule of Operating Expenses

Balance Sheet as of June 30
   Schedule of Accounts Receivable
   Schedule of Accounts Payable

Statement of Changes in Financial Position for the Year
   Schedule of Changes in Working Capital

THE INCOME STATEMENT

The income statement and schedule of cost of goods sold for the year ended June 30, 19--, are reproduced on pages 467 and 468. They were prepared from information provided by the Income Statement columns of the work sheet reproduced on pages 448 and 449. The income statement was arranged to show the sales, cost of goods sold, and the gross margin on sales for each department as well as in total. The manner of handling sales discounts should be noted: The amount of sales discounts taken by customers during the year, $7,835, had been recorded in one account (Sales Discount, No. 043). In preparing the income statement, the amount was allocated to the two departments in proportion to the sales less sales returns of each department. In the case of Department A, the amount is $721,583 ($733,025 − $11,442). For Department B, it is $77,689 ($78,921 − $1,232). The total is, accordingly, $799,272. Sales of Department A were 90.28 percent of the total and those of Department B, 9.72 percent. The amount of the sales discount was allocated in this proportion, that is, $7,073 to Department A and $762 to Department B. The schedule of cost of goods sold shows the components that entered into the cost for each department and the total.

The schedule of operating expenses reproduced on page 469 was prepared from information provided by the operating expenses work sheet shown on page 452. It should be evident that the purpose of the schedule is to provide the detail of what makes up the total amount of operating expenses ($102,162) shown on the income statement. If there had been only ten or twelve accounts for operating expenses it is probable that (1) there would have been no subsidiary ledger for them and (2) the comparatively few items would have been included in the income statement — no schedule would have been needed. It must be understood that there is wide variation in the form and content of financial statements. Some accountants, for example, might have thought that it would have been better to show the components of cost of goods sold in the income statement instead of in the "supporting" schedule.

HOLLING & RENZ

Income Statement

For the Year Ended June 30, 19--

	Dept. A	Dept. B	Total
Sales...............................	$733,025	$ 78,921	$811,946
Less: Sales returns and allowances...	(11,442)	(1,232)	(12,674)
Sales discounts................	(7,073)	(762)	(7,835)
Net sales.............................	$714,510	$ 76,927	$791,437
Cost of goods sold....................	551,131	57,593	608,724
Gross margin on sales.................	$163,379	$ 19,334	$182,713
Operating expenses....................			102,162
Operating income......................			$ 80,551
Other revenue:			
Interest earned.....................			163
			$ 80,714
Other expenses:			
Interest expense....................			(109)
Charitable contributions expense.....			(655)
Net income............................			$ 79,950

Holling & Renz — Income Statement

Interpreting the income statement: percentage analysis

In order of importance, the most significant items shown by the annual income statement are the total amounts of (1) net income, (2) sales, (3) cost of goods sold and gross margin (taken together because of their interrelationship), and (4) operating expenses. The dollar amounts take on added meaning if their proportionate relationship to each other is computed. The customary way of expressing this is to consider net sales ($791,437) to be the base, 100 percent. Cost of goods sold ($608,724) is, then, 76.9 percent of net sales and gross margin, 23.1 percent. Operating expenses equal 12.9 percent of net sales and operating income equals 10.2 percent of net sales. When the relatively minor amounts of other revenue and other expenses are considered, net income is just slightly more than 10 percent of net sales. Each dollar of net sales resulted in ten cents of net profit.

HOLLING & RENZ

Schedule of Cost of Goods Sold

For the Year Ended June 30, 19--

	Dept. A	Dept. B	Total
Merchandise inventory, July 1, 19--....	$174,494	$ 17,380	$191,874
Purchases.............................	$569,910	$ 61,360	$631,270
Less: Purchases returns and allowances..................	(2,668)	(174)	(2,842)
Purchases discounts...........	(9,836)	(1,057)	(10,893)
Net purchases.........................	$557,406	$ 60,129	$617,535
Freight in...........................	4,591	772	5,363
Delivered cost of purchases...........	$561,997	$ 60,901	$622,898
Merchandise available for sale.........	$736,491	$ 78,281	$814,772
Less Merchandise inv., June 30, 19--.	185,360	20,688	206,048
Cost of goods sold...................	$551,131	$ 57,593	$608,724

Holling & Renz — Schedule of Cost of Goods Sold

The same type of analysis can be applied to the data for the net sales, cost of goods sold, and gross margin of each department. For example, considering net sales for each department as the base (100 percent), gross margin was 22.9 percent of the net sales of Department A and 25.1 percent in the case of Department B.

Merchandise turnover; comparative analysis

The data reported in the income statement make it possible to compute the *turnover* of merchandise during the year. For the business as a whole, the average inventory was $198,961 (beginning inventory, $191,874, plus ending inventory, $206,048, divided by two). Since the total cost of goods sold was $608,724, the turnover was slightly more than 3 times ($608,724 ÷ $198,961). This means that, on the average, goods remained in stock for almost four months. Making the same type of calculation for each department reveals that the turnover in Department A was 3.063, and in Department B, 3.026.

Added meaning is given to the information supplied by an income statement if it is compared with statements for past periods. In this way answers will be provided to such vital questions as: Are sales growing or shrinking? How much has net income increased or decreased (both absolutely and relatively)? Has the gross margin percentage become larger or smaller? It may be assumed that the first thing that each partner did after looking at the income statement for the year just ended was to compare it with the statement for the preceding year — probably for several preceding years. Often, income statements and other financial statements are prepared in comparative form to aid in their interpretation.

HOLLING & RENZ
Schedule of Operating Expenses
For the Year Ended June 30, 19—

Selling expenses:

Advertising expense..	$ 3,537
Store clerks salary expense..............................	18,720
Truck drivers wage expense..............................	8,400
A. G. Renz, salary expense..............................	18,000
A. G. Renz, traveling expense..........................	1,318
Truck, gas, and oil expense............................	1,583
Truck repairs expense..................................	258
Garage rent expense....................................	360
Freight out..	22
Merchandise insurance expense..........................	350
Delivery equipment insurance expense...................	288
Store equipment insurance expense......................	39
Store supplies expense.................................	1,539
Posting expense (selling)..............................	587
Depreciation of store equipment........................	313
Depreciation of delivery equipment.....................	1,374
Miscellaneous selling expense..........................	286
Total selling expenses.............................	$ 56,974

Administrative expenses:

Rent expense...	$ 6,600
T. L. Holling, salary expense..........................	18,000
Office salaries expense................................	11,160
Light and water expense................................	144
Telephone expense......................................	251
Uncollectible accounts expense.........................	2,642
Property tax expense...................................	516
Office supplies expense................................	1,415
Postage expense (administration).......................	636
Office equipment insurance expense.....................	66
Depreciation of office equipment.......................	464
Payroll taxes expense..................................	2,969
Miscellaneous general expense..........................	325
Total administrative expenses......................	$ 45,188
Total operating expenses...............................	$102,162

Holling & Renz — Schedule of Operating Expenses

Rounded Amounts in Statements and Schedules. All of the amounts in the foregoing income statement and the two schedules were "rounded" to the nearest dollar. This widespread practice will be illustrated in all of the financial statements that follow. The rule for rounding is: If the cents in the amount are 50 or more, raise the first figure to the left of the decimal by one. If the cents in the amounts are 49 or less, drop them. Thus, $23.62 would be rounded to $24; $23.35 would be rounded to $23.

Very often, the cents that are added in rounding up some of the amounts are largely offset by the cents that are dropped in rounding down other amounts. If this is the case, the rounded total of a column of figures will be the same as the total of the amounts after each has been rounded. Sometimes there will be a discrepancy of a dollar or two — rarely more than that. This is a nuisance if the total amount appears in one statement and the details appear in a supporting schedule. For example, suppose that the income statement showed Operating Expenses to be $14,562 (which, before rounding, was $14,562.47). In the schedule of operating expenses each amount was rounded and their total was found to be $14,563. While a footnote could be used to explain that there was a $1 discrepancy due to rounding, most accountants would merely lower by $1 one of the amounts in the list (probably the amount of miscellaneous expense) so that there would be no discrepancy. The doctrine of materiality allows such trivial "plugging" of the figures.

**Report
No. 19-1**

> Complete Report No. 19-1 in the study assignments. Do not submit the report at this time. Since Reports Nos. 19-1, 19-2, and 19-3 are related, you should retain the working papers until you have completed all three reports. Continue with the textbook discussion until Report No. 19-2 is required.

THE BALANCE SHEET

The balance sheet of Holling & Renz as of June 30, 19--, is reproduced on page 471. It was prepared from information provided by the Balance Sheet columns of the work sheet reproduced on pages 448 and 449. The statement was arranged in "report form" since the data could be arranged better in that fashion on the page. In the asset section, the conventional practice of placing the current assets at the top was followed. The current assets were arrayed in their probable order of liquidity. Government bonds were shown just below cash since these bonds are regarded as temporary investments which can be liquidated readily if a shortage of cash should occur. Receivables — accrued interest and accounts (less the allowance for doubtful accounts) — logically followed. The inventories of merchandise (in terms of dollar amount, by far the most important assets of the firm) were shown last, except for a small amount of supplies and prepayments. These latter items are included as current assets because the fact that they are now owned means that less money will have to be spent for such purposes in the near future. It is not expected that these

items will be directly converted into cash. The long-lived assets of Holling
& Renz are shown last arrayed in columnar form (not illustrated before).

HOLLING & RENZ
Balance Sheet
June 30, 19--

Assets

Current assets:

Cash..........................		$ 7,754	
Government bonds..............		5,000	
Accrued interest receivable...		13	
Accounts receivable..........	$ 19,395		
Less allowance for doubtful accounts.................	2,658	16,737	

Merchandise inventories:

Department A................	$185,360		
Department B................	20,688	206,048	
Supplies and prepayments......		1,060	
Total current assets........			$236,612

Long-lived assets:

	Cost	Accum. Depr.	Undepr. Cost	
Store equipment...............	$ 3,126	$1,044	$2,082	
Delivery equipment...........	5,496	4,236	1,260	
Office equipment..............	5,338	1,354	3,984	
Total long-lived assets.....	$13,960	$6,634		7,326
Total assets...................				$243,938

Liabilities

Current liabilities:

Notes payable................	$4,500	
Accrued interest payable......	59	
Accounts payable.............	8,551	
Accrued and withheld payroll taxes.....................	1,077	
Total current liabilities...		$ 14,187

Owners' Equity

	T. L. Holling	A. G. Renz	
Capital, July 1, 19--..........	$114,329	$73,095	
Net income ($79,950, divided 60% - 40%)................	47,970	31,980	
Less withdrawals............	(21,486)	(16,137)	
Capital, June 30, 19--........	$140,813	$88,938	229,751
Total liabilities and owners' equity.....................			$243,938

Holling & Renz — Balance Sheet

The liabilities of the firm are all of the current variety. The owners' equity section is arranged to show the nature and amount of the change in each partner's equity during the year.

The balance sheet is supported by schedules of accounts receivable and of accounts payable as of June 30, 19--. These schedules, reproduced below, are really just trial balances (with all amounts rounded to the nearest dollar) of the subsidiary accounts receivable and accounts payable ledgers as of the close of the year.

HOLLING & RENZ

Schedule of Accounts Receivable

June 30, 19--

Atlas Hardware..	$ 544
Baden Paint Co..	470
Beyers Lumber Co..	978
Branneky & Sons...	2,921
Brod—Dugan Co...	4,953
County Lumber Co..	1,185
Don V. Davis..	624
Famous—Barr Company.....................................	2,619
Hoffman Paint Co..	258
Kaplan Lumber Co..	1,484
Joe Miller Lumber Co....................................	105
Morris Hardware...	127
St. John Hardware.......................................	1,240
United Lumber Co..	62
Warson Village Hardware.................................	1,067
Wittenberg Lumber Co....................................	758
	$19,395

Holling & Renz — Schedule of Accounts Receivable

HOLLING & RENZ

Schedule of Accounts Payable

June 30, 19--

Celucoat Corporation....................................	$5,109
Glidden Company...	724
Morris Paper Co...	43
Office Equipment Co.....................................	693
Phelan—Faust Paint Manufacturing Co.....................	620
Sunbrite Supply Co......................................	69
U.S. Paint Co...	1,141
Vane—Calvert Paint Co...................................	152
	$8,551

Holling & Renz — Schedule of Accounts Payable

Interpreting the balance sheet

One use of the balance sheet is to aid in judging the *current position* of a business — that is, the ability of the enterprise to pay its debts promptly. Not only the relative amounts of current assets and current liabilities, but the composition of these resources and obligations must be considered. The ratio of the current assets ($236,612) to current liabilities ($14,187) is almost 17 to 1. This is very good, but of equal or greater significance is the fact that the "quick" assets (cash, temporary investments, and current receivables) total $29,504 — more than twice the current liabilities. This indicates that the firm more than passes the *acid test* (a ratio of quick current assets to total current liabilities of at least 1 to 1).

It must be remembered that the *undepreciated cost* of the long-lived assets (the difference between the cost of these assets and the depreciation so far charged off as an expense), does not indicate what those assets would bring if they were sold. They are not expected to be sold. The difference ($7,326, in total) represents the amount, less any expected scrap or salvage value, that is to be charged against future revenues.

As in the case of income statements, a comparison of current and past balance sheets may be informative. Comparative balance sheets are often presented. In some cases, an analysis that involves expressing one amount as a percent of another may be helpful. For example, it is interesting to note that on June 30, 19--, the current assets of Holling & Renz amounted to 97 percent of the total assets. The liabilities (all current) were equal to only 5.8 percent of the total of both liabilities and owners' equity.

Analysis of profitability

The amount of annual net income does not mean too much by itself. When this amount is contrasted with the volume of sales, the total amount of the assets, or the total of the owners' equity element of the business, a better indication of profitability is provided. It has been noted (see page 467) that Holling & Renz had net income equal to 10 percent of net sales. The net income of $79,950 was equal to nearly 33 percent of total assets. The total owners' equity was $187,424 ($114,329 + $73,095) at the start of the fiscal year. The net income for the year was equal to almost 43 percent of that amount. In judging these relationships, however, it must be remembered that no income tax is taken into consideration, since partnerships, as such, do not pay income taxes. In his individual income tax return, each partner must include his share of the partnership net income along with any "salary" payment or allowance. (The amount of any cash or other assets received from the firm is not relevant to the calculation of his taxable income.) The amount of income tax that each partner must pay depends upon the total amount of his income from various sources, the amount of various deductions that he may take, and the number of exemptions to which he is entitled.

Report
No. 19-2

> Complete Report No. 19-2 in the study assignments. Do not submit the report at this time. Since Reports Nos. 19-1, 19-2, and 19-3 are related, you should retain the working papers until you have completed all three reports. Continue with the textbook discussion until Report No. 19-3 is required.

THE STATEMENT OF CHANGES IN FINANCIAL POSITION

The annual report of Holling & Renz includes a *statement of changes in financial position* for the year. Since this type of statement has not been discussed or illustrated in earlier chapters, its nature and purpose will be explained before the one for Holling & Renz is considered.

Nature and purpose of the statement

The managers of a business have the dual objective of generating net income and of keeping the enterprise solvent. It would seem that success in the matter of profitability would automatically assure solvency. Net income brings in cash — either at once, or as soon as receivables are collected. To assure solvency is not that simple, however. The cash inflow resulting from profitable operations may be used to acquire more long-lived assets, to discharge long-term indebtedness, or it may be withdrawn by the owners. Many profitable and growing businesses suffer from a continual shortage of *working capital* (current assets minus current liabilities). Sometimes the reverse is the case. There may be little or no net income, and yet by occasional sales of long-lived assets, by borrowing on a long-term basis, or by additional investments by the owners, the business maintains ample working capital. The increase or decrease in working capital is the result of the interplay of various management actions and outside influences.

In analyzing the affairs of a business, it is helpful to know the reasons for an increase or a decrease in working capital during the period under review (often a year). To provide this information, a special type of financial statement that explains the change in working capital has been developed. It is called the *statement of changes in financial position*, the *statement of source and application of funds*, the *statement of application of funds*, the *fund-change statement*, or the *statement of changes in working capital*.

In this connection, the word "funds" means working capital. The word has other meanings. In a semislang sense, "funds" is sometimes used as a synonym for cash. The term "fund" (singular) is used to describe cash or other assets set aside for a specified purpose such as a *petty cash fund*. In government finance and accounting, a fund is a segregated collection of cash and other assets (and, sometimes, related liabilities) held or used for a certain purpose, such as a *highway construction fund*. A statement of changes in financial position, however, usually is a statement explaining the increase or decrease in the working capital of a business during a specified period of time. (It may be noted that the term "financial position" can be used to encompass more and, sometimes, less than working capital, but the prevailing practice is to limit the statement to an explanation of working capital, i.e., "funds," changes.)

The question may arise as to why a statement of source and application of cash would not better serve to explain what has been happening to the business. For certain purposes, periodic statements of cash receipts and disbursements are needed. However, in judging the current position and the changes in it that have occurred, it can be very misleading to look only at what has happened to cash. To illustrate, consider the following comparative statement of the current assets and current liabilities of a business at the start and close of a year:

	Beginning of Year	End of Year
Current Assets		
Cash...	$ 10,000	$ 50,000
Temporary investments............................	20,000	5,000
Receivables (net)..................................	40,000	30,000
Inventories and prepayments........................	30,000	35,000
Total...	$100,000	$120,000
Current Liabilities		
Notes, accounts, and taxes payable....................	25,000	80,000
Working capital....................................	$ 75,000	$ 40,000

Cash increased 400 percent but the current position of the company deteriorated seriously. The current ratio changed from 4 to 1 to only 1.5 to 1, and the acid-test ratio from 2.8 to 1 to 1.06 to 1. In analyzing what has been happening in the business, the reasons for the $35,000 decrease in working capital are of far more concern than the explanation of why cash is $40,000 greater. Thus, a statement of changes in financial position based on working capital is much more informative than such a statement based on cash receipts and disbursements.

Sources of funds

Funds may be secured or obtained in four ways:

Investments by Owners. If the owners invest cash or other current assets in the business, working capital is increased.

Profitable Operations. If there has been net income for an accounting period, the increase in cash and receivables due to sales (and, sometimes, due to other revenue) must have been more than the total of the decrease in inventory (because of goods sold) and either the decrease in cash or the increase in current payables that took place when most expenses were incurred. (The special problem of depreciation and a few other expenses that do not reduce working capital when incurred will be discussed at a later point.)

Long-Term Borrowing. When money is borrowed and the promised date of repayment is many years in the future, working capital is increased. (Short-term borrowing does not affect working capital because the increase in cash is exactly offset by the increase in a current liability — usually notes payable.)

Sale of Long-Lived Assets. Selling long-lived assets, such as land, buildings, equipment, or trucks, usually increases either cash or current receivables.

Applications of funds

Funds may be applied or used in four ways:

Withdrawals by Owners. When the owners of a business take money out (either because there has been a profit or as a withdrawal of their capital investment) working capital is reduced. In the case of corporations, the payment of cash dividends is the usual example of this type of application of funds.

Unprofitable Operations. Working capital is reduced if the decrease in inventory (because of goods sold) and either the decrease in cash or the increase in current payables that takes place when most expenses are incurred are, in total, larger than the addition to cash and receivables due to sales (and, sometimes, due to other revenue).

Repayment of Long-Term Borrowing. When long-term liabilities, such as mortgages payable, are paid, cash (and, thus working capital) is reduced. (The discharge of short-term obligations does not affect working capital because the decrease in cash is offset by an equal decrease in a current liability.)

Purchase of Long-Lived Assets. When a long-lived asset (land, building, equipment, etc.) is purchased, usually either cash is reduced or accounts payable is increased. In either case, working capital is diminished.

Example of statement of changes in financial position

The statement of changes in financial position is prepared from information supplied by the balance sheets at the beginning and end of the accounting period involved, plus certain other data found in the income statement. To illustrate, assume that the balance sheets of Whitney & Walters at the beginning and end of the year 19–– were as shown below.

	BEGINNING OF YEAR	END OF YEAR
Assets		
Cash..	$ 30,000	$ 40,000
Receivables..	90,000	80,000
Inventory..	100,000	90,000
Total current assets..............................	$220,000	$210,000
Building and equipment.............................		110,000
Land..	20,000	20,000
	$240,000	$340,000
Liabilities and Owners' Equity		
Notes payable.....................................	$ 20,000	$ 30,000
Accounts payable..................................	90,000	60,000
Total current liabilities...........................	$110,000	$ 90,000
Mortgage payable..................................		60,000
Whitney, capital	70,000	100,000
Walters, capital...................................	60,000	90,000
	$240,000	$340,000

During the year Whitney and Walters each invested an additional $10,000. Neither partner withdrew anything. The net income for the year was $40,000.

The amount of working capital at the start of the year was $110,000 ($220,000 − $110,000). At the end of the year the amount was $120,000 ($210,000 − $90,000). The change, then, was an increase of $10,000. The statement of changes in financial position must explain how this happened.

Comparison of the two balance sheets reveals that building and equipment increased from nothing to $110,000. (A building was constructed during the year. It was completed just before the year ended. At that time the equipment was purchased.) This was a $110,000 application of funds. Mortgage payable increased from nothing to $60,000 — a source of funds. (The money was borrowed on a long-term basis by giving a note secured by a mortgage on the land and building.) The owners' equity in the business increased from $130,000 ($70,000 + $60,000) to $190,000 ($100,000 + $90,000). This $60,000 increase in funds was from two sources: **(1)** the net income for the year, $40,000, and **(2)** the partners' additional investment of $20,000. These findings can be classified to produce the statement at the top of page 478.

WHITNEY & WALTERS

Statement of Changes in Financial Position

For the Year Ended December 31, 19--

Sources of funds:

Net income for the year..................................	$ 40,000	
Investments by partners.................................	20,000	
Long-term borrowing...................................	60,000	$120,000

Application of funds:

Purchase of building and equipment.......................		110,000
Increase in working capital.................................		$ 10,000

Whitney & Walters — Statement of Changes in Financial Position

Assembling the data for statement of changes in financial position

There are various techniques for assembling and organizing data to produce a statement of changes in financial position. If the calculations are likely to be complicated, it may be advisable to use a special form of work sheet. If no special problems are involved, the use of a work sheet is not warranted. The first step is to summarize, in comparative form, the balance sheets at the beginning and end of the period. The accountant for Holling & Renz used the balance sheet at the close of the preceding year (not reproduced in this textbook) and the balance sheet at the close of the year just ended (reproduced on page 471). He summarized the statements and noted the changes in each element, as follows:

	BEGINNING OF YEAR	END OF YEAR	INCREASE (DECREASE)
Cash..	$ 5,539	$ 7,754	$ 2,215
Government bonds..............................		5,000	5,000
Receivables (net)...............................	12,825	16,750	3,925
Merchandise inventories........................	191,874	206,048	14,174
Supplies and prepayments......................	820	1,060	240
Total current assets...........................	$211,058	$236,612	$25,554
Long-lived assets (less accumulated depreciation)...	8,784	7,326	(1,458)
Total assets.................................	$219,842	$243,938	$24,096
Notes and interest payable.......................	$ 10,200	$ 4,559	($ 5,641)
Accounts payable..............................	21,305	8,551	(12,754)
Accrued and withheld payroll taxes..............	913	1,077	164
Total current liabilities........................	$ 32,418	$ 14,187	($18,231)
Owners' equity.................................	187,424	229,751	42,327
Total liabilities and owners' equity.............	$219,842	$243,938	$24,096

The first fact to be noted from the foregoing summary is that working capital increased $43,785 (the current assets increased $25,554 and the current liabilities decreased $18,231). The purpose of the statement of changes in financial position will be to explain this $43,785 increase. (It should be observed that cash only increased $2,215. This was overshadowed by the increase in temporary investments, the increase in inventories, and the substantial reduction in the amount of the current liabilities. It was mentioned earlier that the change in the amount of cash is not nearly so significant as the change in working capital.)

In order to be sure that nothing was missed, the accountant mentally went over the list of sources and applications of funds to see which ones applied to this case. As enumerated on pages 475 and 476, the possible sources are (1) investments by owners, (2) profitable operations, (3) long-term borrowing, and (4) sale of long-lived assets. Items (1), (3) and (4) could be ignored: the partners had made no investments during the year, there had been no long-term borrowing, and no sales of long-lived assets. The only source of funds for the year under review was No. (2), profitable operations. This source of funds will be examined in the following section. As enumerated on page 476, the possible applications of funds are: (1) withdrawals by owners, (2) unprofitable operations, (3) repayment of long-term borrowing, and (4) purchase of long-lived assets. Item (2) did not apply since the year had been very profitable, and item (3) was eliminated since Holling & Renz had not started the year with any long-term debt that could have been repaid. Item (1) certainly applied since both partners had made substantial withdrawals, and item (4) was relevant because two pieces of office equipment had been purchased. These applications of funds will be considered shortly.

Funds provided by operations

The income statement of Holling & Renz for the year ended June 30, 19--, revealed a net income of $79,950. Did this mean that the working capital of the business had been increased by that amount during the year? The answer is: "Yes — and then some." There were two types of revenue: sales and interest earned. In both cases, either cash was collected or a current receivable (accounts receivable, or accrued interest receivable) was increased. In any event, the current assets (and, accordingly, working capital) were increased by the amount of both types of revenue.

Almost every type of expense that was incurred caused working capital to be reduced. Cost of goods sold reduced the merchandise inventory — an important current asset. Prepaid Insurance, a current asset, was reduced by an amount equal to the cost of the insurance that expired during the period. The provision for doubtful accounts was, in effect, a reduction of current receivables. Nearly every one of the many sorts of expenses caused an immediate reduction in cash or an increase in a current payable of some sort. Whether the current assets were reduced or the current liabilities were increased, working capital was reduced.

The single exception (in this case) to the foregoing analysis of the effect of expenses upon working capital is the matter of *depreciation expense*. When the depreciation of the three types of long-lived assets was recorded (refer to adjustments (n), (o), and (p) in the work sheets on pages 448 and 449) the offset to the depreciation expense debit was a credit to the proper accumulated depreciation account. Accumulated depreciation represents the amount of asset cost so far charged to operations. An addition to accumulated depreciation is a reduction in the undepreciated cost of the long-lived asset — *not a reduction in a current asset*.

The total amount of Holling & Renz's depreciation expense for the year was $2,151 ($313 + $1,374 + $464). Since this expense did not reduce working capital (funds), for statement of changes in financial position purposes the amount of the net income for the year, $79,950, was augmented by the amount of the depreciation expense for the year and reported as follows:

Funds provided by operations:
Net income (per income statement)................................ $79,950
    Add expenses not requiring funds:
      Depreciation.. 2,151
Total funds provided by operations............................... $82,101

It is unfortunate that a great deal of misunderstanding has arisen about depreciation in the statement of changes in financial position. The idea that "depreciation is a source of funds" is widely accepted. This notion is entirely incorrect. Depreciation, while difficult to measure on a periodic basis, is a very real expense. It differs from most other expenses only in that most others reduce working capital, while depreciation expense is a reduction in certain long-lived assets. In the long run, depreciation *is* just like other expenses. When the assets that are being depreciated were bought, cash was disbursed. In point of time, the disbursement may have been years before. In the case of most other expenses, the disbursement of cash is closely related. In most instances, the money is spent in the same period that the expenses arises; in a few cases the money was spent in the preceding period (such as payments for inventory and supplies that are not sold or used until the next period); and in some cases the money will not be disbursed until the next period (for example, employer's payroll taxes that relate to one year but are not paid until the next). Depreciation is too often misunderstood because the point in time that the money was spent for the depreciable asset and the point in time when the outlay becomes expense may be far apart.

Another method of showing "funds provided by operations" that could be used would be to show total revenue that increased working capital (sales and interest earned) and deduct therefrom "expenses that reduced working capital." In the present case the difference would be $82,101 — just as shown on page 480. Nothing would need to be said about depreciation if this method were used. The reason that this treatment is not followed is that it is considered desirable to have the statement of changes in financial position start with the amount shown as the net income in the income statement. It is felt that this treatment serves to tie the financial statements together in a more desirable manner.

Another argument that may be used to show that depreciation is *not* a source of funds is as follows: Suppose that depreciation expense had been overlooked in calculating the net income for a period. Would the funds provided by operations be any less? The answer, clearly, is "no." If the accountant for Holling & Renz had failed to record the depreciation expense totalling $2,151, the net income for the year would have been incorrectly calculated to be $82,101. In the statement of changes in financial position, that amount would be shown as funds provided by operations, just as it is when the net income calculation includes the depreciation expense.

It should be mentioned that there are a few other expenses that have the same characteristics as depreciation. They, too, arise when something that was purchased is gradually written off as an expense over a number of succeeding years. A good example is the case of a patent. Patents have a legal life of 17 years. A company may have purchased a patent soon after it was issued. The management of the acquiring company may not think that the patent will be valuable for 16 to 17 years, but it may believe that ownership of the patent will be of benefit, perhaps, for 10 years. Accordingly, one tenth of the cost may be charged to an expense for each of the ten years. This is described as *amortizing* the cost. The portion written off each year is described as *amortization expense*. The asset, patent, is classed as long-lived. As portions of its cost are taken into expense, no decrease in working capital is involved. Accordingly, amortization expense, like depreciation expense, must be "added back" to determine the amount of funds provided by operations.

Occasions may arise when the net income figure must be further modified to arrive at funds provided by operations. If, for example, a piece of land that cost $10,000 some years before was sold for $12,000 and the $2,000 profit was reported in the income statement, that amount ($2,000) would have to be excluded from funds provided by operations for the current year. (Unless the business was engaged in buying and selling land, such a transaction would not be considered a part of regular operations.) The $12,000 received from the sale of the land would be reported separately as a source of funds in the statement of changes in financial position.

Regular operations were the only source of funds for Holling & Renz during the year ended June 30, 19--. The two types of funds applications during that year will be considered next.

Applications of funds: owner's withdrawals

Reference to the owners' equity section of the balance sheet for the year ended June 30, 19-- (reproduced on page 471) shows that during the year, T. L. Holling withdrew $21,486 and A. G. Renz, $16,137. These amounts are shown in the *applications* section of the statement of changes in financial position.

Applications of funds: purchase of long-lived assets

In the analysis of the changes in the balance sheets of Holling & Renz shown on page 478, it will be noted that there was a decrease in the total undepreciated cost (cost less accumulated depreciation) of the long-lived assets in the amount of $1,458. A decrease in the total undepreciated cost amounting to $2,151 was due to the amounts of cost written off as depreciation expense for the year. This amount of depreciation has already been taken into consideration in preparing the statement. If the decrease in undepreciated cost due to depreciation for the year was $2,151, but the total decrease was only $1,458, it must be that there was an application of funds in the amount of $693 to purchase some new long-lived assets. An examination of the long-lived asset accounts revealed that on June 9, a desk calculator was purchased at a cost of $603, and that on June 30, a new checkwriter was purchased at a net cost of $90. (The list price of the checkwriter was $95 but a $5 trade-in allowance was given for the old one.) As it happens, both of these items had been purchased from the Office Equipment Co., and since neither had yet been paid for, the amount of accounts payable on June 30, 19--, included $693 due to that company. (See the schedule of accounts payable on page 472.) Since an increase in a current liability is just as effective as a decrease in cash in reducing working capital, the purchases of office equipment certainly were applications of funds for the year. These acquisitions were so reported in the statement of changes in financial position.

Statement of changes in financial position with supporting schedule of changes in working capital

The annual report of Holling & Renz includes a statement of changes in financial position with a supporting schedule of changes in working capital. These are reproduced on page 483. The statement of changes in financial position explains the net change in working capital that occurred between the start and the close of the fiscal year. The supporting schedule shows the amounts of the changes in the elements that comprise working capital (current assets and current liabilities). The balance sheets as of the beginning and end of the year provided the data for the schedule.

Statements of changes in financial position are not always presented in the form illustrated. Various other arrangements of the data are possible.

HOLLING & RENZ

Statement of Changes in Financial Position

For the Year Ended June 30, 19--

Sources of funds:

Funds provided by operations:

Net income (per income statement)....................	$79,950
Add expenses not requiring funds:	
Depreciation......................................	2,151
Total funds provided by operations...................	$82,101

Application of funds:

Partners' withdrawals:

T. L. Holling...............................	$21,486	
A. G. Renz..................................	16,137	
Purchase of office equipment...................	693	
Total funds applied.........................		38,316
Increase in working capital....................		$43,785

Holling & Renz — Statement of Changes in Financial Position

HOLLING & RENZ

Schedule of Changes in Working Capital

For the Year Ending June 30, 19--

	Beginning of Year	End of Year	Working Capital Increase	Working Capital Decrease
Cash.........................	$ 5,539	$ 7,754	$ 2,215	
Government bonds..............		5,000	5,000	
Receivables (net).............	12,825	16,750	3,925	
Merchandise inventories.......	191,874	206,048	14,174	
Supplies and prepayments......	820	1,060	240	
Notes and interest payable....	10,200	4,559	5,641	
Accounts payable..............	21,305	8,551	12,754	
Accrued and withheld payroll taxes......................	913	1,077		$ 164
			$43,949	$ 164
Increase in working capital...				43,785
			$43,949	$43,949

Holling & Renz — Schedule of Changes in Working Capital

One form sometimes used begins with the amount of working capital at the beginning of the period (usually a year). To this is added the amount of funds secured, appropriately classified. The applications of funds are then shown and their total is subtracted to show the amount of working capital at the end of the period. It was mentioned that titles other than "statement of changes in financial position" sometimes are used. By whatever name it may be called, the inclusion of the statement in the annual report has now become standard practice.

**Report
No. 19-3**

Complete Report No. 19-3 in the study assignments and submit your working papers for Reports Nos. 19-1, 19-2 and 19-3 for approval. Continue with the textbook discussion in Chapter 20 until Report No. 20-1 is required.

Chapter 20

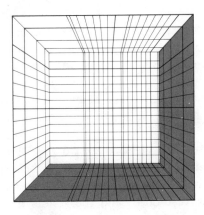

INTERIM
FINANCIAL
STATEMENTS

In accounting for business operations, it has become a nearly universal practice to determine income or loss on an annual basis and to prepare balance sheets at annual intervals. While the calendar year is widely used as the fiscal year, the practice of adopting a so-called *natural business year* (meaning a year that starts and ends at the time when business activity is the lowest) is increasing. In any case, a year is the basic time interval. It is easy to understand, however, that interested parties — notably owners and managers — may have reason to wish for more frequent reports of the affairs of a business. For this reason, it is more and more becoming the practice to prepare *interim financial statements*. Interim means "between." An income statement shorter than, and within the limits of, the fiscal year is an interim income statement. A balance sheet as of a date other than the close of the fiscal year is an interim balance sheet.

Interim periods

It would be possible to prepare interim statements for any segment of a year. Two circumstances, however, make it impractical to use a very short period (such as a day or a week): **(1)** the considerable amount of work involved in producing the statements, and **(2)** the fact that the shorter the period, the more unreliable the determination of income. Many of the problems of accounting (in contrast to pure data gathering, recording, and storing) arise because numerous items of value are acquired in one period, but are not sold or used entirely within that period. Two important examples are **(1)** the problem of allocating cost between goods sold (or used) and goods unsold (or unused) at the end of the period, and **(2)** the problem of cost allocation in the case of most long-lived assets — the matter of depreciation. The shorter the period, the greater the problem.

The constraints just mentioned combine to cause the month to be the smallest time segment generally used for interim-statement purposes. Monthly time segments have the advantage of being universally understood. A disadvantage of using monthly segments is the fact that they are uneven in length. February has only 28 days (29 once every four years), four months have 30 days, and seven months have 31 days. This unevenness may be further accentuated by the dates on which weekends and holidays happen to fall. These circumstances should be kept in mind when comparing the results of successive months and the results of a certain month compared with the same month of the preceding year (or years).

Interim statements often are prepared on a quarterly (three months) basis. In contrast to monthly statements, much less effort is required, the longer time interval gives somewhat more reliability, and quarters are more comparable in length. Quarterly statements in very condensed form commonly are furnished to the stockholders of large business corporations.

In the majority of cases, interim statements must be regarded as very provisional or tentative in nature. At the end of the fiscal year, physical inventories may be taken to determine (or, in some cases, to verify) the quantities of merchandise inventory and various supplies on hand. The procedure is likely to be time consuming and, thus, expensive. It cannot be done every month — or even every three months. Estimates may have to be used for interim-statement purposes. However, even with their imperfections, interim financial statements can be useful.

PRODUCING INTERIM FINANCIAL STATEMENTS WITH THE AID OF WORK SHEETS

It has been shown that the end-of-year work sheet (or work sheets, if circumstances require) is a useful device to **(1)** assist in the production of the annual income statement and the year-end balance sheet, and **(2)** aid in the year-end process of formally adjusting and closing the accounts. For interim-statement purposes the same type of work sheet can materially assist in the statement-production function. (No aid is needed in formally adjusting and closing the accounts because this is not done at the close of interim periods.)

To illustrate the use of interim period work sheets, an example is presented. The example relates to the Mason & Son Wholesale Drug Company owned and operated as a partnership by Peter C. Mason and his son, John H. Mason. They share profits and losses in a 50-50 ratio. (The determination of net income takes partners' "salaries" into account.) The firm uses the calendar year as its fiscal year. The accountant for the company prepares monthly income statements and what are called "year-to-date" income statements, as well as balance sheets, as of the last day of each month. (The income statement for January is, actually, a year-to-date statement in which the "date" is January 31. The income statement for January and February together is a year-to-date statement in which the date is February 28, and so on.) For purposes of this illustration, the business is not departmentalized, and the general ledger contains comparatively few accounts. There is no subsidiary operating expenses ledger. It may be assumed that appropriate books of original entry and auxiliary records are used.

Work sheet for the first month of a fiscal year

This work sheet is reproduced on pages 490 and 491. Actually, a ten-column work sheet was used, but to conserve space the Adjusted Trial Balance columns are not shown. To further conserve space, the amounts are rounded to the nearest dollar. The amounts in the Trial Balance columns were taken from the general ledger after the posting for the month of January had been completed. The reasons why certain of the accounts had no balance will become apparent in the discussion that follows.

The adjustments enumerated starting below were made in the second pair of amount columns.

Entry (a): The amount of the beginning inventory of merchandise, $2,047,921, was transferred by a debit to Cost of Goods Sold, Account No. 531, and by a credit to Merchandise Inventory, Account No. 141.

Entry (b): The amount of the purchases for the month, $1,206,903, was transferred by a debit to Cost of Goods Sold, Account No. 531, and by a credit to Purchases, Account No. 511.

Entry (c): The amount of the purchases returns and allowances for the month, $15,016, was transferred by a debit to Purchases Returns and Allowances, Account No. 051, and by a credit to Cost of Goods Sold, Account No. 531.

Entry (d): The amount of the purchases discount for the month, $26,184, was transferred by a debit to Purchases Discount, Account No. 052, and by a credit to Cost of Goods Sold, Account No. 531.

Entry (e): The amount assigned to the merchandise inventory at January 31, $1,965,000, was taken into account by a debit to Merchandise

Inventory, Account No. 141, and by a credit to Cost of Goods Sold, Account No. 531. Note that an amount rounded to the nearest thousand dollars was used. This is because the figure was, in part, an estimate. The firm of Mason & Son maintains a stock record of certain "high value" items. That record provided the quantities of those items that were presumed to be on hand at January 31. (No physical count was made. The record was considered reliable, since careful physical control of these items is enforced. Very little discrepancy had been found when a physical count was made at the end of the last year.) The quantities were costed by reference to recent purchase invoices. The amount of various low value items was estimated. Accordingly, the cost assigned to the entire inventory was considered to be a reliable estimate. Nevertheless, to avoid the appearance of great precision and accuracy, a round-amount figure was used. For interim-statement purposes, this is considered to be satisfactory.

Entry (f): The interest accrued since January 1, $11,250, on the mortgage payable was debited to Interest Expense, Account No. 811, and was credited to Accrued Interest Payable, Account No. 261. It will be noted that Mason & Son has a $2,000,000 mortgage payable. (Actually it is a note payable that is secured by a mortgage on the real estate — land and building — of the firm. Custom sanctions referring to such a liability as a *mortgage payable*.) This long-term liability is of the type that is to be paid off in full at a distant maturity date — not in monthly installments. Interest at 6¾ percent per annum is payable semiannually each January 1 and July 1. Interest for the six months ended last December 31 ($67,500) was paid on January 2 (since January 1 was a holiday). The determination of net income (or loss) for January must take into account the interest that has accrued during that month.

Entry (g): The amount of the insurance expense for January, $3,542, was debited to Insurance Expense, Account No. 615, and was credited to Prepaid Insurance, Account No. 152. The insurance policy file kept by Mason & Son provided the information needed to calculate the amount.

Entry (h): The estimated cost of store supplies used during the month, $3,086, was debited to Supplies Expense, Account No. 621, and was credited to Store Supplies, Account No. 151. The amount was determined by subtracting the estimated cost of the store supplies on hand January 31, $7,200, from the balance of the store supplies account, $10,286. It will be noted that the firm uses the asset method of accounting for supplies.

Entry (i): The calculated amount of depreciation for the month, $10,832, was debited to Depreciation Expense, Account No. 614, with credits to Accumulated Depreciation — Furniture and Equipment, Account No. 016, $1,810, Accumulated Depreciation — Delivery Equipment, Account No. 017, $2,513, and Accumulated Depreciation — Building, Account No. 018, $6,509. The firm uses straight line depreciation calculated at the following *annual* rates: furniture and equipment, 6 1/4 percent; delivery equipment, 25 percent; and building, 2 1/2 percent. Since no long-lived assets had been purchased during January, these rates were applied to the cost of the assets as shown in the trial balance, and 1/12 was taken as the amount for January.

Entry (j): The amount of the doubtful accounts provision for the month, $7,345, was debited to Uncollectible Accounts Expense, Account No. 622, and was credited to Allowance for Doubtful Accounts, Account No. 013. Experience has indicated that uncollectible account losses average 1/2 of 1 percent of net sales. Net sales for January amounted to $1,469,002 ($1,516,392 − $15,042 − $32,348). One half of one percent of $1,469,002 is $7,345. While it may be assumed that the allowance account had a credit balance on January 1, it should be noted that the January 31 trial balance shows that the account had a debit balance of $2,469. Evidently the write-offs of uncollectible accounts receivable used up the January 1 balance and related to some of the charge sales made in January. It is possible that the January 1 balance of the allowance for doubtful accounts was insufficient, but if the sum of the January 1 balance and the $7,345 provision prove to be adequate to take care of losses relating to sales on account to January 31, no error in prior provisions will be indicated.

Entry (k): The property tax assignable to January, $7,519, was debited to Property Tax Expense, Account No. 616, and was credited to Accrued Property Tax Payable. It will be noted that the latter title had to be added to the list and that no account number is shown. The reason is that there is no need for such an account in the general ledger of Mason & Son Wholesale Drug Company. Property taxes pose a special accounting problem. Such taxes do not accrue in the conventional sense. The tax relates to certain property that is owned *on a specific date* — usually on a specified day in the spring of the year. (It does not matter whether the property has just been purchased or has been owned for many years.) Usually the amount of the tax is not known until the tax bill is received several months after the assessment date. Frequently the tax may be paid in two installments: one half by a specified day late in the year (a day in November or December), and the other half by a specified day in the following spring. (If not paid by the due date, penalties and interest are assessed.)

Property tax expense commonly is accounted for on a cash basis; that is, no record is made until a payment occurs. By the end of the year, the property tax expense account shows the amount of tax actually paid during the year. Mason & Son follows this practice: In the year just ended they

MASON & SON

Work

For the Month Ended

Account	Acct. No.	Trial Balance Debit	Trial Balance Credit
First National Bank	111	47 215	
Accounts Receivable	131	255 916	
Allowance for Doubtful Accounts	013	2 469	
Merchandise Inventory	141	2 047 921	
Store Supplies	151	10 286	
Prepaid Insurance	152	14 379	
Furniture and Equipment	161	347 520	
Accumulated Depreciation — Furniture and Equipment	016		115 742
Delivery Equipment	171	120 624	
Accumulated Depreciation — Delivery Equipment	017		59 318
Building	181	3 124 320	
Accumulated Depreciation — Building	018		1 572 106
Land	191	750 000	
Accounts Payable	211		301 146
Employees Income Tax Payable	221		14 318
FICA Tax Payable	231		12 136
FUTA Tax Payable	241		506
State Unemployment Tax Payable	251		2 731
Accrued Interest Payable	261		
Mortgage Payable	271		2 000 000
Peter C. Mason, Capital	311		1 361 549
Peter C. Mason, Drawing	031	7 682	
John H. Mason, Capital	321		1 121 323
John H. Mason, Drawing	032	5 814	
Sales	411		1 516 392
Sales Returns and Allowances	041	15 042	
Sales Discount	042	32 348	
Purchases	511	1 206 903	
Purchases Returns and Allowances	051		15 016
Purchases Discount	052		26 184
Cost of Goods Sold	531		
Salaries and Commissions Expense	611	101 138	
Payroll Taxes Expense	612	9 305	
Partners' Salaries Expense	613	6 000	
Depreciation Expense	614		
Insurance Expense	615		
Property Tax Expense	616		
Utilities Expense	617	2 774	
Telephone Expense	618	821	
Delivery Expense	619	3 645	
Supplies Expense	621		
Uncollectible Accounts Expense	622		
Miscellaneous Expense	623	6 345	
Interest Expense	811		
		8 118 467	8 118 467
Accrued Property Tax Payable			
Net Income			

WHOLESALE DRUG COMPANY

Sheet

January 31, 19—

Adjustments Debit	Adjustments Credit	Income Statement Debit	Income Statement Credit	Balance Sheet Debit	Balance Sheet Credit
				47 215	
				255 916	
					4 876
(e) 1 965 000	(j) 7 345			1 965 000	
	(a) 2 047 921			7 200	
	(h) 3 086				
	(g) 3 542			10 837	
				347 520	
	(i) 1 810				117 552
				120 624	
	(i) 2 513				61 831
				3 124 320	
	(i) 6 509				1 578 615
				750 000	
					301 146
					14 318
					12 136
					506
					2 731
	(f) 11 250				11 250
					2 000 000
					1 361 549
				7 682	
					1 121 323
				5 814	
			1 516 392		
		15 042			
		32 348			
	(b) 1 206 903				
(c) 15 016					
(d) 26 184					
(a) 2 047 921	(c) 15 016	1 248 624			
(b) 1 206 903	(d) 26 184				
	(e) 1 965 000				
		101 138			
		9 305			
		6 000			
(i) 10 832		10 832			
(g) 3 542		3 542			
(k) 7 519		7 519			
		2 774			
		821			
		3 645			
(h) 3 086		3 086			
(j) 7 345		7 345			
		6 345			
(f) 11 250		11 250			
	(k) 7 519				7 519
5 304 598	5 304 598	1 469 616	1 516 392	6 642 128	6 595 352
		46 776			46 776
		1 516 392	1 516 392	6 642 128	6 642 128

Work-Sheet for One-Month Period

paid $43,318 in April, and $45,114 in December. Another $45,114 must
be paid in April of the current year. Since it seems reasonable to allocate
the total expense for the year over twelve months and it may be reasoned
that the April payment relates to the first half of the year, one sixth of the
amount is assigned to each of the first six months. Entry (k) accomplishes
this by a debit to the expense account and a credit to the liability. The
real purpose of the entry is to cause January to bear a reasonable share
of the year's property tax expense. The credit to the liability is incidental.
(During the second half of the year, the amount must be estimated until
the tax bill arrives in late October or early November and the exact
amount is shown. Usually, however, the estimate can be fairly accurate.)
It should be mentioned that not all accountants would treat property tax
expense in precisely this manner, but some procedure would be followed
to cause a reasonable amount to be included in the income determination
for each interim period.

MASON & SON WHOLESALE DRUG COMPANY

Income Statement

For the Month of January, 19--

Sales...			$1,516,392
Less: Returns and allowances....................................			(15,042)
Sales discounts..			(32,348)
Net sales..			$1,469,002
Cost of goods sold:			
Merchandise inventory, January 1...............................	$2,047,921		
Purchases..	1,206,903		
Less: Returns and allowances..................................	(15,016)		
Purchases discounts......................................	(26,184)		
Cost of merchandise available for sale...........................	$3,213,624		
Less merchandise inventory, January 31........................	1,965,000	1,248,624	
Gross margin on sales...		$ 220,378	
Operating expenses:			
Salaries and commissions expense...............................	$ 101,138		
Payroll taxes expense...	9,305		
Partners' salaries expense......................................	6,000		
Depreciation expense...	10,832		
Insurance expense..	3,542		
Property tax expense...	7,519		
Utilities expense...	2,774		
Telephone expense...	821		
Delivery expense...	3,645		
Supplies expense...	3,086		
Uncollectible accounts expense.................................	7,345		
Miscellaneous expense..	6,345		
Total operating expenses..................................		162,352	
Operating income...		$ 58,026	
Interest expense...		11,250	
Net income...		$ 46,776	

Mason & Son Wholesale Drug Company — Income Statement

The work sheet was completed by **(1)** totaling the adjustments columns to prove their equality, **(2)** extending the amounts (as adjusted, in many cases) into the Adjusted Trial Balance columns (not shown) and totaling those columns to prove their equality, **(3)** showing each amount in the proper Income Statement or Balance Sheet columns, **(4)** footing the last four columns to determine the net income for the month and entering this amount, $46,776, in the Income Statement Debit and the Balance Sheet Credit columns, and **(5)** entering the totals and making the rulings.

The interim statements for January

The income statement for the month of January, 19--, for Mason & Son Wholesale Drug Company is reproduced on page 492. The balance sheet as of January 31, 19--, is shown below and on page 494. It will be observed that, in the owners' equity section, the net income for the month was apportioned between the partners in the agreed ratio: 50%-50%.

The procedure followed in the production of these interim financial statements was almost identical to the steps that normally are followed at the end of the year. At year-end, however, the end-of-period work of the accountant would not have ceased with statement preparation. The adjusting entries would have been journalized and posted, followed by the

MASON & SON WHOLESALE DRUG COMPANY

Balance Sheet

January 31, 19--

Assets

Current assets:

Cash..		$ 47,215	
Accounts receivable..............................	$ 255,916		
Less allowance for doubtful accounts..............	4,876	251,040	
Merchandise inventory..		1,965,000	
Store supplies..		7,200	
Prepaid insurance..		10,837	
Total current assets..			$2,281,292

Long-lived assets:

Furniture and equipment...........................	$ 347,520		
Less accum. depreciation.........................	117,552	$ 229,968	
Delivery equipment................................	$ 120,624		
Less accum. depreciation.........................	61,831	58,793	
Building...	$3,124,320		
Less accum. depreciation.........................	1,578,615	1,545,705	
Land...		750,000	
Total long-lived assets........................			2,584,466
Total assets...................................			$4,865,758

Mason & Son Wholesale Drug Company — Balance Sheet
(*continued on next page*)

Liabilities

Current liabilities:

Accounts payable..	$ 301,146
Employees income tax payable...............................	14,318
FICA tax payable...	12,136
FUTA tax payable..	506
State unemployment tax payable.............................	2,731
Accrued interest payable...................................	11,250
Accrued property tax payable...............................	7,519
Total current liabilities......................................	$ 349,606

Long-term liability:

Mortgage payable..	2,000,000
Total liabilities...	$2,349,606

Owner's Equity

Peter C. Mason, capital:

Capital, January 1................................	$1,361,549	
Add net income (50% of $46,776)................	23,388	
Less withdrawals...............................	(7,682)	
Capital, January 31..		$1,377,255

John H. Mason, capital:

Capital, January 1................................	$1,121,323	
Add net income (50% of $46,776)................	23,388	
Less withdrawals...............................	(5,814)	
Capital, January 31..	1,138,897	
Total owners' equity...		2,516,152
Total liabilities and owners' equity.................................		$4,865,758

Mason & Son Wholesale Drug Company — Balance Sheet (*concluded*)

journalizing and posting of the needed closing entries. It is likely that a post-closing trial balance would have been taken. In many cases, certain reversing entries would have been journalized and posted. At the end of each interim period, none of these bookkeeping steps is involved.

Work sheet for the first two months of a fiscal year

This work sheet is reproduced on pages 498 and 499. The amounts in the Trial Balance columns were the balances of all of the general ledger accounts after the posting for the month of February had been completed. A comparison of the January 31 trial balance on page 490 with the trial balance for February 28 on page 498 reveals that there were no changes in the balances of several accounts. The balance of the merchandise inventory account (No. 141) will remain unchanged until the accounts are adjusted at the end of the year. There were no changes in the balances of the delivery equipment and land accounts (Nos. 171 and 191) because none of these types of assets had been acquired, nor disposed of during February. None of the accumulated depreciation accounts (Nos. 016, 017 and 018) received any debits, since none of the related assets were retired or sold during February, and the accumulated depreciation accounts will receive no credits until the year-end adjustments are recorded.

Accrued Interest Payable, Account No. 261, had no balance at the end of either month since the accrual is not recorded on a monthly basis. There was no transaction during February that affected the balance of Mortgage Payable, Account No. 271. The partners' capital accounts (Nos. 311 and 321) were unchanged, since neither partner made any additional investment in February, and the accounts will be unaffected by withdrawals and net income (or loss) until the annual closing entries are posted at the end of the year. The accounts for Depreciation Expense (No. 614), Insurance Expense (No. 615), Supplies Expense (No. 621), and Uncollectible Accounts Expense (No. 622) had no balances at the end of either month, since they normally are not debited until the year-end adjustments are recorded. Property Tax Expense, Account No. 616, and Interest Expense, No. 811, had no balances at the end of either month, since no payments of property taxes had been made during either month, and the payment of mortgage interest on January 2 had discharged the liability recorded at the end of the previous year. Cost of Goods Sold, Account No. 531, and Expense and Revenue Summary, Account No. 331 (not shown), had no balances at either date, since these accounts are used solely in the end-of-year process of formally adjusting and closing the accounts.

The entries in the Adjustments columns of the work sheet for the two months ended February 28 involved exactly the same accounts as the entries on the work sheet for the month ended January 31:

Entry (a): Cost of Goods Sold, Account No. 531, was debited and Merchandise Inventory, Account No. 141, was credited for exactly the same amount, $2,047,921, as on the earlier work sheet, since the January 1 inventory was involved in the calculations of cost of goods sold both for January alone and for the two-month period ended February 28.

Entries (b), (c), and (d): The balances of Purchases, Account No. 511 ($2,152,795), Purchases Returns and Allowances, Account No. 051 ($28,530), and Purchases Discount, Account No. 052 ($49,751) were transferred to Cost of Goods Sold, Account No. 531. In every case, the balance represented the amount for the two months.

Entry (e): Merchandise Inventory, Account No. 141, was debited and Cost of Goods Sold, Account No. 531, was credited for $1,750,000, the estimated amount of the inventory on February 28.

Entry (f): Interest Expense, Account No. 811, was debited and Accrued Interest Payable, Account No. 251, was credited for $22,500, the mortgage interest accrued for the two months.

Entry (g): Insurance Expense, Account No. 615, was debited and Prepaid Insurance, Account No. 152, was credited for $7,029, the share of insurance premiums applicable to the two months. (The amount was not exactly twice the amount for January alone because one policy expired early in February and was renewed at a slightly lower rate.)

Entry (h): Supplies Expense, Account No. 621, was debited and Store Supplies, Account No. 151, was credited for $5,925, the calculated cost of supplies used during the two months. That amount was determined by subtracting the estimated cost of supplies on hand February 28, $6,800, from the amount of the balance of the store supplies account on February 28, $12,725.

Entry (i): Depreciation Expense, Account No. 614, was debited for $21,664, and Accumulated Depreciation — Furniture and Equipment, Account No. 016, was credited for $3,620, Accumulated Depreciation — Delivery Equipment, Account No. 017, was credited for $5,026, and Accumulated Depreciation — Building, Account No. 018, was credited for $13,018. In every case the amount was exactly twice that for January alone. During February, $42,653 had been added to the furniture and equipment account and $2,067 to the building account, but depreciation was not considered on assets owned for less than one month. There had been no change in the amount of delivery equipment.

Entry (j): Uncollectible Accounts Expense, Account No. 622, was debited and Allowance for Doubtful Accounts, Account No. 013, was credited for $13,956. This amount was determined by taking 1/2 of 1 percent of the net sales for the two months, $2,791,100 ($2,881,145 − $28,579 − $61,466).

Entry (k): Property Tax Expense, Account No. 616, was debited and Accrued Property Tax Payable was credited for $15,038. This amount represented the share of property tax expense for two months. It was exactly twice the amount of the adjustment for January.

It should be noted that in calculating the amounts of insurance expense, depreciation expense, interest expense, and property tax expense, the fact that January had more days than February was ignored. The month — not the number of days — was the unit of time used.

The work sheet was completed in the usual manner. Net income for the two-month period ended February 28, 19--, in the amount of $77,872 was disclosed.

MASON & SON WHOLESALE DRUG COMPANY

Income Statements

	For Two Months Ended February 28, 19—	For January, 19—	For February, 19—
Sales....................................	$2,881,145	$1,516,392	$1,364,753
Less: Returns and allowances.............	(28,579)	(15,042)	(13,537)
Sales discounts..........................	(61,466)	(32,348)	(29,118)
Net sales................................	$2,791,100	$1,469,002	$1,322,098
Cost of goods sold:			
Merchandise inventory, beginning of period..	$2,047,921	$2,047,921	$1,965,000
Purchases................................	2,152,795	1,206,903	945,892
Less: Returns and allowances.............	(28,530)	(15,016)	(13,514)
Purchases discounts......................	(49,751)	(26,184)	(23,567)
Cost of merchandise available for sale....	$4,122,435	$3,213,624	$2,873,811
Less merchandise inventory, end of period....	1,750,000	1,965,000	1,750,000
	2,372,435	1,248,624	1,123,811
Gross margin on sales....................	$ 418,665	$ 220,378	$ 198,287
Operating expenses:			
Salaries and commissions expense........	$ 198,230	$ 101,138	$ 97,092
Payroll taxes expense....................	18,237	9,305	8,932
Partners' salaries expense...............	12,000	6,000	6,000
Depreciation expense....................	21,664	10,832	10,832
Insurance expense.......................	7,029	3,542	3,487
Property tax expense....................	15,038	7,519	7,519
Utilities expense........................	5,409	2,774	2,635
Telephone expense......................	1,605	821	784
Delivery expense........................	7,144	3,645	3,499
Supplies expense........................	5,925	3,086	2,839
Uncollectible accounts expense..........	13,956	7,345	6,611
Miscellaneous expense...................	12,056	6,345	5,711
Total operating expenses...............	318,293	162,352	155,941
Operating income........................	$ 100,372	$ 58,026	$ 42,346
Interest expense.........................	22,500	11,250	11,250
Net income..............................	$ 77,872	$ 46,776	$ 31,096

Mason & Son Wholesale Drug Company — Income Statements

MASON & SON

Work

For the Two-Month

Account	Acct. No.	Trial Balance Debit	Trial Balance Credit
First National Bank	111	66 346	
Accounts Receivable	131	324 575	
Allowance for Doubtful Accounts	013	6 184	
Merchandise Inventory	141	2 047 921	
Store Supplies	151	12 725	
Prepaid Insurance	152	14 957	
Furniture and Equipment	161	390 173	
Accumulated Depreciation — Furniture and Equipment	016		115 742
Delivery Equipment	171	120 624	
Accumulated Depreciation — Delivery Equipment	017		59 318
Building	181	3 126 387	
Accumulated Depreciation — Building	018		1 572 106
Land	191	750 000	
Accounts Payable	211		188 507
Employees Income Tax Payable	221		13 114
FICA Tax Payable	231		11 651
FUTA Tax Payable	241		991
State Unemployment Tax Payable	251		5 352
Accrued Interest Payable	261		
Mortgage Payable	271		2 000 000
Peter C. Mason, Capital	311		1 361 549
Peter C. Mason, Drawing	031	27 925	
John H. Mason, Capital	321		1 121 323
John H. Mason, Drawing	032	23 741	
Sales	411		2 881 145
Sales Returns and Allowances	041	28 579	
Sales Discount	042	61 466	
Purchases	511	2 152 795	
Purchases Returns and Allowances	051		28 530
Purchases Discount	052		49 751
Cost of Goods Sold	531		
Salaries and Commissions Expense	611	198 230	
Payroll Taxes Expense	612	18 237	
Partners' Salaries Expense	613	12 000	
Depreciation Expense	614		
Insurance Expense	615		
Property Tax Expense	616		
Utilities Expense	617	5 409	
Telephone Expense	618	1 605	
Delivery Expense	619	7 144	
Supplies Expense	621		
Uncollectible Accounts Expense	622		
Miscellaneous Expense	623	12 056	
Interest Expense	811		
		9 409 079	9 409 079
Accrued Property Tax Payable			
Net Income			

WHOLESALE DRUG COMPANY

Sheet

Period Ended February 28, 19—

Adjustments Debit	Adjustments Credit	Income Statement Debit	Income Statement Credit	Balance Sheet Debit	Balance Sheet Credit
				66 346	
				324 575	7 772
(e) 1 750 000	(j) 13 956			1 750 000	
	(a) 2 047 921			6 800	
	(h) 5 925				
	(g) 7 029			7 928	
				390 173	
	(i) 3 620				119 362
				120 624	
	(i) 5 026				64 344
	(i) 13 018	3 126 387			1 585 124
				750 000	
					188 507
					13 114
					11 651
					991
					5 352
	(f) 22 500				22 500
					2 000 000
					1 361 549
				27 925	1 121 323
				23 741	
			2 881 145		
		28 579			
		61 466			
(c) 28 530	(b) 2 152 795				
(d) 49 751					
(a) 2 047 921	(c) 28 530	2 372 435			
(b) 2 152 795	(d) 49 751				
	(e) 1 750 000				
		198 230			
		18 237			
		12 000			
(i) 21 664		21 664			
(g) 7 029		7 029			
(k) 15 038		15 038			
		5 409			
		1 605			
		7 144			
(h) 5 925		5 925			
(j) 13 956		13 956			
		12 056			
(f) 22 500		22 500			
	(k) 15 038				15 038
6 115 109	6 115 109	2 803 273	2 881 145	6 594 499	6 516 627
		77 872			77 872
		2 881 145	2 881 145	6 594 499	6 594 499

Work-Sheet for Two-Month Period

The work sheet reproduced on pages 498 and 499 assembled the data needed for an income statement covering the two-month period ended February 28, 19--, and a balance sheet as of the same date. The accountant for Mason & Son Wholesale Drug Company uses the same procedure to develop a succession of year-to-date income statements and month-end balance sheets. Income statements of this type are valuable for comparative purposes. Owners and managers are interested in learning how the progress in the current year compares with that of preceding years.

In addition to the cumulative, year-to-date income statement, an interim income statement is needed for each period by itself. Little effort is required to produce such statements using the year-to-date information. The technique is illustrated on page 497. At the left is the income statement of the company for the two-month period ended February 28, 19--. (This was prepared from the Income Statement columns of the work sheet reproduced on pages 498 and 499.) Next shown is the income statement for January, 19--. This statement is exactly the same as the one shown on page 492 (developed from the Income Statement columns of the January work sheet on pages 490 and 491). At the right is the income statement for February,

MASON & SON WHOLESALE DRUG COMPANY

Balance Sheet

February 28, 19--

Assets

Current assets:

Cash..		$ 66,346	
Accounts receivable.............................	$ 324,575		
Less allowance for doubtful accounts...............	7,772	316,803	
Merchandise inventory...		1,750,000	
Store supplies.......................................		6,800	
Prepaid insurance...		7,928	
Total current assets..			$2,147,877

Long-lived assets:

Furniture and equipment...........................	$ 390,173		
Less accum. depreciation..........................	119,362	$ 270,811	
Delivery equipment................................	$ 120,624		
Less accum. depreciation..........................	64,344	56,280	
Building...	$3,126,387		
Less accum. depreciation..........................	1,585,124	1,541,263	
Land..		750,000	
Total long-lived assets...................................			2,618,354
Total assets..			$4,766,231

Mason & Son Wholesale Drug Company — Balance Sheet
(continued on next page)

19--, that was derived by subtracting the amounts in the January statement from those in the January-February statement (with the two exceptions noted in the following paragraph).

Since the income statements show the manner in which cost of goods sold was calculated, the amounts of the beginning and ending merchandise inventories shown in the February statement were not derived by subtraction. The beginning inventory for February, $1,965,000, was the ending inventory for January. The ending inventory for February, $1,750,000, was also the ending inventory for the two-month period.

The balance sheet as of February 28, 19--, is reproduced on page 500 and below. This was prepared from the Balance Sheet columns of the work sheet on pages 498 and 499. It should be noted that the owners' equity section shows each partner's equity as of January 1, plus his share of the net income for the two-month period, less his withdrawals during the two-month period, to arrive at the amount of his equity on February 28. If desired, each calculation could have started with his equity on January 31 (as shown in the balance sheet on pages 493 and 494), with

Liabilities

Current liabilities:

Accounts payable..	$ 188,507	
Employees income tax payable.................................	13,114	
FICA tax payable..	11,651	
FUTA tax payable...	991	
State unemployment tax payable.............................	5,352	
Accrued interest payable...................................	22,500	
Accrued property tax payable...............................	15,038	
Total current liabilities..		$ 257,153

Long-term liability:

Mortgage payable...		2,000,000
Total liabilities..		$2,257,153

Owners' Equity

Peter C. Mason, capital:

Capital, January 1...............................	$1,361,549	
Add net income (50% of $77,872)...............	38,936	
Less withdrawals................................	(27,925)	
Capital, February 28..		$1,372,560

John H. Mason, capital:

Capital, January 1...............................	$1,121,323	
Add net income (50% of $77,872)...............	38,936	
Less withdrawals................................	(23,741)	
Capital, February 28..	1,136,518	
Total owners' equity...		2,509,078
Total liabilities and owners' equity................................		$4,766,231

Mason & Son Wholesale Drug Company — Balance Sheet (*concluded*)

his net income share for February added and his February withdrawals deducted. The result would have been the same.

It should be evident that a similar procedure would have been employed if quarterly, rather than monthly, interim statements had been prepared.

Report No. 20-1	Complete Report No. 20-1 in the study assignments and submit your working papers to the instructor for approval. The instructor will then give directions as to the work to be done next.

Chapters 16-20

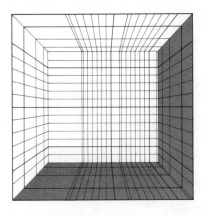

PRACTICAL ACCOUNTING PROBLEMS

Problem 16-A   On May 1, G. E. Bronson organized a photographic equipment and supplies enterprise and opened a new set of books. Following is a list of the assets that he invested in the business:

Cash...	$12,843
Office equipment..	6,280
Store equipment...	7,436
Delivery truck..	6,850
Total...	$33,409

He owed $1,850 on the delivery truck that had been purchased on account.

REQUIRED: Prepare the opening entry in general journal form.

Problem 16-B   Robert Snell, who has been conducting a wholesale wallpaper and paint enterprise, decides to install a formal set of books as of January 2.

REQUIRED: Prepare the opening entry in general journal form. The Balance Sheet is shown on page 504.

ROBERT SNELL
Balance Sheet
December 31, 19 ——

Assets			Liabilities		
Cash.....................		$ 5,434	Accounts payable..........	$ 6,495	
Accounts receivable.........	$ 9,468		Social security tax payable..	164	
Less allow. for doubtful			Employees income tax pay-		
accounts..............	826	8,642	able...................	97	
Mdse. inventory............		19,273	Total liabilities............		$ 6,756
Prepaid insurance..........		412	Owner's Equity		
Store equipment...........	$ 8,000		Robert Snell, capital........		34,245
Less accum. depr.	760	7,240	Total liabilities and owner's		
Total assets..............		$41,001	equity................		$41,001

Problem 16-C   S. F. Tinnin is engaged in the wholesale leather goods business. After closing his revenue and expense accounts for the calendar year ended December 31, his expense and revenue summary account, No. 321, had a credit balance of $22,576. At the same time his capital account, No. 311, had a credit balance of $68,430 and his drawing account, No. 031, had a debit balance of $18,000.

REQUIRED: **(1)** Using the four-column account form of ledger paper, open Mr. Tinnin's capital account, drawing account, expense and revenue summary account, and enter the December 31 balances. **(2)** Assuming that Mr. Tinnin wishes to have the balances of both the expense and revenue summary and drawing accounts transferred to his capital account, journalize and post the required entries. After completing the posting, account Nos. 321 and 031 should show "zero" balances, and account No. 311 should show Mr. Tinnin's present equity.

Problem 16-D   F. W. Human has been operating a wholesale hardware business as a single proprietor. His balance sheet prepared as of September 30 is shown on page 505. On October 1 of the current year he admits James T. Human as a partner with a 40 percent interest in the business to be conducted under the firm name of Human Bros. Hardware. Under the partnership agreement, James T. Human invests $16,863 in cash. The assets of F. W. Human become the property of the partnership and his liabilities are assumed by the partnership.

REQUIRED: Assuming that a new set of books is installed by the partnership, prepare the necessary opening entries in general journal form to record the investments of the partners.

F. W. HUMAN
Balance Sheet
September 30, 19 – –

Assets			Liabilities		
Cash......................		$ 8,420	Notes payable............	$ 7,000	
			Accounts payable..........	6,540	
Accounts receivable........	$10,280		Social security tax payable..	180	
Less allow. for doubtful			Employees income tax pay-		
accounts..............	920	9,360	able...................	120	
Mdse. inventory............		16,354	Total liabilities............		$13,840
Store equipment...........	$ 6,200		Owner's Equity		
Less accum. depr.	1,200	5,000	F. W. Human, capital.......		25,294
			Total liabilities and owner's		
Total assets..............		$39,134	equity.................		$39,134

Problem 16-E   Marsha D. Howard and Susan M. Mello have been competitors in the wholesale drug business. On July 1 of the current year they form a partnership to be operated under the firm name of Howard & Mello. Their balance sheets as of June 30 are reproduced below and on page 506. The partnership agreement provides that the assets are to be taken over at their book value and that the liabilities are to be assumed by the partnership. The agreement also provides that Ms. Mello is to contribute a sufficient amount of additional cash to make her investment equal to Ms. Howard's investment. It is also agreed that the partners will share profits and losses equally.

REQUIRED: Assuming that a new set of books is installed by the partnership, prepare the necessary opening entries in general journal form to record the investments of the partners.

MARSHA D. HOWARD
Balance Sheet
June 30, 19 – –

Assets			Liabilities		
Cash......................		$ 8,250	Notes payable............	$ 3,500	
Accounts receivable........	$ 6,732		Accounts payable..........	5,475	
Less allow. for doubtful			Social security tax payable..	186	
accounts..............	227	6,505	Employees income tax pay-		
Mdse. inventory............		10,279	able...................	160	
Delivery equipment.........	$ 7,200		Total liabilities............		$ 9,321
Less accum. depr.	1,400	5,800	Owner's Equity		
Office equipment..........	$ 3,400		Marsha D. Howard, capital...		23,913
Less accum. depr.	1,000	2,400	Total liabilities and owner's		
Total assets..............		$33,234	equity.................		$33,234

SUSAN M. MELLO
Balance Sheet
June 30, 19 ——

Assets			Liabilities		
Cash.....................		$10,680	Accounts payable..........	$ 9,925	
Accounts receivable.........	$ 5,483		Social security tax payable..	174	
Less allow. for doubtful			Employees income tax pay-		
accounts..............	186	5,297	able...................	158	
Mdse. inventory............		8,721	Total liabilities............		$10,257
Delivery equipment.........	$ 7,400				
Less accum. depr.	1,800	5,600	Owner's Equity		
Office equipment..........	$ 3,200		Susan M. Mello, capital		22,641
Less accum. depr.	600	2,600			
			Total liabilities and owner's		
Total assets..............		$32,898	equity................		$32,898

Problem 16-F   The Willner Upholstering Co., a partnership, is engaged in the whole-sale upholstering business. Ownership of the firm is vested in Ross A. Willner, D. J. Casey, C. L. Mayer, and J. M. Montgomery. Profits and losses are shared equally.

Mr. Mayer died on July 5. His widow is entitled to receive his share in the distribution of the partnership assets. The remaining partners agreed to buy his widow's interest at 95% of its book value. When the books were closed as of the date of Mr. Mayer's death, his capital account had a credit balance of $22,560. On August 15, a partnership check was issued to Mrs. Mayer in final settlement.

REQUIRED: Compute the amount to be paid Mrs. Mayer under the agreement and prepare the general journal entry required to record the check on the books of the partnership.

Problem 16-G   On January 2. The Mohawk Carpet Co. was incorporated with an authorized issue of 3,000 shares of common capital stock, par value $100 per share. Subscriptions were received from the following:

C. B. Nadel, 900 shares, $90,000
J. A. Nagel, 900 shares, $90,000
J. M. Hale, 600 shares, $60,000
J. A. Carstens, 600 shares, $60,000

On January 6, all subscribers paid the amounts due. The stock certificates were issued on January 10.

Following is a list of the corporate accounts to be kept:

Capital Stock   Capital Stock Subscribed
Subscriptions Receivable

REQUIRED: Prepare the general journal entries required to record **(1)** the stock subscriptions received, **(2)** cash received to apply on subscriptions, and **(3)** the capital stock issued.

Problem 16-H   August 28. The board of directors of The Reiss Rolling Mill Co. declared a cash dividend of $4 per share on its 8% preferred stock, payable October 16 to holders of record September 15. There were 43,530 shares of this stock outstanding.

October 16. The company mailed dividend checks amounting to a total of $174,120 to stockholders.

REQUIRED: Using standard two-column general journal paper, record **(1)** the dividend declaration on August 28 and **(2)** the dividend payment on October 16.

Problem 16-I   Ted Feldman, Stephen Mestres, and Terry Seiler were in business as a partnership under the firm name of Feldman, Mestres, & Seiler. On January 2, The Gateway City Distributing Co., with an authorized capital of $125,000, consisting of 5,000 shares of common capital stock, par value $25 per share, was organized to take over the business formerly conducted by the partnership. The following balance sheet of the partnership was prepared at the time of incorporating the business:

FELDMAN, MESTRES, & SEILER
Balance Sheet
December 31, 19 — —

Assets			Liabilities		
Cash.....................		$16,450	Accounts payable..........	$ 8,327	
Accounts receivable.........	$18,875		Social security tax payable..	183	
Less allow. for doubtful			Employees income tax pay-		
accounts..............	1,985	16,890	able..................	162	
Mdse. inventory............		26,252	Total liabilities............		$ 8,672
Office equipment..........	$6,400		Owner's Equity		
Less accum. depr.	2,150	4,250	Ted Feldman, capital.......	$22,438	
Delivery equipment.........	$8,800		Stephen Mestres, capital.....	20,157	
Less accum. depr.	4,800	4,000	Terry Seiler, capital........	16,575	59,170
			Total liabilities and owner's		
Total assets..............		$67,842	equity................		$67,842

The partners subscribed for capital stock of the corporation as follows:

Ted Feldman, 2,000 shares at $25 a share...........................	$50,000
Stephen Mestres, 2,000 shares at $25 a share.......................	50,000
Terry Seiler, 1,000 shares at $25 a share..........................	25,000

The partners, as individuals, received credit toward their subscriptions for their respective equities in the assets of the partnership and gave their personal checks for the balance of their respective subscriptions. A new set of books is to be installed by the corporation.

REQUIRED: Prepare entries in general journal form to record the following: **(1)** The subscriptions to the capital stock of the corporation, **(2)** the transfer of the assets and liabilities of the partnership to the corporation, **(3)** the receipt of cash in settlement of the balances due on the respective subscriptions, and **(4)** the issuance of stock certificates.

Problem 16-J   David G. Deppen has been operating a wholesale grocery business as a single proprietor. His balance sheet prepared as of April 30 is shown below. On May 1 of the current year he admits David O. Musgrave as a partner with a one-half interest in the business to be conducted under the firm name of Deppen & Musgrave. Under the partnership agreement, Mr. Musgrave invests merchandise inventory valued at $24,788, store equipment valued at $8,000, and $21,592 in cash. The assets of Mr. Deppen become the property of the partnership and his liabilities are assumed by the partnership.

DAVID G. DEPPEN

Balance Sheet

April 30, 19 — —

Assets			Liabilities		
Cash......................		$17,798	Notes payable............	$14,000	
Accounts receivable.........	$22,910		Accounts payable..........	12,000	
Less allow. for doubtful			Social security tax payable..	290	
accounts..............	2,320	20,590	Employees income tax pay-		
Mdse. inventory............		34,862	able..................	230	
Store equipment...........	$10,200		Total liabilities............		$26,520
Less accum. depr.	2,550	7,650	Owner's Equity		
			David G. Deppen, capital...		54,380
			Total liabilities and owner's		
Total assets..............		$80,900	equity................		$80,900

REQUIRED: Assuming that a new set of books is installed by the partnership, prepare the necessary opening entries in general journal form to record the investments of the partners.

There are no Practical Accounting Problems for Chapter 17.

Problem 18-A   Leff & Bohler are partners in a wholesale mercantile business. Their accounts are kept on a fiscal year basis, with the year ending on June 30. The accounts with customers, suppliers, and operating expenses are kept in subsidiary ledgers with control accounts in the general ledger. Any necessary adjustments in the operating expense accounts are made at the end of each year after a trial balance is taken. Since the accountant is required to prepare annual financial statements, he follows the practice of preparing a ten-column summary work sheet and a three-column supplementary operating expenses work sheet at the end of each year as a means of compiling and classifying the information needed in financial statement preparation.

The following accounts in the operating expense ledger require adjustment as of June 30:

Insurance Expense	6121	
Store Supplies Expense	6123	
Postage Expense	6124	
Depreciation of Store Equipment	6125	
Depreciation of Delivery Equipment	6126	
Fuel Expense	6134	$ 771.52
Uncollectible Accounts Expense	6136	
Office Supplies Expense	6138	
Depreciation of Office Equipment	6141	
All others (to balance)		181,595.38
		$182,366.90

The trial balance of the general ledger taken as of June 30 is shown on page 510. To conserve space, the accounts primarily involved in the adjusting and closing process are given. To make it possible to complete the work sheet, in two cases the balances of several accounts are shown as one amount.

REQUIRED: Assuming that you are employed as the accountant for Leff & Bohler, you are required to prepare a ten-column summary work sheet for the year ended June 30, 19—, and a supplementary work sheet for operating expenses. Use as your guide the model work sheets reproduced on pages 448, 449, and 452. Allow 3 lines for Cost of Goods Sold on the summary work sheet. The following data provide the information needed in adjusting the general ledger accounts and the operating expenses ledger accounts.

Merchandise inventory, June 30	$163,133.44
Estimated uncollectible accounts expense should be	396.92
Store supplies inventory, June 30	190.00
Office supplies inventory, June 30	185.00
Fuel inventory, June 30	80.00
Postage inventory, June 30	168.10
Insurance expense	856.15

Depreciation of store equipment		317.17
Depreciation of delivery equipment		1,584.10
Depreciation of office equipment		528.72
Interest accrued on government bonds, June 30		56.25
Interest accrued on notes payable, June 30		72.00

Retain the solution to this problem for use in Problems 18-B, 19A and 19B.

LEFF & BOHLER

Trial Balance

June 30, 19--

Mercantile Bank	111	11,987.10	
Government Bonds	121	7,500.00	
Accrued Interest Receivable	122		
Accounts Receivable	123	15,930.80	
Allowance for Doubtful Accounts	013		1,510.14
Merchandise Inventory	151	159,051.86	
Store Supplies	161	1,485.20	
Office Supplies	163	1,454.90	
Fuel	164	624.10	
Postage Stamps	165	1,001.13	
Prepaid Insurance	166	1,302.40	
Long-lived assets (cost)		14,795.30	
Accumulated Depreciation — Store Equip.	017		813.63
Accumulated Depreciation — Del. Equip.	018		1,584.10
Accumulated Depreciation — Off. Equip.	019		944.00
Accrued Interest Payable	241		
Other current liabilities			14,642.12
R. C. Leff, Capital	311		83,496.47
R. C. Leff, Drawing	031	12,210.80	
R. A. Bohler, Capital	321		81,226.49
R. A. Bohler, Drawing	032	11,951.20	
Sales	411		1,192,658.40
Sales Returns and Allowances	041	8,558.15	
Sales Discount	042	7,419.06	
Purchases	511	940,205.15	
Purchases Returns and Allowances	051		5,808.70
Purchases Discount	052		5,148.13
Freight In	531	9,869.23	
Cost of Goods Sold	551		
Operating Expenses	611	182,366.90	
Interest Earned	711		168.75
Interest Expense	811	287.65	
		1,388,000.93	1,388,000.93

Problem 18-B   The work sheets for Leff & Bohler for the year ended June 30, 19--, completed in Problem 18-A, will be used to solve this problem.

REQUIRED: **(1)** Prepare the entries necessary to adjust the general ledger accounts and the operating expense ledger accounts as of June 30, 19––. Use as your guide the model general journal illustration reproduced on page 458. **(2)** After making the required entries, foot the amount columns of each general journal page to prove the footings. **(3)** Prepare the entries required to close the following types of accounts in the general ledger: revenue accounts, expense accounts, the expense and revenue summary account, No. 331, and the partners' drawing accounts. Distribute the balance of the expense and revenue summary account equally between the two partners. Use as your guide the model general journal illustration reproduced on page 460. **(4)** Prepare the necessary entries to reverse the accrual adjustments as of January 1, 19––. Use as your guide the model general journal illustration reproduced on page 464. **(5)** After making the required entries, foot the amount columns of each general journal page to prove the footings. **(6)** Assuming that the individual posting to the general ledger accounts and the operating expense ledger accounts has been completed, insert the necessary check marks in the general journal. Enter the totals of the amount columns on each page and rule each page of the general journal. Assuming that the summary posting has been completed, make the necessary notations in the general journal.

Problem 19-A   The summary work sheet for Leff & Bohler for the year ended June 30, 19––, completed in Problem 18-A, will be used to solve this problem.

Long-lived assets (cost):

Store equipment	$ 3,171.70
Delivery equipment	6,336.40
Office Equipment	5,287.20
	$14,795.30

Other current liabilities:

Notes payable	$ 6,000.00
Accounts payable	7,821.70
Accrued and withheld payroll taxes	820.42
	$14,642.12

REQUIRED: **(1)** Prepare an income statement for the firm of Leff & Bohler for the year ended June 30, 19––. Since the business is not departmentalized, a separate schedule of cost of goods sold is not needed. Use as your guide the statement for Boyd's Clothiers illustrated on page 238. However, insufficient data are lacking to either itemize the operating expenses or to prepare a separate schedule of them. (Round all amounts to the nearest dollar.) **(2)** Prepare a balance sheet for Leff & Bohler as of June 30, 19––. Use as your guide the balance sheet illustrated on page 471. Above is some detail regarding the summary amounts that were shown on the work sheet.

While the firm maintains subsidiary ledgers of accounts receivable and accounts payable, trial balances of these are not provided and, thus, the preparation of schedules is not possible.

Round all amounts to the nearest dollar.

Retain the solution to this problem for use in Problem 19-B.

Problem 19-B   REQUIRED: Using the work sheets of Leff & Bohler from Problem 18-A or the balance sheet from Problem 19-A and the information given below prepare **(1)** a statement of changes in financial position for the year ended June 30, 19–– supplemented by **(2)** a schedule of changes in working capital for that year. Use as your guide the statement and schedule illustrated on page 483.

BEGINNING OF YEAR BALANCE SHEET INFORMATION

Cash..	$ 4,531
Government bonds and accrued interest...........................	—
Accounts receivable (net).......................................	11,127
Merchandise inventory..	159,052
Supplies and prepayments.......................................	1,217
Total current assets.......................................	$175,927
Long-lived assets (less accumulated depreciation)....................	11,453
Total assets...	$187,380
Notes and accrued interest payable...............................	$ 10,893
Accounts payable..	11,051
Accrued and withheld payroll taxes...............................	714
Total current liabilities.....................................	$ 22,658
Owners' equity..	164,722
Total liabilities and owners' equity...........................	$187,380

Problem 20-A   The Millman Sisters are partners in the wholesale grocery business. They share profits and losses in the following ratio: Julia Millman, senior partner, 65%; Janet Millman, junior partner, 35%. "Salaries" are included in the profit shares. The calendar year is used as a fiscal year.

Millman Sisters' accountant prepares quarterly and "year-to-date" income statements, as well as balance sheets as of the last day of each quarter. The completed trial balance for Millman Sisters for the quarter ended March 31, 19–– is shown on the next page.

REQUIRED: **(1)** Using the trial balance on page 513 and the data and information given, prepare a work sheet for Millman Sisters for the quarter ended March 31, 19––. Use as your guide the model work sheet reproduced on pages 490 and 491 (which is complete except for the Adjusted Trial Balance columns). Enter the trial balance in the trial balance columns

MILLMAN SISTERS
Trial Balance
For the Quarter Ended March 31, 19--

Account	No.	Debit	Credit
First Commercial Bank	111	27,437	
Accounts Receivable	131	72,162	
Allowance for Doubtful Accounts	013	1,239	
Merchandise Inventory	161	564,843	
Store Supplies	181	4,046	
Prepaid Insurance	183	6,354	
Furniture and Equipment	211	98,507	
Accumulated Depreciation — Furniture & Equip.	021		35,991
Delivery Equipment	221	34,913	
Accumulated Depreciation — Delivery Equip.	022		15,348
Building	231	862,105	
Accumulated Depreciation — Building	023		420,781
Land	251	198,000	
Accounts Payable	311		89,584
Employees Income Tax Payable	312		3,569
FICA Tax Payable	313		2,142
FUTA Tax Payable	314		95
State Unemployment Tax Payable	315		642
Accrued Interest Payable	316		—
Mortgage Payable	411		660,000
Julia Millman, Capital	511		369,802
Julia Millman, Drawing	051	2,810	
Janet Millman, Capital	521		257,363
Janet Millman, Drawing	052	2,127	
Sales	611		340,320
Sales Returns and Allowances	061	3,256	
Sales Discount	062	6,644	
Purchases	711	281,557	
Purchases Returns and Allowances	071		2,774
Purchases Discount	072		5,601
Cost of Goods Sold (allow 3 lines)	721		
Salaries and Commissions Expense	811	23,798	
Payroll Taxes Expense	812	1,808	
Partners' Salaries Expense	813	8,910	
Depreciation Expense	814	—	
Insurance Expense	815	—	
Property Tax Expense	816	—	
Utilities Expense	817	717	
Telephone Expense	818	296	
Delivery Expense	819	928	
Supplies Expense	821	—	
Uncollectible Accounts Expense	822	—	
Miscellaneous Expense	823	1,555	
Interest Expense	911	—	
		2,204,012	2,204,012
Accrued Property Tax Payable			—

of a ten-column work sheet. Then, enter the necessary adjustments in the adjustments columns of the ten-column work sheet as follows:

    (a) Transfer the beginning merchandise inventory to Cost of Goods Sold.

    (b) Transfer the purchases for the quarter to Cost of Goods Sold.

    (c) Transfer the purchases returns and allowances for the quarter to Cost of Goods Sold.

    (d) Transfer the purchases discounts for the quarter to Cost of Goods Sold.

    (e) Amount of ending merchandise inventory, $558,195.

    (f) Interest accrued on mortgage since January 1, $2,750.

    (g) Insurance expense for quarter, $964.

    (h) Store supplies used during quarter, $1,257.

    (i) Depreciation of furniture and equipment, $547.
        Depreciation of delivery equipment, $727.
        Depreciation of building, $1,796.

    (j) Estimated uncollectible accounts expense for quarter, $1,652.

    (k) Property tax assignable to quarter, $2,196.

(2) Extend the adjusted amounts to the adjusted trial balance columns and foot the columns as a means of proof. **(3)** Complete the work sheet, determine the amount of net income or net loss, and foot the income statement and balance sheet columns as a means of proof.

The solution to this problem will be needed in solving Problem 20-C.

Problem 20-B   This is a continuation of Problem 20-A. The completed trial balance for Millman Sisters for the six-month period ended June 30, 19--, is shown on the next page.

REQUIRED: **(1)** Using the trial balance on page 515 and the data and information given below and at the top of page 516, prepare a work sheet for Millman Sisters for the six-month period ended June 30, 19--. Use as your guide the model work sheet reproduced on pages 498 and 499 (which is complete except for the Adjusted Trial Balance columns). Enter the trial balances in the trial balance columns of a ten-column work sheet. Then, enter the necessary adjustments in the adjustments columns of the ten-column work sheet as follows:

    (a) Transfer the beginning merchandise inventory to Cost of Goods Sold.

    (b) Transfer the purchases for the six-month period to Cost of Goods Sold.

    (c) Transfer the purchases returns and allowances for the six-month period to Cost of Goods Sold.

    (d) Transfer the purchases discounts for the six-month period to Cost of Goods Sold.

MILLMAN SISTERS

Trial Balance

For the Six-Month Period Ended June 30, 19––

First Commercial Bank	111	30,573	
Accounts Receivable	131	81,545	
Allowance for Doubtful Accounts	013	2,766	
Merchandise Inventory	161	564,843	
Store Supplies	181	5,004	
Prepaid Insurance	183	6,916	
Furniture and Equipment	211	111,564	
Accumulated Depreciation — Furniture & Equip.	021		35,991
Delivery Equipment	221	34,913	
Accumulated Depreciation — Delivery Equip.	022		15,348
Building	231	862,105	
Accumulated Depreciation — Building	023		420,781
Land	251	198,000	
Accounts Payable	311		95,179
Employees Income Tax Payable	312		3,511
FICA Tax Payable	313		2,106
FUTA Tax Payable	314		189
State Unemployment Tax Payable	315		1,275
Accrued Interest Payable	316		—
Mortgage Payable	411		660,000
Julia Millman, Capital	511		369,802
Julia Millman, Drawing	051	5,988	
Janet Millman, Capital	521		257,363
Janet Millman, Drawing	052	4,561	
Sales	611		600,504
Sales Returns and Allowances	061	6,195	
Sales Discount	062	12,735	
Purchases	711	534,958	
Purchases Returns and Allowances	071		5,301
Purchases Discount	072		10,674
Cost of Goods Sold (allow 3 lines)	721		
Salaries and Commissions Expense	811	47,206	
Payroll Taxes Expense	812	3,588	
Partners' Salaries Expense	813	17,820	
Depreciation Expense	814	—	
Insurance Expense	815	—	
Property Tax Expense	816	—	
Utilities Expense	817	1,538	
Telephone Expense	818	557	
Delivery Expense	819	1,731	
Supplies Expense	821	—	
Uncollectible Accounts Expense	822	—	
Miscellaneous Expense	823	2,918	
Interest Expense	911	—	
		2,538,024	2,538,024
Accrued Property Tax Payable			—

    (e) Amount of ending merchandise inventory, $553,740.

    (f) Interest accrued on mortgage since January 1, $5,500.

    (g) Insurance expense for six-month period, $1,921.

    (h) Store supplies used during period, $2,324.

    (i) Depreciation of furniture and equipment, $1,094.

        Depreciation of delivery equipment, $1,454.

        Depreciation of building, $3,592.

    (j) Estimated uncollectible accounts expense for period, $3,208.

    (k) Property tax assignable to period, $4,392.

(2) Extend the adjusted amounts to the adjusted trial balance columns and foot the columns as a means of proof. **(3)** Complete the work sheet, determine the amount of net income or net loss, and foot the income statement and balance sheet columns as a means of proof.

The solution to this problem will be needed in solving Problem 20-C.

Problem 20-C   This is a continuation of Problems 20-A and 20-B. The ten-column work sheets completed in these two previous problems will be used here.

REQUIRED: **(1)** Using the income statement columns of the work sheets completed in Problems 20-A and 20-B, prepare a year-to-date income statement for the six-month period ended June 30, 19––, an income statement for the quarter ended March 31, 19––, and an income statement for the quarter ended June 30, 19––. Use as your guide the model comparative income statement reproduced on page 497. **(2)** Using the balance sheet columns of the work sheet completed in Problem 20-B, prepare a balance sheet in report form as of June 30, 19––. Use as your guide the model balance sheet reproduced on pages 493 and 494.

Problem 20-D   Burgess and Graves are partners in the wholesale hardware business. They share profits and losses in the following ratio: Richard C. Burgess, senior partner, 60%; Joseph S. Graves, junior partner, 40%. "Salaries" are included in the profit shares. The fiscal year of this business runs from July 1 to the following June 30.

Burgess & Graves' accountant prepares quarterly and "year-to-date" income statements, as well as balance sheets as of the last day of each quarter. The completed trial balance for Burgess & Graves for the quarter ended September 30, 19––, is shown on page 517.

REQUIRED: **(1)** Using the trial balance on page 517 and the data and information given on page 518, prepare a work sheet for Burgess & Graves for the quarter ended September 30, 19––. Use as your guide the model work sheet reproduced on pages 490 and 491 (which is complete except for the Adjusted Trial Balance columns). Enter the trial balance in the trial

BURGESS & GRAVES

Trial Balance

For the Quarter Ended September 30, 19--

Wellston State Bank	111	18,291	
Accounts Receivable	131	48,108	
Allowance for Doubtful Accounts	013	826	
Merchandise Inventory	161	376,562	
Store Supplies	181	2,697	
Prepaid Insurance	183	4,235	
Furniture and Equipment	211	65,671	
Accumulated Depreciation — Furniture & Equip.	021		23,994
Delivery Equipment	221	23,275	
Accumulated Depreciation — Delivery Equip.	022		10,232
Building	231	574,735	
Accumulated Depreciation — Building	023		280,520
Land	251	132,000	
Accounts Payable	311		59,722
Employees Income Tax Payable	312		2,379
FICA Tax Payable	313		1,428
FUTA Tax Payable	314		64
State Unemployment Tax Payable	315		428
Accrued Interest Payable	316		—
Mortgage Payable	411		440,000
Richard C. Burgess, Capital	511		246,535
Richard C. Burgess, Drawing	051	1,873	
Joseph S. Graves, Capital	521		171,575
Joseph S. Graves, Drawing	052	1,418	
Sales	611		226,880
Sales Returns and Allowances	061	2,171	
Sales Discount	062	4,432	
Purchases	711	187,704	
Purchases Returns and Allowances	071		1,849
Purchases Discount	072		3,733
Cost of Goods Sold (allow 3 lines)	721		
Salaries and Commissions Expense	811	15,865	
Payroll Taxes Expense	812	1,206	
Partners' Salaries Expense	813	5,940	
Depreciation Expense	814	—	
Insurance Expense	815	—	
Property Tax Expense	816	—	
Utilities Expense	817	478	
Telephone Expense	818	197	
Delivery Expense	819	619	
Supplies Expense	821	—	
Uncollectible Accounts Expense	822	—	
Miscellaneous Expense	823	1,036	
Interest Expense	911	—	
		1,469,339	1,469,339
Accrued Property Tax Payable			—

balance columns of a ten-column work sheet. Then, enter the necessary adjustments in the adjustments columns of the ten-column work sheet as follows:

(a) Transfer the beginning merchandise inventory to Cost of Goods Sold.

(b) Transfer the purchases for the quarter to Cost of Goods Sold.

(c) Transfer the purchases returns and allowances for the quarter to Cost of Goods Sold.

(d) Transfer the purchases discounts for the quarter to Cost of Goods Sold.

(e) Amount of ending merchandise inventory, $372,130.

(f) Interest accrued on mortgage since July 1, $1,834.

(g) Insurance expense for quarter, $642.

(h) Store supplies used during quarter, $838.

(i) Depreciation of furniture and equipment, $365.
Depreciation of delivery equipment, $485.
Depreciation of building, $1,197.

(j) Estimated uncollectible accounts expense for quarter, $1,101.

(k) Property tax assignable to quarter, $1,464.

(2) Extend the adjusted amounts to the adjusted trial balance columns and foot the columns as a means of proof. (3) Complete the work sheet, determine the amount of net income or net loss, and foot the income statement and balance sheet columns as a means of proof. Rule all of the amount columns.

The solution to this problem will be needed in solving Problem 20-F.

Problem 20-E   This is a continuation of Problem 20-D. The completed trial balance for Burgess & Graves for the six-month period ended December 31, 19--, is shown on page 519.

REQUIRED: (1) Using that trial balance and the data and information given below and on page 520, prepare a work sheet for Burgess & Graves for the six-month period ended December 31, 19--. Use as your guide the model work sheet reproduced on pages 498 and 499 (which is complete except for the Adjusted Trial Balance columns). Enter the trial balance in the trial balance columns of a ten-column work sheet. Then, enter the necessary adjustments in the adjustments columns of the ten-column work sheet as follows:

(a) Transfer the beginning merchandise inventory to Cost of Goods Sold.

(b) Transfer the purchases for the six-month period to Cost of Goods Sold.

(c) Transfer the purchases returns and allowances for the six-month period to Cost of Goods Sold.

BURGESS & GRAVES
Trial Balance
For the Six-Month Period Ended December 31, 19—-

Account	No.	Debit	Credit
Wellston State Bank	111	20,382	
Accounts Receivable	131	54,364	
Allowance for Doubtful Accounts	031	1,845	
Merchandise Inventory	161	376,562	
Store Supplies	181	3,335	
Prepaid Insurance	183	4,610	
Furniture and Equipment	211	74,376	
Accumulated Depreciation — Furniture & Equip.	021		23,994
Delivery Equipment	221	23,275	
Accumulated Depreciation — Delivery Equip.	022		10,232
Building	231	574,735	
Accumulated Depreciation — Building	023		280,520
Land	251	132,000	
Accounts Payable	311		63,452
Employees Income Tax Payable	312		2,342
FICA Tax Payable	313		1,405
FUTA Tax Payable	314		125
State Unemployment Tax Payable	315		849
Accrued Interest Payable	316		—
Mortgage Payable	411		440,000
Richard C. Burgess, Capital	511		246,535
Richard C. Burgess, Drawing	051	3,992	
Joseph S. Graves, Capital	521		171,575
Joseph S. Graves, Drawing	052	3,040	
Sales	611		440,335
Sales Returns and Allowances	061	4,130	
Sales Discount	062	8,490	
Purchases	711	356,639	
Purchases Returns and Allowances	071		3,534
Purchases Discount	072		7,116
Cost of Goods Sold (allow 3 lines)			
Salaries and Commissions Expense	811	31,471	
Payroll Taxes Expense	812	2,391	
Partners' Salaries Expense	813	11,880	
Depreciation Expense	814	—	
Insurance Expense	815	—	
Property Tax Expense	816	—	
Utilities Expense	817	1,025	
Telephone Expense	818	372	
Delivery Expense	819	1,154	
Supplies Expense	821	—	
Uncollectible Accounts Expense	822	—	
Miscellaneous Expense	823	1,946	
Interest Expense	911	—	
		1,692,014	1,692,014
Accrued Property Tax Payable			—

(d) Transfer the purchases discounts for the six-month period to Cost of Goods Sold.

(e) Amount of ending merchandise inventory, $369,160.

(f) Interest accrued on mortgage since July 1, $3,668.

(g) Insurance expense for the six-month period, $1,280.

(h) Store supplies used during period, $1,549.

(i) Depreciation of furniture and equipment, $730.
Depreciation of delivery equipment, $970.
Depreciation of building, $2,394.

(j) Estimated uncollectible accounts expense for period, $2,138.

(k) Property tax assignable to period, $2,928.

(2) Extend the adjusted amounts to the adjusted trial balance columns and foot the columns as a means of proof. (3) Complete the work sheet, determine the amount of net income or net loss, and foot the income statement and balance sheet columns as a means of proof. Rule all of the amount columns.

The solution to this problem will be needed in solving Problem 20-F.

Problem 20-F

This is a continuation of Problems 20-D and 20-E. The ten-column work sheets completed in these two previous problems will be used here.

REQUIRED: (1) Using the income statement columns of the work sheets completed in Problems 20-D and 20-E, prepare a year-to-date income statement for the six-month period ended December 31, 19--, an income statement for the quarter ended September 30, 19--, and an income statement for the quarter ended December 31, 19--. Use as your guide the model comparative income statement reproduced on page 497. (2) Using the balance sheet columns of the work sheet completed in Problem 20-E, prepare a balance sheet in report form as of December 31, 19--. Use as your guide the model balance sheet reproduced on pages 493 and 494.

Appendix

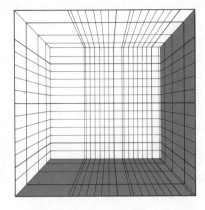

COMPUTER-BASED ACCOUNTING SYSTEMS – DESIGN AND USE

Structure of accounting systems

    The design of a system of forms, records, and reports depends in large measure on the nature of the business by which the system is used. The number of transactions to be recorded in a given time period has much to do with the planning and arrangement of the chart of accounts and of the procedures for gathering and processing transaction information. Physical location of factory buildings, warehouses, stores and offices, and the transaction volume at each location also influence the design of an accounting system.

    The nature of the business, the plan of organization, the kinds of transactions to be recorded and summarized, the transaction volume, and the location of physical facilities together comprise the *structure* of an accounting system. All of these factors together make careful systems planning essential.

The language of computer-based systems

    The original or *source documents* for many kinds of business transactions have been presented in this textbook. The source document is always the key record in a computer-based accounting system just as it is in a manual accounting system. Whether a source document is prepared by hand or by machine, the data it contains must be collected and the recording process started by people.

    Some modern businesses are quite large, and this relative size affects their accounting systems. Modern systems for relatively large businesses include computer equipment (hardware) that operates without human guidance other than pressing one or more buttons. The use of such equipment in an accounting system makes it a *computer-based accounting system*.

Computer-based accounting has brought about the development of a new language as well as new procedures. In computer-based accounting, facts and figures such as ledger account titles, dollar amounts, and physical quantities are known as *data*. The use of these data in different ways for different business purposes is known as *data processing*. Accounting involves the processing of data in several different forms. In fact, the original preparation of the source document for a business transaction is a form of data processing. Likewise, the recording of transactions in books of original entry, posting to ledger accounts, taking trial balances, and preparing financial statements are also forms of data processing.

Those who use computer equipment to process accounting records must apply accounting principles to each step. The same principles of debit and credit apply whether the work is done with computer equipment, with conventional accounting machines, or by the manual bookkeeper. Equipment and machines reduce routine manual work, increase the speed of producing records, and permit more accurate financial reporting.

Data processing is usually described in two ways. The processing of business transactions by means of simple office machines with card punches or tape writers attached is known as *integrated data processing* (IDP). The processing of business transactions by means of an electronic computer is known as *electronic data processing* (EDP).

Accounting systems review

No one can design and install an accounting system for a business that will function properly without a thorough knowledge of the operations of that business. When a business is first established this may not be possible. What is more, expansion of a business into new areas of operation, new personnel, or increased transaction volume may cause its accounting system to become inadequate.

For any one of the foregoing reasons, a business may decide to review its accounting system on an almost continuous basis, and to change one or more parts of the system at frequent intervals. Accounting systems review subdivides into three essential phases: **(1)** systems analysis, **(2)** systems design, and **(3)** systems implementation.

Systems analysis

Systems analysis has three major objectives:

    (a) The determination of business needs for information.
    (b) The determination of sources of such information.

(c) The shortcomings in the accounting systems and procedures presently in use.

The first step in systems analysis usually is a review of the organizational structure and the job descriptions of the personnel involved. The second step in systems analysis usually is a study of forms, records, and reports, and the processing methods and procedures used by the business. In this connection, a *systems manual*, which details instructions to employees and procedures to be followed, is extremely valuable to the systems analyst if it is available. The third step in systems analysis is to project management's plans for changes in such operational matters as sales volume, products, territories, salesmen, or customers into the near future.

Systems design

Accounting systems design changes are the result of systems analysis. A good systems designer needs to know the relative merits of various types of computer hardware, and be able to evaluate the various alternatives open to the business, which may or may not involve computer hardware.

Creativity and imagination are important attributes of a successful systems designer. The following general principles also are important:

(a) The value of information produced by an accounting system should never be less than the cost of obtaining it, and preferably the value should be greater than the cost.
(b) Any accounting system needs sufficient built-in internal control to safeguard business assets and protect data reliability.
(c) Any accounting system needs to be flexible enough to absorb data volume increases and changes in procedures and data processing techniques without disruption of the system.

Systems implementation

A newly created or revised accounting system is worthless without the ability to carry out, or implement, the recommendations of the systems analyst. The new or revised forms, records, reports, procedures, and hardware recommended by the systems analyst must be installed, and obsolete items must be removed. Each and every employee who will have a hand in operating the system must be thoroughly trained and adequately supervised until the new system is operating smoothly.

A major systems change, such as from a manual accounting system to a computer-based accounting system, usually is spread over a rather long period of time. For a while during the changeover period, the old and new systems must function side by side at least in part, and care must be taken to avoid seriously affecting the reliability of the data produced by the system(s).

Flowcharts

One of the major tools of the systems analyst in the design of computer-based accounting systems is called the *flowchart*. In a flowchart, the major steps to be undertaken in processing a particular accounting transaction or series of closely related accounting transactions are shown in graphic form. The symbols most commonly used in preparing flowcharts are:

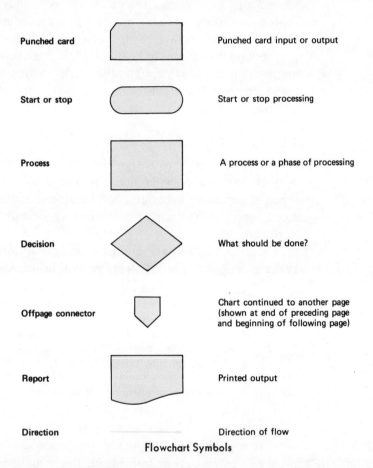

Punched card	Punched card input or output
Start or stop	Start or stop processing
Process	A process or a phase of processing
Decision	What should be done?
Offpage connector	Chart continued to another page (shown at end of preceding page and beginning of following page)
Report	Printed output
Direction	Direction of flow

Flowchart Symbols

Flowcharts usually are prepared to be read from left to right and from top to bottom, with the direction of the flow being shown by lines and arrows. A brief description of each step in processing usually is written inside each flowchart symbol. When one or more decisions are required at some stage in data processing, the questions to be answered usually are printed inside or next to each decision symbol. Most decisions involve comparison of two data items. If the items match, the decision is to go on with the process; if the two items do not match, the decision usually is to retrace some of the previously completed steps in the process.

The process involved in manually posting information from employee check stubs to a payroll register is shown in the flowchart on page A-5.

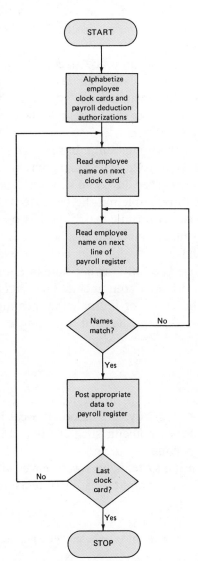

START

Alphabetize
employee
clock cards and
payroll deduction
authorizations

Read employee
name on next
clock card

Read employee
name on next
line of
payroll register

Names
match?   No

Yes

Post appropriate
data to
payroll register

No   Last
clock
card?

Yes

STOP

**Flowchart—Posting Employee Clock Cards
and Deduction Authorizations
to Payroll Register**

This flowchart correlates with the discussion on pages 75–77 in Chapter 4. The employee doing the work begins by arranging the completed clock cards and payroll deduction authorization forms in alphabetical order and clipping the related forms together for each employee. (The clock cards were in clock number or social security number order.) The name on the first clock card and the name on the first line of the payroll register are examined. If they match, the appropriate data is posted to the payroll register. If they do not match, each succeeding line of the register is examined until the right one is found. After posting the appropriate data to the right line, the name on the next clock card is matched to the register and the process is repeated until all clock cards have been posted. This assumes that there is only one clock card and set of related payroll deduction authorization forms per employee, and that each time a new employee is hired, a new clock card is prepared, related payroll deduction authorization forms are completed, and the payroll register listing of employees is revised. Otherwise, the flowchart would have to be extended to include the necessary correctional steps.

The amount of detail shown in a flowchart depends upon its purpose and the amount of detail desired. In implementing a computerized version of the payroll system illustrated above, information concerning hardware would have to be added, and more detailed information about adding new employees, dropping old employees, etc., would have to be included. The punched card symbol for input or output and the report symbol for printed output would then be pressed into use, as well as the connector symbol for flowcharts occupying two or more pages.

In a computer-based payroll system, the flowchart would be the basis for the development of the computer program. Each labeled symbol in the flowchart would constitute a programming step. A collection of computer programs is known as a *software* package.

**The write-it-
once principle
as a labor-
saving device**

A source document, such as a purchase invoice or a sales ticket, usually is prepared manually by handwriting or typing on the document at the time of the transaction. The first step in computer-based accounting is the preparation of a punched card or a section of magnetic tape by a machine operator from a source document. (Optical character recognition (OCR) equipment that can read data from source documents directly into computers is rapidly emerging.)

If the operator types the source document on an office machine with a card punching or tape encoding attachment, the card or tape is being prepared at the same time that the source document is being typed. If the office machine used is not an integrated data processing machine, the card or tape must be prepared later as a separate operation.

The process of recording the basic information about a business transaction in a form that makes later hand copying unnecessary has been called the *write-it-once principle*. This first step in computer-based accounting makes it possible to save labor in completing the later steps of the accounting cycle. Once a punched card or a magnetic tape has been prepared by a machine operator or a source document has been "read" directly into the computer, the recorded information can be used over and over again when and where needed. The only further human effort needed is to feed the cards or tape into computer equipment. This equipment then performs automatically the functions of journalizing, posting, taking trial balances, preparing financial statements, and adjusting and closing ledger accounts.

Importance of locating errors in the write-it-once operation

If errors in the punching of cards, encoding of magnetic tape, or preparation of source documents are not discovered before the cards, tape, or documents are fed into computer equipment, such errors will be repeated in each step of the automated accounting cycle.

Designers of computer-based accounting systems have recognized the seriousness of the error problem. Errors in computer-based systems are normally located in either of two ways:

(a) Transaction information is verified as soon as it has been recorded.
(b) Automatic error-locating procedures built into the computer equipment are used later on in the accounting cycle.

Verifying transaction information already punched into cards is a process of running the cards through manually operated machines a second time. A different machine operator reads the information from the source document and goes through the same punching motions as did the original operator. If each punching stroke hits a hole in the card, the card passes right on through the machine. If a punching stroke hits a solid section of card, an error is indicated, and the machine notches the edge of the card next to the error. Notched cards are set aside and corrected later.

Businesses that find errors very difficult to control may decide not only to verify source document information before cards are processed but also to use automatic error-locating procedures later in the accounting cycle. Computer equipment also may be set up to locate certain errors electronically. When such errors are so located, an error light on the equipment usually goes on, and if the computer operator is not able to remedy the difficulty, the equipment stops running.

Basic phases of automated data processing

The automated processing of any data in the completion of the accounting cycle consists of five basic phases. These five phases are common to all computer equipment, regardless of manufacturer. They are:

(a) Input
(b) Control
(c) Storage

(d) Arithmetic and logic
(e) Output

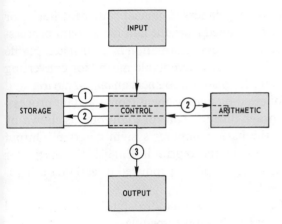

Diagram of Basic Computer System

A diagram of a basic computer system is shown at the left.

Input. In order that computer equipment may complete the accounting process, the source document may have to be rewritten in a form that the equipment can interpret. Information about a business transaction in a form acceptable for use in automated data processing equipment is known as *input*. Any acceptable means for presenting this information to a computer is known as an *input device*.

Control. *Control* is the nerve center, or "action central" of the computer-based accounting system. It is like the central hall in a home or the lobby of a hotel. People must pass through the lobby of a hotel to get to their rooms. In the same way, transaction information must be routed through control in each step of automated data processing. Transaction information received as input is sent by control to storage, as shown by the flow line labeled "1" in the diagram above.

Storage. Transaction information stops in *storage* to await further use in computer-based accounting. Storage is often called the CPU (central processing unit) by computer people. Because storage holds information for future use just as does the human mind, it is often referred to as "memory." But unlike the human mind, storage must be told in great detail what to do with each item of transaction information that it holds. A detailed list of steps to be followed in completing the computerized accounting cycle is known as a *program*. A person who designs programs is called a *programmer*. The detailed work of arranging transaction information in the most efficient manner for computer processing is called *programming* and is usually preceded by a flowchart, as mentioned earlier.

Arithmetic and Logic. The primary work of computer-based accounting is done in the *arithmetic and logic* phase. Transaction information is routed from storage through control to arithmetic and logic. In the arithmetic phase, addition, subtraction, multiplication, or division is performed as needed; and the result is returned by control to storage. This round trip is shown by the flow line labeled "2" in the basic computer system diagram. The logic phase can compare two numbers and tell whether the first number is smaller than, equal to, or larger than the second number. This feature is useful in controlling inventories and expenses.

Output. When ledger account balances, financial statement items, or other data are desired, they are obtained from the automated data processing system in the output phase. Business information in a form acceptable for human use is known as *output*. Any acceptable means for converting coded machine information into English is known as an *output device*.

Business information requested by management from the data processing system is routed from storage through control to output, as shown by the flow line labeled "3" in the basic computer system diagram. Output devices are prepared which are used later to print in English the particular business information requested, or output is produced directly on a high-speed printer attached to the CPU.

Input and output may be and often are handled by the same physical equipment, called I-0 equipment by computer people.

The punched card as an input device

At present, the punched card is the most frequently used initial input device. One form of punched card is the IBM (International Business Machines Corporation) card, illustrated at the top of page A-9.

Utility companies, oil companies, magazine publishers, and mail order houses use punched cards as statements of account. The federal government and many large private companies use punched cards for payroll checks and other remittance checks.

The small figures on the IBM card show that it has 80 columns, numbered from left to right. The large figures on the card show that it has ten rows, numbered 0 to 9 inclusive from top to bottom. In addition, as the above illustration shows, the blank space at the top of the card provides room for two more rows, called the "twelve row" and the "eleven row."

As shown by the punches in the illustration, a single numerical digit may be formed by punching a small hole in a column at one of the ten posi-

Standard IBM Card

tions numbered zero through nine A single letter or symbol may be formed by punching two holes in a column. One of these holes is punched through a position numbered one through nine. The other hole is punched through a position numbered twelve, eleven, or zero, as shown in the illustration above. The three top rows on the card are called the "zone" rows, and a hole punched in one of these rows is called a "zone" punch.

Planning the Use of the Punched Card. The first step in the use of a punched card as an input device is to plan the arrangement of the information on the card. A punched card that is to be used as a statement of account will contain the following information:

(a) Customer's name and address   (e) Current sales to the customer
(b) Customer's account number   (f) Amount received on account
(c) Billing date   (g) Sales returns and allowances
(d) Customer's previous balance   (h) Customer's new balance

Each item of information requires that several holes be punched into the card. An estimate is made of the longest group of letters or numbers required for each of the eight items to be placed on any statement of account. The punched card (or cards if two are needed) is then subdivided into eight groups of columns of sufficient size.

A group of columns used for a single item of information on a punched card is known as a *field*. There is a field for the customer's name and address, and a field for each of the other seven items of information.

Punching Information Into the Punched Card. After the information for preparing a customer's statement of account has been provided by the computerized accounting system, a machine operator enters this information into a machine which in turn punches information holes into the card. One field on the card is used for each of the eight information items.

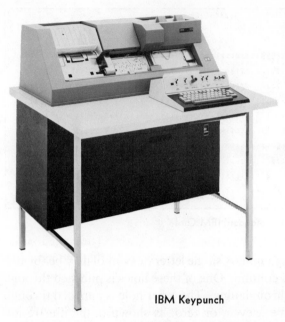

IBM Keypunch

A machine used to punch information holes into punched cards from source documents is known as a *keypunch*. An IBM keypunch machine is illustrated here.

Verifying the Information on the Punched Card. As soon as a batch of cards has been punched, the cards are checked in an attempt to avoid errors. A machine that looks exactly like a keypunch and is used to find punching errors is called a *verifier*. As mentioned earlier, another operator reading from the same source document as the keypunch operator enters the data into the verifier. The IBM verifier machine "feels" each card electronically to determine whether the correct holes have been punched. Each correct card is notched in a special "verify" position. If the verifier machine "feels" a missing hole or a hole in the wrong position, it notches a special "error" position on the card and the keyboard on the machine locks up.

Printing the Information on a Punched Card. The punched information on each IBM card is printed on a two-part statement card consisting of a statement and a stub. The printing is done by running the punched cards through an automatic printing machine that lists, totals, and prints information previously punched onto cards. This machine is called a *tabulator* or *high-speed printer*. The information may either be printed on the same punched card from which it comes or on a separate sheet of paper.

Completing a Punched Card Statement of Account. After each of the two-part statement cards has been tabulated, the customer's account number and balance due are punched into the stub portion of the card. The statement card is then ready to be mailed to the customer. A completed two-part statement card is illustrated at the top of the next page.

Sorting Customer Remittance Stubs. When the customer receives a statement like the one illustrated on page A-11, the stub is detached and returned with the remittance. When a remittance arrives, the amount received is keypunched into the stub that comes with the remittance. The stubs are then grouped into piles and run through a machine which sorts them by customer's account number.

A machine that automatically groups all punched cards of a similar kind and arranges them in some order is called a *sorter*. The stubs received

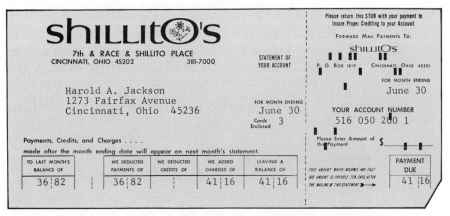

Punched Card Statement of Account

from customers are placed in the hopper of the sorter. The sorted stubs drop into pockets. There is a "reject" pocket for cards that the machine is unable to sort.

Posting Customer Remittance Stubs. The final process in accounting for customer remittances is to run the stubs through the printer or tabulator in account number order. This machine process posts the remittances to individual customers' ledger account cards and determines the new account balances.

The same basic operations are followed in processing punched card checks, except that cash payment transactions are involved rather than cash receipt transactions. The transaction information must still be keypunched, verified, printed, sorted, and posted. These are basic data processing operations in computer-based accounting systems.

Magnetic tape as an input device

Magnetic tape usually is used as a repeat input device in EDP systems. It is prepared for input by depositing small magnetized spots on reels of tape. This tape comes from the factory coated with a magnetic metal substance.

The chief advantage of magnetic tape is the speed with which it can be used as input. It is easy to carry and compact to store.

Magnetic ink symbol numbers as input devices

As discussed in Chapter 3, the American Bankers Association recommends the use of symbol numbers printed in magnetic ink on each bank check. The use of these magnetic ink symbol numbers permits the automated processing of checks.

The use of magnetic ink symbol numbers in the processing of bank checks is called *magnetic ink character recognition*. The common abbreviation for this process is *MICR*. A bank check with magnetic ink symbol numbers printed across the bottom of the check is illustrated below:

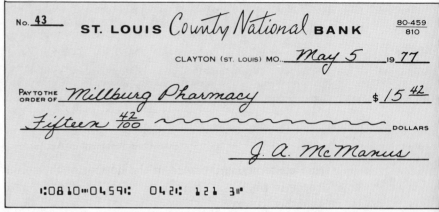

Bank Check with Magnetic Ink Symbol Numbers

Note that the symbol numbers at the bottom of the check use a style that is different from regular Arabic numerals. This is because these numbers are read by a device that "feels" the surface area of each number and recognizes its shape. Regular Arabic numerals, especially 2, 5, 6, and 9, are too much alike to be easily distinguished one from the other by an electronic reading machine.

Encoding Symbol Numbers on Bank Checks. Magnetic ink symbol numbers are printed on checks using special printing machines. A machine for printing magnetic ink characters on checks is called an *encoder*.

Encoding may be done by the company that prints the blank checks, or by the bank that supplies the blank checks to its depositors.

Clearing Encoded Bank Checks Through the Federal Reserve System. The first series of encoded numerals in the check illustration (0810-0459) is adapted from the ABA number in the upper right-hand corner of the check. Notice that the number 80, which represents the State of Missouri, has been dropped from the encoded symbol number. This is because 0810 locates the bank in the Eighth Federal Reserve District (08) and the Greater St. Louis area (10), and the State of Missouri is understood.

The Federal Reserve system sorts checks encoded with magnetic ink symbol numbers as follows:

Step 1. The bank in which the check is deposited forwards it to the Federal Reserve clearing house in its district.

Step 2. The Federal Reserve clearing house sorts the check along with other checks received from banks in its district on special sorting equipment using the first two encoded symbol numbers (08 in the illustration)

This results in twelve batches of checks for the twelve Federal Reserve districts.

Step 3. Each Federal Reserve clearing house forwards the checks drawn on banks in other Federal Reserve districts to the proper districts. In this process, the check illustrated on the previous page is forwarded to the Eighth Federal Reserve District clearing house in St. Louis.

Step 4. The clearing house in St. Louis sorts on the next two encoded symbol numbers (10 in the illustration) for distribution of the checks to regional clearing houses. Since the bank on which the illustrated check is drawn is a Greater St. Louis bank, this check is not forwarded to a regional clearing house.

Step 5. Each district or regional clearing house sorts on the next four symbol numbers (0459 in the illustration) for distribution to individual banks. These four symbol numbers are individual bank numbers.

Step 6. Batches of sorted checks are forwarded to the banks on which they were drawn. The illustrated check is sent to St. Louis County National Bank.

Processing Encoded Bank Checks in Individual Banks. The second series of encoded numerals on the illustrated check (121-077-3) is the account number of the individual depositor at the bank. The depositor's bank sorts its own checks by account number. It uses the same type of MICR sorting equipment as that used in the Federal Reserve clearing houses. This equipment can sort as many as 90,000 checks per hour.

In smaller banks, checks sorted by depositor's account number are posted by using conventional bank posting machines. Larger banks having encoders of their own print the amount of each check in magnetic ink under the signature line. Encoding amounts of individual checks makes it possible to sort and post electronically to depositors' ledger accounts in one operation.

OCR Readers as Input Devices. As mentioned earlier, the use of optical character recognition (OCR) machines to "read" directly from source documents into computers is a growing practice, especially in conjunction with the major credit-card systems discussed in Chapter 6. Special type is required, but it is not as stylized as MICR type. The only requirement is that all characters be printed at right angles and that all curves and diagonal lines be eliminated.

The control phase in automated accounting

The control phase of an electronic system receives electronic commands from input devices and sees that they are carried out. Each command refers to some item of transaction information which is in storage. The control phase searches storage locations one by one in carrying out commands from input devices and keeps track of the location of each command as it is carried out. This avoids skipping program steps.

The storage phase in automated accounting

In manual accounting, the journal, the ledger, and the trial balance are methods of temporarily storing transaction information. This information is stored permanently on the financial statements.

In computerized accounting, means of storage must be used which make it possible to complete the accounting cycle automatically. Means of storing journal entries, ledger account balances, and trial balance information must be found. Any means of storing accounting information in between the steps of the computerized accounting cycle is known as a *storage device.*

External Storage Devices. Storage devices physically removed from a computer system from which data can be fed into the system when desired are known as *external storage devices.* Both punched cards and magnetic tape are able to retain transaction information for long periods of time. For this reason, as well as the fact that they can be physically removed from the system, these input devices are used also as data (external) storage devices. (Magnetic disks, contained in a "phonograph-type" unit, are also used as external storage devices.)

Externally Stored Journal Entries. External storage devices may be used either for temporary storage or for permanent storage of transaction information. Punched cards are excellent storage devices for journal entries. This is because a separate punched card can be used to record each debit element of a journal entry and a separate punched card can be used to record each credit element of a journal entry. The cards can then be machine sorted by ledger account titles for machine posting.

Journal entries may also be stored on magnetic tape. However, reels of tape cannot be sorted in the same way that punched cards are sorted. Journal entries on reels of tape must be machine posted in the order in which they were recorded. This is the same order in which journal entries would be posted manually. The only advantage of machine posting is that it is faster and relatively free of error.

Internal Storage Devices. The internal storage phase of a computer system is contained within the machinery. The storage phase receives instructions from control, which have been passed on from input. These instructions are of four types:

(a) Take data from input   (c) Receive data from arithmetic
(b) Send data to arithmetic   and logic
     and logic   (d) Send data to output

Devices for temporarily storing accounting information within a computer are known as *internal storage devices.*

Internally Stored Ledgers. Internal storage devices are used in computerized accounting to keep ledger accounts up-to-date. Each account in the ledger is assigned a storage address. Debits and credits are fed in on punched cards or reels of tape. Control instructs input to transfer a debit or a credit amount into storage from a card or tape reel.

The incoming debit or credit amount must go to a storage address different from the address assigned to the related ledger account. Since this address is needed only for the current posting operation, it is not permanently assigned. However, the accountant must keep a chart of storage addresses (corresponding to a chart of accounts) in order to know at all times which addresses are assigned and which are open.

Automatic Posting. Automatic posting requires the following steps:

Step 1. Control instructs input to read the old balance of the ledger account from a master magnetic ledger tape into its assigned address in storage.

Step 2. Control instructs storage to transfer the old balance of the ledger account from its assigned address to the arithmetic and logic unit.

Step 3. Control instructs storage to transfer the related debit or credit amount, which has just come into storage from a punched card or transaction tape to arithmetic and logic.

Step 4. Control instructs arithmetic and logic either to add the debit amount to or subtract the credit amount from the old balance of the account.

Step 5. Control instructs storage to receive the new ledger account balance from arithmetic and logic and to store it in the assigned storage address for the particular ledger account. This is the same address in which the old ledger account balance was stored.

Step 6. Control instructs storage to transfer the new ledger account balance out to an updated master magnetic ledger tape.

In a computer-based accounting system, when a new item is stored electronically in the same internal storage address as a previous item, the new item replaces the old item at that address.

To illustrate the automated posting process, suppose that the cash account is assigned storage address number 10. The beginning cash balance, a debit of $1,200, becomes input by means of a punched card and is sent to address number 10 by the control unit. Suppose also that a debit to the cash account, in the amount of $50, is placed in input by means of another punched card and is sent by control to address number 100 for temporary storage.

The posting process will proceed as follows:

Step 1. Control instructs storage to transfer the beginning cash balance of $1,200 from address number 10 to arithmetic and logic.

Step 2. Control instructs storage to transfer the $50 debit to the cash account from address number 100 to arithmetic and logic.

Step 3. Control instructs arithmetic and logic to add the $50 cash debit to the beginning balance of $1,200.

Step 4. Control instructs storage to receive the new cash balance, $1,250, and to store it back in address number 10, the address temporarily assigned to the cash account.

Limitations of Internal Storage. The illustration of automated posting demonstrates that internal storage may be used both for temporary storage of debits and credits to ledger accounts and for semipermanent storage of ledger account balances. A small business having relatively few ledger accounts could get along with a rather small amount of internal storage. However, a large business having a great many ledger accounts would need a rather large amount of internal storage. Internal storage either must be large enough to handle the ledger accounts and the posting operations of the computer-based accounting system in which it is used, or ledger account balances will have to be stored externally on magnetic tape, punched cards, or magnetic disks.

The arithmetic and logic phase in automated accounting

The arithmetic and logic phase of an electronic system receives instructions from control to add, subtract, multiply, or divide, or to compare two numbers. Arithmetic and logic works with only two numbers at a time, having received them from different storage locations. To avoid returning subtotals or partial products to storage, however, arithmetic and logic has a temporary electronic storage unit of its own. The electronic storage device in the arithmetic and logic phase of a computer system used to store subtotals and partial products for further processing is known as an *accumulator*.

The output phase in automated accounting

In many ways, the output phase in automated accounting is just the reverse of the input phase. Punched cards and magnetic tape have already been described as input devices and as storage devices. Cards and reels of tape may also be used effectively as output devices.

Upon request, control will instruct storage to punch out cards or to write on magnetic tape any information desired. This might be journal entries, ledger account balances, trial balances, or financial statements. The cards or tapes must then be converted to English language information.

The Tabulator as an Output Device. The tabulator has already been discussed in connection with the use of the punched card. As indicated, it can list, total, or print journal entries, ledger account balances, trial balances, or financial statements whenever desired. The tabulator prints a line at a time and can handle up to 90 lines a minute.

The High-Speed Printer as an Output Device. High-speed printing machines are now available into which punched cards, magnetic tape, or electronically readable source documents may be fed. These machines are capable of printing in excess of 900 lines of information per minute.

Index